Intratextuality and Latin Literature

Trends in Classics – Supplementary Volumes

Volume 69

Intratextuality and Latin Literature

Edited by
Stephen Harrison, Stavros Frangoulidis and
Theodore D. Papanghelis

DE GRUYTER

ISBN 978-3-11-071018-2
e-ISBN (PDF) 978-3-11-061102-1
e-ISBN (EPUB) 978-3-11-061023-9
ISSN 1868-4785

Library of Congress Control Number: 2018950601

Bibliographic information published by the Deutsche Nationalbibliothek
The Deutsche Nationalbibliothek lists this publication in the Deutsche Nationalbibliografie; detailed bibliographic data are available on the Internet at http://dnb.dnb.de.

This volume is text- and page-identical with the hardback published in 2018.
Editorial Office: Alessia Ferreccio and Katerina Zianna
Logo: Christopher Schneider, Laufen
Printing and binding: CPI books GmbH, Leck

www.degruyter.com

Prologue

The present volume consists of twenty-seven papers, most of which were originally presented at the conference on 'Intratextuality and Roman Literature' held at the Aristotle University Research Dissemination Center from May 25–27, 2017. The event was co-organized by the Department of Classics-School of Philology at the Aristotle University of Thessaloniki and the Corpus Christi College Centre for the Study of Greek and Roman Antiquity at the University of Oxford.

On account of the multifaceted character of the approaches adopted by the authors in the volume, editorial standardization was limited to formatting the papers in accordance with the general *Trends in Classics* style. Authors were free to choose the textual and translation reference system they considered most appropriate for the elaboration of their argument, using either US or UK spelling.

We take here the opportunity to thank all invited speakers, chairpersons and participants for a stimulating conference, which raised many interesting ideas and generated lively discussions. Much of the conference's success was also due to the assistance of departmental colleagues, Aristotle University administration personnel and both graduate and undergraduate students.

The University Research Dissemination Center and the head of its Public Relations Office, Mr. Dimitrios Katsouras, are to be thanked both for hosting the event and for offering invaluable support and technical assistance.

Many thanks also go to the conference sponsors and kind supporters for eagerly embracing and funding our endeavor: The University Studio Press; The School of Philology at the Aristotle University; the Aristotle University Research Committee; and The J.F Costopoulos Foundation. Mrs. Meni Strongyli, Project Manager of the Foundation, undertook every effort to ensure that assistance reached us in time for the opening of the event.

A special and most cordial word of thanks must be reserved for the Welfare Foundation for Social and Cultural Affairs (KIKPE) and particularly its vice chairman, Mr. Manos Dimitracopoulos, not only for supporting the event but also for sponsoring the *Trends in Classics* conference series project in general from 2012 onwards. Through this continued collaboration, the Foundation has forged a unique relationship with the long-term research activity of *Trends in Classics*, held annually in Thessaloniki.

We are much indebted to our fellow co-organizer, Antonios Rengakos, for helping us in numerous ways to run a successful event. What is more, his subsequent invaluable counsel in the preparation of the volume reduced the editorial workload and saved us from infelicities. Any errors or emissions are, of course, entirely our responsibility.

https://doi.org/10.1515/9783110611021-202

Invaluable assistance in compiling the indices was kindly provided by our former and current undergraduate students: Anastasia Pantazopoulou (University of Florida, Gainesville), Maria Leventi (University of California, Santa Barbara) and Vasilis Sazaklidis (Aristotle University of Thessaloniki). Maria Leventi in particular kindly offered notable assistance in proof-reading. The students mentioned above are to be warmly thanked.

Here we also wish to record our gratitude to both Franco Montanari and Antonios Rengakos, General Editors of *Trends in Classics*, for their support and encouragement, as well as for readily agreeing to include the present collection of essays in the *Trends in Classics* – Supplementary Volumes series.

Last but not least, we would like to thank everyone at Walter de Gruyter, and especially Marco Michele Acquafredda, Project Editor, and Katerina Zianna, in charge of typesetting, for their meticulous editorial work at various stages of the publication process.

Stephen Harrison, Stavros Frangoulidis and Theodore D. Papanghelis
Oxford and Thessaloniki

Contents

Introduction: The Whats and Whys of Intratextuality

When in the first paragraph of the opening article in the present volume Alison Sharrock writes that

> [i]ntratextuality is the phenomenon and the study of the relationship between elements within texts: it is concerned with structures such as ring composition, continuities, discontinuities, juxtapositions, story arcs and other repetitions of language, imagery, or idea, including gaps both in the hermeneutic circle and in the form of absent presences and roads not taken. It is interested in the problem of how texts are put together, by authors and readers, as unified wholes, or occasionally in creative disunities, and divided up into sections for ease of consumption or for other purposes

she puts on the plate much that classical scholars, whether of the undertheorised or the overtheorised variety, will one way or another recognize as familiar fare. Apart from the 'ring composition' of our *prima aetatis elementa*, here are the 'imagery' and 'repetitions of idea' beloved of good old New Criticism, here are the gaps to be filled by the reader as celebrated in various brands of reader response theories, here are the silences and 'roads not taken' promoted to paramount ideological significance by many a Marxist critic. On the basis of Sharrock's wording one might feel at liberty to surmise the presence of the leading lights of hermeneutics, phenomenology or even of Roland Barthes officiating and juggling with units and fragments in his uninhibited poststructuralist phase. Is intratextuality an attempt to reckon with features and patterns of a work's internal organization under a new banner? Is there a discernible peculiarity in intratextuality's ways with texts? And is the 'cognitive turn' cautiously canvassed by Sharrock herself pointing in a new 'positivist' direction, away from the twists, turns and aporias of Theory?

Meanwhile, the present volume will hopefully show some of the trails tested under the sign of its title.

The chapters in the present volume

The contributions are grouped together on the basis of either internal intratextual allusions across a single genre or allusions from one work of an author to another work by the same author or a different one; and, what is more, almost all engage with a fruitful combination of intertextual and intratextual poetics.

The opening paper, by Alison Sharrock, 'How Do We Read a (W)hole?: Dubious First Thoughts about the Cognitive Turn', considers the phenomenon of intratextuality within the frame of the so-called 'cognitive turn' in recent literary studies, and what, if anything, cognitive approaches can offer towards greater

https://doi.org/10.1515/9783110611021-001

understanding of how texts fit together and of how readers construct their interpretations of texts. Sharrock probes the idea of what a reader is, asks whether insights about the workings of memory offer anything to intratextual study, and whether recent formulations of the embodied and extended mind (via digital databases and the like) can illuminate the work of critics of ancient texts. Sharrock further stresses that all reader groups, whether ancient or modern, are hypothetical, and argues that readers can be seen as heuristic tools to generate interpretations which can then be put to a larger interpretative community for discussion and potential validation; initial cognitive impressions may be insufficient for such purposes, which may require re-reading and reflection, especially when it comes to making intratextual links. In the end, cognitive approaches, with their emphasis on the diverse experiences of different readers, seem more like useful tools in interpretation rather than constituting an independent hermeneutic methodology.

The first part, 'Latin Republican and Augustan Lyric Poetry and Elegy', groups together papers dealing with the poetry of Catullus, Tibullus and the Corpus Tibullianum.

Gail Trimble, 'Echoes and Reflections in Catullus' Long Poems', explores how repetitions of sounds, images and words in Catullus 61–68 engage the reader's memory in different ways. This highly original thesis is developed in several sections. The first part is devoted to the reoccurrence of aural and musical 'echoes', such as refrains, rhythms, and onomatopoeia, that appeal to hearing as they come to be heard more for their sound than their meaning. The emphasis then falls on 'reflections' of colours and images that appeal to sight or visual imagination by inviting readers to remember something they have previously 'seen'. The final section focuses on the reiteration of specific terms, in which the aural and visual may also be involved. This skilful combination of different kinds of intratextuality, as compellingly argued by Trimble, neatly ties in with the poet's overall aim to explore different kinds of artistic form.

In 'Credula *Spes*: Tibullan Hope and the Future of Elegy', Laurel Fulkerson looks at the concept of *Spes,* as explored in Tibullus 2.6, and suggests that this is a key emotion in the world of elegy, given the centrality of hope and disappointment for the elegiac lover, whose life is one of misery punctuated by occasional joy; the elegiac *puella* is also subject to deceptive hopes. Fulkerson argues further that it might be worthwhile to conceptualize 'elegy' as a single unified text or corpus given its limited volume, number of authors and range of content, and that Tibullus 2.6 itself can be seen as a farewell to the corpus of Tibullan elegy. Fulkerson also points to the role of hope and disappointment in Ovid's exile poetry, continuing this elegiac tradition.

Jacqueline Fabre-Serris, 'Intratextuality and Intertextuality in the *Corpus Tibullianum* (3.8–18)', shows how intratextual and intertextual approaches assist us in understanding the arrangement of the poetic cycle presented in the third book of the *Corpus Tibullianum*. The argument falls into two parts: in the first section, Fabre-Serris offers a thorough comparison of elegies in the third and first person (8, 10, 12 vs. 9, 11, 13–18) with a view to demonstrating the way in which the unidentified poet engages with and responds to Sulpicia's work. In these poems, it is convincingly argued, the *amicus* praises Sulpicia as a poet in accordance with Augustan moral principles, to an extent not displayed by the voice of the poet herself. The homage thus paid to Sulpicia may in part explain why the elegies alternate with those of Messalla's supposed relative. Fabre-Serris then moves on to examine the arrangement of Sulpicia's so-called 'Garland', consisting of elegies 8–12. In addition to providing further support for Parker's view about the authorship of the cycle (first-person poems by Sulpicia, third-person by the so-called *amicus*), it is argued that allusions to both the *amicus* and Sulpicia in Ovid's *Heroides* back up the hypothesis that the poems of the *amicus* were written soon after those of Sulpicia, and that the 'Garland' poems had already been composed by that time.

The second group, 'Didactic, Bucolic and Epic Poetry', focuses on intertextual and intratextual poetics in the poetry of Lucretius, Vergil as well as the latter's influence on Prudentius' allegorical epic.

George Kazantzidis, 'Intratextuality and Closure: The End of Lucretius' *De rerum natura*', looks at how the plague at the end of Lucretius' *DRN* is construed through intratextual links with the language of disease (*morbus*) in the endings of Book 3 and 4. Unlike the predominant view in scholarship, which promotes the plague's symbolic potential and Lucretius' emphasis on its 'psychological' side-effects, Kazantzidis argues that closure is achieved mainly by means of a growing emphasis on the biological aspects of disease throughout the poem, reaching its culmination in 6.1138–286. At the same time, Kazantzidis shows how the intratextual thread which he is proposing can actually be supported by an intertextual reading of the plague in the light of Callimachus' sixth hymn (*In Cererem*), which brings to an end an analogous collection of six units through Erysichthon who is similarly plagued by a terrible disease.

Alison Keith, '*Pascite boues, summittite tauros*: Cattle and Oxen in the Virgilian *Corpus*', investigates Vergil's deployment of the lexicon of cattle and oxen both within individual poems and across the poet's oeuvre as a reflection of his strategic use of programmatic intratextuality, a key compositional technique and counterpart to his intertextual invocation of his literary antecedents. This highly original thesis is elucidated in several sections. The first part concentrates on

In her contribution, 'Figures of Discord and the Roman Addressee in Horace, *Odes* 3.6', Michèle Lowrie argues that a reader steeped in the cultural values common to all Romans would easily have picked up the language of civil discord emerging from the pervasive inter-and intratextual allusions in this ode, which lend unity to its seemingly disjoined textual surface. References to historical events surrounding Antony, layered allusions to other texts, including Horace's other works, and the representation of prostitution within the context of marriage, all direct attention to the collapse of society, made manifest through the employment of the metaphor of adultery as a trope for civil discord. In the context of shared values, Horace's address to the ideal Roman reader (*Romane*) in 3.6 implies a culturally informed addressee, equipped with the hermeneutic skills to perceive the potential for marital breakdown to serve as a strong trope for civil war and the greater truth of political disturbances, a truth implied rather than explicitly stated in the *Ode*.

Stephen Harrison, 'Linking Horace's Lyric Finales: *Odes* 1.38, 2.20 and 3.30', suggests that the common metre of *Odes* 1.1 and *Odes* 3.30 presents them as the bookends of the collection of *Odes* 1–3, while *Odes* 2.20 is clearly linked to them as the middle term of the three book-finales. The addressees of the three poems rise interestingly in importance, matching a pattern of ascent found in Horace's poetic output as a whole, from the slave-*puer* of 1.38 through Maecenas in 2.20 to the Muse of 3.30. *Odes* 1.38, 2.20 and 3.30, Harrison claims, share some details (references to garlands with their poetic symbolism, references to distant or Italian geographical locations in connection with epic poetry) and especially Callimachean metapoetic colour: 1.38 is a manifesto for the short and non-overelaborate poem, 2.20 recalls the envious *Phthonos* of the *Hymn to Apollo*, while 3.30 claims to have Callimacheanised the looser texture of Aeolian lyric; similarly, all of them also allude by contrast to grander poetic predecessors: 1.38 to Choerilus, 2.20 to Argonaut epics, and 3.30 (perhaps) to Vergil's *Aeneid*.

In the next section, 'Intratextual Ovid', the interest shifts to intratextuality as seen mainly yet by no means exclusively in Ovid's elegiac poetry.

Giuseppe La Bua, 'Intratextual Readings in Ovid's *Heroides*', interestingly argues that all the heroines in both single and paired letters in Ovid's work are fraught with intratextual associations. This writing strategy adopted by the *afflictae puellae* in the *Heroides* allows for an ideological re-evaluation of the female lament as unsuccessful. This thesis is well demonstrated by a detailed discussion of the epistles of Phaedra (*Her.* 4), Oenone (*Her.* 5), Hypsipyle (*Her.* 6) and Ariadne (*Her.* 10): all operate on various intratextual levels, equally ineffective in achieving their erotic goals. In contrast, as La Bua argues, Helen (*Her.* 17), a richly intratextual character, effectively capitalizes on earlier stories of *afflictae puellae* and acts as a *praeceptrix amoris*, underscoring the contradictions of love-elegy as well as the unproductiveness of weeping and lamenting over unfaithful lovers in the single epistles.

Thea S. Thorsen, 'Intrepid Intratextuality: The Epistolary Pair of Leander and Hero (*Heroides* 18–19) and the End of Ovid's Poetic Career', argues that the complex intratextuality in *Heroides* 18–19 represents a particular climax of Ovid's poetic career, which highlights the poet's artistic courage. According to Thorsen, the intratextual dialogue is underscored by the fact that Daedalus and Icarus, mentioned as they are by Leander, play an important role throughout Ovid's entire output, and especially in the *Ars Amatoria* narrative. What is more, the intratextual references to both the *Ars Amatoria* and the *Remedia Amoris* are strengthened through the resonance of Hero's letter with these works. These intratextual instances, as convincingly argued by Thorsen, may be read as a meta-dramatic characterisation of the poet himself, exhibiting significant markers of artistry, boldness, learning, gender-transgression, etc. The biographical theme of exile, closely associated with the banished poet, is also reflected in the portrayal of Leander's and Hero's resentment towards their *patria*. From this meta-poetic perspective Leander and Hero may offer an oblique glimpse of an Ovid who is different from the one known from the poetry of exile: banished, yet exhibiting courageous resistance throughout his self-distancing from Augustus' Rome.

Focusing on book 3 of Ovid's *Fasti*, S.J. Heyworth, 'Some Polyvalent Intra- and Inter-Textualities in *Fasti* 3' argues that the *Fasti* offers a particularly rich field for intratextual readings because of the dual timing of its composition: as a late pre-exilic work, originally composed alongside the *Metamorphoses*, the *Fasti* explores earlier parts of Ovid's poetry; yet the poem was also revised during the poet's exile. Heyworth illuminates these complex aspects of intratextuality by examining two narratives. The discussion begins with the analysis of the Numa episode to which the *Tristia* alludes when it presents the poet as attempting to converse with divinities (including members of the imperial household); but the emphasis in the course of Ovid's exile on the limits of the notion of the permissible (*fas, licet*) in turn informs the reading of the Numa narrative, darkening as it does the overall tone of the poem. Then the focus shifts to the story of Anna, Dido's sister. The episode reworks material from *Heroides* 7 as well as the *Aeneid*, and plays with genre (epic and elegy, tragedy and mime); it collaborates with the *Metamorphoses* in telling the story of Aeneas, who, like Anna, is about to become a deity. The bidirectional relationship of the *Fasti* and the *Tristia*, based on shared themes and phraseology, enables Ovid to cast himself as an Anna driven into exile and Anna as the poet: each becomes immortal.

Much scholarship on the fourth book of Ovid's *epistulae ex Ponto* suggests that these elegies were arranged and published posthumously and haphazardly. Tristan Franklinos, 'Ovid, *ex Ponto* 4: An Intratextually Cohesive Book', compellingly argues against this, taking the view that the poems which constitute *ex Ponto* 4 are far from disordered. Franklinos grounds this thesis in a meticulous reading of the book's opening sequence (4.1–6) from an intratextual perspective which adds considerable support to those who have argued for a carefully arranged *libellus* with a clear authorial architecture and order. A sense of cohesiveness results from the recurrence of themes and lexical terms across the poems of the *libellus* which points to an internal correspondence between parts of the collection. This intratextual unity implies that Ovid himself is more than likely to be responsible for the overall arrangement of his final book of *epistulae*.

The ensuing section, 'Seneca: Prose and Poetry', deals with intertextuality along with intratextuality in Seneca's oeuvre. In terms of intertextuality, Greek tragic antecedents are also brought to the fore.

In '*nulla res est quae non eius quo nascitur notas reddat* (*Nat.* 3.21.2): Intertext to Intratext in Senecan Prose and Poetry', Christopher Trinacty examines the different ways Seneca employs intertextual linguistic markers in his tragedies and philosophical works. He illuminates this thesis by focusing on two intertexts, from *Thyestes* and the *Naturales Quaestiones* respectively, in order to examine how the intratextual repetition of intertextual language functions in each genre. The dramatic genre invites a more 'open' interpretation of the intertexts. This is evidenced by the presence of Horace *C.* 1.24 throughout the narrative of *Thyestes*. The characters endorse their own views of the Horatian intertext, correcting it and testing its limits. This ultimately demonstrates the bold generic and thematic variation of Augustan poetry that Seneca practices in his tragedies. Seneca's prose works, on the other hand, often follow a more 'closed' hermeneutics, as intertextuality and the intratextual repetitions of the same language are made to elucidate the philosophical issues under consideration. This becomes evident in *Naturales Quaestiones* in which intertexts from Ovid's Pythagoras (*Metamorphoses* 15) are repeated throughout the work to underscore the workings of Stoic *natura*. Seneca's quotations of Pythagoras' speech reveal a more recognizable authorial control over the Ovidian model and work hand-in-hand with the intertexts to accomplish his philosophical objectives. In doing so, Seneca shows how logic (in this case, the rhetoric of the work) acts to unite physics and ethics and provide a microcosmic view of Stoic *natura* in the form of this book.

Stavros Frangoulidis, 'Intertextuality and Intratextuality: Euripides' *Iphigenia at Aulis* and Seneca's *Troades*', argues that in his *Troades* Seneca may not simply be drawing on Euripides' *Hecuba* and *Troades* but also alluding to the latter's *IA* to convey the horror of human sacrifice. The sustained presence of *IA* within the play, he argues, helps to provide a notable unifying thread to the play's two sub-plots, one focusing on Astyanax and the other on Polyxena. In terms of Seneca's intratextual discourse, this engagement with the text of *IA* in the Astyanax and Polyxena narratives further renders the latter an intratext of the former and vice versa, insofar as both seem to re-work the Euripidean *virgo*. This doubling of horror with the sacrifice of two innocent young people as a reworking of the *IA* text thus intensifies the calamity that has befallen Trojans in the aftermath of the fall of Troy.

The following section, 'Neronian and Flavian Intratextual Poetics', concentrates on aspects of intratextuality and intertextuality in the poetic production under the Neronian *principatus* and the Flavian emperors.

David Konstan, 'Praise and Flattery in the Latin Epic: A Case of Intratextuality', takes a leaf out of Sharrock's formulation of intratextuality, alerting the reader not just to relations among parts but also to the impossibility of assimilating the parts into a unified whole. Konstan skilfully applies this conception to Lucan's effusive eulogy of Nero in *Bellum Civile*, situated at the beginning of the epic, and offers an illuminating analysis of this set piece from an intratextual as well as an intertextual perspective. The *laudatio* of Nero belongs to the tradition of hymnic composition. As such, it is detachable from the larger epic even as it forms part of the poet's overall poetic plan. In Konstan's formulation, the reader is invited to extract the panegyric from its context and so keep it independent of the whole, of which it nevertheless forms a part. Such a reading differs from an intertextual approach, which demands that the reader incorporate the borrowed element seamlessly into the text. This 'defiance' of unity, Konstan argues, whereby the parts maintain their separate character even as they work towards an overall objective, is closer to classical conceptions of literature than to modern ideals of internal coherence and consistency.

Evangelos Karakasis, 'Lucan's Intra/Inter-textual Poetics: Deconstructing Caesar in Lucan', examines the techniques used by Lucan, as the extra-diegetic epic narrator, in order to deconstruct Caesar's initial positive image as a new Aeneas/Augustus, borne out by his prayer to the Roman pantheon before crossing the Rubicon. By means of various intertexts from Homeric, Vergilian and Ovidian epic, Cicero's oratorical production, Livy's historical work and Seneca's tragedies and philosophical writings, Caesar is eventually depicted as an anti-Aeneas (Achilles, Turnus), as a *hostis patriae* like Cicero's Catiline, as an unwise Ovidian Fabius, as an authoritarian and detached Ovidian Jupiter/Augustus, as a polluted Senecan Oedipus, or as a barbarian. This subversion of Caesar's voice is further secured, as Karakasis compellingly argues, on the intratextual level (e.g. through the association of Caesar's words with Pompey's treacherous attitude towards the Parthians in book 8 of the *B.C.*). This 'deconstruction' of Caesar as Aeneas/Augustus may bear contemporary political connotations as well, as Nero crucially fashions himself in terms of an *imitatio Augusti*. The crossing of a swollen and rushing Rubicon is finally read by Karakasis as a meta-linguistic comment on the narrative transition from the introductory lines to the main epic action of *B.C.*'s first book.

Theodore Antoniadis, 'Intratextuality via Philosophy: Contextualizing *ira* in Silius Italicus' *Punica* 1–2', makes the case for the importance of Seneca's treatise on anger (*De Ira*) as a Stoic subtext in the narrative technique and the character portrayal of Silius Italicus' *Punica* 1–2. More specifically, Antoniadis argues that Silius employs the semantics of anger and revenge as intratextual indicators that mark the excessive cruelty of Hannibal and Hasdrubal against the people of Spain/Saguntum as a typical paradigm of Carthaginian 'ethics'. Seneca's concept of *ira*, as Antoniadis claims, is also exemplified by the gory account of the Fall of Saguntum, an event that has been much discussed for its programmatic function and ethical value in the epic as a whole. Thus the question of Silius' multifaceted Stoicism is re–addressed and new light is shed on the emerging discussion concerning not only the *inter*textual but also the *intra*textual dynamics of the *Punica*.

The connection of each poem to the next through thematic and lexical links has been proposed for Catullus' *liber* in 2002. A sequential reading of an entire book of Martial from the perspective of structural devices such as concatenation and parallel arrangement remains a desideratum in research. Christer Henriksén, 'Inside Epigram: Intratextuality in Martial's *Epigrams*, Book 10', shows the potential of such a reading by looking at the first twenty epigrams of Martial's Book 10, up to the famous poem addressed to Pliny the Younger (10.20). This case study reveals that the opening of Book 10 contains two interconnected series of epigrams, viz. 2–9 (with no. 1 serving as an introductory poem) and 10–19. The former highlights the theme of literary *fama* and its conditions, while the latter presents variations on the themes of wealth and friendship, thus preparing the way for the poem to Pliny. The recurrence of thematic patterns and lexical links discloses the tightly woven arrangement of Martial's books of epigrams on a macrostructural level.

The penultimate section, 'Roman Prose and Encyclopedic Literature', groups together papers by Gesine Manuwald, Therese Fuhrer and Ulrike Egelhaaf-Gaiser. The first two examine intratextuality in Roman prose of the early republic while the last focuses on intratexts in the prose of the high imperial age.

Gesine Manuwald, '"Political Intratextuality" with regard to Cicero's Speeches', views the statesman's orations and the texts alluding to them as a single *opus*, which allows an analysis from an intratextual perspective as a result of shared themes and the recurrence of concepts and ideas. The chapter consists of four sections, demonstrating this compelling thesis of unity within the corpus, which comprises both Cicero's speeches and further Ciceronian texts engaging with them. The first part examines intratextuality in individual speeches or groups of orations. Discussion next moves to the intratextual web between later speeches and earlier oratorical activity. The third section analyses cross-references across genres and the mention of speeches in the letters. The final part focuses on references to speeches in the rhetorical treatises. The realization of rich intratextual resonances of the orations throughout the work of the politically active writer, as illuminated by Manuwald, corroborates the impression of unity and adds considerably to the literary texture of the *oeuvre*; moreover, such a method of composition can be shown to be a convenient strategy for controlling audience response and, in Cicero's case, of self-representation.

Employing a term from Manfred Pfister's theory of *Informationsvergabe*, Therese Fuhrer, 'On the Economy of 'Sending and Receiving Information' in Roman Historiography', sheds light on the technique of positioning statements that give information about a particular historical occurrence in Sallust's *Bellum Catilinae* with a view to exploring the new meaning generated by the interconnection of textual elements within a specific textual framing or larger narrative segments within it, not easily evidenced through cross-referencing. This illuminating thesis is skilfully shown through a detailed analysis of the short Fulvia sub-narrative which has not been a focus of interest in recent scholarship. This is first displayed by means of Fulvia's depiction as decisively instrumental in Cicero's election as the consul of 63 BCE, despite her showing a similar opportunistic and venal conduct, as previously in the Sallustian narrative of her affair with Q. Curius; and secondly by the overall behavior of Q. Curius, who also shifts his support from the conspirators to the consul in order to afford his high-maintenance mistress. By manipulating Fulvia and Curius' greed, Cicero eventually develops into a replica of Catiline when employing tactics similar to those of his opponent; yet Cicero does so in the worthier interest of both the *respublica* and himself as its consul.

Ulrike Egelhaaf-Gaiser, 'Saturnalian Riddles for Attic Nights: Intratextual Feasting with Aulus Gellius', focuses on the various forms of intratextuality in the four *commentarii* on riddles of the *Noctes Atticae*, and the way they work for the reader. Egelhaaf-Gaiser views these narratives as exemplary because they may be read as cases of *mise en abyme* regarding Gellius' overall intratextual poetics: the *praefatio* guides the hasty reader through helpful paratexts towards the expected information, while the commentaries on the riddles fulfil the expectations and the reading aspirations of the diligent reader: by leaving various issues unresolved and offering parts of the information located in a number of different textual segments, they challenge the reader to reconstruct the underlying meaning that transcends the limitations imposed by single commentaries and books. Thanks to this sophisticated 'play with supplementation', as convincingly argued by Egelhaaf-Gaiser, the reader is invited not simply to look for quick answers, but to react to a work as a whole, immersing her/himself ever deeper in its complex synthesis and structure.

The concluding paper by Richard Hunter, '*Regius urget*: Hellenising Thoughts on Latin Intratextuality', argues that the modern discussion of intratextuality in Latin literature draws both explicitly and implicitly on reading practices and critical methods theorised and practised in Greek antiquity. This thesis is illuminated by looking at three case-studies of this interaction of theory and practice: Horace's use of Empedocles in the *Ars Poetica*, Plato's importance for all intratextual discussion, and finally the idea of literary and narrative 'necessity'.

Through a detailed examination and analysis of combined instances of intra- and intertextual poetics, the present volume hopes to enrich the intent of contemporary interest in and modern discussions of Roman intratextuality, and to shed light on the evolution of this reading process from Republican Latin literature up to Prudentius across a wide range of authors, genres and historical periods.

Theodore D. Papanghelis, Stephen Harrison
and Stavros Frangoulidis

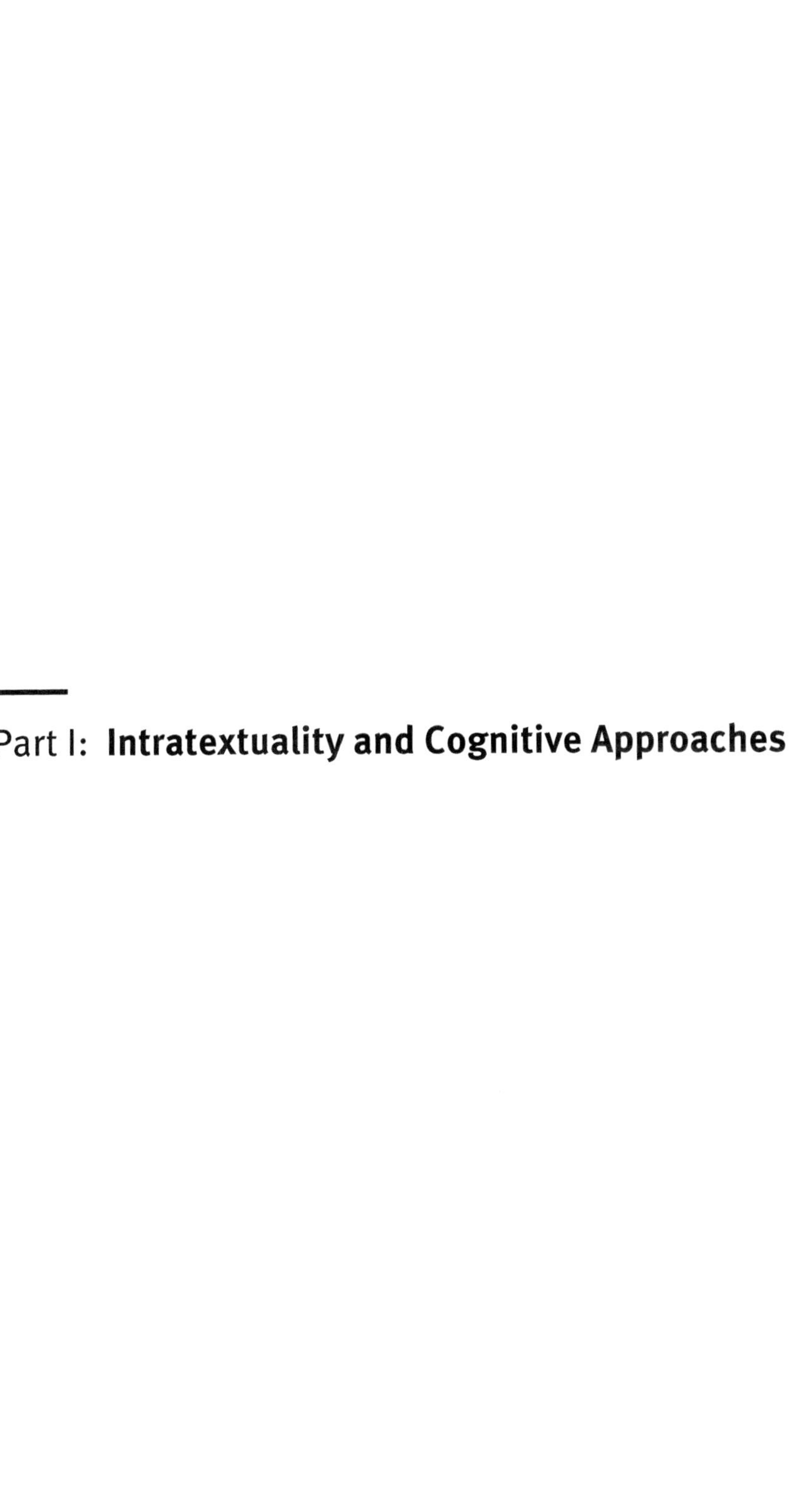

Part I: Intratextuality and Cognitive Approaches

Alison Sharrock

How Do We Read a (W)hole?: Dubious First Thoughts about the Cognitive Turn

1 Intratextuality

Intratextuality is the phenomenon and the study of the relationship between elements within texts: it is concerned with structures such as ring composition, continuities, discontinuities, juxtapositions, story arcs and other repetitions of language, imagery, or idea, including gaps both in the hermeneutic circle and in the form of absent presences and roads not taken. It is interested in the problem of how texts are put together, by authors and readers, as unified wholes, or occasionally in creative disunities, and divided up into sections for ease of consumption or for other purposes. It interacts closely with intertextuality (relationship *between* texts), paratextuality (the *edges* of texts which create one form of interface between the text and the world),[1] and with what might be called 'extratextuality', that is, the way texts point *outside* of themselves, whether to real or fictional worlds. Like intertextuality, intratextuality is concerned, crucially, with the interpretability of links, contrasts, and other textual elements once they have been identified. Just as not all source criticism is intertextual, so not all juxtaposition is intratextual: rather, it becomes so when it functions as the basis for interpretation. Intratextuality is not inherently limited to one side or other of the hermeneutic battle (if so it is) between author and reader, since it is as validly concerned with echoes and structural patterns identified as signs of (and even evidence for) the controlling mind of an author[2] as it is with both widespread and idiosyncratic tendencies towards divisional ('bite-sized chunks') and unificatory

1 Genette's 1997 paratexts are literal edges such as preliminary notices, perhaps as close to the core as prefaces and dust jackets, whereas Alden 2000 uses the term 'para-narratives' (perhaps with greater etymological justification) for paradigmatic narrative diversions in Homeric poems, a phenomenon which I would regard as one of the central examples of intratextuality, although she does not use the term. In the volume edited by Jansen 2014, ancient paratexts stand somewhere in between, in several cases closer to the intratextual than in Genette, for practical reasons of survival, for intra-, para-, and extra-textual reading. Intratextual criticism predates the explicit development of a theory: when I first discussed the theory in Sharrock 2000, I failed to note the use of this terminology, in ways entirely in keeping with my understanding of the phenomenon, in Landolfi 1997. Sharrock 2000, 4 n. 8 discusses the history of the term, including reference to an early example in Frangoulidis 1997.

2 As is often argued for Homer, examples being Alden 2000, 4, and Minchin 2001, 70.

https://doi.org/10.1515/9783110611021-002

strategies in the phenomenology of reading. Since intratextuality begs questions about how the literary mind works, it might seem profitable to consider whether any light can be shown by other forms of investigation into the human mind.

2 The 'cognitive turn'

In recent years, particularly since the new millennium brought about an artificial but powerful barrier between the 20th and 21st centuries, scholars interested in Theory, myself included, have been wondering where we go next, now that post-structuralism has undergone a mixture of debunking and naturalisation, and totalising theories have become somewhat tarred, at least in their most explicit forms, with the damaging brush of 20th century totalitarianism. I remain convinced that one of the most interesting questions to be asked in our field is how meaning happens, what counts as a valid reading, how we communicate it, and what we think it is that we are doing with our 2000-year-old texts. Some scholars in recent years have looked to the cognitive sciences for help in exploring the phenomenon of literature.

The terminology of the 'cognitive turn', however, is (tellingly) unfortunate, both in that the language and its underlying actuality pertain to a kind of insecure aping of our scientific masters in the contemporary STEM world, and also by an implication of radical newness, as if reading, writing, and telling stories had not always been cognitive processes. The history of literary scholarship's interaction with a range of relevant disciplines (primarily cognitive linguistics, cognitive psychology, and neuroscience) can be and has been told in a number of different ways. For me, the best work in cognitive literary criticism is that which is most firmly grounded in its literary history and which tempers its claims for the newness and significance of what cognitive sciences can contribute to the understanding and appreciation of literature. My story of cognitive literary criticism would be the one which traces its history in reader-response criticism, including especially the phenomenology of Iser 1974, whose work is regarded by some as cognitive *avant la lettre*.[3] I would single out in particular a book by Terence Cave,

3 See Fludernik 2014, an afterword to a special issue of the journal *Style* on cognitive approaches to literature. Fludernik usefully shows the continuity between cognitive approaches and mainstream literary criticism. For example: 'the Russian formalist notion of defamiliarisation is, basically, a cognitive concept'. Barthes' reality effect and Iser's phenomenology of reception and gaps are described as looking, from a present-day perspective, 'suspiciously "cognitive"'. See also the introduction to Bernearts *et al.* 2013. That volume is worthwhile for its explicit interest

a literary critic with extensive knowledge of 'cognitive approaches', but free from the fundamentalist evangelising that mars some studies in this area. He begins: 'it [*cognitive literary criticism*] should be a literary criticism worthy of the name, resisting integration into extraneous agendas for which literature would provide mere illustrative examples, but at relevant points inflected by frames of reference, terminology, conjectures, and the like drawn from across the spectrum of cognitive disciplines.'[4]

'Cognitive approaches' can be divided into two broad categories: scientific/empirical and reflective. The first includes both neural imaging (science) and participant-observation/questionnaires (social science), while the second (reflective) is closer to traditional humanities methodologies but draws in a secondary manner on insights from other disciplines. The reflective methodology is, I believe, both the most practically useful for Classics and yet also holds the greatest risks of overstatement. As a number of scholars have warned, transference of (perhaps improperly understood) concepts from one field to another may be at best metaphorical and at worst misleading.[5] The question for this paper is what, if anything, 'cognitive approaches' can offer towards greater understanding of how texts fit together and of the work of readers in constructing interpretations of texts. While this paper cannot hope to do justice to the full range of literary readings that could justifiably be called 'cognitive', the following issues have seemed to me to be of relevance to intratextual enquiry. What do we mean when we talk about 'readings', and about the engagement of 'readers' with texts? Can insights about the workings of memory offer anything to intratextual study? How

---

in narrative and narratology, though I found it sometimes a bit over-zealous. The introduction is good on situating cognitive narratology in relation to its forerunners in phenomenology, reception theory, and classical narratology.

4 Cave 2016, vi. I would mention also (with some reservations) Burke and Troscianko 2017, *Style* 2014, *Poetics Today* 2011, Zunshine 2015, Bernearts *et al.* 2013. For an account of the relevant neuroscience written by a literary scholar, see Armstrong 2013. Ryan 2010 exposes, from a position of knowledge, some of the pitfalls of cognitive literary work. For an example of specifically classical cognitive criticism, see Budelmann and Easterling 2010. The work of Douglas Cairns on metaphor is very valuable in this important subarea of the cognitive, which I am not addressing in this paper. See for example Cairns 2016. Lakoff and Johnson 1999 relates to this tradition, but I found it rather too committed to a particular manifestation of 'embodiment' (see further below), for which they make extravagant claims.

5 Bruhn 2011 is a major introductory article to a special issue of *Poetics Today* on cognitive approaches to literature, and is helpfully sceptical about some of the wilder claims of the cognitive turn: 'central principles and terms of scientific enquiry, such as reproducibility and falsification, apply to literary studies only in an "approximative" sense at best' (418).

can recent formulations of the embodied and extended mind reflect on our work as critics of ancient texts?

3 What is a reader?

Allow me for a moment to draw you into a fantasy, which I hope will illustrate not only what neuroscience cannot do but also what counts as the reading of an ancient text. Imagine, if you will, a research project, in collaboration between a classical literary critic and a real live scientist, in which a large number of people are wired up to an fMRI machine, while they read some Latin poetry, to see whether their brains light up in the same way. To take an intratextual example, we might like to try to find out what proportion of people have a brain-reaction, without being told to look out for it, to the resonance between *dum conderet urbem* at Virg. *Aen.* 1.5 and *ferrum...condit* at 12.950. If so, would this *actually prove* the rightness of a reading which interprets the death of Turnus as the inevitable but despicable consequence of Roman imperialism?

Of course not. Not only would there be all sorts of practical difficulties in such an experiment, but also the recognition of a connection is only a preliminary to interpretation, which in such a case could go in any of several different, even opposing, directions. Neural imaging is very non-specific (shared by a vast range of activities, in animals as well as humans) and is currently unable to tell us anything about the subjective experience of literature.[6] My example is a parody, but it raises questions that I think are important.

The greatest benefit for me in considering opportunities and threats raised by the empirical study of literature is being forced to think in detail about what we mean by a 'reader'. On the empirical side of cognitive literary studies, scholars attempt and discuss experiments with 'civilians' as readers, rather than literary specialists. For us readers of ancient texts, in a language which has no native

6 Caracciolo 2014, 385 poses the problem well: 'how is it possible to reconcile literary interpretation as a specifically cultural form of meaning-making with the generalised aims and reductionist methods of the cognitive sciences?' This goes to the heart of the problem. Anything that we might measure using scientific methodologies is unlikely to tell us anything interesting in response to humanities research questions. The risk, as noted here also, is that the object of study is the human brain/nature, rather than the work of literature. Caracciolo suggests (399) that the gap may not be susceptible to closing, but that it might be possible to bridge it, which I found less convincing. For a polemical attack on humanities academics' over-interpretation of neuroscientific phenomena, see Tallis 2008.

speakers, we would have an additional difficulty in any such undertaking, arising from the fact that we have no 'lay' or 'civilian' readers.[7] Even if such an experiment as my disingenuous bit of Virgilian ring composition were possible, for any outcome to be meaningful – in the statistical terms on which such experiments are predicated – one would need to have a large evidence-base. Our first problem would be that although we could in theory wire up all the competent Latin readers in the world and probably thereby acquire a meaningful sample, it is impossible to imagine someone with sufficient linguistic competence who would never have heard of the possibility of ring composition, or of the debate surrounding the end of the *Aeneid*. Although one might be able to design questionnaire-based experiments which would have the potential to create useful data, we would not be able to test them on lay readers. But useful for what? I can imagine that it might be interesting to see how widely a particular reaction is shared, whether the information is sought by neural imaging or by self-reported response, but I suspect that the interest would be greater for the student of contemporary psychology and sociology than it would be for the literary critic. If it were possible (currently, I believe, it is not) to get meaningful data on all competent readers over a period of time, the extent to which those data change over time might have a contribution to make to literary theory about the embeddedness of any particular reading in its own historical moment. Most likely it would only tell us what we already believe to be the case.

But the crucial point, and the fundamental difference between empirical studies of readers and literary criticism, is this: even if we could devise an experiment using readers who are neither specialists nor students (or former students), how far would we regard the outcome of their brain-responses, whether neural or self-reported, as 'proof' of the rightness of the interpretation? I suggest that the answer is — not very far at all. Although some people might feel that this is an elitist and even arrogant attitude, my intention is not to undermine the validity of any individual's reaction to an ancient poem. Rather, it is to describe what we actually do. Burke and Troscianko claim that the benefit of cognitive literary science (their term) is 'that instead of basing conclusions about textual effects on the singular experience of the critic-as-reader disguised as the generic reader, or accumulating new interpretations without acknowledgement of the cognitive factors on which they depend, we can understand interpretations as cognitive

7 Kuzmičová 2013, 121 is a rare explicit acknowledgement that empirical literary studies are limited to contemporary readers. The paper goes on to attempt a study of ancient responses via ancient rhetoric.

effects, and investigate their natural variations in others as well as ourselves'.[8] I am not convinced that cognitive literary science is able to deliver in this way, but, be that as it may, my argument in this paper is intended to suggest that the experience of the critic-as-reader is neither 'singular' nor 'disguised as the generic reader'. Anyone's reading might be valid for him or herself, but readings which we come to accept as powerful and original (and therefore publishable) tend to be precisely those which stand outside the cloud.[9]

The ancient reader, obviously, cannot be either wired up to an fMRI machine or asked to fill in a questionnaire. Once we begin to think about real readers, we must consider the question of how far our 'reader' is to be identified with an 'ancient reader'. There are some 21st-century scholars of classical literature who would say that what they are interested in is the 'original reader', some who regard their main interest as the 'modern reader', and some who would want to think of a complicated, perhaps fuzzy, but often creative, combination of the two. I regard all these approaches as valid in their own terms, but as requiring careful scrutiny as to their underlying assumptions. For example, when we start thinking about readers in experimental terms, we have to become much more explicit about the evidence-base. By 'ancient reader' of the *Aeneid*, do we include every competent reader of/listener to the Latin language from the 20s BC up to the fifth century AD? Or do we mean the elite group of people who may have been present at preliminary readings of parts of the poem before its completion, if indeed those took place? Virgil's fellow poets and friends? All first century BC readers? My contention, to cut it short, is that all our so-called readers are hypothetical. It may indeed be critically acceptable for us to construct details of and constraints around our hypothetical reader, and (this is crucial) to do so differently for different purposes, but we should not deceive ourselves into imagining that we could ever meaningfully describe a real ancient reader.[10]

In conversation with my colleague Andrew Morrison, I have come to the following conclusion about the 'reader', as regards interpretation, one which would entail a stronger rejection of the role of empirical initial responses by 'real readers': interpretation is more than reading, and 'readers' in criticism are always heuristic tools, which we use to help us conceptualise the effects of a text, and in

---

8 Burke and Troscianko 2017, 11. See also Gibbs 2017 on the relationship between expert and general readers.

9 Up to a point, of course. The literary critic has to tread a careful line between 'originality' and 'situation within the scholarship'.

10 The partial exception might appear to be an ancient reader who also writes, as in the case of Virgil's best reader, Ovid, but then the hermeneutic process begins again in the same way and with the same problems.

turn to help create larger interpretations, which in their own turn depend for their success on their acceptance, at least partial, by interpretative communities. Andrew pointed out that the kind of fleeting impressions texts leave us as we read are not really interpretations (though they can lead to them, or be turned into them, in conversation, study, and written expression). A significant difference between what we are doing in reading ancient texts and the kind of empirical 'first impressions' that some cognitive scholars aim to learn from their civilian readers is that the process described as interpretation in this paragraph comes not only from reading but also, especially, from rereading. For us to be willing to think that a feature is 'there in the text', surely we would not expect it always to be available on first reading? More information about the range of first impressions, and indeed second and third impressions, might help us formulate readings, but never substitute for them.[11]

Moreover, there are great differences between the way we read ancient texts now and the ways in which they were originally received, not to mention the differences over the intervening millennia. Many of these differences are well known, including those relating to the technology of the book, levels of personal literacy, contexts of reading, and wider socio-political backgrounds. What is perhaps less often considered are some of the peculiarities of the way we read now (and here I mean primarily scholars of classical literature). First, most of our reading of classical literature is rereading, as rarely do we have the luxury of reading a new text for the first time. Second, we are not native speakers of Latin. Third, much of our reading is not linear, in the form of uninterrupted or even episodic but continuous cover-to-cover reading of complete texts. To speak for myself, while I do periodically read major works such as the poems of Virgil and Ovid in a 'straight-through' manner, I spend a great deal more time jumping about, reading individual passages, studying repetitions of words and phrases from disparate parts of poems, and thinking about imagery, themes, and words from the poems which I put together in different ways in my mind. My impression from speaking to younger colleagues is that 'straight-through' reading is becoming even less common. The realities of our changing habits of reading should not be regarded, I suggest, as lapsarian inadequacy, but rather as part of the dynamic of

11 Gibbs 2017, 221, acknowledges that cognitive studies have traditionally used 'naive readers' first-time pass through'. They tend to be interested in 'fast-acting unconscious processes', but he claims that we can move beyond this point because of the 'important communalities' between recreational and critical readers (his terms). His argument is that both naive and critical reading involve embodied simulation, which is no doubt true as far as it goes.

literature.[12] We could regard the common non-linearity of practice as in continuity with an essential intratextual feature, which is the ability of what Barthes calls 'connotation' to 'spread like gold dust on the apparent surface of the text'.[13] In describing Barthes' connotation as 'that aspect of the reading text which allows meaning to break free from a linear, consecutive order',[14] Allen explicates an intertextual mechanism which, I suggest, has even greater significance for intratextuality. I shall have more to say on the diachronic dynamic of literature below, but first I should like to reflect a little on an elephant in the room of this section: memory.

4 Memory

An important point that we should all learn, for our lives as well as our criticism, from recent work on memory in cognitive psychology and neuroscience, as well as cultural studies, is the extent to which memory is more like a re-creation based on traces in the brain, than it is like the computer model of data to be retrieved.[15] When we remember something, be it accurately or inaccurately, we do not just pull a piece of information out of somewhere in our brains, but rather we construct a new piece of information, to which the memory laid down by initial intake via our senses contributes, alongside many other associations whether conscious or unconscious. Memory is also highly susceptible to suggestion and is affected by prior expectations and beliefs of the memoriser. The study of memory has played an important role in some of the earliest examples of empirical work on classical literature, as in the researches of Lord and Parry, more recently revisited in the light of developments in cognitive science by Minchin.[16] While these

---

12 Indeed, while linear reading has played a larger role in the past than it does today, we also have reason to suppose that beginning-to-end experience was not the only manner of even first-time reading in antiquity, as is indicated by the story of Virgil's performance before Augustus of selected books of the *Aeneid* (the literal truth or otherwise of the story is irrelevant).

13 Barthes 1974, 9.

14 Allen 2000, 83–5.

15 See Kukkonen and Caracciolo 2014, 261, who explain how first-generation theories in the cognitive sciences perceived and discussed the mind as like a computer, whereas second-generation approaches 'reject previous models of the mind as unduly limited to information processing, placing mental processes instead on a continuum with bio-evolutionary phenomena and cultural practices'.

16 Lord 1960, Parry 1971. Minchin 2001 argues for revision of the Parry-Lord view of the building blocks of Homeric epic as requiring a high level of intensive memorising, replacing it with

studies are focused on the memory of the poet, there has also been a growing interest in literary studies in the workings of memory in the reader.[17]

Since intratextuality's interest includes the question of how disparate parts of texts fit together, and how the presence of an element in one part of the text may make itself felt in the realisation of a far-distant place, an apparently obvious way in which cognitive science might be beneficial to intratextual study is with regard to the workings of memory. An all-too-easy objection to intratextual arguments which depend on linking disparate parts of texts, particularly large texts, is the claim that the reader/listener would not remember the earlier instance when she/he reaches the later one. My impression is that there is indeed something to be learned here from empirical studies, but that the problems identified in my previous section remain at issue, the greatest of which is that empirical studies of memory for text are almost always based on non-specialist readers' first-time pass through a piece of writing. As I have stressed, this is not in fact how we read and interpret our texts. Nonetheless, there are aspects of such work that may have a role in guiding our methodology. In this section, I shall suggest both that there are things we can learn from studies of memory, but on the other hand that interpretation is not based on the weakest link of memory.

Tillman and Dowling make the case, based on empirical study, that memory for surface details of prose falls off with delay, but with music it does so much less. It is important to stress that this discussion is concerned with surface details, such as vocabulary-choice and exact phrasing. They then investigated poetry, as something in between prose and music, to try to help explain the difference. They say: 'if the important factor explaining the difference between memory for prose and music is just that of verbal versus musical material (i.e., the presence or absence of semantic content), poetry should show a pattern of results that is the same as that for prose and different from that for music. If the temporal structure is the important factor, poetry should produce results like those from music and different from those for prose.'[18] What they found was that memory-response to poetry was more like that to music than that to prose. While it seems likely that we would indeed expect memory for surface details in poetry to be greater than that in prose, given the need for vocabulary to fit the meter, this finding offers

insights gained from late 20th-century understandings of memory, in which the role of existing schemas (or 'scripts', in the sense of a play-script, not in the written sense) drawn from ordinary experience enables more creative use of the building blocks. Further developments of memory studies in the last 20 years would support this direction of travel, away from simple information-retrieval and towards memory-as-reconstruction.

17 Lyne 2016 is an example of the interaction between memory and intertextuality.

18 Tillman and Dowling 2007, 629.

corroboration of the intuition that there is a value in thinking about metrical shape and line-position of words involved in an intratextual connection.[19] When I mentioned the study to my colleague Roy Gibson, he remarked that this would fit with his impression from work on the *Ars Amatoria* and prose texts. He believes that the intertext with the greatest *intellectual* significance is the first book of Cicero's *De Officiis*, and yet overwhelmingly the authors most frequently 'alluded to' in *Ars* 3 are Propertius and Virgil, followed by Lucretius. He suggests that this might be because Ovid expected his readers to be able to remember Virgil and Propertius (elegant phrasing and strict metrical structures) but was much less confident about what he calls 'Cicero's rather hurried prose'.

The relationship between surface details and semantic content is of great importance for intratextual study. At first sight, the finding that memory for surface details is relatively poor compared with that for semantic content might seem like a problem for our regular practice of drawing attention to repetition of specific words as a basis for interpretation (although perhaps it might support our practice of drawing on thematic connections). Bortolussi and Dixon 2013 discuss a study which aimed to investigate whether memory for the substitution of a word by a near-synonym could be influenced by various factors. When attention was drawn to the place where the change was to occur by means of some form of *semantic* (as opposed to stylistic) foregrounding, memory, as tested by the recall of exact wording versus synonym, was actually reduced. This, it was presumed, was because the foregrounding caused concentration on content, to the detriment of surface details. Other studies reported in that volume have also suggested that readers' memory for details is less accurate than we would like to think. I suggest, however, that the problem for interpretation is a mirage, not only because of the first-time reader issue, but also because all the studies were concerned with prose texts, generally complex novels, in which reading for the plot will have been almost overwhelming. And yet the test was for surface details, not plot.

But whether the focus is on individual words or some other kind of textual element, such as repeated imagery, parallel scenes, topoi, or allusive mini-narratives, these linkages are at the core of intratextuality. Contemporary studies of memory may not initially seem to give much support for the inevitability of interpretations based on such linkages, but, I suggest, this is because these interpretations are not inevitable – they are constructed. (The fact that memory is itself more re-creation than pure retrieval may be helpful here.) Ovid's *Metamorphoses* is one of the most intratextually rich and difficult of ancient poems, with its

---

19 The case for the metrical role in greater memorability, intuitively obvious, is empirically supported also by the studies reported in Hanauer 2001.

superabundance of characters and dazzling complexity of narrative line, such that it can be difficult even for experts to keep everything in place. And yet we regularly base interpretations on disparate parts of the poem.[20] Juxtaposed episodes like the rape and metamorphoses of Daphne (tree), Io (cow), and Syrinx (reed pipe) tell one kind of intratextual story, but equally powerful (if not so immediately accessible) are all the stories of women turned into trees, from Daphne's dubious escape to Myrrha's agonising parturition, and culminating in the reverse-metamorphosis of Aeneas' wooden ships into sea-nymphs. Likewise, great critical benefits have come from intratextual matching up of disparate stories, from Narcissus and Pygmalion,[21] Narcissus and the missing Oedipus,[22] the 'intratextual footnotes' of tragic characters in the epic,[23] to the Golden Age in books 1 and 15.[24] In a recent paper, I brought together Narcissus and Orpheus (six books apart), not because anything to link them occurred to me on one of my periodic reads-through of the whole poem, but because I was looking for cases where the storyline splits into two and continues with its protagonist beyond his or her death – of which these two cases turned out to be the most marked.[25] Although I would not suggest that the point I am about to make is crucial for acceptance of widely-spaced intratextual links, it seems to me worth mentioning that, in practice, episodic reading of the *Metamorphoses* not only is more common than linear reading, but also reflects early experience of the poem by most of its readers. Most people today will have read Narcissus and at least some of Orpheus before they have read the poem as a whole. I suggest, therefore, that initial memory is subordinate to creative study in the development of intratextual responses to texts.

This is not to say, however, that we should ignore questions of memorability. Bortolussi and Dixon also discuss some quite old empirical studies which show that syntactical completion (end of sentence or clause) causes a reduction in memory: 'When the phrase to be recalled was in the current sentence, recall was substantially better than when the same words were from a preceding sentence, even when the serial position was precisely controlled.'[26] This finding was then reproduced more recently with children's reading 'even when the number of

---

20 Fulkerson and Stover 2016.

21 Rosati 1983.

22 Gildenhard and Zissos 2000. Hardie 2002 is paradigmatic for the Ovidian absent presence.

23 Curley 2013, chapter 6.

24 Ntanou 2018.

25 Sharrock 2018. Likewise, Oliensis' 2004 excellent intratextual reading of *disiecta membra* in/of the *Aeneid* is dependent on repetitions and citations widely spread through the poem.

26 Bortolussi and Dixon 2013, 26.

intervening words was the same'. It seems reasonable to suppose that for us, as non-native speakers of Latin, it would be particularly true that we would hold words closely in mind until they are syntactically complete. It would be surprising if this were not the case for native speakers of Latin, if it is even true for speakers of the relatively syntactically impoverished contemporary English. Does this information help us with anything? While I was working on this paper, I was asked by a recent PhD student, Helen Dalton, who was preparing an article on *arma uirumque* in Statius, what I thought about how far apart we should allow the two words to be for them to be on the list for consideration as significant. She had been looking at just a single line, but had read an article looking at a similar idea in Silius Italicus, where the author allowed up to five lines of intervening text. She was particularly concerned that any decision about the range was arbitrary. As so often with attempts to create a formula for a textual effect, each example has to be considered in its own terms, but we need some parameters in order to be able to start thinking about the question, so I suggested that it would be worth trying the search by sense unit. What we are doing with the initial search (how many lines apart, etc.) is simply to draw up a list of possibles from which one chooses examples that work, by means of what we can only call expert subjectivity, or good, old-fashioned judgement. I would not by any means suggest that collocations of words are irrelevant for interpretation if they belong to separate sense units, but it nonetheless seems to me that the knowledge, however limited, that memory falls off at the end of the sense unit can help us make less-arbitrary decisions about how we do our initial searches.

Here lies a point underappreciated (at least, by me initially) regarding the contribution of cognitive approaches to literary reading. Much of what the cognitive has to offer is at the level of stylistics rather than semantics, of surface features rather than interpretation.[27] It is perhaps better regarded as a tool towards interpretation, rather than a methodology for interpretation in its own right.

5 Minding the gap

It has been axiomatic in Classics, before we heard of the cognitive turn, that ancient readers had better memories than do their modern counterparts, who are weakened by the easy availability of abundant printed texts, dictionaries, and most recently the resources of full-text searching and the Internet. Such a story

27 Stockwell 2009 is a strong statement of this point.

of decline would fit with contemporary neuroscientific understanding of brain plasticity, that we must 'use it or lose it', but before we condemn ourselves for our literary laziness, we might also consider that we are in fact using these tools in new and creative ways which will mean that the brain which reads Ovid or Virgil now has significant positive differences from, as well as continuities with (and indeed no doubt negative differences from), that which first read or heard the *Metamorphoses* and the *Aeneid*.

This leads me to another way in which cognitive developments can help us think about readers, via the notion of the 'extended mind'. This is the idea, not unconnected with the great effort to oppose the Cartesian mind-body dichotomy, that the mind should be conceived of as in continuity with any tools it may use. I have been excited, though not without reservations, by recent improvements in digital tools such as *tesserae* and *musisque deoque*, which allow us to explore the corpus of Latin literature more creatively even than we could with searches of the PHI Disk and before that with concordances. While people most often mention the intertextual use of these tools, there is also huge potential for them to contribute to an intratextual study. Although we still need to use subjective literary judgement to produce a reading, nevertheless these tools do enable us to identify candidates with intertextual and intratextual potential at a speed and with an ease which is much greater than that of 19th-century readers of Latin literature, to say nothing of first century readers. Should we be worried that these mechanisms (affordances, as they would be called in the cognitive jargon) might be encouraging us to construct readings of textual connection that would not be available to earlier readers? Although one response to this concern would be to draw attention to the better memories of premodern readers, another answer (from the other end of the spectrum regarding the nature of the 'reader') would be to say that digital databases are simply part of the extended contemporary mind and that if we are at all interested in contemporary readers (something which I would say we cannot avoid), then we must allow for and include all the affordances available to them.

The 'extended mind' forms part of a nexus of images in cognitive literary study, which is sometimes described as the 4Es: enactive, embedded, embodied, and extended (with optional additions in the form of experiential and emotional). One part of embodied reading puts stress on the 'kinesic', or sensorimotor, aspects of reading also regarded by many of its proponents as 'cognitive'. A significant role in the cognitively-inspired kinesic approaches to literature is the story of 'mirror neurons'. In brief, mirror neurons, whose existence is proven for some primates and strongly suspected for humans, are elements in the brain which light up in response to observation of certain movements, in the same way as they light up for the performance of those movements. The mirror neurons are highly susceptible to overinterpretation by humanities scholars, but the interest which they have provoked can usefully encourage attention to textual elements which we might have missed.[28] Although not everyone (myself included) will want to sign up to the 4E theory and its jargon, I suggest that there are elements in these studies that can remind us to pay attention and help us look at details in a new way. They work, it seems to me, a bit like a Shklovsky's stone for critics, helping to trip us up and make us look at literature more carefully.

This potential usefulness is true of a cognitive cluster I perceive surrounding 'mind-reading, mentalising, theory of mind'. Mind-reading might sound rather futuristic, but as it is used by cognitive critics it is, at its most basic level, simply an explanation of the way communication works. Someone, a character or author, says something, which a receiver, internal or external, interprets by trying to work out what the speaker means, is trying to say, and is thinking. In doing so, the receiver posits a mind, be it fictional or factual or somewhere in between, which is different from the receiver's own. That, in cognitive psychology, is 'theory of mind'. This is not incompatible with theories of literature which stress the role of the reader in the construction of meaning, and even those which would not regard authorial intention, stated or otherwise, as having complete control over the meaning of the text.[29] Likewise, what the speaker omits to say – the gaps – provokes an even greater activity of mind-reading on the part of the receiver.

---

28 See Kukkonen and Caracciolo 2014, 264: 'the so-called mirror neurons in the brain... fire in imitation when we perceive an action; similar claims have been made for their role in mirroring actions we hear or read about in the linguistic communication'. The example given, however, suggests to me that ordinary literary interpretation is more useful. Kukkonen and Caracciolo discuss Squire Allworthy in Fielding's *Tom Jones*, where we are following the Squire's movement up to the pinnacle of his self-pride. As a way of talking about how the text can draw the reader in, the account works quite well, but my immediate reaction to the passage is at one step removed, where I am interacting with the narrator, who is observing and communicating to me the arrogance and self-importance of the character, rather than making me engage with the movement of said character. I don't know which neurons would be firing for that! Furthermore, Kukkonen and Caracciolo notice the problem of historical literature, but claim that 'historical practices and embodiment as a biological and cognitive condition are not opposed but, on the contrary, caught in a dialectic relationship, so that exploring the background of bodily invariants can improve our understanding of historical specificities, and vice versa.' A problem for me is how sure we can be that these bodily features are indeed invariant across time and place. Brain plasticity might suggest significant differences.

29 See Abbot 2011, who argues for the role of the implied author against the actual one. Bernini 2014 makes a case for cognitive literary criticism as bringing authorial intention back into centre stage. I did not find this convincing, except at the trivial level that authors have intentions and those intentions affect their work.

Moreover, many critics would say that the need for readers to fill in the gaps is precisely central to literature.[30] Indeed, evidence from cognitive psychology and empirical studies with readers indicates that the mind of the reader, any reader, will see different gaps and fill them in in different ways.[31] While I am not suggesting that cognitive science can prove the rightness of any particular reading, and I would answer negatively my question about whether the cognitive turn can control how we read wholes and holes, I would nonetheless take its evidence of the wide range of human responses to the same text as encouragement to keep reading.

6 Epilogue

It is a common (and in my view justified) complaint against approaches to literature which call themselves 'cognitive', that the term and its revolutionary claims are at best excessive, in that the results seem to be not massively different from what can be achieved by traditional methods. Many examples of cognitive work are asking different questions from those which are of concern to classical literary critics. At its worst, there is a tendency in cognitive literary criticism to overinterpretation of neurological notions such as mirror neurons and synapses, which tell us very little about texts, human readers, or readers as heuristic tools. On the other hand, however, thinking harder about thinking can certainly help us to be more precise about the theoretical underpinning for what we do, as well as drawing our attention to aspects of texts which we might otherwise simply read over without noticing. Having spent considerable time investigating the issue, I cannot recommend the 'cognitive turn' as revolutionary for the study, intratextual and otherwise, of classical texts, but I for one shall be keeping my ear to the ground as the story develops.

Latin poets seem to be particularly interested in gaps, including back stories, alternative versions, and missing expectations. While Ovid is the master of this phenomenon, it is manifested in poets from Plautus to Catullus to Statius. Perhaps what the ancient literary culture can indicate is that poets and readers who

---

30 Iser's work is central to this notion (see Iser 1974). See also Bernearts *et al.* 2013, 2–4 (quotation on p.3), who note that subjective experience would not register at neural level, but that: 'there is a profound awareness amongst theorists of mind as well as theorists of narrative that the construction and interpretation of narratives as coherent wholes paradoxically require gaps, empty spaces, and hidden information.'
31 See for example Gibbs 2017.

are working with an enclosed or even limited corpus of both myth and generic expectation are in a strong position to communicate things unspoken. It might perhaps not be unreasonable for us to take this possibly self-evident truth about Latin poetry as justification for making ourselves especially attuned to what is not said.

Bibliography

Abbot, H.P. (2011), 'Reading Intended Meaning Where None is Intended: A Cognitivist Reappraisal of the Implied Author', *Poetics Today* 32.3, 461–87.

Alden, M. (2000), *Homer Beside Himself: Para-Narratives in the Iliad*, Oxford.

Allen, G. (2000), *Intertextuality*, London.

Armstrong, P.B. (2013), *How Literature Plays with the Brain: The Neuroscience of Reading and Art*, Baltimore.

Barthes, R. (1974), *S/Z*, (trans. R. Howard), New York.

Bernearts, L./de Geest, D./Herman, L./Vervaeck, B. (2013), 'Introduction: Cognitive Narrative Studies: Themes and Variations', in: *eidem* (eds.), *Stories and Minds: Cognitive Approaches to Literary Narrative*, Lincoln/London, 1–20.

Bernearts, L./de Geest, D./Herman, L./Vervaeck, B. (eds.) (2013), *Stories and Minds: Cognitive Approaches to Literary Narrative*, Lincoln/London.

Bernini, M. (2014), 'Supersizing Narrative Theory: On Intention, Material Agency, and Extended Mind-workers', *Style* 48.3, 349–66.

Bortolussi, M./Dixon, P. (2013), 'Minding the text: memory for literary narrative', in: Bernearts, L./de Geest, D./Herman, L./Vervaeck, B. (2013) (eds.), *Stories and Minds: Cognitive Approaches to Literary Narrative*, Lincoln/London, 23–38.

Bruhn, M.J. (2011), 'Introduction: Exchange Values: Poetics and Cognitive Science', *Poetics Today* 32.3, 403–60.

Budelmann, F., and Easterling, P. (2010), 'Reading Minds in Greek Tragedy', *Greece and Rome* 57.2, 289–303.

Burke, M./Troscianko, E. (eds.) (2017), *Cognitive Literary Science: Dialogues between Literature and Cognition*, Oxford.

Burke, M./Troscianko, E. (2017), 'Introduction: A Window onto the Landscape of Cognitive Literary Science', in: Burke, M./Troscianko, E. (eds.) (2017), *Cognitive Literary Science: Dialogues between Literature and Cognition*, Oxford, 1–13.

Cairns, D. (2016), 'Mind, Body, and Metaphor in Ancient Greek Concepts of Emotion', *L'Atelier du Centre de recherche historique* 16: http://acrh.revues.org/7416.

Caracciolo, M. (2014), 'Interpretation for the Bodies: Bridging the Gap', *Style* 48.3, 385–403.

Cave, T. (2016), *Thinking with Literature: Towards a Cognitive Criticism*, Oxford.

Curley, D. (2013), *Tragedy in Ovid: Theatre, Metatheatre, and the Transformation of a Genre*, Cambridge.

Fludernik, M. (2014), 'Afterword', *Style* 48.3, 404–10.

Frangoulidis, S. (1997), 'Intratextuality in Apuleius' *Metamorphoses*', *L'Antiquité Classique* 66, 293–9.

Fulkerson, L./Stover, T. (eds.) (2016), *Repeat Performance: Ovidian Repetition and the Metamorphoses*, Madison.

Genette, G. (1997), *Paratexts: Thresholds of Interpretation*, trans. J. Lewin, Cambridge.
Gibbs, R. (2017), 'Embodied Dynamics in Literary Experience', in: Burke, M./Troscianko, E. (eds.) (2017), *Cognitive Literary Science: Dialogues between Literature and Cognition*, Oxford, 219–37.
Gildenhard, I./Zissos, A. (2000), Ovid's Narcissus (*Met.* 3.339–510): Echoes of Oedipus', *American Journal of Philology* 121, 129–47.
Hanauer, D. (2001), 'What we Know about Reading Poetry: Theoretical Positions and Empirical Research', in: D. Schram/G. Steen (eds.), *The Psychology and Sociology of Literature: In honor of Elrud Ibsch*, Amsterdam, 107–28.
Iser, W. (1974), *The Implied Reader: Patterns of Communication in Prose Fiction from Bunyan to Beckett*, Baltimore/London.
Jansen, L. (ed.) (2014), *The Roman Paratext: Frame, Texts, Readers*, Cambridge.
Kukkonen, K./Caracciolo, M. (2014), 'Introduction: What is the Second Generation?', *Style* 48.3, 261–74.
Kuzmičová, A. (2013), 'The Words and Worlds of Literary Narrative: The Trade-off between Verbal Presence and Direct Presence in the Activity of Reading', in: Bernearts, L./de Geest, D./Herman, L./Vervaeck, B. (eds.) (2013), *Stories and Minds: Cognitive Approaches to Literary Narrative*, Lincoln/London, 107–28.
Lakoff, G./Johnson, M. (1999), *Philosophy in the Flesh: The Embodied Mind and Its Challenge to Western Thought*, New York.
Landolfi, L. (1997), 'Le molte Arianne di Ovidio. Intertestualità e intratestualità in *Her.* 10; *Ars* 1.525–564; *Met.* 8.172–182; *Fast.* 3.459–516', *Quaderni Urbinati di Cultura Classica* 57, 139–17.
Lord, A.B. (1960), *The Singer of Tales*, Cambridge MA.
Lyne, R. (2016), *Memory and Intertextuality in Renaissance Literature*, Cambridge.
Minchin, E. (2001), *Homer and the Resources of Memory: Some Applications of Cognitive Theory to the Iliad and the Odyssey*, Oxford.
Ntanou, E. (2018), *Ovid and Virgil's Pastoral Poetry*, PhD Diss. University of Manchester.
Oliensis, E. (2004), 'Sibylline Syllables: The Intratextual *Aeneid*', *Proceedings of the Cambridge Philological Society* 50, 29–45.
Parry, M. (1971), *The Making of Homeric Verse: The Collected Papers of Milman Parry* (ed. A. Parry), Oxford.
Rosati, G. (1983), *Narciso e Pigmalione: illusione e spettacolo nelle Metamorfosi di Ovidio*, Florence.
Ryan, M.-L. (2010), 'Narratology and Cognitive Science: A Problematic Relation', *Style* 44.4, 469–95.
Sharrock, A. (2000), 'Intratextuality: Parts and (W)holes in Theory', in: Sharrock, A./Morales, H. (eds.), *Intratextuality: Greek and Roman Textual Relations*, Oxford, 1–39.
Sharrock, A. (2018), 'Till death do us Part... Or join: Love Beyond Death in Ovid's *Metamorphoses*', in: S. Frangoulidis/S. Harrison (eds.), *Life, Love and Death in Latin Poetry*, Berlin/Boston, 125–36.
Stockwell, P. (2009), *Texture: A Cognitive Aesthetics of Reading*, Edinburgh.
Tallis, R. (2008), 'The Neuroscience Delusion', *TLS* 9 April 2008.
Tillman, B./Dowling, W.J. (2007), 'Memory Decreases for Prose but not for Poetry', *Memory and Cognition* 35,4, 628–39.
Zunshine, L. (ed.) (2015), *The Oxford Handbook of Cognitive Literary Studies*, Oxford.

Part II: Late Republican and Augustan Lyric Poetry and Elegy

Gail Trimble

Echoes and Reflections in Catullus' Long Poems

What kind of connection between different parts of a text might we be trying to capture with the word 'intratextuality'? One plausible answer might be that intratextuality should be thought of as something comparable to intertextuality. Specifically, the cognitive process for the reader might involve memory over some appreciable distance: something in the text reminds me of something I previously encountered in the same text, long enough ago that I want to say that I am 'remembering' that other moment rather than that it is still in my immediate experience because my eyes encountered it a line or two further up on the same page, or, as I read aloud, I have not yet taken a breath since I uttered it. If this is along the right lines, then it makes sense to talk about Catullus' *longer* poems under the heading of intratextuality. By 'long poems', specifically, I mean those grouped in the corpus as we have it under the numbers 61 to 68.[1] Their actual length varies from the 24 elegiac lines of poem 65 to the 408 or so hexameters of poem 64,[2] but it is generally true for them as it is not for Catullus' other poetry that each of them is long enough in principle to produce intratextual effects in the way just outlined.

Their relative length, however, is not the only prompt for an intratextual investigation of these poems. In a rich chapter in Sharrock/Morales 2000, Theodorakopoulos discusses intratextuality in Catullus 64, reading that longest and densest of the long poems as a labyrinth, a lake of ink, a textile woven of crisscrossing threads:[3] hers is one of many attempts, to which I am adding in my forthcoming commentary on the poem,[4] to respond to its complex structure and texture – one story inside another, dense tangles of chronological confusion – and its perplexing tone – is it a sensuous celebration of the heroic past and/or a lament for historical decline? My approach here, however, draws more closely on work on Catullus 64 that has looked, without the label of intratextuality, at some of the specific means by which the poem creates these complexities: namely, its networks of repetition. This is a frequent theme in criticism of the poem, and I

1 Unless otherwise specified all references are to Catullus. I use the text of Goold 1989 and adapt his translations.
2 The final line is numbered 408, but there is at least one lacuna, after line 23.
3 Theodorakopoulos 2000.
4 Trimble forthcoming.

https://doi.org/10.1515/9783110611021-003

mention only two significant examples. Duban 1980 discusses these networks in terms of 'verbal links', particular words or patterns of language which, by being used perhaps for the abandoned Ariadne *and* the fields around Peleus' house, or for the sea at the beginning of the poem *and* the earth at the end,[5] suggest 'comparison and contrast between various persons, actions, and states of mind'.[6] Duban particularly explores 'verbal links' which help to create the network of imagery or 'imagistic undercurrent' observable in the poem: 'the sea, agriculture, departure, winds/whirlwinds, fire, etc.'[7] Meanwhile, McKie 2009 casts his net more widely to look for *any* individual words (except for extremely common words such as conjunctions or pronouns) which are repeated across some distance in the poem, whether or not their repetition immediately suggests significance.[8] While admitting the subjectivity of his list, McKie finds about 118 cases of such repetition, demonstrating quite how pervasive is the poem's habit of using specific verbal connection to invite a reader to disrupt her linear reading experience by recalling a different moment in the poem. Yet McKie carefully differentiates this 'apparently random' repetition in poem 64 from other repetitious effects in Catullus' other poetry, including specifically the other long poems. I hope to show, however, that it may be fruitful to look at the 'iterations' and other kinds of 'verbal links' in 64 alongside exactly the kinds of repetition in the other long poems that McKie sets to one side: the refrains and amoebean effects in the wedding-songs 61 and 62 (not forgetting that 64 itself contains a wedding-song with a refrain), the more obviously thematic repetition of words for 'seas, woods, fury, darkness, wandering' in the Attis poem, 63, and the 'concentric responsion' or ring-composition of 68b (and 68a).[9]

This investigation will soon lead to observations about links *among* the various long poems: and naturally, when connections between different works by the same author are under consideration, it will always be debatable whether 'intratextuality' or 'intertextuality' is the better term. This is particularly the case with Catullus, his long poems above all, because we know so little about the original textual contexts in which any of them might have been read, and especially about whether Catullus might have arranged them and intended them to be read in the order in which they now stand.[10] Perhaps 64 was 'published' by itself, as the

---

5 Repeated *non* 'not', 64.39–41, 63–5; *imbuere* 'soak', 'initiate', 64.11, 397.

6 Duban 1980, 778.

7 Duban 1980, 779.

8 McKie 2009, 84–92.

9 McKie 2009, 89–90.

10 On the history of this problem, see Skinner 2007.

Smyrna of Cinna seems to have been according to Catullus 95; perhaps it circulated as part of a *libellus* with poems 61–63; perhaps poems 65–68 were the opening of a separate *libellus* of all Catullus' elegiac poetry.[11] Possibly the effects discussed below are ones that Catullus' first readers might have noticed as they remembered passages they had read in an earlier part of the scroll they were still holding, or in a different one; and maybe the fuzzy boundary between intratext and intertext is not best placed too securely either at the point of separation between individual books or – again a point of difficulty with Catullus' long poems, given the debate over the unity or otherwise of what we still tend to call Catullus 68 – at the point of separation between individual poems.[12]

My focus is not on the potential thematic unity of the long poems,[13] nor on such related questions as Catullus' attitude to marriage or the optimism or pessimism of poem 64. Rather, this chapter looks at some of the *ways in which* intratextuality can work: and it is for this reason above all that this group of poems makes an interesting subject. All intratextual connections are textual: they can only work by means of words. But literary texts can and do emulate other art forms which engage with specific senses, and this emulation, I argue, can play a particular part in intratextuality. It is certainly important in Catullus' long poems: 64 contains an extremely extended (and extremely strange) ecphrasis, a mimesis of a work of visual art, while 61 and 62 are – and 64 again contains – mimeses of song, and we will also find mimesis of instrumental music. Some of the intratexts in these poems come as close as a text can to the way in which a picture might exhibit intratextuality – as, to take an imaginary example, a figure dressed in red and white in the bottom left-hand corner of a huge Baroque painting might remind the viewer that when scanning the top right-hand corner he had seen a bloodstained white flag, and might invite him to make and attempt to interpret a connection. I call these 'reflections'. Other examples might have more in common with the effect on a listener either of a repeated leitmotif in a Wagnerian opera or of the recurring theme in a Mozartian rondo. These are 'echoes'. These intratextual appeals via words to our sight and hearing – or at least to our visual and aural imagination – are not limited to the ecphrasis or to the songs, but the presence of the ecphrasis and the songs helps to sensitise us to their appearance

11 The latter two hypotheses have often been presented together as part of an argument that Catullus personally arranged his work into three books: see esp. Baehrens 1876–85, vol. 2, 57–61; Quinn 1972, 9–20. *libellus* 'little book' is a term used twice by Catullus in poem 1 to refer to some collection of his poetry.

12 For an introduction to the bibliography on whether 'Catullus 68' is one poem or two (or three), see Lowrie 2006, 116 n. 5, and for a cogent new argument Leigh 2016.

13 See Skinner 2007, esp. 43–5. Most 1981 offers one stimulating reading in such terms.

elsewhere. Finally, I shall look again at some examples of intratextuality in which what the reader remembers gives a particularly important role to the *words* themselves. This will take us back to an intratextuality very close, simply, to textuality.

1 Echoes: I've heard this before

I begin with aural 'echoes', and with a particularly obvious kind of repetition: the refrain. Refrains are characteristic of song, and thus, in the Greco-Roman literary tradition, characteristic of lyric poetry; it is therefore not surprising that Catullus uses them in his lyric wedding-song, poem 61. However, refrains also enter the hexameter tradition via their use in Theocritus 1 and 2 for the imitation of song,[14] and this underlies the presence of refrains in both of Catullus' hexameter poems, 62 and 64. In these two poems, the respective refrains are used relatively simply, both in the utterances of the groups of boys and girls in 62 and in the song of the Fates in 64.[15] As in Theocritus, the refrain in both cases is almost always just a grammatically independent single line, although the first appearance of the refrain in 62 is preceded by *iam dicetur hymenaeus* 'now will be uttered the wedding-song', which suggests the singers or the author self-consciously flagging it up (62.4), and the first appearance of the Fates' refrain in 64 is attached syntactically by the preceding half-line to produce the extended command *sed uos, quae fata sequuntur, | currite ducentes subtegmina, currite, fusi* 'but you, drawing the threads which the fates follow [or: which follow the fates], run on, spindles, run on' (64.326–7). In subsequent appearances, neither refrain is attached or highlighted in this way, and so a tension develops. On the one hand, the refrain becomes drained of meaning by its frequent repetition, so that the pattern of sounds that the reader hears becomes more important than the meaning that the words convey; on the other, the lines surrounding the refrain on its later recurrences may offer opportunities for new meaning.[16] So, at the end of 62 as the boys apparently win the argument about whether marriage is on balance a good thing for the bride, and the bride herself appears as an addressee (62.49–66), the final appearance of the refrain may be much more clearly understood as an address to the god needed for the marriage, implying 'come here now, Hymen, and get on

14 Theoc. 1.64ff., 2.17ff, 69ff.

15 62.5 = 10, 19, 25, 31, 38, 48, 66 *Hymen o Hymenaee, Hymen ades o Hymenaee* 'Hymen o Hymenaeus, Hymen, come, o Hymenaeus'; 64.327 = 333, 337, 342, 347, 352, 356, 361, 365, 371, 375, 381 *currite ducentes subtegmina, currite, fusi* 'run on, drawing the threads, spindles, run on'.

16 On this effect in 64, see Beyers 1960.

with your task!'. In 64, as the Fates sing of events following the death of Achilles (64.362–71), it becomes suddenly more obvious that in their refrain they are encouraging the threads of his life to run on towards its end.

This understanding may help us to appreciate the much more complex situation in poem 61. Here the two main refrains, like that in 62, centre on the words *Hymen* and *Hymenaee*. The internal repetition across those two words helps to make these refrains more purely musical 'echoes', as does the obscure history of what is internally repeated, the disyllabic sound *hymen*, which may have originated as a ritual cry without denotative meaning before both it and its extended form *hymenaeus* came to be understood either as the name of a god or as a word meaning 'wedding-song'.[17] In the first refrain, *Hymen* and *Hymenaee* appear with the vocative marker *o*, and alongside other second-person language which usually makes it clear that the god is being addressed (61.4–5, 39–40, 49–50, 59–60).[18] But in the second refrain the repeated *o* is replaced by a repeated *io* – still a word associated with invoking the divine,[19] but in a much less straightforwardly vocative way – and the refrain appears amidst addresses to human addressees (61.117–18, 137–8, 142–3, 147–8, 152–3, 157–8, 162–3, 167–8, 172–3, 177–8, 182–3). *io* and *hymen*, probably even *hymenaee* despite its 'vocative' ending, are heard primarily as non-denotative exclamations.

Elsewhere in 61, however, other utterances much more directly motivated by their context become refrains by repetition. In the admiring comment and question addressed (again) to Hymen, *at potest* | *te uolente. quis huic deo* | *compararier ausit?* 'but if you are willing, he/she can. Who would dare to be compared with this god?' (61.63–5, 68–70, 73–5), the final occurrence varies the diction (if the text is right)[20] by using a synonym for 'can', *queat* instead of *potest* (61.73). This detail plays with the question whether this is a directly motivated utterance or a less motivated refrain – and with whether we are listening for sound or sense.[21] Every refrain in 61 appears at the end of a stanza, but the address to the *concubinus* (the former boy favourite of the groom) that occupies the final line of two

17 See further Agnesini 2007 on 62.4, 5.

18 Compare *o* and *ades* 'come' in the refrain in 62 (n. 15).

19 *OLD* s.v.

20 Catullus' text as transmitted requires a great deal of conjectural emendation. For an introduction to the issues, see Butrica 2007.

21 For the replacement of a single word one could compare the first shift in the refrain in Theocritus 1, when ἄρχετε βουκολικᾶς, Μοῖσαι φίλαι, ἄρχετ' ἀοιδᾶς 'begin, dear Muses, begin bucolic songs' (64ff.) is succeeded by ἄρχετε βουκολικᾶς, Μοῖσαι, πάλιν ἄρχετ' ἀοιδᾶς 'begin, Muses, begin again bucolic songs' (94ff.). But this clearly marks the progress of the song: at 61.73 the 'motivation' for the change is much less clear.

consecutive stanzas at 61.128 and 133 in the form *concubine, nuces da* 'favourite, scatter nuts' is a compressed version of the more motivated or meaningful command that opened the first of those stanzas at 61.124–5 *da nuces pueris, iners / concubine* 'scatter nuts to the boys, idle favourite'.[22] Rather similarly, the address to the bride, first introduced in the last two lines of a stanza at 61.90–1 *sed moraris, abit dies: / prodeas, noua nupta* 'but you delay, the day is going by; come out, bride', is echoed in the repetition of *prodeas, noua nupta* at both the beginning and the end of the next stanza (61.92, 96) before it settles into the slightly shorter form *sed abit dies: / prodeas, noua nupta* at the end of two subsequent stanzas (61.105–6, 112–13). It is becoming a refrain, losing much of its meaningful impact; yet it is recalled once more, sixteen stanzas later, when *sed abit dies* 'the day is going by' recurs at 61.192, in the same place in the stanza (the end of the penultimate line), but addressed this time to the groom. The fact that this phrase was part of a musical refrain earlier in the poem now makes it *more* meaningful later, as it provides for the reader who remembers its earlier occurrences an effective mimesis of, precisely, time going by.[23]

If refrains become more purely 'musical' as they are repeated, this effect is likely to be particularly strong in lyric poetry, especially in Latin, in which lyric forms are rare: focusing less on the meaning of the words, the reader becomes more aware of the relatively unfamiliar metre. This may lead to echoes whose strongest element is, quite simply, the echo of that metre. For a reader who remembers the rhythm of poem 61 – not unlikely after 47 rhythmically identical stanzas – there will be an extra depth to Ariadne's regretful reference at 64.141 to the wedding to Theseus that she had hoped for. This hexameter has a very unusual shape, resolvable, as Goold points out in the notes to his edition, into glyconic + pherecratean:[24]

64.141 sed conubia laeta, sed
optatos hymenaeos.

'but a happy marriage, but a longed-for wedding'

---

22 The final appearance of *concubine, nuces da* at 133 is also preceded by 132 *miser ah miser*, producing the sense, 'ah, poor, poor favourite ...'. Compare the treatment of the Fates' refrain in 64, discussed above, p. 38.

23 Some of the effects described in this paragraph find parallels in Bion's *Lament for Adonis*, which uses several components to create lamenting refrains which are sometimes independent of, sometimes more closely motivated by, their immediate surroundings: see Estevez 1981. However, the hexameter poem cannot make the same use of stanzaic form.

24 Goold 1989, 252.

That pattern is the end of a stanza from 61, just the place, in fact, for a refrain, the two most frequently repeated of which, as we have just seen, end not quite *hymenaeos* but *hymenaee*. And yet *hymenaeos*, which Ariadne uses synecdochically to mean 'wedding', more straightforwardly names exactly what 61 is: a wedding-song.

Although poem 62 makes less sophisticated use of its single refrain than 61, it does much more with another technique characteristic of Theocritean hexameters: amoebean responsion.[25] This is not limited to the individual lines in which the boys use classic amoebean technique to 'cap' a point made by the girls at the equivalent stage of the preceding stanza. Consider the opening and closing lines of one of the girls' stanzas, followed by the 'capping' lines from the beginning and end of the answering stanza from the boys:

62.20 Hespere, quis caelo fertur crudelior ignis?
62.24 quid faciunt hostes capta crudelius urbe?

'Hesperus, what crueller fire rides in the sky? ... What crueller deed do foes commit when a city is captured?'

62.26 Hespere, quis caelo lucet iucundior ignis?
62.30 quid datur a diuis felici optatius hora?

'Hesperus, what kinder fire shines in the sky? ... What gift from the gods is more longed-for than this happy hour?'

The comparative *crudelior*/*crudelius* is repeated from one point made by the girls to another. The boys' response to line 24 in line 30 is not as precisely responsive in vocabulary or theme as some amoebean pairs, but instead uses clever syntactical echoes after the opening *quid* – the neuter comparative at the same place in the line, sandwiched by an ablative of comparison rather than an ablative absolute – and also, in its use of *hora* to refer to the hour of evening, makes a thematic connection to the star, *ignis*, which appears as the last word of the boys' line 26 as well as the girls' line 20. These complex patterns of responsion and echo sensitise us to every detail in these lines – and therefore, I believe, cause us to notice another 'echo' in another of the long poems, when Berenice's lock complains at 66.47 *quid facient crines, cum ferro talia cedant?* 'what will tresses do, when such

25 Although reference dictionaries tend to define amoebean predominantly in terms of 'antiphonal singing' and competition (*BNP* s.v. 'Amoibaion', *OCD* s.v. 'amoebean verse'), I follow the usage which associates the word with the sort of large-scale repetition and variation typical of dialogue song in Theocritus and acutely described by Dover 1971, xlv–l.

things yield to iron?' If we are thinking of 61 as well as 62 as we read 66, then not many lines earlier in that poem we may have heard an echo of one of 61's hymeneal refrains: 66.31 *quis te mutauit tantus deus?* 'which god had power enough to change you?'.[26]

The role played by 'echoes' in establishing intertextuality among the long poems may also be observed when we turn from the imitation of song to the imitation of instrumental music. Catullus' long poems contain descriptions of the music involved in the worship of Cybele (63.8–10, 21–2, 29) and of Bacchus (64.259–64). These descriptions are connected thematically, since similar activities and similar musical instruments are associated, especially in literary representations, with these two broadly 'Eastern' orgiastic cults,[27] but they are also connected by their use of techniques appealing to the reader's hearing. The first of these is simply onomatopoeia: the nouns and verbs referring to instruments and sounds often exemplify those sounds (e.g. *ty(m)panum* 'drum', *tibia, tibicen* 'pipe, piper', *stridebat* 'shrieked'), and Catullus underlines this by assembling them with other words to create onomatopoeic alliteration and assonance, often in contrasting groups (e.g. 64.262 *tereti tenuis tinnitus aere ciebant* 'stirred shrill tinklings on [cymbals of] rounded bronze', 64.263 *raucisonos efflabant cornua bombos* 'horns blared out hoarse-sounding booms'). The second, however, is again internal repetition: sensitised by the obvious onomatopoeia to listen to the sound of these passages, we *hear* the epanalepsis of *typanum* in 63.8–9 (a repetition suggesting the beating of this drum, especially when developed by the alliteration of *t* in lines 9–10), and we remember that epanalepsis and the further characterisation of the *typanum* as Cybele's *initia* when, at 64.259–60, we encounter the epanalepsis of *orgia*, a word meaning more or less the same as *initia*, 'sacred objects/sacred rites'.[28] The point here is partly the one which forms the central thesis of Wills 1996, that repetitive patterns in themselves, even when the repeated word is different, can create 'figures of allusion' or of intertextuality,[29] here between one of Catullus' long poems and another; but it is also that such inter- or intratextual effects may be helped by the aural quality of repetition.

Finally, I suggest that an appreciation of Catullus' intra- and intertextual use of echoing refrains may provoke a new reading of the repetition across several of

26 Cf. 61.46–7 *quis deus magis anxiis / est petendus amantibus?* 'which god is more fit to be invoked by anxious lovers?', which echoes *quis huic deo / comparier ausit?* in the refrain discussed above, p. 39. On poem 66 and the intratextuality of the long poems see further below, p. 50.

27 See Trimble forthcoming on 64.261–4.

28 *orgia* seems to mean 'sacred objects' in 64.259 but 'sacred rites' in 64.260, the epanalepsis shifting the meaning: see Trimble forthcoming, *ad loc.*

29 Wills 1996; see esp. 132–3 on epanalepsis in Catullus 64.

his elegiac poems of his laments for his dead brother. At 65.5–12, 68.19–24, 91–100 and in poem 101, the central address to the brother, *frater*, usually repeated, is surrounded by words for being 'taken away' (65.8 *ereptum*, 68.20 *abstulit*, 68.93 *ademptum*, 101.5 *abstulit*), which are sometimes precisely echoed, sometimes varied from passage to passage;[30] three lines are exactly repeated from 68.22–4 to 68.94–6,[31] and the extended address ending with *frater adempte mihi* appears, in the transmitted text, to occur in three different forms: 68.20 *o misero frater adempte mihi*, 68.92 *ei misero frater adempte mihi*, 101.6 *heu miser indigne frater adempte mihi*, 'o/ah/alas, [poor] brother [cruelly] taken away from [poor] me'. As in poem 61, we may ask ourselves whether this is textual corruption to be emended, or provides different versions of a refrain.[32] Reading these repetitions as a refrain might invite us to see them as intratextual rather than intertextual connections, supporting the arguments of those who see Catullus' elegiac corpus as a unity.[33] It would connect Catullus' repeated laments to refrains in the lament tradition.[34] And it might even justify any reading that sees Catullus' protestations of sorrow as somehow losing their impact with repetition, if my argument above is accepted that repeated refrains begin to be heard more for their sound than their meaning.[35]

2 Reflections: I've seen this before

I turn now from moments that provoke the reader's memory of something she has already 'heard' in the text to those that encourage her to remember something she has already 'seen'. My argument is that intratextuality may work by evoking at different points in a text the reader's mental visualisation of the same or a

30 *ademptum* is also connected to the vocative *adempte* at 68.20, 92, 101.6, while *abstulit* is echoed in sound and reversed in sense at 68.92 *attulit* 'brought towards' (indirect object: the brother; direct object: death).

31 These passages occur respectively in the sections of poem 68 often separated as 68a and 68b (see above, n. 12); Dániel Kiss reminds me that the repetition may be used in arguments both that 68 cannot be one poem, and that it must be one poem.

32 See above, p. 39.

33 Cf. above, p. 37 and n. 11. For this view see esp. Skinner 2003.

34 See Alexiou 2002, 131–7. In the Theocritean hexameter tradition, lamenting refrains appear in Bion *Epit. Adon.* (cf. n. 23) and, more straightforwardly, in [Mosch.] *Epit. Bion.*

35 See above, pp. 39–40.

similar image. The words which create that image may also be the same,[36] but my point is particularly clear from examples in which they are not. A virtuoso case occurs in Catullus 64, at a moment when that poem's complex play with the conventions of ecphrasis is particularly highlighted. At the end of the lengthy series of narrative 'digressions' (64.71–248) which actually comprise most of the poem's central section, conventionally called the 'ecphrasis', and just before the explicit return to the ecphrastic mode at 64.251 *at parte ex alia* 'but in another part [of the coverlet]', Ariadne is described for a second time, looking out at Theseus' ship from the shore on which he has abandoned her:

> 64.249–50 quae tum prospectans cedentem maesta carinam
> multiplices animo uoluebat saucia curas.

> 'And she at that time, sadly looking out at the departing keel, was turning over manifold woes, stricken in her mind.'

This description closely evokes another pair of lines, very near the beginning of the poem's initial description of Ariadne as depicted on Peleus' and Thetis' bridal coverlet:

> 64.53–4 Thesea cedentem celeri cum classe tuetur
> indomitos in corde gerens Ariadna furores

> 'Ariadne watches Theseus departing with his swift craft, bearing unconquerable furies in her heart.'

Yet although there are similarities in syntax and word placement as well as sense, only one word (*cedentem*) is repeated from one passage to the other. This intratextual connection, important for the structure of the poem, works primarily by creating the same image in the reader's mind – in fact, by inviting her to visualise the image which exists as an artistic depiction within the poem's primary narrative.[37]

More typically than repeatedly describing what is supposed to be 'literally' the same scene, however, Catullus' long poems create for the reader intratextual networks of visual associations among descriptions of different things. Further, as we noticed in the case of 'echoes', such a network may be strongly enough

---

36 Hence the connection made by Duban 1980 between 'verbal links' and 'imagistic undercurrent': see above, p. 36.

37 Propertius' description of Ariadne at 1.3.1–2 combines diction from both Catullan passages, suggesting that at least one ancient reader of Catullus appreciated the intratextual link. I owe this point to Stephen Heyworth.

established within one poem that its effects are also felt when reading the others. Poem 64 contains a repeated colour contrast between white and red:[38] the coverlet is reddish-purple on an ivory bed (48–9), Ariadne imagines washing Theseus' white feet and laying a red-purple cloth on *his* bed (162–3), the Fates are dressed in white clothes with a red-purple border, and have red fillets on their white hair (307–9), and the bloodily sacrificed Polyxena has white limbs (364, 368). This network is again created more visually than verbally (several words for 'red' and 'white' are used; ivory does not need to be *called* white, nor blood red). It connects different characters, different objects, different moments in both the poem's inner and outer stories in often unexpected and multiply interpretable ways. But it also sets up connections among other motifs that recur in connection with the contrasted red and white: textiles (49, 163, 225, 234, 307-9), skin (162, 351, 364), hair (224, 309, 350), the earth which stains or is stained (224, 344, 397), a bull (181, 230, 389), a sacrifice (362–71, 389, 393), brothers (181, 399). This means that we may be reminded of this network when it is briefly reflected in the other long poems: for example, when Attis, staining the ground with blood, picks up a drum in his/her white hands (63.7–8), when a blush spreads over a girl's face in a simile (65.24), when marriage demands the bloody sacrifice of bulls (66.34, 68.75–6, 79).

Even more all-pervasive in the long poems, and even harder to list exhaustively, is another network of images that centres on a colour contrast, or perhaps rather a colour assimilation, between white and yellow.[39] This colour group is strongly established as an intratextual feature in poem 61, where its wider associations are with Hymen (6–15), feet (10, 14, 108, 160), the marriage bed (108, 185), flowers (6–7, 21–5, 87–9, 187–8), and above all daylight (11, 85), torchlight (15, 77–8, 94–5, 114), explicit 'shining' (21, 186) and the bride's arrival (especially 84–6, 159–61, 185–8). We are regularly reminded of it in the other 'bridal' poems: 62 adds the light of the evening star (1–2, 7, 20–37 *passim*) and complicates the traditional flower comparison (39–47),[40] 64 uses it to underline the brightness of Peleus' and Thetis' wedding day (25, 31, 44–5, 302, 325) while ironically emphasising the failed bridal potential of Ariadne (63–5, 98–100), and 66 employs a verbal link, the repetition of *optatus* 'longed-for', to connect bridal torchlight to bridal daylight via a reminiscence of a line from 64: 64.31–2 *quae simul optatae finito tempore luces | aduenere* 'as soon as at the appointed time that longed-for daylight arrived', 66.79 *uos, optato quas iunxit lumine taeda* 'you, whom with its

38 A popular colour contrast in Latin poetry generally (André 1949, 346–7), but not typically used on such a large scale.

39 Cf. Clarke 2003, 175–97.

40 The conventional comparison of a beautiful woman with a flower (Rohde 1900, 164 n.3) was particularly associated with wedding-songs, apparently since Sappho (Michael Italicus, *Or.* 2.69).

longed-for light the torch has united'.[41] The same colours highlight the very different change of state experienced by Attis in poem 63, as the sun with golden face and shining eyes surveys the white sky in the dawn that restores Attis' sanity (63.39–40). And the full nexus of yellow, white and related motifs returns strongly in poem 68, especially in its restaging of the 'bride's arrival' as Catullus' adulterous mistress, *candida diua* ('white goddess'), places her foot across the threshold of Allius' house (70–2), accompanied by a Hymen-like Cupid shining white in a yellow tunic (133–4). Whatever our belief about the original publication contexts of the long poems, it is very tempting here to see an intratextual thread connecting them in the order in which modern copies of Catullus' work invite us to read them, ending, in ring-composition, with a powerful reflection of the images with which they opened.

I conclude this section with two further examples of the intratextual and intertextual use of more specific images. Firstly, another body part: women's bare breasts. Catullus depicts these three times in poem 64, connecting the Nereids gazed at by the Argonauts (17–18) with the abandoned Ariadne, gazed at by the viewers of the coverlet (64–5) and the mourning mothers of Achilles' victims, prophesied by the Fates (351). In each case the breasts are referred to by a different word (18 *nutricum*, 65 *papillas*, 351 *pectora*); all are seen in unusual, epic situations compared to the breasts glimpsed in the marriage beds of other poems (61.101, 66.81). Secondly, it is not just Ariadne who stands looking out over the sea, miserable (64.53–4, 60–2, 249–50), but also Aegeus, who similarly looks at Theseus' ship (64.241–5) and Attis, who looks over a vast, empty sea (63.48) – as Ariadne also does at a slightly later moment in her story (64.127). In both of these examples, the similarities cause the depictions of human (or nearly human) figures with contrasting characteristics (male/female, old/young, lusty/weak, beautiful/ugly) to be overlaid upon each other in the reader's mind. This may provoke comparison, contrast, and further interpretation: but it works by means of visual memory.

3 'Verbal links': I've read this before

The final section examines the most 'textual' of the three kinds of intratextuality identified in this chapter. The term used by Duban 1980, 'verbal links', is a useful one for cases in which the reader is prompted to remember not so much his hearing of a sound or visualisation of an image as his reading and understanding of a

41 See below, p. 48, and cf. also above, p. 42.

word or words. Literary critics and their readers are, obviously, used to dealing with words, and arguments for interpretable inter- and intratextualities are very often based on close verbal similarities, in Catullan criticism as elsewhere. I therefore focus on some of the ways in which, I believe, this kind of intratextuality works differently from the kinds involving 'echoes' and 'reflections'.

In the previous section I argued that different points in the text may be connected by the 'reflection' of a visual idea, such as a colour or an object, even if that thing is referred to in different places by several different words. 'Verbal links' are particularly *verbal* when the converse is true: a 'key word', for instance, may be repeated, and its repetition interpreted, in more than one different sense. These senses may be closely related, as with the significant recurrences of *domus* in poem 68, which may mean 'house', 'home', or 'household/ family'.[42] But the reader's mind is kept even more engaged with the word itself when it appears in a wider variety of senses, even if interpretation is usually easier when these senses may be broadly understood as 'literal' and 'metaphorical' variations on a core idea. This is true for most of the examples in poem 64 discussed by Duban, who, for instance, examines all the appearances in the poem of compounds of *sternere*, 'spread out', 'cast down' (64.71, 110, 163, 332, 355, 403), and argues that they suggest connections between Theseus' destructive effects on the Minotaur and on Ariadne.[43] It is often difficult, however, to advance an interpretation in similarly straightforward terms of 'thematic significance' that will convincingly cover every instance of a word's repetition. Forsyth, discussing the recurrences of *uertex* 'head', 'summit' in 64, points to a noticeable feature of the text, the repeated word connected with the visual or conceptual idea of 'descent',[44] but her interpretation in terms of Catullan pessimism seems rather reductive. Moreover, such an instance of 'key word' intratextuality may extend beyond the boundaries of poem 64: we may remember again the recurrent use of *uertex* within that poem when we encounter the lock leaving Berenice's *uertex* in 66 (8, 39, 76) and two examples of 'descent', again with *uertex*, among the similes of 68 (57, 107). McKie therefore seems to me on safer ground when he focuses less on the 'significance' of any one word's repetition than on the overall 'rhetoric of repetition' or 'aesthetics of linkage' created by the 'all-pervasive' use of verbal iterations in Catullus 64;[45] but I would wish to argue that this effect of intratextuality is not, within

42 *domus* in 68 is much discussed in modern scholarship: see Leigh 2016, 207–13, esp. 208 n.43.
43 Duban 1980, 786–8.
44 Forsyth 1975, 44–6.
45 McKie 2009, 92.

Catullus' long poems, restricted to 64 in the way that McKie thinks, and that it operates not just with verbal links but with echoes and reflections too.

Before proceeding to such a conclusion I offer further cases of more complex verbal intratextuality in the long poems. All involve psychological description: as a preliminary point, it is notable that some repeated 'key words' in the long poems are those conveying affective ideas, hard to visualise (one particularly important example is *optare*, 'long for', which appears at 64.5, 22, 31, 82, 141, 328, 372, 401 but also at 62.30, 42, 44, 66.79).[46] In poem 63, however, intratextuality is one of the means used to assimilate to each other the physical and psychological aspects of Attis' situation. Among the obsessively repeated themes of the poem are mental disturbance and wandering:[47] these are connected, very early on, in the memorable metaphor *uagus animi* 'wandering in mind' (63.4). This phrase primes the reader to notice *uagus* in its physical sense throughout the text, whether applied to Attis and companions (25, 31) or to Cybele's animals (13, 72, 86), and also to note all the occurrences of words for 'mind', *animus*, *mens* and *pectus* (18–19, 38, 45–7, 57, 61, 89). The character is assimilated to the surrounding environment and its denizens, and his/her mind is a battleground: the intratextual network developed from *uagus animi* thus reinforces the poem's portrayal, on both mental and physical levels, of helpless movement within a trap.

Finally, in two poems, Catullus uses pairs of intratextually connected passages to describe a mental event. Attis falls asleep, then wakes up free of madness:

> 63.38 abit in quiete molli rabidus furor animi
>
> 'to gentle peace gives way the frenzied fury of their mind'
>
> 63.44 ita de quiete molli rapida sine rabie
>
> 'so after gentle peace and lacking restless frenzy'

As a result of Ariadne's curse, Theseus forgets the instructions Aegeus had given him on departing from Athens (on either side of a flashback to the giving of those instructions, this event is described twice):

> 64.207–9 ipse autem caeca mentem caligine Theseus
> consitus oblito dimisit pectore cuncta,
> quae mandata prius constanti mente tenebat

---

46 Cf. above, p. 45–6.

47 Cf. McKie 2009, 89–90; above, p. 36.

'But Theseus himself, his mind sown thick with blinding mist, let go from his forgetful heart all the instructions which he had previously held fast in constant mind'

64.238–40 haec mandata prius constanti mente tenentem
Thesea ceu pulsae uentorum flamine nubes
aerium niuei montis liquere cacumen.

'These instructions, which he had previously been holding fast in constant mind, left Theseus, as clouds driven by the blast of winds leave the crest of a snowy mountain.'

In these examples, echo, reflection and verbal link all play a part. In both pairs of passages some words are repeated in exactly the same forms, at the same points in the line, so that they are heard as much as read (especially in the unusual galliambic metre of poem 63): yet *rabidus* is transformed into *rapida* ... *rabie*, and *tenebat* into *tenentem*, possibly to illustrate that this is either a different moment (Attis) or the same moment described in a different narrative context (Theseus). In the passages from poem 64 the two images for forgetting are almost opposite, yet connected by their opposition: Theseus' mind is like ground sown with dark cloud (*caligine*), or the instructions that leave it are like clouds blown away from a white mountain. The image of descent from a mountain summit recurs,[48] but the word for 'summit' is now *cacumen*, not *uertex*. The fact that similarly intratextual techniques are used for a similar purpose in both 63 and 64 makes an intertextual connection between the two poems, even between the two characters of Attis and Theseus. It is probably not surprising that one of the most complex cases in which Catullus uses aural, visual and verbal intertextuality to work on the various cognitive faculties of his readers turns out to be his representation of the kind of mental events (a return to sanity, a moment of forgetting) of which it is extremely difficult to have self-aware cognition.

4 Conclusions

Although it began with the suggestion that we might understand intratextuality as involving the reader's memory over some distance, this chapter has shown, I think, that repetitions of words, sounds and images in much closer proximity often make their own contributions to larger-scale intratextual effects. In particular, we have seen how often in Catullus' long poems an intratextual pattern is built up within one poem, and then allows us to observe traces of it in another –

48 Cf. above, p. 47.

perhaps just a single trace. This will certainly mean that such an isolated reminiscence invites more interpretation than would otherwise have been the case; perhaps, also, that such an echo, reflection or verbal recurrence can properly be called 'intratextual' as well as 'intertextual' – not necessarily as a result of taking all the long poems as a group, or all Catullus' oeuvre as one text, but in the sense that such an intertextual moment crucially relates to intratextuality in another poem.

Interestingly, this effect is particularly noticeable in poem 66. I discussed above two echoes of the wedding-songs (one recalling a refrain from 61, the other a piece of amoebean responsion from 62),[49] and one reflection of an image which is strongly intratextual in 64 (bare breasts).[50] The last of these occurs in a passage which may have been added by Catullus to his translation of Callimachus' original 'Lock of Berenice', and the same may also be true of the first,[51] while for 47 *quid facient crines?* we do have Callimachus' original Greek: Call. fr. 110.47 Harder τί πλόκαμοι ῥέξωμεν; 'what are we locks to do?'. Catullus has changed the word order, and the person, mood and tense of the verb – possibly for metrical or idiomatic reasons, but possibly also for intratextual ones. Catullus' translation of Callimachus, then, becomes particularly his own as it reflects or echoes motifs that are well established as intratextual in his other long poems. On the other hand, one of the long poems appears to be significantly less intratextual than the others: 67, the scandalous dialogue with a gossiping door, is clearly linked thematically to the other long poems, with its focus on the door/threshold (an important theme in 61 and 68) and on marriage, yet it lacks patterns of echo, reflection or verbal link within itself, and does not, as far as I can see, offer connections by any of these means to such patterns in other poems.[52] 67 may stand as a counterexample among the long poems demonstrating that I have identified something present in the others.

As I suggested at the outset, I believe that this may be connected with the concern observable in most of these poems with different kinds of artistic form. Catullus seems to be exploring how close a text can come to working in the same way as a piece of visual art, or a piece of music. Whether they appeal to our vision,

---

49 66.31, 47: above, pp. 41–2.

50 66.81: above, p. 46.

51 Neither has an extant equivalent in our one papyrus source for Callimachus' poem: see Harder 2012 on Call. fr. 110.15–32, 79–88.

52 The father who violates his son's marriage bed at 67.23–6 evokes the possibly similar desires (the text is disputed and confusing) of the father at 64.401–2; but that is a single passage, and the connection is thematic rather than being based on aural or visual similarities or on the repetition of any word except *natus* 'son'.

our hearing or even our verbal understanding, all of the kinds of intratextuality I have discussed have a tendency to work against the linearity of a text by inviting us to link different parts of that text to one another. We are freed, to some extent, from having to follow the text straightforwardly from beginning to end in time: it is instead as if we were looking at a picture and able to choose the order in which we examine its different areas, or as if we were listening to a song and experiencing the sense of a timeless present moment every time we hear the chorus.[53] The 'literary' device of ring-composition actually works like this as well, particularly when there is a series of rings within rings, as in poem 68b:[54] as the old metaphor of a nested set of 'Chinese boxes' makes clear, ring-composition invites the reader to consider the text from above, as a whole, as an artefact with 'spatial form'.[55]

Finally, I have begun to wonder about the extent to which these poems or their author are self-aware about all this, or ask us to notice that self-awareness. In poem 61, the mysterious speaker who describes, prescribes and perhaps creates the proceedings of the wedding asks the bride a question, *uiden? faces | aureas quatiunt comas* 'Do you see? The torches shake their golden tresses' (94–5), immediately after making her a request: *audias | nostra uerba* 'hear our words' (93–4). Both utterances have antecedents in one of Callimachus' 'mimetic' *Hymns* (Call. *Hymn* 2.4 οὐχ ὁράᾳς; 'don't you see?', 17 εὐφημεῖτ' ἀίοντες ἐπ' Ἀπόλλωνος ἀοιδῇ 'be quiet, listeners, for the song to Apollo'), but Callimachus' speaker did not address them consecutively to the same person.[56] Juxtaposed in Catullus, they raise the question whether anyone, bride or reader, can simultaneously both see the torches and hear the poet.

In Catullus 64, this question of the accessibility of the world evoked by the text is much at stake. That poem is about trying to reach the content of a picture or the content of the mythical past in which gods mingled freely with humans. At the end, we learn that now, the gods are no longer seen, yet the poem's very last words evoke light: 64.408 *nec se contingi patiuntur lumine claro* 'nor do they let themselves be touched by clear *lumen*'. *lumen* is recurrent in the long poems. It

53 Have you ever forgotten, while listening to (or singing) the chorus of a song, which verse is coming next?

54 See e.g. Courtney 1985, 92–9. Goold 1989 indicates one possible scheme with subheadings in his translation.

55 The term 'spatial form' was introduced in the 1940s by Joseph Frank to describe a characteristic of some modernist texts (see Ryan, 'Space' 2.4 'The spatial form of the text'). Though rarely used by Classicists, it usefully describes the kind of features that they call attention to by, for instance, producing structural diagrams of the arrangement of poems in a collection.

56 For the first, singular address the identity of the addressee is particularly unclear: see Hunter 1992, 12–13 for some of the complexities created for the reader of this mimetic text.

means 'light', whether of day or torches[57] or the stars (another divine realm);[58] but it also refers to eyes, which are *oculi* and *ocelli* (63.37, 39, 48, 64.17, 60, 65.8), but also *lumina* (64.86, 92, 122, 188, 220, 233, 242, 66.30, 68.55). There is a genuine ambiguity in the final line of 64 as to whether the reference of *lumine claro* is more what we see *by*, *lumine*, 'light', or what we see *with*, *lumina*, 'eyes', *lumine*, 'gaze'. How much, then, *can* we come to see, through this poetry in which we keep reading or hearing this ambiguous word, *lumen*, yet also reading and learning to see through other words for eyes, other words for light? It must matter, not least because we learn at the end of 68, the very end of the long poems, in potential ring-composition,[59] that for Catullus, his divine light – *lux* this time – is what makes life worth living.

> 68.160 lux mea, qua uiua uiuere dulce mihist.
>
> 'my light, whose living makes life happiness for me.'

Abbreviations

BNP: H. Cancik/H. Schneider/C.F. Salazar (eds.) (2002–), *Brill's New Pauly: Encylopaedia of the Ancient World*, Leiden.
OCD: S. Hornblower/A. Spawforth/E. Eidinow (eds.) (2012), *Oxford Classical Dictionary*, fourth edition, Oxford.
OLD: P.G.W. Glare (ed.) (1968–82), *Oxford Latin Dictionary*, Oxford.

Bibliography

Agnesini, A. (2007), *Il carme 62 di Catullo: edizione critica e commento*, Quaderni di Paideia 5, Cesena.
Alexiou, M. (2002), *The Ritual Lament in Greek Tradition*, 2nd edition, rev. D. Yatromanolakis and P. Roilos, Lanham, MD/Oxford.
André, J. (1949), *Études sur les termes de couleur dans la langue latine*, Paris.
Baehrens, E. (1876–85), *Catulli Veronensis liber*, 2 vols., Leipzig.
Beyers, E. (1960), 'The Refrain in the Song of the Fates in Catullus C. 64', *Acta Classica* 3, 86–9.
Butrica, J.L. (2007), 'History and Transmission of the Text', in: M.B. Skinner (ed.), *A Companion to Catullus*, Oxford, 13–34.
Clarke, J. (2003), *Imagery of Colour and Shining in Catullus, Propertius and Horace*, New York.

---

57 66.79, 90; cf. 68.93 (above, p. 43), where *lumen* is the light of life. For the image of shining light reflected throughout the long poems, see above, pp. 45–6.
58 66.1, 59, 66; cf. 62.2.
59 61 began with the appearance of a god, shaking a torch: see above, pp. 45–6.

Courtney, E. (1985), 'Three Poems of Catullus', *Bulletin of the Institute of Classical Studies* 32, 85–100.
Dover, K.J. (1971), *Select Poems: Theocritus*, London.
Duban, J. (1980), 'Verbal Links and Imagistic Undercurrent in Catullus 64', *Latomus* 39, 777–802.
Estevez, V.A. (1981), 'Ἀπώλετο καλός Ἄδωνις: A Description of Bion's Refrain', *Maia* 33, 35–42.
Forsyth, P.Y. (1975), 'Catullus 64: The Descent of Man', *Antichthon* 9, 41–51.
Goold, G.P. (1989), *Catullus*, 2nd edition, London.
Harder, A. (2012), *Callimachus: Aetia*, 2 vols., Oxford.
Hunter, R. (1992), 'Writing the God: Form and Meaning in Callimachus, *Hymn to Athena*', *Materiali e discussion per l'analisi dei testi classici* 29, 9–34.
Leigh, M. (2016), '*Illa domus, illa mihi sedes*: On the Interpretation of Catullus 68', in: R. Hunter/S.P. Oakley (eds.) (2016), *Latin Literature and Its Transmission: papers in honour of Michael Reeve*, Cambridge, 194–224.
Lowrie, M. (2006), '*Hic* and Absence in Catullus 68', *Classical Philology* 101, 115–32.
McKie, D.S. (2009), *Essays in the Interpretation of Roman Poetry*, Cambridge.
Most, G.W. (1981), 'On the Arrangement of Catullus' *carmina maiora*', *Philologus* 125, 109–25.
Quinn, K.F. (1972), *Catullus: An Interpretation*, London.
Rohde, E. (1900), *Der griechische Roman und seine Vorläufer*, 2nd edition, Leipzig.
Ryan, M.-L. 'Space', in: P. Hühn et al. (eds.), *The Living Handbook of Narratology*, Hamburg. http://www.lhn.uni-hamburg.de/article/space [accessed 25 March 2018]
Sharrock, A./Morales, H. (eds.) (2000), *Intratextuality: Greek and Roman Textual Relations*, Oxford.
Skinner, M.B. (2003), *Catullus in Verona: A Reading of the Elegiac Libellus, Poems 65–116*, Columbus, Ohio.
Skinner, M.B. (2007), 'Authorial Arrangement of the Collection: Debate Past and Present', in: M.B. Skinner (ed.), *A Companion to Catullus*, Oxford, 35–53.
Theodorakopoulos, E. (2000), 'Catullus 64: Footprints in the Labyrinth', in: Sharrock, A./Morales, H. (eds.), *Intratextuality: Greek and Roman Textual Relations*, Oxford, 115–42.
Trimble, G.C. (forthcoming), *Catullus: Poem 64*, Cambridge.
Wills, J. (1996), *Repetition in Latin Poetry: Figures of Allusion*, Oxford.

Laurel Fulkerson

Credula Spes: Tibullan Hope and the Future of Elegy

1 Introduction

This chapter oscillates between the small and traditional, in its close reading of a particular lexical item in a specific corpus, with implications (2 and 3), and the fairly untraditional, in its expansion of the notion of a 'corpus' beyond most definitions of it (4), and in its raising broader questions about the nature of elegy. As a thought experiment, I will be suggesting that it might be worthwhile to conceptualize 'elegy' as a single unified text or corpus. The genre seems like a worthwhile test case because its practitioners are few in number, likely to have known one another's work intimately (so intimately that the chronology of individual books is hotly disputed), and also because elegiac poetry is so relentlessly focused in on itself and on its generic constraints. So too, amalgamating elegy might help us to think more carefully about which poems we tend to include and exclude when we make generalizations about the genre (i.e. elegy is 'poetry about love'): section 4 therefore treats Ovid's exile poetry as a single text which responds to Tibullus' two books of poetry. And this discussion will also involve an exploration of how and when we can legitimately speak of an end (or a 'death') of elegy.[1]

My starting point is the emotions in elegiac poetry, specifically the emotion of hope, or *spes*, which I posit as central to elegy's worldview, and therefore also as deserving of more careful attention than it has heretofore received in the scholarship.[2] I begin with an outline of the fundamental framework of elegy. The

Many thanks to my amazing hosts in Thessaloniki for the opportunity to think through these issues, and to the audience there who helped me to do so – I single out Steve Heyworth, Michèle Lowrie, Alison Sharrock, and Thea Thorsen as having raised questions I am still struggling to answer.

1 The bibliography here (and throughout) could be enormous; I cite only the work that has directly influenced my own thinking. On the brevity of elegy, see Miller 2004; on the repetitiveness of elegy Sharrock 1993. The chronological problems that beset elegy, especially Ovidian elegy, are also relevant; see Martelli 2013 and Thorsen 2014.

2 There is, however, growing interest in elegiac emotions: on elegiac jealousy, see Caston 2012; on male desire in elegy, Greene 1998 (though the latter is not specifically focused on emotions).

https://doi.org/10.1515/9783110611021-004

elegiac situation is a delicate emotional equilibrium in which the basic condition of misery is occasionally punctuated by bursts of joy. There are, in fact, precisely the requisite number of moments of joy to keep the relationship alive: generally speaking, the elegist is either unhappy, deeply unhappy, angry, or elated. At any given moment, both the elegiac poet and his beloved know on some level how much more misery he is able to bear. Just as the *amator* is ready to give up the relationship as lost, the *puella* relents the tiniest bit, throwing him a crumb of affection, and the cycle continues. For such an unsatisfying cycle to work, hope is necessary; in fact, it may well be the key mechanism which allows elegy to function. Because things in elegy are usually pretty bad, there is always the possibility that they could get better, and they *have* in the past gotten just enough better with just enough frequency to make it seem plausible, likely even, that they might get better again. And, as with much else in elegy, the emotions portrayed are deeply repetitive, replicating from one author to another, such that even a novice elegist and *amator* can have points of reference for judging his brand-new relationship. This is part of what inclines me to think about elegy as a single body of material: while all narrative is repetitive, and many love-stories are similar, elegy seems to be much more insistently interested in its own cyclical nature than other genres are.

For most modern readers, the elegiac situation is peculiar, distasteful. The genre as a whole seems to be predicated upon deception, manipulation, and selfishness. We might even characterize the elegiac relationship as a hopeless one, doomed from the start. And yet, despite his intermittent resolutions to walk away, and what looks from the outside like the inevitable conclusion that this relationship costs far more than its value, the elegist continues, most of the time, to find it worth his while. He hopes despite knowing better, or hopes and therefore does not always notice that he knows better. So, even though the lexical markers for hope do not permeate elegy, I posit that the genre is nonetheless grounded in the twin concepts of hope and despair.[3]

For me, one of the most fascinating aspects of ancient conceptions of hope is precisely the slippage that we find in elegy between the *feeling* of hope, which can be entirely subjective, and the potentially more objective, externalized assessment of a situation as being one in which hope is or is not an appropriate emotion. And this points to a key difference between ancient and modern hope:

3 Occurrences of *spes/sperare* in (standard, amatory) elegy: Prop. 1: 0; Prop. 2: 4; Prop. 3: 3; Prop. 4: 2; Tib. 1: 3; Tib 2: 1; Ov. *Am.* 1: 3; *Am.* 2: 5; *Am.* 3: 0; *Ars* 1: 5: *Ars* 2: 1; *Ars* 3: 4; *RA*: 3. It also appears in the *Heroides* and even more frequently in the double *Heroides* (where the relationships are newer, and so, perhaps, where there is greater cause for hope). See also n. 14.

ancient hope seems to be ambiguous at best in both Greek and Latin literature: mentions of *elpis* and *spes* very often carry the suggestion that there has been a failure of some kind, or the implication that it is at least potentially blameworthy to have landed oneself in a situation in which hope is necessary.[4] Hope, that is, often comes to be a rough synonym for the failure to foresee consequences. This can look to modern eyes like blaming the victim, but I think there are important ways in which the ancients got it right: it is sometimes the case that individual perceptions function in ways that are sharply at odds with how the world works, such that hope can be an objectively inappropriate emotion, and may even indicate a larger character flaw. So, for instance, we might not *blame* someone who has his heart set upon winning a race, who spends a lot of time estimating his chances of winning, and who plans what he will do with the prize money, but who has not undertaken any kind of training program in order to improve his chances at winning. But we would probably also have little sympathy for his profound disappointment when he does not win.

Indeed, it is just that disjunction between what one reasonable person would consider a plausible future outcome and what some other person might (nonetheless) hope for that makes it such a fruitful topic. Hope sits right where rational calculations about probability meet personal desires: *elpizo* and *spero* can signify both the emotion of hope and something closer to 'expect' (they can even be used to denote something we dread). And Greek and Roman instances of hope tend to focus more on unreasonable, or at least unrealized, hopes than on stories of triumph. When a character expresses a hope in a narrative context in Greco-Roman literature, it means one of two things: once in a great while, it is a hint of the success that awaits her or him, but much more often, it is a foreshadowing of disappointment and failure. In fact, we might do well to think of ancient hope as the linguistic equivalent of scary music in a horror film, alerting the audience that Something Bad is about to happen.

Back to elegy, a genre in which something bad is nearly always about to happen. Hope occurs right at the start of the elegiac relationship, for both parties. Ovid assures the neophyte that he should hope for all girls (*Ars*. 1.343, *ergo age, ne dubita cunctas sperare puellas*). And, because talk is cheap, the *amator* is encouraged to manipulate the *puella*'s hope for gifts since promises cost him nothing (Ov. *Ars* 1.445–6, *spes tenet in tempus, semel est si credita, longum:/ Illa quidem fallax, sed tamen apta dea est*). So too, any initial reverses should be met with hope and persistence (Ov. *Ars* 1.469–70, *si non accipiet scriptum, inlectumque remittet, / lecturam spera, propositumque tene*). Things are not a lot better for

4 See Fulkerson 2015, 2016, and 2017.

the *puella*: once in a while, she is given a voice, and she expresses her own disappointed hopes, as when the dead Cynthia berates Propertius for his disloyalty at 4.7.13–14. But for the most part, she is simply warned that she is a fool to hope for gifts from poets, who are notoriously cash-poor (Ov. *Ars* 3.551).

Once the poet has entered into the elegiac relationship, and has acquired the habit of hopefulness, it becomes a more destructive emotion. Because the elegiac relationship is by its nature a hostile one, with each of its two main participants pursuing fundamentally different goals (James 2003), the *amator*'s hopes are often disappointed (Prop. 2.5.3, 2.22b.45–6). Hope impedes the lover's judgment (Ov. *Am.* 1.6.52, *Her.* 17.234, *RA* 685) and affects his behavior (Ov. *Am.* 1.11.13). It drives him to drink (Prop. 3.17.11–12). In sum, it leads to his disillusionment and disappointment, again and again, and yet, he continues to come back for more.

I have suggested that the rules of elegy inevitably generate hopes, which are almost-inevitably disappointed. Indeed, the elegists themselves sometimes recognize this, as at Propertius 2.9a7–8: *visuram et quamvis numquam speraret Ulixem, / illum exspectando facta remansit anus.* This passage is key to understanding elegiac hope: it features Penelope, who embodies the extremes to which the elegist will go in his devotion. She waits for twenty years for her husband to return; her situation is, any reasonable person would agree, a hopeless one. And yet, her implausible, extreme hopefulness is rewarded by the eventual return of her husband. The elegist chooses to imagine that his own persistence will be similarly rewarded, however preposterous his behavior looks to others. The implicit comparison – Propertius is like Penelope in his shining fidelity and moral goodness – is presumably as deliberate as it is misleading, placing the blame for any flaws in the relationship on the *puella*. The truth, hinted at only occasionally, is more complicated: no elegiac relationship can (should?) exist without the creation and encouragement of deceptive hopes by both parties. Ovid, typically, is more straightforward about both the game and the stakes than Propertius or Tibullus: for him, the tantalizing and frustrating nature of elegiac hope is part of its appeal, and, as usual, he manages to have it both ways, encouraging the *puella* to trick him into hoping (Ov. *Am.* 2.9b.43–4, 2.19.5–6 and 49–50, *Ars* 3.477–8, 3.592) as he simultaneously bemoans her faithlessness and cruelty.

2 Tibullan *spes*

Tibullan elegy is usually understood to differ in a number of key ways from that of Propertius and Ovid, and his treatment of hope is no exception to this principle. On average, he mentions hope about as often as the other two (see above

n. 4), but his hopes are less central to the primary concerns of elegy. His first poem expresses what I have elsewhere called an 'agricultural hope',[5] one which focuses on obtaining sustenance in sufficient quantity from a part of nature that may or may not choose to grant it: Tib. 1.1.9–10, *nec spes destituat, sed frugum semper acervos / praebeat et pleno pinguia musta lacu.* This is an example worth paying attention to, as I will suggest that it connects to Tibullus' final evocation of hope. Tib. 1.9 features two instances of *spes*, the first of which suggests a conventional, anti-elegiac view of morality: at Tib. 1.9.23–4, *nec tibi celandi spes sit peccare paranti: / est deus, occultos qui vetat esse dolos*, Tibullus warns us that there is no point in plotting, because tricksters will be discovered. His motive is a selfish one, and the poem goes on to show us that his advice falls upon deaf ears, since Marathus continues to deceive him. But later in that poem, he again undermines the elegiac paradigm, claiming to have provided pleasure for Marathus with the latter's own *puella* even beyond Marathus' hopes, through his own largesse: Tib. 1.9.43, *saepe insperanti venit tibi munere nostro*. Elegiac love always comes at a cost, but here, the cost is all Tibullus' and the benefit is all Marathus'. Tibullus' naïveté leads the *puer* to take advantage of him, but also, Marathus is thereby deprived of elegiac suffering, and so, we might say, of a genuinely elegiac relationship (which might, of course, be just fine with him). The three examples of *spes* in the first book of Tibullus, then, are anything but conventional: one is not about elegy at all, and the other two undermine its premises. If I am right about the centrality of *spes* to (the rest of) elegy, then Tibullus is doing something rather different, using the concept to think through his dissatisfaction with the existing rules of elegy.

We see this putative dissatisfaction even more clearly in Tibullus' most extensive, and final, treatment of the subject, the '*spes*-interlude' of Tib. 2.6.19–28:

> iam mala finissem leto, sed credula vitam
>   spes fovet et fore cras semper ait melius.
> spes alit agricolas, spes sulcis credit aratis
>   semina, quae magno faenore reddat ager;
> haec laqueo volucres, haec captat arundine pisces,
>   cum tenues hamos abdidit ante cibus;
> spes etiam valida solatur conpede vinctum:
>   crura sonant ferro, sed canit inter opus;
> spes facilem Nemesim spondet mihi, sed negat illa;
>   ei mihi, ne vincas, dura puella, deam.

5 Fulkerson 2017, 217.

This passage details a number of vignettes in which people hope – farming, fowling, fishing, being a slave – and compares the situation of the elegist to each. Tibullus, he tells us, would have ended it all long ago, but *credula spes* kept him hanging on. So too she encourages others, seemingly deceitfully. While the passage ends on a nominally positive note, in which Tibullus encourages Nemesis not to disobey the wishes of a personified Spes, he has already made clear that she herself refuses (*negat*).

It is difficult to know how to interpret this passage, which is our first extant poetic excursus on hope in Latin.[6] Those critics who connect the appearance of the goddess Spes in this poem with the name of Nemesis must be on to something, but the point of this connection remains obscure. Is it, as Murgatroyd suggests, that Nemesis, despite her powerful name, should not contend with real goddesses (1989: 138)? Does it, as Bright opines, clarify that Spes, seen as a potentially powerful force in book 1, turns out to be no real competition for Nemesis (1978: 221–2)? Or does it fulfil some as-yet-undetermined function? I am persuaded by the second option: to me, and to others (Lee-Stecum forthcoming), there is a pointed circularity between the invocation of hope in 1.1 and its occurrence in this poem, where it is undermined by Nemesis. Despite (or perhaps because of) its idyllic (anti-elegiac) start, the Tibullan corpus ends in despair of the elegiac situation.

3 Tibullus 2.6 in its context

This seeming ring-composition raises the question of what we should make of Tib. 2.6, particularly whether we should understand it as a 'last poem', a farewell to elegy, rather than simply the place where Tibullus' poetry trails off. There is a sizeable scholarly industry from the 1980's which focuses on the arrangement of Augustan poetry books, but it usually dodges the peculiar situation of Tib. 2.[7]

6 Smith 1913 and Murgatroyd 1994 *ad loc.* discuss similar passages (including Ov. *EP* 1.6, treated below). There is also the pseudo-Senecan *De Spe* which touches upon similar points at greater length.

7 Dettmer argued in 1980 that the connections between poems in book 2 and between 2.6 and book 1 provide 'strong, if not conclusive, evidence that Book 2 is complete and was arranged by Tibullus himself' (82). But in general, those who subscribe to this ring-composition view (e.g. Bright 1978: 216, 220, 222, Veremans 1981, 790–2, Maltby 2002 *ad loc.*) do not explicitly connect it to the narrative of Tibullus' untimely death. For dissenting opinions, see Ullrich 1889 and Reeve 1984.

Because we think we know that Tibullus died fairly young, the majority of the interest in book-organization focuses on the first book, where the likelihood is greater of deliberate ordering.

I have not unearthed any exciting new evidence about the date of Tibullus' death, but it seems to me that 2.6 is an eminently suitable last poem, and further, that it can even serve to explain the rather truncated length of book 2. First, there is the ring-composition noted above: although elegiac hope inevitably turns out to be deceptive, for the inexperienced Tibullus, way back at the start of book 1, it might still have seemed like a good place to start. Sixteen poems and two disappointing *puellae* (and a *puer*) later, he has learned his lesson. Second, 2.6 begins with Macer's abandonment of the world of love for the world of war and ends with the post-mortem visitation of Nemesis' dead sister; both of these motives, change of genre and death, are standard closural devices, which incline the scales toward reading the poem as a last poem. Finally, the very fact that Tib. 2 is so much shorter than Tib. 1 might be taken as evidence of the death of its author – as it usually is – but it might also powerfully illustrate Tibullus' growing realization of the fruitlessness of further poetic discourse: after 2.6, the blinkers are off, and Tibullus has nothing more to say.[8] The date of Tibullus' death is one of the few fairly secure chronological points in elegy, and my aim is not to provoke a revision of it.[9] I am more interested in the authorial point that 2.6, however it happened to become Tibullus' last poem, makes a fitting end to Tibullus' oeuvre and perhaps even to elegy as a whole.

In that light, let's return to the *spes*-discursus in 2.6. Within this passage, Tibullus refers to the most common metaphors for the elegiac relationship, which is notoriously self-reflexive in its language. In addition to being occasions on which people might feel hope, each of these Tibullan examples – farming, fowling, fishing, being a slave – adumbrates a potential role that the lover can embody in metaphor, and in each scenario, hope needlessly prolongs his sufferings. Because such analogies are in elegy always meant simultaneously to stand on their own and to be seen-through, each vignette brings the lover right back to his own unfortunate situation. His imaginative rehearsal of the doomed hopes of

8 Gestures toward this argument at Murgatroyd 1989, 135 (the poem 'depicts a man at the end of his tether' who 'finally runs out of ideas'); cf. Murgatroyd 1994 *ad loc.* And Ball suggests that we might even read the poem as a suicide note (1983: 219).

9 Domitius Marsus' epigram (fr. 7 Morel) about the deaths of Tibullus and Vergil suggests that they died at roughly the same time. Vergil died in September 19, so Tibullus' death is usually dated to 19 or early 18. For discussion, see Avery 1960 and 1961, Levin 1967, McGann 1970; Knox 2005 explores the implications of the traditional dates for our understanding of Propertius' and Tibullus' relationship to one another, suggesting that Tibullus' first book predates Propertius'.

others, who also serve as alternate selves, helps Tibullus to realize that he is no better off than these others, none of whom, from his vantage-point, has any good reason to continue hoping. Tibullus proceeds to negotiate and to appeal to Nemesis' better instincts, but in the end he comes to a clear understanding of the elegiac situation, which, as I have suggested, is *by definition* one in which hopes are always disappointed.

Scholarship on elegy has long been interested in the fact that Tibullus breaks the unspoken rule of having a single *puella*, instead switching from Delia to Nemesis in his second book, and including in the first book a *puer*, Marathus.[10] If we look at that fact through the lenses of hope and despair, we can see Tibullus, always a bit different from Propertius and Ovid, as also savvier than they, in that he learns the lesson elegy *really* teaches. Disappointed by his experiences with Delia, Tibullus turns to Marathus, and then, when this proves equally unsatisfying, tries to start fresh with a new *puella* in book 2. This is good elegiac practice, even if it smacks of indecent haste. But – the name of Nemesis foreshadows his failure – the poet must eventually face the fact that switching *puellae* does not mend matters. It turns out to be elegy in general, not in particular, that is the problem. The examples in 2.6 make this clear: as Tibullus searches for appropriate metaphors to characterize his elegiac relationship, he comes to see that every one of them confirms his situation as one in which hope and despair alternate in an ever-worsening spiral. So it may not be accidental that 2.6 (and therefore, the poetry of Tibullus as a whole) ends in *aporia*, trailing off into disappointed or angry or depressed silence.

4 Ovidian *spes*

And yet, elegy does not end with Tibullus, even if you accept the argument that he thinks it should have. We might connect this to competitiveness between the elegists, to a real or playful wish to have Ovid's *Amores* unwritten.[11] Many have noticed that Ovid's elegiac poetry betrays a sense of its own belatedness; some of the reason for this may be that he has fully understood the lessons of Tib. 2.6: elegy is over. There is nothing more to say. This ought to deter your typical would-be elegiac poet. But it seems instead to free Ovid: the recognition of elegy as

10 See especially Gibson 2013 on the elegist's monogamy.
11 This may extend to parts of Propertius' poetry as well – I sidestep, for reasons of space and simplicity, issues of chronology.

mostly-dead enables his own increasingly wild deviations from it (e.g. the *Heroides*, the didactic works, and perhaps even the exile poetry). Perhaps, then, the standard narrative of literary history in which Ovid takes the blame for ruining elegy should be edited slightly to include Tibullus, who had at least hinted at the end Ovid would later make explicit. Indeed, this repetitive cycle of death and rebirth might prove to be central to the genre's self-conception. Ovid could not have killed elegy, and neither could Tibullus, because it was always already dead, but also always already not dead yet.[12]

The topics of death and elegy bring us, inevitably, to Ovid's exile poetry.[13] The two collections from exile have regular recourse to notions of hope, and for good reason: like the elegiac lover at the threshold, a cold and lonely Ovid finds himself in a situation partly of his own making but entirely out of his control, from which he can neither extricate himself nor receive satisfaction.[14] As in more traditional elegiac poetry, the lover's oscillation between hope and fear therefore recurs in the exile poetry, but in a different way, revisiting his earlier revision of the hopeless cycle of elegy and descending still further into despair. So, for instance, at *Tristia* 1.1.101–2, Ovid cautions a friend who wants to help him, since *tantum ne noceas, dum vis prodesse, videto/ nam spes est animi nostra timore minor.* This is a reversal of the elegiac situation, in which hope manages to triumph over fear, but the two emotions nonetheless remain central to Ovid's elegiac persona in exile (see too their juxtaposition at *EP* 1.2.61–4).

A number of situations, or moods, either give hope to Ovid in exile,[15] or take it away.[16] He understands that his exile poetry will disappoint the hopes of those who used to enjoy reading him (*Tr.* 1.11.36). He hopes for death, as the only cure

---

12 While the ideas behind this paragraph owe their inspiration to Thea Thorsen and Steve Heyworth, the formulation is stolen from elsewhere (Princess Bride: 'Mostly dead is slightly alive'; Monty Python and the Holy Grail: 'I'm not dead ... I'm getting better'); see Wheeler 2004–5 for the continued partial life of elegy after Ovid.

13 The arguments of this section are in some ways an expansion of Barchiesi's argument that Ovid's double *Heroides* provide an encapsulated history of elegy, with each pair representing a stage in the transition from epic to Hellenistic poetry, to the natural end point of elegy (1999).

14 Occurrences of *spes* in the exile poetry: *Tr.* 1: 5, *Tr.* 2: 6; *Tr.* 3: 4; *Tr.* 4: 5; *Tr.* 5: 3; *EP* 1:9; *EP* 2:6; *EP* 3: 7; *EP* 4: 4.

15 In addition to those discussed in the main text, see *Tr.* 3.3.24, 3.5.25, 43 and 53, 4.7.8, 4.8.13, 4.9.13, 5.4.17 (placed into a third party's voice), 5.8.22, *EP* 1.3.4, 2.3.68, 2.7.79, 2.8.14 (hope of seeing the imperial family almost realized, through a gift of their statues), 2.8.72, 3.1.140 (Ovid's wife is to approach Livia carefully, so as not to destroy Ovid's hopes of alleviation), 3.3.92 (an epiphanic Cupid assures Ovid that there is still hope).

16 In addition to those discussed in the main text, see *Tr.* 1.2.33, 2.182, 4.3.12, 5.12.29, *EP* 3.5.58 (his friends should not encourage his hope if there is no possibility of return).

for his ills (*Tr.* 4.6.49). *Tristia* 2.145–54 provides a more extended example of how Ovid's exilic hope works: it fluctuates, irrationally, as he takes into consideration various features of his situation. The passage ends in a kind of *aporia*.

In the *Epistulae ex Ponto*, Ovid offers an extended discussion of hope:

> spes igitur menti poenae, Graecine, levandae
> non est ex toto nulla relicta meae.
> haec dea, cum fugerent sceleratas numina terras,
> in dis invisa sola remansit humo.
> haec facit ut vivat fossor quoque compede vinctus,
> liberaque a ferro crura futura putet.
> haec facit ut, videat cum terras undique nullas,
> naufragus in mediis bracchia iactet aquis.
> saepe aliquem sollers medicorum cura reliquit,
> nec spes huic vena deficiente cadit.
> carcere dicuntur clausi sperare salutem,
> atque aliquis pendens in cruce vota facit.
> haec dea quam multos laqueo sua colla ligantis
> non est proposita passa perire nece!
> me quoque conantem gladio finire dolorem
> arcuit iniecta continuitque manu,
> 'quid' que 'facis? lacrimis opus est, non sanguine' dixit,
> 'saepe per has flecti principis ira solet.'
> quam vis est igitur meritis indebita nostris,
> magna tamen spes est in bonitate dei. *EP* 1.6.27–46

Here Ovid expands upon the point of Tib. 2.6 (commentators are unanimous in referring these lines to the earlier passage) and also makes clear in retrospect that Tibullus actually had nothing to complain about. Elegiac love is indeed hopeless, and a poet is indeed much like a slave or a sick man. But elegy, Ovid now suggests more insistently than he did before, was always a lifestyle choice and so could always be un-chosen or rejected, as I have suggested Tibullus finally did. The post-exilic Ovid, according to his poetry, is now in a situation in which hope really is his last refuge – this is real despair, folks, and real suffering! Ovid's notion of hope as a last resort, incidentally, strikes a strikingly modern tone which is not much found elsewhere in ancient literature; as noted above, Greco-Roman hope is mostly of the kind found in Tibullus 2.6, providing a temporary comfort that is inevitably shown to be deceptive and not worth the cost it exacts.

As Ovid continues to write from exile, his mood continues to darken:

> Spem iuuat amplecti, quae non iuuat inrita semper,
> et, fieri cupias si qua, futura putes.
> proximus huic gradus est bene desperare salutem
> seque semel uera scire perisse fide.

curando fieri quaedam maiora videmus
vulnera, quae melius non tetigisse fuit.
mitius ille perit, subita qui mergitur unda,
quam sua qui tumidis bracchia lassat aquis.
cur ego concepi Scythicis me posse carere
finibus et terra prosperiore frui?
cur aliquid de me speravi lenius umquam?
an fortuna mihi sic mea nota fuit? *EP* 3.7.21–32

In this poem, Ovid apologizes for bothering his friends and suggests that he has given up on hope entirely. The rest of *EP* 3 confirms this mood of hopelessness. Given the Tibullan precedent, we might reasonably expect silence hereafter. Once there is no hope, there is no point in going on, certainly no point in going on writing.

And yet – as with the silence that might have happened after Tibullus 2, but didn't – there is more poetry, a fourth book of *Epistulae ex Ponto*. It returns to the previously-rejected hope in four passages (4.6.15–16, 4.8.21, 4.12.41–2, 4.14.61–2). The first of these, written after Augustus' death, claims that the emperor was just about to relent and pardon the exiled Ovid; however intrinsically implausible a claim, it is certainly a reasonable one for Ovid to make. Indeed, it is tempting to connect the changed mood of the earlier part of *EP* 4 to the death of Augustus. But what Ovid actually says is that Augustus' demise puts an end to his hopes, since the emperor was just on the brink of forgiving him (*coeperat Augustus deceptae ignoscere culpae,/ spem nostram terras deseruitque simul, EP* 4.6.15–16). The poet might well have expected that he would fare better under the putative successor Drusus, and even the actual emperor, Tiberius, might have seemed like an improvement. In any case, the death of Augustus –however much Ovid denies it – seems to infuse the book with new hope; in 4.8 he urges his relation-by-marriage Suillius to try again, issuing a direct appeal of the kind we have not seen for many books. Several poems later, he directs a similar request to Tuticanus. But the poet's final word on hope, also written to Tuticanus, is equivocal at best, Ovid wishing he could hope for peace and warmth (*di modo fecissent, placidae spem posset habere/ pacis, et a gelido longius axe foret, EP* 4.14.61–2).

In Ovid's first eight books of exile poetry, we see a repetition-and-expansion of the elegiac cycle of hope and despair, which ends, as it inevitably must, in silence. But this cycle then repeats all over again in miniature in the last book, trying one last time to see whether hope might provide a way forward. In the end, elegiac hope fails. In this it is little different from other ancient manifestations of this deeply troubling emotion. At the same time, and despite its repeated exposure as a deeply problematic, frustrating emotional response to the world, it continues to be available (like elegy itself) to those who have nothing else, who can manage to convince themselves that this time, for them, it might be different.

Bibliography

Avery, W.T. (1960), 'The Year of Tibullus' Death', *CJ* 55, 205–9.
Avery, W.T. (1961), 'Tibullus' Death Again', *CJ* 56, 229–33.
Ball, R.J. (1983), *Tibullus the Elegist: A Critical Survey*, Göttingen.
Barchiesi, A. (1999), 'Vers une Histoire à Rebours de l'Élégie Latine: Les Héroïdes "Doubles" (16–21)', in: J. Fabre-Serris/A. Deremetz (eds.), *Élégie et Épopée dans la Poésie Ovidienne (Héroïdes et Amours) en Hommage à Simone Viarre*, edd., Villeneuve, 53–67.
Bright, D.F. (1978), Haec Mihi Fingebam: *Tibullus in His World*, Leiden.
Caston, R.R. (2012), *The Elegiac Passion: Jealousy in Roman Love Elegy*, Oxford.
Dettmer, H. (1980), 'The Arrangement of Tibullus Books 1 and 2', *Philologus* 124, 68–82.
Fulkerson, L. (2012), 'Sad Ovid, Angry Augustus', in: C. Deroux (ed.), *Studies in Latin Literature and Roman History* vol. XVI, Brussels, 339–66.
Fulkerson, L. (2015), 'Plutarch and the Ambiguities of 'Ελπίς', in: D. Cairns/ L. Fulkerson (eds.), *Emotions Between Greece and Rome*, *BICS* Supplement, 67–86.
Fulkerson, L. (2016), 'Torn Between Hope and Despair: Narrative Foreshadowing and Suspense in the Greek Novel', in: R.R. Caston/R.A. Kaster (eds.) *Hope, Joy and Affection in the Classical World*, Oxford, 75–91.
Fulkerson, L. (2017), 'The Vagaries of Hope in Vergil and Ovid', in: D. Cairns/D. Nelis (eds.), *Emotions in the Classical World: Methods, Approaches, and Directions*, Stuttgart, 207–230.
Gibson, R. (2013), 'Loves and Elegy', in: T. Thorsen (ed.), *The Cambridge Companion to Latin Love Elegy*, Cambridge, 209–23.
Greene, E. (1998), *The Erotics of Domination: Male Desire and the Mistress in Latin Love Poetry*, Baltimore.
James, S.L. (2003), *Learned Girls and Male Persuasion: Gender and Reading in Roman Love Elegy*, Berkeley.
Knox, P.E. (2005), 'Milestones in the Career of Tibullus', *CQ* 55, 204–16.
Lee-Stecum, P. (forthcoming), 'Present Memory and Frustrated Desire (Tibullus 2.1, 2.5, and 2.6)', in: I. Goh (ed.), *Tibullus the Idealist.*
Levin, D.N. (1967), 'The Alleged Date of Tibullus' Death', *CJ* 62, 311–14.
Maltby, R. (2002), *Tibullus*: Elegies. *Text, Introduction and Commentary*, Cambridge.
Martelli, F. (2013), *Ovid's Revisions: The Editor as Author*, Cambridge.
McGann, M.J. (1970), 'The Date of Tibullus' Death', *Latomus* 29, 774–80.
Miller, P.A. (2004), *Subjecting Verses: Latin Love Elegy and the Emergence of the Real*, Princeton NJ.
Murgatroyd, P.N. (1989), 'The Genre and Unity of Tibullus 2.6', *Phoenix* 43, 134–42.
Murgatroyd, P.N. (1994), *Tibullus* Elegies II, Oxford.
Reeve, M. (1984), 'Tibullus 2.6', *Phoenix* 38, 235–9.
Smith, K.F. (1913), *The Elegies of Albius Tibullus*, New York.
Thorsen, T. (2014), *Ovid's Early Poetry: From His Single Heroides to his Remedia Amoris*, Cambridge.
Ullrich, R. (1889), *Studia Tibulliana: de libri secondi editione*, PhD Diss., Berlin.
Veremans, J. (1981), 'L'anaphore dans l'oeuvre de Tibulle', *AC* 50, 774–800.
Wheeler, S. (2004-5), 'Before the *Aetas Ovidiana:* Mapping the Early Reception of Ovidian Elegy', *Hermathena* 177/8, 9–26.

Jacqueline Fabre-Serris

Intratextuality and Intertextuality in the *Corpus Tibullianum* (3.8–18)

The reception of [Tibullus] Book 3.8–18 in learned commentaries since 1475 is now well documented.[1] I will not discuss in detail the various hypotheses about Sulpicia's authorship and style published since Santirocco's (1979) seminal article. Poems 8–18 are considered to form a self-contained unit, but, according to the opinions of different critics, these poems are either attributed to one author (Tibullus, Ovid, an anonymous poet or Sulpicia, the niece of Messalla),[2] or divided in two parts attributed to two different authors. The *communis opinio* assigns poems 8–12 to an anonymous poet, generally called the *amicus Sulpiciae,* and poems 13–18 to Sulpicia. Parker (1994), however, has argued that the poems in the first person (9, 11, 13–18) were by Sulpicia and the poems in the third person (8, 10, 12) were by an unnamed poet.[3]

In this paper, I would like to demonstrate that intratextual and intertextual approaches can help us understand how this poetic cycle has been created. First, by pursuing Parker's claim that the poems sharing a single authorial view are by Sulpicia, I will compare the poems in the third person (8, 10, 12) with the poems in the first person (9, 11, 13–18). I want to examine how their unidentified author engages with and responds to Sulpicia's poems 13–18, but also to poem 11. As noted by Hinds, scholars generally agree that the elegies ascribed to the *amicus* are 'picking up and expanding themes adumbrated in the short group'.[4] I shall argue that the *amicus* aims to praise Sulpicia as a poetess, but by presenting her in a manner more consistent with Augustan Roman morality than she did herself. In my opinion *how* the *amicus* has paid homage to Sulpicia could explain in part *why* his poems have been intercalated with those of the niece of Messalla. I will try also to explain how the unit 8–12 and the unit 13–18 have been created by offering some assumptions about the arrangement of the poems that could support Parker's positions. Finally, I will argue that Ovid is referring to Sulpicia *and* to the *amicus* in the *Heroides* and that this immediate reception, when the

1 Skoie 2002.

2 The identification with Tibullus or someone impersonating Tibullus is proposed by Holzberg 1998–9 and Hubbard 2004, with Ovid by Bréguet 1946, and with Sulpicia by Hallett 2002.

3 See also Fabre-Serris 2009. Except for epigram 15, this repartition was initially proposed by Heyne in his commentary on the *Corpus Tibullianum* published between 1755 and 1798 (Skoie 2002, 128).

4 Hinds 1987, 41.

https://doi.org/10.1515/9783110611021-005

members of Messalla's circle were still active, allows the supposition that the poems of the *amicus* were written soon after those of Sulpicia and that the entire 'Garland' was probably already constituted at that time.

1 Intratextual and extratextual allusions in the poems by the *amicus*: 8, 10 and 12

I will focus on poem 8 in arguing that this poem, placed at the beginning of the Sulpician cycle, constitutes an 'oriented' introduction, to be compared with poem 13, placed at the beginning of the epigrammatic sequence in the first person.

1.1 Poem 3.8 or the response of the *amicus* to poem 3.13

In poem 8, Sulpicia is praised while she attends the Matronalia. The public rites celebrated on the Kalends of March, a day sacred to Juno, were performed by Roman matrons, but other women were probably present at the temple. We do not know the social status of Sulpicia, presumably an unmarried woman, perhaps widowed or divorced.[5] The *amicus* asks Mars to come and see Sulpicia, elegantly clad for him: *Sulpicia est tibi culta tuis, Mars magne, kalendis; / spectatum e caelo, si sapis, ipse ueni* (Sulpicia is dressed for you, great Mars, on your Kalends. If you have wit, come yourself from heaven to look at her, 1–2). He develops a curious triangular scenario whose protagonists are Sulpicia, Mars, and Venus, asked to forgive Mars for coming to see Sulpicia (*hoc Venus ignoscet*, 3). The *amicus* warns Mars not to drop his weapons when overwhelmed at the sight of the girl: *at tu, uiolente, caueto/ ne tibi miranti turpiter arma cadant* (but you, violent one, have a care lest to your shame your weapons drop as you marvel, 3–4). When Amor wants to inflame the gods, he kindles both his torches from the fire of her eyes: *illius ex oculis, cum uult exurere diuos,/ accendit geminas lampadas acer Amor* (5–6).

In previous papers,[6] I have argued that this potential erotic scene is inspired by the one described by Sulpicia in poem 13. At last Love has come (*tandem uenit amor,* 1). Sulpicia had implored Venus in her poems; in return the goddess has brought her lover and placed him in her embrace: *exorata meis illum Cytherea Camenis / attulit in nostrum deposuitque sinum* (3–4). The situation described

5 Hallett 2010, 84–5.
6 Fabre-Serris 2014, 2017.

(Cerinthus received *in nostrum sinum*, a word synonymous with *gremium*, according to Adams),[7] is indeed – or so I believe – a variation on the famous scene at the beginning of the *De rerum natura*, where *Mavors armipotens* comes into the *gremium* of Venus (33), *aeterno deuictus uolnere amoris* (defeated by the eternal wound of love, 34). As highlighted by Sedley, at the beginning of the *De rerum natura*, Lucretius is imitating Empedocles' proem.[8] I have argued that Lucretius, in order to refer to the *Peri phuseos* and provide an Epicurean and Roman reception of the cosmological Empedoclean principle of Love, had inserted some Varronian etymologies of Venus, like *uenire, uis, uincere* and *uincire*, in his proem, and particularly in the love scene between Mars and Venus (imitated from the Homeric episode (*Od.* 8.266–366), philosophically read as staging the victory of Empedoclean Love). These etymologies, as a way of exploring various philosophical dimensions of Venus,[9] are recalled either by words (*tua* ui, 13, *aeterno deuictus uolnere amoris*, 34) or through the situations described: Venus is coming (*uenire*), she is embracing Mars (*uincire*) while seeking peace for the Romans. My main thesis is that Gallus had handled the Homeric episode by referring to Lucretius' *prooemium* and used some Varronian etymologies of Venus to develop various motifs related to the power of love, like the 'victory' of Amor (*uicit amor*), the tight embrace of lovers when having sex (*uincire*), the love bonds (*foedera amoris*) or the antagonism between love and war.

In poem 13, Sulpicia is alluding both to Sappho's *Ode to Aphrodite*,[10] successfully implored by the Greek poetess for help, and to Gallus. With *Tandem uenit amor* Sulpicia refers indeed to the papyrus of Qaṣr Ibrîm, more precisely to the power of the Muses (tandem *fecerunt carmina Musae/ quae possem domina deicere digna mea*, At last the Muses have made poems that I could utter as worthy of my mistress, 6–7), but also to a (probably) Gallan *iunctura*,[11] alluding to one of the etymologies of Venus (*uenire*). Then she reworks the Lucretian love scene when claiming that Venus, moved by her Muses, has brought her lover into her embrace.

In poem 8, the *amicus* pays tribute to Sulpicia while making explicit her allusion to the Lucretian staging of the *amores* between Mars and Venus. Sulpicia had replaced Mars by Cerinthus, he replaces Cerinthus by Mars. As in poem 13, Venus is mentioned but she is herself, in a way, replaced by Sulpicia. The *amicus*

7 Adams 1990, 90.
8 Sedley 2007.
9 Hinds 2006.
10 Piastri 1998, 139–40; Merriam 2006, 12; Fabre-Serris 2009, 150–1.
11 See below p. 76.

uses in turn some Varronian etymologies of Venus, alluded to in the *De rerum natura*: *uenire* (*ueni*, 2), *uis* (*uiolente*, 3), *uincere* (*ne tibi miranti turpiter arma cadant*, 4). He adds two other etymologies of Venus: *uenia* (*hoc Venus ignoscet*, 3) and *ueneror*. This latter etymology is very indicative of what he intends to do: *ueneranda* is placed at the end of lines 7–10, where he uses two other words with strong moral connotations *Decor* and *decet* when describing Sulpicia's attractiveness and its effect on men (7–10):

> Illam, quidquid agit, quoquo uestigia mouit,
> componit furtim subsequiturque Decor;
> seu soluit crines, fusis decet esse capillis:
> seu compsit, comptis est ueneranda comis.

> Whatever she does, wherever she goes, attractiveness (with a dose of decency) adorns and secretly follows her; if she loosens her hair, flowing tresses become her; if she dresses it, she is worthy of respect with her hair up.

It is equally significant that the *amicus* is not echoing words employed by Sulpicia in her provocative statement about her first night of love: *pudor, fama, iuuat, taedet*. He does propose a suitable *retractatio* of the opening scene: Mars comes to see Sulpicia, who is dressed in his honor, without Venus becoming jealous. If Sulpicia can be called *digna* in poem 8, the word conveys a different sense than it has in poem 13, where she claims: *cum digno digna fuisse ferar* (Let it be said that I have been with a man worthy of me, as I was worthy of him, 10). For the *amicus* Sulpicia is *digna* because she is a *puella culta* in both senses of the word. She is the only girl (*sola puellarum digna*) who deserves luxurious clothing, Arabian perfumes, and to be bedecked with Eastern gems (15–20). As a poet, she is particularly worthy to be welcomed in the chorus of the Muses and of Apollo: *dignior est uestro nulla puella choro* (no girl is more worthy of your chorus, 24). To conclude, the *amicus* is playing a very ingenious game with Sulpicia and her intertextual interlocutors, Gallus, Lucretius, and Sappho, who knew better than anybody how to praise women's beauty and refined clothing. The moral perspective of the *amicus* is confirmed when we continue our comparative reading of poems 10 and 12, in the third person, and poems 14, 15, 16, 17, and 18, in the first person.

1.2 The selections of the *amicus* in poems 10 and 12

In poem 10, the *amicus* asks Phoebus to come and to cure the illnesses of a sweet girl, unnamed. After having described Cerinthus' despair, the *amicus* gives him back his confidence: *Pone metum, Cerinthe* (leave your concern, Cerinthus, 15) by claiming: *deus non laedit amantes* (the god does not hurt lovers, 15). Cerinthus merely needs to keep on loving his girlfriend: *tu modo semper ama* (16). She is going to get better. There is no reason to cry as long as she is in love with him. Apparently the *amicus* has intended to give a reassuring reply to poem 17, and implicitly to poem 16. In poem 17, Sulpicia, who is sick, explains that she would wish to be cured only if she could think that this would also be the wish of Cerinthus: *A ego non aliter tristes euincere morbos/ optarim, quam te si quoque uelle putem* (Ah! I would not otherwise wish to overcome my grievous illness than if I thought you too wished it, 3–4). As, in poem 16, she is alluding to the unfaithfulness of Cerinthus, we can understand that in poem 17 she is expressing doubts about the strength of his love.

The birthday of Sulpicia or of Cerinthus (the issue is debated) is a central element in poems 14 and 15, where Sulpicia is afraid of a —foreseen (14) but finally cancelled (15)— journey imposed by her uncle, Messalla, which would result in the separation of the lovers. In poem 12, written on the occasion of Sulpicia's birthday, the *amicus* begs Juno to keep anybody from separating the two lovers: *At tu, sancta, faue, neu quis diuellat amantes,/ sed iuueni, quaeso,* mutua *uincla para* (But you, venerable one, be favorable! Prevent anybody from separating the lovers, but I beg you, prepare chains and make them be shared with the young man, 7–8). If the first part of this request is alluding to the situation feared in poem 14, the motif of *mutuus amor* and the image of shared *uincla* are referring to the request addressed to Venus in poem 11, written in the first person (7,13–4):

> mutuus adsit amor (...)
> Nec tu sis iniusta, Venus: uel seruiat aeque
>   uinctus uterque tibi uel mea uincla leua.
>
> make our love be mutual (...) Let's not be unfair, Venus: May each of us be equally slave and chained or make my chains lighter.

As in poem 8 (*componit* (...) *Decor*), the *amicus* uses the verb *componere*, employed in a provocative context by Sulpicia in poem 13: ... *uultus componere famae/ taedet: cum digno digna fuisse ferar* (composing a face for my reputation disgusts me, let it be said that I have been with a man worthy of me, as I was worthy of him, 9–10). In poem 12, *componere*, positively connoted (*bene*), is associated with Juno, praised for having created the couple by choosing the two partners extremely well (*dignior*): *Sic bene compones: ullae non ille puellae/ seruire aut cuiquam dignior illa uiro* (You will provide a good match: there was no woman he deserved more to serve, there was no man she deserved more to serve, 9–10). The *amicus* is also alluding to a motif central in poem 18: Sulpicia's ardent love: *uritur, ut celeres urunt altaria flammae, / nec, liceat quamuis, sana fuisse uelit* (she is burning, as the flames are burning the altar, and, even if it were possible, she would not want to be cured, 17–18). In poem 18, Sulpicia is apologizing for having abandoned her lover in the night because she wanted to hide her excessive *ardor* (6). In poem 12, this sexual context has been erased. Because she is *natae* (...) *studiosa* (concerned about her daughter, 15), like Messalla (*mei studiose* in 14.5), the mother of Sulpicia advises her to make (aloud) a vow in accordance with her own wishes (*praecipit* (...) *quod* optat, 15). But Sulpicia is silently (*tacita*, 16) making another vow. The *amicus* is probably alluding to poem 11, where Cerinthus is silently making his vow (17–18, 20):

... sed tectius optat:
nam pudet haec illum dicere uerba palam.
(...) quid refert, clamne palamne roget?

... but he makes his wish more secretly; he is indeed ashamed of saying openly these words (...) Does it matter if he is asking in secret or openly?

To conclude, the three poems written in the third person share some common (intratextual) features.[12] First they include in the first two lines the name of a god (Mars, Phoebus, and Juno), to whom the poet is about to make a request. Secondly they are focused on Sulpicia, portrayed as praiseworthy, because she is a *puella culta*, but also *pia* (poems 8 and 12) and a perfect lover (poems 10 and 12). Her love is burning, faithful, and totally shared by Cerinthus. On this point their author has taken as a model poem 11 that contains a declaration of love expressed in a less erotically explicit manner than poem 13. The *amicus* has reused motifs and images from all the poems in the first person except from poem 16 and poem 9. The former is focused on a presumed infidelity of Cerinthus and the reply of Sulpicia, who suggests that he could be wrong to be so sure of her own faithfulness. The second includes a feminine variation on the Gallan motif of hunting as *seruitium amoris*, ending with a sexual union in the open! The *amicus* has systematically avoided any allusion to erotic passages or contexts, and tried to give a respectable image of Sulpicia in accordance with her social status. Therefore, I suggest, Sulpicia wrote not only poems 13–18, but also poem 11, to which the *amicus* refers, and poem 9, a poem 'excluded', like poem 16, by the *amicus*, for its 'immorality'. Obviously the latter was guided by the concern of correcting the scandalous image that Sulpicia had presented of herself. Anyway it would have been impossible for a poet of Messalla's circle to impersonate the identity of his niece and frankly evoke her illicit love affair and erotic enjoyments. To be sure, in poem 13 Sulpicia proposes to someone said to be without his or her own joys

12 My analysis is the counterpart of that of Parker (1994, 55), who points out that '3.9 and 3.11 reveal several stylistic and syntactic features that are shared with Sulpicia's poems 3.13–8 and are infrequent or absent in poems 3.8, 10, and 12'.

to recount her *gaudia*, but this is a quite provocative proposal and that does not mean that this individual is supposed to write texts in the first person as if he or she was Sulpicia herself. In fact the *amicus* should rather be compared to the *amici* of poem 16, *solliciti pro nobis* (concerned about us, 5), who would feel great sorrow if Sulpicia yielded to any unknown lover (*quibus illa dolori est/ ne cedam ignoto maxima causa toro*, 5–6).

2 Order and date of the Sulpician cycle

2.1 The hypothesis of the 'Garland'

In her paper on the different critical trends in interpreting Sulpicia in 2006, regarding the Sulpician cycle, Keith[13] considers that 'Parker does not attempt to offer an explanation for the arrangement of the Sulpician poems in the Tibullan corpus as it has come down to us (3.8, 10, and 12 describing Sulpicia and her love for Cerinthus in the third person; 3.9, 11, and 13–18 in the first-person voice of Sulpicia), though he notes the precedent of Hellenistic Greek poetry collections such as Meleager's Garland, in which the author's poems are interwoven with those of other authors, often in thematic groupings'. In order to support Parker's assumption, I would initially observe that he has rightly suggested that one 'principle of arrangement may simply be the length'.[14] Poem 8 has 24 lines; poem 9 24 lines, poem 11 20 lines, poem 12 20 lines, poems 13, 14, 15, 16, 17, 18 taken together as forming an epigrammatic cycle written in the first person, 34 lines. I will argue that one can discern another principle of arrangement, generally used to organize a narrative cycle thematically. It consists in telling successive stories by taking up some motifs from one narrative in another, but also by combining them differently in order to create continuity while respecting the stylistically and intellectually enjoyable principle of variety.[15] I have highlighted and italicized words that emphasize the different motifs. In poem 8, written on the occasion of the Matronalia, the *amicus* makes *a request* to Mars: he asks the god to *come* and see Sulpicia. He is praising Sulpicia as a *puella culta* (she is elegantly dressed and a poetess worthy to be celebrated). In minor mode, as a *puella culta*, Sulpicia is also praised for *inflaming the desire of all men*. In poem 9, Sulpicia makes a request:

13 Keith 2006, 5.
14 Parker 1994, 50.
15 The 'alternation of author, combined with contrast of theme' has already been proposed by Parker (1994, 50), but he has not made the demonstration in detail.

she asks the boar to spare her lover in the hunt. Then she makes successive wishes. She imagines herself going hunting with Cerinthus and she says that she would like it if they were surprised making love in front of the nets, without being disturbed by the boar. As for now Cerinthus is hunting without her, she wishes that he will remain chaste (and then *faithful)* and come back soon into her embrace (*in nostros sinus*). In case any *rival* tries to seduce him, she wishes this woman will perish by being torn apart by hunting dogs. In poem 10, the *amicus* makes a *request* to Apollo: he asks the god to *come* and *cure* Sulpicia, who is *sick*. Her lover is very concerned and makes innumerable wishes for her recovery. That means he is *faithful* (and implicitly that the fear of Sulpicia in poem 9 was unfounded). The *amicus* explains to him that Sulpicia is a *constant lover*, although she is courted by a *credula turba* (a variation on the motive of the *rival*). Cerinthus should not cry; she will *be cured* by Apollo. In poem 11, written on the occasion of his *birthday*, Sulpicia praises Cerinthus as a very attractive man, who is *inflaming the desire of all young girls*. Sulpicia, who describes herself as the *most ardent girl*, makes a request to the Genius of Cerinthus: she asks him to *welcome the incense* and to be *favorable* and wishes that Cerinthus will not be *unfaithful*. She makes also a *request* to Venus. She wishes that their love affair will *always last* by using the image of the *shared chains*. She adds that this is also the wish of Cerinthus, but he does not dare express it openly, and she asks the Genius to accomplish this *secret* wish. In poem 12, written in the occasion of Sulpicia's *birthday*, the *amicus* makes a *request* to Juno. He asks her to *welcome the incense* offered by Sulpicia (as in poem 8 the young girl *se compsit* for the deity) and to be *favorable*. He wishes that their love will *always last*, using also the image of the *shared chains* (8) and that nobody will force them apart (an allusion in minor mode to the motive of the *rival*). Sulpicia is described *as burning with love* and *secretly* wishing that she will never *be cured* (a variation in minor mode on the motif of the *sickness* treated in poem 10). What about poems 13–18? Taken together, they form a miniature epigrammatic love cycle. I have tried to show that poems 8, 10 and 12 have been written in response to epigrams 13–18. But this miniature cycle is also in itself thematically arranged. The first and the last poems are focused on a night of love. In poem 13, Sulpicia is claiming that *amor has come* (an illicit love affair) and that she has no regrets. Poems 14 and 15 are alluding to a possible *separation*, planned but finally cancelled, which allows Sulpicia to celebrate with Cerinthus her or his *birthday*. In poem 16, Sulpicia is expressing her concern about the possible *infidelity* of Cerinthus (she has perhaps a *rival*), too sure that she could not be so stupid[16] (*inepta*) to prefer to him someone less valuable. In

16 I refer to Heyne's interpretation (Skoie 2002, 134–5).

poem 17, Sulpicia, who is *sick*, asks her lover if he is *always in love* with her, in other terms, if he is *faithful* or not. She explains that she wishes to *be cured* only if he wishes the same thing, in other words if he is *always in love* with her. In poem 18, Sulpicia wishes not to *be loved* any more by Cerinthus, if she has acted stupidly (*stulta*) (and she regrets that) when she has left him in the night in order to hide from him her excessively *burning passion*. The thematic arrangement of the entire Sulpician cycle had the added advantage that Sulpicia's sexually provocative statements in poems 9 and 11 were framed by more suitable descriptions of her *persona*.

2.2 What may be inferred from the reception of the Sulpician cycle?

Assuming that Sulpicia was composing her poems when the circle of Messalla was flourishing (and probably before the enactment of the Julian laws), when were the poems of the *amicus* written? If it is agreed that poems in the third person are elegiac answers to poems in the first person, in accordance with the usual practice of the elegists, it may be presumed that these 'gifts' to the niece of Messalla were more relevant if they were written shortly after those of Sulpicia. When was the Sulpician cycle arranged? There is no evidence that enables us to respond to this question. Critics have reported many verbal and thematic similarities between Ovid, the *amicus* and Sulpicia, but they have come to different conclusions.[17] It is indeed difficult to be rigorous in interpreting apparent parallels. We have to be careful, as noted by Parker, about a twofold methodological fallacy: 'First, when two poets share a word or trope, it is assumed that one must be imitating the other, rather than both drawing on a third or a set of common topoi. Second, it is always assumed that the less famous poet must be imitating the more famous'.[18] Personally, as a woman myself, I don't have any problem in challenging the second assumption and believe that a male author could find inspiration from a female poet, or that an immensely talented poet could have drawn on one with lesser gifts. Parker's first objection raises a real difficulty, inasmuch as, in addition, a poet may refer both to another poet and to his model. I will try to show that this is probably the case in *Heroides* 4: Ovid is referring to Gallus, but by taking into account Sulpicia's variations on Gallan motifs.

---

17 See, about *Rem. am.* 199–200, *Met.* 1.508–9, 593, 10.545, compared with some similarities in poem 9, Bréguet 1946, 269–72, who argues for one and the same author, Ovid, and Hinds 1987, 36–7, who thinks that the author of elegy 9 (according to him, the *amicus*) has imitated Ovid.

18 Parker 2006, 26 n. 31.

Two verbal features in lines 19–20: *Venit amor grauius, quo serius. Vrimur intus; / urimur et caecum pectora uulnus habent* (Came love all the more heavy as it came latter. I am burning inside; I am burning inside, and my breast holds a hidden wound) are also used by Sulpicia in poem 13: *uenit amor* (1), and in poem 11: *Vror ... uror* (5). The *iunctura uenit amor* is also found in Propertius 1.7.26: saepe uenit *magno faenore tardus* Amor (often when Amor has been slow to come, he gets paid with high interest rates), and in Propertius 2.3.45–6: ...*aut mihi, si quis,* / acrius *ut moriar,* uenerit *alter* amor (...or if for me another love came more ardently so that I die). It is likely that Sulpicia, Propertius and Ovid are referring to a prior poet who would have used *uenit amor* with an adverb. When verbal similarities are found in several elegists, critics usually conclude that the best candidate is the founder of the elegiac genre, Gallus.[19] The verb *uro(r)* in an erotic sense is used by Tibullus (2.4.6), by Propertius (2.3.44, 24.8), by the *amicus* (12.17), by Sulpicia (11.5), and by Ovid in *Amores* (1.1.26, 2.43, 2.4.12), in *Heroides* (3.138, 4.19–20, 52, 7.25; 15.9), and in *Ars amatoria* (3.448, 573). I leave aside the *Fasti*, the *Metamorphoses* and the double *Heroides*, composed after 18 BCE. However *uror*, probably a Gallan word,[20] is repeated only in poem 11 and in *Heroides* 4, and within the same context: when a girl is proclaiming her love. This suggests that these texts by Sulpicia and Ovid are interrelated but there is no way to know who has imitated whom. In *Heroides* 4, we find two other words present in poem 13: *pudor* and *fama*: *Qua licet † quitur †*, pudor *est miscendus* amori (as much as possible, we must mix modesty with love, 9); Fama, *uelim quaeras, crimine nostra uacat* (my reputation, I wish you to inquire about it, is free from accusation, 18). In similar contexts (they are talking freely about their loves), Propertius (2.24.1–4) and Ovid (*Am.* 3.1.21–2) associate *pudor* with *fabula*. *Fabula* is probably a Gallan word, as can be inferred also from Tibullus (1.4.83; 2.3.31) and from Lygdamus (4.68).

Later in *Heroides* 4 (87–104), Ovid reworks another Gallan motif, the hunt as *seruitium amoris*, by focusing on its ending: a sexual union performed in the open, as in Sulpicia, 9.15–16. If we compare the treatment of the hunt motif in Virgil, Tibullus, Propertius, Sulpicia and *Heroides* 4, without going into detail, *aper* is employed only in *Eclogue* 10.56 (*acris ... apros*), in *Heroides* 4, and in poem 9, and considered as dangerous, because of its *dentes*, only in poem 9 and *Heroides* 4, where the word is at the same place in the verse: *ne ueneris cupidae gaudia turbet, aper* (without disturbing the pleasures of an eager passion, the boar, 9.19; ... *neque obliquo dente timendus* aper, nor the boar formidable because

19 For detailed discussion about *uenit amor*, see Fabre-Serris 2017.
20 Fabre-Serris 2017, 131–2, n. 39.

of its oblique tusks, 4.104). This later detail also leads us to think that one of the two poets is referring to the other. At this point, I believe we have to look at the issue in a different way: by taking gender into account.[21] If we consider the fact that Ovid is a man, it is more likely that he borrows the words of a *real* girl, if this girl is a poet, when imagining how a *fictive* female character could declare her love rather than the reverse. I personally find it intellectually rather odd that the first treatment in the feminine voice of the most famous Gallan *exemplum* of *seruitium amoris*, the hunt, was attributed by some critics to Ovid, a man, rather than to a woman, Sulpicia, whose poems are all proposing a feminine transposition of the (male) elegiac genre. Of course, as noted previously, it is not paradoxical (especially for a man) to have difficulty in conceiving that a male author, a great poet, could find inspiration from a female poet, almost unknown. But Sulpicia was from Rome's highest social class and the niece of Messalla. Since Ovid frequented the circle of her uncle as a young man, he probably knew her. If a poet of this circle, the *amicus*, composed some poems in response to Sulpicia's poetry, according to the usual practice between elegists, probably improved in Messalla's circle by the *recitationes*, why would Ovid not have considered Sulpicia in the same manner, i.e. as an elegiac poet with whom he could engage in dialogue? Especially in *Heroides* 4, when he was trying to give an authentic sounding manner of speaking to a fictive female letter writer? Some verbal echoes have been listed also between Ovid and the *amicus*. Four expressions in poem 10 can be found also in different poems of Ovid: *pone metum* (15 and *Fast.* 2.759); *tu … semper ama (*16 and *Her.* 17.256); … in uno/ corpore *seruato restituisse* duos (19–20) and … *et* in un*a parce* duo*bus* (*Am.* 2.13.15) and *uiue nec* uni*us* corpore *perde* duos (*Her.* 11.62); *lacrimis* erit aptius *uti* (21) and aptius *impressi*s *fu*era*t liuere labellis*, *Am.* 1.7.41); aptius e*st deceatque magis potare puellas* (*Ars am.* 3.761). As noted by Bréguet, we find this last prosaic expression in poetry only in Ovid and Statius.[22] These four expressions are particularly adapted to the context in poem 10, but, as we well know,[23] this is not a sufficient argument. Furthermore, Ovid is the only poet besides the *amicus* (in poem 12) to use the verb *componere*[24] in the

21 In regard to the negative effects of Gender perspective on some male critics, see Farrell (2001, 57). As noted by Parker (2006, 27, n. 32), Farrell points out that, when Sulpicia was no longer considered 'a bad poet', who has written short texts, lacking the polish expected from a professional author, some critics 'can no longer believe she was a woman'.

22 Bréguet 1946, 139.

23 See, against this argument, Most (1987, 203–4), who uses, as counter-examples, the Catullan line: inuit*a*, o regina, tuo de *uertice* cessi (66.39) and its imitation by Virgil: inuit*us*, regina, tuo de *litore* cessi (*Aen.* 6.460).

24 Bréguet 1946, 181.

absolute sense of 'match': *sic bene* compones (9) and *Hoc* bene compositos, *hoc firmos soluit amores* (*Ars am.* 2.385). As a comparison between the poetic contexts does not allow us to reach a conclusion other than that one of the two poets is referring to the other, I suggest taking another perspective and wondering *why* a collection of poems like the Sulpician cycle could have been created. By this, I mean: for which audience? The simplest – and then most likely – answer is: for readers able to understand and appreciate both Sulpicia's complex poetry and the *amicus*' subtle variations, in other terms, for members of Messala's circle and more broadly for other contemporary poets – like the young Ovid. The accurate, ingenious way in which all these poems have been gathered to create such a refined composition makes sense only if Sulpicia was alive, and if the purpose of the collection was to offer this 'Garland' to the female poet who has inspired the answers of the *amicus*. Another final argument is that the arrangement of Sulpicia's and the *amicus*' poems into a small collection could have made both more famous and also account for Ovid's frequent references to *both* the former *and* the latter. Conversely, assuming that the Sulpician cycle is later than Ovid,[25] why would someone have created this refined collection of poems at a time when all the protagonists, Messalla included, were dead? To conclude, I am aware that I have proposed some more or less convincing reconstructions: intratextuality and intertextuality are subtle and fascinating tools that give us the impression that we can enter the genesis of poetic creation and become as ingenious as Roman poets, a delightful temptation!

25 See Hinds 1987, Tränkle 1990, Hubbard 2004.

Bibliography

Adams, J.N. (1990), *The Latin Sexual Vocabulary*, Baltimore.

Bréguet, E. (1946), *Le roman de Sulpicia, Elégies IV, 2–12 du* Corpus *Tibullianum*, Genève.

Dolansky, F. (2011), 'Reconsidering the Matronalia and Women's Rites', *CW* 104.2, 191–209.

Fabre-Serris, J. (2009), 'Sulpicia: An/other Female Voice in Ovid's *Heroides*. A New Reading of Letters 4 and 5', *Helios* 36.2, 149–72.

Fabre-Serris, J. (2014), 'La réception d'Empédocle dans la poésie latine: Virgile (*Buc.* 6), Lucrèce, Gallus et les poètes élégiaques', *Dictynna* 11.

Fabre-Serris, J. (2017), 'Sulpicia, Gallus et les élégiaques. Propositions de lecture de l'épigramme 13', *Eugesta* 7, 115–39.

Farrell, J. (2001), *Latin Language and Latin Culture*, Cambridge.

Flaschenriem, B. (1999), 'Sulpicia and the Rhetoric of Disclosure', *CP* 94.1, 36–54.

Hallett, J. (2002), 'The Eleven Elegies of the Augustan Poet Sulpicia', in: L.J. Churchill/P.R. Brown/J.E. Jeffrey (eds.), *Women Writing Latin from Roman Antiquity to Early Modern Europe*, 1: *Women Writing Latin in Roman Antiquity, Late Antiquity and the Early Christian Era*, New York/London, 45–65.

Hallett, J. (2009), 'Sulpicia and her Resistant Intertextuality', in: D. van Mal-Maeder/A. Burnier/L. Núñez (eds.), *Jeux de voix. Enonciation, intertextualité et intentionnalité dans la ittérature antique*, Bern, 141–55.

Hallett, J. (2010), 'Scenarios of Sulpiciae: Moral Discourses and Immoral Verses', *Eugesta* 1, 79–97.

Hinds, S. (1987), 'The Poetess and the Reader. Further Steps towards Sulpicia', *Hermathena* 143, 29–46.

Hinds, S. (2006), 'Venus, Varro and the *uates*: Toward the Limits of Etymologizing', *Dictynna* 3.

Holzberg, N. (1998–1999), 'Four Poets and a Poetess or a Portrait of the Poet as a Young Man? Thoughts on Book 3 of *Corpus Tibullianum*', *CJ* 94, 169–91.

Hubbard, T. (2004–2005), 'The Invention of Sulpicia', *CJ* 100, 177–94.

Keith, A. (1997), '*Tandem venit amor*: A Roman Woman Speaks of Love', in: J. Hallett/M. Skinner (eds.), *Roman Sexualities*, Princeton NJ, 295–310.

Keith, A. (2006), 'Critical Trends in Interpreting Sulpicia', *CW* 100.1, 3–10.

Lowe, N.J. (1988), 'Sulpicia's syntax', *CQ* 38, 193–205.

Luck, G. (1959), *The Latin Love Elegy*, London.

Merriam, C (2006), 'Sulpicia, Just Another Poet', *CW* 100.1, 11–15.

Milnor, K. (2002), 'Sulpicia's (Corpo) reality: Elegy, Authorship, and the Body in {Tibullus} 3.13', *Clas. Ant.* 21.2, 259–82.

Most, G. (1987), 'The 'Virgilian' *Culex*', in: P. Hardie/M. Withby (eds.), *Homo uiator.* Classical essays for John Bramble, Bristol, 199–209.

Parker, H.N. (1994), 'Sulpicia, the *auctor de Sulpicia,* and the Authorship of 3.9 and 3.11 of the *Corpus Tibullianum*', *Helios* 21, 39–62.

Parker, H.N. (2006), 'Catullus and the *Amici Catulli.* The Text of a Learned Talk', *CW* 100.1, 17–29.

Piastri, R. (1998), 'I carmi di Sulpicia e il repertorio topico dell'elegia', *Quad. Fil. Ling. Trad. Class.* 11, 137–70.

Piastri, R. (2013), 'Sulpicia e la sua fama', *B StudL*, 2013, 16–25.

Santirocco, M. (1979), 'Sulpicia Reconsidered', *CJ* 74, 229–39.

Sedley, D. (2007), 'The Empedoclean Opening', in: M. Gale (ed.), *Oxford Readings in Classical Studies, Lucretius*, Oxford, 48–87.

Skoie, M. (2002), *Reading Sulpicia: Commentaries 1475–1990*, Oxford.

Tränkle, H. (1990), *Appendix Tibulliana*, Berlin/New York.

Treggiari, S. (1991), *The Roman marriage*: Iusti Conjuges *from the Time of Cicero to the Time of Ulpian*, Oxford.

Part III: **Didactic, Bucolic and Epic Poetry**

George Kazantzidis

Intratextuality and Closure: The End of Lucretius' *De rerum natura*

'All plots tend to move deathward ... We edge nearer death every time we plot.'
Don DeLillo, *White Noise* (1985)

1 Introduction

In a well-known essay, entitled 'The Problematic of Ending in Narrative', J. Hillis Miller states that:

> Attempts to characterize the fiction of a given period by its commitment to closure or to open-endedness are blocked from the beginning by the impossibility of ever demonstrating whether a given narrative is closed or open. Analysis of endings leads always, if carried far enough, to the paralysis of this inability to decide.[1]

The author supports this claim by arguing against Aristotle's rigid conception of a 'critical turning point' in the tragic plot. Every tragedy, Aristotle says, falls into two parts, 'complication' (δέσις) and 'unraveling' (λύσις). The incidents lying outside the drama proper, and often certain of the incidents within it, form the complication; the rest of the play constitutes the unraveling (*Po.* 1455b24–6).[2] Where does the complication, folding up, or tying together end and the untying start, according to this model? 'Aristotle', as Hillis Miller observes, 'suggests the possibility of a narrative which would be all unraveling or denouement, in which the "turning-point" from tying to untying would be the beginning of the narrative proper and all the complication would lie prior to the action as its presupposition'.[3] The problem of the ending here becomes displaced to the problem of the beginning and the 'turning-point' spreads across, and adds meaning to every instance of the action.

At the same time, it should be noted that emplotment, which governs the sequence of information in the course of a narrative and integrates disparate events with the overall story,[4] foreshadows also an impending end. 'All plots tend to

1 Hillis Miller 1978, 7.
2 See Belfiore 1992, 128–31.
3 Hillis Miller 1978, 4.
4 See Ricoeur 1980.

https://doi.org/10.1515/9783110611021-006

move deathward', as one of the characters proclaims in the excerpt by Don DeLillo cited in the epigraph. Just as 'writing is the destruction of every voice' and presents itself as a 'neutral, oblique space where our subject slips away [and] all identity is lost',[5] so the idea of an overarching, finite structure bears the marks of an ultimate undoing. On this interpretation, closure is always imminent in a text,[6] if not a necessary precondition without which a story cannot have its beginning.

In the present chapter, I would like to discuss this 'deathward movement' in Lucretius' poem. In so doing, I wish to consider closure not as a section of the text that is formally placed and contained at the end of the narrative but as a trope which is disseminated – as Hillis Miller would have it – *throughout* the text.[7] I would like to see closure, in other words, as that process by which the poem's ending, whether we consider it to be 'satisfying' or not, is foregrounded, but can also be constantly redefined through various sections in the narrative and through the interrelations which we as readers impose on them; we may call these sections 'intratexts'.

Intratextuality is an elusive concept. In Alison Sharrock's words, it is a way of looking at texts by focusing on 'how parts relate to parts, wholes and holes'.[8] Indeed, one could conceive of intratextuality in opposition to the notion of 'wholeness' as outlined by Aristotle in *Poetics* 1451a31–35: the plot should be a *mimesis* of 'one action and that a whole one', with the different sections so arranged 'that the whole is disturbed by the transposition and destroyed by the removal of any one of them' (οὕτως ὥστε μετατιθεμένου τινὸς μέρους ἢ ἀφαιρουμένου διαφέρεσθαι καὶ κινεῖσθαι τὸ ὅλον); for if it makes no visible difference whether a thing is there or not, 'that thing is no part of the whole' (οὐδὲν μόριον τοῦ ὅλου ἐστίν).[9] By contrast, intratextuality encourages fragmentation[10] and a virtually endless network between different parts of the text, which produces a variety of meanings and, one may add, a multiplicity of unities.[11] To quote Sharrock again:

5 Barthes 1977, 142. cf. Derrida 1982, 44.
6 Cf. Fowler 1997, 21: '[i]t is frequently easier to say where the beginning ends than where the end begins'.
7 See Fowler 1989, 78.
8 Sharrock 2000, 5.
9 See Bittner 1992.
10 Fragments resist integration; they are defiant of form and order: see Barthes 1989, 94.
11 For the use of the 'labyrinth' model in intratextual readings, see Theodorakopoulos 2000; cf. Fowler 2000a.

> It is only when we pull texts apart, and look at the myriad ways of their putting-together… that we can fully engage with the whole range of epistemological, historical, philosophical, aesthetic, and critical exegeses that constitute our response to literary texts and cultural poetics.[12]

Intratextuality not only is comfortable with a text's resistance to (a single) meaning, but it actually seeks uncertainty: an important element of the theory is that 'sometimes parts *don't* relate to each other in tidy and significant ways but stick out like sore thumbs'.[13] Unlike Aristotle who is obsessed with unity, intratextuality finds its thrill in contradictions, repetitions, digressions and other 'anomalies', viewing them as creative, even though contested, sites of interpretation. In this model, meaning is construed on the condition that it can be constantly reviewed: a given relation (that we as readers determine) between this and that part of a text can always be called into question by another intratextual thread. The situation becomes more complicated when such networks are built with a view to a text's ending. Intratextuality in this case can work in the following ways: it can either be used so as to present a closural script that makes the end look 'satisfying' or, alternatively, it can be used to highlight the text's open-endedness– or both at the same time. The premise that closure extends beyond a text's concluding section and spreads across the narrative can easily fit to a dynamic reading predicated on a never-ending network of intratexts which signify the ending in multiple, and often contradictory, ways.

Lucretius' plague at the end of *DRN* (6.1138–286) is considered a notoriously anomalous passage in Latin literature; it sticks out like a sore thumb denying us the comfort of closure. As I will attempt to show, several sections dispersed throughout the narrative foreshadow the end and make it look less abrupt and chaotic. However, considering that these intratexts are mostly about disease and death's ever-increasing presence in the poem, they will be shown to imbue the text with a sense of growing decay and unraveling.[14] What we encounter here is a paradox which is brilliantly captured in 3.472: *morbus* is called in that case 'the architect of death' (*leti fabricator*) and the phrasing clearly suggests that, although by nature a sign of deterioration and decline towards an end, disease can operate simultaneously as a principle which guarantees cohesion and structure.[15] Rather than take 3.472 as an incidental reference to death, I will argue that one of

---

12 Sharrock 2000, 3.

13 Sharrock 2000, 6.

14 On death as a closural device in Latin literature, see P.G. Fowler 1997, 114–18.

15 *Fabricator*: 'a maker, fashioner'; see Cic. *Luc.* 120; Verg. *A.* 2.264, Ov. *Tr.* 5.12.47. The word is also applied to God as 'the maker of the world'; see Cic. *Tim.* 6; Ov. *Met.* 1.57.

the major pathways which give unity to Lucretius' poem has to do with how its chaotic ending is disseminated throughout the narrative. But in a sense, this is precisely what intratextuality claims to be interested in: it is concerned both with 'wholes' and 'holes' and how the difference between the two collapses; what may be giving unity to a text can also be used to engineer its demise.

2 (W)holeness in decay: Disease as a closural device in Lucretius

In book 5.146–55 Lucretius rejects strongly the false assumption that the gods' residence can be found *in mundi partibus ullis*, 'in any part of the world' (5.147).[16] They are too far away, and they 'cannot possibly touch anything that we can touch'. Therefore, 'their abodes also must be different from ours, being thin in accord with their bodies', *tenues de corpore eorum* (5.154). 'This', as Lucretius promises to Memmius, 'I will prove to you later in an ample discourse', *posterius largo sermone probabo* (5.155).[17] As it happens, the promise remains unfulfilled and many scholars have traced in this 'gap' an indication that the poem was left unfinished: had Lucretius had the time to complete his work, so it is argued, he would have concluded the poem with a comforting description of the gods' serene residence and not with a scene of earthly chaos and destruction as we have it now.[18]

What is it about the plague, though, that makes it look so unfit for an ending? The answer should be pretty obvious: a scene of tremendous catastrophe is not the best conclusion to a poem which seeks, time and again, to eliminate the fear of death from people's lives. Lucretius' plague is characterised by profound violence (which exceeds, by and large, that of the original account found in Thucydides, 2.47.3–54) and, more importantly, it offers no final word of consolation. Scholars have tried to deal with the difficulties posed by the plague by invoking three types of explanation: (a) some have seen it as a kind of ultimate 'test' for the reader: if we have been listening carefully to Lucretius in the previous six books we should then be able to encounter the scene and stay calm, bearing in mind that 'death is nothing to us'.[19] (b) Others have read the plague as being

16 Translation of Lucretius is based on Smith 1992, with modifications at points.
17 See Gale 2009, on lines 146–55; cf. O'Hara 2007, 55–76.
18 See Sedley 1998, 160–5 and Volk 2002, 82 with n.4. Contra: P.G. Fowler 1997 and Penwill 1996.
19 See Clay 1976, 222–3 and Müller 1978, 217–21.

designed to generate a new reading of Lucretius' work: the striking presence of death at the end of the poem can only be counterbalanced by the emphasis on birth and creation in the opening hymn to Venus (1.1–49); it is there that we as readers are consequently driven to seek comfort, by starting to read the poem all over again.[20] The third explanation, introduced by Steele Commager in a seminal article published in 1957, has been the most influential. Lucretius has been shown to display a strongly revisionist attitude towards Thucydides: while the latter's emphasis lies on the devastating physical symptoms of the disease,[21] Lucretius describes physical ills with a psychological vocabulary; he treats clinical symptoms as emotionally motivated actions and intertwines medical data with an ethical kind of commentary, thus broadening the plague's symbolic potential in defiance of historical fact. Fear of death and desire become central in Lucretius' recasting of the disease, and this allows the poet effectively to turn a natural catastrophe into an image of life itself.[22]

Despite their differences, the three explanations are not incompatible with each other. One of the common features they clearly share is the fact that they treat the plague as a section of the text which does not *relate* to the rest of the poem in a tidy way. In what follows, I will focus instead on how the plague is actually anticipated by specific sections throughout the narrative. I propose to show that we can better understand the ending scene as the final stage of a progressive culmination which revolves around the notion of death; by culmination I refer to a forward, escalating movement which should not be necessarily linked to a (positive) sense of resolution. My second point will be that this culmination, once traced through different parts in the text, reveals that in the poem's final scene emphasis is placed on the biological aspects of the disease–and not the psychological ones, which is currently the predominant view in scholarship. Finally, the process which I have in mind requires a committed intratextual reading, relying especially on the endings of book 3 and 4.

There are many formal reasons why one should look at the endings of book 3, 4 and 6 together. Joseph Farrell has recently shown how Lucretius' six-book epic was designed as a sequence of three pairs of books while being divided at the same time into two distinct halves, each one consisting of three books.[23] According to this structural model, the endings of 3 and 4 can be examined side by side since they provide closure to the central pair of books. The endings of 3 and

20 See Schrijvers 1970, 324.

21 See Craik 2001.

22 Commager 1957; cf. Segal 1990, 228–37.

23 Farrell 2007.

6 constitute the points where each of the two halves of the poem comes to an end; and the endings of 4 and 6 stand as the conclusions to the first and the final book of the second triad (book endings, one may argue, resemble intratexts in that they are open to multiple networks of internal connections).

The one common feature between the endings of 3, 4 and 6 (which seems to be missing from the remaining three books) is the poet's emphasis on disease. In 3.1053–75, Lucretius speaks of an elusive 'weight', *pondus* (3.1054),[24] that is constantly pressing on people's minds and whose cause remains unknown (3.1053–7); in fact, a close reading of the text suggests that not knowing the cause is the most unsettling part of the condition, perhaps even what makes it a disease in the first place.[25] Book 4 (1037–287) is about the disease of love and sexual desire, a long-established metaphor in earlier literature which, in the hands of Lucretius, turns into a concrete, clinical reality: love is literally a 'wasting' disease that consumes our bodies from the inside, almost to the point of death, e.g. in 4.1068–9: *ulcus enim vivescit et inveterascit alendo, / inque dies gliscit furor atque aerumna gravescit.*[26] Finally, book 6 (1138–286) becomes as clinical as possible; in fact, we could say that, unlike the allegorical readings that have been proposed, what makes the plague so disturbing has to do precisely with the fact that there is no space left for metaphor. Lucretius, as we shall see below, capitalizes on a heavy and thorough use of medical language to flesh out the point that death is now present as a hard, biological fact.

The endings of books 3, 4 and 6 communicate with each other on multiple levels. In the course of his argumentation against the fear of death in book 3, Lucretius mentions two medical conditions side by side, *furor* and *lethargus* (3.828–9); the point that is made there is that the soul is subject to disease and therefore to annihilation. It is very tempting to see these two clinical registers returning and defining the endings of book 3 (a lethargic patient who spends most of his life sleeping and vainly attempting to get rid of the 'weight' which bothers him) and book 4 (a manic immersion in the world of sexual desire). The clinical picture in book 3 is one of self-alienation and disgust (1068–70): 'each man tries to flee from himself, but to that self, from which of course he can never escape, he clings against his will, and hates it, because he is a sick man who does not know the cause of his complaint'. What appears in this case as an impossibility of 'splitting' from one's self, becomes in book 4 an impossibility of merging two 'halves' into a single physical body. In a passage that is reminiscent of Aristophanes' speech

24 Cf. *gravitate* (3.1054); *moles* (3.1056); *onus* (3.1059) and *gravis* (3.1066).

25 See, especially, 3.1070: *morbi quia causam non tenet aeger*, with Bailey 1947, 1170.

26 See Langslow 1999, 202–5.

in Plato's *Symposium*,[27] Lucretius describes the lovers 'greedily pressing against each other and joining their salivas, drawing deep breaths and crushing lips with teeth. But all is in vain, for they can rub nothing off nor can they penetrate and be absorbed body to body' (4.1108–11). Another point of contrastive contact between the two closing sections relates to the idea of wandering, *errare*, which appears in both passages as a manifestation of discontent and lack of fulfilment: in 3.1058 erratic movement is attributed to the absence of a specific object of desire (*quid sibi quisque velit nescire et quaerere semper*); what generates that same movement in book 4 is, surprisingly, the possession of that object (4.1076–7): 'indeed, in the very time of possession, lovers' ardor is storm-tossed, uncertain in its course', *fluctuat incertis erroribus*.

As we move from book 3 to 4 Lucretius' clinical focus becomes more specific: both conditions remain frustratingly incurable, but in the latter case, that of book 4, there seems to be at least an attempt at 'containing' it within the limits of the physical body. The wound of love may remain invisible for those involved (*volnere caeco* in 4.1120), but we as readers get a chance to have a good, close look at the sore which grows within (see 4.1068–9, cited above). This process of 'physicalisation' becomes more manifest as we move from book 3 to book 6. Here I will mention one characteristic example: a key term in book 3 is the word *oblivia* (3.1066), the 'forgetfulness' one seeks in sleep, in an attempt to escape reality. The plague in book 6 makes use of the same word but in a more sinister context; in that case it is not a desired state but a grim pathological side-effect of the disease: those who were affected by the plague, Lucretius says, were seized by 'a complete loss of memory', *oblivia rerum cunctarum* (6.1213). *Oblivia* in 3.1065–6 is combined with the image of a wearied man returning home: 'the moment he has reached the threshold of his house, he yawns, or falls into heavy sleep and seeks oblivion'. This image is echoed in 6.1248–9, in the description of the relatives of the dead patients, 'as they take to bed wearied with tears and mourning'. Book 3 operates in a semi-metaphorical, semi-literal mode: what is described in its closing section as a life of restlessness and aimless wandering, is introduced by Lucretius as *mortua vita* (3.1046), 'a dead life'. Once more, the concept recurs in the plague invested with a clinical sense: in 6.1268 Lucretius describes how 'you could see bodies half-dead with fainting limbs', *semanimo cum corpore*. Here too we have a state on the verge between existence and non-existence, but this time literally.

Book 4 also interacts with book 6. Fire and thirst occupy a central position in Lucretius' account of erotic desire (4.1097–9): 'as when in dreams a thirsty man

27 See, especially, 191a5–8.

seeks to drink, and no water is forthcoming to quench the burning in his frame, but he seeks the image of water, *laticum simulacra*, striving in vain', so does the lover seek to satisfy his desire to no avail. The plague is quite similar in this respect (after all Lucretius has already eroticized death by translating lines from Sappho fr.31 LP at 3.152–8,[28] a passage which speaks about fear and foregrounds at the same time several of the symptoms that will occur in book 6):[29] although the patients have access to water and consume it in large quantities (6.1163–76), their disease prevents them from enjoying it: 'dry thirst beyond all quenching drenched their bodies, and made a flood of water no more than a drop', *aequabat multum parvis umoribus imbrem* (6.1176). What we first encounter as a dream – and dreams are conceptually linked to metaphors already in Aristotle[30] – becomes a nightmarish reality at the end of the poem. Earlier in book 6 Lucretius has talked about 'erysipelas', a creeping disease that takes hold of the body and makes it 'burn': *existit sacer ignis et urit corpore serpens* (6.660). The 'burning', which dominates with its presence the pathology of the plague,[31] should be located in the same clinical index. The poem's final scene can of course be allegorized (even though, as Paul de Man would hasten to add, allegory by definition fails to accomplish symbolic closure);[32] nonetheless, its most striking effect derives from the clinical tone that pervades it, conveying a sense of finality that seems as irreversible as biological death itself.

Perhaps the most important thread which connects the three closing sections is the anxiety about the way in which disease tests the limits of our knowledge. In book 3, as I have pointed out, part of the problem is that we do not know what exactly the complaint is about: *nec reperire potes tibi quid sit saepe mali* (3.1050), 'you cannot tell what is bothering you'. In book 4 the notion returns: this time, the disease may have become more tangible but what cannot still be found is a means to fight it: *nec reperire malum id possunt quae machina vincat* (4.1119). In book 6 the secrets of the disease, its so-called *ratio*, have been fully revealed, but medicine cannot do anything about it: 'it mutters and stays silent', *mussabat tacito medicina timore* (6.1179). By way of a paradox, the more we get to know about a *morbus*, the harder it becomes to fight. The plague is a lethal condition, and

---

28 See Fowler 2000b, 23–4.

29 See especially 3.156: *caligare oculos, sonere auris, succidere artus*, and compare it with the obstructed vision (6.1146), the buzzing ears (6.1185) and the faltering tongue (6.1147–50) in the plague scene.

30 See Worman 2015, 25–6.

31 *ardore* (6.1163), *fervescere* (6.1164), *tepidum* (6.1165), *sacer ignis* (6.1167), *flagrabat* (6.1169), *flamma* (6.1169).

32 De Man 1979, 205.

unlike Thucydides in whose narrative there are survivors, in Lucretius everyone seems to die.

3 Intratexts and intertexts

Intratextuality, however, can never work on its own. Just as a text's fabric is determined by limitless threads of internal connections between its various parts, so we need to assume that the same text is defined by an endlessly expanding number of intertexts. As Julia Kristeva has shown, the intersection of textual surfaces in a literary wor(l)d can never be circumscribed since it is open to never-ending dissemination.[33] What I have been outlining in the section above is an intratextual hypothesis according to which the plague 'makes sense' as an ending. It is now time to see how in this closural script intratexts cooperate with intertexts.

In one of the most medicalised passages in book 6, the faces of those patients who are about to die are described as follows (6.1192–6):

> item ad supremum denique tempus
> conpressae nares, nasi primoris acumen
> tenue, cavati oculi, cava tempora, frigida pellis
> duraque, in ore iacens rictum, frons tenta manebat.
> nec nimio rigida post artus morte iacebant.

> Moreover, as life's final hour approached, the nostrils were compressed, the tip of the nose grew sharp, the eyes were sunken, the temples hollow, the skin cold and hard, the mouth agape and grinning, the forehead remaining tense. Soon afterwards the limbs lay stretched in the stiffness of death.

In these lines, Lucretius translates [Hipp.], *Prog.* 2 [2.114 L.],[34] a passage concerned with the signs of imminent death: ῥὶς ὀξεῖα, ὀφθαλμοὶ κοῖλοι, κρόταφοι ξυμπεπτωκότες, ὦτα ψυχρὰ καὶ ξυνεσταλμένα, καὶ οἱ λοβοὶ τῶν ὤτων ἀπεστραμμένοι, καὶ τὸ δέρμα τὸ περὶ τὸ μέτωπον σκληρόν τε καὶ περιτεταμένον καὶ καρφαλέον ἐόν. Medical language is present throughout the *DRN*. What we notice, however, is its calculated use by the poet in his attempt to stress the ever-increasing presence of death in the narrative. Thus, while the medical intertexts for *pondus* at the end of book 3 remain fairly ambiguous, the account of sexual

33 Kristeva 1980, 65–6.
34 See Langslow 1999, 209.

desire at the end of book 4 invites considerably more extensive allusions to medical texts: not only is the 'wound' of love conveyed in a language which imparts a tone of clinical observation (4.1068–9), but, on a broader level, Lucretius' emphasis on female excitement in sex and the female's contribution of seed to the conception of the child reflects medical lore.[35] Such use of medical language reaches its point of culmination in book 6, manifesting itself occasionally as an actual translation of Hippocratic texts, such as the one cited above. What I have been describing in the ends of books 3, 4 and 6 as a growing emphasis on the clinical aspects of disease can thus be seen to be both intratextually sustainable as a hypothesis, but also intertextually dependent on the increasing use of medical literature.

A possible risk that we run when too much emphasis is placed on intratextual readings is to end up treating the text as a 'self-enclosed' unity; as an endless network of associations *contained* within it. But as I have noted above, intratexts cannot but be seen as operating in constant association with intertexts, and acquiring extra layers of meaning through them. Let me finish this discussion by pointing out one such important intertext which has long been overlooked.

In an article published in 2008, Joseph Farrell has proposed that one of the main structural models for the six books of Lucretius – more specifically, for the composition of the *DRN* in three groups of two books each – was Callimachus' collection of six hymns. Farrell argues convincingly and in detail, laying particular emphasis on the hymnic form of Lucretius' proems. Obviously, one important consequence of accepting Farrell's hypothesis (and one which Farrell does not pursue at all in his article) is the fact that the end of Lucretius' book 6 should engage with the sixth – and final – hymn of Callimachus, the story of Erysichthon's eventual self-consumption, which is inflicted as a divine punishment by Demeter because of the hero's blasphemous behaviour and his violation of the goddess's sacred grove. The close similarities between Erysichthon's pathology and what we find in Thucydides' account of the plague (Lucretius' main model in 6.1138–1286) invite such a reading.

Echoes of Thucydides' plague can already be detected in Callimachus' Erysichthon; assuming that Lucretius displays a good knowledge of the hymns[36] (and a remarkably thorough knowledge of Thucydides' text) it seems unlikely that this would have escaped his attention. Of particular significance, in this respect, is the use of the adjective ἡμιθνῆτες at line 59, which describes Erysichthon's companions becoming 'half-dead' because of the terror caused by Demeter's divine epiphany:

35 See Lonie 1981, 120–1.
36 See Brown 1982.

οἱ μὲν ἄρ' ἡμιθνῆτες, ἐπεὶ τὰν πότνιαν εἶδον,
ἐξαπίνας ἀπόρουσαν ἐνὶ δρυσὶ χαλκὸν ἀφέντες.

When they saw the goddess they started away, half-dead with fear, leaving their bronze implements in the trees.[37]

This is an extremely rare adjective in Greek literature and it is not coincidental that among its very few occurrences it can be found in Thucydides 2.52: 'The bodies of dying men lay one upon another, and half-dead creatures reeled about the streets and gathered round all the fountains in their longing for water', ἡμιθνῆτες τοῦ ὕδατος ἐπιθυμίᾳ. Although Callimachus does not apply it to Erysichthon, it nonetheless anticipates the disease by which he is going to be afflicted later in the narrative.

Erysichthon's sickness in Callimachus not only is invested with thoroughly crafted medical details; it also bears striking resemblances to the general pathology outlined by Thucydides, especially with regard to the feelings of hunger and thirst, which in both cases remain unsatisfied (compare e.g. Call., *Cer.* 87–90 with Th. 2.49.5). As a result, the question as to whether Lucretius engages directly with the Greek historian or, occasionally, by using the Hellenistic poet as an intermediary is not always easy to settle. That said, there are significant clinical details in the Latin text which are missing from Thucydides' description but are, intriguingly enough, present in both Callimachus and Lucretius. One such detail concerns Lucretius' emphasis on the victims' extreme state of emaciation moments before they die (6.1267–71), captured in the phrase *pelli super ossibus una* in 6.1270 ('the only thing that was left to them was skin on their bones'). This detail is absent from Thucydides' text: rather than speak of emaciation, the Greek historian comments instead on the bodies' marvelous endurance during the disease: ἀλλ' ἀντεῖχε [sc. τὸ σῶμα] παρὰ δόξαν τῇ ταλαιπωρίᾳ (2.49.6). Erysichthon's ravenous hunger, on the other hand, makes his body shrink (87–93):

ἐνδόμυχος δήπειτα πανάμερος εἰλαπιναστὰς
ἤσθιε μυρία πάντα: κακὰ δ' ἐξάλλετο γαστὴρ
αἰεὶ μᾶλλον ἔδοντι, τὰ δ' ἐς βυθὸν οἷα θαλάσσας
ἀλεμάτως ἀχάριστα κατέρρεεν εἴδατα πάντα.
ὡς δὲ Μίμαντι χιών, ὡς ἀελίῳ ἔνι πλαγγών,
καὶ τούτων ἔτι μεῖζον ἐτάκετο μέσφ' ἐπὶ νευράς:
δειλαίῳ ἶνές τε καὶ ὀστέα μῶνον ἔλειφθεν.

37 Translations of Callimachus are from Hopkinson 1984.

> Meanwhile, closeted in the house, he banqueted all day long and consumed countless things. His wretched belly leapt as he ate more and more, and all his food flowed down into him as if into the depths of the sea. Like snow on Mimas or a wax doll in the sun – even more quickly than these he wasted away to the very sinews: only skin and bone were left to the wretch.

Lucretius' *pelli super ossibus una* could be a nice translation of Callimachus, *Cer.* 93: ἶνές τε καὶ ὀστέα **μῶνον**, 'only skin and bone were left to the wretch'. What is more, the poet's emphasis on filth at 6.1269–70 (*horrida paedore et pannis cooperta perire, / corporis inluvie, pelli super ossibus una*) – another element that is entirely absent from Thucydides' plague – could be linked with similar expressions in Hellenistic poetry which seem to inform the stress put by Callimachus on emaciation; cf. e.g. Apollonius Rhodius, *Arg.* 2.200–1: πίνῳ δέ οἱ αὐσταλέος χρὼς/ ἐσκλήκει, ῥινοὶ δὲ σὺν ὀστέα μοῦνον ἔεργον. Finally, (*corporis*) *inluvie* in 6.1270 lies very close to the Greek λῦμα (in line 115, Callimachus describes Erysichthon begging for 'scraps of food', ἔκβολα λύματα δαιτός): the word's semantic origin in Latin is that of a 'wash' of water which gathers impurities, and it can therefore mean either 'inundation' or 'dirt on the body'.

Monica Gale notes that one important difference between Thucydides and Lucretius is that the first treats the plague as a historical event, whereas in the latter case the disease is placed within a timeless, mythological setting.[38] Indeed, a close comparison between Thucydides and Lucretius reveals that in the Roman poet's imagination the Athenians have been (mythically) 'enlarged' – they seem to have a superhuman quality in them. Thucydides (2.49.5) observes crisply that the diseased were burning on the inside and could not satisfy their thirst. Lucretius' description, on the other hand, has a magnifying effect: in 6.1168–9 we read that the 'flame in the stomach was blazing like a flame in a furnace', *ut fornacibus intus*, a phrase that has been used earlier in book 6 for the description of Aetna's 'vast furnace' (6.680–82). Equally interesting, in this respect, is Lucretius' depiction of the diseased while they are trying to satisfy their thirst. Thucydides (2.49.5) mentions the fact that they were seized by an 'insatiable' thirst, plunging themselves into the city's 'rain-tanks': 'What they would have liked best would have been to throw themselves into cold water; as indeed was done by some of the neglected sick, who plunged into the rain-tanks in their agonies of unquenchable thirst'. The Greek text is imitated closely by Lucretius but, once more, the people's agony becomes intensified as they are shown to throw themselves, 'from high above' and into the wells with 'gaping mouths', but to no avail (6.1172–5). *Ore*

38 Gale 1994, 112–3; 225.

patente in 6.1175 recalls death's huge 'gaping maw', *vasto hiatu*, which awaits to devour the world in its final moment of destruction in 5.373–75.

The Athenians' bodies are magnified during the plague in Lucretius: this magnification is fleshed out by association with the mythical figures in book 3 whose suffering transcends the boundaries of human pain, and whom Lucretius implicitly evokes at the end of his poem. Once more, Callimachus' Erysichthon fits well in this context. The Hellenistic poet is toying with the mythical version according to which Erysichthon is a giant (his friends in line 34 are identified as ἀνδρογίγαντας); this is hinted also in the enormous quantities of food devoured by the afflicted patient in 87–90 (cite above).

Lucretius' enlarged bodies have more in common with Erysichthon than they do with Thucydides' normal-sized people. The connection between Lucretius and Callimachus can be drawn a bit further. Erysichthon's suffering has profoundly self-reflexive undertones; the scraps of food which he consumes at line 115 (ἔκβολα <u>λύματα</u> δαιτός) are meant to evoke what is dismissed as (poetic) 'filth' in the second hymn of the collection (recall Apollo's words in 108–9, ἀλλὰ τὰ πολλά / λύματα γῆς καὶ πολλὸν ἐφ' ὕδατι συρφετὸν ἕλκει.). In the same way, Lucretius' imagery of the plague creates a tension with ideas of poetic purity: seeing the Athenians jumping into the wells *ore patente* and consuming large quantities of (contaminated and filthy) water, reminds us of *DRN* 1.412 where Lucretius promises to Memmius 'copious drafts from the large springs that fill his breast', *largos haustus e fontibus magnis*. The end of the *DRN*, however, holds in store a 'muddying' of waters, similar to the one we find when we compare the endings of Callimachus' second and sixth hymn.

4 Conclusion

In intratextual terms, the plague makes sense as an ending, more specifically as an escalation of the clinical colour assigned to disease throughout the poem. Sections of the text can thus be put into a 'certain order' so as to present a convincing script of closure. However, just as intratextual threads can be endlessly expanding, intertexts should also be located in a setting of limitless dissemination. It is indeed very likely that Lucretius conceived of the plague as a point of culmination, and that many of his previous references to disease scattered across various book-endings have been designed to build towards it. At the same time, this culmination could be imitating, structurally, another book collection, that of Callimachus' hymns: Callimachus too, for his own reasons, brings to an end a six-unit structure with an emphatic description of disease. Whether the plague pathology presented to us in book 6 is modeled on earlier references to disease in the poem or whether it is linked at points with Erysichthon's pathology in Callimachus' *final* hymn of his collection should remain an open question. Intratexts and intertexts are constantly overlapping, so much so that it is often futile, but also misleading, to try and prioritize between them.

Bibliography

Bailey, C. (1947), *Lucretius. De Rerum Natura: Edited, with Prolegomena, Critical Apparatus, Translation and Commentary*, 3 vols., Oxford.

Barthes, R. (1977), *Image, Music, Text* (transl. S. Heath), London.

Barthes, R. (1989), *Roland Barthes* (transl. R. Howard), New York.

Belfiore, E.S. (1992), *Tragic Pleasures: Aristotle on Plot and Emotion*, Princeton.

Bittner, R. (1992), 'One Action', in: A. Oksenberg Rorty (ed.), *Essays on Aristotle's* Poetics, Princeton, 97–110.

Brown, R.D. (1982), 'Lucretius and Callimachus', *ICS* 7, 77–97.

Clay, D. (1976), 'The Sources of Lucretius' Inspiration', in: J. Bollack/A. Laks (eds.), *Études sur l'epicurisme antique: Cahiers de Philologie*, Lille, 203–227.

Commager, H.S. (1957), 'Lucretius' Interpretation of the Plague', *HSCP* 62, 105–118.

Craik, E.M. (2001), 'Thucydides on the Plague: Physiology of Flux and Fixation', *CQ* 51, 102–108.

De Man, P. (1979), *Allegories of Reading: Figural Language in Rousseau, Nietzsche, Rilke and Proust*, New Haven.

Derrida, J. (1982), *Positions* (transl. A. Bass), Chicago.

Farrell, J. (2007), 'Lucretian Architecture: The Structure and the Argument of *De Rerum Natura*', in: S. Gillespie/P. Hardie (eds.), *The Cambridge Companion to Lucretius*, Cambridge, 76–91.

Farrell, J. (2008), 'The Six Books of Lucretius' *De rerum natura*: Antecedents and Influence', *Dictynna* 8 (http://dictynna.revues.org/385).

Fowler, D. (1989), 'First Thoughts on Closure', *MD* 22, 75–122.

Fowler, D. (1997), 'Second Thoughts on Closure', in: D.H. Roberts/F.M. Dunn/D. Fowler, 3–22.

Fowler, D. (2000a), 'Epic in the Middle of the Wood: *Mise en abyme* in the Nisus and Euryalus Episode', in: A. Sharrock/H. Morales, 89–113.

Fowler, D. (2000b), *Roman Constructions: Readings in Postmodern Latin*, Oxford.

Fowler, P.G. (1997), 'Lucretian Conclusions', in: D.H. Roberts/F.M. Dunn/D. Fowler, 112–38.

Gale, M. (1994), *Myth and Poetry in Lucretius*, Cambridge.

Gale, M. (2009), *Lucretius, De rerum natura V: Edited with Translation and Commentary*, Oxford.

Hillis Miller, J. (1978), 'The Problematic of Ending in Narrative', *Nineteenth-Century Fiction* 33.1, 3–7.

Hopkinson, N. (1984), *Callimachus: Hymn to Demeter*, Cambridge.

Kristeva, J. (1980), *Desire in Language: A Semiotic Approach to Literature and Art* (transl. T. Gora *et al.*), New York.

Langslow, D.R. (1999), 'The Language of Poetry and the Language of Science: The Latin Poets and 'Medical Latin'', in: J.N. Adams/R.G. Mayer (eds.), *Aspects of the Language of Latin Poetry*, Oxford, 183–225.

Lonie, I.M. (1981), *The Hippocratic Treatises 'On Generation', 'On the Nature of the Child', 'Diseases IV': A Commentary*, Berlin.

Müller, G. (1978), 'Die Finalia der sechs Bücher des Lukrez', in: O. Gigon (ed.), *Lucrèce*, Geneva, 197–231.
O'Hara, J. (2007), *Inconsistency in Roman Epic: Studies in Catullus, Lucretius, Vergil, Ovid and Lucan*, Cambridge.
Penwill, J.L. (1996), 'The Ending of Sense: Death as Closure in Lucretius Book 6', *Ramus* 25, 146–69.
Ricoeur, P. (1980), 'Narrative Time', *Critical Inquiry* 7, 169–90.
Roberts, D.H./Dunn, F.M./Fowler, D. (eds.) (1997), *Classical Closure: Reading the End in Greek and Latin Literature*, Princeton.
Schrijvers, P.H. (1970), *Horror ac divina voluptas: Études sur la poétique et la poésie de Lucrèce*, Amsterdam.
Sedley, D.N. (1998), *Lucretius and the Transformation of Greek Wisdom*, Cambridge.
Segal, C. (1990), *Lucretius on Death and Anxiety: Poetry and Philosophy in De Rerum Natura*, Princeton.
Sharrock, A. (2000), 'Intratextuality: Texts, Parts and (W)holes in Theory', in: A. Sharrock/H. Morales, 1–39.
Sharrock, A./Morales, H. (eds.) (2000), *Intratextuality: Greek and Roman Textual Traditions*, Oxford.
Smith, M.F. (1992), *Lucretius: De rerum natura*, Loeb Classical Library 181, Cambridge MA.
Theodorakopoulos, E. (2000), 'Catullus 64: Footprints in the Labyrinth', in: A. Sharrock/H. Morales, 115–41.
Volk, K. (2002), *The Poetics of Latin Didactic: Lucretius, Vergil, Ovid, Manilius*, Oxford.
Worman, N. (2015), *Landscape and the Spaces of Metaphor in Ancient Literary Theory and Criticism*, Cambridge.

Alison Keith

Pascite boues, summittite tauros: Cattle and Oxen in the Virgilian Corpus

In this chapter, I analyse Virgil's deployment of the lexicon of cattle husbandry in his poetry and ask what we can learn about his poetic designs from the prominence of cattle and oxen in his oeuvre. The pastoral and georgic care of cattle is a prominent theme of his first two poetic collections, and the poet often draws analogies between cattle and their human herders. Even in the *Aeneid*, Virgil likens his mythological characters to bulls as he updates the classical epic tradition of similes comparing heroic figures to animals in the natural and georgic worlds. The primary focus of my study, accordingly, is on Virgil's investment of the lexicon of pastoralism and cattle husbandry with a metapoetic, or literary-critical, dimension.[1] I argue that the Augustan poet introduces cows and bulls at programmatic moments in all three of his poetic works as he articulates his generic commitments in the *Bucolica*, *Georgica*, and *Aeneid*. His self-citations of bucolic and taurine material, both within individual poems and across the whole oeuvre, bear exemplary witness to his strategic deployment of programmatic intratextuality, an important compositional technique and counterpart to his intertextual invocation of literary models.

1 *Boues*

The manuscript tradition of Virgil's first collection of poetry confirms that it circulated in antiquity under the title *Bucolica* ('cattle-herding songs'), while individual poems were called 'eclogues', literally 'extracts' from the collection.[2] The special significance of the collection's title *Bucolica* is underlined by a series of programmatic statements in the first poem's opening exchange (*Buc.* 1.1–10):[3]

1 On Virgilian metapoetics, see most recently Henkel 2014, with full bibliography.

2 Horsfall 1981, 108–9; Clausen 1994, xx n. 23; Perutelli 1995, 27–8. On the MS tradition of Virgil, including the *Bucolics*, see Reynolds 1983, 433–6.

3 Quotations of Virgil's works are from Mynors 1969; translations adapt Fairclough rev. Goold 1999.

https://doi.org/10.1515/9783110611021-007

M. Tityre, tu patulae recubans sub tegmine fagi
siluestrem tenui Musam meditaris auena;
nos patriae finis et dulcia linquimus arua.
nos patriam fugimus; tu, Tityre, lentus in umbra
formosam resonare doces Amaryllida siluas.
T. O Meliboee, deus nobis haec otia fecit.
namque erit ille mihi semper deus, illius aram
saepe tener nostris ab ouilibus imbuet agnus.
ille meas errare boues, ut cernis, et ipsum
ludere quae uellem calamo permisit agresti.

Meliboeus – Tityrus, reclining beneath the canopy of a spreading beech, you practise woodland music on a slender oaten straw; we are leaving the bounds of our fatherland and our sweet fields. We are going into exile from our fatherland; you, Tityrus, relaxing in the shade, teach the woods to re-echo 'Beautiful Amaryllis'.
Tityrus – O Meliboeus, a god gave us this leisure. For he will always be a god to me, and a tender lamb from our sheepfold will often stain his altar. He allowed my cattle to roam, as you see, and me to play what I wish on the rustic pipe.

Meliboeus, who delivers the opening words, bears a speaking name derived from a Greek verb meaning to 'care for' (μέλω; cf. its derivatives μελεδαίνω and μελετάω) and 'cow' (βοῦς, cognate with Latin *bos*);[4] and the first element of Meliboeus' name also puns on the Greek word for 'song' (μέλος). His name thus encapsulates the thematic focus of Virgil's bucolic collection in its collocation of cattle-herding and cattle-song. Meliboeus' interlocutor Tityrus, moreover, has been granted permission to 'pasture his cattle and play what he wants on his rustic pipe' (9–10). Tityrus thus lays explicit claim to practise the twin foci of Virgilian bucolic, cow-herding and bucolic song, and he later reports that a youthful god has instructed him precisely to 'pasture cattle as before, and raise bulls' (*Buc.* 1.45): *'pascite ut ante* ***boues****, pueri; summittite* ***tauros****'*.[5]

In explaining the god's injunction here, J.E.G. Wright (1983, 114) drew 'attention to the well-established convention in ancient literature of describing the author as doing that about which he writes', in order to suggest that 'on the literary

4 In the headnote to his commentary on *Buc.* 1, Servius remarks that Meliboeus' name is fashioned from his rustic duties, 'because he has care (μέλει) of the cattle (βοῶν)', and he glosses this Greek explanation with a Latin translation (*id est quia* ***curam*** *gerit* ***boum***) that emphasizes the genre's descent from cattle-herding songs and underlines the bilingual ethos of Virgil's collection.

5 On the bucolic program articulated in *Buc.* 1, see Wright 1983; for the special significance of line 45, see *ibid.* 114–17. Cairns 1999 proposes an alternate program for the first eclogue, prompted by the etymological association of the name 'Tityrus' with a Doric word for 'reed'; he does not adduce 1.10 in his discussion, nor does he consider the prominence of cattle-herding in *Buc.* 1.

level, the god's instructions are all about the kind of poetry [i.e., bucolic] which Tityrus-Virgil composes'.[6] In support of his claim, he adduced, as Virgil's likely source for his programmatic focus on *boues* in these two lines (*Buc.* 1.9 and 1.45), a passage at the opening of Theocritus' ninth idyll (Theocr. *Id.* 9.1–6):[7]

> **Βουκολιάζεο**, Δάφνι· τὺ δ'ᾠδᾶς ἄρχεο πρᾶτος,
> ᾠδᾶς ἄρχεο, Δάφνι, ἐφεψάσθω δὲ Μενάλκας,
> μόσχως **βουσὶν** ὑφέντες, ἐπὶ στείραισι δὲ **ταύρως**.
> χοἰ μὲν ἁμᾷ **βόσκοιντο** καὶ ἐν φύλλοισι πλανῷντο
> μηδὲν ἀτιμαγελεῦντες· ἐμὶν δὲ τὺ **βουκολιάζευ**
> ἐκ τόθεν, ἄλλοθε δ'αὖτις ὑποκρίνοιτο Μενάλκας.

> Bucolicize, Daphnis. And begin your father's strains, begin
> his strains, Daphnis, and let Menalcas follow after, putting the
> calves beneath the cows to suckle and mating the bulls with
> the uncalved. And let them pasture the while and wander among
> the flowers, in no way straying. But you, bucolicize for me
> from there, and on the other side let Menalcas in turn reply.

Virgil's re-elaboration of Theocritus' passage, in his opening eclogue, marks his intertextual adherence to the Greek pastoral tradition and its most celebrated exponent, Theocritus, whose characters use the verb **βου**κολιάσδεσθαι, 'bucolicize' (literally 'play the cowherd'), to describe their music-making and song-exchange (Theocr. *Id.* 5.60, 7.36),[8] and the adjectival phrases **βου**κολικαὶ μοῖσαι / ἀοιδαί (Theocr. *Id.* 1.20; cf. *Id.* 7.49–51: 'bucolic music/songs') to describe the songs themselves. Indeed, Virgil seems to emphasize his recuperation of an earlier poetic project (Theocritean bucolic?) in the pregnant phrase *ut ante*, which intervenes between the cattle (*boues*) and oxen (*tauri*) that constitute the most significant intertextual markers of his adaptation of *Id.* 9.3 in *Buc.* 1.45.[9]

Elsewhere too throughout his Latin collection of 'cow-songs', Virgil offers self-conscious comment on his transfiguration of the specifically bovine poetics of Theocritus' *Idylls*. For example, in the opening question of the third eclogue, Menalcas insultingly asks Damoetas whose herd he's pasturing (*Buc.* 3.1–6):

---

6 Wright 1983, 115.

7 I quote Theocritus' *Idylls* from Gow 1950, and adapt his translations, often with reference to Hunter 1999.

8 For the meaning of the verb, see Hunter 1999, 6–7.

9 I am grateful to Sarah McCallum for the suggestion, *per litteras*, of metapoetic reference in the temporal phrase *ut ante* (*Buc.* 1.45).

M. Dic mihi, Damoeta, cuium **pecus**? an Meliboei?
D. Non, uerum Aegonis; nuper mihi tradidit Aegon.
M. Infelix o semper, **oues, pecus**! ipse Neaeram
dum fouet ac ne me sibi praeferat illa ueretur,
hic alienus **ouis custos** bis mulget in hora,
et sucus **pecori** et lac subducitur **agnis**.

M. Tell me, Damoetas, whose herd? Meliboeus'?
D. No, Aegon's; recently Aegon handed it over to me.
M. O wretched flock of sheep, always unlucky! While he
cuddles Neaera and worries that she prefers me to him,
this stranger milks his sheep twice an hour, stealing vital
sap from the flock and milk from the lambs.

The opening exchange between Virgil's herdsmen closely reworks the opening of Theocritus' fourth idyll, where Battos accuses Korydon of stealing another herdman's cattle and milk (Theocr. *Id.* 4.1–3, 13):

B. Εἰπέ μοι, ὦ Κορύδων, **τίνος αἱ βόες**; ἦ ῥα Φιλώνδα;
K. οὔκ, ἀλλ᾽ Αἴγωνος· βόσκειν δέ μοι αὐτὰς ἔδωκεν.
B. ἦ πᾷ ψε κρύβδαν τὰ ποθέσπερα πάσας ἀμέλγες;
δείλαιαί γ᾽ αὗται, τὸν **βουκόλον** ὡς κακὸν εὗρον.

B. Tell me, Korydon, whose are the cattle? Philondas'?
K. No, rather Aegon's. He gave them to me to pasture.
B. And maybe you milk them on the sly in the evening?
...They're wretched as they've found a bad cowherd.

Virgil translates his Theocritean model's βόες ('cattle') as *pecus* (*Buc.* 3.1), lit. 'herd of livestock',[10] in the same metrical *sedes* of his line. This constitutes another programmatic gesture towards Theocritean 'bucolic', even though the Virgilian Menalcas goes on to specify the animals in Damoetas' keeping as 'sheep', *oues* (3.3, 5; cf. *agnis*, 'lambs', 3.6).[11] Virgil's intertextual acknowledgement of Theocritean inspiration at the opening of the third eclogue thus also hints at his divergence from a purely Theocritean program of bucolic poetry. Nonetheless, in this early eclogue, the herdsmen's wagers for the ensuing song contest, like the exchange of insults and the singing match itself, are drawn from Theocritus. And in proposing the contest, Damoetas stakes a heifer (*Buc.* 3.28–31), which we may

10 For the association of *pecus* with cattle, see Varr. *Rust.* 2.1.12, *pecus maius et minus ... de pecore maiore in quo sunt ad tres species natura discreti, boues, asini, equi*; V. *Geo.* 3.64; and cf. *OLD* s.vv. *pecuaria*[1] and *pecuaria*[2]; *pecuarius*[1] and *pecuarius*[2]; and *pecus*[1].
11 Cf. Jones 2011, 157 n. 3.

interpret as a metaliterary acknowledgement of the tradition of Theocritean 'bucolic' at the same time as it constitutes an intratextual gesture to Virgil's own poetic program of 'pasturing cattle and raising bulls' (*Buc.* 1.45), i.e., of composing cow-songs.

Many of the details of the singing match also contain such intratextual resonances. Damoetas demands the presence of both Phyllis and her mate with none too subtle sexual innuendo (*Buc.* 3.76–7): *Phyllida mitte mihi: meus est natalis, Iolla;/ cum faciam* ***uitula*** *pro frugibus, ipse uenito.* ('Send Phyllis to me: it's my birthday, Iollas; when I sacrifice with a heifer for the crops, come yourself'.) Wendell Clausen found Damoetas' proposed sacrifice of a heifer 'pretentious for someone in [his] position',[12] but we may interpret the very specificity of a bovine sacrifice as an implicit metapoetic commentary on Virgil's generic commitments in his *Bucolica*. As the herdsmen continue, moreover, they supplement the themes of love and pasturage with that of poetic rivalry (*Buc.* 3.84–7):

> ***D.*** Pollio amat nostram, quamuis est rustica, Musam:
> Pierides, **uitulam lectori pascite uestro.**
> ***M.*** Pollio et ipse facit noua carmina: **pascite taurum**,
> iam cornu petat et pedibus qui spargat harenam.

> ***D.*** Pollio loves our Muse, though she's a country girl:
> Pierian Muses, pasture a heifer for your reader.
> ***M.*** Pollio too composes new poems: pasture a bull
> who now butts with his horn and kicks sand with his feet.

Both singers honour Virgil's patron Pollio, not only by naming him (3.84, 86; cf. 3.88) but also by repeating the god's injunction from the first eclogue to pasture a heifer (3.85; cf. *pascite ut ante boues*, 1.45) or a bull (3.86, cf. *summittite tauros*, 1.45)–i.e., write a bucolic poem–for him (to read).[13] Damoetas emphasizes Pollio's love of his rustic song, and by extension of the poet's bucolic verse, and self-consciously alludes to its circulation in written form (3.85),[14] while Menalcas compliments Pollio on his own poetry (3.86), which we learn elsewhere was in the tragic genre (Hor. *Sat.* 1.10.42–3, *C.* 2.1.9–12), and thus outdoes Damoetas' bucolic heifer (*uitulam*, 3.85; cf. his sacrifice of a heifer at 3.77, quoted above) with Dionysus' tragic bull (*taurum*, 3.86).[15]

---

12 Clausen 1994, 110, *ad loc.*

13 Cf. Wright 1983.

14 On literacy and orality in the *Bucolics*, see Breed 2006.

15 For the bull as the sacrificial animal of Dionysus *par excellence* (and in whose form the god himself often appeared), see Dodds 1960, xviii, citing Eur. *Ba.* 618, 922, 1017; Ar. *Frogs* 357; Plut.

In the sixth eclogue too, Virgil offers metapoetic commentary on the bovine etymology of bucolic poetry. The eclogue is often interpreted as a 'proemio nel mezzo' for the collection because of the programmatic opening lines (1–12), which rehearse the polemical poetics of Callimachus' *Aetia* Prologue and decline to celebrate the dedicatee in grand epic.[16] Here the Latin poet articulates his literary program by reworking Callimachus' account of the god Apollo's literary instructions, newly adapted to a pastoral setting (*Buc.* 6.3–5): *cum canerem reges et proelia, Cynthius aurem/ uellit et admonuit: 'pastorem, Tityre, pinguis/ pascere oportet ouis, deductum dicere carmen'*. ('When I would sing of kings and battles, Cynthian Apollo plucked my ear and advised: "Tityrus, the shepherd should fatten his sheep but sing a refined song".') Apollo's concern about Tityrus' sheep here recalls Damoetas' shepherding (rather than cowherding) in the third eclogue, and continues Virgil's revision of Theocritean pastoral. But in the rest of the eclogue, the Latin poet rehearses a self-consciously bucolic song of Silenus in support of his programmatic rejection of martial epic. Silenus' song features scientific poetry (in an Apollonian-Lucretian cosmogony at lines 31–40) and Alexandrian learning (in a Callimachean-neoteric catalogue of obscure erotic and metamorphic myth at lines 41–81),[17] but at the centre of his song, Pasiphae claims the singer's attention most prominently (45–60):

et fortunatam, si numquam **armenta** fuissent,
Pasiphaen niuei solatur amore **iuuenci.**
a, uirgo infelix, quae te dementia cepit!
Proetides implerunt falsis **mugitibus** agros,
at non tam turpis **pecudum** tamen ulla secuta
concubitus, quamuis collo timuisset aratrum
et saepe in leui quaesisset **cornua** fronte.
a! uirgo infelix, tu nunc in montibus erras:
ille latus niueum molli fultus hyacintho
ilice sub nigra pallentis **ruminat** herbas
aut aliquam in magno sequitur **grege.** 'claudite, Nymphae,
Dictaeae Nymphae, nemorum iam claudite saltus,

Q.Gr. 36.299B; Ant. Lib. *Met.* 10; Athen. 476A. The god's Greek cult titles reflect his close association with the bull: δίκερως, ταυρωπός, ταυρομέτωπος, κερασφόρος. As Dodds (1960, xviii n. 5) observes, some of his worshippers were called βουκόλοι, while at Argos the god himself was worshipped as βουγενής (Plut. *Is. Et Os.* 35, 364F). On the Virgilian passage, see especially Wright 1983, 123–4; Farrell 1991, 282; Nauta 2006, 316, who reads the line in connection with the *Opfervergleich* motif of Augustan *recusatio*; and Henkel n.d., 7, who offers a metaliterary reading of the lines broadly similar to, though independent of, my own.

16 On the 'proem in the middle', see Conte 1992.

17 On the program of *Buc.* 6, see Ross 1975, 18–38 (= Volk 2007, 189–215).

si qua forte ferant oculis sese obuia nostris
errabunda **bouis** uestigia; forsitan illum
aut herba captum uiridi aut **armenta** secutum
perducant aliquae **stabula** ad Gortynia **uaccae**.'

And he consoles Pasiphae—fortunate had there never been herds—for her love of a snow-white bullock. Ah, unhappy maiden, what madness possessed you! Proetus' daughters filled the fields with feigned mooing, but yet not one of them followed such shameful beddings with the herd, even though she had feared the plough for her neck and had often looked for horns on her smooth forehead. Alas, unhappy maiden, now you wander on the mountains, while he, supporting his snowy flank on soft hyacinth beneath the black holm-oak, chews the yellow grasses or follows some cow in a great herd. 'Nymphs of Cretan Dicte, Nymphs, shut off the glades in the woods, shut them off, if by chance any errant traces of a cow should present themselves to meet my view; perhaps some cows may lead him to Gortyn's stalls, if he's been captivated by the lush grass or he followed the herd'.

Particularly striking is the singer's sympathy for Pasiphae and her deluded passion for Minos' bull (45–7): she too might have enjoyed happiness had Minos not reneged on his vow to sacrifice to the sea-god the beautiful white bull the god had sent. Silenus suppresses the backstory of her husband's impiety and the god's resulting vengeance, however, in order to focus on the lovelorn Pasiphae, and rightly so in a bucolic collection, as Virgil embellishes a myth already featuring Minos' bull (46, 58), with the addition of herds (45), cattle (49), and cows (60). Indeed, the play of cow-myths continues in Silenus' allusive account, embedded in his recital of Pasiphae's unhappy history, of the daughters of Proetus, who insulted Hera and were maddened by her with the hallucination that they had been transformed into cows (48–51).

Silenus frames his allusive treatment of the Proetides' delusions with apostrophes to Pasiphae in her erotic madness (*Buc.* 6.47, 52): *a uirgo infelix, quae te dementia cepit!/ .../ a uirgo infelix, tu nunc in montibus erras* ('Alas, unhappy maiden, what madness possessed you! ... Alas, unhappy maiden, now you wander on the mountains'.) Both apostrophes begin with a half-line quoted from another cow-song, the epyllion *Io*, composed a generation earlier by Catullus' friend Calvus (Fr. 20 Hollis): *a uirgo infelix, herbis pasceris amaris!* ('Ah, unhappy maiden, you will pasture on bitter grasses!'). But it is notable that in the first apostrophe, Virgil has united the Calvan intertext with his very own Corydon intratext, as Silenus marries the first hemiepes of Calvus' line, addressed (perhaps by the neoteric poet himself) to the unhappy cow-maiden Io, to Corydon's pathetic self-apostrophe at the end of his song in the second eclogue (2.69): *a, Corydon, Corydon, quae te dementia cepit!* ('Ah, Corydon, what madness has seized you, Corydon!')[18] Unlike Corydon, however, who discovers a limit to love at the end of his song in the second eclogue (2.70–3), Pasiphae seems doomed to erotic obsession. Like Io, transformed into a heifer and maddened by the gadfly's sting, she wanders on the mountains tracking an elusive, not to say delusory, love (6.52–60). In Silenus' first, simultaneously inter- and intratextual, apostrophe, we can see Virgil consciously manipulating the controlling bucolic metaphor of his collection, as he recalls Io's bovine career and merges it with the moment of Corydon's insight into his erotomania. For the latter's self-diagnosis is inspired very precisely at the sight of plough-oxen returning at the end of the day (2.66–9):

> aspice, **aratra iugo** referunt suspensa **iuuenci**,
> et sol crescentis decedens duplicat umbras;
> me tamen urit amor: quis enim modus adsit amori?
> a, Corydon, Corydon, **quae te dementia cepit!**
>
> Look, the bullocks bring back the plough suspended from their yoke,
> and the setting sun redoubles the growing shadows;
> yet love burns me still: for what limit might there be to love?
> Alas Corydon, Corydon, what madness possessed you!

In the labour of animal husbandry, Corydon (unlike Pasiphae) locates the possibility of finding a limit to the madness of erotic passion.[19]

Elsewhere in the *Bucolica*, Virgil keeps intratextual metapoetic reference briefer and more pointed. In the third eclogue, for example, where we have already seen Virgil set the scene for the singing competition that dominates the action with intertextual play on Theocritean bucolic (τίνος αἱ βόες;, Theocr. *Id.* 4.1 ~

---

18 Cairns 1993, 112–14, suggests that Gallus too may have treated the Io myth, in imitation of Calvus. Sarah McCallum notes, *per litteras*, that the potential intertext deepens the connections between the elegiac Corydon of *Buc.* 2, the wandering Gallus of *Buc.* 6, and Gallus' madness in *Buc.* 10.

19 I am grateful to Sarah McCallum for drawing to my attention, *per litteras*, the intratextual relationship of this passage with a passage in the seventh eclogue, where Corydon invites Galatea to come to him when her oxen have returned to their stalls from pasture (*Buc.* 7.39–40): *cum primum pasti repetent praesepia* ***tauri***, */ si qua tui Corydonis habet te cura, uenito*. Virgil forges a strong intratextual relationship between Corydon's song in the second eclogue and these verses of Corydon in the seventh eclogue, as both are based on Polyphemus' song in Theocritus' *Idyll* 11: see Coleman 1977, 107–8 on *Buc.* 2, and 217 ad 7.37; Clausen 1994, 62–3 ad *Buc.* 2, and 226 ad *Buc.* 7.37–40.

cuium pecus, V. *Buc.* 3.1), the neatherd Damoetas laments the lovelorn emaciation both he and his bull suffer (*Buc.* 3.100-1): *Heu heu, quam pingui macer est mihi* ***taurus*** *in eruo!/ idem amor exitium* ***pecori pecoris****que magistro.* ('Oh dear, oh dear—how thin is my bull in the vetch! Love is alike deadly for the herd and its master'.) We may interpret the slenderness of the afflicted beast and his herdsman programmatically, as evidence of Virgil's commitment, in his bucolic collection, to the stylistic principle of Callimachean refinement. For the scrawny bull, like his emaciated master, wittily figures the 'slender Muse' (τὴν Μοῦσαν λεπταλέην, Call. *Aet.* Fr. 1.24 Harder)[20] espoused by Callimachus in lines we have seen Virgil adapt at the beginning of the sixth eclogue (*Buc.* 6.5, quoted above). A similarly programmatic use of the lexicon of animal husbandry, combining *boues* and *tauri*, occurs in the fifth eclogue, where the herdsmen Menalcas and Mopsus lament the death of Daphnis, the archetypal cow-herder and bucolic singer of Theocritus' first idyll (Theoc. *Id.* 1.64–145).[21] At his death, grief consumes the bucolic landscape and the pastoral routine is suspended (*Buc.* 5.24–6): *non ulli pastos illis egere diebus/ frigida, Daphni,* ***boues*** *ad flumina; nulla neque amnem/ libauit quadripes nec graminis attigit herbam.* ('None drove their cattle to pasture in those days, or to the rills; no four-footed beast drank from the stream or touched the grassy bank'.) For Daphnis was the first and best exponent of pastoralism, the glory of herding and cow-song (and so, by implication, the best subject for bucolic poetry), comparable to the first-fruits of the pastoral world (*Buc.* 5.32–4): *uitis ut arboribus decori est, ut uitibus uuae,/ ut gregibus* ***tauri****, segetes ut pinguibus aruis,/ tu decus omne tuis.* ('As the vine is the glory of the orchard, the grapes of the vine, the bulls of the flocks, and the crops of the rich fields, so you are the glory of all of them'.)

A final example of Virgil's investment of metapoetic significance in his intratextual deployment of the lexicon of bucolic comes in the eighth eclogue where he gives to one of the singers whose songs he reports the etymologically resonant name of Alphesiboeus. Although the masculine form of the name, an adjective which means 'producing a good yield of oxen',[22] does not appear in earlier bucolic, in his third idyll Theocritus rehearses a myth in which the feminine form of the name, 'Alphesiboia', appears (*Id.* 3.43–5), in an adaptation of a Homeric tale of cattle-rustling (*Od.* 11.288–92). The Virgilian Alphesiboeus, in his song, impersonates a woman performing a magic rite to draw her absent husband home, at

20 I cite Callimachus' *Aetia* from Harder 2012, and adapt her translations.

21 On Daphnis in Theocritus' first *Idyll*, and Theocritus' manipulation of the Daphnis-tradition (insofar as we can discover it), see Gow 1950, 2.1–2; Hunter 1999, 63–8.

22 *LSJ* s.v. 'ἀλφεσίβοιος'; cf. Gow 1950, 2.74 and Hunter 1999, 125, both ad *Id.* 3.45.

one point comparing her situation to that of a heifer exhausted by her search for her partner bullock (*Buc.* 8. 85–9):

> talis amor Daphnin qualis cum fessa **iuuencum**
> per nemora atque altos quaerendo **bucula** lucos
> propter aquae riuum uiridi procumbit in ulua
> perdita, nec serae meminit decedere nocti,
> talis amor teneat, nec sit mihi cura mederi.
>
> Such a love as when a heifer, tired out from seeking her
> bullock through glades and thick groves, lies down beside a
> green riverbank on the sedge, lost, and does not remember
> to yield to late night—let such a love hold him, nor let it
> be my concern to cure him of his madness.

By embedding in Alphesiboeus' song a bovine comparandum for the situation of the human lovers, Virgil retains an intratexual trace of the bovine program of his bucolic poetry, even as he varies the lexicon of 1.45 from *boues* to *bucula* and *tauri* to *iuuencus.*

2 *Boues et tauri*

Just as Virgil's revision of the genre of Theocritean bucolic demands the pasturing of cattle and oxen, so the didactic genre of georgic, to which Virgil ascends after the bucolic collection,[23] requires vigilant attention to their care and breeding (*Geo.* 1.1–5):

> Quid faciat laetas segetes, quo sidere terram
> uertere, Maecenas, ulmisque adiungere uitis
> conueniat, quae cura **boum**, qui cultus habendo
> sit **pecori**, apibus quanta experientia parcis,
> hinc canere incipiam.
>
> What makes the crops fertile, Maecenas; at what constellation,
> it is fitting to turn the soil and join vines to elms;
> what care belongs to cattle, what tending there is for the
> possession of a herd; what skill is required for thrifty bees—
> thence shall I begin my song.

23 On Virgil's career, see Theodorakopoulos 1997 and Farrell 2002.

The opening lines of the *Georgics* sketch the subject of each of the four books in their order of presentation over four lines. It is significant that animal husbandry is introduced, already at the outset of the poem, under the sign of cattle (*cura boum*, 1.3), as if to emphasize his new project's literary succession to the *Bucolics*. Even before the poet-preceptor reaches the third book, moreover, it is notable that plough-oxen—variously *boues*, *iuuenci*, and *tauri* in Virgilian usage—repeatedly recur in the first two books.[24] For the poem proper, and the farmer's labours, begin early in the spring with oxen put to the plough (*Geo*. 1.43–6):

> Vere nouo, gelidus canis cum montibus umor
> liquitur et Zephyro putris se glaeba resoluit,
> depresso incipiat iam tum mihi **taurus aratro**
> ingemere et sulco attritus splendescere uomer.
>
> In the early spring, when cold moisture flows from the snowy mountains and the crumbly clod loosens at Zephyr's breath, already then let my bull begin to groan at the deep pressure of the plough and the ploughshare, worn in the furrow, gleam.

The didactic poet signals the significance of his own commitment to didactic georgic with the personal pronoun in the dative of interest (*mihi*, 1.45), juxtaposed to his programmatic plough-ox (*taurus*).[25] The opening passage concludes, moreover, with the return of the farmer's plough-oxen in ring composition (*Geo*. 1.63–6): ... *ergo age, terrae/ pingue solum primis extemplo a mensibus anni/ **fortes** inuertant **tauri**, glaebasque iacentis/ puluerulenta coquat maturis solibus aestas.* ('Come then, and let your strong oxen turn the rich soil of the earth immediately from the first months of the year, and let the dusty heat bake the clods of earth lying under the increasing intensity of summer sunshine'.)

Still more significant is Virgil's introduction of the overarching theme of his didactic poem, *labor*, in close conjunction with plough-oxen (*Geo*. 1.118–24):[26]

---

24 *Boues*: 1.118, 285, 325; 2.470, 515; *iuuenci*: 2.237, 357, 515; *tauri*: *Geo*. 1.45, 65. On *iuuencus* as *uerbum proprium* for plough-ox, see Thomas 1991, 214–15.

25 Mynors (1990, 11 *ad loc.*) notes that Virgil improperly calls the plough-ox *taurus* here, and uses singular for plural.

26 Sarah McCallum reminds me, *per litteras*, that the passage is replete with intratextual links to the final eclogue, which is the only one in which *labor* appears (10.1): *Extremum hunc, Arethusa, mihi concede **laborem**.* ('Permit me this last labour, Arethusa [i.e., one last eclogue]'.) The didactic reminder that the shade of trees may be harmful (*Geo*. 1.121) also recalls the final lines of the last eclogue (10.75–6): *solet esse grauis cantantibus **umbra**,/ iuniperi grauis **umbra; nocent** et frugibus **umbrae**.* ('The evening shadows are commonly burdensome to singers, burdensome to juniper; the evening shadows harm the fruits of the farm too'.)

Nec tamen, haec cum sint **hominumque boumque labores**
uersando terram experti, nihil improbus anser
Strymoniaeque grues et amaris intiba fibris
officiunt aut umbra nocet. pater ipse colendi
haud facilem esse uiam uoluit, primusque per artem
mouit agros, curis acuens mortalia corda
nec torpere graui passus sua regna ueterno.

Nor yet, after all that the toil of men and oxen has attempted in turning the earth, does the wicked goose do no mischief, or the Strymonian cranes, or the bitter fibres of endive; nor is the shade of trees harmless. The great Father himself has willed that the path of husbandry should not be easy, he who first roused the fields through skill, sharpening mortals' hearts with cares, nor letting his realm slumber in heavy lethargy.

Commentators note the Homeric source (*Od.* 10.98: οὔτε βοῶν οὔτ᾽ ἀνδρῶν ... ἔργα) of Virgil's calque *hominumque boumque labores* (*Geo.* 1.118), 'the toil of men and plough-oxen', but see it as a conflation of the Homeric tag ἔργα ἀνδρῶν / ἀνθρώπων[27] with the Hesiodic phrase ἔργα βοῶν (*Erga* 46),[28] in an exemplary instance of Virgil's combinatorial intertextuality.[29] In my view, Hesiod's programmatic use of the phrase ἔργα βοῶν early in the *Works and Days* confirms the thematic primacy of the Hesiodic reference for Virgil's didactic program. For in setting out the program of his poem to his addressee, Perses, Hesiod bitterly observes that the fields worked by plough-oxen and sturdy mules would run to waste if man could sustain himself for a year on a day's toil (*Erga* 42–6). Indeed, the argument of Hesiod's poem is precisely that the farmer can do no such thing, that he must rather engage the unremitting toil of plough-oxen and sturdy mules, along with his own, to sustain himself. Thus, Virgil's adoption of the Greek hexameter formula 'of men and plough-oxen' explicitly marks the generic alignment of his 'poem of the earth'[30] with Hesiodic didactic, rather than Homeric epic. Moreover, Virgil recuperates Hesiod's didactic program along with his agricultural lexicon in the introduction of his own didactic theme of the relentless toil of

---

27 For Homeric usage of both phrases, see Cunliffe 1924[1963], 155 s.v. ἔργον (12) (c).

28 Quotations of Hesiod are from West 1978; translations are adapted from Evelyn-White 1914. West 1978, 154 ad *Erga* 46, notes that at *Od.* 10.98 the same phrase is used in the concrete sense of 'tilled fields', but he suggests that Hesiod's use here is 'less concrete'. On the extended sense of Virgil's calque *boum labores* as 'crops', see Mynors 1990, 25–6, ad *Geo.* 1.118, where the phrase first appears; cf. *Aen.* 2.306, with Horsfall 2008, 262 *ad loc.*

29 Thomas 1988, 1.87 ad *Geo.* 1.118; cf. Mynors 1990, 25–6.

30 The phrase is the title of Putnam 1979.

the georgic life (*Geo.* 1.145–6): ***labor** omnia uicit | improbus et duris urgens in rebus egestas* ('unrelenting toil has overwhelmed everything, and pressing need in harsh circumstances').[31] In this way, Virgil's emphasis at the outset of the *Georgics* on the primacy of *labor*—both of oxen and of men—functions intertextually, as an extended programmatic allusion to Hesiod in the Greek poet's role as the founder of didactic georgic in the *Works and Days*,[32] and intratextually, conjoining the toil of oxen with the labour of man in the leitmotif of his own didactic poem and also enacting the formal and thematic continuation of his agricultural poem with the *Bucolica*.

A programmatic concern with textual models and literary forms is clearly at issue in Virgil's repetition of the Hesiodic phrase later in the first book (1.324–6): *ruit arduus aether/ et pluuia ingenti sata laeta **boum**que **labores**/ diluit.* ('High heaven bursts and washes away the fertile crops and toil of oxen in the huge downpour'.) Although this description of the storm is indebted not only to Homeric simile (*Il.* 16.384–92) but also to Lucretian physics (*DRN* 1.271–6, 6.253–61), in addition to Hesiod's didactic treatment of the effects of storm on cultivation (*Erga* 507–16), the repetition of the Hesiodic motif both intertextually confirms the *Works and Days* as 'code' model[33] for Virgil's didactic poem on farming and intratextually reinforces his own thematic focus on toil in the *Georgics* and on cattle husbandry in his georgic continuation of the *Bucolics*.

So too, when Virgil instructs his reader about the best time to break oxen to the plough, he draws on specifically Hesiodic style and precept in his reiteration of the importance of the task (1.284–6): *septima post decimam felix et ponere uitem/ et prensos domitare **boues** et licia telae/ addere. nona fugae melior, contraria furtis.* ('The seventeenth is lucky for planting the vine, for yoking and breaking in oxen, and for adding loops to the warp. The ninth is better for the runaway but opposed to the thief'.) These instructions come at the close of Virgil's 'Days' (1.276–86), a passage which opens with the first attested reference in Latin to the title of Hesiod's poem (1.276–7): *Ipsa **dies** alios alio dedit ordine luna/*

---

31 In his presentation of the importance of toil (*labor omnia uicit*) to the *Georgics* here, Virgil intratextually revises his intertextual adaptation of the Gallan motto *omnia uincit amor* in the *Bucolics* (10.69: 'Love conquers all things'), where it emblematizes the importance of love both to Gallan elegy and to Virgilian pastoral.

32 Farrell 1991 does not discuss the programmatic relationship between the passages, though his discussions of both Virgil's '*Ascraeum carmen*' (27–60) and his 'Allusive Style' (61–127, especially 70–6), as well as that of 'Hesiod' (131–68, especially 131–57 and 163–8), are important for an appreciation of the significance of his formal debts to Hesiod's didactic poem on farming.

33 Following Hinds 1998, 41–2, and Curley 2013, 14–18, I use the term 'code' model after Conte 1986, 31.

felicis ***operum***...[34] ('The moon herself has allotted some days favourable for work in some order...') Richard Thomas (1988, 1.114) has observed the 'ostentatiously Hesiodic' character of the passage, which pointedly recalls the Greek poet's *Days* (*Erga* 765–828), 'from which at first sight V. appears to give a straightforward translation, apparently excerpting 802–13, treating the fifth, seventeenth, and nin(eteen)th [days]'. Indeed, Virgil not only couches his passage in the style of Hesiod's *Days*, but also draws from it the emphasis on toil (cf. *Erga* 773: βροτήσια ἔργα, 'the works of man').

A similar concern to signal his poem's formal generic alignment with Hesiodic georgic animates Virgil's disavowal of the fire-breathing bulls of martial epic, as distinct from the plough-oxen of didactic georgic, in the *laudes Italiae* (*Geo.* 2.140–2): *haec loca non* ***tauri*** *spirantes naribus ignem/ inuertere satis immanis dentibus hydri,/ nec galeis densisque uirum seges horruit hastis.* ('Fire-snorting bulls have not ploughed these fields for the sowing of a great dragon's teeth, nor has a crop of helmets and serried lances of men bristled in Italian lands'.) Virgil caps this implied rejection of the heroic themes of Homero-Apollonian mythological epic with a ringing endorsement of a distinctively Hesiodic allusive program in the closing line of the *laudes Italiae* (2.176): *Ascraeumque cano Romana per oppida carmen.* ('I sing an Ascraean [i.e., Hesiodic] song through Roman towns'.)[35] The closing movement of the second *Georgic* as a whole likewise reflects Virgil's programmatic alignment of his poem of the earth with Hesiodic didactic (as opposed to Homeric martial epic) in its famous praise of the farmer and farming life (2.458–60, 467–71, 513–15):

O fortunatos nimium, sua si bona norint,
agricolas! quibus ipsa, **procul discordibus armis**,
fundit humo facilem uictum iustissima tellus...
at secura quies et nescia fallere uita,
diues opum uariarum, at latis otia fundis,
speluncae uiuique lacus, at frigida tempe
mugitusque boum mollesque sub arbore somni
non absunt...

---

34 Thomas 1988, 1.115 *ad loc.*

35 Farrell 1991, 27–60. The line closes Virgil's statement of poetic primacy in adapting Hesiodic georgic into Latin (*Geo.* 2.174–6): *tibi res antiquae laudis et artem/ ingredior sanctos ausus recludere fontis,/ Ascraeumque cano Romana per oppida carmen.* ('For thee I embark on a subject and craft of ancient glory, having dared to disclose the holy sources, and I sing a Hesiodic song through the Roman towns of Italy'.) In his reuse of the adjective *Ascraeus* from *Buc.* 6.70, Virgil seems to link his own Hesiodic project in the *Georgics* with the poetic investiture of Gallus in the Hesiodic tradition at the climax of the sixth eclogue (*Buc.* 6.69–71).

> agricola incuruo terram dimouit aratro: 513
> hinc anni **labor**, hinc patriam paruosque nepotes
> sustinet hinc **armenta boum** meritosque **iuuencos**.

> O farmers, happy beyond measure, could they but know their blessings! For them, far from the clash of arms, most righteous Earth pours forth from her soil an easy sustenance...
> And they have leisure free from anxiety, a life free of deceit and rich in a variety of resources. Nor do they lack the peace of broad holdings, caverns, and natural lakes, cool valleys, and the lowing of oxen, and soft slumbers beneath the trees...
> The farmer cleaves the soil with his crooked plough; thence the year's toil, thence he sustains his country and small grandsons, thence he sustains his herds of cows and deserving bullocks.

In drawing the idyllic contours of the farming life, Virgil underlines the farmer's distance from the world of war (2.459), and that of his georgic poem from martial epic, and emphasizes his close relation, in the work and produce of the farm, to his plough oxen (2.513–15), and thereby his own literary commitment to didactic georgic. Thus, the two sets of *laudes* in the second *Georgic*—the praise of Italy and the farmer—underline the Latin poet's generic allegiance in his didactic poetry to Hesiodic georgic in their contrasting presentation of heroic bulls and the farmer's plough-oxen.

Virgil's final intratextual recuperation of the phrase *boumque labores* comes in the *Aeneid* and confirms his sensitivity to generic propriety, for here it occurs in a simile set during the sack of Troy (*Aen.* 2.304–8):

> in segetem ueluti cum flamma furentibus Austris
> incidit, aut rapidus montano flumine torrens
> sternit agros, sternit sata laeta **boumque labores**
> praecipitesque trahit siluas; stupet inscius alto
> accipiens sonitum saxi de uertice pastor.

> Just as when fire falls on a cornfield when the south winds rage, or a swift torrent from a mountain river lays low the fields, lays low the fertile crops and work of oxen,
> and drags the woods headlong, so the shepherd, all unawares, is amazed to hear the sound from the crag's lofty height.

Likening the Greeks' unexpected night attack on Troy (*Aen.* 2.309–10) to the devastation of sudden fire or flood to fields, crops, and forests, Virgil elevates the agricultural specificity of 'the work of oxen' (here perhaps, more than anywhere else in his oeuvre, to be understood in the concrete Homeric sense of 'crops')[36] to the decorum of martial epic, by resituating his georgic turn of phrase within an epic simile.

3 *Tauri*

The *laudes Italiae* introduce the bull's other central role in ancient Italian culture (*Geo.* 2.146–8): *hinc albi, Clitumne, greges et maxima taurus/ uictima, saepe tuo perfusi flumine sacro,/ Romanos ad templa deum duxere triumphos.* ('Hence come your bulls, Clitumnus, the snowy herd and noblest of victims, which, often bathed in your sacred stream, have led Roman triumphs to the gods' temples'.) The bullock, as sacrificial beast *par excellence*,[37] inaugurates the third Georgic and its subject of animal husbandry with the ritually prescribed sacrifice that concludes an imagined triumphal procession to the poet's temple of Caesarian song (3.21–3): *ipse caput tonsae foliis ornatus oliuae/ dona feram. iam nunc sollemnis ducere pompas/ ad delubra iuuat caesosque uidere iuuencos...*[38] ('My head wreathed with leaves of cut olive, I myself will award the prizes. Even now I long to escort the stately procession to the shrine and witness the slaughter of the steers'.)

The third book's didactic program proper then begins with a discussion of cattle-breeding, as the poet-preceptor recommends that the farmer select a dam with a taurine demeanor in order to breed strong plough oxen (3.50–8):

---

36 See n. 28 above.

37 Cf. *Aen.* 2.201–2, 223–4; 3.20–1, 219–49; 5.58–63, 472–84; 8.182–3; 11.197. The emphasis on sacrifice in the *Aeneid* is another way in which Virgil illustrates his epic poem's continuity with the taurine themes of his earlier poetry. This is especially visible in Laocoon's death struggle, likened by the poet to that of a sacrificial bull (*Aen.* 2.223–4), as he officiates at the sacrifice of a bull to Neptune (*Aen.* 2.201–2): on the episode, see Lehr 1934, 75; Kleinknecht 1944, 438; Luterbacher 1967; Zintzen 1979, 61–2; Harrison 1990, 51–4, esp. 54 n. 38. On cattle as the most expensive sacrificial animal, cf. Clausen 1994, 110, ad *Buc.* 3.77; and see especially McInerney 2010.

38 On the vexed relationship between Virgil's intratextual association of the end of the golden age with the slaughter and eating of oxen (*Geo* 2.536–8), where the phrase *caesis iuuencis* first appears, and the propitious slaughter of sacrificial oxen depicted in the proem to the next book where the phrase recurs (*Geo.* 3.22–3; cf. *Geo.* 4.284, *Aen.* 8.719), see Habinek 1990; Thomas 1991; Dyson 1996; and Morgan 1999, 108–16. I accept the latter's argument that, while the calamitous slaughter of the bullocks in *Geo.* 2 is not specifically sacrificial (1999, 113), Virgil's intratextual repetition of the phrase *iuuencis caesis* elsewhere in his corpus assimilates the social collapse outlined in this passage (*Geo.* 2.536–8) to the socially regenerative bull sacrifice of later passages in which the phrase appears (1999, 115).

pascit ... seu quis **fortis ad aratra iuuencos**
corpora praecipue matrum legat. optima **toruae**
forma bouis cui turpe caput, cui plurima ceruix,
et crurum tenus a mento palearia pendent;
tum longo nullus lateri modus: omnia magna,
pes etiam, et camuris hirtae sub cornibus aures.
nec mihi displiceat maculis insignis et albo,
aut iuga detrectans interdumque aspera **cornu**
et faciem **tauro** propior ...

... or whether a man breeds strong bullocks for the plough, let him select the mothers' bodies especially carefully. The best-formed cow is fierce looking, her head ugly, her neck thick, and her dewlaps hanging down from chin to legs; then there is no limit to her long flank; all points are large, even the feet, and under the crooked horns are shaggy ears. Nor would I dislike one marked with white spots, or impatient of the yoke, at times fierce with the horn, and more like a bull in her demeanour ...

The best-formed cow (*bos*), the poet instructs us in an etymological wordplay, is *torua* ('fierce')—nearly a *taurus* already, as Virgil explains in the phrase *faciem tauro propior* (3.58, 'closer to a bull in demeanor'). Here the poet links his earlier focus on plough oxen (in the preceding two books) to the new theme of (the third book, on) animal husbandry, and the role of breeding in the farmer's care of his livestock, through intratextual echo. The passage opens with an emphasis on the need for bullocks' strength at the plough (***fortis** ad **aratra** iuuencos*, 3.50; cf. 1.65, quoted above) and ring composition underlines the importance of breeding stock strong enough for the plough in the poet's specification of the period of the dam's fertility (3.60–2): *aetas Lucinam iustosque pati hymenaeos/ desinit ante decem, post quattuor incipit annos;/ cetera nec feturae habilis nec **fortis aratris***. ('The age to bear motherhood and lawful marriage ends before the tenth year and begins after the fourth; the rest of their life is neither fit for breeding nor strong for the plough'.) Virgil therefore concludes his discussion of breeding with an injunction to the farmer to begin by sending his cattle to mate (3.64, *mitte in Venerem **pecuaria** primus*), and here again he reminds us of the primacy of *labor* in agriculture (3.66–8): *optima quaeque dies miseris mortalibus aeui/ prima fugit; subeunt morbi tristisque senectus/ et **labor**, et durae rapit inclementia mortis*. ('Life's best age is always the first to flee from wretched mortals; diseases come upon us and gloomy old age, and toil; and harsh death's relentless advance snatches us away'.) But the passage also introduces the theme of illness (*morbi*, 3.67), and thereby anticipates the plague of Noricum with which the book concludes.

Even before we reach the plague narrative at the end of the third *Georgic*, however, Virgil presages the plague with a series of afflictions (*pestes*) that beset the farmer's cattle. The first is the gadfly (3.146–53):

est lucos Silari circa ilicibusque uirentem
plurimus Alburnum uolitans, cui nomen asilo
Romanum est, oestrum Grai uertere uocantes,
asper, acerba sonans, quo tota exterrita siluis
diffugiunt armenta; **furit mugitibus aether**
concussus siluaeque et sicci ripa Tanagri.
hoc quondam monstro horribilis exercuit iras
Inachiae Iuno pestem meditata iuuencae.

Around the groves of Silarus and the green holm-oaks of Alburnus swarms a fly, whose Roman name is *asilus*, but the Greeks have called it in their language *oestrus*. Fierce, it has a high-pitched whine and scatters whole herds, terrified, in the woods; and the air rages, struck with their bellowings, the groves too, and the riverbank of dry Tanager. With this monster Juno once wreaked her terrible anger, having devised this plague for Inachus' daughter in the form of a heifer.

The commentators have well discussed Virgil's multiple intertexts here and the sophisticated etymological underpinnings of his account of the gadfly, in a passage that, like the Pasiphae myth in the sixth eclogue, must look back to Calvus' *Io*.[39] But the intratextual resonances of this richly allusive passage have received rather less attention. We may note, in particular, Virgil's emphasis on the gadfly as a 'plague' (*pestem*, 3.153) afflicting the transformed cow-maiden Io. For the poet-pastoralist articulates the successive thematic panels of the third georgic in intratextual deployment of this term. Virgil intensifies the threat to the farmer's livestock from the gadfly afflicting the bovine Io here, its Greek name (*oestrum*, 3.148) hinting at the metaphorical plague constituted by unchecked sexual desire later in the book (*caeci stimulos amoris*, 3.210); through the snake that threatens his cattle (*pestis acerba boum*, 3.419); to the plague that decimates his stock (3.470–1): *non tam creber agens hiemem ruit aequore turbo/ quam multae pecudum pestes.* ('Not so frequently does a whirlwind rush from the sea, driving on a storm, as plagues swarm among herds'.) We can already hear *pestis* as an intratextual marker on its first appearance in the third book if we remember Virgil's reference to the many 'agents of destruction' that harass the farmer in the first book (1.181): *tum uariae inludunt pestes.* ('Then diverse pests mock him'.)

39 Thomas 1988, 2.66–70; Mynors 1990, 205–7.

Moreover, the shrill hum of the gadfly (*asper, acerba sonans*, 3.149) is itself an intertextual echo of Lucretius (*DRN* 5.33, *asper, acerba tuens*), who uses it of the mythical snake guarding the apples of the Hesperides, an allusion activated in Virgil's simultaneously inter- and intratextual echo later in the book, where *pestis acerba boum* (3.419) recombines various elements of his earlier description of the gadfly in application to the fauna (snakes) described in his intertextual source passage.

The gadfly's shrill hum seems, even more than its bite, both to anticipate and to provoke, onomatopoetically, the furious bellowing of the cattle, which re-echoes around the groves of Silarus and Alburnus (3.150–1, quoted above). Further resonances of the gadfly passage, instantiated in more bellowing cattle, recur later in the book, in the heat of the second affliction that assails the herd (3.209–26):[40]

Sed non ulla magis uiris industria firmat
quam Venerem et caeci stimulos auertere amoris
siue **boum** siue est cui gratior usus equorum.
atque ideo **tauros** procul atque in sola relegant
pascua post montem oppositum et trans flumina lata,
aut intus clausos satura ad praesepia seruant.
carpit enim uiris paulatim uritque uidendo
femina, nec nemorum patitur meminisse nec herbae
dulcibus illa quidem inlecebris, et saepe superbos
cornibus inter se subigit decernere amantis.
pascitur in magna Sila formosa **iuuenca**:
illi alternantes **mu**lta ui proelia miscent
uulneribus crebris; lauit ater corpora sanguis,
uersaque in obnixos urgentur cornua uasto
cum gemitu; re**boant** siluaeque et longus Olympus.
nec mos bellantis una stabulare, sed alter
uictus abit longeque ignotis exsulat oris,
multa gemens ignominiam ...

But no husbandry strengthens their powers so as to keep
them from sexual desire and the sting of blind passion,
whether one's preference is to deal with cattle or horses.
And so men exile the bull to lonely pastures far away,
beyond a mountain barrier and across wide rivers, or keep
him shut up within, at his full mangers. For the sight of the

40 On the passage and its sources, see Thomas 1988, 2.79–86; Hunter 1989; and Mynors 1990, 214–19.

> female slowly wastes his strength and inflames him,[41] nor indeed does she let him remember the groves or the pastures with her sweet enticements; and often she drives her proud lovers to decide the contest between themselves with their horns. A beautiful heifer grazes on great Sila: the bulls join battle with great force, inflicting frequent wounds. Black blood washes their bodies, and they press their lowered horns against each other with a mighty groan; the forests and far-off Olympus resound. Nor is it their custom to herd together, but the conquered one goes far off, an exile on unknown shores, groaning deeply at his shame ...

Virgil documents the destructive force of oestrus by turning up the intratextual volume, as it were, in a battle of bulls that he explicitly characterizes as cosmic in its acoustic reach (3.223). He emphasizes the intratextual relationship of this passage to his discussion of the gadfly not only by setting both herds on Mt Sila (3.146 ~ 3.219), but also by intensifying the herds' bellows. In the gadfly passage, Virgil had applied the noun *mugitus* to the bellowing of the cattle harrassed by the gadfly (3.150).[42] In the agonistic frenzy of *oestrus*, however, the Virgilian bulls' resonant bellowing can be heard, re-doubled and re-echoed in the woods, as ***multa** ui* (3.220) turns into ***multa** gemens* (226); the bulls' groaning in combat (*cum **gemitu***, 223) turns into the loser's groaning in shame (***multa gemens***, 226); and the woods reiterate (*re**boant***, 223) their cries in a Greek loan-word (βοάω) that seems to embody the word for the bellowing cattle (***boum***, 211) in both Greek (βοῦς) and Latin (*boues*). The passage closes, moreover, with another pun that exemplifies Virgil's concern for intratextual consistency, as well as generic propriety, as the defeated bull 'trains his strength with every care' in preparation for a rematch with his rival (3.229): *ergo* **omni cura** *uiris exercet*. The echo of Virgil's poetic project in the third *Georgic*, 'the care of cattle' (*cura boum*, 1.3) in the defeated bull's training regimen is comic, but nonetheless apposite in its intratextual alignment of subject matter and didactic program.

The intratextual resonances of the passage, moreover, reach well beyond the *Georgics*, all the way to the end of the *Aeneid* (12.713–24):

> dat gemitum tellus; tum crebros ensibus ictus
> congeminant, fors et uirtus miscetur in unum.
> ac uelut ingenti Sila **summoue** Taburno

---

41 We may recall Damoetas' bull, wasted with love like his master (*Buc.* 3.100–1), discussed above.

42 In this he is fully consistent with the Latin etymological tradition: see Keith 2017, 56–7 and 61 n. 15.

cum duo conuersis inimica in proelia tauri
frontibus incurrunt, pauidi cessere magistri,
stat pecus **omne metu mutum, mussantque** iuuencae
quis **nemori** imperitet, quem tota armenta sequantur;
illi inter sese **mul**ta ui uulnera miscent
cornuaque obnixi infigunt et sanguine largo
colla armosque lauant, **gemitu nemus omne remugit**:
non aliter Tros Aeneas et Daunius heros
concurrunt clipeis, ingens fragor aethera complet.

The earth gives a groan; then with their swords they redouble
their frequent blows, with chance and courage mixed together.
And just as, on lofty Sila or the peak of Taburnus, when two
bulls rush against each other, heads lowered in deadly combat,
the fearful herdsmen draw back, the whole herd stands silent
with fear, and the heifers whisper about who may rule the
grove, whom all the herds will follow; with great force the
bulls exchange wounds and gore each other, thrusting their
horns, and bathe their necks and shoulders with flowing
blood; the whole grove resounds with their groans.
So Trojan Aeneas and the Italian hero rush together
with their shields, and the mighty crash fills the sky.

The scene is much discussed in Virgilian scholarship, not only because of its place at the climax of the *Aeneid*, in a simile likening Aeneas and Turnus, fighting to decide the outcome of the Italian War, to a pair of bulls competing for a heifer and thence rule over the herd; but also because this is one of the most striking instances of intratextuality in the Virgilian corpus, as the poet transposes the georgic contest of bulls over a heifer into a martial arena that bears acoustic witness to the epic import of the contest between Aeneas and Turnus for rule over Latium.[43] The poet heralds the momentous occasion in the alternation between an unnatural silence and the low rumbling of the cow-spectators (12.718); and in the successive repetition of the onomatopoetic phoneme *mu-* in *mutum, mussantque ... gemitu nemus omne remugit* (12.718, 722), Virgil offers a punning acoustic commentary not only on the magniloquence of the bulls' roars, but also on their intratextuality. The sound effects are amplified as the intratextual resonances increase from one passage to the next, first within the *Georgics* and then in the climactic passage in the *Aeneid*.

43 On the relationship between the two passages, see Klingner 1967, 289; Briggs 1980, 49–50; Miles 1980, 187–90; Ross 1987, 158–63; Townend 1989, 86–7; Nelis 2001, 368–9; Niehl 2002, 116 and 192–3; Murray 2011, 76–7.

I have argued that Virgil deploys the lexicon of cattle and bulls intratextually, in both the *Bucolics* and the *Georgics*, in order to instantiate his poetic commitments to the genres of Theocritean bucolic and Hesiodic georgic, respectively, and we may likewise interpret the bull simile in *Aeneid* 12 in metapoetic terms. For here again, Virgil recontextualizes a didactic description (of the mating contest between bulls from the third *Georgic*) in an epic simile, adapting the agricultural scene to one of the most prominent formal features of the classical epic tradition. Richard Tarrant notes that 'the germ of the simile is found'[44] already in Apollonius' comparison, in the *Argonautica*, likening Amycus and Polydeuces in their boxing match to two bulls competing for a grazing heifer (*Arg.* 2.88–9): ἂψ δ' αὖτις συνόρουσαν ἐναντίω, **ἠύτε ταύρω**/ φορβάδος ἀμφὶ βοὸς κεκοτηότε δηριάασθον. ('Then they fell on each other once more, like two bulls tussling in grim rivalry for a fattened heifer'.) Thus, in the last book of the *Aeneid*, Virgil intratextually redeploys his own intertextual adaptation of this simile from the *Georgics*, returning it to its original home in heroic epic and thereby delineating the single combat between Turnus and Aeneas in the generic contours of Apollonian, and ultimately Homeric, martial epic.[45] Virgil's self-citation in *Aeneid* 12 thus marks his generic rise from didactic georgic to heroic epic at the same time that it bears witness to his earlier achievements in georgic (and bucolic) poetry.

Further intratextual continuity with the theme of animal husbandry in the *Bucolics* and *Georgics* is on display in the Hercules and Cacus episode in *Aeneid* 8, which features another quintessentially epic theme, in the succession of cattle thefts narrated by Evander.[46] For from Homer on, cattle-rustling had been a constituent of epic action,[47] taken up in a lower poetic register in Theocritean and Virgilian bucolic, as we have seen (*Id.* 4.1–3, *Buc.* 3.1–6). Hercules opens the sequence by stealing Geryon's cattle (*Aen.* 8.201–4): *nam maximus ultor/ tergemini nece Geryonae* ***spoliisque*** *superbus/ Alcides aderat* ***taurosque*** *hac uictor agebat/* ***ingentis***, *uallemque* ***boues*** *amnemque tenebant.* ('For the greatest avenger was

---

44 Tarrant 2012, 272, ad *Aen.* 12.715–22; cf. Thomas 1988, 2.81–2, ad *Geo.* 3.217–18; Mynors 1990, 215–16, ad *Geo.* 3.215–41. See also Briggs 1980, 49–50; Niehl 2002.

45 Homer is thus the 'code' model, Apollonius the 'local' model for Virgil's bull simile here: see Curley 2013, 16 n. 54, for this terminology, and my n. 33 above.

46 The episode has occasioned much discussion: in addition to the commentators, see Galinsky 1966 and 1972, 429–49; Hardie 1986, 110–18.

47 E.g., the cattle raiding ambushes between the Eleans and Pylians reported in Homeric epic by Nestor (*Il.* 11.668–762) and Odysseus (*Od.* 11.281–97; cf. 15. 230–8); the infant Hermes' theft of Apollo's cattle in the *Homeric Hymn to Hermes*; and the Hesiodic report of Hercules' slaughter of Geryon and theft of his cattle (Hes. *Theog.* 287–94). For cattle-rustling in the earliest strata of Greek myth, see further McInerney 2010, 68–172.

here, Hercules, proud of slaying triple-bodied Geryon and taking his spoils; victorious, he was driving his huge bulls this way, and his cattle held the valley and stream'.) Cacus' subsequent theft thus constitutes an intratextual reduplication of Hercules' heroic feat, which exposes the Italian monster as an inferior epigone in his mimetic desire to challenge the maximal hero of Greek myth (8.207–8):[48] ***quattuor*** *a stabulis* ***praestanti corpore tauros****/ auertit,* ***totidem*** *forma superante* ***iuuencas***. ('He turned four bulls of exceptional strength away from their pastures and the same number of heifers of outstanding beauty'.) Virgil self-reflexively signals his own epigonal status, as an author of 'secondary' epic, in the twice-stolen cattle: Hercules' theft of Geryon's cattle was one of the Greek hero's most famous labours (attested already in Hesiod, *Theog.* 287–94), while Cacus' secondary theft redevelops the Herculean motif along the lines of the treatment, in the *Homeric Hymn to Hermes*, of Hermes' theft of Apollo's cattle.[49]

Karl Galinsky (1966, 35) has demonstrated the intratextual connections between the Hercules and Cacus episode and the simile comparing Aeneas and Turnus to bulls fighting for leadership of the herd in *Aeneid* 12.

> The fight [between Hercules and Cacus] in VIII takes place over the same object. Its setting is a grove filled with the plaintive lowing of the cattle (215–16): *discessu mugire boues atque omne querelis/ impleri nemus et colles clamore relinqui.* ['At their departure the cattle bellowed; the grove was filled with complaints and the hills were left behind with their cries'.] The scene in XII is not very different. The outcome of the combat will decide who will rule over the grove, which in VIII is identified with the site of Rome (XII, 719 ... 722 [quoted above]). Both times the effect of the fight is heightened by the echo it finds in nature. The verbal similarity of the descriptions is again very close: ... *impulsu quo maximus intonat aether.* (VIII, 239 ['At the onslaught, the sky thundered mightily'.]) ... *ingens fragor aethera complet.* (XII, 724 ['A huge crash filled the sky'.])

Through its intratextual connection with the simile in *Aeneid* 12, moreover, the Hercules and Cacus episode is also linked to the description of the effects of *oestrus* on the herd in *Georgics* 3. Nor, however, is that the only intratextual link between this cattle-rustling episode in the *Aeneid* and the agricultural precepts of the *Georgics*. For in his theft of the choicest bulls and cows from Hercules' stolen stock (*Aen.* 8.207–8, quoted above), Cacus follows the injunctions of the nymph Cyrene to her son Aristaeus in the fourth *Georgic* to slaughter his best bulls and

---

48 On mimetic desire, see Girard 1965. On the maximal, or 'totalizing', ambitions of the classical epic hero, see Hardie 1993, developing the insights of Nagy 1979.

49 Virgil's sources for the episode are nearly contemporary with his own poetic career: Livy 1.7.5–15 and Dionysius of Halicarnassus (1.39, 42.2–3). See Galinsky 1966, and 1972, 129–49; Eden 1975, 74–92; Gransden 1976, 106–8; Fordyce 1977, 223–7.

heifers, in order to generate a new hive of bees through the *bugonia* ritual (*Geo.* 4.538–40): ***quattuor*** *eximios* ***praestanti corpore tauros,***/ *qui tibi nunc uiridis depascunt summa Lycaei,/ delige, et intacta* **totidem** *ceruice* **iuuencas**. ('Select four bulls outstanding for their exceptional strength, which now pasture among your herds on the summit of green Mt Lycaeon, and the same number of heifers with necks unbroken to the yoke'.) In Cacus' theft, Virgil thus reworks an important passage from the closing panel of the *Georgics*, a highly metapoetic section of the poem on any reading, and one associated in antiquity with (presumably intertextual) praise of his contemporary, friend and fellow poet, Gallus.[50]

4 *Bugonia*

The complex nexus of relationships linking the myth of Orpheus and Eurydice (*Geo.* 4.453–527), reported to Aristaeus by the old man of the sea in explanation for the loss of the former's hive (4.315–558), to the practice of *bugonia* (4.281–314), the culture of bee-keeping (4.1–280), and thence to the fourth book of the *Georgics* as a whole, has occasioned critical debate for over two millenia and I do not attempt to resolve the issues here.[51] I wish rather, in conclusion, to draw attention to the continuing metapoetic significance of cattle and oxen in Virgil's account of the birth of a hive from slaughtered cattle at the end of the *Georgics*. For, following his mother's advice to the letter, Aristaeus regenerates his bees in a ritual *bugonia*, 'birth from cattle' (4.548–51):

> haud mora, continuo matris praecepta facessit:
> ad delubra uenit, monstratas excitat aras,
> quattuor eximios praestanti corpore tauros
> ducit et intacta totidem ceruice iuuencas.
>
> Without delay, he immediately performed his mother's precepts: he went to the shrines, kindled the altars she'd shown him, led four bulls outstanding for their exceptional strength, and the same number of heifers, necks unbroken to the yoke.

50 Servius ad *Buc.* 10.1 and *Geo.* 4.1. I follow Griffin 1979, 75–6 (= 1985, 180–2), Thomas 1988, 1.13–16, and Mynors 1990, 296, in rejecting the biographical interpretation of Servius' notice while accepting, with Coleman 1962 and Thomas 1988, 1.15–16, that, in the second half of *Georgics* 4, Virgil acknowledged his appreciation of Gallus' poetry in allusions to the formal features and subject matter of Gallan verse.

51 On the passage, see Griffin 1979 (= 1985, 163–82); Morgan 1999; and the extensive bibliography discussed by Volk 2008, 9–10.

Cyrene's instructions differ from those of the didactic poet somewhat earlier in the book, where only one bull is required for the rite (4.299–300): *tum* ***uitulus*** *bima curuans iam* ***cornua*** *fronte/ quaeritur.* ('Then they seek a bullock whose horns are just now arching on his two-year old forehead'.) But the results of both Aristaeus' performance of the *bugonia*, and the poet-preceptor's account of the rite, are the same. Nine days after the slaughter of his cattle, Aristaeus finds a hive miraculously generated from their liquified entrails (4.554–8):

hic uero subitum ac dictu **mirabile** monstrum
aspiciunt, liquefacta boum per uiscera toto
stridere apes utero et **ruptis** efferuere costis,
immensasque trahi **nubes**, iamque arbore summa
confluere et lentis uuam demittere ramis.

But here they see a sudden prodigy, marvellous to report, as
bees buzz through the liquefied entrails of the cattle in the
whole belly and seethe in the broken ribs; they're drawn out
in huge clouds, and converge now at the top of a tree, and
hang in a cluster from the pliant boughs.

Similarly, the didactic poet explains that by leaving a ritually slaughtered bullock to rot we can regenerate a lost hive (4.308–13):

interea teneris tepefactus in ossibus umor
aestuat, et uisenda modis animalia **miris**,
trunca pedum primo, mox et **stridentia** pennis,
miscentur, tenuemque magis magis aëra carpunt
donec ut aestiuis effusus **nubibus** imber
erupere ...

Meanwhile, the moisture, warming in the softened bones,
seethes; and creatures of wondrous ways can be seen, at
first without feet, but soon, buzzing on wings, they swarm
together and tentatively take to the light air until,
like rain pouring from summer clouds, they burst out ...

Virgil draws on Egyptian lore (4.281–94) to present the birth of bees from a slaughtered bullock as an eastern marvel.[52] In both *bugonia* passages, which

52 On the tradition, see Shipley 1918; Whitfield 1956; Thomas 1988, 2.196–201 and Mynors 1990, 293–300, both ad *Geo.* 4.281–314; Habinek 1990; Thomas 1991; Stephens 2004, with full bibliography. Antigonus of Carystus (19.23) includes the *bugonia* in his *paradoxa*, while Philitas connects the adjective βουγενής ('cowborn') to the practice of *bugonia* (Fr. 14a Spanoudakis):

frame the Aristaeus exemplum that closes the *Georgics*, the poet emphasizes the miraculous results (*modis miris*, 4.309; *mirabile monstrum*, 4.554) of the liquefaction of the slaughtered bullock's body (*umor*, 4.308; *liquefacta*, 4.555), and the buzzing (4.310, 556) of the bees as they leave the carcass for the air.

Many readers have looked for a deeper significance in the *bugonia* beyond the natural behaviour of bees, since Virgil presents the *bugonia* as a marvel and Servius reports that the passage replaced an encomium of his friend and fellow poet, Gallus. In this regard, it is perhaps instructive to consider the traditional associations of bees in classical literature. Callimachus, for example, had drawn on the metaphorical connection of bees with poets and poetry in concluding his second hymn with an explicit endorsement of 'slender verse', embodied in the bee-priestesses of Demeter (Call. *Hymn* 2.110–12): Δηοῖ δ'οὐκ ἀπὸ παντὸς ὕδωρ φορέουσι μέλισσαι,/ ἀλλ' ἥτις καθαρή τε καὶ ἀχράαντος ἀνέρπει/ πίδακος ἐξ ἱερῆς ὀλίγη λιβὰς ἄκρον ἄωτον. ('Not from every spring do the Bees carry water to Demeter, but the pure, unsullied, trickling stream that springs up from a holy fountain, the choicest of its kind'.) In his commentary on these lines, Frederick Williams (1978, 92–4) assembles the abundant evidence for the conventional association of poets, and their poems, with bees in the Greek literary tradition, and shows that Demeter's bee-priestesses act in accordance with Callimachus' precepts about the kind of poetry he values, in offering the goddess pure water from small, undefiled streams. Virgil knew Callimachus' oeuvre well and endorses his poetics elsewhere, as we have seen (e.g., *Buc.* 6.3–5, quoted above); moreover, the metaphorical association of bees with poets and poetry was current at Rome in his day.[53] It is tempting, therefore, to interpret the Latin poet's *bugonia* metapoetically, and all the more so as this study has documented Virgil's pervasive investment of the lexicon of cattle and oxen with a metapoetic valence. We might thus interpret the *bugonia* as figuring the generation of georgic poetry from bucolic verse or even, still more broadly, the generation of Virgilian poetry from the 'cattle and oxen' granted to the poet by the god of the first eclogue.[54] On

βουγενέας ... μελίσσας ('cowborn bees'); see Spanoudakis 2001, 184–6, *ad loc.* Callimachus (himself writing in Egypt, at the Ptolemaic court) applies the same adjective to Io's descendant Danaus (Call. *Aet.* Fr. 54.4 Harder) in a passage that introduces the Apis bull (Call. *Aet.* Fr. 54.16 Harder), with which Danaus' ancestor, Io's son Epaphus, was associated. See Harder 2012, 2.400–1 and 2.412–13 respectively.

53 See the evidence collected and discussed in Davies 1973 and Roessel 1990.

54 Christopher Trinacty and Sarah McCallum, among others, have suggested to me that, as Acosta-Hughes and Stephens (2012, 243 n. 102) put it in tracing intertextual connections between Callimachus' Epaphus/Apis bull and Virgil's *bugonia*, there is 'an implied bilingual pun as the cowborn Apis in Callimachus becomes "cowborn" *apes* in Virgil', through its metonymic relation

such a reading, Virgil's intratextual adaptation of Cyrene's instructions for *bugonia* in Cacus' cattle-rustling in *Aeneid* 8 confirms the metapoetic importance of the latter episode in articulating the poet's new commitment in the *Aeneid* to composing Homeric epic even as, once again, he adapts bovine material to hexameter verse.

If we ask why cattle and oxen should play so large a role in Virgil's articulation of his poetic undertakings, it is surely enough, on the one hand, to point to the extraordinary importance of cattle as movable wealth in the ancient Mediterranean.[55] But we may also wish to consider the importance of cattle specifically in ancient Italy.[56] For a very prominent school of thought in classical antiquity derived the name of the peninsula, *Italia*, from the Latin word for bullock, *uitulus*.[57] Varro, in his *Res Rustica* (an important source for Virgil's *Georgics*),[58] disputes the etymology (2.1.9): *denique non Italia a uitulis appellata est, ut scribit Piso* ('Indeed, Italy was not named from bullocks, as Piso writes'.) Nonetheless, he elsewhere provides evidence of both the antiquity and contemporary currency of this etymology (*Rust.* 2.5.3):

> Graecia antiqua, ut scribit Timaeus, tauros uocabant italos, a quorum multitudine et pulchritudine et fetu uitulorum Italiam dixerunt. Alii scripserunt, quod ex Sicilia Hercules persecutus sit eo nobilem taurum, qui diceretur italus.

> In ancient Greece, as Timaeus writes, they used to call bulls 'italos', and they named Italy from the great number, beauty and fertility of these bullocks.[59] Others have written that Hercules followed here from Sicily a noble bull, which was [*or* so that it was] called 'Italus'.

Somewhat later in the first century BCE, Dionysius of Halicarnassus reports the same etymology with additional detail, identifying Hellanikos of Lesbos as the author of this version and specifying Hercules' naming activity as occurring while

---

to Io's son Epaphus, himself 'equated with the Egyptian Apis bull (who is mentioned at *Victoria Berenices* 16)'. Cf. Stephens 2004, 158–60, who sees in Virgil's description of the Egyptian rite of *bugonia* a resemblance to the famous Egyptian ritual 'of the death, mummification, and "rebirth" of the Apis bull' 'that functioned to insure the fertility of Egypt' (159). She notes (160) that 'for Virgil the transformation may have been even more obvious, since the Greek name for the Egyptian bull (Hapi), "Apis", was a word that in Latin already meant "bee".'

55 McInerney 2010.

56 Morgan 1999, 130–4, reviews the etymological association of 'Italy' with cattle in his discussion of the *bugonia* as a redemptive and regenerative rite, allegorically reflecting 'the death and rebirth of Roman *Italia* during the Civil Wars' (134).

57 Maltby 1991, 314 s.v. 'Italia' (a).

58 Kronenberg 2009, with extensive bibliography.

59 Cf. Colum. 6 *praef.* 7; Gell. *N.A.* 11.1.1.

he was herding Geryon's cattle in Italy (1.35.2). The bovine etymology may thus be felt to resonate throughout the Hercules and Cacus episode in *Aeneid* 8, a book that focuses intensively on the question of local names.[60] On this interpretation, Italia is as much an 'Ox-land' as the Greek Boeotia.[61] The etymology deriving Italy from *uituli* was apparently in wide circulation in the first century BCE, when Virgil composed his *Bucolica*, *Georgica* and *Aeneid*, each work more Italocentric than the last. While the very titles of his poems imply the intratextual continuity of cattle-song, cattle-husbandry, and cattle-rustling in their action, the thematic continuity of his poetry is enhanced by the etymological resonance of *boues* and *tauri* in the name of Italy, the setting of each of Virgil's works.[62]

Bibliography

Acosta-Hughes, B./ Stephens, S.A. (2012), *Callimachus in Context*, Cambridge.
Breed, B.W. (2006), *Pastoral Inscriptions: Reading and Writing Virgil's Eclogues*, London.
Briggs, W.W. Jr. (1980), *Narrative and Simile from the Georgics in the Aeneid*, Leiden.
Cairns, F. (1993), 'Imitation and Originality in Ovid, *Amores* 1.3', *PLLS* 7, 101–22.
Cairns, F. (1999), 'Vergil *Eclogue* 1.1–2: A Literary Programme?', *HSCP* 99, 289–93.
Clausen, W. (1994), *A Commentary on Virgil, Eclogues*, Oxford.
Coleman, R. (1962), 'Gallus, the *Bucolics*, and the End of the Fourth *Georgic*', *AJP* 83, 55–71.
Coleman, R. (ed.) (1977), *Vergil, Eclogues*, Cambridge.
Conte, G.B. (1986), *The Rhetoric of Imitation: Genre and Poetic Memory in Virgil and Other Latin Poets*, ed. C. Segal, Ithaca NY.

---

60 So Morgan 1999, 133, especially 133 n. 80, adducing *Aen.* 8.321–2, and 329; cf. O'Hara 1996, 207–8. Virgil himself rehearses an alternate etymology, preserved by Dionysius of Halicarnassus (1.35.1), deriving the name of Italy from that of an Italian king, Italos, early in the *Aeneid* (1.532–3 = 3.165–6): ... *Oenotri coluere uiri; nunc fama minores/ Italiam dixisse ducis de nomine gentem.* ('Oenotrian men cultivated the land; now the story goes that his descendents called the people Italian from the name of their leader'.) Cf. Maltby 1991, 314 s.v. 'Italia' (b), citing Hyg. *Fab.* 127.3; Paul. Fest. 106; Serv. ad *Aen.* 1.2, 533, 8.328; Isid. *Orig.* 14.4.18, 14.5.18; and see also O'Hara 1996, 128. Servius, however, reports the widespread acceptance of the taurine etymology in his commentary on these very lines (Servius auct. ad *Aen.* 1.533): *alii Italiam a bubus quibus est Italia fertilis, quia Graeci boues ἰταλούς, nos uitulos, dicimus.* ('Others derive [the name] Italy from cattle, with which Italy is fertile, since the Greeks call cattle "italoi", we "uituli".')
61 Maltby 1991, 82 s.v., citing Hyg. *Fab.* 178.6: *ex boue ... quem secutus fuerat Cadmus Boeotia est appellata* ('Boeotia ["Oxland"] was named from the ox which Cadmus had followed'); cf. Ov. *Met.* 3.10–13.
62 I am grateful to the organizers of the conference on 'Intratextuality' for the invitation to contribute a paper to the proceedings, and to the participants for their comments on an earlier version of this chapter. Thanks also to Brad Hald, for his bibliographical industry in his own research on the *bugonia*; to John Henkel for discussion about Virgilian metapoetics; and to Sarah McCallum for her comments on this chapter. I alone am responsible for any remaining errors.

Conte, G.B. (1992), 'Proems in the Middle', *YCS* 29, 147–59.
Cunliffe, R.J. (1924), *A Lexicon of the Homeric Dialect*, Glasgow/Bombay, Repr. Norman OK, 1963.
Curley, D. (2013), *Tragedy in Ovid*, Cambridge.
Davies, C. (1973), 'Poetry in the Circle of Messalla', *B&R* 20, 25–35.
Dodds, E.R. (ed.) (1960), *Euripides, Bacchae*,[2] Oxford.
Dyson, J.T. (1996), '*Caesi Iuvenci* and *Pietas Impia* in Virgil', *CJ* 91.3, 277–86.
Eden, P.T. (1975), *A Commentary on Virgil: Aeneid VIII*, Leiden.
Evelyn-White, H.G. (1914), *Hesiod, The Homeric Hymns and Homerica*, Cambridge MA.
Fairclough, H.R., rev. G.P. Goold (1999), *Virgil: Eclogues, Georgics, Aeneid*, 2 vols. Cambridge MA.
Farrell, J. (1991), *Vergil's Georgics and the Traditions of Ancient Epic*, Oxford.
Farrell, J. (2002), 'Greek Lives and Roman Careers in the Classical *Vita* Tradition', in: P.G. Cheney/F.A. De Armas (eds.), *European Literary Careers: The Author from Antiquity to the Renaissance*, Toronto, 24–46.
Fordyce, C.J. (1977), *Virgil, Aeneid VII–VIII*, edited by J.D. Christie, Oxford/Glasgow.
Galinsky, G.K. (1966), 'The Hercules-Cacus Episode in *Aeneid* VIII', *AJP* 87.1, 18–51.
Galinsky, G.K. (1972), *The Herakles Theme: The Adaptations of the Hero in Literature from Homer to the Twentieth Century*, Oxford.
Girard, R. (1965), *Deceit, Desire, and the Novel: Self and Other in Literary Structure*, (trans. by Y. Freccero), Baltimore MD.
Gow, A.S.F. (1944), 'BOUGONIA in *Geoponica* XV.2', *CR* 58.1, 14–15.
Gow, A.S.F. (ed.) (1950), *Theocritus, with Translation and Commentary*, 2 vols., Cambridge.
Gransden, K.W. (ed.) (1976), *Virgil, Aeneid, Book VIII*, Cambridge.
Graßl, H. (1982), 'Zur norischen Viehseuche bei Vergil (Georg. III 478-566)', *RhM* 125, 67–77.
Griffin, J. (1979), 'The Fourth *Georgic*, Virgil, and Rome', *G&R* 26, 61–80.
Griffin, J. (1985), *Latin Poets and Roman Life*, London.
Habinek, T. (1990), 'Sacrifice, Society, and Virgil's Ox-Born Bees', in: M. Griffith/D. Mastronarde (eds.), *Cabinet of the Muses: Essays on Classical and Comparative Literature in Honour of Thomas G. Rosenmeyer*, Atlanta, 209–23.
Harder, A. (ed.) (2012), *Callimachus, Aetia*, 2 vols., Oxford.
Hardie, P. (1986), *Virgil's Aeneid: Cosmos and Imperium*, Oxford.
Hardie, P. (1993), *The Epic Successors of Virgil*, Cambridge.
Harrison, E.L. (1990), 'Divine Action in *Aeneid* Book 2', in: S.J. Harrison (ed.), *Oxford Readings in Vergil's* Aeneid, Oxford, 46–59.
Henkel, J. (2014), 'Vergil Talks Technique: Metapoetic Arboriculture in *Georgics* 2', *Vergilius* 60, 33–66.
Henkel, J. n.d. *Metanarrative Allegory in Vergil's Eclogues and Georgics*.
Hinds, S. (1998), *Allusion and Intertext*, Cambridge.
Hollis, A.S. (ed.) (2007), *Fragments of Roman Poetry c. 60 BC –AD 20*, Oxford.
Horsfall, N. (ed.) (1981), 'Some Problems of Titulature in Roman Literary History', *BICS* 28, 103–14.
Horsfall, N. (1995), *A Companion to the Study of Virgil*, Leiden.
Horsfall, N. (ed.) (2008), *Virgil,* Aeneid 2, Mnemosyne Suppl. 299, New York/Leiden.
Hunter, R. (1989), 'Bulls and Boxers in Apollonius and Vergil', *CQ* 39, 557–61.
Hunter, R. (1999), *Theocritus: A Selection*, Cambridge.
Jones, F. (2011), *Virgil's Garden: The Nature of Bucolic Space*, London.
Keith, A. (2017), 'Cattle, Oxen, and Hercules' Labors: Response to the 2017 ACL Affiliated Group Panel at SCS on Latin Epic', *Classical Outlook* 92.2, 54–62.
Kleinknecht, H. (1944), 'Laokoon', *Hermes* 79, 66–111.

Klingner, F. (1967), *Virgil: Bucolica Georgica Aeneis*, Zurich/Stuttgart.
Kronenberg, L. (2009), *Allegories of Farming from Greece and Rome*, Cambridge.
Lehr, H. (1934), *Religion und Kult in Vergil's Aeneis*, PhD Diss., Giessen.
Liebeschuetz, W. (1965), 'Beast and Man in the Third Book of Virgil's *Georgics*', *G&R* 12, 64–77.
Luterbacher, F. (1967), *Die Prodigienglaube und Prodigienstil der Römer*, repr., Darmstadt.
Maltby, R. (1991), *A Lexicon of Ancient Latin Etymologies*, Leeds.
McInerney, J. (2010), *The Cattle of the Sun: Cows and Culture in the World of the Ancient Greeks*, Princeton.
Miles, G.B. (1980), *Virgil's Georgics: A New Interpretation*, Berkeley.
Morgan, L. (1999), *Patterns of Redemption in Virgil's* 'Georgics', Cambridge.
Murray, J. (2011), 'Shipwrecked Argonauticas', in: P. Asso (ed.), *Brill's Companion to Lucan*, Leiden, 57–80.
Mynors, R.A.B. (ed.) (1969), *P. Vergili Maronis, Opera*, Oxford.
Mynors, R.A.B. (ed.) (1990), *Virgil, Georgics*, Oxford.
Nagy, G. (1979), *The Best of the Achaeans*, Baltimore MD.
Nauta, R.R. (2006), 'Panegyric in Virgil's *Bucolics*', in: M. Fantuzzi/T. Papanghelis (eds.), *Brill's Companion to Greek and Roman Pastoral*, Leiden/Boston, 301–32.
Nelis, D. (2001), *Virgil's Aeneid and the Argonautica of Apollonius Rhodius*, Cambridge.
Niehl, R. (2002), *Vergils Vergil: Selbstzitat und Selbstdeutung in der Aeneis. Ein Kommentar und Interpretationen*, Frankfurt am Main.
O'Hara, J.J. (1996), *True Names: Vergil and the Alexandrian Tradition of Etymological Wordplay*, Ann Arbor MI.
Perutelli, A. (1995), '*Bucolics*', in: Horsfall 1995, 27–62.
Putnam, M.C.J. (1979), *Virgil's Poem of the Earth: Studies in the Georgics*, Princeton.
Reynolds, L.D. (ed.) (1983), *Texts and Transmission: A Survey of the Latin Classics*, Oxford.
Roessel, D. (1990), 'The Significance of the Name Cerinthus in the Poems of Sulpicia', *TAPA* 120, 243–50.
Ross, D.O., Jr. (1975), *Backgrounds to Augustan Poetry: Gallus, Elegy and Rome*, Cambridge.
Ross, D.O., Jr. (1987), *Virgil's Elements: Physics and Poetry in the Georgics*, Princeton.
Sharrock, A./Morales, H. (eds.) (2000), *Intratextuality: Greek and Roman Textual Relations*, Oxford.
Shipley, A.E. (1918), 'The Bugonia Myth', *Journal of Philology* 67, 97–105.
Spanoudakis, K. (2002), *Philitas of Cos*, Leiden.
Stephens, S.A. (2004), 'Whose Rituals in Ink?', in: A. Barchiesi/J. Rüpke/S. Stephens (eds.), *Rituals in Ink*, Stuttgart, 157–60.
Tarrant, R. (ed.) (2012), *Virgil, Aeneid Book XII*, Cambridge.
Theodorakopoulos, E. (1997), 'Closure: the Book of Virgil', in: C. Martindale (ed.), *The Cambridge Companion to Virgil*, Cambridge, 155–65.
Thomas, G.T. (1978), 'Religious Background for Virgil's Bee Symbol in the *Georgics*', *Vergilius* 24, 32–6.
Thomas, R.F. (ed.) (1988), *Virgil, Georgics*, 2 vols., Cambridge.
Thomas, R.F. (1991), 'The "Sacrifice" at the End of the *Georgics*, Aristaeus, and Vergilian Closure', *CP* 86.3, 211–18.
Townend, G.R. (1989), 'Some Animal-Similes in the *Aeneid*', in: A. Bonanno/H.C.R. Vella (eds.), *Laurea Corona: Studies in Honour of Edward Coleiro*, Amsterdam, 84–8.
Volk, K. (ed.) (2007), *Oxford Readings in Vergil's Eclogues*, Oxford.
Volk, K. (ed.) (2008), *Oxford Readings in Vergil's Georgics*, Oxford.
West, M.L. (ed.) (1978), *Hesiod, Works & Days*, Oxford.

Wheeler, S.M. (1993), 'Lost Voices: Vergil, *Aeneid* 12.718-19', *CQ* 43.2, 451–4.
Whitfield, B.G. (1956), 'Virgil and the Bees', *G&R* 3, 99–117.
Williams, F. (1978), *Callimachus, Hymn to Apollo*, Oxford.
Wright, J.E.G. (1983), 'Virgil's Pastoral Programme: Theocritus, Callimachus and *Eclogue* 1', *PCPS* 29, 107–60.
Zintzen, C. (1979), *Die Laokoonepisode bei Vergil*. Abh.Adak.Mainz 10, Mainz.

Martin Korenjak

Contradictions and Doppelgangers: The Prehistory of Virgil's Two Voices

As Alison Sharrock underlines in her introduction to *Intratextuality*, the seminal collected volume which was a major inspiration for the 11th *Trends in Classics* conference, we all tend to read for unity – whether it be unity of features in a work's content, such as plot or message, or of formal features like narrative stance or style.[1] Confronted with texts whose unity is not apparent at first sight, readers have developed various strategies to look for it more closely and systematically, some of which are exemplified in the essays that make up the body of *Intratextuality*. Unity, and the intratextual phenomena working towards it, thus appear not only as properties of a given text, but also as results of what its readers do to it.

But what if the quest for unity is ultimately frustrated? In what follows, I would like to show that readers have also developed strategies for coping with such failure, and to exemplify this by having a closer look at one particular coping strategy. My starting point is the widely influential notion formulated by Adam Parry in his famous 1963 article on 'The Two Voices of Virgil's *Aeneid*'. Throughout his epic, we are told, Virgil speaks in two different voices – one loud and dominant, the other harder to hear – that are fundamentally opposed to each other. As Parry himself summarized his findings:

> The *Aeneid*, the supposed panegyric of Augustus and great propaganda-piece of the new régime, has turned into something quite different. The processes of history are presented as inevitable, as indeed they are, but the value of what they achieve is cast into doubt. Virgil continually insists on the public glory of the Roman achievement, the establishment of peace and order and civilization, that *dominion without end* which Jupiter tells Venus he has given the Romans:
>
> *Imperium sine fine dedi.*

I am much indebted to Stephen Harrison for putting at my disposal a pre-publication version of his paper on the 'Harvard School', to Gail Trimble for pointing out James Kenneth Stephen's sonnet to me, and to all participants in the conference for a lively discussion of my paper. Simon Wirthensohn and William Barton have provided helpful criticism of its penultimate version; William has also corrected my English.

1 Cf. Sharrock 2000, esp. 2, 13, 17, 21–4, 38.

https://doi.org/10.1515/9783110611021-008

> But he insists equally on the terrible price one must pay for this glory. More than blood, sweat and tears, something more precious is continually being lost by the necessary process; human freedom, love, personal loyalty, all the qualities which the heroes of Homer represent, are lost in the service of what is grand, monumental and impersonal: the Roman State.[2]

This two-voices-theory, as it soon came to be known, is usually seen as an approach born from leftist political concerns, from a New Critical tendency to separate literature from its historical context and from a postmodern fascination with ambiguity. Along with this view goes the tacit assumption that Parry's theory is *sui generis* in the sense that it has been invented in order to tackle problems which are specific to Virgil and the *Aeneid*.[3]

There clearly is some truth to these notions: Parry has indeed much in common with other critics from the so-called 'Harvard school' who were influenced by New Criticism, reacted to the political climate in post-war America and proposed new readings of Virgil foregrounding ambiguities, dark aspects and sinister political implications.[4] Parry's core idea of Virgil's two opposing voices, however, sets him apart from his contemporaries and immediate predecessors.[5] Rather, it has a longer pedigree which has not been sufficiently recognised so far,[6] as I would like to show in the following: it is informed not only by modern and postmodern concerns, but can also be seen as a late offshoot of a considerably older literary critical strategy. In short, this strategy starts from the diagnosis that a certain poem contains, alongside its overtly proclaimed message, a number of elements which point in the opposite direction. This fact is then ascribed to an inner conflict, a kind of split, within the soul of its author, a half-suppressed impulse which opposes his/her conscious efforts and aims.

---

2 Parry 1963, 78.

3 For a convenient summary of these assumptions, see Thomas 2014.

4 O'Hara 2014. – As the term 'Harvard School' is problematic (the movement was neither exclusively connected to Harvard, nor a school), it appears in inverted commas throughout this article.

5 It is absent from all earlier or contemporary classical specimens of the 'Harvard School' such as Brooks 1953 or Clausen 1964 as well as from 'pre-Harvard' papers such as Bowra 1933/34.

6 Things are complicated by the fact that the 'Harvard School' as a whole has its own long prehistory, whose key notions, Virgil's melancholy character and literature as a vehicle of political dissidence, may be tracked back as far as Arist. *Pr.* 30.1 (why are all outstanding intellectuals melancholiacs?) and as the turmoils of the late Republic / early Principate respectively. A good deal has recently been written on this prehistory (e.g., Thomas 2001; Kallendorf 2007; Harrison 2018), whose latest phase in the 19th and 20th centuries to some degree contextualizes the subject of the present paper and interacts with it. In order not to wander from the overall theme of this volume, I will however focus as much as possible on the more specific notion of the two voices.

In order to substantiate these claims, let us now consider three prominent earlier examples. From a classicist's point of view, the first one that comes to mind is Lucretius. Since antiquity, numerous readers had admired the poetry of the *De rerum natura* and at the same time loathed its contents: what a terrible mistake on the part of Lucretius to put his poetic powers at the service of such a base doctrine as Epicureanism! An influential reaction to this attitude is a piece of pseudo-biography, which goes back to Suetonius and is recorded in a famous entry in St. Jerome's *Chronicle*:

> Titus Lucretius poeta nascitur. Qui postea amatorio poculo in furorem versus, cum aliquot libros per intervalla insaniae conscripsisset, quos postea Cicero emendavit, propria se manu interfecit anno aetatis XLIV.
>
> The poet Titus Lucretius is born. Later, he became mad because he was given a love potion. Having written a few books (emended afterwards by Cicero) in the intervals between his fits, he committed suicide, aged 43.[7]

In itself, this spectacular tale – taken up in the so-called 'Borgia Life' at the end of the 15th century, widespread through early modern times, later popularised in Alfred, Lord Tennyson's 'Lucretius' (1868) and intensely discussed in modern scholarship[8] – does *not* aim at coming to terms with tensions or contradictions within the *De rerum natura* but simply tries to discredit the poem's content. Its message is clear: as the very case of Epicureanism's most eloquent advocate demonstrates, this philosophy does not live up to its promises, proving unable to guarantee one's peace of mind if the latter comes under attack. In fact, the very idea of championing this philosophy could occur only to a madman.

In the course of the 19th century, however, readers began to project the tormented, mentally instable Lucretius of this story back onto his poem, so to speak: more and more signs of melancholy and despair were discovered in the *De rerum natura* and explained in terms of the author's own misery. Moreover, the image of Lucretius underwent considerable changes in the process and he came to look quite different from the victim he had been in Jerome: now, his problems were no longer due to harmful influences from the outside, they were part and parcel of his own psyche.[9] In the end, the poet appeared as a veritable split personality –

7 Suet. *Poet.* 16.1 Rostagni = Hieronymus, *Chronicon* ad *Ol.* 171.1–3.

8 For an overview of the story's reception, see Bailey 1947, 2, 8–12. 'Lucretius': Tennyson 1868. The scholarly discussion has abated during the last decades due to the general demise of biographism.

9 This process lasted over decades and did not follow a linear development: in the 1860s, for example, Matthew Arnold still mentioned the poisoning and did not explicitly deny its

torn by an inner struggle between two parts of himself which he was unable to reconcile.

What these parts of Lucretius' personality actually stood for varied in accordance with the nature of the rupture perceived in the fabric of the poem. In probably the earliest and at the same time most emphatic statement of the notion, an essay published in 1868 (the same year as Tennyson's poem) and programmatically entitled 'L'Antilucrèce chez Lucrèce', the French classicist Henri Patin presented Lucretius as an *anima naturaliter Christiana* whose religious convictions had unfortunately been strangled by his strong belief in Epicureanism but whose 'spiritualité involontaire'[10] surfaced time and again beneath the poem's cold, godless rationality:

> Je viens de vous montrer par quelle heureuse inconséquence Lucrèce, se corrigeant luimême, éclaircit quelquefois les tristes ombres dont il a enveloppé les destinées du monde et de l'homme.
> N'est-il pas remarquable que ce poème, d'où la divinité devait être absente, nous la fasse rencontrer si souvent dans ces idées de suprême sagesse, de suprême puissance, de suprême bonté auxquelles s'élèvent, en dépit de son système matérialiste et athée, la forte intélligence, le cœur aimant, l'imagination du poète?[11]

Less pious critics rather perceived a pessimistic undercurrent pervading the *De rerum natura* alongside its overt optimistic message and accordingly saw its author as a passionate and melancholy personality whose emotional upheaval and despair again and again clashed with Epicurean dogma. A classic representative of this strand was Cyril Bailey. Concluding a comparison between Epicurus and Lucretius in the introduction to his monumental commentary, he wrote:

> It does not need this comparison with his master to be sure that Lucretius' temperament was ardent, vehement, and passionate; he longed for the 'tranquil mind', but the poem is enough to show that he did not attain it. His very ardour combined with the melancholy already noticed brought it about, as Giussani has well put it, that 'the Epicurean comedy of nature became in Lucretius a tragedy'.[12]

---

historicity: 'In reading him, you understand the tradition which represents him as having been driven mad by a poison administered as a love-charm by his mistress, and as having composed his great work in the intervals of his madness.' (Arnold 1868–9, 312). Yet already in the 1830s, John Keble had proclaimed that 'we feel throughout the whole poem that the man is tortured' without dropping any hint at poisoning (Keble 1912, 266).

10 Patin 1868, 132.

11 Patin 1868, 125.

12 Bailey 1947, 16. The citation is from Giussani 1896, xxiii.

The basic pattern underlying both Patin's and Bailey's reading of the *De rerum natura* did however not emerge within Lucretian studies, and not even within classical studies in general. Dante's *Divina Commedia* is a somewhat earlier case in point.[13] The overall structure of the poem is clearly intended as climactic, as it rises from the depths of Hell to Purgatory and culminates in Paradise. It first and foremost celebrates God's infinite might and goodness as they manifest themselves in the beatitude He bestows on those who do His will. Hell is meant above all to provide a dark background against which Heaven's joy and glory can stand out all the brighter. The experience of readers, at least of modern readers, has often been at odds with this, however. To most people, it is the *Inferno* that strikes them as the strongest part of the *Commedia* by far while the *Purgatory* and *Paradise* remain pale in comparison.[14]

Again, this tension between the programme of the poem and its execution has been projected back onto the poet himself since the early 19th century: strong emotional forces were thought to be working against Dante's conscious intentions and to prevent their full realisation. The origin of this dark psychic energy was sought in Dante's innate character, in his grim personal destiny marked by the early death of his parents, the loss of Beatrice and his exile from Florence, or in a combination of both as the idea was elaborated by the English Romantics (the Florentine poet as a Promethean character who refused to compromise with his enemies and accepted his sad fate with fierce defiance).[15] In any case, Dante was seen as a personality so profoundly embittered that his description of Hell turned out to be uniquely vivid and powerful in spite of himself; the same embitterment obfuscated the splendors of Heaven and the author was unable to fully realize his poetic potential in the last part of his work. In the following extract from an early essay (1825) by the later English cabinet minister and peer Thomas Babington Macaulay, the emphasis lies on the poet's character predisposition:[16]

> The character of Milton was peculiarly distinguished by loftiness of spirit, that of Dante by intensity of feeling. In every line of the *Divine Comedy* we discern the asperity which is produced by pride struggling with misery. There is perhaps no work in the world so deeply and uniformly sorrowful. The melancholy of Dante was no fantastic caprice. It was not, as far as at this distance of time can be judged, the effect of external circumstances. It was from within. [...] The gloom of his character discolours all the passions of men, and all the face

13 For a general overview of Dante's afterlife, see Caesar 1989.

14 For some 19th century testimonies to this sentiment, see Caesar 1989, 468–9, 528, 539; for the German speaking world, Hölter 2002, 91–116.

15 Caesar 1989, 54; Crisafulli 2003, 126–9.

16 Macaulay 1825, 322 (Caesar 1989, 482).

> of nature, and tinges with its own livid hue the flowers of Paradise and the glories of the eternal throne.

On the other hand, Dante's misfortunes are foregrounded in an overview of his life and genius given in 1854 by the French critic Ferjus Boissard:[17]

> Son père et sa mère moururent tandis qu'il était encore jeune; ces premières et terribles douleurs imprimèrent peut-être, dans l'âme de l'enfant, cette mélancolie sombre et presque sauvage qu'il garda toute sa vie, dont chacun de ses vers a porté l'empreinte et qui laissa gravé sur son visage un cachet ineffaçable.

After a review of the following stages of Dante's anguished life, Boissard again comments on his physiognomy,[18] which is taken to reflect his 'fier génie': 'C'est comme le fantôme de toutes les douleurs réservées à l'humanité, comme le spectre de la colère, de l'indignation et du mépris'; after that, he proceeds to exemplify the poet's rancour and acrimony by his attacks on popes and kings in the *Inferno*. Writing in the same year as Boissard, Heinrich Heine summarises the close connection perceived between Dante's biography and his poetry in a nutshell when he calls him the 'Dichter der Hölle und des Exils'.[19] To demonstrate the persistence of this thought pattern, one further, later example may suffice. In 1921, Werner von der Schulenburg again analyses Dante's facial features, making the connexion to the parts of the *Commedia* even more explicit than Boissard and Heine: 'Spricht [...] sein Antlitz davon, dass er nach der Hölle den Himmel geschaut hat? Nein. Der Himmel [...] muss als Abglanz vorübergegangen sein; ein zartes Bild, das das Grauen der Hölle nicht verscheuchen konnte.'[20]

As for my last example, the second great poem on heaven and hell in Western literature, John Milton's *Paradise Lost*, I can be brief, since much relevant material has already been collected and analysed by Meyer Howard Abrams.[21] Among the most remarkable features of *Paradise Lost* is the captivating portrait that Milton paints of Satan. He traces his psychology in such depth and detail that the reader is hard pressed not to feel some understanding, and even sympathy, for the epic's villain. It is difficult to experience the same kind of compassion for God the Father and the Son or for the archangels Raphael and Michael. As early as the

---

17 Boissard 1854, 43–61; for the following citations and paraphrases, see 43, 51, 52–53.

18 In general, Dante's image was influenced to an unusual degree by the iconographic tradition (Hölter 2002, 118–22).

19 Heine 1854, 163. Cf. already de Staël 1807, 56 (Caesar 1989, 434): '... l'enfer s'offre à lui sous les couleurs de l'exil.'

20 Von der Schulenburg 1921, 9–10 (Hölter 2002, 119).

21 Abrams 1953, 250–6.

first years of the 1790s, William Blake ascribed this sympathy for Satan to the author himself in his *Marriage of Heaven and Hell.* In the course of an allegorical reading of *Paradise Lost* which equated God with cold reason, Satan with passion and energy, Blake argued that Milton went against his better, if unconscious, instincts as a poet when he defined his goal in the proem as to 'justifie the wayes of God to men': 'Note: The reason Milton wrote in fetters when he wrote of Angels & God, and at liberty when of Devils and Hell, is because he was a true poet and of the Devil's party without knowing it.'[22] Since the early 19th century, Milton's un- or subconscious sympathy for the Devil became something of a critical commonplace. It was taken up and varied by writers such as Shelley (1792–1822), William Hazlitt (1778–1830), John Stirling (1806–44) and, more recently, E.M.W. Tillyard (1889–1962). As early as 1825, John Keble testified to the popularity that the notion of Milton's satanic leanings had gained by his lifetime, and at the same time gave the idea a political twist:

> What again can be said [...] of the too attractive colours, in which, perhaps unconsciously, the poet has clothed the Author of Evil himself? It is a well-known complaint among many of the readers of Paradise Lost, that they can hardly keep themselves from sympathizing, in some sort, with Satan, as the hero of the poem. The most probable account of which surely is, that the author himself partook largely of the haughty and vindictive republican spirit, which he has assigned to the character, and consequently, though perhaps unconsciously, drew the portrait with a peculiar zest.[23]

Milton criticism provides the earliest attempt of which I am aware to explain a perceived lack of ideological unity in a poem with recourse to two conflicting impulses in the soul of its author. While the actual existence of earlier examples of this critical stance cannot be categorically excluded, there are two good reasons to assume that it is indeed a child of Romanticism. Firstly, it was romantic criticism that elevated the notion's most important precondition, namely the concept of the poem as an emanation of the poet's soul (rather than as a true image of the real world), to the dominant model of poetic production.[24] Secondly, the motif of the split personality, the doppelganger, belongs to the very core of the romantic and post-romantic imagination, from Jean Paul's *Siebenkäs* (1796) to Dostoyevsky's *The Double* (1846/66) and Robert Louis Stevenson's *Dr. Jekyll and Mr. Hyde* (1886).[25]

---

22 Blake 1979, plate 6.

23 Keble 1825, 229.

24 Abrams 1953.

25 Forderer 1999; Bär 2005. Dostoyevsky's novel is an especially suggestive case, since the falling apart of its protagonist is illustrated by the disintegration of his language.

Adam Parry was presumably aware of at least two of the cases just discussed when he wrote his celebrated article: Lucretius, whose personality was analysed in standard works of philology, such as Bailey's commentary, and Milton, commonly acknowledged as the second greatest English poet. In connection with Lucretius, one may in addition note the striking circumstance that Parry apparently borrowed his title from Alfred, Lord Tennyson whom I have already mentioned as the author of a poem on Lucretius' inner conflicts and his suicide: as early as in 1842, Tennyson had published another poem entitled precisely 'The Two Voices', where he had tried to lay open his own torn soul in a dialogue between the poet's 'I' and a 'still small voice' urging him, again, towards suicide.[26] All in all then, it seems probable that the two-voices-theory was indeed, to a substantial extent, inspired by the critical stance just sketched.

True, Parry's Virgil appears less as a puppet of his unconscious impulses than Patin's Lucretius or Blake's Milton, and more as a sovereign poet, who carefully balances out the victories and losses of Roman history. Having been raised, as already noted, in the tradition of New Criticism, Parry was careful not to reduce the *Aeneid* to a simple outpouring of Virgil's life-experience and feelings – probably one reason why he chose to talk not of Virgil's two souls or minds, but of his two voices. All said and done, however, it is often hard to see what substantive difference this makes. When Parry writes, for example, of 'the continual opposition of a personal voice which comes to us *as if* it were Virgil's own to the public voice of Roman success',[27] few of his readers will know exactly what to make of the 'as if' and resist the impression that the 'personal voice' expresses indeed what Virgil the man, or one part of him, thought and felt.

Of course, none of this means that Parry is wrong or outdated – quite the contrary: fifty years after the publication of his article, most classicists would agree that he has indeed captured a pivotal aspect of Virgil's art and worldview and made a lasting contribution to Virgilian scholarship.[28] It just means that his insights do not stem exclusively from postwar politics, New Criticism and postmodernism, but also from a romantic concern with the author's soul as it expresses itself in poetry. In present-day critical discourse, romantic criticism often appears as the Other, encapsulating such abominable practices as biographism,

---

26 Tennyson 1842. On top of this, James Kenneth Stephen wrote a parodic sonnet beginning with the very same words 'Two voices'; in the course of the poem, these voices are specified as 'of the deep' and 'of an old half-witted sheep' and ascribed to William Wordsworth at his best and worst respectively (Stephen 1891). Whether this piece relates to Tennyson and Parry, and if so, in which way, I do not know.

27 Parry 1963, 69 (my italics).

28 E.g. Thomas 2014, 1311: 'the binary approach led to progress'.

unreflective empathy and neglect of theory – everything we define ourselves by no longer doing. However, the case of the two-voices-theory seems to indicate that this negative self-definition may involve a good deal of delusion. Insofar as we are Parry's heirs when seeking further voices in the *Aeneid* or pervasive ambiguities in Augustan literature as a whole, we may still be more romantic than we would like to believe.

By way of conclusion, let us briefly return to Alison Sharrock's introductory thoughts on intratextuality. While Sharrock acutely analyses *how* we read for unity and how much trouble we take to find it in a text, she does not touch on the question *why* we experience such a desire for textual wholeness in the first place. This withholding of judgement is of course a prudent attitude, since the problem is not one that will likely allow for a definitive solution. Yet, the critical stance reviewed in this article suggests at least one partial answer: textual unity, we might suppose, matters so much to us because it represents personal unity, while a fragmented text represents one of our deepest fears – the disintegration of our very self.

Bibliography

Abrams, M.H. (1953), *The Mirror and the Lamp. Romantic Theory and the Critical Tradition*, Oxford.

Arnold, M. (1868–9), 'On the Modern Element in Literature', *Macmillan's Magazine* 19, 304–14.

Bär, G. (2005), *Das Motiv des Doppelgängers als Spaltungsphantasie in der Literatur und im deutschen Stummfilm*, Amsterdam/New York.

Bailey, C. (1947), *Lucretius: De rerum natura libri sex. Edited with Prolegomena, Critical Apparatus, Translation, and Commentary*, vol. 1, Oxford.

Blake, W. (1979), *The Marriage of Heaven and Hell*, in: M.L. Johnson/J.E. Grant (eds.), New York.

Boissard, F. (1854), *Dante révolutionnaire et socialiste, mais non hérétique*, Paris.

Bowra, C.M. (1933/34), 'Aeneas and the Stoic Ideal', *G&R* 3, 8–21.

Brooks, R.A. (1953), '*Discolor Aura*. Reflections on the Golden Bough', *AJPh* 74, 260–80.

Caesar, M. (1989), *Dante. The Critical Heritage*, London/New York.

Clausen, W. (1964), 'An Interpretation of the *Aeneid*', *HSCPh* 68, 139–47.

Crisafulli, E. (2003), *The Vision of Dante. Cary's Translation of the Divine Comedy*, Market Harborough.

Forderer, Ch. (1999), *Ich-Eklipsen. Doppelgänger in der Literatur seit 1800*, Stuttgart/Weimar.

Giussani, C. (1896), *T. Lucreti Cari De rerum natura libri sex: revisione del testo, commento e studi introduttivi*, vol. 1: Studi lucreziani, Torino.

Harrison, St. (2018), 'Reflections on the Harvard School', *CW* 111.

Heine, H. (1854), 'Die Libelle', in: *Vermischte Schriften*, vol. 1, Hamburg, 161–4.

Hölter, E. (2002), *'Der Dichter der Hölle und des Exils'. Historische und systematische Profile der deutschsprachigen Dante-Rezeption*, Würzburg.

Kallendorf, C. (2007), *The Other Virgil. 'Pessimistic' Readings of the Aeneid in Early Modern Culture*, Oxford.

Keble, J. (1825), 'Review of Josiah Conder, The Star in the East, with other Poems', *Quarterly Review* 32, 211–32.

Keble, J. (1912), *Keble's Lectures on Poetry 1832–1841*, trans. by E.K. Francis, vol. 2, Oxford.

Macaulay, Th.B. (1825), 'Review of: Joannis Miltoni, Angli, de Doctrina Christiana libri duo posthumi ..., translated from the original by Charles R. Sumner', *Edinburgh Review* 84, 304–47.

O'Hara, J.J. (2014), 'Harvard School', in: R.F. Thomas/J.M. Ziolkowski (eds.), *The Virgil Encyclopedia*, vol. 2, 588–9.

Parry, A. (1963), 'The Two Voices of Virgil's *Aeneid*', *Arion* 2/4, 66–80.

Patin, H.J.G. (1868), 'L'Antilucrèce chez Lucrèce', in: *Études sur la poésie latine*, vol. 1, Paris, 117–37.

Schulenburg, W. von der (1921), *Dante und Deutschland. Euopäisches Denken und die deutsche Kaiseridee im XIV. und XX. Jahrhundert*, Freiburg i.B.

Sharrock, A. (2000), 'Intratextuality: Texts, Parts and (W)holes in Theory', in: eadem and H. Morales (eds.), *Intratextuality. Greek and Roman Textual Relations*, Oxford, 1–39.

Staël, Germaine de (1807), *Corinne ou l'Italie,* Tome premier, Paris.

Stephen, J.K. (1891), 'A Sonnet', in: *Lapsus Calami* (Fourth Edition, August), Cambridge, 83.

Tennyson, A. (1842), 'The Two Voices', in: *Poems*, vol. 2, London, 116–47.

Tennyson, A. (1868), 'Lucretius', *Macmillan's Magazine* 18, 1–9.

Thomas, R.F. (2001), *Virgil and the Augustan Reception*, Cambridge.

Thomas, R.F. (2014), '"Two Voices" Theory', in: idem and J.M. Ziolkowski (eds.), *The Virgil Encyclopedia*, vol. 3, 1310–1.

Christine Perkell

Intratextuality and the Case of Iapyx

Iapyx and Aeneas are intertwined figures in an enigmatically and elliptically told episode in *Aeneid* 12. Their stories are told in such a way as to foreground the theme of *pietas*, among others.[1] *Pius* Aeneas is, of course, famous as a model of *pietas* for saving his elderly father from falling Troy, a legend that goes back to at least the sixth century BC.[2] Iapyx, too, is read by some scholars as a model of *pietas* because he preferred (*maluit*) the (un)offered gift of medicine –in order to postpone his terminally ill father's death– over the possibilities of Apollo's *offered* gifts of music, archery, and prophecy for himself and others. Nevertheless, as this paper will argue, *gaps* in Iapyx' story suggest that his relationship to *pietas* may be more complicated and less accessible than has been assumed. The several crucial gaps in the story have been filled by different scholars in different ways, with the result that no critically accepted interpretation of the whole episode exists. The centrality of *pietas* in Roman ideology, the climactic importance of the twelfth book of the *Aeneid* —the last and the longest in the poem—, and the seeming fact that Vergil created the character and history of Iapyx for this singular role suggest that something of significance inheres in this brief episode. It might be sufficient to hypothesize that the posing of questions about *pietas* (amongst other things) is the very point of this episode.[3] This paper will attempt to push somewhat further in interpretation, however, by reading the Iapyx and Aeneas threads of the narrative against each other to see what meaning might emerge for each of the threads separately and together from such an intratextual reading. In this context we will find that the long recognized Iliadic intertexts are fruitful for interpretation of the Aeneas thread and, at minimum, suggestive for interpretation

I wish to thank Professors Stavros Frangoulidis and Stephen Harrison for including me in the 11th Trends in Classics Conference: *Intratextuality in Roman Literature* in Thessaloniki and for being most extraordinarily generous hosts and supportive colleagues.

1 Other puzzles include the non-appearance of Apollo, the appearance of Venus as a healer, and what, if anything, is being implied about Roman medicine. The scene of Aeneas' treatment by Iapyx is famously represented in a Pompeian wall painting, Casa di Sirico at the Museo Archeologico Nazionale in Naples.

2 See O'Hara (2014, vol. 1, 16–19).

3 In this essay Fish (1976) argues that scholars err in trying to *resolve* ambiguities or sites of critical dispute in a text by trying to find the true answer in the text. Ambiguities in the text are meant to be provocative. Responsibility for interpretation should, in these instances, be given to the reader, not the text.

https://doi.org/10.1515/9783110611021-009

of the Iapyx thread as well. As a result of these readings, Iapyx, it will be argued, contraty to most critical readings, is opposed and not parallel to Aeneas in terms of *pietas.*

In *Aeneid* 12.311 after the breaking of the treaty by the Latins, Aeneas, taking off his helmet, extends his open right hand in appeal to the troops for order and compliance with the treaty. His appeal fails, as he is struck by an arrow shot by an unknown actor and must be escorted, limping, from the field by Ascanius, Mnestheus, and Achates. In the camp he is met by, amongst others, the healer Iapyx. Paying Iapyx no apparent mind, Aeneas, furiously urgent to return to battle, struggles to rip out the arrowhead, demanding to be given the most expeditious treatment for the purpose, i.e., cutting out the arrowhead with a broadsword:

> saevit et infracta luctatur harundine telum 12.387
> eripere auxilioque viam, quae proxima, poscit:
> ense secent lato vulnus telique latebram
> rescindant penitus, seseque in bella remittant.

> He struggled furiously to pull out the head of the broken
> shaft, and called for the quickest means of assistance:
> to cut open the wound with a broadsword, lay open
> the arrow-tip's buried depths, and send him back to war.

Iapyx attempts repeatedly but in vain to extract the arrowhead; meanwhile, tension rises as the enemy advances. Apollo does not come, the narrator says (405–6), thereby drawing emphatic attention to this non-event, while allowing the inference that Apollo's coming was a reasonable expectation on the part of someone(s).

Venus, then, offended by the illegitimacy of Aeneas' wound, comes to the rescue, first visiting Crete for dittany (an herb known within the poem's story world to help ease the expulsion of arrows embedded in goats). This, along with two other medicines (*ambrosia, panacea*), she (in a cloud, unseen) adds to the balm that Iapyx is using to bathe the wound. Miraculously, the arrowhead now slips out–following Iapyx' hand, without human help (*nullo cogente*): the pain abates; the bleeding stops; Aeneas regains his strength.

> hoc Venus obscuro faciem circumdata nimbo
> detulit, hoc fusum labris splendentibus amnem
> inficit occulte medicans, spargitque salubris
> ambrosiae sucos et odoriferam panaceam.
> fovit ea vulnus lympha longaevus Iapyx
> ignorans, subitoque omnis de corpore fugit

quippe dolor, omnis stetit imo vulnere sanguis.
iamque secuta manum nullo cogente sagitta
excidit, atque novae rediere in pristina vires.

This Venus brought, her face veiled in dark mist,
this, with its hidden curative powers, she steeped
in river water, poured into a glittering basin, and sprinkled
there healing ambrosial juice and fragrant panacea.
Aged Iapyx bathed the wound with this liquid,
unknowing of its effects, and indeed all pain fled
from Aeneas' body, all the flow of blood ceased deep
in the wound, following the motion of his hand,
and fresh strength returned to Aeneas, such as before.

Recognizing that this cure was the work of something great(er), a god,[4] and not of his own right hand, Iapyx exhorts the men to hasten to take up their arms in Aeneas' great cause:

'arma citi properate viro! quid statis?' Iapyx
conclamat primusque animos accendit in hostem.
'non haec humanis opibus, non arte magistra
proveniunt, neque te, Aenea, mea dextera servat:
maior agit deus atque opera ad maiora remittit.'

Iapyx cried: 'Quickly, bring our hero weapons. Why are you
standing there?' and was first to inflame their courage against
the enemy. 'Aeneas, this cure does not come by human means,
nor medical art, it is not my right hand that saved you: a god,[5]
a greater one, did this, and sends you out again to greater deeds'.

Iapyx now becomes commanding, showing a commitment to Aeneas' mission that was not (by implication) previously felt or so expressed. Restored to health, Aeneas rearms and, addressing Iulus for the only time in the poem –and possibly for the last time in their fictional lives– instructs him to model himself after his father Aeneas and his uncle Hector. Thus concludes this episode, which starts with Aeneas' taking off his helmet and will end with his rearming and kissing Iulus farewell through his helmet, now again placed on his head. Similarly, where Iapyx' right hand (*dextera*) fails (428), Aeneas' right hand, which failed to persuade combatants to adhere to the treaty, will succeed in securing life and

4 For this translation see Servius and Tarrant *ad loc.*
5 The motto of French surgeon Ambroise Paré (1510–90) was: '*je le pensai, Dieu le guarist*' (I treated him, God cured him.)

future for Iulus (436). Helmets and right hands make a frame for this ecphrastic episode.

Let us turn now to the curious back story of Iapyx. The *Aeneid* narrator recounts that the young Iapyx had been at one time the favorite of Apollo. Joyfully enamored of Iapyx, the god tried to give (*dabat* is conative)[6] to Iapyx his gifts of archery, music, and prophecy.[7] Iapyx, however, preferred (*maluit*) the gift of medicine (the powers of herbs and empirical treatments), apparently indifferent to the consequent lack of glory (*inglorius*, 397), in order to postpone the death of his father (*depositi proferret fata parentis*), who was already 'laid out' (*depositi*) before the door, i.e., despaired of, because his death was perceived as imminent.

> iamque aderat Phoebo ante alios dilectus Iapyx
> Iasides, acri quondam cui captus amore
> ipse suas artis, sua munera, laetus Apollo
> augurium citharamque dabat celerisque sagittas.
> ille, ut depositi proferret fata parentis,
> scire potestates herbarum usumque medendi
> maluit et mutas agitare inglorius artis.

> Now Iapyx, Iasus's son, was present, dearest of all to Apollo,
> to whom the god himself, struck by deep love, once
> tried to give with delight his own arts, his own gifts,
> his powers of prophecy, his lyre, and swift arrows.
> But Iapyx, in order to delay the fate of his dying father,
> preferred knowledge of the virtues of herbs, and the use
> of medicine, and, without fame, to practice the silent arts.

The term *depositi* (395) indicates that the father is grievously ill, deemed incurable. Servius (*ad loc.)* explains that the ancients, once a person's life was despaired of, would place the body outside the door, either so that the dying person could give his last breath to the earth, or so that he might be helped by a passer-by experienced with similar cases.

Some provocative *gaps* in this account are: does Apollo in fact give Iapyx the UNoffered gift of medicine? Many readers assume so, but this is not stated. We do

6 *Dabat* is conative (Servius *ad* 394): *vera lectio est* 'dabat'*: nam non dedit.*

7 The original three gifts in Callim. *hymn. Ap.* are archery, song, and prophecy. Medicine comes fourth: 'None is so abundant in skill as Apollo. To him belongs the archer, to him the minstrel; for unto Apollo is given in keeping alike archery and song. His are the lots of the diviner and his, the seers; and from Phoebus do doctors know the deferring of death.' (42–46) (trans. G.R. Mair). Interestingly, Servius *ad* 394 says that the lyre and archery are *artes*, skills; but prophecy is not only an *ars*, but a divine gift.

know that Iapyx' treatment of Aeneas' wound fails (405). This might suggest that Iapyx is an ordinary healer, with no divine gift. Does Iapyx succeed in extending his father's life? or not? We do not know. Given that Iapyx himself is now an old (*longaevus*) man, his father presumably would have died, in either case, decades before the narrative present. Are we to read any brief extension of the ill old man's life as an endorsed act of *pietas*? Or are we, in retrospect at least, to question Iapyx' preference for more time in life for his old and ill father as an unnatural and short-term goal? Too small a gain to compensate for loss of glory (*inglorius*) or of possibilities through other arts that are not mute (*mutas artis*)?[8] Given the implicit reservations of the narrator, this is a difficult question to answer.[9]

The next we hear of Iapyx' story, he is a healer in Aeneas' army during the Trojans' struggle against the Latins. He is present amongst others who meet the wounded Aeneas on his return to camp. Though Aeneas asks for a definitive, brutal surgery with a *broadsword* to cut out the arrowhead and implicitly rejects something more delicate, Iapyx proceeds tentatively, unassertively (*trepidat.. ...sollicitat prensat*, this last conative, per Servius) to try to extract the arrowhead with *forceps* (the better procedure medically, surely, but likely a violation of epic decorum).[10] However, his efforts fail, and although Iapyx is dressed in healer garb

8 Servius *ad* 396 reviews possible meanings of 'mute'. Traina *ad loc.* suggests it simply refers to the preceding arts that do not give renown. Traina adds that Stok's argument that it refers to doctors' vain mutterings during the plague (in allusion to Lucr. *DRN* 6.1179: *mussabat tacito medicina timore*) is *poco probabile*.

9 Vergil makes the relationship between love, the good, and *pietas* a vexed one in the *Aeneid*. W.R. Johnson (1965, 362) points to examples where *pietas* is shown to be objectively unethical or inhumane. Conte (2007, 163–4) discusses *pietas* as it illustrates Vergil's strategy of 'divided truth': Aeneas tells Lausus that his *pietas* is tricking him: *fallit te incautum pietas tua* (*Aen.* 10.812). Lausus loves a bad father, therefore is his *pietas* ill-directed? or is it unadvisable for him to act with *pietas* if he might be killed? '*quo moriture ruis maioraque viribus audes*?' (*Aen.* 10.811).

10 I believe that this discrepancy has not been noted previously. I suggest that it is a function of (medical) epic decorum, which derives from the medical treatment scenes –the first in western literature– that appear in the *Iliad* (4.210–19, 11.841–6, 16.513–31). These scenes show Machaon pulling the arrow out of Menelaus' wound, sucking out the blood, applying healing medicines; Patroclus cutting out the arrow from Eurypylus, washing away the blood, applying bitter root; Glaucus, suffering pain and bleeding in both arms, praying to Apollo, who stops the pain and bleeding. As Noonan (1997) explains, epic decorum eschews professional doctors with advanced instruments that would suggest medical sophistication beyond what (poets thought) epic heroes could have known in ancient times. Aeneas proposes a most primitive technique (cutting with a broadsword) for removing the arrowhead from his thigh. (Servius *ad* 389: *lato ita dictum accipiunt, ut, quasi ipso iubente, ne scapello aut aliquo ferramento minore, sed ense, et hoc lato.*) Iapyx pursues a more sophisticated (if less manly) technique with a fine surgical instrument (forceps or tweezers), for which the Romans became renowned. Further, healers in epic must be warriors

(*Paeonium in morem*) and is using Apollo's powerful herbs, Apollo does not come to help.

> ille retorto
> Paeonium in morem senior succinctus amictu
> multa manu medica Phoebique potentibus herbis
> nequiquam trepidat, nequiquam spicula dextra
> sollicitat prensatque tenaci forcipe ferrum.
> nulla viam Fortuna regit, nihil auctor Apollo
> subvenit.
>
> The aged Iapyx, his robe rolled back
> in Paeonian fashion, worked in vain with healing fingers
> and Apollo's powerful herbs: in vain he worked at the arrow
> with his right hand, and tugged at the metal with tightened pincers.
> No luck guided his course, nor did Apollo his patron
> come to aid.

Why does Apollo not come to help Iapyx treat Aeneas? Did Iapyx' preference for an UNoffered gift put him at odds with the god? Is Apollo angry with Iapyx for rejecting his (i.e., a god's) gift? or for wanting his father to live beyond nature/fate? Or has Apollo perhaps had a change of heart about *Aeneas*? This is a stubborn question. Why is it Venus who comes instead? She is not known as a healing goddess. And why does she first acquire dittany, in this context a medication, since gods do not need drugs to cure (if they care to) those in need (Noonan 1997)? An example of this last is Apollo's curing of Glaucus in the *Iliad* (*Il.* 16.513–29). Glaucus, weakened and bleeding in both arms, calls on Apollo and is cured of pain. He assumes that it is indeed Apollo who has answered his prayer, although the god does not show himself. Two other healing scenes in the *Iliad* show warrior healers succeeding in managing wounds, using natural poultices learned from teachers who learned from gods. Machaon *Il.* 4.210–19 applies gentle drugs learned from Cheiron to treat Menelaus' wound; Patroclus *Il.* 11.842–8 treats Eurypylus with a drug learned from Achilles. In Homeric epic, gods are the originary source of cures, even if at some distance in time or place, and healers are warriors first.

Iapyx' story invites completion by readers and also judgment. For many of the questions provoked by the gaps in this episode, scholars have suggested

---

first, not professional doctors, with healing knowledge based on experience (empiricism), not *ratio* (theory). Note that trained doctors, who were not also warriors, did not accompany Roman armies until after 125CE. Therefore, in this as in other ways, Iapyx is an un-epic figure. See also Byrne (1910), Schlager and Lauer (2001, *passim*), Gabriel (2012).

answers: Harrison (1981) had suggested that Venus comes to the rescue because Vergil is giving her a chance to, as it were, amend the record. In *Iliad* 5.311–74 she had failed in her attempt to rescue Aeneas from Diomedes when, wounded herself, she dropped him! (Aeneas gives his perspective on this event in *Aeneid* 1.92–101.) Apollo then comes to the rescue, while Aphrodite runs crying to her mother Dione in Olympus. Casali (2009, 318 n.43) suggests that Apollo fails to come because he has by now become alienated by Aeneas' savagery that aligns him with Achilles, Apollo's enemy at Troy. As to Venus' bringing drugs, Hawkins 2004 argues that, first, Venus does have a relevant association with healing, even if it is insufficiently recognized, and, further, that Vergil wishes to support Augustus' agenda of elevating Roman (vs. Greek) medicine by showing Roman Venus' effective methods. As to the very presence of Venus as healer, Skinner (2007) argues that Venus, as goddess of passion, is more suited to the passions of the battlefield than is Apollo, whose comparatively chaste, controlled, and pedagogic relationship with Iapyx unfits him for the impassioned battlefield. Venus, therefore, takes Apollo's place. Miller (2009), in his comprehensive review of the questions and the scholarship, especially as they relate to possible causes for Apollo's absence from the scene, comes to no conclusion that he finds satisfying. Tarrant (2012) understands Iapyx' presence in the poem as a means to exemplify *pietas*, thereby aligning him with Aeneas as an exemplar of *pietas*.[11]

Nicoll (2001, 193–4) is a provocative outlier in proposing that there is something problematic in Iapyx' actions. He suggests that Iapyx lacks high aspirations, has an unheroic character, and therefore chooses to pursue, *inglorius*, the silent or mute arts (*Aen.* 12.397). 'Virgil's disapproval is plain' he says (193). Skinner (2007, 91), contesting Nicoll directly, says 'the young man's motive for becoming a physician should be viewed as commendable, and the adjective *inglorius* must rather acknowledge his willing sacrifice of fame in the interests of *pietas*.' Further on she adds: '... Apollo deals honorably with his beloved...he shows self-restraint and employs persuasion rather than force, offering the youth an array of desirable gifts and finally bestowing on him an art that enables him to succor his father...' (91). Skinner fills the major gaps in the story in the most

11 Quoting Tarrant *ad* 391–7: 'His (Iapyx') principal functions in the scene are to provide a model of filial devotion which parallels that of Aeneas and Iulus and to certify the necessity of divine intervention in curing Aeneas'. Again *ad* 391–7: when Iapyx puts his father's survival above all else, 'the element of *pietas* is thereby strongly highlighted'; *ad* 425–9 Tarrant mentions Iapyx' 'role as a surrogate for A.' Tarrant also contests Nicoll, saying 'it is not clear, though, why a physician should be required to be a heroic character'. Tarrant's objection seems to reverse Nicoll's proposed idea of cause (Iapyx is unheroic in aspiration) and effect (he therefore becomes a healer).

positive way. However, even if she assumes correctly that Iapyx does get Apollo's gift of medicine, Iapyx' failure to help Aeneas remains an implicitly unexpected outcome. Nicoll has raised legitimate questions not easily answered about Iapyx' choices, as Iapyx' preference for the (unoffered) gift of medicine, his indifference to glory, and his failure to cure Aeneas' wound are all anomalies that require interrogation, not normalization. Skinner argues, as above, that 'willing sacrifice of fame in the interests of *pietas*' is commendable.' But, is it reasonable, even for one to whom being 'inglorious' is thoroughly acceptable, to decline incalculable opportunities for the future (at least for oneself if not for others) in order to postpone the death of an elderly father, already at the point of death? Is this an appropriate valuing of the father's life? Or an excessive valuing of the father's life? Or can such devotion to one's father ever be considered excessive? Possibly consequential for interpretation are hints that Iapyx is retiring and unassertive by nature. In Aeneas' camp he is simply present (*aderat*, 391), not in authority. He is not a warrior-healer, like Patroclus (*Il.*11.842–8) or Machaon (*Il.*4.210–19). Dressed in medical garb, he appears to have made a profession of healing and is now healer on staff, as it were, to Aeneas. His attempt at extractive surgery is described with weak verbs (*trepidat, sollicitat, parat* [conative]); he pursues an ineffective procedure without changing course. He is modest and honest in admitting that a god, not his own hand, effected the cure. The coming of a god (note that *Iapyx* does not say it was *Apollo,* though Servius thinks he thinks so) persuades him of Aeneas' cause; he then becomes an ardent supporter, exhorting others to take up arms. At this point, of course, he himself would be too old (*longaevus*) to take up arms.

To summarize: Iapyx was once Apollo's favorite before others, but not now. He preferred a gift not offered. He fails to treat Aeneas' wound successfully. Although it might have been thought by someone that Apollo would come to help, he does not. No reason for this absence is stated or implied. This provocative and perplexing picture is a challenge to interpretation. Readers can legitimately wonder if Iapyx is to be read as authorially endorsed in his preference to prolong his dying father's life and THEREFORE as an exemplar of a *pietas* that aligns him with Aeneas, as Tarrant, for example, explicitly proposes. *Pietas*, according to Cicero, requires the performance of what one owes to the gods, the *patria*, and those related by blood.[12] Does Iapyx' lack of other, further concerns– beyond his father–

12 Cicero's definitions of *pietas* encompass what one owes to gods, fatherland, parents, and blood relatives. From Brill's New Pauly, s.v. *pietas. De inventione* 2.22.66 *pietatem, quae erga patriam aut parentes aut alios sanguine coniunctos officium conservare moneat*; Latin 'dutiful behaviour' towards the gods (Cic. *Nat. D.* 1,116 *est enim pietas iustitia adversum deos*; Ter. *An.* 869;

for, e.g., gods or *patria*, suggest not so much dutiful *pietas* as, more simply, love, on a personal level, for his father and grief at his impending loss? Perhaps, because of love for his father Iasius (Iapyx is *Iasides*, 392), Iapyx always and only wanted to be a healer.[13] Does love for one's father, in and of itself, qualify as *pietas*? Such questions about what *pietas* is are provoked by this passage.

If a disconsolate reader wishes to search for some firmer, more specific grounds for interpretation of the Iapyx thread of the episode, s/he might look within the poem for an intratext, i.e., a passage that overlaps this 'target' passage in some thematic or other aspect.[14] Redfield speaks of a function of an intratext (as one might call it now) in commenting on how one scene or passage, because it shares themes or context with another passage, can illuminate the meaning of the target passage. He points to a scene from *Iliad* 20 wherein an overly audacious Hector is warned by Apollo to retreat into the crowd to avoid Achilles, who is simply better. As Redfield (1975, 155) explains: 'Hector, who might at this moment (20.371–80) have died bravely and thoughtlessly, is saved by the god for another death [i.e., in *Iliad* 22], less brave and more thoughtful. The whole incident is one of those nonevents which in poetry often serve to clarify later events. (It is the special privilege of the tragic hero that he meets his own death in the fullness of reflective self-knowledge.)' The space of *difference* between the two scenes clarifies the meaning of each one. Easily enough we find an intratext for Iapyx' story precisely in the previously noted Aeneas thread with which the Iapyx thread is intertwined. This thread also encompasses themes of *pietas*, father/ son relationship, and a gift from a god or a call to mission from a god. Thus the Iapyx and Aeneas threads are as tightly intertwined thematically as they are visually in terms of lines on the page. On my reading, intratextual study suggests that Iapyx and Aeneas are most significantly related, not by parallelism or similarity, but by contrast. While both Aeneas and Iapyx have fathers and are sons, their

---

one's mother country (Cic. *Rep*. 6,16; Liv. 39,9,10); and later the emperor. *Pietas* was translated into Greek as *eusébeia* [2]. *Pietas* is frequently linked to other virtues: e.g. *clementia* ('mercy'), *concordia* ('harmony'), *constantia* ('constancy'), *fides* ('fidelity'), *virtus* ('courage'). Maharam, s.v. *Pietas*. See also Fratantuono (2014, vol.3, 1007–8) where all citations of Aeneas as *pius* are cited.

13 For the likelihood we are concerned with a medical family, see O'Hara (1996, 234–5): both name and patronymic of *Iapyx Iasides* suggest the Greek word for healing *iaomai* to cure.

14 On the interpretive value of intratextual reading, see Brooks (1953, 261): 'It is not only possible but necessary to view the Golden Bough as part of the *Aeneid*'s structure, to evolve its meaning primarily from its context and from what Vergil says about it, not from what we know and from what he may have known about its origins'. See also n.21, below. See also Sharrock (2000, 6) on intratextuality and reading of relationships between parts.

relationship to *pietas* –i.e., to gods and *patria,* in addition to blood relatives– is not parallel, but largely inverse.

Aeneas, of course, is famous for his dedication to Anchises, carrying him out of burning Troy on his shoulders. There are multiple variants of the Aeneas legend,[15] and all feature Aeneas' exceptional devotion to his father. Further, images in both material and literary art characteristically show Aeneas not only with his father, but also with others, as in the *Aeneid* itself, which describes Aeneas escaping from Troy leading his son by the hand, while his father carries the Penates. His wife Creusa is to follow *longe* behind.[16] The *Tabula Iliaca* also shows a wife following behind Aeneas, his father with the Penates on his shoulders, and his son at his side.[17] These images, encompassing two or three generations, represent the enactment of *pietas* as implicated in the survival of the family. Further, the reverence for the Penates implies engagement in larger religious practices and social/political entities. While dedication to the Italian/Roman future *patria* is a later accretion to the Aeneas legend, as definitively shaped for the ages by Vergil, there is implicit in the ideology of *pietas* a commitment to a communal future. In the *Aeneid* Aeneas' mission comes to him from outside, through visions or divine epiphanies of various kinds: the dream of Hector tells Aeneas that Troy is lost and that he must lead the surviving Trojans to a new *homeland* (2.289–95). Later Venus appears, rebukes him for forgetting his *family* (2.594–620), and leads him home, where divine signs (flame around Iulus' head, shooting star), solicited from *Jupiter* by Anchises (2.689–91), convince Anchises that their escape is divinely authorized. Homeland (*patria*), blood relatives, and the gods are embraced in the mission that Aeneas gradually accepts in full. He does not choose the mission, but nor does he 'prefer' another.

As we join Aeneas' story in *Aeneid* 12, we find Aeneas in an extravagantly fine moment, bare-headed, his right hand extended, insisting on the treaty and the right to fight Turnus and thereby end the war.[18] After his wounding by the anonymous arrow-shot, Aeneas' every gesture shows his heroic *pietas*: he is indomitable, stoic, enduring of pain, dedicated to the Trojan/Roman mission, voicing no

---

15 See O'Hara (2014, vol.1, 16–19).

16 See Perkell (1981, 201–223): Aeneas' actions in departing from Troy (*Aen.*2.699–804) are in harmony with Cicero's definition of *pietas* (above, n.12), in that he makes good flight plans for the *penates* and blood relatives (father and son), which together signify the future of Rome, but not for his wife Creusa (not related by blood), whom he instructs to follow at a distance and never thinks of or looks back for (2.741) until he reaches the designated meeting place outside of the city.

17 See Petrain (2014, 1241): in the early first century CE *Tabulae Iliacae* Aeneas appears three times: receiving the *penates*, fleeing with his family, and setting sail for Hesperia (i.e., the new *patria*).

18 *Aen.* 12.311–7.

weakness or fear. Everything about his behavior shows him to be a *vir fortis* who behaves with *dignitas* (Servius *ad* 12.387). This heroic portrait includes his struggling to pull the arrowhead out of his thigh himself, as he calls for the quickest treatment to return to battle. What he suggests as a procedure (cutting out the arrow with a broadsword) shows his disregard for his own comfort (*ense secent lato vulnus telique latebram, / rescindant penitus, seseque in bella remittant,* 12.389–90). In the event, Iapyx tries extraction, not cutting, and with forceps, not a broadsword.[19]

Aeneas' fortitude is further shown by his remaining *standing*, leaning on his spear, throughout the treatment of the wound (Servius *ad loc.*). Alone in the crowd he stands unmoved by others' tears (Iulus' specifically).

> stabat acerba fremens ingentem nixus in hastam
> Aeneas magno iuvenum et maerentis Iuli
> concursu, lacrimis immobilis. (398–400)

> Aeneas stood leaning on his great spear, raging bitterly,
> amongst a vast assembling of youths and Iulus sorrowing,
> himself unmoved by tears.

The term *concursu* implies the young warriors, in their concern, ran to see their wounded heroic commander. With this almost inhuman lack of expectable affect, Aeneas exemplifies for onlookers the *pietas* of the Roman hero/general in war.

Iliad 4.148ff. is a commonly cited (from Servius to Williams, Traina, and Tarrant) Iliadic intertext (4.148ff.) for this scene of Aeneas' wounding: Menelaos, too, is struck by an arrow from an unknown (to him) assailant that interrupts the formalizing of an agreement, in this case between Priam and Agamemnon, to a duel between Menelaos and Paris to settle the war. Here, significantly, according to Homeric scholiasts,[20] we find Menelaus and Agamemnon acting badly, as they are represented as frightened by the blood, fearing death, and relieved the wound is not fatal. Agamemnon is openly distraught by the possibility of losing Menelaus, who, though he is the wounded one, tries to encourage (literally) his brother.

---

19 See n.10 above on healers in epic. Aeneas' heroic epic request for the broad sword correlates with his heroic *pietas*; Iapyx' use of forceps, alien to epic decorum, hints at his ethical difference from Aeneas.

20 On Menelaus and Agamemnon as 'insufficiently heroic' in *Il.*4.184–7, see Tarrant *ad* 387–90; he cites further Schlunk (1974, 90–91) and Schmit-Neuerberg (1999, 155–61).

ῥίγησεν δ' ἄρ' ἔπειτα ἄναξ ἀνδρῶν Ἀγαμέμνων
ὡς εἶδεν μέλαν αἷμα καταρρέον ἐξ ὠτειλῆς:
ῥίγησεν δὲ καὶ αὐτὸς ἀρηΐφιλος Μενέλαος.
ὡς δὲ ἴδεν νεῦρόν τε καὶ ὄγκους ἐκτὸς ἐόντας
ἄψορρόν οἱ θυμὸς ἐνὶ στήθεσσιν ἀγέρθη.
τοῖς δὲ βαρὺ στενάχων μετέφη κρείων Ἀγαμέμνων
χειρὸς ἔχων Μενέλαον, ἐπεστενάχοντο δ' ἑταῖροι:
φίλε κασίγνητε θάνατόν νύ τοι ὅρκι' ἔταμνον
οἶον προστήσας πρὸ Ἀχαιῶν Τρωσὶ μάχεσθαι,
ὥς σ' ἔβαλον Τρῶες, κατὰ δ' ὅρκια πιστὰ πάτησαν.

ἀλλά μοι αἰνὸν ἄχος σέθεν ἔσσεται ὦ Μενέλαε
αἴ κε θάνῃς καὶ πότμον ἀναπλήσῃς βιότοιο.

τὸν δ' ἐπιθαρσύνων προσέφη ξανθὸς Μενέλαος:
θάρσει, μηδέ τί πω δειδίσσεο λαὸν Ἀχαιῶν:
οὐκ ἐν καιρίῳ ὀξὺ πάγη βέλος, ἀλλὰ πάροιθεν
εἰρύσατο ζωστήρ τε παναίολος ἠδ' ὑπένερθε
ζῶμά τε καὶ μίτρη, τὴν χαλκῆες κάμον ἄνδρες.

Then Agamemnon, lord of men, shuddered, seeing the dark blood flow from the wound, and Menelaus, beloved of Ares, blanched likewise, but finding the arrow-head and its binding had failed to penetrate, his heart grew calm. Nevertheless the king grasped his hand, and groaning heavily among his groaning companions, said: 'Was it your death, then, I caused by swearing this truce, sending you out alone to fight the Trojans, who in wounding you have trampled their solemn oaths underfoot? (148–57)

But Menelaus if you died, if that was your present fate: what dreadful sorrow would be mine? (169–70)

But red-haired Menelaus comforted him: 'Be calm, and say nothing to worry the men. The bright arrow missed my vital parts, stopped by the metal belt, my corselet and the apron fashioned by coppersmiths.' (183–7)

From the Roman perspective, this behavior would be unheroic, weak, undignified; but it is not so in the Homeric perspective. Homer loves Menelaus and addresses him directly (e.g., 4.127, 146). Menelaus and Agamemnon love each other and express their emotions unguardedly. Aeneas' control of personal feelings, therefore, and his focused purpose and fearlessness are rendered emphatic by their contrast with the emotional openness of the sons of Atreus.[21] Roman readers, we assume, were educated to see expression of such tender emotion as

21 Clausen (1966, 67) '....but he [a reader coming upon such a model and hypertext] would also be aware of a difference, and this is the meaning of the allusion.'

weakness; but other readers, at other times, saw and might continue to see therein humanity, love, and care, and think these to be goods. Important to see here, then, are the contrasting behaviors, both of which have virtues and costs.

With the medical issue resolved, Aeneas, immediately rearmed, speaks a farewell injunction to Ascanius (as already noted above, the only words to his son in the poem), describing in words what he had just shown in actions, i.e., what *pietas* is. Aeneas sets out responsibilities for his son, whom he embraces with armored arms, kisses through his helmet, and addresses only as *puer*.[22] The boy (here a function) is to learn courage, manliness, hard work, and hardship from his father Aeneas. The implicit expectation is that the boy will be a public actor, with responsibilities for others. Good luck (therefore happiness (?)) he is to learn from others.[23] Aeneas' right hand (*dextera* 12.436), Aeneas says, will protect Iulus in war and endow him with victory's rewards. When grown the boy is to see to it that he is mindful of, seeks, and is inspired by the *exempla* of his male ancestors. Aeneas refers even to himself in third person by his role as father and equally to Hector as uncle.

postquam habilis lateri clipeus loricaque tergo est,
Ascanium fusis circum complectitur armis
summaque per galeam delibans oscula fatur:
'disce, puer, virtutem ex me verumque laborem,
fortunam ex aliis. nunc te mea dextera bello
defensum dabit et magna inter praemia ducet.
tu facito, mox cum matura adoleverit aetas,
sis memor et te animo repetentem exempla tuorum
et pater Aeneas et avunculus excitet Hector.'

Once the shield was fixed at his side, the chain mail
to his back, he clasped Ascanius in armed embrace,[24]
and kissing his lips lightly through the helmet, said:
'My son, learn courage from me and true labor,
good fortune from others. Now my (right) hand will protect you
in battle, and lead you to great rewards. Be mindful,
and when your years have reached maturity,
when you seek models among your people,
let your father Aeneas and your uncle Hector
inspire your soul.'

---

22 So Anchises famously calls his son *Romane* at *Aen.* 6.851, with the similar injunction *memento.*

23 Cf. Servius *ad* 436 on what verb, we are to infer, governs *fortuna.*

24 O'Hara (1996, 236–7 *ad Aen.* 12.433–4 ambiguity of *armis* (arms or shoulders) and *fusis* (abl. absolute or instrumental).

In this emotionally distant, impersonal way, Aeneas instructs Ascanius on the Roman ethic of tradition, *mos maiorum*, courage, and dedication to the *patria*—with no expectation of good fortune or, by extension, happiness. *Exempla* is the key word: Iulus is to model himself after his (heroic) father and uncle. Aeneas makes no allowance for Ascanius' fear and tears at the sight of his father wounded (398) or for approval of any different values going forward.

The Iliadic intertext for this (possibly) farewell speech is the famous scene at the end of *Iliad* 6.391–529.[25] Andromache with the baby Astyanax and Hector meet at the Scaean gate. In parting Hector moves to embrace the baby who, terrified by the nodding feathers of his father's *helmet*, cries. Hector *korythaiolos* 'of the shining helm' removes his helmet to solace his son and dandle him in his arms.

> αὐτίκ' ἀπὸ κρατὸς κόρυθ' εἵλετο φαίδιμος Ἕκτωρ, 472
> καὶ τὴν μὲν κατέθηκεν ἐπὶ χθονὶ παμφανόωσαν·
> αὐτὰρ ὅ γ' ὃν φίλον υἱὸν ἐπεὶ κύσε πῆλέ τε χερσὶν
> εἶπε δ' ἐπευξάμενος Διί τ' ἄλλοισίν τε θεοῖσι·
>
> And at once glorious Hektor lifted from his head the helmet
> and laid it in all its shining upon the ground. Then taking
> up his dear son tossed him about in his arms, and kissed him,
> and lifted his voice in prayer to Zeus and the other immortals:

Hector *removes* his helmet, symbol of his very identity as a warrior, to embrace his son, to express love, closeness, solace. No armor comes between him and the baby. Aeneas, by contrast, kisses Iulus *through* his helmet, as he offers emotionally distant instruction. Here, as with the prior Iliadic intertext, Vergil is contrasting the unreserved emotional expression of the Greeks and Trojans with the Romans' revered emotional control and prioritizing of mission. A further meaningful contrast appears in Hector's generous wish for his son to be *better* than he is (at fighting). Hector wishes preeminence and rule like his own for his son (*Il.* 6.477), but *not* as a limiting model. He prays:

25 Tarrant *ad* 435–40 sees a dual allusion, to both Homer's Hector and Sophocles' *Ajax*: 'o child, may you be luckier than your father but like in other things and may you not be *kakos*'. There is also a line from Accius' *Armorum iudicium* 156R^2: *virtuti sis par, dispar fortunis patris* cited by Macrobius (*Sat.* 6.1.58). Page and Conington also see an allusion to Ajax. One could not say this is *wrong*, but given the subject of this episode, the predominance of allusions in this book to the *Iliad*, and the spectacular specificity of the HELMET *on* and so touchingly *taken off*, this is an allusion above all to the most touching scene in the *Iliad*, wherein Hector puts off the helmet and the war and plays with his son.

Ζεῦ ἄλλοι τε θεοὶ δότε δὴ καὶ τόνδε γενέσθαι
παῖδ' ἐμὸν ὡς καὶ ἐγώ περ ἀριπρεπέα Τρώεσσιν,
ὧδε βίην τ' ἀγαθόν, καὶ Ἰλίου ἶφι ἀνάσσειν·
καί ποτέ τις εἴποι πατρός γ' ὅδε πολλὸν ἀμείνων
ἐκ πολέμου ἀνιόντα.

'Zeus and you other immortals, grant that this boy, who is my son,
may be as I am, pre-eminent among the Trojans, great in strength as I am,
and rule strongly over Ilion; and someday let them say of him: 'He is
better by far than his father,' as he comes in from the fighting.'

Aeneas' instruction to Ascanius is prescriptive: the boy is to look to his past, to seek and follow– implicitly not to exceed or transcend–his father's and uncle's *exempla*. This reverence for established tradition and past models is a defining feature of Roman culture.[26] In sum, based on the differences between the *Aeneid* passages and their Iliadic models, we see that Vergil is contrasting and elevating Aeneas' Roman fortitude and *dignitas* over the Iliadic characters who express unheroic love and fear without reserve. Whether or not readers endorse the Roman way and see love as distraction and weakness, they are asked to judge afresh the character, costs, and benefits of *pietas* vs. love, affection, or closeness, independent of duty or heroic or cultural aspiration.

To resume, it has been suggested by some that Aeneas and Iapyx are parallel in relation to *pietas*. This paper has argued, alternatively, that Iapyx and Aeneas are essentially opposites in their relationship to this paradigmatic Roman value. Iapyx is consistently portrayed as an un- or post-epic figure whose love for his father is personal and separate from other values associated with *pietas*. Menelaus, Agamemnon, and Hector are recalled intertextually in similarly unheroic, touching moments of deep sentiment; by contrast Vergil has made Aeneas unmoved by distraction, pain, or fear, focused unwaveringly on the mission for the *patria* to be. Therefore, with respect to interpretation of Iapyx, I suggest that this character differs from Aeneas as do the emotional Greeks Agamemnon and Menelaus and Trojan Hector. Iapyx himself may come from Crete (cf. Servius on *Aen.* 3.332).[27] Iapyx' dedication to his father appears to come from love and not from felt *duty* to the larger heroic *pietas*. His preference for the unoffered gift of

---

26 e.g., Livy *AUC* proem [10] 'There is this exceptionally beneficial and fruitful advantage to be derived from the study of the past, that you see, set in the clear light of historical truth, examples of every possible type. From these you may select for yourself and your country what to imitate, and also what, as being mischievous in its inception and disastrous in its issues, you are to avoid.' *Livy. History of Rome*, trans. Rev. Canon Roberts New York, 1912.

27 I owe this reference to Prof. Stephen Harrison.

medicine to defer the death of his dying father appears narrow and regressive when set against Aeneas' *pietas* that encompasses gods, *patria*, family, and a purpose for the *future*. This contrast magnifies Aeneas as a public actor, but also hints at his emotional isolation, the constraints of duty, and the absence of private happiness. Thus, an intratextual reading of the Iapyx story thread against the Aeneas story thread, as illuminated by the latter's Iliadic intertexts, sharpens questions about what *pietas* is and requires by problematizing the 'preference' and surprising failure of Iapyx.

Bibliography

Brooks, R. (1953), '*Discolor Aura*. Reflections on the Golden Bough', *AJP* 74, 260–80.

Byrne, E.H. (1910), 'Medicine in the Roman Army', *CJ* 5, 267–72.

Casali, S. (2009), 'The Theophany of Apollo in Virgil *Aeneid* 9: Augustanism and Self-Reflexivity', in: L. Athanassaki/R.P. Martin/J.F. Miller (eds.), *Apolline Politics and Poetics*, Athens, 299–327.

Clausen, W. (1964), 'An Interpretation of the *Aeneid*', *HSCP* 68, 139–47; repr. 1966. in: S. Commager (ed.) *Virgil: A Collection of Critical Essays*, Englewood Cliffs, 75–88.

Conington, J./Nettleship, H. (eds.) (1858–83), *Works of Virgil*, 3 vols., repr. 2008, Exeter, U.K.

Conte, G. (2007), 'The Strategy of Contradiction', in: *The Poetry of Pathos, Studies in Virgilian Epic*, Oxford, 150–69.

Fish, S.E. (1976), 'Interpreting the Variorum', *Critical Inquiry* 2, 465–85.

Fratantuono, L. (2014), '*Pietas*', in: Thomas/Ziolkowski, vol. 3, 1007–8.

Gabriel, R.A. (2012), *Man and Wound in the Ancient World: A History of Military Medicine from Sumer to the Fall of Constantinople*, Dulles, Virginia.

Harrison, E. (1981), 'Vergil and the Homeric Tradition', in: F. Cairns (ed.), *Papers of the Liverpool Latin Seminar*, vol.3. ARCA Classical and Medieval Texts, Papers, and Monographs 7, Liverpool, 209–25.

Hawkins, J. (2004), 'The Ritual of Therapy. Venus the Healer in Virgil's *Aeneid*', in: A. Barchiesi/J. Rüpke (eds.), *Rituals in Ink: A Conference on Literature and Literary Production in Ancient Rome*, Stanford, 77–97.

Johnson, W. (1965), 'Aeneas and the Ironies of *Pietas*', *CJ* 60, 360–64.

Maharam, W.-A. (2006), 'Pietas', in: *Brill's New Pauly*, Antiquity volumes edited by: H. Cancik/H. Schneider, English edition by: C.F. Salazar, Classical Tradition volumes edited by: M. Landfester, English Edition by: F.G. Gentry. Consulted online on 14 May 2018 http://dx.doi.org.proxy.library.emory.edu/10.1163/1574-9347_bnp_e925180.

Mair, A.W. (ed.) (1921), *Callimachus: Hymns and Epigrams, Lycophron and Aratus*, Loeb Classical Library No. 129, London.

Miller, J. (2009), *Apollo, Augustus, and the Poets*, Cambridge.

Nicoll, W. (2001), 'The Death of Turnus', *CQ* 51, 190–200.

Noonan, J. (1997), 'The Iapyx Episode of *Aeneid* 12 and Medical Tales in Myth and Mythography', *Phoenix* 51, 374–92.

O'Hara, J. (1996), *True Names: Vergil and the Alexandrian Tradition of Etymological Wordplay*, Ann Arbor MI.

O'Hara, J. (2014), 'Aeneas', in: Thomas/Ziolkowski, vol.1, 16–19.

Perkell, C. (1981), 'On Creusa, Dido, and the Quality of Victory in Virgil's *Aeneid*', *Women's Studies* 8, 201–223.
Petrain, D. (2014), '*Tabulae Iliacae*', in: Thomas/Ziolkowski, vol.3, 1241.
Rammelt, C. (2014), 'Flight from Troy in Art', in: Thomas/Ziolkowski, vol.2, 489–91.
Redfield, J. (1975), *Nature and Culture in the Iliad: The Tragedy of Hector*, Chicago.
Schlager, N./J. Lauer (eds.) (2001), 'The Military Medicine of Ancient Rome', in: *Science and Its Times*, vol.1, Gale World History in Context, http://link.galegroup.com/apps/doc/CV2643450064/WHIC?u=lith7757&xid=faf176fe
Schlunk, R.R. (1974), *The Homeric Scholia and the Aeneid. A Study of the Influence of Ancient Homeric Literary Criticism on Vergil*, Ann Arbor MI.
Schmit-Neuerburg, T. (1999), *Vergils Aeneis und die antike Homerexegese: Untersuchungen zum Einfluss ethischer und kritischer Homerrezeption auf Imitatio und Aemulatio Vergils*, Berlin.
Sharrock, A. (2000), 'Texts, Parts, and (W)holes in Theory', in: A. Sharrock/H. Morales (eds.), *Intratextuality: Greek and Roman Textual Relations*, Oxford, 1–42.
Skinner, M. (2007), 'Venus as Physician: *Aen*. 12.411–19', *Vergilius* 53, 86–99.
Stok, F. (1988), *Percorsi dell'esegesi virgiliana: due ricerche sull' Eneide*, Pisa.
Tarrant, R. (ed.) (2012), *Virgil* Aeneid *Book* 12, Cambridge.
Thilo, G. (ed.) (1881–7), *Servii Grammatici in Vergilii Aeneidos librum duodecimum Commentarius*, Leipzig.
Thomas, R./J. Ziolkowski (eds.) (2014), *The Virgil Encyclopedia*, 3 vols., Malden, MA.
Traina, A. (ed.) (1997, rev.2004), *Il libro XII dell' Eneide*, Turin.
Williams, R.D. (ed.) (1972), *The Aeneid of Virgil*, 2 vols., Basingstoke/London.

Philip Hardie

Augustan and Late Antique Intratextuality: Virgil's *Aeneid* and Prudentius' *Psychomachia*

1 Introduction

Virgil's *Aeneid* must be one of the most intricately and intensely intratextual texts in Latin literature, echoing and reflecting on itself from start to finish.[1] Beginnings, middles, and endings construct and deconstruct patterns of expectation. Overlapping structures of continuity and contrast are built up through the twelve books of the poem, books which both aspire to the status of self-contained unity as Aristotelian wholes, and interact either contiguously or at a distance with other books, in a manner which readers have reached for analogies both architectural and musical to describe. Intratextuality, as a textual phenomenon, maps on to the construction of relationships between different levels of reality, between microcosm and macrocosm, between the divine and the human, between psychology and politics. Relationships are also established diachronically between different periods of history, between the legendary present of the main narrative and the deeper mythological past, and between both of these chronological layers and more recent Roman history.

Prudentius' *Psychomachia* is a one-book epic narrative in 915 hexameters following an iambic *Praefatio*. It tells of the battle in the soul between personified Virtues and Vices, followed by the building of the Temple of Wisdom. It is a profoundly Virgilian text. Its Virgilianism is flagged in the first hexameter, one of the poem's closest adaptations of a Virgilian line. *Christe, graues hominum semper miserate labores* ('Christ, who have always pitied the heavy toils of men') rewrites the first line of Aeneas' prayer to Apollo in his interview with the Sibyl at Cumae, *Aeneid* 6.56, *Phoebe, grauis Troiae semper miserate labores* ('Apollo, who have always pitied the heavy toils of Troy'). The *Kontrastimitation* is clear: Christ, the Sun of Righteousness (Malachi 4:2),[2] replaces the pagan sun-god Apollo, and the prayer is on behalf not of Troy and Troy's Roman descendants, but of all men: the *Psychomachia* is an epic about the soul of Everyman. But beyond this, the placing of the line at the start, rather than in the middle, of an epic triggers Virgilian

1 See e.g. Oliensis 2004.
2 For extended solar imagery of Christ see above all Prud. *Cathem.* 5.

https://doi.org/10.1515/9783110611021-010

intratextualities: *labores* at the start of an epic will put us in mind of Virgil's programmatic use of *labores* at the start of the *Aeneid*, 1.10 *tot adire labores*. Aeneas' reminder of this to Apollo in book 6 is but one of the many recurrences of the theme through the *Aeneid*. The initial placing of *miserate* reminds the reader of an appeal to pity at the beginning of another of Virgil's works, the poet's address to another man-god, Caesar Octavian, at the beginning of the *Georgics*, 1.41 *ignarosque uiae mecum miseratus agrestis* ('taking pity together with me on the countryfolk ignorant of the path'). Finally, within the *Aeneid* Aeneas' promise, in his prayer to Apollo and the Sibyl at the beginning of book 6, to build a temple to Apollo and Diana anticipates, intratextually, the description of the newly built Palatine Temple of Apollo at the end of book 8, the climax of the Shield of Aeneas. The Virgilian vow to build a temple is reflected intertextually in the building of the Temple of Wisdom[3] that forms the major closure of the *Psychomachia*, and which is the consequence of the successful defeat of the Vices in the human soul, instruction on which had been the burden of the opening prayer to Christ.

This reading of Prudentian intertextuality and intratextuality in the opening line of the poem already suggests that we are embarking on a text that will yield readily to reading strategies now standard for Virgil and other early imperial texts.

This is a kind of reading that is in line with some recent studies of Prudentian intertextuality,[4] and it is the kind of reading to which I myself find that the text of Prudentius responds. In this paper I want to test that impression further, with reference to two kinds of question. Firstly, is there something distinctly late antique about Prudentian intratextuality? Secondly, is there something distinctly Christian about it? To anticipate my conclusions, the answers will be no, and yes (up to a point).

Firstly, on the general question of late antique poetics. Successive attempts to define such a beast have emphasized the episodic and the fragmentary, whether to make a vice or a virtue out of what is presented as qualitatively different from an earlier, let us call it classical, drive towards unity and organic wholes.[5] There are certainly differences between the management of speech and narrative in the *Aeneid* and the *Psychomachia*. The action is interrupted by lengthy speeches, often homiletic or paraenetic in tone. In part this is because the range of actions open to specific personifications of Virtues and Vices is limited, but in part too it is a reflection of the strongly didactic quality of this epic

3 A Christian *Sapientia* to replace the pagan god of wisdom, Apollo, perhaps.
4 Lühken 2002; Heinz 2007.
5 Roberts 1989, index s.vv. 'Episodes', 'Fragmentation'.

narrative: Christ is called on as a teacher to give instruction on how to conduct the war within one's soul.[6]

In the matter of the management of narrative, whereas the outbreak and sequence of the war in Latium in the *Aeneid* is clearly motivated, each battle or duel logically following the other, the single combats in the *Psychomachia* have the appearance of a catalogue, as matched pairs of a Virtue and Vice step up to the plate in succession to do battle. 'A recurrent feature of late antique poetry is the enumeration, catalog, or list.'[7] So Michael Roberts in his influential book *The Jeweled Style*, who then goes on to say that 'it is Ovid in the *Metamorphoses* who can claim to have inaugurated the systematic use of enumeration as a technique of composition and amplification.' But if the *Metamorphoses* is a *Kataloggedicht*, it is one whose components are in a constant and intensive intratextual dialogue with each other of a kind that is not the least important mark of affinity between the hexameter narrative poems of Virgil and Ovid. A closer look at the seven single combats in the *Psychomachia* reveals intratextual structuring of several kinds that go beyond the superficial observations of a striving for variety, and of the progressive increase in length of each of the first six encounters. So, for example: 1. The recurrent use of two Virgilian models for the depiction of the forces of evil, the Fury Allecto,[8] and Hercules' killing of Cacus, provides continuity to the series of combats. 2. In a ring composition *Fides* dispatches the first and last in the series of Vices, *Veterum Cultura Deorum* and *Discordia* (in both cases stopping the passage of their throat, respectively to breath, 33–5, and voice, 716–18). This is also a historical progression, from the defeat of pagan superstition, the achievement of the heroic age of the martyrs, to the championing of orthodoxy against Heresy in the recent history of the Church.

In the rest of this paper I focus on two aspects of Virgilian and Prudentian intratextuality: 1. beginnings and endings, and 2. typology.

6 With 5–6 *dissere, rex noster, quo milite pellere culpas | mens armata queat nostri de pectoris antro*: cf. Lucr. 1.54–5 *nam tibi de summa caeli ratione deumque | disserere incipiam et rerum primordia pandam.*

7 Roberts 1989, 59.

8 Allecto is the model for combats 2, *Pudicitia* vs *Libido*, 3, *Ira* vs *Patientia*, and 7, *Concordia* vs *Discordia*. *Ira* and the *Eumenides* are companions of *Auaritia* in combat 6.

2 Beginnings and endings

The *Psychomachia* deploys Virgilian intertextuality to articulate its own pattern of repeated beginnings and endings, and its own interplay between closure and open-endedness. The *Aeneid* falls into two halves, each of which is motivated by an eruption of demonic energy from dark spaces below, the winds of Aeolus in book 1 and the Fury Allecto in book 7. Prudentius alludes to both opening sequences in the prayer to Christ that forms a second prologue (after the iambics) within the hexameter section of the *Psychomachia*, 7–11:

> exoritur quotiens turbatis sensibus intus
> seditio atque animam morborum rixa fatigat,
> quod tunc praesidium pro libertate tuenda
> quaeue acies Furiis inter praecordia mixtis
> obsistat meliore manu.

> Whenever our senses are disordered and rebellion arises within us and strife of diseased passions distresses the soul, what help is there then to guard her liberty, what army with superior force is there to oppose the Furies invading our heart?

seditio, referring to the civil war in the soul, is the word used for the civil unrest calmed by the statesman in the first simile in the *Aeneid*, applied to Neptune's calming of the storm, 1.148–9 *ac ueluti magno in populo cum saepe coorta est | seditio saeuitque animis ignobile uulgus* ('Just as when rebellion has often arisen in a great people, and the lowly mob rages in its spirits').[9] The personified *Furiis* points to the appearance of the Fury Allecto to motivate the second half of the *Aeneid*.[10]

The narrative of the *Psychomachia* is also structured as the recurrence of hellish violence to remotivate a plot that seems to have run its course, and whose completion is marked by ring composition. The defeat of what appears to be the last of the Vices to be confronted, *Auaritia*, is accompanied by a threefold ring composition that works on an intratextuality through intertextualities Virgilian and Lucretian:

Ring no. 1 (Virgilian): *Operatio*, Good Works, here specifically Almsgiving, finally intervenes to defeat *Auaritia*, the most dangerous Vice, described as 480–1 *uictrix | orbis*, and so end the series of combats, 574–6 *pugnamque capessit |*

---

9 With *coorta* cf. *Psychom.* 7 *exoritur*; with *animis Psychom.* 8 *animam*; with *praecordia* cf. *A.* 7.347 *inque sinum praecordia ad intima subdit.*

10 Note also *Aen.* 1.51 *furentibus Austris*, 150 *furor arma ministrat.*

militiae postrema gradu, sed sola duello | impositura manum, ne quid iam triste supersit ('she enters the battle, posted last in the order of fighting, but destined singly to put a finishing hand to the war, so that there is no more pain to come').[11] *Operatio* is *postrema* where *Fides* had been *prima* (21) to enter the field.[12] Having given away all her wealth, *Operatio* is 'enriched in faith', 582 *ditata f/Fidem*, and is thus working in collaboration with the Virtue, *Fides*, who had won in the first encounter against *Veterum Cultura Deorum*. Like *Fides*, *Operatio* crushes the life out of her opponent by strangling her, in a repetition of Hercules' throttling of Cacus in *Aeneid* 8.

Ring no. 2 (Lucretian): Hercules' defeat of Cacus in *Aeneid* 8 is a replay of the Lucretian Epicurus' defeat of the monster *Religio* or *Superstitio*, as Ingo Gildenhard has shown.[13] From a Christian point of view superstition goes by the name of *Veterum Cultura Deorum*. Prudentius knew his Lucretius well, and in the detail of *Fides* trampling underfoot her opponent in the first encounter, 32 *pede calcat*, I would see an allusion to the conclusion of Epicurus' contest with *Religio*, Lucr. 1.78–9 *quare religio pedibus subiecta uicissim / obteritur* ('Therefore *religio* in turn is placed under our feet and crushed'). After what seems the final victory, a Christian version of *Religio* is established in the heavens, 640–3:

agmina casta super uultum sensere Tonantis
adridere hilares pulso certamine turmae,
et Christum gaudere suis uictoribus arce
aetheris ac patrium famulis aperire profundum.[14]

The squadrons, gladdened by the ending of contention, see the face of the Thunderer smiling on their unstained forces from above, and Christ in the height rejoicing in the victory of his followers and opening for his servants his Father's home in the deep of heaven.

---

11 Cf. *Aen.* 7.572–3 *nec minus interea extremam Saturnia bello | imponit regina manum.*

12 Cf. *Operatio*'s call to cease operations and rest, 608 *requiescere*. The cessation of war is an allegory of the defeat of *Auaritia* and of her ever-restless desire for more, leading to an Epicurean~Christian *quies*, 612 *expletumque modum naturae non trahat extra.*

13 Gildenhard 2004.

14 Prudentius' choice of the pagan *Tonans* to refer to the Christian supreme god reminds us that *fulmina* inspire the religious dread from which Epicurus frees mankind (*DRN* 1.68–9). But the new, Christian, sky religion welcomes mankind to the heavens, rather than keeping it in oppression on earth: *DRN* 1.79 *nos exaequat uictoria caelo* is indeed the message of the *Psychomachia*. Christ's gladness that as a result of the victory *patrium famulis aperire profundum* alludes to *Aen.* 8.681 *patriumque aperitur uertice sidus*: false pagan beliefs in apotheosis are superseded by a true Christian path to the heavens. *aperire profundum* also alludes punningly to the passage of the Red Sea a few lines later.

Unlike the hostile and menacing thunderings of the imaginary *Religio* which oppresses mankind from the heavens in Lucretius (1.64–5 *quae caput a caeli regionibus ostendebat | horribili super aspectu mortalibus instans*, 'which revealed her head in the reaches of the sky, standing over mortal men and terrible to see'), this Christian version of *Iuppiter Tonans* smiles from above (*super*) on his followers.

Ring no. 3 (Virgilian): After the happy Virtues see the smiling face of the Thunderer, *Concordia* gives the signal to return to camp in triumph. In the only formal extended epic simile in the poem (650–64), the return of the Virtues is compared to the successful crossing of the Red Sea by the Israelites in their exodus from Egypt, leaving behind them the Egyptians destroyed by the waters which come together again after the Israelites' safe passage. The language alludes to the storm that launches the Virgilian epic narrative *in medias res* in *Aeneid* 1,[15] and so, within the text of the *Psychomachia* takes us back to the inaugural allusion to the *seditio* of the Virgilian storm in the opening prayer to Christ.

This is the point of the beginning of a fresh outburst of evil violence, corresponding to the fresh eruption of chaos at the beginning of the second half of the *Aeneid*. On the threshold of the Virtues' camp there is a sudden turn of events, a new storm, 667–8 *nascitur hic inopina mali lacrimabilis astu | tempestas* ('here arises a storm unlooked for, through the cunning of a woeful Evil'). This new storm is the assault of another of the avatars of Virgil's Allecto, *Discordia*, who, in disguise, inflicts a wound, but only light, on *Concordia*, before being unmasked, speared in the mouth by *Fides* to stop her heretical babblings, and then torn to pieces by an indignant mob. Once again Prudentius combines Virgilian storm and Virgilian Fury, aware, of course, of the emphatic storm imagery of war later in *Aeneid* 7.

The suddenness of *Discordia*'s terrorist outrage is dramatically effective. It also forms another intratextual link with the opening of the first part of the narrative. The storm is *inopina* (667), disturbing the great triumph with a sudden, *subita*, disaster, 669 *quae tantum subita uexaret clade triumphum*. Sudden also had been the entry on to the field of *Fides*, impelled by a (24) *repentinus laudis calor ad noua feruens | proelia* ('a sudden ardour for praise, ablaze for the new

15 With 654 *mons rueret pendentis aquae* cf. *Aen.* 1.105 *praeruptus aquae mons*; with 655 *fundo deprenderet imo* cf. *Aen.* 1.84 *totumque a sedibus imis*. Cf. also the hyperbolical opening of the sea bottom at *Aen.* 1.106–7 *his unda dehiscens | terram inter fluctus aperit*. The Israelites, unlike the Egyptians, are saved from the storm, 661 *subsistente procella*, protected by a god more powerful than the Virgilian Neptune. For an epicizing narrative of the crossing of the Red Sea, including some allusion to the storm in *Aen.* 1, see Prud. *Cath.* 5.45 ff.

battle').[16] Here there are two versions of the Virgilian sudden *in medias res* opening of his epic.[17] This formal feature in the allegory is also motivated by the realities veiled by the allegory: Faith's impetuosity in defence of the faith is the spirited impulse of the martyr to bear witness to his or her faith.[18] The sneaky and unexpected attack of a disguised *Discordia* is the ungrateful – and unexpected – assault of heresy within a Church which had appeared Triumphant.

From beginnings to endings. The *Aeneid* contains multiple points of closure, which co-exist in a tension between closed and open. The narrative trajectories of the grand passages of prophecy, the Speech of Jupiter in book 1, the Parade of Heroes in 6, the Shield of Aeneas in 8, stand in obvious and much-discussed contrast to the actual ending of the *Aeneid*, heavily closural as a death, but leaving open both the unresolved anger of Aeneas and questions of morality and ideology. A typological openness too: the killing of Turnus prefigures Romulus' killing of Remus, and a further series of fratricidal civil-war killings extending into the future.

Within the main narrative of the *Psychomachia*, the triumphal closure that is thwarted by the intervention of *Discordia* is succeeded by the definitive establishment of *Concordia* and *Pax*, and by the building of a Temple that will last because, in the end, it is the Celestial Jerusalem. In the end, eschatology trumps everything else, at the Last Trump. But because the *Psychomachia* is the story not just of sacred history, from the expulsion from Eden to the New Jerusalem, but also the story of Everyman, there will always be new wars to fight in the soul, new backslidings to overcome by the individual, as in the personification allegory there was a backsliding when *Discordia* interrupted the peace that followed the triumph over the Vices, in historical terms the appearance of heresies to disrupt the 'Peace of the Church' established by Constantine with the Edict of Milan in 313.

These repetitions of psychomachia within the individual are laid out, in the closing thanksgiving to Christ, at 899–904:

> o quotiens animam, uitiorum peste repulsa,
> sensimus incaluisse Deo! quotiens tepefactum
> caeleste ingenium post gaudia candida taetro
> cessisse stomacho! feruent bella horrida, feruent
> ossibus inclusa, fremit et discordibus armis
> non simplex natura hominis.

---

16 The suddenness of this *laudis calor* explains why Faith wears no weapons, of which, allegorically, she has no need.

17 With 641 *hilares* of the forces of the Virtues cf. *Aen.* 1.35 *uela dabant laeti.*

18 Cf. Perist. 3.31 ff. Eulalia's urge to martyrdom, *infremuit sacer Eulaliae | spiritus, ingeniique ferox | turbida frangere bella parat …*

How often, when the plaguing sins have been driven away, have we felt our soul aglow with the presence of God! How often after these pure joys, felt our heavenly nature grow cool and yield to foul desire! Savage war rages hotly, rages within our bones, and man's two-sided nature is in an uproar of rebellion.

quotiens refers us back to 7–8 *exoritur quotiens turbatis sensibus intus | seditio ... discordibus armis*, a Virgilian phrase from the *Georgics* (2.459–60 *procul discordibus armis ... iustissima tellus*),[19] and points to the interruption of *gaudia candida*, once thought achieved, by *Discordia*, as in the main narrative. *feruent bella horrida, feruent* echoes both the Sibyl's prophecy of a second round of *bella, horrida bella* at *Aen.* 6.86,[20] and the programmatic reference in the invocation at the beginning of *Aeneid* 7 to the *horrida bella* (41) that will result from the renewed outburst of hellish violence.[21] The imagery and sound of (902–4) *bella ... ossibus inclusa, fremit et discordibus armis ...* evokes the Virgilian image of *Furor* chained but alive, and roaring, inside the closed gates of War at the end of the Speech of Jupiter in *Aeneid* 1.294–6 *claudentur Belli portae*; *Furor impius intus ... fremet horridus ore cruento* ('The Gates of War will be closed; inside impious Madness will roar terrifyingly with bloody mouth'). Virgil's *Furor* is not killed, like the Vices in the *Psychomachia*, but lives on to roar at his prison bars, and perhaps one day to escape into a fresh career of the *Discordia* to whom Virgil's *Furor* is closely related. But there will come an end to the resurgences of vice in Prudentius' scheme of things, when Christ comes to our aid and founds his golden temple in the individual human's soul, 908–11:

spiritibus pugnant uariis lux atque tenebrae,
distantesque animat duplex substantia uires,
donec praesidio Christus Deus adsit et omnes
uirtutum gemmas componat sede piata.

Light and darkness with their opposing spirits are at war, and our two-fold being inspires powers at variance with each other, until Christ our God comes to our aid, and puts together all the jewels of the virtues in a purified structure.

donec at 910 has something of the force of *dum* in the first sentence of the *Aeneid*, *dum conderet urbem* (1.5), the achieved goal of foundation, after Aeneas' repeated

19 Echoed at Stat. *Theb.* 11.100–1 (Tisiphone to Megaera) '*ipsae odiis, ipsae discordibus armis | aptemur.*'

20 Wills 1996, 63-4. In context the gemination can signal a repeated outbreak of war.

21 Prudentius' repetition *feruent ... feruent* displaces on to another word the Virgilian repetitions of *bella ... bella* and *Aen.* 7.41-2 *dicam horrida bella, dicam*. Cf. also Stat. *Theb.* 601-2 '*bella horrida nobis, | atque iterum Tydeus*'; 6.457.

experience of sufferings on both land and sea. That final point of rest and closure is also reinforced by the two occurrences of *aeternus* that frame the closing thanksgiving to Christ, 888–9 *reddimus aeternas, indulgentissime doctor / grates, Christe, tibi* ... ('We give everlasting thanks to you, Christ, most kindly teacher'), and 915 (the last line of the poem) *aeternum solio diues Sapientia regnet* ('rich Wisdom reigns for ever on her throne') – *imperium sine fine*, at the end.

Prudentius appears fully in control of his endings, both closed and open: the open endings are provisional, stages on the path to the final closure guaranteed by the presence of a transcendental principle, 910 *donec praesidio Christus Deus adsit*. This is of course an ending held out only to those individuals who are willing to listen to the lessons of the *indulgentissimus doctor* (888), Christ. For those who turn a deaf ear there will be a very different ending, and one no less final.

3 Typology

That is one way in which intratextuality, understood as a text's internal dialogue on the matter of endings, works differently in a text with a Christian message from a text that does not ground itself in transcendental certainties. Another way concerns the intratextual relationships between different events and between different characters. A number of Virgilian scholars have reached for the term 'typology' to refer to the ways in which, within the *Aeneid*, mythological and legendary characters and events anticipate or foreshadow events in later history. The term typology is taken from biblical hermeneutics, where events in the Old Testament are types of events in the New Testament, antitypes of the Old Testament types, the New Testament fulfilment of Old Testament shadows. Biblical typology rests on a particular theology of history, in which events are 'concrete prophecies' of things to come. Looking at it simply in terms of texts, typology operates intratextually between the two Testaments of the Bible viewed as a single text.

The use of the term typology to refer to these historical mirrorings in the *Aeneid* has been criticised on the grounds that pagan antiquity lacks anything that corresponds to the Christian teleological view of history, pivoting round a decisive and transformative event, the Incarnation. Yet viewed purely as a textual phenomenon, a way of perceiving relationships within or between texts, Virgilian and Biblical foreshadowings work in comparable ways.[22]

---

22 I examine elsewhere the extent to which Virgilian 'typology' can be said to converge with Christian typology; here I dwell more on the differences.

Prudentius gives a clear example of how typology works in *Pudicitia*'s address to the fallen *Libido*. The attack of the personified Vice is seen as a hydra-like renewal (58–9 *resumptis / uiribus*: cf. Ovid *Met.* 9.193 (the Hydra) *geminasque resumere uires*), a narrative repetition, of the lust of the Old Testament character Holofernes, whose head was cut off by Judith. That should have been a decisive victory of chastity over lust, 66–9:

> at fortasse parum fortis matrona sub umbra
> legis adhuc pugnans, dum tempora nostra figurat,
> uera quibus uirtus terrena in corpora fluxit
> grande per infirmos caput excisura ministros.
>
> But perhaps a woman still fighting under the shadow of the law had not force enough, though in so doing she prefigured our times, in which the real power has passed into earthly bodies to sever the great head by the hand of feeble agents.

As type, Judith's virago-like heroism finds its fulfilment in the making new of human flesh through the Incarnation of the weak Christ-child in the womb of the Virgin Mary, Christ and the Virgin together enable the final victory of Chastity over Lust, so giving new closural force to the Virgilian tags of *Pudicitia*'s vaunt over her fallen enemy, 53–4 '*hoc habet ... supremus / hic tibi finis erit*' ('She's done for ... this will be your final end').

The longest passage of typological exegesis comes in the iambic *Praefatio*, a paratext that works intratextually to foreshadow and comment on the main hexameter narrative, interweaving typology and moral-psychological allegory.[23] The iambic *Praefatio* places the poem in the contexts of faith and history, the history of the faith, sketching a framework of interpretation that reaches from Genesis to the New Testament, and which provides a template to which Prudentius' individual Christian reader is to conform his or her behaviour. We begin with (1–2) *Senex fidelis prima credendi uia / Abram* ... ('Abram, the faithful old man, who first showed the way to belief ...')[24] The history of Abra[ha]m's military campaign to rescue his nephew Lot is both an *exemplum* (10) of how to behave, in terms of an ethical rhetoric (10 *suasor*, *suasit*), and also part of a typology that foreshadows Christ. The close connection of the typological and the tropological (moral sense) is perhaps signalled in the application of the language of *figura* and of foreshadowing to the moral lesson to be taken away by the reader, 50–1 *haec ad figuram*

---

23 On the *Praefatio* see Smith 1976, 206–22; Charlet 2003; Zarini 2000.

24 Abraham, as the *exemplum* of the *fidelis*, anticipates the first of the Virtues to take the field, 21–2 *prima petit campum dubia sub sorte duelli | pugnatura Fides.*

praenotata est linea, / quam nostra recto uita resculpat pede ('This outline has been drawn beforehand to be a model for our life to carve again with straight steps'). Abraham's fight against the captors of his nephew Lot, with the aid of 318 of his homegrown servants, is allegorized as the fight that we must undertake with our own inner forces to liberate our body from its enslavement to desire. This fight the reader undertakes as one of the faithful (52 *uigilandum in armis pectorum fidelium*) in Christ, who is foreshadowed, typologically, in the number of Abraham's servants, 318,[25] and in Melchisedech, the priest and king whose bringing of bread and wine to Abraham after his victory (Gen. 14:18) is a type of the Eucharist, while the three men who appear to Abraham (Gen. 18:1–5) are a type of the Trinity.

The *Praefatio* thus presents a tightly woven and interconnected set of exegetical approaches that is programmatic for a reading of the main body of the poem. The *Praefatio* starts from an Old Testament narrative and develops typological and moral allegories from it. The agents in the narrative of the main body of the poem are moral personifications, but the moral allegory incorporates exemplary characters from the Old Testament, for example Judith and Job (who accompanies the personification *Patientia*), as well as allusions to New Testament salvation history, and the poem concludes with a foreshadowing of the last things of Revelation in the shape of the Temple of Wisdom.[26] The progress of the individual soul in its struggle to free itself from sin is framed within, and underwritten by, a Christology that works historically through the supersession of the Old Testament age of the law by the New Testament age of grace. As a deeply Virgilian poet, Prudentius will doubtless have been convinced that these biblical fulfilments were of a higher order than the shadowy 'types' that operate intratextually within the *Aeneid*, and which are not grounded on a transcendent theology of history.

Bibliography

Charlet, J.-L. (2003), 'Signification de la preface à la *Psychomachia* de Prudence', *REL* 81, 232–51.

Gildenhard, I. (2004), 'Confronting the Beast – From Virgil's Cacus to the Dragons of Cornelis van Haarlem', *PVS* 25, 27–48.

Heinz, C. (2007), *Mehrfache Intertextualität bei Prudentius*, Frankfurt/Oxford.

Lühken, M. (2002), *Christianorum Maro et Flaccus. Zur Vergil- und Horazrezeption des Prudentius*, Göttingen.

25 In Greek 318 is TIH, T representing the cross, and IH being the first two letters of the name of Jesus.

26 For a useful table of 'the types, their scriptural sources, and their mode of existence in the allegory', see Smith 1976, 179.

Oliensis, E. (2004), 'Sibylline Syllables: The Intratextual *Aeneid*', *PCPS* 50, 29–45.
Roberts, M. (1989), *The Jeweled Style. Poetry and Poetics in Late Antiquity*, Ithaca/London.
Smith, M. (1976), *Prudentius' Psychomachia. A reexamination*, Princeton.
Wills, J. (1996), *Repetition in Latin Poetry: Figures of Allusion*, Oxford.
Zarini, V. (2000), 'Les prefaces des poèmes épico-panégyriques dans la latinité tardive (IVe–VIe siècles: esquisse d'une synthèse', in: *Le Texte préfaciel*, Nancy, 35–47.

Part IV: **Horace's Intratextual Poetics**

Chrysanthe Tsitsiou-Chelidoni

Horace's 'Persona<l> Problems': On Continuities and Discontinuities in Poetry and in Classical Scholarship

1 Prologue

'Horace tells us far more about himself, his character, his development, and his way of life (his *βίος*), than any other great poet in antiquity' —so says Eduard Fraenkel in the opening words of his book on the poet (1957, 1). Since the publication of that monumental work in the late 1950s, major changes have occurred in classical studies. Earlier certainties now appear outdated: for decades now, critics have as a rule viewed the autobiographical rhetoric of texts from Greek and Roman antiquity as being misleading. Poetry, it is claimed, neither refers to its creator's historical personality nor records his or her personal life, but is essentially a product of fiction, an artificial construct following the conventions of literary tradition or the preferences and particularities of the audience being addressed on each occasion. Rather than as individuals, poets speak from behind one or more fictitious poetic masks, which are their *persona* or *personae*.[1]

From an epistemological point of view, just how this critical volte-face came about is an interesting question. Of similar interest as regards literary scholarship is the issue of what conclusions are to be reached when studying those intratextual links across the Horatian oeuvre at large which appear to highlight facets of

I owe the first half of my title to Roland Mayer (2003). Many thanks are due to Dr. Ben Petre, who helped me to achieve a more natural style of English in the writing of this text. I am also very grateful to the editors of this volume, Prof. Stephen Harrison, Prof. Theodore Papanghelis and Prof. Stavros Frangoulidis, and to all the participants at the discussion following the presentation of my thesis for their useful remarks. Any remaining weaknesses are of course my own.

1 In relevant bibliography, the Latin term 'persona' (pl. 'personae') is used in the ancient sense, i.e. a mask worn by actors in the theatre (*OLD* s.v. *persona* 1a); metonymically it refers to the role itself (*ibid.*, 2a); it is also used metaphorically to denote the role, the character one assumes (pretence) (*ibid.*, 2d). The term was introduced into the language of critical discourse in the late 1940s, after Ezra Pound published his *Personae* poems (1909), and Carl Jung used the words 'persona' and 'mask' as terms central to his psychoanalytical theories (see Elliott 1982, 8–9). See also Wright 1960, 6–7, Elliott 1982, 19–32, Mayer 2003, 62–3.

https://doi.org/10.1515/9783110611021-011

the poet's personality. Contrary to the 'masks theory', do they ultimately convey the image of a single, even authentic individual?[2]

2 Critical stances

I shall begin my discussion with a brief and by necessity highly selective account of certain interpretive approaches to Horace's first-person, rhetorically autobiographical poetry, which I see as typical of the trends emerging in late 20th and early 21st century criticism on his works.

In a series of articles published from the mid-1960s to the mid-1970s, William Anderson set out views which marked a sea-change in the existing interpretive paradigm, and had a decisive impact on subsequent criticism of Horace's works. As Anderson argued, in each collection the poet portrays himself in line with the conventions of the genre he is writing for, and with the need to create particular impressions on his audience. In other words, on each occasion he adopts a role or wears a mask: this is the poet's *persona* or *personae*, which ultimately conceals his true face, leaving it in the dark.[3]

Moving on to 1993, Kirk Freudenburg argues in *The Walking Muse* that Horace's so-called 'personal' poetry is not in the least personal; in his *Satires*, the poet fashions a character or persona entirely familiar from earlier satirical tradition in terms of its basic characteristics. Freudenburg then goes on to claim that the person so concerned about the issue of *recte vivere* in both the *Satires* and the

2 On the difficulty involved in answering this specific question see Harrison 2007a, 35, Freudenburg 2010, 271.

3 See esp. Anderson 1982, 29, 50–1, 66, 69. Anderson (*ibid.*, esp. 9–10) mainly refers to Alvin Kernan as the inspiration behind the distinction drawn in the poem between the poet and the 'personal speaker', 'the satirist'. In *The Cankered Muse* (1959), Kernan highlights the artistic dimension in 17th and 18th century English poetic satire, in an attempt to counterbalance the biographical, historical and cultural approach dominating literary studies up until the late 1950s. On the relationship between Anderson's work and the positions taken by Kernan, see Freudenburg 2005, 28. Similar interpretive trends emerged early on in German-language literary criticism: on this see Wili 1948, 306, Knoche 1958, 152. In 1963 Carl Becker expressed the view that Horace's basic aim in the *Epistles* was neither to convey 'personal stories' —some of which he had invented and others not— nor to compile an autobiography, but to pass on enduring lessons in ethics (1963, 46, 48). Anderson's views came in for harsh criticism from Gilbert Highet (1974); for a critical approach to his position see also Mayer 2003, 71–7.

Epistles is not the real poet Horace, but merely a 'Horace', a favourite mask he wears (pp. 4–7, 9).[4]

In her *Horace and the Rhetoric of Authority*, published in 1998, Ellen Oliensis attempts to bridge the gap between the poet (as 'author') and the 'mask' by introducing the term 'face', which 'registers the fusion of mask and self' (p. 2). Via each collection, the poet carefully composes his 'self-image', introducing himself to his varying audience. Horace is none other than the 'faces' he presents, which are not authentic and accurate impressions of his true self (p. 2); these 'faces' 'construct' the image of his self.[5]

Oliensis herself confides that her interest in Horace arises in particular from 'the degree to which he confronts his own implicated and compromised position within society while maintaining the independence of his poems' (p. 14). She thus appears to believe that the poet's single personality is reflected in the entirety of his oeuvre,[6] even if highlighting discontinuity rather than continuity across the collections is what most attracts her interest.[7]

Similarly, in his 2001 book entitled *Horace. Image, Identity, and Audience*, Randall McNeill showed no desire to comment on the possibility of divining any single identity for the poet underlying the points where his collections intersect, despite the fact that he does point out a number of them (pp. 77, 159 n. 28). On the contrary, McNeill is highly insistent on the differences between works, speaking of several identifiable 'Horaces' in the sum total of his oeuvre (pp. 1–2). If the poet assumes various forms (or plays different 'personae' or 'represents a set of created images'), it is in essence because he is addressing various different audiences (pp. 5–7, 69, 76–7).

More recently (2014), Stephen Harrison has directed discussion on the issue of the poet's biography towards recording his poetic development, looking at Horace's path from one genre to another (pp. 13–33). Harrison thus highlights the unity and evolution in Horace's poetic career, without overlooking the differences between the poet's generically coloured 'personae'.

Leaving this literature review aside for a moment, let us now move on to the poetry itself. It is clear, I would say, that some of Horace's compositions –

4 Comparable stances were adopted in earlier studies by Zetzel 1980 and Gold 1992. Freudenburg takes a critical stance towards his own early views in subsequent texts (2005, 2010), though without ever in essence abandoning them (see e.g. 2010, 280).

5 Kirk Freudenberg subsequently also moves in this general interpretive direction (2010, *passim* and mainly 272, 285).

6 See also Oliensis 1998, 3, 7.

7 Besides, as Oliensis herself also points out (1998, 13), her focus 'in this study is on Horace's poems, not on his life or his times or his culture'.

belonging to different genres— enable us to make specific conjectures about details of the poet's life and even about his physical appearance: e.g. that he was born on the borders of Apulia and Lucania (*Serm.* 2.1.34);[8] that he was of humble origin (*Serm.* 1.6.6, 45–6; *Carm.* 2.20.5-6; 3.30.12; *Epist.* 1.20.20–1);[9] that he was physically small (*Epod.* 1.16; 12.3; *Carm.* 3.9.22; *Serm.* 2.3.308–9; *Epist.* 1.20.24); fairly quick-tempered (*Carm.* 3.9.23–4; *Serm.* 1.3.29; *Epist.* 1.20.25); that he had a brilliant education (*Serm.* 1.6.76–8; *Epist.* 2.2.41–5), but an unlucky career in the military (*Serm.* 1.6.47–8; *Carm.* 2.7.9–12; 3.4.26; *Epist.* 2.2.46–9). Furthermore, we learn that he miraculously escaped being killed by a falling tree (*Carm.* 2.13; 2.17.27–9; 3.4.27; 3.8.6–8) and very nearly drowned (*Carm.* 3.4.28). In the first satire of Book 2 the poet even claims to follow Lucilius, who constantly confided his secrets to his books —regardless of how well his life went— looking on them as his faithful friends (*Serm.* 2.1.28–34).[10]

In the framework of the present paper, what I shall be looking for in the lines from Horace that are autobiographical, at least from a rhetorical point of view, are traces of poetic consciousness and psyche. They are what I believe will bring me closer to the mystery of an artistic existence with a specific historical identity, whether genuine or not. From that perspective, my study also originates in what I would term anthropological interest.[11]

Thus, my intratextual analysis represents a conscious return to the old question of whether or not it is possible to uncover features of Horace's personality, and ultimately of his historical identity, from his oeuvre.[12] This enterprise, which is not concerned with a single composition in a specific genre, but rather in principle with the poet's entire oeuvre, also aims to test out earlier positions in scholarship and highlight their own historical identity.

---

8 All references are to the Shackleton Bailey edition (1991).

9 But see Williams 1995.

10 On the possible interpretations of this passage as proof or not of genuine autobiographical writing by Horace the satirist, see Mayer 2003, 62, 73–4 and Anderson 1982, 30, Freudenburg 1993, 6 with n. 10 respectively.

11 On the anthropological significance of autobiography see Gusdorf 1980, 43–4. As Johanna Hanink and Richard Fletcher claim (2016, 5): 'audiences have long desired to ... experience the visual fulfilment of "seeing" great creators of the past at work.'

12 On the vintage of the question see e.g. Graziosi 2016, 56, Becker 1963, 14 with nn. 1 and 2, 25–6 with n. 1. The particular point at issue is inevitably linked to the more general question of the authenticity of Roman personal poetry, on which see Clay 1998 and Mayer 2003.

3 The 'testimony' of poetry

In this initial stage of my commentary on the poetry, and until I reach any firm conclusions, I shall be using the term 'poet' (or the name 'Horace') in inverted commas, so as to distinguish between the first-person voice speaking supposedly from the poet's perspective within the poem, and the man himself as its historical creator.

We are in 30 BCE —more or less the year when the second book of the *Sermones* was published.[13] In the seventh *Satire* in the book, taking advantage of the licence allowed to slaves at the Saturnalia, Davus levels specific accusations against his master; the latter, the person speaking as 'poet', has first permitted him to do so. Davus accuses him of vacillating between what is right and what is depraved; on the one hand, says the slave, you praise the good fortune and behaviour of ordinary Romans of old, and on the other you would put up stout resistance if a god took you back to that time (22–4); when you are in Rome you long for the countryside, and when you are out in the fields you sing the city's praises (28–9). You judge by circumstances: if you do not receive a dinner invitation, you praise humble fare and consider yourself lucky for not having to clink glasses elsewhere, as if invitations were a burden. But if Maecenas sends you an invitation, you race to get ready (29–35). To maintain an illicit affair, you disguise yourself and pretend to be someone else (53–6). While playing master to your slaves, you yourself are a slave to circumstances and individuals, captive to your pathetic fear, a puppet or marionette in others' hands (75–82). 'Yet who is free?' asks the 'poet' (83). Only the wise man, replies Davus, is a free master of his own self, devoid of fears and indifferent towards praise and honours, self-sufficient and well-rounded —you know nothing of such things (83–9). The climax comes in the closing lines: 'you can't bear an hour in your own company, or enjoy your leisure properly, you shun your own self, a fugitive without a roof over your head, you try to cheat your cares with wine and sleep; but they dog your flight' (111–15). The 'poet' reacts to this daring speech in an angry outburst (116–18), as if to imply that the slave's criticisms are right on the mark.[14]

---

13 See Nisbet 2007, 12.

14 According to pseudo-Acron scholia (ad *Serm.* 2.7.1, Keller) *ex persona sua Horatius aliena vitia carpit* ('Horace is castigating others' faults in his own name'), which could be taken as meaning that in this particular satire the poet may simply be impersonating himself. But see also the comment by Porphyrio (ad *Serm.* 2.7.1, Holder): *loquitur enim cum servo Horatius* ('to be specific, Horace is talking to his slave'). On use of the term 'persona' in ancient scholia see Clay 1998, 35–9, Mayer 2003, 75–6.

Davus, who bears a stock comic slave-name,[15] is of course conveying what he himself claims (45) to be the teachings of the doorkeeper of Crispinus, the Stoic philosopher whom the 'poet' has treated with irony from his very first satire (*Serm.* 1.1.120–1).[16] One might say that such self-ridicule is a legitimate literary ploy in this particular genre:[17] the slave charges 'Horace' with possessing habits which the 'poet' himself castigates in other satires as being typical of other individuals. Davus accuses him of adultery (cf. *Serm.* 1.2), implies that his master is profligate (recalling *Serm.* 2.2; 2.6) and finds him unstable and hypocritical (in evocation of *Serm.* 1.1.1–22).[18]

Nevertheless, other poems —admittedly we are still in the *sermo* genre— appear to 'substantiate' at least part of the slave's indictment. In the *Epistles*, published roughly eleven years after his second book of *Satires*,[19] 'Horace' sketches himself partly as described by his (supposed) slave, as if he has admitted the latter was right and taken his advice in the meantime: 'Horace' declares his wish to free himself of all that causes him anxiety,[20] to cease composing for the public and Maecenas —despite the marked irony of the declaration being written in verse—[21] to withdraw from society and dedicate himself to philosophy (*Epist.* 1.1.4–6, 11), so as to attain mental balance, self-control, internal self-sufficiency and calm (27). Indeed, the closing lines of the first letter, which as almost always feature a fair dose of irony and subversion,[22] recall *Serm.* 2.7.83–8:[23] the wise man has gained freedom, overcoming the fear of poverty, death and social ties; he is self-sufficient, indifferent to desires and honours, as Davus argued there; here the 'poet' asserts such a man is rich and free, having tasted recognition and beauty, and is the prudent and healthy master of all —provided he is not suffering from an annoying cold (*Epist.* 1.1.106–8).

Still more striking is the congruence between *Satire* 2.7 and *Epistle* 1.8: here 'Horace' is unusually and disarmingly frank in confessing to a grave psychic and intellectual weakness, which is closely reminiscent of Davus' final diagnosis. The

---

15 Noted as early as pseudo-Acron, ad *Serm.* 2.7.1 (Keller): *Inducitur servus, sicuti in comoedia.* ('A slave is introduced, as in comedy.') See also Freudenburg 1993, 48, 225–6.

16 See Gowers 2012, ad *Serm.* 1.1.120.

17 See Oliensis 1998, 52.

18 See also Muecke 2007, 119.

19 See Nisbet 2007, 15.

20 Cf. also *Epist.* 1.16.63–6.

21 See Harrison 2007a, 33; 2014, 20.

22 See Mayer 1994, ad *Epist.* 1.1.106–8.

23 According to modern commentators, the lines primarily refer to *Serm.* 1.3.124–5. See Kiessling/Heinze 1898, ad *Epist.* 1.1.106, Mayer 1994, ad *Epist.* 1.1.106–8.

tone of the letter is of course no longer comic, though it does remain critical and is quite clearly self-reflective. Besides, the illness is here recorded from the sufferer's perspective, without reference to any moral deficiency similar to that Davus accused his master of having. Despite his many good intentions and great expectations, the 'poet' lives neither properly nor pleasantly (4); it is his weakness of mind, his mental illness (*mente minus validus*), being greater than that of his body, that renders him disinclined to listen to or learn of anything that could relieve him (7–8). He is displeased at faithful doctors, and gets angry with friends who keep him from fatal lethargy (9–10); he does whatever is bad for himself, and avoids whatever he believes could do him good (11); he is as fickle as the wind: in Rome he longs for Tibur, and in Tibur for Rome (12).[24] Here the subject matter and textual style point to the earlier composition:[25]

> Romae rus optas, absentem rusticus urbem
> tollis ad astra levis.
> (*Serm.* 2.7.28–9)

> At Rome you long for the country; in the country, you extol
> to the stars the distant town, you fickle one!
> (transl. by H. Rushton Fairclough)

> Romae Tibur amem ventosus, Tibure Romam.
> (*Epist.* 1.8.12)

> and am fickle as the wind, at Rome loving Tibur, at Tibur Rome.
> (trans. by H. Rushton Fairclough)

Despite the fact that *Epist.* 1.1 shows a somewhat strong-willed 'poet', *Epist.* 1.8 and *Serm.* 2.7.111–15 reveal one who is torn and indecisive. The 'poet's' internal fragmentation may have one fundamental cause (which is analysed into more), but it takes various guises. Davus talks quite clearly of dependencies that have rendered the 'poet' a puppet (*Serm.* 2.7.75–82); he is bogged down emotionally (*Serm.* 2.7.112), feels unhappy (*Serm.* 2.7.115, *Epist.* 1.8.4), engages in self-destructive behaviour (*Epist.* 1.8.9–11) and is altogether inactive (*Serm.* 2.7.114, *Epist.* 1.8.10). His mental impasse finds expression in permanent dissatisfaction

---

24 On the illness plaguing 'Horace' see pseudo-Acron, ad *Epist.* 1.8.1 (Keller), Kiessling/Heinze 1898, ad *Epist.* 1.8.7.

25 This congruence is pointed out as early on as Porphyrio (ad *Serm.* 2.7.28, Holder). See also Becker 1963, 21 n. 12, 25 with n. 22.

with staying in one place. When in the city he longs for life out in the fields, and when there he longs for town life.

In essence, this division means a coming and going between two opposing worlds. *Sermo* 2.6 has much to reveal on this: the simple life in the countryside is associated by the 'poet' with writing (16–17), carefree study (61), sleep and idleness (61), an existence far removed from the worries of the city (62), simple, unpretentious food (63–5), and conversations with familiar people on matters of ethics (71–6). In the city, he is burdened with a busy schedule of commitments, inextricably bound up with his obligations towards his patron; conversations revolve around prosaic, paltry matters, such as who has the best house, and whether a mime performance was good or not (71–2). The city is associated with ambition (18), and is also the place where the 'poet' is envied for his relationship to Maecenas (47–8). The countryside seems to secure him what Rome deprives him of: valuable freedom of movement (61–2), a life far removed from dangers, fears and agitation (78-9, 113–14).[26]

In terms of quality and content, the confrontational relationship between town and country remains the same in the *Epistles*: isolation in the countryside may mean dedication to philosophy (*Epist.* 1.1.1–19) or abstaining from disputes with rival poets and critics (*Epist.* 1.19.39–49). At the end of the day it means enjoying freedom, far from morbid passions, dependencies and commitments (*Epist.* 1.7; 1.10; 1.14). In *Epistles* 1.10; 1.11.8–10; 1.14 and 1.16 the 'poet' actually expresses a clear preference for simple rural life. Nevertheless, 1.4 and 1.5 are redolent of the atmosphere at festive symposiums in the city, via which 'Horace' seeks to join his associates in casting aside the burden of everyday concerns. The final letter in the collection (*Epist.* 1.20) further highlights a turning towards public life and the town, as a trend in the book that the author is ultimately forced to give in to.

In both collections (implicitly in the *Sermones* and explicitly in the *Epistles*), the author thus presents himself as being divided between two lifestyles and two diametrically opposed worlds. That of the countryside is synonymous with a protected, private space; it is the world of freedom, calm, simplicity, pious austerity and humility; the other life in the town is synonymous with an exposed, public arena that is perilous, tiring and uncontrollable, being the world of activity, wealth and reputation, and simultaneously that of envy and dependence.[27] This oscillating between two poles —both of which the 'poet' is powerfully attracted

26 The idea of associating urban living and wealth with fears and dangers is not of course unknown to literary tradition prior to Horace: see Kiessling/Heinze 1921, ad *Serm.* 2.6.79.
27 See also Harrison 2007b.

to nonetheless— is directly linked to his mental and emotional weakness. He is plagued with guilt and permanent anguish, looking and feeling ill both in the town —where he coexists with Davus (*Serm.* 2.7.117–18)— and out in the fields, from where he addresses his letter to Celsus (*Epist.* 1.8.3–6).

Is this confession of internal division, and of the 'poet's' hovering between two opposing worlds merely a literary diversion? Following perhaps in the footsteps of an earlier autobiographical or other tradition, could it be a rhetorical ploy aimed at composing a self-reflective poetry, which gives the impression of functioning in a self-aware and ultimately self-therapeutic manner? Might it be a device enabling the poet to win over his public?

Whatever the case may be, it is interesting that the impression of the 'poet' gained by readers of the *Sermones* and the *Epistles* in line with the above argument does not differ significantly from that revealed by the *Odes*. Although in the *Carmina* 'Horace' does not confess to any internal division, it is reflected in the compositions themselves, which often show contradictory personal preferences. As Stephen Harrison has pointed out (2007b, 242): 'Much of the sympotic colour of the *Odes* is urban, and the majority of the pleasurable celebrations there described seem to take place in Rome. Symposia in the country are not unknown, however, and here again we see the country represented as the antidote to urban excitement and stress in a strikingly modern mode.'[28] Besides, poems that honour the unpretentious enjoyment of life (*Carm.* 1.20; 1.31; 1.38; 2.6; 2.16) or even recommend disdaining wealth (*Carm.* 2.2; 2.18; 3.16) are found alongside others promoting as ideal, if not to excess, the self-indulgent entertainments one should enjoy while still young (*Carm.* 2.3.13–16; 2.11).[29]

Indeed, the 'poet' of the *Carmina* once again appears on some occasions to prefer life in a humble world, far from the commotion of town, and on others to enjoy publicity, which cannot but involve exposure to the hubbub there. In *Carm.* 2.16,[30] to be more specific, he states his preference for a simple, carefree

---

28 In common with other Roman writers, Horace occasionally expresses nostalgia for 'Rome's imagined beginnings as a primitively virtuous rustic community', thus Harrison 2007b, 238–9.

29 See also how in *Epist.* 1.14.32–5 the poet contrasts the world and décor of symposiums with simple rural customs. In *Carm.* 3.14.17–22 he seeks the pleasures of a self-indulgent symposium. The ode, however, features celebrations for the triumphal return of Augustus from Spain; cf. also *Carm.* 4.11.1–20 (grandiose birthday celebrations for Maecenas).

30 Lejay (1911, 555) explicitly associates *Satire* 2.7 with *Ode* 2.16 and *Epistle* 1.8: 'Nous avons son premier aveu. [sc. in *serm.* 2.7] Quelques années après, il écrivait les réflexions mélancoliques d'*Od.*, II, 16, 18–28. La crise commence: nous la verrons dans les *Epîtres* se développer, puis s'apaiser.'

life, far from the anxieties of the *vita activa*.[31] In the first three stanzas, *otium*, 'calm of mind', 'an ideal inward tranquility',[32] is touted as the much coveted counter to the preoccupations and worries of busy activity, which may offer material comforts and honours, but deprives one of peace of mind and equanimity (1–12). Constant travelling cannot make anyone happier, because ultimately it does not distance one from personal problems or one's very essence (18–20). In the background to the rhetorical question *patriae quis exsul / se quoque fugit?* (*Carm.* 2.16.19–20, 'which fugitive from his homeland avoids his own self?') one can 'hear' Davus rebuking *teque ipsum vitas fugitivus et erro* (*Serm.* 2.7.113, 'you flee your own self, a fugitive and wanderer'), along with the *sententia* of *Epist.* 1.11.27 *caelum, non animum, mutant qui trans mare currunt* ('those who cross the sea change skies, not their soul'). 'You, Grosphus,' says the 'poet' in the closing lines of the ode, 'live among riches. Fate dealt me a modest farm, the delicate spirit of the Greek Muse and the power to disdain the malicious rabble' (... *malignum spernere vulgus, Carm.* 2.16.37–40).

The poem's final verse appears to mean that 'Horace' abhors publicity. The same stance towards the masses, for which there are literary and philosophical parallels,[33] is also recorded at other points in the *Carmina*: 3.1.1; 3.2.21–4. Nevertheless, the final poem in the collection lends a rather different impression: it is a proud announcement of the prospect that 'Horace's' achievement —in adapting Aeolian song to Italian melody— will become known to an impressively widespread community of people in his native land, in Apulia; even in later ages his posthumous reputation and he himself will remain vivid and fresh (*Carm.* 3.30.7–8, 10–2).[34] The wide and constantly renewed praise which the 'poet' here acknowledges as an achievement clearly signals a turn towards public life; 'Horace' does ultimately appear to seek publicity. Such a fortune is in many respects reminiscent of distinction in politics and the acquisition of political power, 'achievements' which *Carm.* 2.16 explicitly links with a world foreign and in opposition to the simple environment of 'small fields' and humble life (*Carm.* 2.16.9–11).[35]

---

31 On Horace as poet of the *Carmina* and his preference for rural life (a theme that entered Roman poetry from Ancient Greek lyric and Alexandrian verse) see Nisbet/Hubbard 1970, XX, 215–16; Troxler-Keller 1964, 122 with n. 59. In *Epod.* 2 the respectable and pleasant if humble life in the fields and in nature is contrasted with the busy life and burdensome hubbub of the town from the interesting standpoint of a hypocritical usurer; see Harrison 2007b, 238.

32 Thus Nisbet/Hubbard 1978, 254.

33 See Nisbet/Hubbard 1978, ad *Carm.* 2.16.39; Harrison 2017, ad *Carm.* 2.16.39–40.

34 Thus Nisbet/Rudd 2004, ad *Carm.* 3.30.7–8. See also *Carm.* 2.20.13–20.

35 The tenor in the collection's final poem differs from the Callimachean one in the closing lines of *Carm.* 1.1 (see Nisbet/Rudd 2004, ad *Carm.* 3.30.13–14, Nisbet/Hubbard 1970, ad *Carm.* 1.1.32).

In any case, this type of alternation between a small, hand-picked audience and a clearly larger one addressed via published work is also typical of both the *Satires* and the *Epistles*. The first book of the *Satires* ends with the 'poet' explicitly showing interest in the opinion of relatively few select readers (*Serm.* 1.10.37–9, 73–4). The second opens with a dialogue between the 'poet' and the legal expert Trebatius on the polemic directed against the former for his first book. Are we to suppose that the polemic derives from the close circle of select readers mentioned at the end of *Serm.* 1.10.81–8? Whatever the case is, in lines *Serm.* 2.1.75–7 'Horace' predicts that he will overcome the envy which will be forced to confess that the 'poet' was friend to the prominent men of Rome; 'if it tries to sink its teeth into tender flesh, they will strike against granite' (77–8). This declaration probably concerns individuals associated with the guild critics and poets, such as Pantilius, Demetrius, Fannius and Hermogenes Tigellius (*Serm.* 1.10.78–80),[36] who were not favourably disposed towards the 'poet' – 'Horace' treats them as a *turba*, whose admiration is not worth seeking (*Serm.* 1.10.73). The 'poet' thus appears to anticipate his verses being so widely disseminated that his reputation will transcend the narrow circle of the *docti amici*, provoking the envy of rivals. Besides, Trebatius' recommendation that 'Horace' should take into account the sacred laws that protect everyone against poetic defamation (*Serm.* 2.1.80–3),[37] acquires its full meaning only if the 'poet' is not using his oeuvre to address a closed if numerous group of familiar, hand-picked readers.[38]

Back in the *Epistles*, the 'poet' professes from the very outset that he has decided to retire. In the opening lines of *Epistle* 1 he speaks of Veianius the gladiator, who dedicated his weapons to the temple of Hercules and withdrew to the country, so as not to have to beg the crowd for a favourable decision at the end of every contest (*Epist.* 1.1.4–6). Towards the end of the composition, the 'poet' confesses to the emotional and intellectual gap separating him from the *populus Romanus* (*Epist.* 1.1.70–6): if he were to be asked by the crowd why he did not share their views, he would give the same answer as that once given by the fox to the sick lion: 'What frightens me are the tracks I can see, which all lead into to your den, but none come out.'[39] The people are a many-headed monster of multiple desires: in the end, the 'poet' does not know what or whom to follow.[40] The

36 See Gowers 2012, ad *Serm.* 1.10.78, 79, 80.

37 On this see Kiessling/Heinze 1921, ad *Serm.* 2.1.81.

38 See also Oliensis 1998, 174 and Gowers 2012, ad *Serm.* 1.4.22–3.

39 On the significance of the myth to which Horace alludes, see Mayer 1994, ad *Epist.* 1.1.73.

40 See also *Epist.* 2.2.58–64.

counterpoint to this comes in the collection's closing composition, *Epistles* 1.20, where sending the work out to the broader public appears inevitable.

Such contradictory behaviour calls for an explanation. If in the *Satires*, the *Odes* and the *Epistles* the 'poet' initially chooses to speak to a small, select audience, why does he end up consciously addressing a much larger one by publishing each of the collections? And if he admits in numerous poems to preferring humble life in the country, what eventually thrusts him towards the world of publicity and the crowded city? One might suppose the incentive to be personal ambition,[41] *amor laudis*, which he also attributes to the Greeks —they are only greedy in that respect, as he says (*Ars* 323–4). This is quite possibly amplified by prompting if not direct pressure from his patron (*Epist.* 1.1.1–3), ultimately shielded at least for some time by the need that the 'poet' feels to survive (*Epist.* 2.2.49–52). This incentive may not be a *prava ambitio* (*Serm.* 1.6.51–2),[42] or a *sordidus cupido* (*Carm.* 2.16.15–16), yet as the 'poet' himself admits it does lead him to compromises, concessions and dependencies contrary to his true will. In order to appeal, he is forced to seek the vote of more than a close circle of select friends: 'I endure a great deal so as to humour the excitable tribe of poets, when I scribble to beg for public recognition; for my part, once my endeavour is complete and I recover, I would stop my ears to readers without any repercussions.' (*Epist.* 2.2.102–5).

Nevertheless, contact with figures who were prominent on the Roman literary scene but who did not belong to the 'poet's' intimate circle of friends was far from trouble-free; it was plagued by extreme bad feeling on the part of the critics and powerful emotions on that of the 'poet' (*Epist.* 1.19.41–9).[43] 'Horace' was in any case possessed of a keen sense of responsibility and decency (*Serm.* 1.6.57), as was only to be expected of one inculcated with the importance of restraint and exemplary behaviour (*Serm.* 1.4.120–31), and who had thus learnt both to control himself and to agonize over the control of others (*Serm.* 1.10.89–90; 2.1.6–7). The 'poet's' occasional reluctance to write (*Serm.* 2.3.1–18, 39–40; *Epist.* 2.2.20–1) might well be attributable to these inhibitions. In any case, the distressing compromise with the terms of literary life in Rome proves short-lived: somewhat later

41 See also Kiessling/Heinze 1921, ad *Serm.* 2.6.18.

42 According to C.O. Brink 1982, ad *Epist.* 2.2.206–7, Horace 'regularly uses a critical epithet to delimit the notion of ambition'.

43 In *Epist.* 1.19.37–49 the 'poet' essentially denies taking part in public poetry readings (*recitationes*), while in *Epist.* 2.2.87–105 he admits to having done so. In any case, both letters reveal that 'Horace' detested self-seeking shows of obligatory (pseudo) politeness towards poets and critics. Of course, in *Epist.* 2.2.102–5 he offers what might be termed a cynically frank admission of his own stance, which could possibly be taken as yet another indication of late composition. On dating the letter together with *Epist.* 2.1 and *Ars* see Harrison 2014, 66–7.

the 'poet' chooses isolation, withdrawal from the commotion and stressful dependencies that come with city living (*Serm.* 2.6.16–8; *Epist.* 2.2.65–86, 102–5). Far from the town and its fears, he can devote himself to what he sees as true creation.

All the same, the completion of poetic composition once more occasions a return to the wider public. *Epistles* 1.20 interprets this in an interesting manner: it is not the 'poet's' desire for recognition that leads him to publish his verse for an audience transcending his circle of select, trustworthy friends, but the nature of literature itself, which imposes tradition on the general public; it is the scroll personified which wishes to 'be publicized', despite admonishments and serious objections from the 'poet', who ultimately caves in nonetheless.[44]

There are of course occasions when exposure to the wider public ceases to generate negative feelings: in his last book of *Odes* the 'poet' joyfully professes that he has gained widespread recognition. Lines 13–24 of *Odes* 4.3 are revealing: this is no mere prediction that envy will be forced to admit how powerful 'Horace' has become (*Serm.* 2.1.75–8), or a triumphant announcement that envy will eventually be transcended (*Carm.* 2.20.4), but a discreet, restrained yet masterly acknowledgment that it truly is subsiding and can no longer do him any harm.[45] The 'poet' is now generally recognized as the Roman lyric poet *par excellence*, a fact which 'Horace' essentially appears to attribute to a miracle, to divine intervention by Melpomene.

Thus far I have attempted to sketch out features of 'Horace' and 'fragments' of his personality (even in genuine extra-literary circumstances, is it ever possible to know someone entirely?). In essence I have given the outline of a puzzle pieced together with the aid of various collections by the poet. In the end, a single personality does emerge as the face of the creator himself from within Horace's personal poetry, a literary 'ego'.[46] However, this is a personality clearly riddled with fissures and contradictions. The 'Horace' we know from his literary works is a poet vacillating between life in the clamorous city, where dependencies become suffocating and worries grow out of all proportion, and isolation in the simple countryside, where one can devote oneself to writing, reading and taste freedom, free of morbid ambition.[47] In any case, the 'poet' hovers between the desire for popular acclaim and discriminating acknowledgment by the few. He is a

44 See Tsitsiou-Chelidoni 2012.

45 The 'poet' often refers to the envy others show towards him: *Serm.* 2.3.13, 2.6.47–8, *Epist.* 1.14.37–8. See also Oliensis 1998, 225–6.

46 'io letterario' according to Citroni 1993, 283. See also Nisbet/Rudd 2004, xxvi.

47 See also Harrison 2007b, *passim*, esp. 246.

perfectionist (*Serm.* 2.1.6–7), and at the same time an almost agoraphobic poet of Callimachean character, yet one who had to agree to meeting an ill-disposed wider public,[48] as that was in principle what contemporary rules of life in the limelight demanded of anyone wishing to promote their literary power and worth (*Epist.* 1.1.1–6; 1.20). However, it is the 'poet' himself who owns up to his sense of internal division[49] —once again via his autobiographical rhetoric (*Serm.* 2.7; *Epist.* 1.8)— as the symptom or source of his own mental impasse, thus intimating that there are not several systematically different 'Horaces' or 'personae', each emerging separately in every personal composition, but rather many different aspects of his own person, which might coexist in their historical dimension in a painful manner, and in their literary dimension in a self-aware, self-therapeutic mode.[50] In fact, in a range of different poetic genres the 'poet' himself repeatedly highlights the need to achieve internal equilibrium (*aequus animus*, *Epist.* 1.11.29–30; 18.112) and self-control (*Carm.* 3.29.41–3). Clearly this blissful serenity is the polar opposite of the internal fragmentation or spiritual and intellectual impasse that Davus diagnoses in 'Horace' in *Serm.* 2.7, and which the 'poet' himself confesses to in *Epist.* 1.8. Besides, in *Epist.* 2.2.200 'Horace' discloses that his ideal personal goal is internal intellectual oneness, unaffected by the vicissitudes of fortunes and the trials of life.[51]

One could even argue that the image of the 'poet' outlined in his early works assumes its mature characteristics in the *Epistles* and the final book of the *Odes*.[52]

---

48 In various groups of lines —from compositions of varying genre— the 'poet' either implicitly or explicitly sets out the reasons why he detests the wider public: it is volatile (*Carm.* 1.1.7; 1.35.25; 3.2.17–20; *Epist.* 1.1.82, 90; 1.19.37; 1.20.10–3), makes unsound and erroneous judgements (*Serm.* 1.6.15–17; *Carm.* 2.2.17–21), and is hostile and malicious (*Carm.* 2.16.39–40). The volatility and thoughtlessness of the crowd were of course proverbial in classical literature before Horace, and also preoccupied ancient philosophers: see Otto 1890, 378 s.v. *vulgus*, Nisbet/Hubbard 1970, ad *Carm.* 1.1.7; 1978, ad *Carm.* 2.2.18, Mayer 1994, ad *Epist.* 1.1.70.

49 On the poet's self-portrayal as an internally fragmented person in the *Satires*, and especially in the *Epistles*, see also Citroni 1993, 282–4.

50 According to Richard Heinze, the poet was in principle following the model laid down by Epicurus in quite consciously providing a picture of his soul and personality via his book of epistles (1972, 297–8). This, Heinze points out, was something entirely new not only in Roman literature, but also in the history of the intellect: a milestone in the development of conscious awareness of personality (*ibid.*, 301). See also Pöschl 1985, 43–4.

51 See also *Carm.* 2.3.1–4.

52 See Becker 1963, 10. Earlier on, Heinze 1972, 300 sees a new phase in the poet's life reflected in the first book of the *Epistles*. See also Abel 1969, 34–6, 44; Estévez 1982, 298–9, and here n. 30 on Lejay's views. On the other hand, Harrison (2014, 26) sees a wish on the poet's part to offer an overview of his earlier personal poetry in *Epist.* 2 and particularly in *Ars*, the final book in his career. Oliensis (1998, 4–5) also acknowledges 'the evolution of Horace's distinctive face'.

Besides, from the outset of his poetic career 'Horace' proclaims the need for timely enjoyment of life, within the bounds of human nature, and for abandoning the amusements of youth when old age begins to show its first signs (*Serm.* 1.1.117–19; *Carm.* 1.9.13–24; 2.3.13–16). In the *Epistles* and the fourth book of the *Odes*, works of maturity, the 'poet' applies this same basic principle, elevating it to a fundamental rule of ethics that consistently governs his life (*Epist.* 1.1.4–9; 14.31–6; 2.2.214–16; *Carm.* 4.1). 'Horace' thus presents himself to his audience via different generic codes, but with a single identity. For all its internal rifts – or even occasional generic disguises —it is an identity that shows consistency and continuity.

Nonetheless, the question that remains unanswered is whether the above self-presentation reveals aspects of the poet's genuine historical existence. Do the unity and evolution of the personality attributed to 'Horace' as recorded in his poems guarantee it was a historical identity? Does [the] poetry convey the truth, or merely an illusion of truth? One could of course conjecture that the poet composes his works in such a way that in the end, when viewed together, they merely convey the impression of evolution and coherence, i.e. illusory reflections of life.[53] Nevertheless, as Roland Mayer has argued, it is highly likely that readers in Roman antiquity —poets included— looked on personal poetry as a genuine, reliable deeply personal confession by its creator.[54] Be that as it may, given the rhetoric in the texts (in the first person, thus creating the impression that it is the poet himself speaking) reference to a historical personality as the identity of the creator is both automatic and inevitable; on the level of history (as experience), that personality is ultimately what links together all the works that have survived in Horace's name, especially if despite all its internal rifts it displays coherence and unity. In such a case, the onus on us is not to explain why we can recognize elements of historical referentiality in the personality of the poet recorded in his poetry, but rather why we should not do so. And in poetry with clear historical references, what in fact are the limits of a rhetorical construct, with the possible exception of obvious products of pure imagination (but what does that mean, in the light of personal impressions of experience)?

In answer to the above, one could of course counter that literature is primarily fiction, and in any case imitation and 'representation of natural discourse',[55] and that the question of whether and to what degree Horace's personal history

53 See Bourdieu 2000, 298 on coherence as a characteristic of fundamentally traditional (auto) biographical narrative. See also Becker 1963, 12 and *passim*, Elliott 1982, 71–2.

54 Mayer 2003, 74–6, 78. See also Clay 1998, 10.

55 See Elliott 1982, 89–90.

lies concealed in his compositions is of no interest.[56] Yet in that way all the problems associated with the nature of personal poetry are apparently reduced to cutting the Gordian knot, since we can be certain that literature is never at bottom merely fiction, and that imitation cannot but relate to the object imitated. This holds true even if as a rule it appears impossible to precisely distinguish the share of fiction from that of history, above all in autobiographical poetry.[57]

In any case, both in antiquity[58] and in much later times the biographical approach to Horatian poetry has had significant advocates, including Christoph Martin Wieland, Richard Heinze, Eduard Fraenkel, Gilbert Highet, and Niall Rudd, though naturally enough they do not see a reflection of the poet's historical identity in every composition of a personal nature.[59] This same line of interpretation continues to bear fruit to the present day.[60]

Nevertheless, by the early 20th century G.L. Hendrickson (1900, 122–3) was already arguing that 'the tone and spirit of this composition [sc. *Serm.* 1.4] ... can be imagined'– though the same critic later named Horace 'the earliest considerable autobiographer of Western literature' (1935, 189) –, while in 1919 Lorenz Niedermeier saw the counterpoint to records of genuine experience in the personal testimony reminiscent of earlier rhetorical topoi to be found in Horatian satirical poetry (p. 14).

And yet, *Carm.* 2.13, a *σχετλιασμός* on a falling tree that almost cost the 'poet' his life, necessarily leads us to second thoughts on the relationship between poetry that draws on earlier literary topoi and empirical reality: the poem in question can indeed be seen as belonging to a rich literary tradition. But that fact clearly does not detract from the reality of the accident, which the poet repeatedly refers to at various points in his oeuvre: *Carm.* 2.17.27–9; 3.4.27; 3.8.6–8.[61] All the

56 Cf. Becker 1963, 24 and *passim*, Williams 1968, 674, Davis 1991, 78 and *passim*.

57 See Elliott 1982, 70–1, with references to earlier theory.

58 On the biographical interpretation of Horace's poetry by ancient commentators see Becker 1963, 25–6 with n. 1.

59 In the first quarter of the 20th century, critics (Theodor Birt, Ulrich von Wilamowitz) acknowledged the genuine experiential character of love poetry by Catullus, Propertius and Tibullus. See Knoche 1958, 148 with nn. 3, 4, Clay 1998, 12–14. Peter Levi (*Horace. A Life*, 1997) is generally regarded as the continuer of E. Fraenkel's views – see comment by Harrison 2007a, 35.

60 See Lyne 1995, 1–8 and *passim*, Mayer 1995, Williams 1995, Armstrong 2010. In fact, in 1998 Horsfall noted (somewhat disappointedly) that 'serious scholars still write at length about Horace's life' (1998, 40). On the other hand, recent years have seen a heightened interest in biography in Classics: see Hanink/Fletcher 2016, 5–6. However, what is often underscored is the fictionality of the lives (*vitae*) of ancient poets (see e.g. Lefkowitz 2012) and of biographical traditions (Hanink/Fletcher 2016, 7).

61 See also Nisbet/Hubbard 1978, 201–5, Harrison 2007a, 24; 2014, 29.

same, what of committed and eloquent advocates of the idea that the only truth conveyed by a poem is exclusively its own self? How could they be disabused of the belief that the realism evoked by poetic composition is no more than the masterful mimicry of an imaginary and therefore historically non-existent experience?[62]

Whatever the case may be, the following questions automatically arise, even if they must ultimately go unanswered: does literary form predominate and even determine the content of poetry, or is it personality, temperament and experiences that lead creators to select the literary code that best corresponds to their personal identity? Why should we suppose that a late first century BCE Roman poet would have preferred to indulge in a series of imaginary literary exercises, rather than using verse and its generic conventions to express whatever really concerned him, his personal experiences and his individual concerns?[63]

4 Critiquing criticism

What I have noted so far as autobiographical material in Horace's poetry (at least in rhetorical terms) is certainly not unknown to critics who back the 'masks' or 'various personae' theory of the poet. However, what is as a rule stressed in basically intratextual approaches concerning one collection at a time are the inconsistencies regarding the image Horace gives of himself in different compositions; such inconsistencies are interpreted as markers of different poetic 'masks' or 'faces', rather than (sometimes self-confessed) fractures in a single personality which, at least rhetorically speaking, is clearly identified with the poet. But one truly noteworthy fact is that *Satires* 2.7 and *Epistles* 1.8, texts in which the 'poet' himself acknowledges his inner fragmentation as being characteristic of his personality, have either failed to attract any attention in the bibliography mentioned

62 See e.g. the concern raised by Freudenburg 2010, 283–4 on the poem in question: whether traces of historical truth can be seen in it ultimately depends on the reader.

63 The passages in *Serm.* 1.10.46–9; 2.1.28–34 are not necessarily revelatory of the poet's true motives in writing satiric poetry. However, according to R. Heinze, what led Horace to Lucilius, Archilochus and the Lesbian poets, who were pre-eminent writers of personal poetry, was his intense desire to speak about himself through his compositions (1972, 305). See also Schmidt 1993, 460, 462 (with a reference to Friedrich Leo), 464–5, Harrison 2014, 27. Indeed, in some of his lines 'Horace' makes explicit or implicit reference to his peevish, irascible character (*Serm.* 1.3.29; *Carm.* 3.9.22–3; *Epist.* 1.20.25) —anger is a pervasive emotion in satire (*Serm.* 2.1.44–6, Freudenburg 2005, 24–5) and iambic verse (*Epod.* 6)— added to which, in *Carm.* 1.16.22–5 the 'poet' makes mention of the violent passion that impelled him to compose in iambs.

earlier or, where they have, are not used to validate the basic position of the critical approach adopted.[64]

Why, then, has literary criticism insisted on the theory of masks and varying different personae for the poet, and not on the continuity and consistency in Horace's verse?[65] In the few remaining paragraphs below I shall make what I trust is understandably only a brief reference to the conditions that appear to have shaped the above tendency in the interpretation of Horatian verse (and more besides).

If we accept that we read and understand texts as our cultural identity suggests, then shifts and alterations over the course of time and from one era to the next appear inevitable.[66] Yet what brought about the change in the way Horace's personal poetry is read, ultimately leading to the imposition in recent times of a very different approach to that previously taken?

According to Roland Mayer (2003, 56), 'the use of the mask in modernist lyric' —meaning especially Ezra Pound and Fernando Pessoa— 'prompted critics during the past half century to reread personal forms of classical poetry in the belief that a similar persona or mask could be found in them.' In any case, it is evident that the problem of identity and more specifically the question of 'how to speak the truth about oneself' became uppermost in the thought of important thinkers in the course of the 20th century.[67] Perhaps even more than literature per se it was literary theory that directly or indirectly inspired critics to approach Horace's poetry (and that of others) from a new angle. By this I am referring to the theoretical models that gained ascendancy in the second half of the 20th century, and which initially proved highly fruitful, leading to the production of insightful and sensitive studies that determined the thinking of earlier critics and continue to do so to the present day.[68] In the main, the theories in question are New Criticism, structuralism, deconstructionism or post-structuralism, and new historicism.

64 See also the critical remark by Gilbert Highet 1974, 333 (based especially on *Serm.* 2.7 and *Epist.* 1.8): 'it is not the fictitious and ineffective "tensions" of a satirical *persona* that we see in Horace's satires, but the ethical contradictions of a real man'.

65 See e.g. Muecke 2007, 106–9, Holzberg 2008; 2009, 8 and *passim*, Schlegel 2010, 253–4, Möller 2014, 348–9 for some of the most recent approaches.

66 See Wright 1960, 5.

67 See Elliott 1982, 84 (with particular reference to Jean Paul Sartre's treatment of the question).

68 See Freudenburg 2005, 28. However, see also observations by Harrison 2014, 28 on the 'post-theoretical age'.

From the early-mid 1950s onwards, following in the footsteps of earlier critics inspired by New Criticism,[69] R.C. Elliott (*The Satirist and Society*, 1954; *The Power of Satire: Magic, Ritual, Art*, 1960), proposed that a distinction be drawn between the satirical poet as an individual with a concrete historical identity, and his rhetorical and literary role as society's lampooner, for which he coined the term 'persona'.[70] Alvin Kernan (*The Cankered Muse*, 1959; *The Plot of Satire*, 1965) drew on Elliott's ideas to discuss issues of rhetoric and style in English 17th and 18th century satirical poetry. As we have already pointed out,[71] Kernan's approach was then used by William Anderson to interpret compositions by Horace and Juvenal.

At the start of the following decade, the same line was taken by G.T. Wright (1960, 7–8), in his study *The Poet in the Poem*: 'Poetry, dramatic or lyric, does not present fragments of human experience, but formalized versions of it. The actions represented do not really take place; the persons, including the "I", do not exist outside the poem, or at least do not exist in the same way.' And further on: 'The frequent modern practice of making a clear distinction between a poet and his personae draws attention to the facts that art is formal and that a work of art — even a lyric poem— in which the poet is <...> "too exactly himself" is in danger of not being art at all.' These thoughts lead effortlessly on to the aphorism that 'There is no such thing as "I" ...; there are only specific men who may assume, among others, these particular formal roles.' (p. 15)[72]

Interpretive discourse grows more radical still in Roland Barthes' essay 'The Death of the Author' (1968): 'Writing is the destruction of every voice, of every point of origin. Writing is that neutral, composite, oblique space where our subject [i.e. the author] slips away, the negative where all identity is lost, starting with the very identity of the body writing.'[73] From that standpoint, poetry does not convey any 'truth' beyond that constructed by language itself, or, according to a related view, it conveys nothing beyond the meaning attributed by the reader on each occasion.[74]

69 An interesting discussion of the biographical approach to poetry commenced much earlier on, in the first half of the 20th century: see Highet 1974, 321–2.

70 See Elliott 1982, 3–18, Freudenburg 2005, 27.

71 On the relationship between the positions taken by A. Kernan and the views of W.S. Anderson, see here n. 3.

72 Wright's views closely resemble those previously expressed by Suzanne K. Langer in *Feeling and Form*, London 1953, 211, 256–7, cited by Robert Elliott (1982, 87–8 with n. 30). See also Clay 1998, 15 on the impact of Wayne Booth's *The Rhetoric of Fiction*, Chicago 1961.

73 Barthes 1977, 142.

74 Cf. Wright 1960, 17.

We are still in the 1960s, when Erving Goffman was formulating his views on the 'construction' of the 'face' as an 'image of self' via social structures and rules that govern in every situation the interaction of the individual with the social milieu, though without entirely determining individual behaviour (1967, 6–9, 12). Within such a theoretical framework, one can imagine poetry as performance by the poet, who adopts the face anticipated by the social and cultural rules in his or her environment – and consequently the rules of each poetic genre – which also meet the audience's expectations, in order to 'have, be in, or maintain face'. Thus the poet's 'face', his image may change from case to case, from genre to genre, as the person's face 'is something that is not lodged in or on his body, but rather something that is diffusely located in the flow of events in the encounter and becomes manifest only when these events are read ...' (p. 7).[75]

The issue of identity continued to preoccupy contemporary schools of criticism over subsequent years. For deconstructionism, which without rejecting anything of the above also contends that contrasts, diversity, chaos and disorder are what dominate both our microcosm and our macrocosm, identity does not constitute the hard core of individual existence, which develops through historical change but fundamentally remains unitary. Such an identity is treated as a traditional and outdated rhetorical construct.[76] 'Identities' are built via differences and never display unity.[77] This basic position sits well with new historicism, which likewise highlights the multiplicity and nuance of history, as well as the complexity of literary texts recording history, once again seeing very often a purely rhetorical construct at play.[78]

In the light of the above theories, the search for an artist's unitary and/or historical identity not only appears merely outdated, but is a pointless and ultimately impossible endeavour. Worse still, it risks giving the impression of a barely critical approach to poetry.

Yet what purpose might be served by the modernizing readings of Latin poetry based on the dominant theoretical trends we have mentioned? To start with, the interesting or even charming interpretation of poetic discourse and the creative understanding of it might be considered one gain. In the case of Horace, one could add the use of such theories in overcoming the interpretive difficulties that

---

75 Erving Goffman's theory was made use of by Ellen Oliensis (1998, 1, 3).

76 See Bourdieu 2000, 298.

77 See Hall 2000, 17. It is interesting to note that Robert Elliott (1982, xi–xii, 98 and *passim*), one of the proponents of the persona theory, came out against theoretical statements which 'attempt to abolish the notion of the self as conscious subject altogether'. See also the critical selection of relevant bibliography on autobiography by Gowers 2003, 56 n. 7.

78 See Parker 2011, 245–7.

mark out compositions where the poet attributes provocative behaviour and morals —perhaps just from a modern point of view— to himself (see e.g. *Serm.* 1.2.116–19).[79] Besides, the basic aim of the above approaches is apparently to arrive at a fresh, new view of ancient literature via highly sophisticated treatments, on the one hand so that antiquity can continue to exert charm, and on the other so that classical studies can find communication routes with other modern literatures, offering valuable ways out into the present.

Yet if the authenticity of the original is at stake, the price can occasionally be high —and I believe we can talk of authenticity, even if it is only artificial. The statement 'Do not ask me who I am and do not ask me to remain the same: that is the bureaucratic mentality, which keeps our papers in order' is not (and in spirit could not even be) part of Horatian poetic discourse —it belongs, as is well known, to Michel Foucault (1969, 28). Texts from Greek and Roman antiquity may well exert timeless charm, but historicity is a part of their identity —just as it is a part of every artwork. Antiquity has its own cultural precepts, which when all is said and done are not, in my view, determined by the subsequent or contemporary reader or spectator's perspective. Ancient literature reflects and assists in shaping specific cultural structures. Ultimately, it reflects social mechanisms favouring the normal experience of life as whole and unified —mechanisms which the birth and formation of individual and collective identity are not independent of.[80] And that is the reason why Horace projects the rift within himself as a painful problem —unless (having first admitted to a totally subversive disposition) we accept that he is always speaking ironically. If one wishes, therefore, to read Horace's personal poetry from the viewpoint of subsequent theories, one should at least own up to such an obvious anachronism, if not restrain it.[81]

Of course, the way one approaches literature is not simply a matter of taste, but ultimately of ideology. So if art (and in essence the creator) neither reflects reality nor affords any access to it, or both reflects multiple 'realities' and affords access to each of them —according to those theoretical models that advocate relativism, and deny the possibility of discovering any truth, or one 'truth' alone (in a triumphant revival of the old sophistic principle that 'man is the measure of all things')— then it neither possesses nor can it possess any specific, stable

79 See Freudenburg 2005, 29.

80 See Hall 2000, 17, who regards fragmented, cracked 'identity' as a product of 'late modern times'. Elliott (1982, 92) believes that 'it is impossible to locate precisely the historical point at which erosion of the idea of the unified, autonomous self definitively set in' (see also *ibid.*, 93–5).

81 See also Mayer 2003, 57, 78–9. Cf. Kirk Freudenberg's self-critical stance (2010, 273). Both Oliensis (1998, 1–15) and McNeill (2001, 142 n. 23) make clear reference to the methodological roots of their studies.

ideology,[82] even on issues of aesthetics and poetics,[83] unless it is an ideology of complexity, diversity, inconsistency or even chaos. Essentially, this is the triumph of agnosticism, which sooner or later leads to the inevitable result that anything can be said, provided that certain 'technical' conditions are met. It is interesting to conjecture precisely what those conditions might be, and by which criteria they are defined.[84]

5 Epilogue

In 1997 Alessandro Barchiesi wrote the following on the conflict between formalism and historicism: 'The polemic between formalist and historicist readers has long been exhausted, and the last Japanese snipers isolated in the jungle should have been informed of this by now.'[85] A little over ten years later, in 2009, Denis Feeney commented: ' ... despite the eloquent arguments presented by Barchiesi, ... in fact we can imagine a counter-factual scenario in which those snipers could have been hanging around in the jungle long enough to be dangerous in the next round of conflict.'[86] I hope what I have argued earlier does not create the impression that I belong to such a primitive, aggressive and savage group.

I would however acknowledge the value of the quotation by Fraenkel, with which I opened my chapter, and would simply add the following: if Horace was able to 'make use' of himself in his works, it was because he was a great poet. He thus managed to render individual subject matter universal: among other things he wrote about his own personal problems and his place in society. This he did as a creator who on the one hand sought recognition, but on the other worried about and laid claim to the right to his own individual world view, ethics and freedom, in a world of powerful conventions and dependencies, where the notion and function of life in the limelight kept changing, and the boundaries between

82 Kirk Freudenburg himself acknowledges that in drawing a distinction between the poet as a historical individual and his role as a satirist, formalist literary approaches to Roman satire are incapable of seeing the political dimension and function of the poetry in question (2005, 28–9).
83 See e.g. Zetzel 1980, 62–3, McNeill 2001, 61.
84 See e.g. Parker 2011, 245: ' ... it is a matter of saying that multiple things go, and that we will distinguish among those multiple things on the basis of what interests us ... and on the basis of whether we can put together an interesting argument to back up our interpretation.' See also Fowler 1994, 254.
85 Barchiesi 2001, 147.
86 Feeney 2009, 38 n. 58. See further Hinds 2010.

public and private were blurred. In his verse, his concern over the creation and acceptance of poetry is recorded with particular force: not as an individual, personal struggle, but as a phenomenon with social dimensions and implications.[87] Horace thus managed to achieve what Virginia Woolf regarded as the ultimate challenge for an author: '... never to be yourself and yet always.'[88]

Abbreviations

OLD: Glare, P.G.W. (1968–82), *Oxford Latin Dictionary*, edited by P.G.W. Glare, Oxford.

Bibliography

Abel, K.H. (1969), 'Horaz auf der Suche nach dem wahren Selbst. Ein Vortrag', *A&A* 15, 29–46.
Anderson, W.S. (1982), *Essays on Roman Satire*, Princeton, NJ.
Armstrong, D. (2010), 'The Biographical and Social Foundations of Horace's Poetic Voice', in: Davis (2010), 7–33.
Barchiesi, A. (2001), *Speaking Volumes. Narrative and Intertext in Ovid and Other Latin Poets. Edited and Translated by M. Fox and S. Marchesi*, London.
Barthes, R. (1977), 'The Death of the Author', in: R. Barthes, *Image – Music – Text. Essays Selected and Translated by Stephen Heath*, New York, 142–8 (originally published 1968).
Becker, C. (1963), *Das Spätwerk des Horaz*, Göttingen.
Bourdieu, P. (2000), 'The Biographical Illusion', in: Gay/Evans/Redman (2000), 297–303 (originally published 1986).
Brink, C.O. (1982), *Horace on Poetry. Epistles Book II: The Letters to Augustus and Florus*, Cambridge.
Citroni, M. (1993), 'L'autobiografia nella satira e nell' epigramma latino', in: Gr. Arrighetti/Fr. Montanari (eds.), *La componente autobiografica nella poesia greca e latina fra realtà e artificio letterario, Atti del convegno Pisa, 16–17 maggio 1991*, Pisa, 275–92.
Clay, D. (1998), 'The Theory of the Literary Persona in Antiquity', *MD* 40, 9–40.
Davis, Gr. (1991), *Polyhymnia. The Rhetoric of Horatian Lyric Discourse*, Berkeley *et al.*
Davis, Gr. (2010), *A Companion to Horace*, Malden MA/Oxford.
Elliott, R.C. (1982), *The Literary Persona*, Chicago/London.
Estévez, V.A. (1982), '*Quem tu, Melpomene*: The Poet's Lowered Voice (C.iv 3)', *Emerita* 50, 279–300.
Feeney, D. (2009), 'Becoming an Authority: Horace on His Own Reception', in: L.B.T. Houghton/M. Wyke (eds.), *Perceptions of Horace. A Roman Poet and His Readers*, Cambridge, 16–38.
Fletcher, R./Hanink, J. (eds.) (2016), *Creative Lives in Classical Antiquity. Poets, Artists and Biography*, Cambridge.
Foucault, M. (1969), *L' archéologie du savoir*, Paris.

87 See also Tsitsiou-Chelidoni 2013.
88 Woolf 1925, 222.

Fowler, D. (1994), 'Postmodernism, Romantic Irony, and Classical Closure', in: I.J.F. De Jong/J.P. Sullivan (eds.), *Modern Critical Theory and Classical Literature*, Leiden *et al.*, 231–56.
Fraenkel, E. (1957), *Horace*, Oxford.
Freudenburg, K. (1993), *The Walking Muse. Horace on the Theory of Satire*, Princeton, NJ.
Freudenburg, K. (2005), 'Introduction: Roman Satire', in: K. Freudenburg (ed.), *The Cambridge Companion to Roman Satire*, Cambridge, 1–30.
Freudenburg, K. (2010), '*Horatius Anceps:* Persona and Self-revelation in Satire and Song', in: Davis (2010), 271–90.
Gay, P. du/Evans, J./Redman, P. (eds.) (2000), *Identity: A Reader*, London *et al.*
Goffman, E. (1967), *Interaction Ritual. Essays on Face-to-Face Behavior*, New York.
Gold, B. (1992), 'Openings in Horace's *Satires* and *Odes*: Poet, Patron, and Audience', *YCS* 29, 161–185.
Gowers, E. (2003), 'Fragments of Autobiography in Horace *Satires* I', *ClAnt* 22, 55–91.
Gowers, E. (2012), *Horace. Satires Book I*, Cambridge.
Graziosi, B. (2016), 'Close Encounters with the Ancient Poets', in: Fletcher/Hanink (2016), 51–74.
Gusdorf, G. (1980), 'Conditions and Limits of Autobiography', in: J. Olney (ed.), *Autobiography. Essays Theoretical and Critical*, Princeton, NJ, 28–48.
Hall, S. (2000), 'Who Needs 'Identity'?', in: Gay/Evans/Redman (2000), 15–30 (originally published 1996).
Hanink, J./Fletcher, R. (2016), 'Orientation: What we Mean by "Creative Lives"', in: Fletcher/Hanink (2016), 3–28.
Harrison, S.J. (ed.) (1995), *Homage to Horace: A Bimillenary Celebration*, Oxford.
Harrison, S.J. (ed.) (2007), *The Cambridge Companion to Horace*, Cambridge.
Harrison, S.J. (2007a), 'Horatian Self-representations', in: Harrison (2007), 22–35.
Harrison, S.J. (2007b), 'Town and Country', in: Harrison (2007), 235–47.
Harrison, S.J. (2014), *Horace*, Cambridge, *Greece and Rome*. New Surveys in the Classics 42.
Harrison, S.J. (2017), *Horace. Odes Book II*, Cambridge.
Heinze, R. (1972), 'Horazens Buch der Briefe', in: E. Burck (ed.), *Vom Geist des Römertums. Ausgewählte Aufsätze*, 4., durchges. Auflage, Stuttgart, 295–307 (originally published 1919).
Hendrickson, G.L. (1900), 'Horace, *Serm.* 1.4: A Protest and a Programme', *AJPh* 21, 121–142.
Hendrickson, G.L. (1935), 'Vox Vatis Horati', *CJ* 31, 189–200.
Highet, G. (1974), 'Masks and Faces in Satire', *Hermes* 102, 321–37.
Hinds, St. (2010), 'Between Formalism and Historicism', in: A. Barchiesi/W. Scheidel (eds.), *The Oxford Handbook of Roman Studies*, Oxford, 369–85.
Holzberg, N. (2008), 'A Sensitive, Even Weak and Feeble Disposition? C. Valgius Rufus and His Elegiac Ego', in: Al. Arweiler/M. Möller (eds.), *Vom Selbst-Verständnis in Antike und Neuzeit (Notions of the Self in Antiquity and Beyond)*, Berlin/New York, 21–32.
Holzberg, N. (2009), *Horaz: Dichter und Werk*, München.
Horsfall, N.M. (1998), 'The First Person Singular in Horace's *Carmina*', in: P.E. Knox/C. Foss (eds.), *Style and Tradition. Studies in Honor of Wendell Clausen*, Stuttgart, 40–54.
Kiessling, A./Heinze, R. (1921), *Q. Horatius Flaccus. Erklärt von A. Kiessling*. Zweiter Teil: *Satiren. Fünfte Auflage. Besorgt von R. Heinze*, Berlin.
Kiessling, A./Heinze, R. (1898), *Q. Horatius Flaccus. Erklärt von A. Kiessling*. Dritter Teil: *Briefe. Zweite Auflage. Besorgt von R. Heinze*, Berlin.
Knoche, U. (1958), 'Erlebnis und dichterischer Ausdruck in der lateinischen Poesie', *Gymnasium* 65, 146–65.
Lejay, P. (1911), *Oeuvres d' Horace. Satires*, Paris.

Lefkowitz, M. (2012), *The Lives of the Greek Poets*, 2nd ed., London.
Lyne, R.O.A.M. (1995), *Horace: Behind the Public Poetry*, New Haven/London.
Mayer, R.G. (1994), *Horace. Epistles Book I*, Cambridge.
Mayer, R.G. (1995), 'Horace's *Moyen de Parvenir*', in: Harrison (1995), 279–95.
Mayer, R.G. (2003), 'Persona<l> Problems. The Literary Persona in Antiquity Revisited', *MD* 50, 55–80.
McNeill, R.L.B. (2001), *Horace. Image, Identity, and Audience*, Baltimore/London.
Möller, M. (2014), 'Neues aus der Alten Welt (I). Nähe und Distanz: Antike und moderne Autobiografie', *Merkur* 68, 344–50.
Muecke, F. (2007), 'The *Satires*', in: Harrison (2007), 105–20.
Niedermeier, L. (1919), *Untersuchungen über die antike poetische Autobiographie*, München.
Nisbet, R.G.M. (2007), 'Horace: Life and Chronology', in: Harrison (2007), 7–21.
Nisbet, R.G.M./Hubbard, M. (1970), *A Commentary on Horace: Odes Book I*, Oxford.
Nisbet, R.G.M./Hubbard, M. (1978), *A Commentary on Horace: Odes Book II*, Oxford.
Nisbet, R.G.M./Rudd, N. (2004), *A Commentary on Horace: Odes Book III*, Oxford.
Oliensis, E. (1998), *Horace and the Rhetoric of Authority*, Cambridge.
Otto, A. (1890), *Die Sprichwörter und sprichwörtlichen Redensarten der Römer*, Leipzig.
Parker, R.D. (2011), *How to Interpret Literature. Critical Theory for Literary and Cultural Studies*, 2nd ed., New York/Oxford.
Pöschl, V. (1985), 'Die Suche nach der Individualität des Dichters am Beispiel von Virgil und Horaz', in: D. Bremer/A. Patzer (eds.), *Wissenschaft und Existenz. Ein interdisziplinäres Symposium*, Würzburg, 35–46.
Schlegel, C. (2010), 'Horace and the Satirist's Mask: Shadowboxing with Lucilius', in: Davis (2010), 253–70.
Schmidt, E.A. (1993), 'Öffentliches und privates Ich. Zur Funktion frühgriechischen und alexandrinisch-neoterischen Epochenstils in Horazens Iambik', in: G.W. Most/H. Petersmann/A.M. Ritter (eds.), *Philanthropia και Eusebeia*. Festschrift für Albrecht Dihle zum 70. Geburtstag, Göttingen, 454–67.
Shackleton Bailey, D.R. (ed.) (1991), *Q. Horati Flacci Opera*, 2nd ed., Stuttgart.
Troxler-Keller, Ir. (1964), *Die Dichterlandschaft des Horaz*, Heidelberg.
Tsitsiou-Chelidoni, Chr. (2012), 'Ορατίου *Επιστολή* 1.20. Στα ίχνη μιας πρώιμης "Ποιητικής της Πρόσληψης"', in: D.Z. Nikitas (ed.), *Laus et Gratia. In memoriam Κωνσταντίνου Γρόλλιου*, Thessaloniki, 215–55.
Tsitsiou-Chelidoni, Chr. (2013), 'Horace on the Role of the Poetry's Audience in the Literary Process', *TC* 5, 341–75.
Wili, W. (1948), *Horaz und die Augusteische Kultur*, Basel.
Williams, G. (1968), *Tradition and Originality in Roman Poetry*, Oxford.
Williams, G. (1995), '*Libertino Patre Natus*: True or False?', in: Harrison (1995), 296–313.
Woolf, V. (1925), 'The Modern Essay', in: V. Woolf, *The Common Reader. First Series*, New York, 216–27.
Wright, G.T. (1960), *The Poet in the Poem. The Personae of Eliot, Yeats, and Pound*, Berkeley/Los Angeles.
Zetzel, J.E.G. (1980), 'Horace's *Liber Sermonum*. The Structure of Ambiguity', *Arethusa* 13, 59–77.

Wolfgang Kofler

The Whole and its Parts: Interactions of Writing and Reading Strategies in Horace's *Carmina* 2.4 and 2.8

The connection may not always be explicitly stated, but in the study of literature questions concerning the relationship between the whole and its parts, as well as the relationships between the parts themselves, are hardly different from questions raised by reader-response theory. Overstating my point, one could argue that reader-response theory has just about made possible the recent advances made in the study of intratextual phenomena. That is because the question of how parts of a text relate to each other and are able to form a whole cannot be addressed without taking into account the reader's response: in the end, it is the act of reading which identifies parts of a given text, relates them to each other, and generates what we may call the 'meaning' of a text. This becomes even more obvious if we turn to other concepts developed in the wake of reader-response theory, for example the differentiation between an initial, so-called 'heuristic' reading and a subsequent 'hermeneutic' one.[1] These two acts (or phases) of reading significantly differ, amongst other aspects, in that in the latter the reader is not bound to follow the linear presentation of the text, but is free to read it in blocks, the sequence of which is flexible and often determined by loose thematic associations. One should pay attention to the fact that this division of a text into blocks, performed during a hermeneutic reading, forms the basis of any intratextual analysis.

Of course reader-response theory did not invent intratextuality. In some sense, intratextuality is, on the contrary, much older than reader-response theory: it is already implied in the notion of the hermeneutic circle as set out by the classical philologist Friedrich Ast. In his 1808 book, *Grundlinien der Grammatik, Hermeneutik und Kritik*, he writes:

> Now, it seems as if we can recognize the universal spirit of classical antiquity only by its manifestations in the works of the authors, but the identification of these manifestations in turn presupposes the recognition of that universal spirit. But since we can only perceive one after the other, but never the whole at one and the same time, is an identification of a single instance even possible, given that such an identification presupposes the recognition of the whole? This circle—i.e. that I can only identify a, b, c etc. by means of A, but A in turn only

1 I use these terms in accordance with Riffaterre 1978, 1–22, esp. 4–6.

https://doi.org/10.1515/9783110611021-012

> by means of a, b, c etc.—is irresolvable if we think of A and a, b, c as opposites which entail and presuppose each other, and do not recognize their unity, so that A does not follow from, or is produced by, a, b, c etc. In truth, this unity rather precedes them and permeates them all in the same way, so that a, b, c are nothing other than individual representations of the one A. a, b, c are thus already laid out in A; these members are themselves the individual instances of the one A, therefore A already resides in each one of them, and there is no need to go through the entire, infinite list of individual instances to find their unity.[2]

The 'whole' Ast is referring to here is the 'universal spirit of classical antiquity', in particular the 'works of the authors'. But it did not take long for Ast's circle to be applied to the text itself, and the movement he described soon worked as an instrument to tie together the work and its parts.

Judging from a historical perspective on literary theory, it is obvious that hermeneutics focuses strongly on the reader. But the author also plays an important part. As it were, a differentiation between the author and the reader is always methodically difficult, and not always useful. There are various reasons for this, but in particular a text's author is always also its first reader. According to reader-response theory, composing a text mainly consists in the effort of directing the reader's response, and the author continuously tests his success by reading the text himself.

It is precisely this constant shift between the author's and the reader's perspectives which I wish to illustrate in the following pages, by analysing two love poems from the second book of Horace's *Carmina*. In particular, I wish to inquire into the strategies the author employs to guide the reader through the text, to make him relate the various textual parts to each other correctly, and so produce the intended 'meaning'.

---

2 Ast 1808, 179–80: 'Wenn wir nun aber den Geist des gesammten Alterthums nur durch seine Offenbarungen in den Werken der Schriftsteller erkennen können, diese aber selbst wieder die Erkenntniß des universellen Geistes voraussetzen, wie ist es möglich, da wir immer nur das eine nach dem anderen, nicht aber das Ganze zu gleicher Zeit auffassen können, das Einzelne zu erkennen, da dieses die Erkenntniß des Ganzen voraussetzt? Der Zirkel, daß ich a, b, c u.s.w. nur durch A erkennen kann, aber dieses A selbst wieder nur durch a, b, c u.s.f., ist unauflöslich, wenn beide A und a, b, c als Gegensätze gedacht werden, die sich wechselseitig bedingen und voraussetzen, nicht aber ihre Einheit anerkannt wird, so daß A nicht erst aus a, b, c u.s.f. hervorgeht und durch sie gebildet wird, sondern ihnen selbst vorausgeht, sie alle auf gleiche Weise durchdringt, a, b, c also nichts anderes, als individuelle Darstellungen des Einen A sind. In A liegen dann auf ursprüngliche Weise schon a, b, c; diese Glieder selbst sind die einzelnen Entfaltungen des Einen A, also liegt in jedem auf besondere Weise schon A, und ich brauche nicht erst die ganze unendliche Reihe der Einzelnheiten zu durchlaufen, um ihre Einheit zu finden'. Unless indicated otherwise, the English translations in this article are by myself and Timothy King, who has kindly assisted me in preparing the English version of this article.

Let us turn to the first poem, 2.4, in which the poet addresses a certain Xanthias of Phocis, who has apparently fallen in love with a slave-girl, but is too ashamed to admit it.[3] According to the poet, Xanthias' bashfulness is unwarranted, seeing that even great mythological heroes have fallen in love with slave-girls. The first three stanzas read:

Ne sit ancillae tibi amor pudori,
Xanthia Phoceu: prius insolentem
serva Briseis niueo colore
  mouit Achillem;

mouit Aiacem Telamone natum
forma captiuae dominum Tecmessae;
arsit Atrides medio in triumpho
  uirgine rapta,

barbarae postquam cecidere turmae
Thessalo uictore et ademptus Hector
tradidit fessis leuiora tolli
  Pergama Grais.[4]

Phocian Xanthias, don't be ashamed of love
for your serving-girl. Once before, Briseis
the Trojan slave with her snow-white skin stirred
  angry Achilles:

and captive Tecmessa's loveliness troubled
her master Ajax, the son of Telamon:
and Agamemnon, in his mid-triumph, burned
  for a stolen girl,

while the barbarian armies, defeated
in Greek victory, and the loss of Hector,
handed Troy to the weary Thessalians,
  an easier prey.[5]

In the following two stanzas the poet suggests that Phyllis—such is the girl's name—may even come from a rich family background. Her noble character—she is described as *fidelis* (18), 'true, faithful', and *lucro auersa* (19), 'opposed to making profit' (a reference to the proverbial avarice of courtesans)—certainly points

3 Recent interpretations of this poem may be found in Sutherland 2002, 91–101, Johnson 2004, 147–53, Nadeau 2008, 189–97 and Kovacs 2016.
4 For the Latin, I use Shackleton Bailey's text.
5 For English translations of Horace, I use Kline 2003.

to a high born lady. The poem then quickly draws to an end, and the persona of the poet himself unexpectedly steps onto the scene (21–4).

> Bracchia et uultum teretesque suras
> integer laudo: fuge suspicari
> cuius octauum trepidauit aetas
> claudere lustrum.

> I'm unbiased in praising her arms and face,
> and shapely ankles: reject all suspicion
> of one whose swiftly vanishing life has known
> its fortieth year.

At first sight, these lines appear to add a kind and friendly twist to the end of the poem, which includes an unobtrusive point: the speaker has apparently become aware of his own rather too generous praise of Phyllis, and fears Xanthias may misinterpret his words. So the poet assures his friend that he has no inappropriate interest in the girl. There is no cause for concern. He is too old for anything like that anyway.

Kießling/Heinze have already noted correctly that the poem is a 'lustiger Protrepticus', instructing Xanthias to indulge in love, and that the final statement too is designed to motivate him to finally admit to his feelings. For this purpose, the poet subtly indicates that he himself might have taken a fancy to the girl, if only he were still young.[6] However, Kießling/Heinze do not believe Horace represents any real danger: they claim that the final strophe resumes the light-hearted tone of the preceding stanzas, and that the comical effect is increased by the fact that Phyllis had been called *fidelis* earlier in line 18.[7]

Other classicists disagree. Nisbet/Hubbard, for example, are reluctant to take the speaker and the reference to his age at face value, and argue for their sceptical attitude by pointing to the rather idiosyncratic appearance of the topos underlying the final lines, the *renuntiatio amoris*. Their claim is that the topos here is rather half-hearted: '[...], Horace's modest excuses are not here intended to be convincing'.[8] Kovacs too has doubts about whether a 40-year-old should be immune to erotic attractions, and moreover raises the question as to where the poet has obtained the detailed information given in lines 18–19, about the girl's non-physical qualities: 'how, exactly, can he be sure that Phyllis is faithful to Xanthias and that she is above considerations of gain? Did he attempt to seduce her, with the

6 Kießling/Heinze [13]1968, 176–7.
7 Kießling/Heinze [13]1968, 179.
8 Nisbet/Hubbard 1978, 68.

help of expensive gifts?'[9] Harrison also regards Horace's *renuntiatio* as insincere, and even gives three reasons: (1) The stanza in question is a direct quotation from the first half of an epigram by Philodemus (*AP* 11.41 = 4 Sider), in the second half of which the speaker affirms that he can still be tempted by erotic desires *despite* his advanced age.[10] (2) Throughout the *Odes*, there can be observed a general 'tendency [...] to conclude with the poet's longing'. (3) Readers of the *Odes* are 'familiar with renunciations of love owing to age which are then promptly reversed (cf. e.g. 3.26.1–4, 4.1.1–8)'.[11]

Now, I believe all these reservations are right and proper. I too distrust Horace. However, I distrust him not only for the reasons mentioned above but also because the mythological exempla he lists at the beginning of his poem have certain implications. These implications can be understood if one puts into practice, as I wish to do now, the idea of hermeneutic reading mentioned earlier. It is certainly true that Achilles and Briseis represent a classic example of a love affair between a slave-girl and her master, and they rightfully claim first place in the catalogue.[12] But on the other hand—as we all know—Briseis does not only arouse Achilles' affections but also those of another man, moreover one of his allies, and one who eventually even takes her away from him. This man—Agamemnon—is even explicitly mentioned three lines later—admittedly in a different context, as the 'lover' of Cassandra, but this reference certainly encourages the reader to reflect on the ignoble part Agamemnon played in the quarrel over Briseis. If we complete the story of Briseis for ourselves, then not only does it present an example of a famous mythological hero getting involved with a slave-girl, but it also confirms the suspicion Horace first voices, and then downplays, at the end of the poem—that he himself may have cast an eye on the mysterious lady. What is more, the reference to Agamemnon in particular displays a remarkably subtle and ironic taunt, in that it invalidates the very argument the poet is about to employ to calm Xanthias down: Agamemnon *is* of an advanced age, and must be, given that his daughter Iphigenia had already reached a marriageable age ten years before the present conflict ensued. In any case, in more than one version of

9 Kovacs 2016, 869–870. Nadeau 2008, 189–97 takes this even further and presumes, albeit failing to provide convincing arguments from the text, that Phyllis had had a liaison with the speaker, but was later snatched away by Xanthias.

10 Harrison 2017, 75–6; for the intertextual references to this epigram cf. also Höschele 2009, 83 and 2011, 29.

11 Harrison 2017, 81.

12 This is all the more so since we can note another analogy: as suggested by Johnson 2004, 150, Xanthias points to the addressees' blonde hair, also the hair colour traditionally ascribed to Achilles since Homer (cf. *Il.* 1.197, P.*N.* 3.41).

the Troy myth the quarrel between Achilles and Agamemnon takes on the shape of a generational conflict.

In this context, it is imperative to realise that the story of Briseis and Agamemnon is not a marginal issue in the myth of Troy, but that this event forms the very starting point of the storyline of the *Iliad*, the work of literature which we associate more than any other with the struggle for the city on the Scamander. There, Agamemnon's move against Briseis entails consequences on two levels. As mentioned just before, at first on the level of plot: because Agamemnon takes Briseis into his tent, Achilles goes on strike. But on a second level Agamemnon's misdeed triggers off the *Iliad* itself. In other words: Agamemnon's injustice has spectacular consequences for the history of literature. So if somebody—and especially a poet—puts the Briseis episode on the table, one should beware and pay particularly close attention to possible implications.

This analysis of *Carmen* 2.4 should act as an example of how the meaning of a text can change if one reinterprets the relationship between two of its constituent parts. The following example works in a similar way, but with one difference: here the relationship between the various parts is not direct, but works via an ancillary text, so that we are dealing with a case where intertextuality and intratextuality interact with each other. Or, to be more precise, and at the same time more paradoxical: intertextuality here generates intratextuality.

The poem I have in mind is 2.8. Conspicuously, it is of equal length, the same metre, and found only four poems after the ode to Xanthias. The addressee is a lady called Barine:[13]

> Ulla si iuris tibi peierati
> poena, Barine, nocuisset umquam,
> dente si nigro fieres uel uno[14]
>   turpior ungui,
>
> crederem; sed tu simul obligasti
> perfidum uotis caput, enitescis
> pulchrior multo iuuenumque prodis
>   publica cura.
>
> If any punishment ever visited
> you, Barine, for all your perjuries, if you
> were ever harmed at all by a darkened tooth,
>   a spoilt fingernail,

13 Some recent publications concerned with this poem are Sutherland 2002, 108–13, Nadeau 2008, 206–14 and Spelman 2014.

14 Shackleton Bailey, following Usener's conjecture, prints *albo*.

I'd trust you. But no sooner have you bound your
faithless soul by promises, than you appear
much lovelier, and shine out, as every one's
dearest young thing.

The situation this poem is based on clearly revolves around a promise made to the author by Barine, one which he wishes he could trust, but, given his past experiences with the lady, he simply cannot do so. It seems as if the gods have failed to punish her lies and broken oaths, but have let her escape scot-free. Even worse: the more shamelessly Barine has behaved, the more beautiful and desirable she has become. It is this last point the poet expands upon in the remaining four stanzas: in her case, dishonesty evidently has its uses. Together with her accomplices Venus and Amor she has become a master of deceit, and so has perfected the art of luring even more lovers into her house. Therefore, the poet has no reason to believe she has changed for the better. Quite the opposite: all circumstances indicate that she will continue with her licentious behaviour, seeing that she can even rely on divine protection.

The aesthetic appeal of many of Horace's poems lies in the challenge they present to the reader, who has to reconstruct step by step the dramatic situation the poem presupposes. The reader is enabled to do so by following various, more-or-less evident hints the author has placed into his poem. This kind of decoding of context is familiar to us, mainly from epigram: in a seminal article, Peter Bing has termed this strategy 'Ergänzungsspiel' ('the supplementing game').[15] We have already played this game with our Horatian poem, and have noticed that the speaker is facing an unfaithful lady, who has said something he is reluctant to believe. Now, useful and interesting as this information may be, if we are honest, we really want to know more—especially: what exactly did Barine promise? Porphyrio, participating in our supplementing game as far back as the 3rd century, appears to be in the know and comments on the first line:

> Scaenicum principium. Intellegendum enim aliquos sermones praecessisse, quibus Varine [sic!] haec noctem sui iure iurando interposito repromiserit; dein postquam fefellerit, tum in haec uerba hunc erupisse.

> A beginning as in a comedy. It is to be understood that some talks have already gone before, talks in which Barine, repeatedly and by oath, promised him a night with her; having broken her promise once again, he angrily burst out into these words.

---

15 Bing 1995. Cf. also my remarks in Kofler (forthcoming).

I believe Porphyrio's reconstruction of the situation to be mistaken in two points. First, he believes the persona is speaking in a fit of anger, having noticed that Barine has just been cheating on him once again. If this were true, *crederem* in line 5, which clearly refers to a statement of Barine and not to any action of hers, would be misplaced. But this observation is less important than my second one. Porphyrio actually believes he has a definite answer to the question of what it was that the lady promised: a night of love-making. Now, this is a very particular promise indeed, and the idea that Barine did make such a vow is certainly possible. But if we are honest, we can find no indications in the text which warrant such an assumption.

I therefore wish to pursue a different path. I believe the key to unlocking Barine's promise can be found in the final stanza, where the poet recapitulates the awesome power the lady has received at the hands of the gods in spite of her numerous transgressions (21–4).

> Te suis matres metuunt iuuencis,
> te senes parci miseraeque nuper
> uirgines nuptae, tua ne retardet
>   aura maritos.

> All the mothers fear you, because of their sons,
> and the thrifty old fathers, and wretched brides,
> who once were virgins, in case your radiance
>   makes husbands linger.

It has long been noticed that this stanza echoes lines 51–5 of Catullus 61—one of his famous marriage poems (a continuous line indicates a direct verbal borrowing; a dashed line indicates semantic correspondence).

> Te [sc. Hymenaee] suis tremulus parens
> inuocat, tibi uirgines
> zonula soluunt sinus,
> te timens cupida nouos
>   captat aure maritus.

> You her trembling father
> invokes: for you
> the virgin belt's untied:
> for you the bridegroom waits,
>   fearful with new desire.[16]

16 Transl. Kline 2003.

Especially conspicuous is the correspondence between the anaphorae *te/te/tua* and *te/tibi/te*, the appearance of the *uirgines* in both places, and the semantically different but very similarly sounding junctures *aura maritos* and *aure maritus* at the end. The exact significance of these parallels has long eluded scholars, and comments on the passage have been, even though often correct, ultimately superficial.[17] To quote Nisbet/Hubbard as an example: '[H]e wittingly transfers the anxiety from the young husband to the old fathers and the newly married *virgines*'.[18] Thankfully, some recent and very useful remarks have drawn attention to the fact that this poem evidently represents a parody of a traditionally phrased wedding poem and its typical praise of the wedding god and the bridal couple, which is here applied to a girl of dubious reputation.[19]

But I believe there is more to this intertextual allusion,[20] and nothing less than the answer to the question raised earlier: why should we not assume that Barine, having repeatedly betrayed the speaker, has finally promised to remain faithful, or even to marry him?[21] Now, a first concern may be raised about the legality of a marriage between a free Roman citizen and a *hetaera*, for a *hetaera* is what many critics believe her to be. But at close inspection this concern turns out to be invalid, since such marriages were only prohibited by the *Lex Iulia de maritandis ordinibus*, carried in 18 B.C.,[22] and so after the publication of the first three books of *Odes*. But it isn't even necessary to argue from the law. Judging from Latin elegy, we find that the *puellae* of the Roman poets do not correspond to a type of woman we could expect to meet in a real social setting. Ladies like Cynthia, Delia and Corinna rather combine and incorporate various profiles of women from all steps of the social ladder.[23] For this reason it is never entirely clear whether we are dealing with *hetaerae* or unfaithful married women. Their

17 The first to discuss this parallel in more detail is Ensor 1902, 108–10.

18 Nisbet/Hubbard 1978, 132.

19 Cf. e.g. Holzberg 2009, 140–1 and Putnam 2006, 128–31. If we follow Spelman 2014, esp. 26, the intertextual play is further enhanced by yet another subtext, seeing that Horace also alludes to Alcman 3.61–74 *PMGF*. This fragment formed part of a *partheneion* and *partheneia* were in fact closely connected with the theme of marriage.

20 Another interpretation, which takes this point further, is offered by Ancona 2005. However, her approach is entirely different from mine, and raises the question as to how these two passages reflect different positions about the interplay of marriage, gender and power.

21 Cf. also Putnam 2006, 131 and Nadeau 2008, 206–14, who, however, suggest Barine has only promised faithfulness and not marriage.

22 On this issue cf. Kaser [2]1971, 319 and Mette-Dittmann 1991, 142–6.

23 Cf. Konstan 1994, 150–9, esp. 157–8 and Nadeau 2008, 212–14.

relationship to the poet too can be many-sided, and can occasionally take on the appearance of marriage.

So Barine could indeed have brought up the idea of marriage. The thought is appealing not only because it makes the reference to Catullus act as a key to unlocking the underlying dramatic situation and to provide the puzzled and anxious reader with information about the mysterious promise, but there is more: In order to grasp this point, we need to remember that the poem actually is a *rejection* of Barine's request.

If Barine did indeed commit to everlasting love and has proposed marriage, then the words with which the speaker rejects this proposal are perfectly well chosen, culminating as they do in a quotation which takes one of the most famous wedding songs of Roman literature out of its context and turns it on its head. In other words: The poet rejects Barine's desire for marriage by cynically deconstructing Catullus' wedding song.[24]

But let us return to our initial question: How does the intertextual reference to Catullus affect the meaning of the whole text? The answer is twofold. First, Catullus provides the key for solving the mystery of the request, and so aids us to correctly define the situation on which this text is based. And secondly, the intertextual play with the epithalamium modifies the image of the protagonist, which the reader has acquired during his first heuristic reading. The man has certainly grown in character. Of course he appears as a rather tough person from the outset, seeing that he stands up against Barine, a woman at whose feet other men fall like dominoes. But the rejection of marriage commands even greater respect. What is more: the sophisticated way by which he asserts himself in the face of this vicious girl makes an even deeper impression on the reader. To him he appears as the able and savvy *poeta doctus*, who can at least rely on the love of his audience, if not on the love of Barine. This is certainly a kind of readjustment similar to the one we have found in poem 2.4, where the speaker at first glance presents himself as an innocent admirer of his friend's mistress. But judging from a precise analysis of the textual relationship between the poem's beginning and its end, it emerges that Xanthias does have a cause for concern after all. For if the poet proves to be as skilful in the art of erotic seduction as he is in the practice of

24 In this context one ought to point out that the aforementioned ambiguities concerning a *puella*'s social status are also a common feature in Catullus. The strategy Catullus employs to this purpose—making the relationship appear as a marriage through use of the appropriate language—can even be said to be one of his trademarks. The literary game of hide-and-seek which Horace plays with Barine's promise is therefore *per se* very reminiscent of Catullus. The fact that an intertextual allusion to Catullus should provide the necessary hint to resolve this game is therefore no surprise.

literary allusion, Xanthias truly is in danger of becoming a second Achilles, and of losing his beloved Phyllis.

Bibliography

Ancona, R. (2005), '(Un)constrained Male Desire: An Intertextual Reading of Horace Odes 2.8 and Catullus Poem 61', in: R. Ancona/E. Greene (eds.), *Gendered Dynamics in Latin Love Poetry*, Baltimore, 41–60.

Bing, P. (1995), 'Ergänzungsspiel in the Epigrams of Callimachus', *Antike und Abendland* 41, 115–31.

Ensor, E. (1902), 'Notes on the Odes of Horace', *Hermathena* 12, 105–10.

Harrison, S. (2017) (ed./comm.), *Horace. Odes, Book II* = Cambridge Greek and Latin Classics, Cambridge.

Holzberg, N. (2009), *Horaz. Dichter und Werk*, München.

Höschele, R. (2009), 'Epigrammatizing Lyric: Generic Hybridity in Horace's Odes', in: M.H. Rocha Pereira/J. Ribeiro Ferreira/F. de Oliveira (eds.), *Horácio e a sua perenidade*, Coimbra, 71–88.

Höschele, R. (2011), 'Inscribing Epigrammatists' Names: Meleager in Propertius and Philodemus in Ho-race', in: A. Keith (ed.), *Latin Elegy and Hellenistic Epigram*, Cambridge, 19–31.

Johnson, T.S. (2004), *A Symposion of Praise: Horace Returns to Lyric in Odes IV*, Madison.

Kaser, M. ([2]1971), *Das römische Privatrecht*. Vol. 1: *Das altrömische, das vorklassische und klassische Recht* = Handbuch der Altertumwissenschaft 10.3.3.1, München.

Kießling, A./Heinze, R. ([13]1968), *Q. Horatius Flaccus*. Vol. 1: *Oden und Epoden*, Dublin/Zürich.

Kline, A.S. (2003) (transl.), *Horace (Quintus Horatius Flaccus). The Odes, sine loco*, available online at https://www.poetryintranslation.com/klineashorace.php, 02.04.2018.

Kline, A.S. (2007) (transl.), *The Poems. Catullus, sine loco*, available online at: https://www.poetryintranslation.com/klineascatullus.php, 31.03.2018.

Kofler, W. (forthcoming), 'Briseis an Achill. Rezeptionsästhetische und motivgeschichtliche Überlegungen zu Ovids drittem Heroidenbrief und Joseph Reschs Agamemnon suimet victor', in: M. Schauer/J. Zenk (eds.), *Text, Kontext, Klartext. Festschrift fur Niklas Holzberg zum 70. Geburtstag* = Göttinger Forum für Altertumswissenschaft, Beihefte N.F. 9, Berlin.

Konstan, D. (1994), *Sexual Symmetry. Love in Ancient Novel and Related Genres*, Princeton.

Kovacs, D. (2016), 'Phyllis' High-born Parents: Horace, Odes 2.4.13–20', *Mnemosyne* 69, 866–71.

Mette-Dittmann, A. (1991), *Die Ehegesetze des Augustus. Eine Untersuchung im Rahmen der Gesellschaftspolitik des Princeps* = Historia Einzelschriften 67, Stuttgart.

Nadeau, Y. (2008), *Erotica for Caesar Augustus. A Study of the Love-poetry of Horace, carmina, Books I to III* = Collection Latomus 310, Bruxelles.

Nisbet, R.G.M./Hubbard, M. (1978), *A Commentary on Horace, Odes, Book II*, Oxford.

Poiss, T. (2001), 'Horaz als Erotiker betrachtet. Überlegungen zu carm. 2,8 und carm. 3, 9', *Wiener Studien* 114, 251–66.

Putnam, M.J.C. (2006), *Poetic Interplay: Catullus and Horace* = Martin Classical Lectures, Princeton.

Riffaterre, M. (1978), *Semiotics of Poetry*, Bloomington.

Shackleton Bailey, D.R. ([4]2001) (ed.), *Q. Horatius Flaccus. Opera* = Bibliotheca scriptorum Graecorum et Romanorum Teubneriana 1234, München/Leipzig.

Spelman, H. (2014), 'Alcman 3 PMGF and Horace C. 2.8', *Zeitschrift für Papyrologie und Epigraphik* 192, 23–8.
Sutherland, E.H. (2002), *Horace's Well-Trained Reader. Toward a Methodology of Audience Participation in the Odes* = Studien zur klassischen Philologie 136, Frankfurt a.M. *et alibi*.

Michèle Lowrie

Figures of Discord and the Roman Addressee in Horace, *Odes* 3.6

> Newspaper clipping (309): 'On defenseless people, who ask only to work and be paid honestly for that work, the *carabinieri* rained down blows until the streets of Rupe were splashed with the blood of the inhabitants. The delirium of a civil war was unleashed on the stricken people.'
>
> Anna, on her memoir of her grandfather (313): '"But don't you think I've misread the whole society? I mean, seen sexual struggles where there were other kinds of struggle going on, more important ones, perhaps – social, economic – men and women fighting side by side. For their survival, not their *honor*? Rosa and Tommaso and Davide in it, together. Not romance, but revolution?"'
>
> Fantina, Anna's mother (316–17): '" – but love and jealousy, they don't change that much. In the final count, when you look back you remember those things, not the fights for bread in the queues in the war or the woman who hoarded rations and sold them like daylight robbery when nobody else had anything. It's the people you loved you remember."'
>
> Marina Warner, *The Lost Father* (New York, 1988)

References to civil discord weave Horace's sixth Roman Ode together and undercut its initial promise, that reform will put a time limit on suffering – 'you will pay for the sins of the ancestors, *until* you rebuild the temples' (*Delicta maiorum ... lues / ... donec templa refeceris*, 3.6.1–2). The opening reassurance conflicts with the final stanza that makes generational decline an inescapable reality.[1] Furthermore, logical inconcinnities about the causation of civil war in relation to moral decline and about the possibility of undoing the damage through moral renewal establish irresolution deep in the poem. The way the poem creates its message about civil discord wages internal war on its own initial assertion of a clear

Beyond the conference in Thessaloniki, stimulating discussion with audiences at Wake Forest, in Florence, in Bloomington, and in Chicago have improved this paper. I extend heartfelt thanks to the organizers of these events: Cynthia Bannon, Margaret Foster, Stavros Frangoulidis, Stephen Harrison, Mario Labate, Josh Oskanish, and Gianpiero Rosati. Best wishes and warm feelings go to Mario Citroni, honored in Florence on the occasion of his retirement, May 2017. I have translated all primary texts myself.

1 Kraggerud 1995, 62–3 mitigates the contradiction with an implied 'unless', but see Porter 1987, 170–1. Jal 1963, 234 situates Horace's pessimism here within a shared dark outlook on civil war among writers who lived through it.

https://doi.org/10.1515/9783110611021-013

program for reform, namely through rebuilding the temples, a signal element of the Augustan program.[2]

Almost every detail of the poem can be recuperated through the framework of civil war. To that extent, I believe, to quote Alison Sharrock, 'it must all really be unified.'[3] However, to avoid the 'trap' of totalizing interpretation, I argue that the diverse textual elements create their overwhelmingly consistent meaning not all in the same way: techniques vary from direct naming, indirect reference, inter- and intratextual allusion, and cultural trope, with much overlap.[4] The meaning of these elements is additionally at first glance opaque, so that the dynamism of the poem's hermeneutic challenge and the surface flow from one topic to another counteracts any sense of an aesthetic monolith. The poem's complex system of signification undoes the initial premise of an effective plan of action and challenges our cognitive and affective certainty about any ultimate takeaway. Its metaphorics show that civil war is not 'simply a bug in the system ... that can be either fixed or expelled', but inhabits Rome from within.[5]

With 'the city occupied by sedition' (*occupatam seditionibus ... urbem*, 13–14), canonical vocabulary for intramural disturbance forwards the conventional claim that internal turmoil has exposed the city to foreign attack.[6] But this apparently clear distinction immediately becomes blurred. References to recent theaters of war progress from external to internal conflict. The Parthians under Pacorus defeated Antony's legate in 40 BCE; Monaeses played a role in Antony's withdrawal from Parthia in 36 after the defeat of another legate.[7] The Dacian, who sided with Antony before Actium, marched defeated in the triple triumph of 29 BCE; the Ethiopian refers derogatively to Cleopatra's Egyptian forces at Actium. Horace expresses Roman vulnerability explicitly with the phrase about sedition and through allusion to an earlier poem linking vulnerability to Parthia with civil war: *sed ut secundum vota Parthorum sua / urba haec periret dextera* (but so that this city perish by its own right hand in answer to the Parthian's prayers,

---

2 On the date in relation to Augustus' program to restore 82 urban temples in 28 BCE, see Fraenkel 1957, 261; Kraggerud 1995.

3 Sharrock 2000, 22.

4 Nadeau 1983, 328–31 totalizes the poem as support of Augustus. Jal (1963) 152 n. 2 insists the Augustan poets' celebration of Augustus *qua* peace-bringer postdates the civil wars – they were not partisans.

5 Breed *et al.* 2010, 9.

6 Armitage 2017 cleaves to a strong definition of civil war over, e.g., 'tumult, dissension, or sedition' (57) but literature elides such neat distinctions.

7 For historical details, see Pasquali 1964, 706–7, who emphasizes civil war; Nadeau 1983, 329; NR *ad loc.*

Epodes 7.9–10).[8] That Antony or his delegates participated in all the battles mentioned integrates foreign and civil warfare into a single framework. Monaeses' possible 'double game' folds in indistinction between friend and foe, a basic trope of civil war.[9] Historical references, literary allusion, and the cultural trope collectively support the claim that internal conflict has exposed Rome to external aggression, but Antony's role in both dissolves the distinction. To that extent, the poem makes it hard to sustain the ostensible ideological program, whereby 'the imperialistic program of annexation becomes the erasure of the evils of civil war.'[10] Civil war resists erasure.

A stronger indistinction between friend and enemy, relying similarly on allusion, undermines the apparent clarity of the list of external foes in the ninth stanza. Punic blood, Pyrrhus, Antiochus, and Hannibal nicely render the good old Romans of yore as engaged in a virtuous fight against foreigners. But the bloodstained sea muddies the waters with the memory of Latin and Italian blood on other fields and waters. Horace's *Odes* 2.1, on Asinius Pollio's writing a history of the civil wars, ends with a similar mix (2.1.25–36): North African enemies, Latin blood, waters discolored, and the threat of foreign foes' (Medes) learning of Hesperia's ruin. Both poems urge expiation. The Roman Ode calls for rebuilding the temples. In 2.1, blood conveys the idea: *arma / nondum expiatis uncta cruoribus* (arms smeared with as yet unexpiated gore, 4–5); Juno joins other gods hostile to Rome to placate Jugurtha with the victors' grandsons, namely, with soldiers as human sacrifice (25–8). Any reassuring distinction between Punic and Italian bloodshed in *Odes* 3.6 founders in the swirl of motifs. If reference to the Parthians reaches to an Epode outside the collection, the bloodstained waters trickle in from another poem in the same meter, within the same collection. The difference between textual outside and inside becomes muddled.

Reference to Sabellians elsewhere in Horace also blurs internal and external conflict and thereby shows up the ideological simplification of the image of Samnites as paragons of Italian virtue. Again, apparently irrelevant details link passages from different contexts. *Sermones* 2.1.34–9 treats Venusia's foundation in 291 BCE during the Third Samnite War, when Rome fought against Italian neighbors. The terms question boundary distinctions.[11] Horace's birth on the border of Lucania and Apulia, both originally threats to Rome, makes his identifications unclear. Is he primarily Roman or Italian? Which Italian loyalty would he share?

8 Other parallels to the *Epodes* with an emphasis on civil war at Fraenkel 1957, 285–7.

9 NR 3.6.9–10.

10 La Bua 2013, 270, with a focus on Parthians.

11 Villeneuve 1995, 135.

Reference to a third Italic people, the Sabellians or Samnites, driven out to make a buffer against the fierce Apulians or Lucanians, further confuses. Are they friend or enemy? And to whom? Perplexity keeps Horace's satirical sword in its sheath.

Subordination to the gods sanctions Rome's rule (*imperas*, 3.6.5), but the empire conveyed also crosses boundaries. Depending on the historical frame, the Samnites represent a fierce external enemy or the solid Italian stock that drove out Hannibal. As at *Odes* 2.1.32, *Hesperia* at *Odes* 3.6.8 codes the homeland as Italian. But the combination of an explicitly Roman addressee, *Romane* (3.6.2) with mention of the former Samnite foe, layers the 'evils besetting calamitous Hesperia' (*mala Hesperiae luctuosae*, 3.6.8) over references to Rome's empire during multiple periods of outwardly expanding confrontation: the recent civil wars, the earlier Social Wars, Rome's extension over the Italian peninsula. Distinctions between these internal conflicts collapse so a unified Rome appears monolithic against the foreign foes Pyrrhus, Antiochus, and Hannibal, but the careful reader reconstructs the Italian history.

Horace's methods do not differ substantially whether shared details establish links within the *Odes*, other Horatian works, or works by other authors Greek or Roman, far or near in time. Inter- and intra-textual allusion operate according to shared principles that bind Roman thinking about civil war into a shared cultural framework. Beyond explicit vocabulary denoting conflict among citizens – elements recuperable to conceptual history – a repertory of tropes and literary allusion evokes civil discord without denotation.

Layered allusion from Aratus through Vergil links the decline of the ages in the last stanza to civil war. Horace's dense comparatives *peior, nequiores, vitiosiorem* in the last three lines echo the lament of Dike, Aratus' personified Justice, who leaves the world in disgust at war and bloodshed, also marked with three comparatives of decline (χειροτέρην, worse; κακώτερα, more evil; ὀλοώτεροι, more destructive, *Phainomena* 123–30). An intervening text adds the civil qualification of spilt blood. Justice leaves the farmers last among men at *Georgics* 2.473–4, a passage where discord and fratricidal strife stain violent politics with the tropes of civil discord (*discordibus armis*, discordant arms, 2.459; *infidos agitans discordia fratres*, discord driving faithless brothers, 496; *gaudent perfusi sanguine fratrum*, they rejoice drenched in brothers' blood, 510).[12] Without naming civil war or fratricide per se, Horace counts on his educated reader to remember the relevant contexts in Aratus and Vergil.

12 Fenik's 1962, 83–5 parallels emphasize the ideal countryside despite tracing fratricide in parallels between the *Georgics* and Lucretius (77).

Similarly subtle is the dark background to the ostensibly tranquil image of the shadows cast by the mountains at sunset and the tired oxen's release from the plough (3.6.41–3). Horace's 'friendly time' of the evening recalls Vergil's famous line: *maioresque cadunt altis de montibus umbrae* (and the shadows fall greater from the mountains on high, *Eclogues* 1.83). The first Eclogue closes with Tityrus inviting Meliboeus to a rustic meal at eventide to relieve his flight into exile. The juxtaposition of *discordia* with *civis* steeps Meliboeus' loss of his farm in the vocabulary of civil war: *en, quo discordia civis / produxit miseros*! (look where discord has brought us wretched citizens! *Eclogue* 1.71–2).

My interpretation so far follows the assumptions typically governing the study of inter- and intra-textuality in Latin literature. Specific verbal and semantic similarities transfer associations beyond denotation from an explicit context to one where they appear entirely absent. For such associations to resonate, they must be recognizable and make sense in their new context. In *Odes* 3.6, naming sedition anchors other images and ideas in a network of shared thought that binds this Horatian ode to other poems within the collection, his corpus, and to his contemporaries. Other binding mechanisms, however, operate more fluidly.

The perversion of marriage that starts with a general statement of corruption in line 17 and becomes more vivid in the following stanzas, also serves as a trope for civil discord – one much harder to pin down. It concerns the conditions of a discordant society rather than technical *bellum civile*. It does not work according to allusion, inter- or intratextual, but indicates broad societal dysfunction more generally within the Roman political imaginary. The Augustan marriage legislation speaks to marriage's symbolic importance in societal restitution in the wake of civil war. Horace identifies the effect of marital depravity on the state: it has flowed *in patriam populumque* (into the fatherland and the people, 3.6.20). The fatherland (*patriam*) suggests the senatorial fathers (*patres*) and Horace uses the same phrasing of the people as in the 'SPQR'.

We might ask what the corruption of marriage has to do with civil discord.[13] The Roman *concept* of civil war innovates on Greek terminology (*stasis*) doubly by specifying formal war among citizens,[14] but Latin literature consistently oversteps the juridical bounds of this definition to represent civil war *metaphorically* through violence within the family (fratricide, patricide, filicide) and by the

13 A 'mirabilis coniunctio': Nadeau 1983, 331. The trope does not concern Jal 1963. Syndikus 1973, 92 typifies the link between morals and worship of the gods as Judeo-Christian rather than classical and sees this passage as exceptional.

14 Armitage 2017, 3–27, 37–45.

violation of marital relations.[15] While Aristotle makes coupling between a man and a woman the basis of all further political attachments (*Politics* 1252a30), marriage often binds – or fails to bind – men. Conflict between a father-in-law and a son-in-law consistently evokes Pompey and Caesar in this period. The story of the rape of the Sabines, where daughters and wives reconcile fathers and sons-in-law, endows family bonds with the potential to overcome conflict between opposing sides. Exogamy is one step on the way toward a more inclusive, networked political entity beyond Rome's original borders. Healing a divide that cuts family apart lays the path to Empire as Rome enfolds the Sabines first among its neighbors.

Horace's 'ripe virgin' (*matura virgo*, 3.6.22) links men between generations across the Roman Empire, but rather than building healthy social connections, she perverts the marriage bond in her only complicity with her husband. While love should join father-in-law to son-in-law vertically across generations, her lust connects men laterally through adultery. Horace takes us through progressive degradation. Her illicit desire is first permitted, then even ordered by her husband; her sexual desire, already wrong, devolves into his profiteering. The Empire of political rule in deference to the gods of the second stanza degrades into globalization: mercantile liaisons among lowlife salesmen and traders. The Spanish ship of line 31, no glorious trireme, is a vessel for cargo. Trade symbolizes a moral decline from the noble economy of farming in literature since Cato the Elder's *De agricultura*. This couple's sexual economy has become paradigmatic, befouling not merely an individual, limited marriage; the generic *virgo* and *maritus* stand for the entirety of corrupt Roman society. Fragmentation of the word *concordia*, encrypted through the repetition of disjointed syllables (*cor-* in *coram*; *con-* in *conscio*; *-cor-* again in *dedecorum*, 3.6.29–32), enacts a sonic icon of the discord depicted at the moment where the couple perverts their union.[16] Their failed bond stands for the breakdown of the social virtue *concordia*. Implied *discordia* evokes a standard word for civil war.

The consistent perversion of gender roles also challenges the presupposition of a fundamentally temporal break between good old-fashioned morals and the current age.[17] Corruption is nothing new. The poem's opening attributing sins to

15 Lowrie and Vinken, work in progress.

16 I thank Stephen Heyworth for this observation. For 'lyric cryptography', see Shoptaw 2000, especially 239–44; Ahl 1985.

17 Many take the contrasts – ideal past versus now, good mother versus bad wife – at face value: e.g., Fenik 1962, 83; Pasquali 1964, 707; Syndikus 1973, 86, 94–7; Shumate 2005, 93, 97. Horace challenges sharp temporal and aesthetic distinctions with the paradox of the heap at *Epist.* 2.1.34–49.

the ancestors says as much, but sits in tension with the ostensibly idealized depiction of erstwhile rustic Italian society.[18] We find no restoration of patriarchy with the youth victorious in the Punic Wars. The mothers of the 'male scions of rustic soldiers' (*rusticorum mascula militum / proles*, 3.6.37–8) call the shots: *severae / matris ad arbitrium* (at the command of a stern mother, 3.6.39–40) is strong language. 'Severe' more typically characterizes the likes of Appius Claudius or Manlius Torquatus, real he-men and defenders of senatorial prerogative, the shaggy ancestors of the *mos maiorum*. *Arbitrium* identifies decision-making power. Even when the menfolk left for war, extant agricultural literature leads us to expect a bailiff to run the farm.[19] The sons bear cut rods at her bidding, an inversion of the *fasces* the lictors bore before the consul.[20] Agency here belongs to women. The mother of this poem, however upstanding, jars with Roman ideological norms simply by virtue of being in charge. If she follows the model of the virtuous Spartan mother,[21] she improves on the ripe married virgin who dances to Ionian steps (3.6.21), but any Greek is a far cry from the Roman ideal. Better a virtuous mom than a prostituted wife, but what happened to the father in the fatherland? Horace undermines another apparent sharp divide in his poem between virtue and depravity.

The resulting destabilization performs a different operation from double-speak, which requires a clear-cut distinction between support of and resistance to the Augustan program.[22] The tropological inscription of Rome's historical inability to overcome internal division and to achieve the blessings of patriarchy hardly undermines the vision of aspirational goals. It does, however, offer a bleak prognosis on the goals' potential for realization.

My interpretation of this poem depends on there being a shared interpretive community. For the clearly negative judgment of the adulterous wife and the only apparently positive evaluation of the stern mother to serve as vehicles of Horace's commentary on civil war, a Roman audience must understand prostitution within marriage and a mother's stepping into the symbolic roles of father and consul as tropes for society's collapse. Horace's address of *Romane* in this poem gestures

---

18 Thom 1998, 63: '*delicta maiorum*' (sins of the ancestors, 3.6.1) shocks in contrast to an expected *mos maiorum* (customs of the ancestors).

19 Green 2010, 46: the bailiffs corresponded to magistrates in Varro's allegory of the Roman state as a farm.

20 John Oskanish stresses *per litteras* that *fustis* typically means 'cudgel' elsewhere in Horace, a fact perhaps suggesting more intrafamilial conflict. For *fasces*, see NR at 39–41.

21 I owe the suggestion to Stephen Harrison.

22 Thom 1998 reads the Roman Odes as 'double talk' that covertly advocates for individual freedom over a group perspective and that Horace uses this procedure in response to external pressure.

toward such a community by identifying a cultural addressee. This utterance is peculiar in expressing what normally goes unsaid. Eleanor Dickey avers that when Romans address a Roman in the collective singular, 'these addresses do not have the identifying functions of other ethnics but rather seem to stress some ideal of Roman-ness.'[23] I argue that here it flags the poem's assumption of, first, shared values and, second, conditions of interpretability. Comparative materials will support both aspects.

In the *Aeneid*, Anchises assumes shared values in his famous lines on the Roman arts – rule, the imposition of peace, sparing the subjected and warring down the proud – which are also addressed to a generic *Romane* (6.851–3). The exemplary context of the previous ten lines puts pressure on anyone who identifies as Roman. After a series of addresses to specific exemplary figures from Roman history – an unnamed Julius Caesar, Cato, Cossus, Serranus, the Fabii, but particularly Fabius Maximus – the collective singular Roman sums them all up. Other exemplary figures, the Gracchi, the Scipios, Fabricius, are merely named. If Vergil had wanted, Anchises could convey the same message about the Roman arts without address: after cataloguing the heroes in the third person, he could summarize with 'the Roman art is to rule peoples with empire.' The address adds something more than rhetorical drama. Unlike the named Romans, whose future acts are guaranteed by history, Anchises' generic Roman appears aspirational. The injunction *memento* (remember, 851) makes it unsure that said Roman will in fact embody Dickey's 'some ideal of Roman-ness.' Rather, Anchises articulates the ideals the putative Roman should live up to. Rebecca Langlands has argued that the Romans conceptualized reasoning by *exempla* not necessarily as strict imitation or avoidance, but rather as aspirational.[24] The figure of the Stoic *proficiens*, on the way to wisdom without ever quite achieving the goal, is her model. At the end of the *Aeneid*, the poem's paradigmatic proto-Roman does not spare the subjected, although he does war down the proud. Aeneas, the first recipient of this address, lives up to the ideal only in part.

Anchises' address reaches beyond Aeneas. His son is present and most of the second person singulars in Anchises' speech are directed at him, but Aeneas is not Roman, nor will he ever be. Anchises speaks beyond the man before him, beyond even the poem's original readership, to all contemporary and post-Vergilian Romans, beyond even, I would argue, any Roman-identified reader to us in our

23 Dickey 2002, 210. On the oracular tone, Syndikus 1973, 88. For the address's general applicability, calling on 'cultural pride' with a hint of a 'shadow-figure for Augustus', see Sutherland 2002, 202.
24 Langlands 2015.

own here and now, to share a message that the art of governance entails sparing as much as fighting. By setting the address of a generic Roman in Anchises' mouth, Vergil puts the stamp of Roman identity onto an ideal he hopes all Romans worth the name would recognize. If we embrace this ideal, we too may identify as members of the Roman tradition.

When Horace addresses an auditor or reader as *Romane* in *Odes* 3.6, he also speaks to a cultural context of shared values. Rebuilding the temples is the first step to any expiation that might stem a seemingly inevitable decline. He restates, reinstates what the Romans, who have not lived up to these values, all know to be true: they must restore the temples, surmount sedition to unify and direct their military energies outward, and get sexual morality back on track. As with Anchises' speech, Roman rule depends on respecting the right values; Horace adds subordination to the gods (3.6.5). Where Anchises uses positive *exempla* to spur his readership to virtuous action, Horace displays what is to be avoided. In Livy's famous formulation (*pref.* 10), Vergil shows 'what you may take to imitate for yourself and your republic' and Horace 'what you should avoid, foul in its beginning, foul in its end.'

Horace and Vergil furthermore speak to a community with shared interpretive presuppositions about the conditions of intelligibility. Just as Vergil presupposes his Roman will understand the aspirational drive motivating exemplarity, Horace presupposes a cultural addressee with precise hermeneutic skills, namely one capable of grasping that the metaphor of social collapse expressed through the degradation of the marriage bond reveals the greater truth of the recent political disturbances. While moderns need commentaries to understand the full importance of Anchises' exemplary figures, such background information required no supplementation for an educated Roman. But denotative reference is only the beginning. Roman habits of exemplary thinking make not only the values Anchises articulates intrinsically Roman, but also their mode of presentation. Polybius' description of the deployment of ancestor masks in the Roman funeral, Scipio's dream in Cicero's *De re publica*, the preface to Livy, and the ranks of statues in the *exedrae* of the Forum Augustum are only the most conspicuous evidence cited as parallels to Anchises' catalogue of heroes. Anchises interpellates the generic Roman not only as someone expected to share the values he articulates, but also as an interpreter of their means of articulation. The Roman should know he should put himself next in line.

The message about civil discord communicated with the cultural addressee in *Odes* 3.6 requires shared vocabulary, assumptions, and figurations. These have in the meantime become obscure and require work to bring them into view. Moral and religious renewal, sometimes called the Augustan program, is the antidote provided to the destruction wrought by civil war.[25] I submit that the Roman addressee would understand the perversion of sexuality represented by marital prostitution in *Odes* 3.6 as a trope for civil war. David Armitage, in his recent book on the conceptual history of civil war, emphasizes the Roman origins of this term. *Bellum* denotes formal warfare and *civile* specifies citizen participants. The concept has nothing to do with the relations between husband and wife. Nicole Loraux, however, has emphasized the familial and tribal underpinnings of *bellum civile*'s Greek predecessor: *stasis emphylios*.[26] Blood bonds assert that citizens are bound by more than law. This poem is paradigmatic for how Latin literature reveals the social nature of the collapse of the civil wars through the corruption of the institution of marriage. In Lucan's words, civil war is 'more than civil'; *bella ... plus quam civilia* (1.1) are wars in the family. Latin literature frequently figures civil war as a collapse of family ties.

Odes 3.6 links corruption in marriage to civil war more explicitly than earlier literature, but less so than later. At the end of Catullus 64, a series of images of familial breakdown establishes the social disorder of the age: Justice's exile resulting in fratricide; parents failing to mourn their children's deaths; a father's eliminating his son as a rival for the sexy young stepmother's attentions; incest where – horror of horrors – agency resides in the mom's desire. We can only wonder what happened to his first wife and her husband! Fratricide, which becomes a strong trope for civil war in triumviral poetry, is here one element among others in the general collapse of the social bond. The debasement of all family ties lambasts the social order of the moment. Corruption in child-bearing, of maternal as well as paternal lineage, puts society's future in question. Catullus makes causality clear: our mixing of right and wrong has turned the gods away from us.

In *Odes* 3.6, prostitution within marriage similarly represents the collapse of the social bond. This couple is certainly not bearing children, who would not anyway resemble their father. Additionally, by naming sedition and referring covertly to Actium, Horace links social to political collapse, perverted marriage to civil war. It is hard to tell which category is prior, the political or the social, sedition or marital prostitution. The fifth stanza sets out a chicken-and-egg paradox that questions the chronological priority of social and political categories. Horace first states that the corruption of the age (*fecunda culpae saecula*, centuries fertile

---

25 Shumate 2005 emphasizes the primacy of Augustan gender ideology in light of modern theories of nationalism (90). She reads the Roman Odes as constitutive of ideology and does not read Horace 'against the grain' (92). Ideology, however, encodes what it struggles to contain, so the poem's undercurrent of civil war hardly undermines its ideological function.

26 Loraux 1997a and b; see also Agamben 2015.

in wrongdoing, 17) has defiled 'marriages ... and lineage and houses' (*nuptias/ ... et genus et domos*, 17–18), that is, the political has infused the social. Then he asserts the opposite, that destruction derived from 'this source' has flowed into the 'fatherland and people' (*hoc fonte derivata clades / in patriam populumque fluxit*, 19–20).[27] Do failures in the political sphere – the religion, Empire, foreign and civil wars of the first four stanzas – degrade social relations? Or does social corruption break down the public sphere? Is civil discord cause or effect? In any event, civil war and social discord equally violate divine order; the Roman addressee should refer all beginnings and ends to subordination to the gods (3.6.6). Such a moral determination, however, leaves unresolved logical and consequently representational priority. The metaphorics go both ways. The corruption of marriage passes from a mere symptom of social disorder to a strong trope for the internal breakdown of the political order in civil war, but civil war conversely figures the collapse of the social bond. The link is now firm in the Roman imaginary.

This tropology becomes conventional in retrospect.[28] Tacitus, *Histories* 1.2 conjoins many Horatian images: civil wars mixed with foreign, ruined temples, polluted rites, the Capitoline burned at the hands of citizens, adultery, cliffs dyed with slaughter. Beyond the broken marriage bond, slaves and freedmen betray the family, and friends crush those lacking an enemy. Machiavelli in turn condenses this passage from the *Histories* into a sometimes word for word translation:

> If he then considers minutely the times of the other emperors, he will see them atrocious because of wars, discordant because of seditions, cruel in peace and in war; so many princes killed with steel, so many civil wars, so many external ones; Italy afflicted and full of new misfortunes, its cities ruined and sacked. He will see Rome burning, the Capitol taken by its own citizens, the ancient temples desolate, ceremonies corrupt, the cities full of adulterers. He will see the sea full of exiles, rocks on the shores full of blood.
>
> *Discorsi* 1.10.5

Odes 3.6 sets ruined temples and adultery in a context of sedition and civil war. The reference to Actium reminds us of *Odes* 1.37.6, where Cleopatra threatens the Capitoline. Tacitus and in turn Machiavelli reveal the threat to the Capitoline as internal. Even the blood-stained maritime landscape linked to civil war in *Odes* 2.1 recurs. Tacitus coalesces these elements into a package Machiavelli

---

27 For blaming the woman, who becomes a metaphor for a 'diseased body politic', see Pasquali 1964, 708; Shumate 2005, 97–8; Keith forthcoming. Lyne 1995, 174: 'an arguable absurdity'.

28 Lowrie and Vinken work in progress; Ginsberg 2017; Keith forthcoming.

picked up wholesale. The tradition becomes more explicit with time and spells out what Horace encodes: that adultery provides the social correlate to the political collapse of civil war.[29]

When Horace addresses the Roman public as *Romane*, he speaks to the Roman community somewhere between the individual addressee in relation to a private circle, and the general public. This communication operates within a dynamic cultural field in the process of evolution and to that extent intervenes in a particular moment in the development of the metaphorics of civil war. Catullan tropes of social breakdown begin to attach to civil war without yet being fully conventional. Horace's poem comes at the moment of a tradition's formation, before it has crystallized into a roughly fixed set of figurations. To that extent, the address to *Romane* tilts more toward the coded communication Mario Citroni looks for in poems with specific historical addressees, without going quite that far, than it does toward a more universal public.[30] We should not, however, assume here the accessibility to interpretation we would attribute, say, to passages in the *Aeneid* alluding clearly to Homer. These had already entered the tradition in Vergil's times and have remained canonical to classically educated Western readers, however much their number has shrunk in recent years.

The communicative potential of marital breakdown as a trope for civil war at a particular moment of composition accords with Hans Robert Jauss' insistence on the cues to interpretation a text gives (1982, 23):

> A literary work, even when it appears to be new, does not present itself as something absolutely new in an informational vacuum, but predisposes its audience to a very specific kind of reception by announcements, overt and covert signals, familiar characteristics, or implicit allusions. It awakens memories of that which was already read, brings the reader to a specific emotional attitude, and with its beginning arouses expectations .... The psychic process in the reception of a text is, in the primary horizon of aesthetic experience, by no means only an arbitrary series of merely subjective impressions, but rather the carrying out of specific instructions in a process of directed perception.

Knowledge of the violation of familial norms in Catullus cues the Augustan reader to the general social collapse indicated by Horace's poem. Reference to Actium sets the social collapse within a context of civil war. The 'not absolutely new' awakens memories that orient us with specific instructions. These are to understand civil war's disturbance according to a 'specific emotional attitude' elicited by the horror we good Romans feel at marital prostitution.

---

29 See also sexual depravity when the Flavians take Rome at Tacitus, *Histories* 3.83.2.

30 Citroni 1995, xii–xiii. Pasquali 1964, 706 extends the addressee beyond the present generation.

The system of metaphors that become conventional figures for civil war – fratricide, parricide, adultery – opens up discord's reality to us beyond personal experience. Its horror surpasses what the concept of civil war can capture, as bad as formal warfare among citizens may be. Hans Blumenberg calls a metaphor absolute when what it conveys cannot be reduced to a concept (2010, 14):

> ... we ask once again about the relevance of absolute metaphors, their *historical* truth. This truth is *pragmatic* in a very broad sense. By providing a point of orientation, the content of absolute metaphors determines a particular attitude or conduct [*Verhalten*]; they give structure to a world, representing the nonexperienceable, nonapprehensible totality of the real. To the historically trained eye, they therefore indicate the fundamental certainties, conjectures, and judgments in relation to which the attitudes and expectations, actions and inactions, longings and disappointments, interest and indifferences of an epoch are regulated.

Adultery as a trope for civil war gives us access across historical distance to the affective orientation of Horace's world, to the wounds felt to the political imaginary. It lets us feel Roman revulsion to civil war at a visceral level.

My reading of *Odes* 3.6 as coherently and consistently marshaling the tropes of civil discord relies on a range of critical moves that mostly entail bringing materials outside the poem into engagement with it. In my argument's first part, standard techniques of positive reference and allusion to a variety of texts closer and further at hand support my claim to unity. In the second, however, more distant comparative materials establish a shared semantic field within the broader tradition of Roman social and political thought, one Machiavelli's example shows lived beyond antiquity. As literary critics, we make fine distinctions between these various techniques, but by focusing overly on minute differences between allusion, inter- and intra-textuality, we risk losing sight of the larger picture, that a poem's conditions of readability depend on knowing the conventional figurations of its tradition. The boundaries of a poem's inside and outside are fluid. Without a reader's familiarity with the conventions that civil war made Rome vulnerable to foreign attack, that lengthening shadows offered a moment of pause in civil discord, that various foreign enemies all touch on internal enemies within Rome's expanding Empire, that violating the marital bed and letting the temples decay abut fratricide and civil war in the Roman tropology of socio-political corruption, the poem would reel from one unrelated image to another. Horace's elision of imagistic links from one formal or semantic unit to the next challenges interpretation. His method of overlaying different referential techniques escapes any neat scheme, but they all pull in the same direction.

Having pleaded for unity, I will now push against it. The poem as artifact *does* reel from image to image. Any interpretive concord is of the sort Horace names *concordia discors* (discordant concord, *Epist.* 1.12.19), an Empedoclean mix of harmony and strife that Lucan will apply to the uneasy peace Crassus maintained between Pompey and Caesar before civil war's outbreak (1.98).[31] Perceiving the links across stanzas requires knowledge of Roman conventions in their process of becoming. Tracing the web of this poem's – any poem's – cultural, sense-making network demands a critical toolbox of strategies for bringing diverse comparanda to bear. I have argued that the relations between the various parts of this poem do not differ in kind from the relations each part has with other elucidating texts from closer or farther away. This poem's meaning emerges from a common cultural field. The line between a text's interior and exterior, like that between friend and enemy in civil war, is inherently unstable.

Abbreviations

NR = R.G.M. Nisbet and Niall Rudd, *A Commentary on Horace, Odes, Book III*, Oxford 2004.

Bibliography

Agamben, G. (2015), *Stasis. La guerra civile come paradigma politico,* Homo sacer, II, 2, Torino.

Ahl, F. (1985), *Metaformations: Soundplay and Wordplay in Ovid and Other Classical Poets*, Ithaca NY.

Armitage, D. (2017), *Civil Wars: A History in Ideas*, New York.

Blumenberg, H. (2010), *Paradigms for a Metaphorology*, (trans. by R. Savage) (orig. publ. 1960), Ithaca NY.

Breed, B./Damon, C./Rossi, A. (2010), *Citizens of Discord: Rome and its Civil Wars*, Oxford.

Citroni, M. (1995), *Poesia e lettori in Roma antica*, Rome/Bari.

Dickey, E. (2002), *Latin Forms of Address: From Plautus to Apuleius*, Oxford.

Fenik, B.C. (1962), 'Horace's First and Sixth Roman Ode and the Second Georgic', *Hermes* 90.1, 72–96.

Fraenkel, E. (1957), *Horace,* Oxford.

Ginsberg, L.D. (2017), *Staging Memory, Staging Strife: Empire and Civil War in the Octavia*, Oxford/New York.

Green, C.M.C. (2010), 'Agricultural Treatises', in: M. Gagarin *et al.* (eds.), *The Oxford Encyclopedia of Ancient Greece and Rome*, Oxford, 45–7.

Henderson, J. (1998), *Fighting for Rome*, Cambridge.

Jal, P. (1963), *La guerre civile à Rome*, Paris.

Jauss, H.R. (1982), *Toward an Aesthetic of Reception*, (trans. by T. Bahti), Minneapolis.

Keith, A. (forthcoming), 'Engendering Civil War in Flavian Epic', in: L. Ginsberg/D. Krasne (eds.), *Flavian Literature and Civil War, Trends in Classics-* Supplementary Volumes, Berlin.

Kraggerud, E. (1995), 'The Sixth Roman Ode of Horace: Its Date and Function', *Symbolae Osloenses* 70, 54–67.

31 Horace uses subterfuge compared to the rhetorical extravagance of Lucan as analyzed by, e.g., Henderson 1998, 165–211.

La Bua, G. (2013), 'Horace's East: Ethics and Politics', *Harvard Studies in Classical Philology* 107, 265–96.
Langlands, R. (2015), 'Roman Exemplarity: Mediating between General and Particular,' in: M. Lowrie/S. Lüdemann (eds.), *Exemplarity and Particularity: Thinking through Particulars in Philosophy, Literature, and Law*, Abington/New York, 68–80.
Loraux, N. (1997a), 'La guerre dans la famille', *Clio* 5, 21–62.
Loraux, N. (1997b), *La cité divisée: l'oubli dans la mémoire d'Athènes*, Paris.
Lowrie, M./Vinken, B. (in progress), *Civil War and the Collapse of the Social Bond: The Roman Tradition at the Heart of the Modern*.
Lyne, R.O.A.M. (1995), *Horace: Behind the Public Poetry*, New Haven.
Nadeau, Y. (1983), 'Eloquentes Structurae. Speaking Structures. Horace, *Odes*, 3.1–3.6', *Latomus: revue des études latines* 42, 303–31.
Pasquali, G. (1964), *Orazio lirico*, Florence.
Porter, D.H. (1987), *Horace's Poetic Journey*, Princeton.
Sharrock, A. (2000), 'Intratextuality: Text, Parts and (W)holes in Theory', in: A. Sharrock/H. Morales (eds.), *Intratextuality: Greek and Roman Relations*, Oxford, 1–39.
Shoptaw, J. (2000), 'Lyric Cryptography: A Poetics of Reading', *Poetics Today* 21.1, 221–62.
Shumate, N. (2005), 'Gender and Nationalism in Horace's 'Roman' *Odes* (*Odes* 3.2, 3.5, 3.6)', *Helios* 32.1, 81–107.
Sutherland, E.H. (2002), *Horace's Well-Trained Reader: Toward a Methodology of Audience Participation in the 'Odes'*, Frankfurt am Main.
Syndikus, H.-P. (1973), *Die Lyrik des Horaz*, Darmstadt.
Thom, S. (1998), 'Lyric Double Talk in Horace's Roman *Odes* (*Odes* 3.1-6)', *Akroterion* 43, 52–66.
Villeneuve, F. (1995), *Horace, Satires*, Paris.

Stephen Harrison

Linking Horace's Lyric Finales: *Odes* 1.38, 2.20 and 3.30

1 Introduction

The unit of intratextuality considered in this paper is that of the first three books of Horace's *Odes*. These are usually thought to have been issued together c.23 BCE; though it is possible that the three books were earlier released sequentially as well as later as an ensemble,[1] it is generally agreed that the use of the same metre only in the first and last poems of the eighty-eight in Books 1–3 indicates that they should be considered together as a literary unit. In previous work I have already suggested that the final poem in Horace's next collection, *Epistles* 1.20, self-consciously alludes to and appropriately modifies key elements from the final poems *Odes* 2.20 and 3.30;[2] here I would like to juxtapose that pair of odes with their final lyric counterpart *Odes* 1.38 and suggest links between the three of them.[3] In doing this I hope to show that the final poems in the three-book collection of odes present a common and poetically significant group of features and topics. This would resemble the 'initial grammar' I have recently argued for across the opening poems of Horatian poetry books over his literary career.[4]

2 The poems

For convenience, I here cite the three final poems involved with my translations.

1.38
Persicos odi, puer, apparatus,
displicent nexae philyra coronae,
mitte sectari, rosa quo locorum
  sera moretur.
Simplici myrto nihil adlabores

Many thanks to Philip Hardie for some important comments on my original conference paper.

1 See Hutchinson 2008, 131–61.
2 See Harrison 1988.
3 The three poems are dealt with together by Fraenkel 1957, 297–307, but with little attempt to stress their common elements.
4 See Harrison 2014.

https://doi.org/10.1515/9783110611021-014

sedulus curo: neque te ministrum
dedecet myrtus neque me sub arta
  vite bibentem.

Persian paraphernalia, my boy, I disapprove;
No pleasure to me are bast-fastened garlands;
Don't bother to pursue the select places where
The late rose lingers.
My mandate: take care to add no elaboration
To simple myrtle – it fits you as server
and me too, drinking under
These dense-woven vines.

2.20
Non usitata nec tenui ferar
penna biformis per liquidum aethera
  uates neque in terris morabor
    longius inuidiaque maior
urbis relinquam. non ego pauperum
sanguis parentum, non ego quem uocas,
  dilecte Maecenas, obibo
    nec Stygia cohibebor unda.
iam iam residunt cruribus asperae
pelles et album mutor in alitem
  superne nascunturque leues
    per digitos umerosque plumae.
iam Daedaleo notior Icaro
uisam gementis litora Bosphori
  Syrtisque Gaetulas canorus
    ales Hyperboreosque campos.
me Colchus et qui dissimulat metum
Marsae cohortis Dacus et ultimi
  noscent Geloni, me peritus
    discet Hiber Rhodanique potor
absint inani funere neniae
luctusque turpes et querimoniae;
  conpesce clamorem ac sepulchri
    mitte superuacuos honores.

On no usual or slender wing will I be borne
Through the clear heaven as a biform bard,
Nor will I tarry longer on earth, but
Superior to ill-will, I will leave its cities behind.
I, the issue of poor parents, I, whom you,
Beloved Maecenas, summon to your house,
Will not die, or be constrained
By the waters of the Styx.

Already now skin-patches are shrinking to roughness on my legs
And I am being changed into a white winged one
On top, and light feathers are growing
On my fingers and shoulders.
More celebrated than Icarus son of Daedalus,
I will visit the shores of the lowing Bosphorus
And the African Syrtes as a singing bird,
And the plains of the far North.
I shall be known by the Colchians and by the Dacians
Who hide their fear of the Italian army
And the far-distant Gelonians; I shall be taught to
the learned Spaniard and he who drinks the Rhône.

3.30
Exegi monumentum aere perennius
regalique situ pyramidum altius,
quod non imber edax, non Aquilo inpotens
possit diruere aut innumerabilis
annorum series et fuga temporum.
Non omnis moriar multaque pars mei
vitabit Libitinam; usque ego postera
crescam laude recens, dum Capitolium
scandet cum tacita virgine pontifex.
Dicar, qua violens obstrepit Aufidus
et qua pauper aquae Daunus agrestium
regnavit populorum, ex humili potens
princeps Aeolium carmen ad Italos
deduxisse modos. Sume superbiam
quaesitam meritis et mihi Delphica
lauro cinge volens, Melpomene, comam.

I have executed a monument more lasting than bronze
And loftier than the royal rotting-place of the Pyramids,
That hungry showers and winds without control
Cannot wreck, or the sequence of years
No man can number, or the flight of time.
I shall not wholly perish, and a great part of me
Will escape the goddess of death; I will grow,
Made fresh by the praise of those to come,
For as long as the priest climbs the Capitol with the silent virgin.
I shall be said, where the violent Aufidus roars
And where Daunus, poor in water, ruled over rustic peoples,
To have become great from a humble start
And to have been the first to compose Aeolian song to Italian measures.
Take on the pride earned by my achievements,
Melpomene, and crown me graciously with the Delphic bay.

3 Formal features

Metre. As already noted, *Odes* 1.1 and 3.30 are formally linked: their shared metre found only in these two poems frames them as the start and end of the three-book collection of *Odes* 1–3. This shared metre of the stichic lesser Asclepiad is used several times in poems of Alcaeus, e.g. fr.350 L/P; in Sappho this line is found only as part of longer stanzas, e.g. fr.93 and 96 L/P, but its stichic form seems to have continued in use in Hellenistic lyric (cf. Asclepiades (?) *SH* 215).[5] Thus the metre of *Odes* 3.30 may look back both to archaic Lesbian lyric and more recent Hellenistic practice, both appropriate to Horace's collection, which combines evocation of Sappho and Alcaeus with various elements of Hellenistic poetic refinement. Likewise, the Sapphic stanza of *Odes* 1.38 looks to both archaic and more recent lyric models: this was the metre of the first book of Sappho's poems in the Alexandrian collection of her works and is often seen as her signature form,[6] but was also a metre appropriated by Catullus in the previous generation in two prominent poems (11 and 51) which the Horatian lyric collection knew and used.[7] Thus the two metres of these three poems are emblematic both of Horace's key model of archaic Greek lyric in Sappho and Alcaeus and its subsequent literary history in both Alexandria and Rome which necessarily forms part of its Horatian reception.

Length. These three final poems are relatively short: 8 lines (1.38), 24 lines (2.20) and 16 lines (3.30); this brevity is emphasised in each case by juxtaposition with a longer penultimate poem (1.37 = 32 lines, 2.19 = 32 lines, 3.29 = 64 lines). Such short poems are found in archaic lyric (e.g. Sappho fr.1 L/P, complete at 28 lines, fr.31 L/P, likely to have been complete at 20 lines), but here again we might see the influence of earlier final poems. It is not clear from the exiguous evidence whether previous Greek poetry-books concluded with relatively short poems, though some believe that the elegiac Theognis 237–54 West on the fame of Cyrnus (18 lines) formed the conclusion of a collection.[8] In Roman poetry-books, Catullus 116, if it was indeed a final poem,[9] matches 1.38 in its length of eight lines, while Propertius 1.22 has ten lines; the Gallus papyrus (fr.2) seems to present us

---

5 See West 1982, 151, 167. On the reception of Alcaeus in the Hellenistic period see Acosta-Hughes 2010, 105–40.

6 Cf. Acosta-Hughes 2010, 24.

7 Cf. Nisbet and Hubbard 1970, 265, 273, Harrison 2017, 13–14 and in general Putnam 2006.

8 See e.g. West 1974, 42.

9 See e.g. Macleod 1983, 181–6, Skinner 2003, 2–3.

with a pair of elegies of four lines which looks very much like the end of a book.[10] All these model poems are in elegiacs and have epigrammatic colour, and the characteristically brief form of epigram is similarly a relevant genre for Horace's three short finales as often for the *Odes* in general:[11] 1.38 echoes sympotic epigrams in both theme and length (cf. e.g. *AP* 5.181–5, five similar Hellenistic sympotic epigrams of 12, 8, 6, 8 and 6 lines), while 2.20 picks up Posidippus' autobiographical 'Seal' (*SH* 705 = 118 A/B) in a number of ways as well as echoing Ennius' likely self-epitaph (see further below),[12] and 3.30 may echo a sepulchral epigram of Posidippus (122 A/B).[13]

Addressees. Finally, I have elsewhere considered the addressees of the opening poems of Horatian poetry-books, which begin with Maecenas in *Satires* 1 and end with Augustus in *Epistles* 2,[14] showing an ascending sequence of importance. A similar ascent is visible in the addressees of the three lyric finales: 1.38 is addressed to a slave *puer*, a low-status human, 2.20 to Maecenas, a high-status human, and 3.30 to the lyric Muse, a divinity. These three addressees, I suggest, benefit from being read as a coherent sequence as the collection advances, moving towards an appropriate climax which is both elevated in status and relevant to the collection's literary genre.

4 Thematic features

More substantial are the shared thematic features in the three poems, to which I now turn. Almost all of these are also found elsewhere in the *Odes* outside its finales; what is significant here is their persistent grouping in these poems, which thus gather together in prominent and linked locations a number of important elements which are programmatic for Horace's lyric collection.

The brief finales of Catullus 116, Gallus fr.2 and Propertius 1.22 already mentioned share descriptions of or allusions to the poet and his work as well as brevity. Such an element is a key part of the so-called *sphragis*, a 'seal' set by the poet on his work to identify it as if it were a wine-jar belonging to him (the image comes

---

10 See e.g. Nisbet 1995, 120.

11 See e.g. Harrison 2007, 177–84.

12 Harrison 2017, 236.

13 Nisbet and Rudd 2004, 366.

14 See Harrison 2014 (I take *Epistles* 2 to have been intended to include the *Ars Poetica*: Harrison 2008). On the function of addressees in the *Odes* in general see Citroni 2009.

originally from Theognis 19–38 West, itself more likely to have been a prologue rather than an epilogue).[15] Catullus 116 engages in literary polemic with Gellius and defends the poet's own work,[16] while Gallus fr.2.6–10 describes the poet's work as worthy of his mistress and as likely to receive a positive reception from contemporary critics such as Viscus, and Propertius 1.22 follows the autobiographical tradition of Theognis and Posidippus (see above) by setting out the poet's Umbrian origins. All these elements can be seen in the three Horatian lyric finales.

The Catullan contrast between different types of poetry seems to be brought out in *Odes* 1.38. Though commentators have been sceptical about metapoetical symbolism in this poem,[17] I side with critics who see it here; the garland should represent the poet's own notion of his work.[18] It has been plausibly suggested that this poem looks back to Callimachus *Ep*. 28 Pf. = *AP* 12.43:

Ἐχθαίρω τὸ ποίημα τὸ κυκλικόν, οὐδὲ κελεύθῳ
  χαίρω τίς πολλοὺς ὧδε καὶ ὧδε φέρει,
μισῶ καὶ περίφοιτον ἐρώμενον, οὐδ' ἀπὸ κρήνης
  πίνω· σικχαίνω πάντα τὰ δημόσια.
Λυσανίη, σὺ δὲ ναιχὶ καλὸς καλός—ἀλλὰ πρὶν εἰπεῖν
  τοῦτο σαφῶς Ἠχώ, φησί τις 'ἄλλος ἔχει.'

I hate the poem that belongs to the normal round, nor do I
Take pleasure in the road which carries many here and there.
I loathe too the lover who goes around, and I do not drink from the spring;
I loathe all things that are public property.
Lysanias, you are indeed handsome, handsome - but before Echo has clearly
Repeated this, someone says 'Another possesses him'.

The verbal link *odi* / Ἐχθαίρω has indeed been noted,[19] but the epigram's parallel between poetic and erotic preference may also influence the ode; both poems are addressed to a young male who is a potential sexual partner and whose looks are commented on, and some recent scholarship has stressed the homoerotic colour

15 West 1974, 42.

16 Macleod 1983, 181–6.

17 See most recently Mayer 2012, 227, following Nisbet and Hubbard 1970, 422–3, West 1995, 191 and Syndikus 2001, 332–4.

18 There are suggestions of literary and/or metapoetical symbolism for the poem in Pasquali 1920, 324–5, Fraenkel 1957, 298, Davis 1991, 118, Lowrie 1997, 164–75 and Fedeli 2012, 731; very full on this topic (though not always plausible) is Cody 1976, 15–44.

19 See Cody 1976, 24.

of 1.38 (plausibly in my view).[20] For the present purpose, the key point is that the garland has symbolic and metapoetic value (for poetic garlands see further below).

Plausible too is the view that *Persicos ... apparatus* looks back to the rejection of the Persian chain (measurement of length) as the criterion for poetic quality in the polemical preface to Callimachus' *Aetia* (fr.1 Pf.17–20):[21]

αὖθι δὲ τέχνῃ
κρίνετε,] μὴ σχοίνῳ Περσίδι τὴν σοφίην·
μηδ' ἀπ' ἐμεῦ διφᾶτε μέγα ψοφέουσαν ἀοιδήν
τίκτεσθαι· βροντᾶν οὐκ ἐμόν, ἀλλὰ Διός.

Now judge poetry by its art, not by the Persian chain,
And do not seek from me the birth of a song
Which makes a loud noise; thundering
Belongs not to me, but to Zeus.

Horace's poem joins Callimachus' in rejecting 'Persian' literary quantity through the symbol of the garland; it is not impossible that there is an allusion here to Choerilus' epic *Persica*,[22] written at the end of the 5th C BCE, which would represent the kind of lengthy poetry here targeted.[23]

Thus *Odes* 1.38 like Catullus 116 presents a contrastive defence of the poet's own work, drawn at least partly from Callimachean aesthetics; we recall that the Catullan poem refers to imitating the *Iambi* of Callimachus (116.2 *carmina ... Battiadae*). In the same way, *Odes* 2.20.1 *non usitata* echoes Callimachus' programmatic rejection of the commonplace in poetry (cf. *Ep.* 28.4 Pf. above, σικχαίνω πάντα τὰ δημόσια, 'I loathe all things that are public property'), while 2.20.4 *inuidiaque maior* 'superior to envy' translates Callimachus' self-description at *Ep.* 21.4 Pf. as κρέσσονα βασκανίης. Though *Odes* 3.30 seems not to engage in polemics with other types of poetry, it does reflect on the poet and his work via the metaphor of building for poetry, drawn from Pindar *Pythian* 6.1–13 and the more recent Vergil *Georgics* 3.10–39. It also looks to the *sphragis*-tradition of giving personal details about the poet: the somewhat modest claim that the poet will have a reputation in the region of the Aufidus and Daunus for having risen far from humble origins looks to the Apulian region of the poet's birth, just as Theognis names Megara (23 West), Posidippus Pella (118.17 A/B) and Propertius

20 See e.g. West 1995, 191–2.

21 See Davis 1991, 121.

22 Narrating the expedition of Xerxes to Greece in 480–79 BCE. For the remaining fragments see *Supplementum Hellenisticum* 314–23.

23 So Hutchinson 2008, 169.

Umbria (1.22.9). Unsurprisingly, then, all three Horatian finales engage in comment on the poet and his poetry.

Another element found in all three poems is that of cultural transfer between Italy and the rest of the world. In 1.38, as we have already seen, we find a rejection of incoming Eastern influences (1 *Persicos odi, puer, apparatus*); such foreign luxuries (and poems) can be seen as inappropriate from the native Italian perspective of the poet, seated at home underneath his vine pergola (7–8 *sub arta / uite bibentem*). In 2.20 we find a centrifugal movement, with the poet predicting his future departure from Italy as a bird and his travel to the boundaries of the Roman empire (see further below), while in 3.30 by contrast the movement is centripetal, bringing Greek Aeolian poetry and a Delphic garland to a very localised Italy, looking forward to future fame (as we have seen) in the poet's own specific region of birth. This stress on movement to and away from Rome fits the relationship of the *Odes* with the wider literary world, importing Greek lyric, remaking it, and exporting it to the Roman empire; it also reflects Rome's key role as the centre for international trade and commerce. Poetry, like other commodities, moves freely across the globe within the context of the Roman dominions.[24]

Sometimes a key feature is shared by only two of the three poems. For example, the notion of the poet's later reception, present in the Greek *sphragis*-tradition (see above) and implicit in the lasting poetic fame of 3.30, is not found at all in 1.38 but is explicit in 2.20.17–20: Horace's work will be read by Colchians, Dacians, Gelonians, Iberians and dwellers by the Rhone. This list combines unstable border areas of the contemporary Roman empire with some elements of the mythic Argonautic journey (see below). Similarly, 1.38 and 3.30 share the idea of the garland, not present in 2.20; as already suggested, the apparently sympotic garland of 1.38 has as much poetic significance as that requested of the Muse in 3.30. Indeed, it has been fleetingly proposed that the garland of 1.38 alludes in its metapoetical character to Meleager's famous introduction to his *Garland* anthology of epigrammatic poets, *AP* 4.1.[25] This hint can be followed up in more detail; it is not unlikely that Meleager's prefatory poem might influence Horace's concluding ode in its garland symbolism. I cite its opening (1–4):

> Μοῦσα φίλα, τίνι τάνδε φέρεις πάγκαρπον ἀοιδάν;
>   ἢ τίς ὁ καὶ τεύξας ὑμνοθετᾶν στέφανον;
> ἄνυσε μὲν Μελέαγρος, ἀριζάλῳ δὲ Διοκλεῖ
>   μναμόσυνον ταύταν ἐξεπόνησε χάριν ...

24 For further reflections on Rome as a global centre for cultural import and export see Woolf and Edwards 2003.

25 Davis 1991, 126.

Dear Muse, to whom do you offer this full-fruited song?
Or who is he who wrought this garland of singers?
Meleager accomplished it, and laboured at this graceful object
As a keepsake for the distinguished Diocles ...

Here there are a number of elements which seem to be picked up in the Latin poem. Both poems are addressed to a male friend, potentially an erotic partner, and both involve a metapoetical garland where particular types of flowers are woven in. The Horatian garland, composed simply of myrtle, is evidently different from its multifloral Meleagrian counterpart (Meleager's 58-line poem, enormous for an epigram, goes on to list twenty-five poets, all with their counterpart flower), but may pick up an element in the Greek epigram. As has been noted, later on in Meleager's poem we find myrtle as the flower linked with Callimachus (21–2 ἡδύ τε μύρτον / Καλλιμάχου), and given the double Callimachean allusion already argued for above this is likely to be significant: a recommendation of the flower of Callimachus for a garland in this poem is clearly consistent with its function as a Callimachean manifesto for the *Odes*.

The two garlands of 1.38 and 3.30 correspond in more ways than in their metapoetic symbolism. 3.30 can be said to engage with the issue of 1.38 about what kind of garland the poet needs; in Book 1 the poem debates which plant to use for its material (lime-bast, rose, myrtle), and comes down in favour of Callimachean myrtle, but in Book 3 it is clear that only Apollo's bay is appropriate, the prize for victory at the Pythian Games (the point of 3.30.15 *Delphica*). In this respect, as commentators note,[26] Horace becomes a full match for Pindar, the greatest of the Greek lyric poets, who at *Odes* 4.2.9 is similarly *laurea donandus Apollinari*, 'to be awarded the bay of Apollo', and whose architectural imagery for poetry has already been echoed in this same poem (see above). 1.38 suggests Callimachus' miniature aesthetics in the form of myrtle, appropriately drawn from the brief epigrammatic tradition of Meleager; 3.30 adds in the allusion to Pindaric achievement, suggesting that the collection now completed has successfully combined high Pindaric lyric ambition with Callimachean polish and care. As with the matter of metre (above), older Greek lyric is received in the *Odes* through the filter of later literary developments.

Another element shared by only two of the three poems is the idea that the poet and his work will be immortal. In the Greek *sphragis*-tradition, Theognis (237–54 West) had suggested that the poet's subject Cyrnus would be immortalised, not the poet himself,[27] and Posidippus' 'Seal' concludes with the idea that

---

26 See e.g. Nisbet and Rudd 2004, 378, Thomas 2011, 107.

27 Theognis 19–24 West seems to point to the poet's potential fame in his lifetime, but there is no mention there of his death or the lack of it.

the poet will have a good death in old age and leave his wealth to his children (fr.118.24–28). The Horatian emphasis in both 2.20 and 3.30 on the poet's own immortality through the eternal life of his work (2.20.5–8 *non ego ... / ... / ... obibo*, 3.30.6 *non omnis moriar*) is not in fact unparalleled in Greek poetry,[28] but seems to belong particularly here to the Roman poetic tradition.[29] The emphasis in 2.20.21–4 that there is no need to mourn the eternal poet is drawn from Ennius' self-epitaph (*var.* 17–18 Vahlen): *nemo me lacrumis decoret, nec funera fletu / faxit. cur? uolito uiuus per ora uirum*, where the metaphor of *uolito* is also likely to be one of the elements underlying the bird of *Odes* 2.20;[30] also relevant is Catullus' wish for his own book at 1.10 *plus uno maneat perenne saeclo*, where *perenne* may suggest the Horatian *aere perennius* (3.30.1).[31] Engagement with Ennius is another feature shared between 2.20 and 3.30; for the latter's use of the *Annales* see below.

Finally, I come to a key point which is shared by all three poems – interaction of some kind with the epic tradition. As already suggested above, even the brief 1.38 can be argued to allude to the epic *Persica* of Choerilus in its opening words *Persicos odi, puer, apparatus*. In 2.20, I would argue, we find as yet unnoted allusions to the voyages of the *Odyssey* and the *Argonautica*.[32] When the poet says *urbis relinquam* (2.20.5), this can be seen as a neat inversion of the city-visiting of Odysseus at the start of the *Odyssey*: 1.3–4 πολλῶν δ' ἀνθρώπων ἴδεν ἄστεα καὶ νόον ἔγνω / πολλὰ δ' ὅ γ' ἐν πόντῳ πάθεν ἄλγεα ὃν κατὰ θυμόν, 'and he saw the cities of many men and got to know their mind, and suffered many sorrows in his heart on the sea'. By taking to the air as a bird, Horace avoids the perils of Odysseus on the sea, and leaves rather than visits the cities of men, abandoning rather than embracing the world of humanity; it is the unusual plural *urbis*, strange without a complement, which suggests the Homeric ἄστεα here, matching the use of the same unadorned plural noun in Horace's two versions of this Homeric passage elsewhere (*Epistles* 1.2.19–20 *qui domitor Troiae multorum providus urbes/et mores hominum inspexit latumque per aequor*, *Ars Poetica* 142 *qui mores hominum multorum vidit et urbes*).

Likewise, the locations envisaged as visited by the poet-bird in 2.20.13–20 include a number of places on the route of the Argonauts as found in Apollonius' *Argonautica*: the Bosporus [Ap.Rh.2.168], the Syrtes [Ap.Rh.4.1235], Colchis [Ap.Rh.3], and the Rhone [Ap.Rh. 4.627]. The poet is perhaps here interacting with the lost contemporary Latin version of the Argonaut epic by Varro of Atax, probably from the 30s BCE, admired by Propertius and Ovid and used by Vergil in the

28 For examples going back to Sappho and Hellenistic epigram see Nisbet and Rudd 2004, 371.
29 See especially Thévenaz 2002.
30 See Harrison 2017, 236–7.
31 See Nisbet and Rudd 2004, 368.
32 See Harrison 2017, 238.

Georgics and *Aeneid*.[33] Note how these mythical locations are combined with areas of the Roman empire known for recent military operations (Dacia, Spain, the Geloni);[34] this is perhaps a strategy of competition, suggesting that the bird-poet will match Roman military might in traversing wide stretches of the world as well as retracing and adding to the voyage of the Argonauts.

Odes 3.30 seems to be interacting with Ennius' *Annales* and quite possibly with Vergil's *Aeneid*. Its initial argument, that Horace's poetic monument in the *Odes* is more long-lasting than the architectural self-commemorations of kings (1–5) plainly looks back to Ennius' description in *Annales* 16 of how kings seek to perpetuate themselves through physical monuments (*Annales* 404–5 Skutsch):[35]

> Reges per regnum statuasque sepulcraque quaerunt,
> Aedificant nomen, summa nituntur opum ui ...
>
> Kings seek statues and tombs throughout their reigns:
> They build themselves a name, and strive with the highest force of resources ...

Given that these lines were probably followed soon after by *Annales* 406 Skutsch, *postremo longinqua dies confecerit aetas*, 'in the end a distant age shall have put an end to their days', the Ennian context like *Odes* 3.30 is likely to have cast doubt on the royal strategy of self-commemoration in physical monuments,[36] perhaps even also contrasting it unfavourably in Horatian mode with the greater capacity of poetry to preserve name and reputation over time.

This epic interaction is perhaps paired with another here. As commentators have noted, the Horatian assertion that his poetry will last as long as the Roman occupation of the city's Capitol has a striking parallel in the Vergilian praise of the dead Nisus and Euryalus:

> 3.30.7–9:
> usque ego postera
> crescam laude recens, dum Capitolium
> scandet cum tacita virgine pontifex.
>
> I will grow,
> Made fresh by the praise of those to come,
> For as long as the priest climbs the Capitol with the silent virgin.

33 For the evidence see Hollis 2007, 171–9.

34 See Harrison 2017, 242–3.

35 The parallel is briefly noted by Nisbet and Rudd 2004, 374.

36 See Skutsch 1985, 568–9.

Aeneid 9.446–9:
Fortunati ambo! si quid mea carmina possunt,
nulla dies umquam memori vos eximet aevo,
dum domus Aeneae Capitoli immobile saxum
accolet imperiumque pater Romanus habebit.

Fortunate pair! If my lines have any power,
No day will take you from the memory of the ages,
As long as the house of Aeneas inhabits the immovable rock of the Capitol
And the Roman father holds imperial sway.

Recent commentators have suggested that the resemblances here may derive from a common source in the context of Ennius *Annales* 16 just discussed,[37] but it is also possible (here as elsewhere)[38] that the *Odes* may have had pre-publication access to the *Aeneid*, especially given that *Aeneid* 9 (in which Nisus and Euryalus are formally introduced, 9.176–81) may well have preceded *Aeneid* 5 (in which the two are treated as known characters) in date of composition.[39] Here the fame suggested in Vergil's epic for his characters is modified by the Horatian ode into fame for the poet himself, an appropriate transformation of the recessive epic narrator into the more prominent I-figure of lyric.[40]

5 Conclusion

I hope to have shown that the finales to the three books of Horace's first lyric collection, namely *Odes* 1.38, 2.20 and 3.30, share a number of formal and thematic features which relate significantly to the literary programme of *Odes* 1–3. These features include the relationship of these poems to the metre and length of archaic Greek lyric, their role in the collection's rhetoric of ascent through their addressees, and above all their common thematic aspects: the elements of autobiographical *sphragis*, of literary polemic and Callimachean aesthetics, of cultural relations between Rome and the larger world, and of interaction with epic texts. Taken together, I would argue, these three poems reveal much about the key characteristics of the lyric collection in which they are so prominently placed.

37 Nisbet and Rudd 2004, 373–4.
38 See e.g. Harrison 2007, 214–7.
39 See Berres 1982, 169–88.
40 On the prominence of first-person references to the poet in Horace see e.g. Horsfall 1998.

Bibliography

Acosta-Hughes, B. (2010), *Arion's Lyre: Archaic Lyric into Hellenistic Poetry*, Princeton.

Berres, T. (1982), *Die Entstehung der Aeneis*, Wiesbaden.

Citroni, M. (1983), 'Occasioni e piani di destinazione nella lirica di Orazio', *Materiali e discussioni per l'analisi dei testi classici* 10–11, 133–214 [translated as 'Occasions and Levels of Address in Horatian Lyric' in: M. Lowrie (ed.), *Horace: Odes and Epodes*, Oxford, 2009, 72–105].

Cody, J.V. (1976), *Horace and Callimachean Aesthetics*, Brussels.

Davis, G. (1991), *Polyhymnia: The Rhetoric of Horatian Lyric Discourse*, Berkeley/London.

Edwards, C./Woolf, G. (eds.) (2003), *Rome the Cosmopolis*, Cambridge.

Fedeli, P. (2012), *Orazio: tutte le poesie*, Milan.

Fraenkel, E. (1957), *Horace*, Oxford.

Harrison, S.J. (1988), 'Deflating the *Odes*: Horace, *Epistles* 1.20', *Classical Quarterly* 38, 474–6.

Harrison, S.J. (2007), *Generic Enrichment in Vergil and Horace*, Oxford.

Harrison, S.J. (2008), 'Horace *Epistles* 2: The Last Horatian Book of *Sermones*', *Proceedings of the Langford Latin Seminar* 13, 173–86.

Harrison, S.J. (2014), 'The initial poems in Horace's poetry-books', in: J.-C. Juhle (ed.), *Pratiques latines de la dédicace*, Paris, 243–58.

Harrison, S.J. (2017), *Horace Odes Book II*, Cambridge.

Hollis, A.S. (2007), *Fragments of Roman Poetry c.60 BC – AD 20*, Oxford.

Horsfall, N.M. (1998), 'The First Person Singular in Horace's Carmina', in: P.E. Knox/C. Foss (eds.), *Style and Tradition: Studies in Honour of Wendell Clausen*, Stuttgart/Leipzig, 40–54.

Hutchinson, G.O. (2008), *Talking Books*, Oxford.

Lowrie, M. (1997), *Horace's Narrative Odes*, Oxford.

Macleod, C.W. (1983), *Collected Essays*, Oxford.

Mayer, R. (2012), *Horace Odes I*, Cambridge.

Nisbet, R.G.M. (1982), *Greek Metre*, Oxford.

Nisbet, R.G.M. (1995), *Collected Papers on Latin Literature*, Oxford.

Nisbet, R.G.M./Hubbard, M. (1970), *A Commentary on Horace, Odes* I, Oxford.

Nisbet, R.G.M./Rudd, N. (2004), *A Commentary on Horace, Odes* III. Oxford.

Pasquali, G. (1920), *Orazio Lirico*, Florence.

Putnam, M.C.J. (2006), *Poetic Interplay: Catullus and Horace*, Princeton.

Skinner, M. (2007), *Catullus in Verona*, Columbus.

Skutsch, O. (1985), *The Annals of Quintus Ennius*, Oxford.

Syndikus, H-P. (2001), *Die Lyrik des Horaz* [2 vols; 3rd ed], Darmstadt.

Thévenaz, O. (2002), 'Le cygne de Venouse: Horace et la métamorphose de l'Ode II,20', *Latomus* 61, 861–888.

Thomas, R.F. (2011), *Horace. Odes IV and Carmen saeculare*, Cambridge.

West, D. (1995), *Horace Odes 1: Carpe Diem*, Oxford.

West, M.L. (1974), *Studies in Greek Elegy and Iambus*, Berlin/New York.

Part V: **Intratextual Ovid**

Giuseppe La Bua

Intratextual Readings in Ovid's *Heroides*

In *Amores* 2.18, a programmatic poem addressed to the epic poet Macer[1] and composed for the three-book second edition,[2] Ovid reaffirms his commitment to love-elegy as a lifelong poetic occupation (in contrast to his sporadic pursuit of more serious genres, like tragedy and epic).[3] By rejecting martial epic and drama he stresses the elegiac nature of his poetry and establishes himself as a love-elegist. The poem is not only a formal literary *recusatio*, however. It also constitutes an authorial presentation of love-elegy as a genre encompassing various forms and patterns. The elegiac poem contains the first (by no means exhaustive) catalogue of the single love-letters, the *Epistulae Heroidum*,[4] the fifteen fictional epistles imagined as written by female heroines lamenting their abandonment by and separation (and absence of any reply) from the men they loved (ll. 19–34):[5]

Quod licet, aut artes teneri profitemur Amoris
   (ei mihi, praeceptis urgeor ipse meis),
aut quod Penelopes verbis reddatur Ulixi
   scribimus et lacrimas, Phylli relicta, tuas,
quod Paris et Macareus et quod male gratus Iaso
   Hippolytique parens Hippolytusque legant,
quodque tenens strictum Dido miserabilis ensem
   dicat et † Aoniae Lesbis amata lyrae †
Quam cito de toto rediit meus orbe Sabinus
   scriptaque diversis rettulit ipse locis!

I would like to thank Stavros Frangoulidis and the organizers of the 11th *Trends in Classics* International Conference on 'Intratextuality and Roman Literature' for inviting me to participate as a speaker. Many thanks also to Laurel Fulkerson, Alison Sharrock, colleagues and friends attending the conference for their thoughtful suggestions.

---

1 Macer is also the addressee of Ov. *Pont.* 2.10 and mentioned in *Trist.* 4.10.43–4. About the supposed identification of the Macer referred to in Tib. 2.6 with the poet addressed in Ovid's elegy, see McKeown 1998, 382–3.
2 Hollis 1977, 150–1; McKeown 1998, 384–5.
3 For an exhaustive commentary of the elegy of the *Amores*, see McKeown 1998, 382–405.
4 The term *epistula*, used by Ovid himself in *Ars* 3.345 to designate an individual poem in the collection of the *Heroides*, was later applied to both the single and paired epistles; see Knox 2002, 117. See also Gibson 2003, 238–9 (for the interchangeability of *cantare* and *legere* and the originality, *novitas*, of the *Heroides*).
5 Ovid mentions ten mythological characters (the writers and recipients of the single letters 1–7, 10, 11, and 15): see Björk 2016, 21–2.

https://doi.org/10.1515/9783110611021-015

Candida Penelope signum cognovit Ulixis,
legit ab Hippolyto scripta noverca suo;
iam pius Aeneas miserae rescripsit Elissae,
quodque legat Phyllis, si modo vivit, adest.
Tristis ad Hypsipylen ab Iasone littera venit,
dat votam Phoebo Lesbis amata lyram.

'What I may, I do. I either profess the art of tender love – ah me, I am caught in the snares of my own teaching! – or I write the words Penelope sends her Ulysses, and thy tearful plaint, abandoned Phyllis; what Paris and Macareus are to read, and what ungrateful Jason, and Hippolytus, and Hippolytus' sire; and what pitiable Dido, with drawn blade in her hand, indites, and the Lesbian, loved of the Aonian lyre. How quickly has my Sabinus returned from the ends of the earth and brought back missives writ in far-distant places! Spotless Penelope has recognized the seal of Ulysses; the stepdame has read what was penned by her Hippolytus. Already devout Aeneas has written back to wretched Elissa, and a letter is here for Phyllis to read, if only she live. A missive grievous for Hypsipyle has come from Jason; the daughter of Lesbos, her love returned, may offer to Phoebus the lyre she vowed'.[6]

As Harrison notes, *Amores* 2.18 sheds light on Ovid's tendency towards diversification in erotic elegy.[7] The poet combines didactic elegy, the *Ars Amatoria*, alluded to at l. 19 (*artes amoris*, 'arts of love')[8] with an experimental form of elegy of lamentation, *Heroides* 1–15,[9] a collection of epistolary female complaints showing evident connections with school declamation.[10] Elegy reflects Ovid's poetic versatility. Ovid himself gives voice to his flexibility in exploiting generic possibilities within love-elegy. Later in the poem (*Am.* 2.18.27–34) he informs his potential readers of the planned composition of double epistles, letters from male heroes paired with replies from loved women (*Heroides* 16–21), a poetic collection presumably inspired by the lost male replies written by his friend and colleague

6 I cite the text and English translation of the *Heroides* and *Amores* from the second edition of G. Showerman, revised by G.P. Goold (Cambridge, MA-London, 1977).

7 Harrison 2002, 81–2.

8 McKeown 1998, 385–6.

9 On the *Heroides* as Ovid's early poetry-book, contemporary with the *Amores*, see Knox 1995, 5–6.

10 For the epistolary discourse in the *Heroides*, see Kennedy 2002. On declamation in the *Heroides*, see Knox 1995, 15–17.

poet Sabinus,[11] acclaimed for his ingenuity in devising the reinsertion of the male into traditional love-elegy.[12]

The so-called 'Sabinus-elegy' invites us to look at the *Heroides* (both the single and the paired epistles) as a textual assemblage of individual poems operating on both an inter- and intra-textual level. As mythological and historical figures, the female heroines, members of a poetic fictional community 'created by their shared presence in a poetic book',[13] self-consciously refashion and re-envision previous versions of their stories. They show 'an intrinsic tendency to comment on their nature and their position within past (but also forthcoming) literature'.[14] As competent, well-educated writers, *doctae puellae*, the heroines engage the external readers, already familiar with literary tradition and love-romances, in recollecting specific canonical texts which the epistles allude to (and their reciprocal intersections) and in capturing the strategies of reformulation (and manipulation) of standard narrative (and their effects).

Intertextual play is crucial to our understanding of the love-letters,[15] as modern approaches to the female voice in Ovid's work have fruitfully demonstrated.[16] Ovid himself offers intertextuality as a constructive way of reading his fictional epistles and re-interpreting both literary tradition and the subtext of the female lament. *Scribo*, 'I write', and *lego*, 'I read', are key elements of this intertextual exercise by which the poet reverses the traditional elegiac dichotomy between male deceit and female self-revelation, making writing a female art form and confining the male deceiver to the subaltern role of reader.[17] Exemplary for this intertextual reading is Penelope, the first female lover of the collection, who exploits her traditional role as a faithful spouse and assumes knowledge of the *Odyssey* on the part of the male reader as essential to discern the dissonances between the

11 Heldmann 1994. For Sabinus, cf. also Ov. *Pont.* 4.16.13–14 (see McKeown 1998, 383–4). Rosati 1996, points to disparity in treatment of the absent lover in Penelope's and Sappho's letters (1 and 15) and notes that the final recommendation to Phaon to compose a written reply prompts us to rethink about Ovid's overall design of a collection including both the single, female letters and the paired epistles.

12 McKeown 1998, 399; Harrison 2002, 83.

13 Fulkerson 2005, 2.

14 Spentzou 2003, 18.

15 On intertextuality and Roman literature, see in general Hinds 1998; Edmunds 2001.

16 For a survey of intertextual approaches to the *Heroides* in modern scholarship, see Jacobson 1974, *passim*; Spentzou 2003, 1–12; Fulkerson 2005, 7–16. In general, on intertextuality in the love-epistles, see Barchiesi 1986; 1987; Jolivet 2001; Lindheim 2003; Casali 2009, 345–8; see also Alden Smith 2006. On the love-letters as epistolary and elegiac refashionings of mythological stories and the role of the heroines as past message senders, see Drinkwater 2007.

17 Farrell 1998, 323–6.

intertext and her authorial voice.[18] She warns against masculine epistolarity.[19] The male lovers, the ideal recipients of the letters, are prohibited from writing back. They must only act as external readers, invited as they are to reconsider their role in what is planned to become a revised canonical love-story. In echoing Virgil, reworking and contradicting him, the miserable Dido of *Heroides* 7 recommends herself as a new prototype of elegiac-epic female lover. By adapting the *suasoria* form to epistolary lament,[20] she modifies 'Virgilian material for the purpose of building a good rhetorical case' for herself.[21] The Ovidian Dido vindicates herself. In engaging with Book Four of the *Aeneid* she threatens Aeneas' fame as *pius* and makes herself into a new author and a new heroine of the myth.[22] And in recreating a narrative of her love-story 'she proffers herself to Aeneas as an idealized version of himself'.[23]

As much as the female self-referential letters are very specifically intertextual,[24] the Ovidian heroines adopt intratextual strategies and recreate their stories by means of 'textual experience'. As Laurel Fulkerson has lucidly observed, the female writers 'base their own words on their interpretation of the stories of other abandoned women in their community'.[25] If it is true that they refashion their stories by continuously alluding to previous, traditional, versions of the myth, they portray themselves as abandoned women, *relictae*, by drawing on the stories of other deluded women within the collection. Like the external reader, the heroine-writer of the *Heroides* knows both the inter- and intra-texts, the other voices in the virtual book-poetry of deceived love. She perceives external and internal relationships. The *afflictae* heroines learn about the world of love from reading other letters, written by other female authors. They know their past and foretell their future by using similar stories of erotic deception and failure in the epistolary collection. In other words, they learn lessons from intratextuality.

---

18 Kennedy 1984; Barchiesi 1992, 15–19. On Penelope's letter and its programmatic role within the collection, see Hinds 1985.
19 Farrell 1998, 327.
20 Piazzi 2007, 68–94 (for the rhetorical structure of the epistle).
21 Jacobson 1974, 80.
22 On the Ovidian Dido, see Desmond 1993. For Phyllis-Dido parallels, see Fulkerson 2005, 26–9.
23 Lindheim 2003, 101.
24 On intertextual characters in the *Heroides*, see also Hinds 1993; Bessone 1997, 11–41; Heinze 1997, 25–41 (Medea); Battistella 2010, 7–22 (for an extra-Catullian intertextual reading of Ariadne). For an intertextual interchange between poems and characters throughout the collection and the 'competitive/harmonious interactions' between the single and double epistles, see Rimmel 2009, 156–79.
25 Fulkerson 2005, 5.

As expected, intratextuality serves also as the keyword in Ovid's elegiac reformulation of the female and male-female voice in the paired epistles. As a notion involving structure, textual segmentation, and the interrelations between parts and the whole,[26] intratextuality in the double *Heroides* encourages the reader to discern and appreciate the connections between the epistles, each conceived of as a discrete unit but each needing to be examined through perceived reciprocal interrelationships between male and female arguments. As the Ovidian elegy of the *Amores* makes it clear, Sabinus' and Ovid's recreation of the male author contrast with and complement the female voice, eventually satisfied in its desire for the male revelation of perennial love. Penelope, Phaedra, Dido, Phyllis, Hypsipyle, and Sappho: all are said to receive and read male letters, texts that pointedly respond to their pathetic request for love. *Heroides* 16–21 provide a limpid example of the Ovidian technique of intratextuality. The paired epistles are intrinsically intratextual poems, complementing the self-referential and self-reflexive female monologues through a dialectical interaction between the lovers.[27] They draw attention to the poet's innovative recuperation of a 'regular' male love through interrelated texts, reacting to each other in agonal forms. In creating a clash of opposing characters and viewpoints Ovid replaces the female soliloquy (and self-contained dilemma) with dramatic, rhetorical confrontation. He rewrites and reworks elegiac themes by substituting the unifying motif of the single letters, female lamentation, with topics of erotic pleasure, seduction (Paris-Helen and Acontius-Cydippe), and frustrated love (Hero-Leander) and re-establishing thereby the recognized norms of erotic discourse.[28]

It has been noted that the paired epistles remind us of the Augustan *Gedichtbuch*, 'a collection of poems designed to be read and appreciated both individually and as a literary whole, each poem or group of poems taking on added significance from the rest'.[29] Whether the paired epistles are Ovidian or not,[30] post-exilic Ovidian poems or fruit of one or more imitators,[31] this has no significant impact on intratextuality, the internal principle of organization of the male-

26 On the theory of intratextuality the natural reference text is Sharrock-Morales 2000.

27 Barchiesi 1993, on the *Heroides* as self-reflexive texts and the dialogue between the epistle and the source text.

28 Barchiesi 1999 (for a re-reading of the single epistles in *Heroides* 16–21).

29 Kenney 1996, 20. See also Bessone 2003, 174.

30 On the authenticity of the paired epistles for metrical reasons, see Ceccarelli 2014.

31 In general, on the problem of the authenticity of the *Heroides*, see Knox 1995, 5–14; Farrell 1998, 307–8. See Tarrant 1981 (suspecting the Ovidian authorship of the epistle of Sappho to Phaon); see also Fulkerson 2005, 152–8. Knox 1986; Hinds 1993 (for a discussion of the authenticity of the Medea-letter).

female epistolary exchange. The term 'intratextuality' may also be conveniently applied to the sophisticated relationship of pattern- and meaning-making between the single and the paired epistles. This paper contends that an ironic intratextual reading of the *Heroides* allows for an ideological re-evaluation of the elegiac female lament as unproductive. My focus is especially on Helen's letter (*Heroides* 17), a poetic, 'modern' and subversive reversal of love conflicts, a text that points to the contradictions of love-elegy and shows, in parodic terms, the internal failure of female voice (and the end of elegiac love).

Recent scholarship has successfully concentrated on intratextual relations within the single letter collection and between *Her.* 1–15 and the paired epistles. Fulkerson has provided illuminating examples of Ovid's strategy of intratextuality in the *Heroides* collection.[32] To enlarge upon this point, Phaedra's letter (*Her.* 4), an exploitation of seductive elements which resembles a love-*suasoria* and capitalizes on Ovidian imagery of licentiousness,[33] configures itself as an elegiac refashioning of Ariadne as the exemplar of the deserted woman.[34] Yet in tempting Hippolytus Phaedra elaborates on the classic adultery motif and depicts herself as an elegiac character, not dissimilar from the figure of the seductive lover as embodied in Paris (*Her.* 16).[35] If it is true, as Fulkerson remarks, that 'Phaedra's letter is influenced in profound ways by the atmosphere of abandonment that pervades the *Heroides*',[36] it is beyond doubt that the Ovidian Phaedra speaks as a lover-poet, using a language which any reader of elegy is familiar with. As much as Paris legitimizes adultery, she makes incest a 'moral' thing. Certainly, Phaedra refashions herself as a new Ariadne. Her story offers also clues to the story of Acontius and Cydippe (*Her.* 20–21). But she has learned not only from Ariadne. She has learned also from the *Ars* how to compose a seductive (though ineffective) love-epistle.

Paris' and Helen's character-types operate on multiple intratextual levels in the *Heroides*. The representation of Achilles as an elegiac effeminate lover in Briseis' letter (*Her.* 3. 113–20),[37] a character replicated in that of Hercules in Deianira's epistle (*Her.* 9. 101–118), prefigures Paris' portrait. In an intratextual dimension, the mechanism of ironic anticipation and prefiguration of the future that the heroines will meet is crucial to reading strategy. In the case of Oenone

32 Fulkerson 2005 (*passim*).
33 Landolfi 2000, 16–38 (on Phaedra as *erotodidaskalos*, erotic master teacher).
34 Fulkerson 2005, 122–42.
35 On Paris' rhetoric of seduction in *Her.* 16, see Cucchiarelli 1995.
36 Fulkerson 2005, 135.
37 For Achilles as an elegiac character in the epistle, see Barchiesi 1992, 234–8.

(*Heroides* 5) and Hypsipyle (*Heroides* 6), the characterization of the heroine as a prophet provokes emotional, ironic reactions. As literary figures, they know their own stories and tend to reinterpret them elegiacally. Yet, the heroines fail in their attempt to create a 'positive' love-story. As has been noted, Oenone (in particular) incorporates the examples of Medea and Hypsipyle into her own and successfully competes with Helen in rhetorical skills.[38] Yet she appears to be a powerless figure in the face of her love rival, Helen. Her violent reaction of jealousy at the sight of Helen embracing her new lover prefigures a story of imminent betrayal (*Her.* 5.65–76):

> Dum moror, in summa fulsit mihi purpura prora:
>   Pertimui: cultus non erat ille tuus.
> Fit propior terrasque cita ratis attigit aura:
>   Femineas vidi corde tremente genas.
> Non satis id fuerat: quid enim furiosa morabar?
>   Haerebat gremio turpis amica tuo.
> Tunc vero rupique sinus et pectora planxi,
>   Et secui madidas ungue rigente genas,
> Implevique sacram querulis ululatibus Iden:
>   Illuc has lacrimas in mea saxa tuli.
> Sic Helene doleat desertaque coniuge ploret,
>   Quaeque prior nobis intulit, ipsa ferat.

> 'While I delayed, on the highest of the prow I saw the gleam of purple —fear seized upon me: that was not the manner of your garb. The craft comes nearer, borne on a freshening breeze, and touches the shore: with trembling heart I have caught the sight of a woman's face. And this was not enough —why I was mad enough to stay and see? In your embrace that shameless woman clung! Then indeed did I rend my bosom and beat my breast, and with the hard nail furrowed my streaming cheeks, and filled holy Ida with wailing cries of lamentation: yonder to the rocks I love I bore my tears. So may Helen's grief be, and so her lamentation, when she is deserted by her love: and what she was first to bring on me may she herself endure!'

Oenone's jealousy flares up in full force when she gazes at her rival arriving on board a ship and then becomes conscious that her story is coming to an end. She keeps watching the ship (*morabar*, l. 69). On a metaphorical level, she keeps 'reading' a revised love-text, a text that marks the beginning of Helen's and Paris' adulterous (and celebrated) love. Sensitive to visual and aural experience, like Hypsipyle (*Her.* 6.83–4),[39] the female lover realizes that she will be eventually

---

38 Fulkerson 2005, 40–66. On the contrast between pastoral and epic in the Oenone-letter, see Fabre-Serris 1999.

39 Caston 2012, 79–81 (on Hypsipyle, see Verducci 1985, 56–65).

deleted from literary memory as Paris' lover. Through a paradoxical intratextual reading, Oenone prefigures her destiny as a betrayed woman. And in frustration she puts a curse on her literary rival.

Oenone's letter pre-signals future events.[40] It 'functions as a sort of running commentary on the correspondence of Paris and Helen'.[41] The heroine annihilates herself (and her story) in the face of Paris' other love. She has managed to affect her destiny but the virtual book of Paris' myth envisages a dramatic, ironic reversal of roles. In contrast, Helen, a very 'intratextual character', exploits the moral lessons she has learned from other heroines. As an external reader, she has knowledge of past love experiences. In the guise of a detached observer of erotic passion, Helen revisits and meditates upon the condition of other heroines weeping and lamenting over unfaithful lovers. Helen holds the *Heroides*-book in her hands. Having attentively read previous stories of betrayed women, she is now able to 'instruct' other women (and her male lover) to control excess of love. The lines 189–204 of *Heroides* 17 are illustrative of this intratextual parodic move:

Dum novus est, potius coepto pugnemus amori!
  Flamma recens parva sparsa resedit aqua.
Certus in hospitibus non est amor:[42] errat, ut ipsi,
  Cumque nihil speres firmius esse, fugit.
Hypsipyle testis, testis Minoia virgo est,
  In non exhibitis utraque lusa toris.[43]
Tu quoque dilectam multos, infide, per annos
  Diceris Oenonem destituisse tuam.
Nec tamen ipse negas, et nobis omnia de te
  Quaerere, si nescis, maxima cura fuit.[44]
Adde, quod, ut cupias constans in amore manere,
  Non potes; expedient iam tua vela Phryges.
Dum loqueris mecum, dum nox sperata paratur,
  qui ferat in patriam, iam tibi ventus erit.
Cursibus in mediis novitatis plena relinques
  Gaudia; cum ventis noster abibit amor.

40 Lindheim 2000, 84.

41 Michalopoulos 2006, 37.

42 On the theme of the 'faithless guest' in the *Heroides* (cf. Demophoon, Aeneas, and Theseus) cf. Kenney 1996, 140.

43 So MSS; Kenney 1996 prefers *De non exhibitis utraque questa toris.*

44 'Helen was not fooled by Paris' offhand and disingenuous reference to Oenone (cf. 16.97–8 *nec tantum regum natae petiere ducumque / sed nymphis etiam curaque amorque fui*) and she now reveals that she has been doing some private detective work on her own account' (cf. Dido to Aeneas on the fate of Creusa 7.81–4)': Kenney 1996, 141.

> 'While it is new, let us rather fight against the love we have begun to feel! A new-kindled flame dies down when sprinkled with but little water. Uncertain is the love of strangers; it wanders, like themselves, and when you expect nothing to be more sure, 'tis gone. Hypsipyle is witness, witness is the Minoan maid, both mocked in their unacknowledged marriage-beds. You, too, faithless one, they say have abandoned your Oenone, beloved for many years. Not yet do you yourself deny it; and, if you do not know, to inquire into all concerning you has been my greatest care. Besides, though you should long to remain constant in love, you have not the power. The Phrygians are even now unfurling your sails; while you are speaking with me, while you are making ready for the hoped-for-night, already the wind to bear you homeward will be here. In their mid-course you will abandon joys yet full of freshness; away with the winds will go your love of me.'

'An excellent motto for the whole collection of the *Heroides*',[45] the sentence *certus in hospitibus non est amor* (l. 191) displays Helen's good knowledge of past erotic literature. Meta-literary, ironic intratextuality determines meaning and allows for a reader-response to the theme of love lamentation in the *Heroides*. Reading offers Helen the possibility to question the very concept of *eros-nosos*, love as disease of soul and body. The story of Hypsipyle (and Jason) in *Heroides* 6 and that of Ariadne (and Theseus), in epistle 10, along with the former love-story of Paris (with Oenone) represent, to Helen's eyes, a rich repertoire of mythological *exempla*, which the female lovers may rely on.[46] Acting as a *praeceptrix amoris*, well informed about the erotic pedagogy of the *Ars*, she provides other heroines and readers (and her inept lover) with a new, more realistic vision of elegiac love.[47] Helen's letter interacts with previous stories of failed love and especially with the Sapphic-Catullian concept of love as 'illness'. Intratextuality helps to dismantle the underlying notion which regulates the composition of the single female letters, that is, complaint and lamentation as the essence of Ovid's elegiac world.

Helen's poem is the confession of a woman enjoying her lover's attention but unaffected by passion or false hopes by virtue of her textual experience. Prospecting (and fearing) her condition of exiled woman, Helen draws on Medea's book (*Heroides* 12), the canonical story of the heroine-witch as a deceived and abandoned heroine, to reformulate the traditional lamentation of exile deprived of any paternal aid (*Her*. 17.225–37):

> Da veniam fassae – non sunt tua munera tanti,
>   nescio quo tellus me tenet ipsa modo.
> Quis mihi, si laedar, Phrygiis succurret in oris?

---

45 Michalopoulos 2006, 331.

46 On the use of mythological exempla in the correspondence of Paris and Helen, see Michalopoulos 2006, 41–2.

47 For Paris as far from being 'the polished lover the *Ars* hopes to create', see Drinkwater 2013.

Unde petam fratres, unde parentis opem?
Omnia Medeae fallax promisit Iason:
Pulsa est Aesonia num minus illa domo?
Non erat Aeetes, ad quem despecta rediret,
Non Idyia parens Chalciopeque soror.
Tale nihil timeo, sed nec Medea timebat;
fallitur augurio spes bona saepe suo
Omnibus invenies, quae nunc iactantur in alto,
Navibus a portu lene fuisse fretum.

'Forgive me if I say it —your gifts are not worth so much; I know not how, my land itself still holds me back. Who will succour me on Phrygian shore if I meet with harm? Where shall I look for brothers, where for a father's aid? All things false Jason promised to Medea —was she the less thrust forth from the house of Aeson? There was no Aeetes to receive the scorned maid home, no mother Idyia, no sister Chalciope. Naught like this do I fear —but neither did Medea fear! Fair hope is often deceived in its own augury. For every ship tossed now upon the deep, you will find that the sea was gentle as it left the harbour'.

Medea had no fears for her safety. Jason, the prototype of the false lover, a master of the art of deception, had promised everything to Medea. Nor does Helen fear for her own safety. In elegy hope is expected to be disappointed.[48] Helen would never trust Paris.[49] The virtual book of the *Heroides* reports stories of deception. It especially recounts how deceit and fraudulence are intrinsic to love. *Spes*, the expectation and desire for a faithful, perennial love, is a 'treacherous goddess' (*fallax dea*).[50]

To sum up, within the interconnection of double and paired epistles in the *Heroides* intratextuality allows for an ironic and paradoxical re-assessment of the concept of elegiac love. Helen, the incarnation of the *docta puella*,[51] educated at the school of the poet-lover Ovid, re-establishes the norms of the adulterous, illegitimate love of the *Amores* and the *Ars*, offering a *remedium*, an antidote to the unproductive love lament of the female heroines. As Drinkwater puts it, Helen is a good student of the *Ars*, 'excellent at synthesizing lessons from a variety of sources and proceeding with the appropriate caution'.[52] Intratextual reading is vital to this ironical reformulation of the canonical world of love-elegy. Through

48 On the notion of hope in Ovidian epic, in connection with the general implausibility of the pathetic hopes of the elegiac *amator*, see Fulkerson 2017. See also Gibson 2013.

49 On Paris as a duplication of Aeneas, see Michalopolous 2006, 9–16.

50 Ov. *Ars* 1.445–446. Cf. also *RA* 685; Prop. 4.7.13–14; 3.17.11–12; 2.5.3.

51 On the figure of the *docta puella* in love elegy, see James 2003, 71–107 (and *passim*). On *erotodidaxis* and intertextuality in the *Heroides*, see Kennedy 2006.

52 Drinkwater 2013, 122 (who reformulates Kennedy 2006, 61).

contemplation, from an external point of view, Helen (and the reader of the *Heroides*) prospects the failure of Ovid's elegiac female soliloquy. Intratextuality marks the revitalization of erotic love-elegy. Love is essentially deceit and infidelity. Helen, the *praeceptrix amoris*,[53] exploits literary love-stories to instruct her readers in libertine and licentious love. And Helen's poem teaches the reader how to be a good lover by making the most of the advantages offered by previous stories of *afflictae puellae*.

Bibliography

Barchiesi, A. (1986), 'Problemi d'interpretazione in Ovidio: Continuità delle storie, continuazione dei testi', *Materiali e Discussioni* 16, 77–107.
Barchiesi, A. (1987), 'Narratività e convenzione nelle *Heroides*', *Materiali e Discussioni* 19, 63–90.
Barchiesi, A. (1992), *P. Ovidii Nasonis Epistulae Heroidum* 1–3, Firenze.
Barchiesi, A. (1993), 'Future Reflexive: Two Modes of Allusion and Ovid's *Heroides*', *Harvard Studies in Classical Philology* 95, 333–65.
Barchiesi, A. (1999), 'Vers une Historie à Rebours de l'Élegie Latine: Les *Héroides* 'Doubles' (16–21)', in: J. Fabre-Serris/A. Deremetz (eds.), *Élegie et Épopée dans la Poésie Ovidienne (Héroides et Amours) en Hommage à Simone Viarre*, Villeneuve, 53–67.
Battistella, C. (2010), *P. Ovidii Nasonis Heroidum Epistula 10: Ariadne Theseo*, Berlin/New York.
Bessone, F. (1997), *P. Ovidi Nasonis Heroidium Epistula XII Medea Iasoni*, Firenze.
Bessone, F. (2003), 'Discussione del mito e polifonia narrative nelle *Heroides*. Enone, Paride ed Elena (Ov. *Her.* 5 e 16–7)', in: M. Guglielmo/E. Bona (eds.), *Forme di comunicazione nel mondo antico e metamorfosi del mito: dal teatro al romanzo*, Alessandria, 149–85.
Björk, M. (2016), *Ovid's Heroides and the Ethopoeia*, Lund.
Casali, S. (2009), 'Ovidian Intertextuality', in: P. Knox (ed.), *A Companion to Ovid*, Blackwell, Malden, MA/Oxford, 341–54.
Caston, R.R. (2012), *The Elegiac Passion. Jealousy in Roman Love Elegy*, Oxford.
Ceccarelli, L. (2014), 'Note sul distico delle *Heroides* doppie: contributo alla discussione sull'autenticità', *Materiali e Discussioni* 73, 25–67.
Cucchiarelli, A. (1995), 'Ma il giudice delle dee non era un pastore? Reticenze e arte retorica di Paride (Her. 16)', *Materiali e Discussioni* 34, 135–52.
Desmond, M. (1993), 'When Dido Reads Vergil: Gender and Intertextuality in Ovid's *Heroides* 7', *Helios* 20, 56–68.
Drinkwater, M. (2007), 'Which Letter? Text and Subtext in Ovid's *Heroides*', *American Journal of Philology* 128, 367–87.
Drinkwater, M. (2013), 'An amateur's art: Paris and Helen in Ovid's *Heroides*', *Classical Philology* 108, 111–25.
Edmunds, L. (2001), *Intertextuality and the Reading of Roman Poetry*, Baltimore/London.

53 Wood 2013–2014 (on Helen as an expert in erotodidactic and the relationship between the Ovidian Helen and Euripides' tragedy).

Fabre-Serris, J. (1999), 'L'*Heroide* V d'Ovide. Variation sur un topos de la poèsie romaine: l'opposition monde pastoral/monde héroïque', in: J. Fabre-Serris/A. Deremetz (eds.), *Élegie et Épopée dans la Poésie Ovidienne (Héroides et Amours) en Hommage à Simone Viarre*, Villeneuve, 41–51.

Farrell, J. (1998), 'Reading and Writing the *Heroides*', *Harvard Studies in Classical Philology* 94, 307–38.

Fulkerson, L. (2005), *The Ovidian Heroine as Author. Reading, Writing, and Community in the Heroides*, Cambridge.

Fulkerson, L. (2009), 'The *Heroides*. Female Elegy?', in: P. Knox (ed.), *A Companion to Ovid*, Blackwell, Malden MA/Oxford, 78–89.

Fulkerson, L. (2017), '*The Vagaries of Hope in Vergil and Ovid*', in: D. Cairns/D. Nelis (eds.), *Emotions in the Classical World: Methods, Approaches, and Directions*, Stuttgart, 207–30.

Gibson, R.K. (2003), *Ovid Ars Amatoria Book 3*, Cambridge.

Gibson, R.K. (2013), 'Loves and Elegy', in: T. Thorsen (ed.), *The Cambridge Companion to Latin Love Elegy*, Cambridge, 209–23.

Harrison, S. (2002), 'Ovid and Genre: Evolutions of an Elegist', in: Ph. Hardie (ed.), *The Cambridge Companion to Ovid*, Cambridge, 79–94.

Heldmann, K. (1994), 'Ovids Sabinus-Gedicht (*Am.* 2.18) and die *Epistulae Heroidum*', *Hermes* 122, 188–219.

Hinds, S. (1985), 'Booking the Return Trip: Ovid and *Tristia* 1', *Proceedings of the Cambridge Philological Society* 31, 13–32.

Hinds, S. (1993), 'Medea in Ovid: Scenes from the Life of an Intertextual Heroine', *Materiali e Discussioni* 30, 9–47.

Hinds, S. (1998), *Allusion and Intertext. Dynamics of Appropriation in Roman Poetry*, Cambridge.

Hollis, A.S. (1977), *Ovid Ars Amatoria Book 1*, Oxford.

Jacobson, H. (1974), *Ovid's Heroides*, Princeton.

James, S.L. (2003), *Learned Girls and Male Persuasion: Gender and Reading in Roman Love Elegy*, Berkeley.

Jolivet, J.-C. (2001), *Allusion et fiction épistolaire dans les Héroides. Recherches sur l'intertextualité ovidienne*, Paris/Rome.

Kennedy, D. (1984), 'The epistolary Mode and the First of Ovid's *Heroides*', *Classical Quarterly* 34, 413–22.

Kennedy, D. (2002), 'Epistolarity: The *Heroides*', in: Ph. Hardie (ed.), *The Cambridge Companion to Ovid*, Cambridge, 217–31.

Kennedy, D. (2006), '*Vixisset Phyllis, si me foret usa magistro*: Erotodidaxis and Intertextuality', in: R. Gibson/S. Green/A. Sharrock (eds.), *The Art of Love. Bimillenial Essays on Ovid's Ars Amatoria and Remedia Amoris*, Oxford, 54–74.

Kenney, E.J. (1996), *Ovid. Heroides XVI-XXI*, Cambridge.

Knox, P. (1986), 'Ovid's *Medea* and the Authenticity of *Heroides* 12', *Harvard Studies in Classical Philology* 90, 207–23.

Knox, P. (1995), *Ovid Heroides. Select Epistles*, Cambridge.

Knox, P. (2002), 'The *Heroides*: Elegiac Voices', in: B. Weiden Boyd (ed.), *Brill's Companion to Ovid*, Leiden/Boston/Köln, 117–39.

Landolfi, L. (2000), *Scribentis imago. Eroine ovidiane e lamento epistolare*, Bologna.

Lindheim, S.H. (2000), '*Omnia vincit amor*; Or, Why Oenone Should have Known it would Never Work Out (Eclogue 10 and Heroides 5)', *Materiali e Discussioni* 44, 83–101.

Lindheim, S.H. (2003), *Mail and Female. Epistolary Narrative and Desire in Ovid's Heroides*, Madison.
McKeown, J.C. (1998), *Ovid's Amores*: Vol. III, *A Commentary on Book Two*, Leeds.
Michalopoulos, A.N. (2006), *Ovid Heroides 16 and 17. Introduction, Text and Commentary*, Cambridge.
Piazzi, L. (2007), *P. Ovidii Nasonis Heroidum Epistula VII. Dido Aeneae*, Firenze.
Rimmel, V. (2009), *Ovid's Lovers. Desire, Difference, and the Poetic Imagination*, Cambridge.
Rosati, G. (1996), 'Sabinus, the *Heroides* and the Poet-Nightingale. Some Observations on the Authenticity of the Epistula Sapphus', *Classical Quarterly* 46, 207–16.
Sharrock, A./Morales, H. (2000) (eds.), *Intratextuality. Greek and Roman Textual Relations*, Oxford.
Smith, R. Alden (2006), 'Fantasy, Myth, and Love Letters: Text and Tale in Ovid's *Heroides*', in: P.E. Knox (ed.), *Oxford Readings in Classical Studies. Ovid*, Oxford, 217–37.
Spentzou, E. (2003), *Readers and Writers in Ovid's Heroides. Transgressions of Genre and Gender*, Oxford.
Tarrant, R.J. (1981), 'The Authenticity of the Letter of Sappho to Phaon (*Heroides* XV)', *Harvard Studies in Classical Philology* 85, 133–53.
Verducci, F. (1985), *Ovid's Toyshop of the Heart: Epistulae Heroidum*, Princeton.
Wood, T.J. (2013-2014), 'Didactic Helen: Ovid's *praeceptrix* and Euripidean Proto-Elegy', *Classical Journal* 109 (3), 257–79.

Thea S. Thorsen

Intrepid Intratextuality: The Epistolary Pair of Leander and Hero (*Heroides* 18–19) and the End of Ovid's Poetic Career

1 Introduction

This paper argues that the rich intratextuality of *Heroides* 18–19 establishes an outline of Ovid's literary career, whose closure appears unexpected. *Heroides* 18–19 echo each other as well as (extensively) the *Metamorphoses* and (less so) the *Ars Amatoria* and the *Remedia Amoris* in a way that highlights the characteristic artistry, eroticism, learnedness and gender-inclusivity of Ovidian poetry. While this is expected, it may come as a surprise that the intratextuality of *Heroides* 18–19 may also include Ovid's exile poetry, and that together this complex of internal references offers a surprisingly intrepid twist on Ovid's biographic theme of artistic censorship, which characterizes the end of the poet's career as it is known from his *Tristia* and *Epistulae ex Ponto*.

The present approach to *Heroides* 18–19 presupposes that Ovid's double *Heroides* is a late composition that belongs to the period of Ovid's exile. There are compelling reasons to sustain this view. Firstly, there are certain linguistic and metrical features in this work, which are otherwise observed only in Ovid's later poetry.[1] Next, Ovid, who has a habit of referring internally to one work in another work in his own literary output, does not explicitly mention the double *Heroides* in any other extant poem, which suggests that he did not write much after he composed these poems.[2] Finally, as Alessandro Barchiesi convincingly argues, the work represents a closure of the genre of Latin love elegy itself, reiterating its

I would like to thank Theodore Papanghelis, Stephen Harrison, Antonios Rengakos and Stavros Frangoulidis for kindly inviting me to deliver an earlier version of this paper at the wonderful 11th Trends in Classics Conference that took place in Thessaloniki 25–27th of May 2017. I am also grateful to Alessandro Barchiesi, Laurel Fulkerson, Stephen Harrison, Stephen Heyworth, Andrew Laird, Alison Sharrock and Gail Trimble for helpful comments and criticisms.

1 Cf. Thorsen 2013, 117, n. 10, with references to Platnauer 1951, Courtney 1965 and Kenney 1996.
2 This fact is one important reason why these poems have been regarded as inauthentic. The debate on the authenticity of the double *Heroides* goes at least as far back as Scaliger, whose notes on the *Heroides* are included in Daniel Heinsius' important edition of Ovid's *Opera omnia*, see Thorsen 2014, 21.

https://doi.org/10.1515/9783110611021-016

origins and its history, including Ovid's own erotic-elegiac output.[3] Building on these observations, the present paper argues that the many layers of intratextuality in *Heroides* 18–19 trace a particular trajectory of Ovid's literary career, which culminates in a moment of courage.[4]

2 A rich case of Ovidian intratextuality

Heroides 18–19, the paired epistolary elegies dedicated to Leander and Hero, are famously inserted between Paris and Helen's letters on the one side (*Her.* 16–17), and those of Acontius and Cydippe (*Her.* 20–21) on the other. Unlike the relationships of these two other couples, which in many ways start as they compose their Ovidian letters to each other, the relationship between Leander and Hero will end as soon as they have written their epistles. As we know e.g. from Virgil's *Georgics*, an epigram by Antipater of Thessaloniki and Musaeus,[5] Leander is to drown in the attempt to swim from his side of the strait across the stormy Hellespont, and Hero is to commit suicide by throwing herself from her tower when she discovers his body, washed ashore on her side of the strait. Notably, from the point of view of the Ovidian letters, these events have yet to happen.

2.1 An intratextual match made in heaven

Heroides 18–19 share a striking number of features. Both Leander and Hero address storm-related deities; Leander reproaches Boreas for the strong winds that prevent him from swimming across the Hellespont to his beloved (*Her.* 18.39–40; 209) and Hero blames Neptune for making it impossible for her lover to cross the water (*Her.* 19.139–50). Both perform quasi-soliloquies: Leander about Hero to the Moon while swimming (*Her.* 18.53–82) and Hero about Leander to her nurse while spinning (*Her.* 19.33–54). Furthermore, both relish thoughts of lovemaking;

3 Barchiesi 1993 and 1999, cf. also Ingleheart 2010, 21 and Barchiesi and Hardie 2010, 63.

4 In this I will follow the lead of Stephen Heyworth (2016) who argues for an understanding of *Heroides* 16 as composed in exile.

5 A brief account of the story of Leander and Hero is included in Virgil's *Georgics* (3.258–63), notably as an example of the power of love. Servius attests the popularity of their story by pointing out that Virgil could omit Leander's name, *quia cognita erat fabula* (*ad G.* 3.258–63, 'because the story was well-known'). The Rome-based poet Antipater of Thessaloniki, a contemporary of Ovid, wrote an epigram about the couple (*Anth. Pal.* 7.666), who were also depicted in Roman frescoes, *RE* 8.912. Musaeus (c. fifth century AD) recounts the tale in hexameters.

Leander contemplates past pleasures (*Her.* 18.99–116), while Hero fantasises and dreams about future joys (*Her.* 19.59–68). Leander's and Hero's focus on past and future erotic encounters are due to the fact that they are presently separated, which they both —naturally— lament (*Her.* 18.125–160, 161–182; *Her.* 19.69–118). Moreover, both Leander (*Her.* 18.137–144) and Hero (*Her.* 19.119–128) reflect on the aetiological myth of Phrixus and Helle, who gave her name to the Hellespont that separates them. Along the lines of the erudite sophistication evoked by thoughts on the etymology and aetiology of the Hellespont, Leander parades learned catalogues (*Her.* 18.149–160), one on catasterized heroines, another on distant places, as does Hero, on Neptune's erotic conquests (*Her.* 19.129–138). Finally, both Leander (*Her.* 18.183–214) and Hero (*Her.* 19.191–210) romanticize their tragic and still hypothetical deaths. In short, these poems reflect each other so much so —both in form and content— that it is almost difficult to tell them apart.

2.2 *Heroides* 18–19 and other works by Ovid

At the same time, this pair of epistolary elegies is intratextually linked with a number of other works in Ovid's output. Among the works that both *Heroides* 18–19 evoke are *Heroides* 15, the closing poem of Ovid's collection of single *Heroides*,[6] the third book of Ovid's *Ars Amatoria*, addressed to women,[7] and the tragic story of Ceyx and Alcyone, whose death by drowning is told in Book 11 of the *Metamorphoses*.[8] These intratextual avenues to other works by Ovid, which are thus shared by Leander and Hero, contribute to the twin-like mirroring of the two poems and affirm the general pattern of similarities shared internally between the two epistolary elegies, as outlined above.

There are, however, some intratextual references in *Heroides* 18–19 to other works by Ovid that do not seem to fit this balance of equal parallels. Considering the consistent way in which these two letters draw on and allude to one another, such breaks with the overall pattern may thus call for Alison Sharrock's 'classic intratextual move', that is, 'the relating of apparently disparate parts of the text in order to enhance the reading of both.'[9] In the following it will therefore be argued that an element, which at first appears as an oddity from the point of view

6 Compare. *Her.* 15.153–5 with *Her.* 18.81–2 and *Her.* 15.121 with *Her.* 19.173. I take *Heroides* 15 to be a genuine poem by Ovid, see Thorsen 2014, 96–122.

7 Compare *Ars* 3.83 with *Her.* 18.61–74, and *Ars* 3.381–2 with *Her.* 19.9–14, see also below.

8 Compare *Met.* 11.410–748 with *Her.* 18.81–2, and *Met.* 11.544–5; 562–3 with *Her.* 19.40.

9 Sharrock and Morales 2000, 10.

of the overall pattern, upon closer inspection proves to hold a key to a profounder understanding not only of *Heroides* 18–19, but also of the dynamics of Ovidian intratextuality.

2.3 Leander's explicit reference to Daedalus and Icarus

Leander's evocation of Daedalus and Icarus (*Her.* 18.49–50) is arguably such an intratextual odd one out considering the overall pattern of similarities between the two epistolary elegies, since Hero, while reflecting Leander's letter in numerous ways, does not mention Daedalus, or Icarus. At the same time, Daedalus and Icarus are important and protean figures in Ovid's poetry, whose presence in Leander's letter appears significant.[10]

Indeed, Daedalus and Icarus occur throughout Ovid's entire output, and in a wide variety of contexts, which require a similar variety of approaches and interpretations: some contexts are erotic, as in Leander's letter and the case of Iphis (*Met.* 9.741–4), others are non-erotic, as apparently in Book 2 of the *Ars Amatoria* (*Ars* 2.21–96); some episodes, like these two latter cases, are in elegiac couplets (including *Fasti* 4.284), while others are in epic hexameters, such as the famous account at *Met.* 8.184–235. This occurrence of Daedalus and Icarus, like several others, belongs to mythological excursions and metapoetic discourse – focussing on Daedalus as artist and Icarus as a victim of his hubris. Some explicit mentions of Daedalus and Icarus are therefore fittingly made from the perspective of exile, where artist and victim have become one (e.g. *Tr.* 1.1.90, 3.4.21 and 3.8.6, and the *Ibis* 611).

Among these evocations, Leander's is relatively brief: *nunc daret audaces utinam mihi Daedalus alas/ Icarium quamvis hinc prope litus abest*[11] (*Her.* 18.49–50, 'O, if only Daedalus had given me audacious wings now, even though the Icarian coast is not far away!').[12] Despite this brevity, there are good reasons to dwell on this couplet in particular in the light of the other Ovidian passages in which Daedalus and Icarus are mentioned. Like the Daedalus and Icarus episode of the *Ars Amatoria*, Leander's reference is in elegiac couplets, but unlike the excursus in the *Ars*, which appears surprisingly non-erotic given its erotodidactic

10 See e.g. Sharrock 1994.

11 Here and elsewhere I follow the text of Kenney 1996.

12 All translations, often slightly adapted, are taken from the online Loeb Classical Library, unless otherwise is stated.

context,[13] Leander's evocation clearly has an erotic purpose: were he equipped with wings made by Daedalus, he would fly to Hero and make love to her. Leander's reference to Daedalus and Icarus is thus fulfilling the criteria of the genre of Latin love elegy more directly than the extended episode on the same theme in the *Ars Amatoria*. At the same time, Leander's evocation of Daedalus and Icarus is arguably just as strongly metapoetical as the more extensive passages in the *Ars* and the *Metamorphoses*, if not more, thanks to the epistolary qualities of Ovid's *Heroides*, whose grammatical privileging of the first person singular blurs the distinction between the voice of the Heroidean letter-writer and that of the actual author.[14]

Metapoetics may in fact help explain a feature that has been regarded as somewhat absurd in Leander's reference to Daedalus and Icarus, namely the claim that the Icarian coast *hinc prope ... abest*,[15] since the geographical distance between the Hellespont and the Icarian sea is considerable ('some 180 miles').[16] However, the *Icarium litus* is closer to Leander if the reference is understood not geographically, but metapoetically —as a place within Ovid's own poetry. In that sense Leander is not far from the place where Icarus drowned.

This understanding of Leander's puzzling claim is in line with the many layers of metapoetics otherwise compressed into this couplet. Daedalus —the artist— is for example easily associated with Ovid, since Leander's prayer to Daedalus may in fact be seen as an oblique prayer to the poet, who ultimately controls the destiny of his literary figures, Leander's included.[17] But the creator may also be controlled by his creation: for if Ovid acts like Daedalus and equips Leander with 'audacious wings', then Leander may suffer the fate of Icarus. So Leander may also be seen as a potential Icarus, who too, as the victim of artistry, may be seen as an image of Ovid —especially from the hindsight of exile. For Ovid is like

---

13 The passage in the *Ars* is not in any obvious way about love, except —as Alison Sharrock points out— the love of art, see Sharrock 1994. In Thorsen 2018, I argue that the Daedalus-episode in the *Ars* is linked if not exactly to love, then to another prominent love-related theme in Ovid's *Ars Amatoria*, namely adultery, since the three mythical excursions of more than thirty lines, of which there is just one per book, concern Pasiphae and the bull (Book 1), Daedalus and Icarus (Book 2) and Procris and Cephalus (Book 3), who all have a common denominator in Minoan adulteries.

14 Cf. Fulkerson 2005.

15 No alternative readings are reported in the apparatus of Kenney 1996, 54, however, as Stephen Heyworth kindly pointed out to me at the conference in Thessaloniki, where one finds *abest* one may always suspect *adest*.

16 Kenney 1996, 150.

17 Cf. e.g. Ov. *Am.* 3.12.

Daedalus, the artist who challenges existing confinements, and Ovid is like Icarus, the victim who suffers the consequences. Leander aligns himself closely with both as he prays for the aid of artistic boldness and recognizes the fall that might ensue. Leander's reference to Daedalus and Icarus is therefore strongly metapoetic and as much about the power and dangers of poetry as it is about the speaker's need for inventive means of transportation.

2.4 Hero's subtle evocation of Arachne

Leander's reference to Daedalus and Icarus has no *direct* parallel in Hero's letter. Nonetheless, she does *indirectly* evoke another figure in the *Metamorphoses*, namely the spinner and weaver Arachne. Arachne's transformation is famously described in Book 6 and, like Daedalus and Icarus, she is regarded as a self-referential figure from the point of view of the poet proper —not least in the context of the censorship and punishment of artistic expression, again evoking Ovid's biographical theme of exile.[18]

While the intratextual allusion to Arachne in Hero's letter is less explicit than Leander's evocation of Daedalus and Icarus —for example, in the fact that her name is nowhere mentioned in *Heroides* 19— the evocation of the figure of Arachne is arguably also more extensive, inasmuch as Hero represents herself as spinning, which is one of the activities with which Arachne, the weaver (cf. e.g. *Met.* 6.22),[19] is identified:

...
sic ubi lux acta est et noctis amicior hora
  exhibuit pulso sidera clara die,
protinus in summo vigilantia lumina tecto
  ponimus, assuetae signa notamque viae,
tortaque versato ducentes stamina fuso
  feminea tardas fallimus arte moras.
quid loquar interea tam longo tempore, quaeris?
  nil nisi Leandri nomen in ore meo est.
...
sternuit en lumen (posito nam scribimus illo)
  sternuit et nobis prospera signa dedit.

(*Her.* 19.33–152)

18 See e.g. Harries 1990 and Johnson 2008.

19 I am grateful to Gail Trimble for the precision concerning the vocabulary of spinning and weaving here.

> Thus, when the light is done and night's friendlier hour has driven out day and set forth the gleaming stars, straightway I place in the highest of the abode my watchful lamps, the signals to guide you on the accustomed way. Then, drawing with whirling spindle the twisted thread, with woman's art I beguile the slow hours of waiting. What, meanwhile, I say through so long a time, you ask? Nothing but Leander's name is on my lips. ... My lamp has sputtered, see! —for I am writing with it near— it has sputtered and given us favouring signs.

Spinning —and weaving— is famously an ancient image for text-production, and offers Latin —as well as many modern languages— the very metaphor that lies behind the word 'text'.[20] Hero merges the concrete and metapoetic aspects of spinning and weaving in a strikingly seamless manner. The lamp that has been the leading light for Leander as he swims across the Hellespont, and which, on the very night that Hero is writing her Ovidian letter, will lead to his death as its flame dies down, marks the starting and end point of Hero's act of spinning/ writing. Hero describes how, as soon as the day is over, she usually starts preparing her spinning in order to kill time, and goes on to explain that the *feminea ars* is soon accompanied by the production of words, as she begins to talk, seemingly to her nurse, but really to herself, and finally, she reveals that all of these activities form part of the production of the very text that we are reading, as she again brings the lamp to our attention, explaining *posito nam scribimus illo* (*Her.* 19.151, 'for I am writing with that [lamp] beside me').

2.5 Neptune's erotic conquests

Notably, it is in this long passage, which starts with Hero claiming to be *spinning* beside the lamp and ends with her claiming to be *writing* beside the lamp, that she includes her learned catalogue:

> at tibi flammarum memori, Neptune, tuarum
> nullus erat ventis impediendus amor,
> si neque Amymone nec laudatissima forma
> criminis est Tyro fabula vana tui
> lucidaque Alcyone Calyceque Hecataeone nata,
> et nondum nexis angue Medusa comis
> flavaque Laudice caeloque recepta Celaeno,
> et quarum memini nomina lecta mihi.
> has certe pluresque canunt, Neptune, poetae
> molle latus lateri composuisse tuo.
>
> (*Her.* 19.129–138)

20 Explored e.g. by Scheid and Svenbro 1994.

> Yet, Neptune, were you mindful of your own heart's flames, you would let no love be hindered by the winds – if neither Amymone, nor Tyro much praised for beauty, are stories idly charged to you, nor shining Alcyone, and Calyce, child of Hecataeon, nor Medusa when her locks were not yet twined with snakes, nor golden-haired Laodice and Celaeno taken to the skies, nor those whose names I remember having read. These, surely, Neptune, and many more, the poets say in their songs have mingled their soft embraces with your own.

In terms of intratextuality, this catalogue evokes *one* specific passage in Ovid's output, namely the following from Book 6 of Ovid's *Metamorphoses*:

> te quoque mutatum torvo, Neptune, iuvenco
> virgine in Aeolia posuit; tu visus Enipeus
> gignis Aloidas, aries Bisaltida fallis,
> et te flava comas frugum mitissima mater
> sensit equum, sensit volucrem crinita colubris
> mater equi volucris, sensit delphina Melantho.[21]
>
> (*Met.* 6.115–20)

> You also, Neptune, she pictured, changed to a grim bull with the Aeolian maiden; now as Enipeus you do beget the Aloidae, as a ram deceive Bisaltis. The golden-haired mother of corn, most gentle, knew you as a horse; the snake-haired mother of the winged horse knew you as a winged bird; Melantho knew you as a dolphin.

By discoursing on Neptune's erotic conquests, Hero evokes a part of the tapestry that Arachne produces during her famous contest with the goddess Minerva. Hero's direct address to Neptune replicates that of the poet Ovid —who uniquely apostrophizes only this deity in the description of Arachne's tapestry— in the passage from the *Metamorphoses*. Thus Hero underscores the self-reflective force of her intratextual reference, which is further corroborated by sophisticated variations and an obliqueness typical of the learned poet: Hero elegantly avoids the names of the objects of Neptune's love, which are included in the artistic model, Arachne's tapestry; Medusa is the exception, but even in this case the variation is pointed, as the explicit mention of her name in *Heroides* 19 replaces a periphrastic reference in the *Metamorphoses*. At the same time, the names of the erotic conquests of Neptune included by Arachne might nevertheless be regarded as present in *Heroides* 19 through the *praeteritio* with which Hero closes her catalogue (*Her.* 19.137–8, see quotation above). From a metapoetic perspective, Hero's claim that Neptune has had erotic encounters with these and many more female figures, according to what 'the poets say in their songs', appears ironic and self-referential (much in the same way as does Leander's prayer to Daedalus *qua* Ovid) since it is in Ovid's own works that she may have read about these

---

21 The text is that of Tarrant 2004.

conquests. In fact, by means of intratextuality, Hero prompts a series of associations between the poet and the weaver in general, between Ovid and Arachne in particular, and between both of these figures and herself as she creatively reproduces in her text Ovid's poetic ekphrasis of Arachne's tapestry in his *Metamorphoses*.

The more oblique, yet more extensive intratextual evocation in *Heroides* 19 of Arachne as she is depicted in Ovid's *Metamorphoses* thus activates much the same range of intratextual effects as does Leander's reference to Daedalus and Icarus. Firstly, it involves the elegiac couplets of the *Heroides* with the epic hexameters of the *Metamorphoses*; furthermore, the epic passage in question, though depicting an erotic motive, does not have an erotic purpose, but rather an agonistic one, whereas the purpose of Hero's catalogue of Neptune's conquests is precisely to make it easier to get together with her beloved; finally, Hero's intratextual reference to Arachne intensifies the metapoetic significance of both – with reverberations reaching well into the biographical theme of Ovid's career ending in exile.

2.6 Weaving as writing and non-erotic leisure

Arachne famously doubly offends the gods, firstly by challenging the goddess Minerva, and secondly by irreverently depicting gods in amorous pursuit. For these offences she is severely punished, thus figuratively embodying Ovid in his exile. And as Ovid tells us repeatedly, this exile was partly due to his *Ars Amatoria*.

Notably, there are intratextual connections between *Heroides* 19 and the *Ars Amatoria*, as well as its sequel, the *Remedia Amoris*. These intratextual links do not concern the theme of artistic punishment, but a pervasive claim within Ovid's output, namely that lovers –and poets– tend to transgress stereotypical gender boundaries. It is worthy of note that this claim is only applicable to the following case when the *loci similes* in question are taken together, that is, when regarded intratextually. For gender stereotypes appear to be upheld in Book 3 of the *Ars Amatoria* addressed to women, where *Naso magister* concludes that men have more diversions to be entertained by than women:

> hos ignava iocos tribuit natura puellis;
> materia ludunt uberiore viri.
> sunt illis celeresque pilae iaculumque trochique
> armaque et in gyros ire coactus equus.
> (*Ars* 3.381–4)

> These are the games that indolent nature has given to women; men have richer material for their games. They have swift balls, and javelins and hoops and armour, and the horse that is trained to go in circles.

The implication of this observation, which is that those who do not indulge in sports and leisure activities are more prone to love and to suffer from love sickness —independently of their sex— is rendered more explicit in the *Remedia Amoris*, addressed overtly to men and implicitly to women,[22] where several kinds of diversions, such as hunting and fishing, plus gardening, are recommended in order not to love:

> desidiam puer ille sequi solet, odit agentes:
> da vacuae menti, quo teneatur, opus.
> sunt fora, sunt leges, sunt, quos tuearis, amici:
> vade per urbanae splendida castra togae
>
> rura quoque oblectant animos studiumque colendi:
> quaelibet huic curae cedere cura potest.
> ...
> ipse potes riguis plantam deponere in hortis;
> ipse potes rivos ducere lenis aqua
> ...
> cum semel haec animum coepit mulcere voluptas,
> debilibus pinnis irritus exit Amor.
> vel tu venandi studium cole: saepe ecessit
> turpiter a Phoebi victa sorore Venus
> ...
> lenius est studium, studium tamen, alite capta
> aut lino aut calamis praemia parva sequi,
> vel, quae piscis edax avido male devoret ore,
> abdere sub parvis aera recurva cibis.
> aut his aut aliis, donec dediscis amare,
> ipse tibi furtim decipiendus eris.
>
> (*Rem. Am.* 149–212)

> Where sloth is, that Boy is wont to follow; he hates the busy: give the empty mind some business to occupy it. There are courts, there are laws, there are friends for you to protect: frequent the camps that gleam with the city gown.

> The country also delights the mind, and the pursuit of husbandry: no care is there but must yield to this ... You yourself can plant a shoot in a well-watered garden, you yourself can guide the runnels of gentle water. When once this pleasure begins to charm the mind, on

22 Thorsen 2014, 31.

> maimed wings Love flutters hopelessly away. Or cultivate the pleasures of the chase: Often has Venus, vanquished by Phoebus' sister, beaten a base retreat ... It is a milder pleasure (yet a pleasure it is) to seek a humble prize by snaring birds with net or reed, or to hide beneath the scanty bait the brazen hook, which the greedy fish may swallow to his hurt with ravening mouth. By these or other pursuits, until you unlearn your love, you must craftily deceive yourself.

With these intratextual references in mind it is hard to take the exclusive gender-perspective of Hero's reasoning about her being a woman and therefore more prone to love at face value:

> urimur igne pari sed sum tibi viribus impar:
> fortius ingenium suspicor esse viris.
> ut corpus teneris ita mens infirma puellis:
> deficiam, parvi temporis adde moram.
> vos modo *venando*, modo *rus geniale colendo*
> ponitis in varia tempora longa mora.
> aut *fora* vos retinent aut *unctae* dona *palaestrae*,
> *flectitis aut freno colla sequacis equi;*
> *nunc volucrem laqueo, nunc piscem ducitis hamo*;
> diluitur posito serior hora mero.
>
> (*Her.* 19.5–14)

> We burn with equal fires, but I am not equal to you in strength; men, I suspect, must have stronger natures. As the body, so is the soul of tender women frail —delay but a little longer, and I shall die! You men, now in the chase, and now husbanding the genial acres of the country, consume long hours in the varied tasks that keep you. Either the market-place holds you, or the sports of the supple wrestling-ground, or you turn with bit the neck of the responsive steed; now you take the bird with the snare, now the fish with the hook; and the later hours you while away with the wine before you.

The figure of Ovid —in the pose of *Naso magister* in the *Ars Amatoria* and *Naso legendus* in *Remedia Amoris*[23]— clearly lurks behind the reasoning of Hero, which intratextually – as seen from the italicized words in the passage quoted above – synthesizes and summarizes the only two other *loci similes* in the Ovidian corpus so that together they modify Hero's seemingly gender-exclusive perspective. This perspective is furthermore undercut by the very fact that Leander does not go to a bar (*vel sim.*) in order to kill time while he waits for the storm to die down; instead he resorts to the exact same activity as his beloved: writing.

Similarly, the art of weaving, which Hero dubs *feminea* (*Her.* 19.38), also proves to be more gender-inclusive when seen in the context of Ovid's other

23 Thorsen 2014, 39.

works, such as, again, the *Ars Amatoria* and the *Remedia Amoris*. The explicit suggestion that Ovid too is a weaver is namely embedded —however metaphorically— already at the outset of the *Remedia* in the poet's claim that his new Muse has not unwoven the preceding poem: *nec te, blande puer, nec nostras prodimus artes, / nec nova praeteritum Musa retexit opus* (*Rem. Am.* 11–12, 'Neither you do I betray, sweet boy, nor my own craft, nor does the new Muse unravel the old work'). The implication of this couplet is that Ovid has 'woven' both the *Ars Amatoria* and the *Remedia Amoris*.

What seems and is even represented as gender-exclusive within the narrower context of Hero's letter appears instead as gender-inclusive within the larger context of Ovidian intratextuality: Hero's lack of diversions, which makes her exposed to love, and her spinning and weaving prove to be concerns and activities shared by the poet Ovid.

3 Pontus and *patria*

Furthermore, the larger context of Ovidian intratextuality also offers a key to understanding the significance of the geographical setting of Leander and Hero's letters, which is as accurate as Leander's location of the Icarian sea appears inaccurate.[24] *Heroides* 18–19 has one foot in the (barely) civilized world, namely Abydos, where Leander is from, and another firmly placed on barbarian soil, namely Sestos, where Hero lives. Together they span the strait that forms part of the road, which is partly seaborne and partly goes on land to Pontus, on the shores of which Ovid laments that he spent his last years in relegation. Notably, there is an explicit reference to this significant terminus in Leander's letter:

> est aliud lumen, multo mihi certius istis,
> non errat tenebris quo duce noster amor.
> hoc ego dum spectem, Colchos et in ultima Ponti,
> quaque viam fecit Thessala pinus, eam
> ...
>
> (*Her.* 18.155–8)

There is another light, far surer for me than those [various constellations], and when it leads me through the dark my love leaves not its course; while my eyes are fixed on this, I could

24 I am grateful to Alessandro Barchiesi for stressing this point to me at the conference in Thessaloniki.

> go to Colchis or the farthest bounds of Pontus, and where the ship of Thessalian pine held on its course ...

Embedded in heroic references to Jason and his quest on the ship Argo for the Golden Fleece in Colchis, the expression *ultima Ponti* appears to acquire a less mythical and more biographical ring against the background of the end of Ovid's literary career as we know it. Yet, how far can we push the metapoetic significance of such a ring-composition? To what extent can Leander, who wishes to go to Pontus —with love, as it were— reflect the exiled poet Ovid who incessantly laments his new abodes and pines for his lost homeland, as here, in *Tristia* 3.4b?[25]

> ulterius nihil est nisi non habitabile frigus.
> heu quam vicina est ultima terra mihi!
> at longe patria est, longe carissima coniunx,
> quicquid et haec nobis post duo dulce fuit.
> (*Tr.* 3.4b.51–4)

> Farther still is nothing but a cold that forbids habitation. Alas! how near to me is the margin of the world! But my fatherland is far away, far my dearest wife, and all that after these two was once sweet to me.

Certainly, Ovid explicitly and repeatedly longs for his lost *patria* in the *Tristia* and *Epistulae ex Ponto*.

At the same time, Ovid recognises the close connection between the fatherland and the *pater*, Augustus, a pair that must be approached with utmost care and caution, not to say servility, as for example here: *his, precor, atque aliis possint tua numina flecti, / o pater, o patriae cura salusque tuae!* (*Tr.* 2.573–4 'May this, I pray, and other things have power to bend your will, O father, O protector and salvation of your fatherland')!'[26] But what if the *pater patriae* cannot be persuaded to let Rome be the homeland also of Ovid? Questions such as this increase the relevance of the biographical interpretation not only of Leander's wish to go to Pontus, but also of Hero's claim that *metuo, patria ne laedar* ... (*Her.* 19.99, 'I fear that I may be injured by the *patria* ...'), and even more so Leander's claim that *invitus repeto patriam —quis credere possit?* (*Her.* 18.122 'I am going back to my *patria* against my will— who could believe it?') It is especially this final question —formulated, according to the epistolary genre, in the first person singular— that attenuates the Heroidean guise of the letter-writer so much so that behind it the features of Ovid arguably emerge. For it is precisely Ovid who incessantly

25 Compare also e.g. *Tr.* 4.2.57–64.
26 Cf. Augustus, *Res Gestae* 35.

claims that he wants to go back home and so it is precisely in Ovid's case that a wish *not* to return to one's fatherland must sound most incredible. Thus, through the mouthpiece of Leander Ovid poses a question that may be rhetorical but more probably is real: seriously, who could believe that Ovid would be unwilling to return to Rome? But in the world of fiction, everything is possible, even to alter one's fate.

4 Conclusion

By means of intratextuality the epistolary elegies of Leander and Hero draw attention to artistic censorship and the biographical theme of exile within the context of Ovid's literary career. Some of the richest intratextual instances in this epistolary pair of elegies conjure up the figures of Daedalus and Icarus (*Heroides* 18) and Arachne (*Heroides* 19). Daedalus, Icarus and Arachne are all victims associated with artistic courage under the sway of superior powers, similar to how Ovid represents himself in his relegation from Rome by the emperor Augustus. The significance of the intratextual links between *Heroides* 18–19 and Ovid's *Metamorphoses*, which activates the theme of exile, is further deepened by the fact that Daedalus and Icarus, mentioned by Leander, feature prominently in the *Ars Amatoria*, which Ovid famously refers to as one of the causes of his exile. The relevance of this context for the significance of intratextual links to the *Ars Amatoria*, as well as its sequel the *Remedia Amoris*, within the context of *Heroides* 18–19, is enhanced by the way in which Hero's letter intratextually resonates precisely with these works. The intratextual complex of the epistolary pair of elegies is finally toppled by the evocation of Ovid's exile poetry through the buzz-words 'Pontus' and '*patria*' in *Heroides* 18–19, so that this pair of elegiac epistles emerges as a powerful allegory of Ovid's poetic career in retrospect.

From this perspective Leander and Hero offer oblique portrayals of an Ovid who is different from the one we know from his traditional exile poetry: still exiled, but courageously showing resistance till the end. From every angle, the lives of Leander and Hero are threatened and the love that they share is endangered, yet, the fixation of the presence, which the epistolary genre requires, liberates the two protagonists from any actual closure.[27] However momentarily, this freedom is essentially optimistic in a way that allegorically imbues the end of Ovid's poetic career with an intrepidly bold attitude —a kind of recklessness, even— that is

27 See Thorsen 2013, 127.

absent from his more traditional works of exile. For it is exceedingly important that even in their deeply desperate situation Leander and Hero will not yield: not to the parental disapproval that forced Leander to swim stealthily across the Hellespont to Hero in the first place, not to their hostile fatherlands, not to the ominous tale of Helle, not to the dire doom of Ceyx. Leander is an Ovid who will do whatever it takes: for his love he is even willing to go all the way to *ultima Ponti* and —even as the *patria* is harmful— power-challenging texts continue to be woven by our H/hero.

Bibliography

Barchiesi, A. (1993), 'Future Reflexive: Two Modes of Allusion and Ovid's *Heroides*', *HSCPh* 95, 333–65.

Barchiesi, A. (1995), 'Review of Die Briefpaare in Ovids *Heroides*: Tradition und Innovation by Cornelia Hintermeier', *JRS* 85, 325–7.

Barchiesi, A. (1999), 'Vers un'histoire à rebourse de l'élégie latine: Les *Héroïdes* "Double" (16–21)', in: A. Deremetz/J. Fabre-Serris (eds.), *Élégie et Épopée: Melanges Offerts à S. Viarre*, Lille, 53–67.

Barchiesi, A./Hardie, P. (2010), 'The Ovidian Career Model: Ovid, Gallus, Apuleius, Boccaccio', in: P. Hardie/H. Moore (eds.), *Classical Literary Careers and Their Reception*, Cambridge, 59–88.

Courtney, E. (1965), 'Ovidian and Non-Ovidian *Heroides*', *BICS* 12, 63–66.

Fulkerson, L. (2005), *The Ovidian Heroine as Author: Reading, Writing, and Community in the Heroides*, Cambridge.

Goold, G.P./Wheeler, A.L. (eds.) (2014), *Ovid, Tristia, Ex Ponto*, with an English translation by A.L. Wheeler, new ed./revised by G.P. Goold, Loeb Classical Library, online edition.

Harries, B. (1990), 'The Spinner and the Poet: Arachne in Ovid's *Metamorphoses*', *PCPhS* 36, 64–82.

Heyworth, S. (2016), 'Authenticity and Other Textual Problems in *Heroides* 16', in: R. Hunter/S. Oakley (eds.), *Latin Literature and its Transmission*, Cambridge, 142–170.

Ingleheart, J. (2010), *A Commentary on Ovid, Tristia* 2, Oxford.

Johnson, P.J. (2008), *Ovid Before Exile: Art and Punishment in the Metamorphoses*, Madison, WI.

Kenney, T. (ed.) (1995), *P. Ovidi Nasonis, Amores, Medicamina, Faciei Femineae, Ars Amatoria, Remedia Amoris*, Oxford.

Kenney, T. (ed.) (1996), *Ovid: Heroides* XVI-XXI, Cambridge.

Platnauer, M. (1951), *The Latin Elegiac Couplet*, Oxford.

Scheid, J./Svenbro, J. (1994), *Le métier de Zeus: mythe du tissage et du tissu dans le monde gréco-romain*, Paris.

Sharrock, A. (1994), *Seduction and Repetition in Ovid's Ars Amatoria II*, Oxford.

Sharrock, A./Morales, H. (2000), *Intratextuality: Greek and Roman Textual Traditions*, Oxford.

Shipley, F. (ed.) (2014), *Compendium of Roman History, Res Gestae Divi Augusti*, with an English translation by F.W. Shipley, Loeb Classical Library online edition.

Tarrant, R. (ed.) (2004), *P. Ovidi Nasonis Metamorphoses*, Oxford.

Thorsen, T.S. (2013), 'Ovid the Love Elegist', in: T.S. Thorsen (ed.), *The Cambridge Companion to Latin Love Elegy*, Cambridge, 114–32.

Thorsen, T.S. (2014), *Ovid's Early Poetry*, Cambridge.

Thorsen, T.S. (2018), 'The Second Erato and the Deeper Design of Ovid's *Ars Amatoria*: Unravelling the Anti-Marital Union of Venus, Procris and Romulus', *Exemplaria Classica* 10, 140–65.

S.J. Heyworth

Some Polyvalent Intra- and Inter-Textualities in *Fasti* 3

The voluminous nature of Ovid's corpus lends itself to the study of intratextuality, as does the poet's self-aware style. The *Fasti* is a particularly rich field for such examination, partly because it appears late in the poet's life so there is a large amount of material to recall, but especially because the poem itself belongs to two periods. Initial composition was alongside the *Metamorphoses* – these were the works Ovid was working on before he was dispatched to Tomi,[1] and each shows awareness of the other;[2] but the published version, addressed to Germanicus, is Tiberian, and explicitly refers to his exile in book 4 (79–84). Consequently, by the time he issued the work readers were in a position to observe any links with most of the books of exile poetry. We cannot know in most cases whether the text of the *Fasti* has been left unchanged since the departure from Rome in A.D. 8; but leaving a text unchanged is an authorial decision, and it is quite possible for a passage of the *Tristia* to allude to the *Fasti* and the same passage of the *Fasti* to allude to the same passage of the *Tristia*.[3]

One place where we can see such developments is in the aetion for the Salii and the *ancilia* in *Fasti* 3.259–392. King Numa is depicted as a man of peace, author of a calendar, keen to promote legal and religious order, dealing with thunderbolts, and engaging in conversation with various gods: he offers numerous

1 Note the parallel phrasing at *Tristia* 2.552 *sors mea rupit opus* ('my fate interrupted the work') of the incomplete *Fasti* and 1.7.14 *fuga rupit opus* ('exile interrupted the work') of the *Metamorphoses*. The difference is that the *Met.* is published and available in Rome as *Tristia* 1.1, 1.7 and the *iubeas legi* ('have it read to you') of 2.558 demonstrate, whereas there is no evidence that *Fasti* has been issued: in *Tristia* 2 he says only *scripsi* ('I have written').

2 Nicely established by Hinds 1987, e.g.

3 There is some similarity in the relationship between the *Amores* and the other early works. In book 3 the first and the final poem both express the intention to write tragedy; but 2.18 refers to tragedy as already having grown through the poet's efforts (*cura*, 13). The implication is that this poem was written for the second edition, and so can refer back to the *Medea* as already composed. However, the effect is less interesting and creative in this case: we do not have a text of the *Medea* from which to trace allusions in either direction; and there is no other solid evidence for late composition in the *Amores*, nor any crucial biographical or historical event to inform our reading. The same is true of the references to *Ars amatoria* and *Heroides* in 2.18.19–20 and 21–6. More expressive is the implied dating of the revised first book of *Ars amatoria* to autumn 2 B.C. (Hollis 1977, xiii and 150–1), which pointedly places it in the year of the exile of the elder Julia. But the political edge is more significant than intratextual complexities.

https://doi.org/10.1515/9783110611021-017

analogies for Ovid himself, as the peaceful poet, erstwhile *decemvir*, and author of the *Fasti*. When banished Ovid is himself the victim of a lightning strike; and in exile he writes *Tristia* 2 and other passages addressed to Caesar, and thus becomes, like Numa, a 'man not to be excluded from conversation with the gods' (*Fasti* 3.344). The analogy in situation may originate in coincidence, but he exploits it in the *Tristia*, and by the time the *Fasti* was published in its revised form, the intratextualities have become significant.

Two words expressing what is 'permissible' play a key role in the passage: *fas* (3.314) and *licet* (3.326).[4] From its very title the *Fasti* is a poem that concerns itself with what is permitted: the term implies a calendrical list of the days on which one may 'speak', i.e. legal action is allowed: cf. 1.48 *fastus erit per quem lege licebit agi* (n.b. 47–62), and Varro, *Ling. Lat.* 6.29 *dies fasti, per quos praetoribus omnia uerba sine piaculo licet fari*.[5] Some instances of the words reflect on the poet's access to arcane knowledge and divine inspiration, e.g. 3.167 *si licet occultos monitus audire deorum / uatibus* ('if poets are allowed to hear the secret advice of gods') and 6.7–8:

> fas mihi praecipue uultus uidisse deorum,
> uel quia sum uates, uel quia sacra cano.[6]

However, *licet* is a key term in the exile poetry from the first couplet on (*Trist.* 1.1.1–2):

> Parue, (nec inuideo) sine me, liber, ibis in Vrbem,
> ei mihi, quo domino non licet ire tuo.[7]

The terms thus come to evoke the restrictions placed on Ovid as an exile; and all the more so given that *licet* and *fas* appear as a pair together in a couplet marked as late because it is addressed to Germanicus (*Fasti* 1.25–6):

4 Cf. also 3.325 *scire nefas homini. nobis concessa canentur* ('<these things> it is not right for a man to know. We shall sing what is permitted').

5 Varro has similar formulations at *Ling. Lat.* 6.30, 53. Ovid reprises the diction at *Fasti* 1.289 *quod tamen ex ipsis licuit mihi discere fastis* ('what it has been possible for me to discover from the *Fasti* themselves'). For discussion of the theme see Feeney 1992.

6 'It is right for me in particular to have seen the faces of the gods, both because I am a poet and because I sing of holy ritual.'

7 'Little book, you shall go to Rome without me (I am not envious); alas that is a place where it is not permitted to your master to go.' Cf. e.g. 1.1.16, 57; 1.3.67-8; 3.12.26, 3.14.12; 5.4.3; *Ex Ponto*2.2.8, 3.4.68, 4.4.45. *fas* appears e.g. at *Tristia* 2.515, 3.1.81, *Ex Ponto* 4.8.55, 4.16.45.

si licet et fas est, uates rege uatis habenas,
auspice te felix totus ut annus eat.[8]

In asking gods for forgiveness because of the known innocence of his character, the Ovid of exile is figured as Numa addressing first Picus and Faunus (*Fasti* 3.309–10):

tum Numa: di nemorum, factis ignoscite nostris
si scelus ingenio scitis abesse meo.[9]

and then Jupiter himself (3.333–6):

ut rediit animus, da certa piamina, dixit,
fulminis, altorum rexque paterque deum,
si tua contigimus manibus donaria puris,
hoc quoque quod petitur si pia lingua rogat.[10]

Forgiveness is a theme already at *Trist.* 1.1.71 *ignoscant augusta mihi loca dique locorum* ('may I be pardoned by the august place and the gods of the place'); and the poet's lack of wickedness and fundamental innocence is repeatedly asserted. Both appear together at *Trist.* 1.2.97–105 when he appeals to the gods of the Adriatic to let him pass through the storm:

si tamen acta deos numquam mortalia fallunt,
a culpa facinus scitis abesse mea.
immo ita si scitis, si me merus abstulit error,
stultaque mens nobis, non scelerata fuit, ...
... ita parcite, diui![11]

Some of the language precisely recalls that of the Numa episode, especially *scitis abesse mea*. Ovid aggrandizes his situation by associating himself with an esteemed hero as he does throughout *Tristia* 1 with the evocations of Aeneas,

8 'If it is permitted by human law and divine, as a poet guide the reins of a poet so that the whole year may pass propitiously under your auspices.'

9 'Then Numa says: "Gods of the woods, pardon our actions, if you are aware that my mind is free from wickedness." '

10 'Once his wits returned he said, "Give us a sure way of expiating the thunderbolt, king and father of the lofty gods, if we have touched your sanctuary with unsullied hands, if it is a pious tongue that makes this request too." '

11 'However, if mortal acts never escape the notice of the gods, you know that villainy is absent from my fault. In fact, if that is what you know, if I was carried away by a simple mistake and my mind was foolish not wicked ... then spare me, gods'.

Ulysses and the like; he wistfully evokes a figure who was able to use his wit to charm a threatening deity. Ovid can only address his Jupiter in absence, and is doubtful whether he has the right to do so at all (*Tristia* 5.2.45–6):

> alloquor en absens absentia numina supplex,
> si fas est homini cum Iove posse loqui.[12]

But when the exiled Ovid has established his own distinctive identity, the parallels between Numa and the poet darken the tone in the *Fasti*: having *fas* and legality on your side is insufficient in the world of Augustus.

The Ides of March was in the traditional lunar calendar the first full moon of the year, an event marked by celebration of Anna Perenna. Though the cult was an established part of the calendar, and thus sanctioned by the state, Ovid's account at *Fasti* 3.523–696 says nothing about formal rites, but emphasizes the popular participation in the day and the obscene entertainment enjoyed by the crowds. Anna is to us a rather obscure goddess, and was apparently so in antiquity too. Ovid presents a series of different accounts of her identity: she is a symbol of on-going time (the moon or the year), a nymph of flowing water, a deity of food and fertility. But he gives the greatest space to a story that casts her as Anna the sister of Dido, familiar to us as a sympathetic figure from book 4 of the *Aeneid*. The narrative begins where Vergil's finishes, with Dido's death. Driven from her new homeland in Carthage by the intrusion of Iarbas, the local king, Dido's rejected suitor, Anna finds sanctuary with Battus on Malta; but her vindictive brother Pygmalion threatens to attack and she is forced to flee again, this time towards Italy. Just as the ship approaches the shores of the Gulf of Tarentum, a sudden storm drives them far away. Finally, she is ship-wrecked on the coast of Latium, and actually finds Aeneas there, walking barefoot with Achates. Recognizing her, he offers regrets and hospitality, and takes her home. He commends her to the care of Lavinia, but the queen is suspicious of the exotic arrival from her husband's past, and plots to kill her. The ghost of Dido warns Anna to escape; she leaps from the window, runs across the fields, and finds a permanent home in the waters of the Numicius. When the locals search for her, a voice is heard from the river (3.653–4):

12 'See, as a suppliant, in absence I address the absent gods, if a man has the right to be able to speak to Jupiter.'

ipsa loqui uisa est: placidi sum nympha Numici:
amne perenne latens Anna Perenna uocor.[13]

Anna's drowning in the ever-flowing river has immortalized her: as a result of the union *amnis* becomes *Anna*, and she becomes *perennis*. The perennial river symbolizes the ever-flowing nature of time, and thus of the goddess of the year.

Analogies with the *Aeneid* are obvious: exiled from her home in Tyre, like the Trojans after the sack of Troy, Anna's attempts to settle are repeatedly thwarted by events: the episode 'at first sight appears to be a continuation, completion, and replica of the *Aeneid*' (Barchiesi 1997, 21), and virtually every couplet can be related to something within the *Aeneid*.[14] But there is considerable play with the elegiac here, and the opening lines (545–50) give a very Ovidian twist[15] to *Aeneid* 4:

arserat Aeneae Dido miserabilis igne,
arserat exstructis in sua fata rogis,
compositusque cinis, tumulique in marmore carmen
hoc breue, quod moriens ipsa reliquit, erat:
PRAEBVIT AENEAS ET CAVSAM MORTIS ET ENSEM:
IPSA SVA DIDO CONCIDIT VSA MANV.[16]

The anaphora *arserat ... arserat* brings out the theme of fire that dominates Vergil's book: here we can see Ovid the literary critic, producing in one evocative couplet the significance that a modern critic might elucidate in several pages of a learned journal. There is a kind of syllepsis as the force of the verb changes from psychological in the hexameter to physical in the pentameter. This matches the move in the *Aeneid* from the metaphor of love as fire to the reality of Dido's pyre, constructed and set alight towards the end of book 4, and seen burning from the sea by Aeneas at the start of book 5. From love and death he naturally moves to the funeral, another elegiac topic, and commemoration through an epitaph, a

---

13 'She herself was heard to speak: "I am the nymph of the calm Numicius. Hidden in the perennial stream, I am called Anna Perenna.' "

14 Like the Ariadne story (3.459–516) this self-aware sequel, engaging in insightful reading of a predecessor, has received much critical attention: see Döpp 1969, 56–76; Porte 1985, 144–8; Brugnoli 1991; Pfaff-Reydellet 2002, 955–8; Murgatroyd 2005, 105–6, 114–15, 121–31; Tronchet 2014; Chiu 2016, 72–86. It too marks its imitation with reference to, and evocation of, repetition (545–6, 554, 563, 613) and memory (553, 612, 623).

15 The reduction of the whole book to a single couplet is reminiscent of the epigrammatic synopses of *Aeneid* 4 and 6 at *Met*. 14.78–81, 116–19.

16 'Unhappy Dido had burned with fire for Aeneas, she had burned on the pyre constructed for her end, and the ash had been collected, and on the marble of her tomb there was this epigram, which she had herself left when she died: AENEAS PROVIDED THE CAUSE OF DEATH AND THE SWORD; BUT DIDO FELL USING HER OWN HAND.'

'short' poetic form (n.b. *breue*), and one that reprises not Virgil's epic, but, in an audacious moment of literary one-upmanship, Ovid's own elegiac letter. He quotes as Dido's the epitaph that he himself had written at the climax of *Heroides* 7 (193–6):

nec consumpta rogis inscribar Elissa Sychaei;
  hoc tantum in tumuli marmore carmen erit:
PRAEBVIT AENEAS ET CAVSAM MORTIS ET ENSEM:
  IPSA SVA DIDO CONCIDIT VSA MANV.[17]

The *Fasti* lines confirm that Dido's instructions have been carried out precisely (note the echo of *in tumuli marmore carmen*, *Ep.* 7.194); presumably this has been done by Anna, the explicit addressee at *Ep.* 7.191. The syllepsis PRAEBVIT ... ET CAVSAM MORTIS ET ENSEM emphasizes the fact that the sword with which Dido kills herself is the one left by Aeneas in her bedroom. The epitaph answers the question Aeneas had posed to her ghost when they met in the underworld at *Aen.* 6.458 *funeris heu tibi causa fui?* ('Alas, was I the cause of your death?'). Next Iarbas invades (551–2), but even he is cast in the role of a spurned lover (553–4):

protinus inuadunt Numidae sine uindice regnum,
  et potitur capta Maurus Iarba domo,
seque memor spretum, thalamis tamen, inquit, Elissae
  en ego, quem totiens reppulit illa, fruor.[18]

The Carthaginians' flight is described with an epic simile (555–6):

diffugiunt Tyrii quo quemque agit error, ut olim
  amisso dubiae rege uagantur apes.[19]

However, the picture of bees dispersing when their queen dies takes us, via the simile comparing Carthage to the hard-working, organized hive of spring-time in *Aeneid* 1.430–6, back to the small scale of *Georgics* 4, and especially the grimmer picture of 4.212–14:

17 'Nor when consumed by the pyre shall I be inscribed as Elissa wife of Sychaeus; only this couplet will be on the marble of the tomb: AENEAS etc.'

18 'Immediately the Numidians invade the kingdom that lacked a protector, and Moorish Iarbas occupied the house he had captured, and, remembering that he had been scorned, said "Behold I whom she rejected so often yet enjoy the bedroom of Elissa." '

19 'The Tyrians flee where their wandering takes each of them, as sometimes bees wander uncertainly when the queen is lost.'

> rege incolumi mens omnibus una est;
> amisso rupere fidem, constructaque mella
> diripuere ipsae et cratis soluere fauorum.[20]

As Anna says farewell to her sister's ashes (559–64), the quasi-funeral is once again conducted in elegiac language. Her voyages, first to Malta, then to Italy, inevitably provide more epic material (including a simile at 584), but unlike epic heroes she travels without divine intervention or guidance,[21] she does not visit the land of Mars[22] nor Jupiter's birthplace Crete, nor does she encounter monsters like the Harpies, Polyphemus, or Scylla and Charybdis; but for three years she lives on Malta, small as it is (572), the guest of Battus, an unwarlike king, whose name recalls Callimachus (son of Battus), and who hates arms and speaks only in pentameters.[23] However, Anna's wicked brother Pygmalion restores the epic tone, threatening war. Once again she sets sail, to be driven off course by a great storm. Like Aeneas and Odysseus she wishes she had died on land (597–8). Once she reaches Latium, however, there is no magic cloud to obscure her identity (contrast *Od.* 7.14–17, *Aen.* 1.411–14), and the recognition scene happens with comic immediacy (*Anna est, exclamat Achates*, 607). Aeneas reminisces about his epic past (613–20), but he has the bare feet of an actor from low-brow drama (604), and he speaks elegiacs, notably mannered ones at 623–4:

> multa tibi memores, nil non debemus Elissae:
> nomine grata tuo, grata sororis eris.[24]

Though the appearance of Dido's ghost to warn Anna seems an epic moment and there is a final simile at 646, the generic affiliations as the story plays out are contested between tragedy (the traveller is threatened by the local queen, as Menelaus and Orestes by the local king in Euripides' *Helen* and *Iphigenia in Tauris*) and adultery mime: mime wins, as Anna jumps out of the window half-dressed (643–5) and comes to a happy end in the waters of the Numicius (653–6). Unlike Aeneas — no one tells stories about Indiges — she retains her identity and has life as a goddess, tricking Mars into confusing her with Minerva, and enjoying the joke (677–96).

---

20 'When the queen is unharmed, they share a single mind; when she is lost, they break their bond, and themselves tear apart the honey they have made and dissolve the construction of the honeycomb.'

21 Tronchet 2014 §52.

22 Aeneas describes Thrace as *terra Mauortia* at *Aen.* 3.13.

23 Barchiesi 1997, 22.

24 'We owe much to you, everything to Dido, I remember: you will be welcome in your own name, and your sister's.'

I turn now to verses 557–9:

tertia nudandas acceperat area messes,
inque cauos ierant tertia musta lacus:
pellitur Anna domo; ...[25]

After the general dispersal of the Carthaginians (*diffugiunt Tyrii*, 555), the narrative turns its focus to the key individual. But why should Anna delay three years, especially when the aggressive Iarbas is sleeping in her sister's bedroom? Murgia 1987 saw that the lines do not belong where transmitted, but with 575–6, where the length of Anna's stay with Battus is described as lasting into the third year:

tertia nudandas acceperat area messes, 557
inque cauos ierant tertia musta lacus; 558
signa recensuerat bis sol sua, tertius ibat 575
Annus, et exilio terra paranda noua est:
frater adest belloque petit.[26]

Compare the similar account given by Silius, at *Punica* 8.61–3:

atque ea, dum flauas bis tondet messor aristas,
seruata interea sedes: nec longius uti
his opibus Battoque fuit.[27]

The *Punica* has had no delay in Carthage: in 8.54–5 (*regnis se imponit Iarbas / et tepido fugit Anna rogo*) Iarbas arrives, and immediately Anna leaves, while Dido's pyre is still warm. Reducing to one the groups of three years also fits the chronology of the *Aeneid*. In Jupiter's speech of consolation to Venus in book 1, he describes the period of Aeneas' reign in Latium in similar terms (1.263–7):

bellum ingens geret Italia populosque ferocis
contundet moresque uiris et moenia ponet,
tertia dum Latio regnantem uiderit aestas

---

25 'For the third time the threshing floor had received the harvest to strip it of its husk, and for a third time the new vintage had gone into hollow vats: Anna is driven from her home ...'
26 'For the third time the threshing floor had received the harvest to strip it of its husk, and for a third time the new vintage had gone into hollow vats; the sun had twice reviewed the signs of the zodiac and the third year was progressing, and she had to find a new land for her exile: her brother comes and seeks her through war.'
27 'And that home is kept while the reaper twice shears the golden corn; but it was not possible any longer to use Battus and the resources there.'

> ternaque transierint Rutulis hiberna subactis.
> at puer Ascanius ...[28]

Aeneas shall fight the locals when he arrives in Italy, and he shall win, Jupiter reveals; then he shall start establishing his city —until three years have passed. He does not spell out to Venus what happens then, but that is simply tact: he can move on to the positive image provided by the succession of Iulus, and his descendants, the Julian *gens*. But the clear implication is that Aeneas will die, as he does, for example, in the account of Dionysius of Halicarnassus.[29] If Anna only reaches Italy in the sixth year, Aeneas should be dead, on Vergil's, and on the traditional, chronology; the emphatic way in which the passing of three years is again expressed by Ovid strongly implies that he is following Vergil, whereas confusion is all that results from our maintaining 3.557–8 in their transmitted position.[30] Anna thus sails on from Malta in the third year after her sister's death.

When she is ship-wrecked on the coast of Latium, and meets Aeneas, he is described in 603–5 as going on a secret journey barefoot, accompanied only by Achates:

> litore dotali solo comitatus Achate
> secretum nudo dum pede carpit iter,
> aspicit errantem ...[31]

The passage never explains the couplet, and we should ask what the strange details imply. Scholars have offered a variety of explanations for the lack of shoes:

28 'He shall wage a great war in Italy and crush fierce races and establish practices and a city for the people, until the third summer has seen him reigning in Latium and the third winter has passed since he subjugated the Rutulians. The boy Ascanius ...'

29 *Rom. Ant.* 64.3–5: three years after the war against Turnus, and three years into his reign. In other respects the account is different: Aeneas becomes king only after the death of Latinus in the same war.

30 Monhardt 1994 observes that the sequence produced by Murgia's transposition is a strange one, in which three years had apparently passed (557–8), but then only two (575). The rhetoric is odd, but the sequence is in fact logical. If we suppose that Anna has reached Malta in spring, by the time she has seen the third harvest and the third vintage, the sun has completed two full years, and is now making progress through the third. There are some further points that may be made in favour of the authenticity of 557–8, but for my current purposes, what matters is that the couplet does not belong where transmitted.

31 'On the shore that came as his wedding gift, accompanied by Achates alone, while he was treading a secluded path, barefoot, he spies <Anna> wandering, ...'

it is a sign of primitive simplicity,[32] or turns Aeneas into a mime or pantomime performer,[33] just as his mother wears the buskin of tragedy when she meets Aeneas and Achates at *Aen.* 1.314–405. In addition nudity of the feet may indicate informality, and hint at erotic encounters;[34] though these are usually set in the bedroom, Ovid depicts a number of heroines barefoot as they are about to be taken up by gods: Ariadne (*Ars* 1.530), Persephone (*Fasti* 4.426), and Ilia (*Am.* 3.6.50).[35] The evocation of Ilia is particularly important because she is a model for Anna: her story ends with her throwing herself into the river Anio and becoming a nymph. Here, however, it is Aeneas who is like Ilia. What of the *secretum ... iter*? Is Aeneas keen to get away from the burdens of rule? Now he has found a settled home, does he (like Tennyson's Ulysses) hanker after his old life as a traveller? Or is there a purpose here that Anna's sudden arrival interrupts?

One possible answer is that he was heading to a meeting with his mother at the mouth of the river Numicius, an event that is described at 14.596–604 in the *Metamorphoses*, a poem that has so far played no part in my discussion:

gaudet gratesque agit illa parenti
perque leues auras iunctis inuecta columbis
litus adit Laurens, ubi tectus harundine serpit
in freta flumineis uicina Numicius undis.
hunc iubet Aeneae quaecumque obnoxia morti
abluere et tacito deferre sub aequora cursu;
corniger exsequitur Veneris mandata suisque
quicquid in Aenea fuerat mortale repurgat
et respersit aquis; pars optima restitit illi.[36]

32 So Peter 1889, *ad loc.*; Littlewood 1980, 311; and Delz 1994, 90 n.5: cf. *Aen.* 7.689, Hor. *Ep.* 1.19.12–13 *siquis uultu toruo ferus et pede nudo | ... simulet ... Catonem* ('if some wild individual were to imitate Cato with grim mien and bare feet ...').

33 Barchiesi (1995, 8); cf. the noun *planipes* (= 'barefoot'), and the implication of Seneca, *Ep.* 8.8 *quam multa Publilii non excalceatis sed coturnatis dicenda sunt* ('how many of Publilius' lines are fit to be spoken not by shoeless comedians but by booted tragic actors').

34 E.g. *Am.* 3.7.82, Hor. *Serm.* 1.2.132.

35 Cf. also the Nymphs at *Fasti* 1.410 *impediunt teneros uincula nulla pedes.* Of course, the Romans did enjoy walking barefoot in relaxed situations: Pliny, *Ep.* 2.17.15.

36 '<Venus> rejoices and thanks her father, and carried by yoked doves through the light breezes she approaches the Laurentine coast where the Numicius, covered in reeds, snakes with his river waters into the neighbouring sea. Him she tells to wash off whatever in Aeneas is liable to death and to carry it down to the sea in his silent flow; the horn-bearing god carries out Venus's instructions and purges whatever was mortal in Aeneas and washed him with his waters: his best part remains.' Verses 607–8 report his cult title, *Indiges.*

The two passages are immediately connected by the phrase *Laurens litus* (*Fasti* 3.599); and this is reinforced by the diction used to describe the Numicius in each episode, *corniger* in particular (*Fasti* 3.647). It may be relevant to this line of interpretation that ritual can require the absence of one shoe or both;[37] and that gods are often depicted barefoot.[38]

In the *Aeneid* Jupiter reveals in book 1 that Aeneas will reign for three years in Latium, and at 12.794–5 the god tells Juno that she will accept him into heaven as the god Indiges:

> Indigetem Aenean scis ipsa et scire fateris
> deberi caelo fatisque ad sidera tolli.[39]

The Sibylline prophecy in Tibullus 2.5 has the same combination of information as *Metamophoses* 14: Aeneas deified in the Numicius and becoming Indiges (2.5.39–44):

> 'Impiger Aenea, uolitantis frater Amoris,
> Troica qui profugis sacra uehis ratibus,
> iam tibi Laurentes adsignat Iuppiter agros,
> iam uocat errantes hospita terra Lares.
> illic sanctus eris, cum te ueneranda Numici
> unda deum caelo miserit Indigetem. ...'[40]

The *Fasti* has three years passing after the death of Dido, and a deification in the river Numicius —but of Anna, not Aeneas. Or not explicitly of Aeneas: but a reader of the *Fasti* who combines the information given there with that from Ovid's intertexts may feel that there is something to be said for Lavinia's suspicions. Both Aeneas and Anna will become gods associated with the river Numicius, and in the same year. If we ask where Aeneas was going when they met, the answer is surely 'to the Numicius'; and if 'why does he disappear from the narrative? why does he play no part in the group hunting for Anna?', we may suppose that 'he is already there'. The upshot is succinctly given in Silius' description of

37 E.g. Dido at Verg. *Aen.* 4.518; Medea at Ov. *Met.* 7.183; Columella 11.3.64.

38 E.g. Bacchus at Prop. 3.17.32 *feries nudos ueste fluente pedes*; Mars Ultor on coins and gems; the Prima Porta Augustus, on which see Squire 2013, 266–7.

39 'You yourself know, and admit you know that Aeneas is owed to the heavens as Indiges, and to be raised to the stars according to fate.'

40 'Heroic Aeneas, brother of winged Cupid, you who carry sacred Trojan objects in migrant boats, Jupiter has already assigned the Laurentine fields to you, already the hospitable land summons your wandering Lares. There you will be sanctified when the holy water of the Numicius sends you to heaven as the god *Indiges*. ...'

Anna at *Punica* 8.39, *diua Indigetis castis contermina lucis* ('the goddess who is neighbour to the chaste groves of Indiges'). In the account offered by Dionysius, it is Aeneas' disappearance that leads to his apotheosis, and the reported inscription actually equates him with the river Numicius (*Rom. Ant.* 1.64.5):

> μάχης δὲ γενομένης καρτερᾶς οὐ πρόσω τοῦ Λαουϊνίου καὶ πολλῶν ἑκατέρωθεν ἀπολομένων τὰ μὲν στρατεύματα νυκτὸς ἐπελθούσης διελύθη, τὸ δὲ Αἰνείου σῶμα φανερὸν οὐδαμῇ γενόμενον οἱ μὲν εἰς θεοὺς μεταστῆναι εἴκαζον, οἱ δ' ἐν τῷ ποταμῷ παρ' ὃν ἡ μάχη ἐγένετο διαφθαρῆναι. καὶ αὐτῶι κατασκευάζουσιν οἱ Λατῖνοι ἡρῶιον ἐπιγραφῆι τοιᾶιδε κοσμούμενον, «Πατρὸς θεοῦ χθονίου, ὃς ποταμοῦ Νομικίου ῥεῦμα διέπει».[41]

An intra- and intertextual reading thus has Anna and Aeneas, Perenna and Indiges, ending up as the deities of the Numicius, happy ever after.

Anna's story is fashioned from Aeneas's, but it is also at points significantly akin to Ovid's: both have crossed stormy seas to dangerous locations. A key word of his exile recurs at the start and end of the journey: the Carthaginians head wherever *error* sends them (3.555), and Anna gives an account of her *errores* at 3.626. The tale of Anna's exile is introduced, as we have seen, with the emphatic anaphora *arserat ... arserat* (3.545–6); in moments of wild fantasy, I do find myself wondering whether we might be intended to read this also as *ars erat ... ars erat*, and thus a statement of the existence of the *Ars amatoria* that was the motivation for the poet's relegation. He certainly plays on the *Ars* in his account of the exile of the *tibia* on the *Quinquatrus minores* in June (6.649–710). This passage of *Fasti* 6 is marked as exilic, both by the polysyllabic pentameter ending *funeribus* at 660, and by the poignant *exilium quodam tempore Tibur erat* ('once upon a time exile meant Tibur'), describing the destination of the *tibicines*, at 666.[42] At 701 Minerva says of the *tibia* she has invented: *ars mihi non tanti est; ualeas, mea tibia* ('the art is not worth so much to me; farewell, my flute'), phrasing that in context recalls Ovid's frequent rejection of his own *Ars*.

As we proceed through Anna's story, we keep finding reminders of Ovid's departure from Rome and his journey to Tomi. Consider *Fasti* 3.563–4, as she leaves Carthage:

---

41 'A major battle took place not far from Lavinium, and many were killed on each side. The armies separated as night came on, and when the body of Aeneas was nowhere to be seen, some concluded that it had been translated to the gods, some that it had disappeared in the river besides which the battle took place. The Latins made a shrine for him, adorned with an inscription of this kind: "<Shrine> of the native father god [= Indiges], who guides the stream of the river Numicius." '

42 Courtney 1965, 63.

terque uale dixit, cineres ter ad ora relatos
  pressit, et est illi uisa subesse soror.[43]

The anaphora of *ter* ... *ter* recalls the attempts of epic figures to embrace ghosts, but the context is closer to a line describing Ovid's own departure for exile from his home, *Trist.* 1.3.55–6:

ter limen tetigi, ter sum reuocatus, et ipse
  indulgens animo pes mihi tardus erat.[44]

Moreover, the phrase *uale dixit* echoes the following couplet from *Tristia* 1.3 (57–8), which begins *saepe uale dicto*; *saepe* reworks *ter*:

saepe uale dicto rursus sum multa locutus,
  et quasi discedens oscula summa dedi.[45]

In 3.565 *moenia respiciens* is a quotation from *Aen.* 5.3, of Aeneas departing from Carthage. But by the time that Ovid publishes the *Fasti* he has used the participle of his own departure from his home and family at *Tristia* 1.3.60 *respiciens ... pignora cara*, and of the group of captives seized by marauders at *Tristia* 3.10.62 *respiciens frustra rura Laremque suum.*

A number of details in the storm that hits Anna's ship recall the storms that afflict Ovid on his way to Tomi, described in *Tristia* 1.2, 1.4, 1.11. I shall concentrate on 3.591–6:

adsiliunt fluctus imoque a gurgite pontus
  uertitur, et canas alueus haurit aquas.
uincitur ars uento nec iam moderator habenis
  utitur, at uotis is quoque poscit opem.
iactatur tumidas exul Phoenissa per undas
  umidaque opposita lumina ueste tegit.[46]

43 'And three times she said farewell, three times she brought the ashes to her face and pressed them, and she felt her sister was at hand.'
44 'Three times I touched the threshold, three times I was called back, and my very foot was slow, indulging my mind's wish.'
45 'Often, having said farewell, I again said much more and gave final kisses as if departing.'
46 'Waves leap up and the sea is churned from its depths, and the hull drinks in the foaming waters. Craft is conquered by wind and the helmsman no longer uses the strings on the rudder but even he seeks aid with prayers. The Phoenician exile is tossed on the swollen waves and hides her damp eyes behind her clothing.'

In 595 the epithet *tumidus* is a conventional marker of epic, especially when applied to the sea: cf. e.g. Propertius 3.9.35 *non ego uelifera tumidum mare findo carina*. But in this context, where the word is juxtaposed with *exul*, a series of instances of *tumidus* in *Tristia* 1 and 2 is equally important: 1.2.23–4 *pontus ... fluctibus ... tumidus*, 1.5.77 *tumidis ... undis*, 2.18 *tumidas ... aquas*. Two striking details are shared with *Tristia* 1.11.17–18, 21–2:

saepe maris pars intus erat; tamen ipse trementi
   carmina ducebam qualiacumque manu. ...
ipse gubernator tollens ad sidera palmas
   exposcit uotis, immemor artis, opem.[47]

Both passages visualize the sea within the boat and a helmsman who gives up steering in order to raise his hands in prayer (an allusion to Aeneas at *Aen.* 1.93).[48] In the *Tristia* the helmsman is pointedly contrasted with Ovid himself, the one forgetful of his art, the other still writing poems despite the storms that assail him. These storms are both real and metaphorical, the effect of the wind on the sea and of banishment on his heart, as is made clear in verses 1.11.9–10, 33–4:

ipse ego nunc miror tantis animique marisque
   fluctibus ingenium non cecidisse meum. ...
cumque sit hibernis agitatum fluctibus aequor,
   pectora sunt ipso turbidiora mari.[49]

The shared phrasing *uotis poscit opem* interconnects the two poems; but so does the presence of the noun *ars*. Anna is like Ovid in facing the storms of sea and exile. However, though Ovid's *Ars amatoria* may have been overwhelmed by the storm of exile (cf. *uincitur ars uento, Fasti* 3.593), his poetic craft has not been. Encyclopaedia entries retain Jerome's date of A.D. 17 for the poet's death, and 2017 was replete with conferences to celebrate the supposed bimillennium; but there is no solid evidence for Ovid's death, and with the final words of the *Metamorphoses* he himself claimed *per omnia saecula ... uiuam*. The intratextuality

---

47 'Often some of the sea was inside the boat; but I myself with trembling hand was composing poems, whatever their quality ... The very helmsman, raising his hands to the stars, seeks aid with prayers, forgetful of his craft.'

48 The helmsman has vain recourse to prayer at *Met.* 11.537–42; his *ars* fails also at *Trist.* 1.2.31–2, 1.4.11–12.

49 'I myself am now amazed that my poetic creativity has not submitted to the enormous disturbance of mind and sea. ... And though the sea is stirred up with winter waves, my heart is more storm-tossed than the sea itself.'

should help us remember that like Anna he was an exile, and like her he is immortal.

Bibliography

Barchiesi, A. (1995), 'Genealogie: Callimaco, Ennio e l'autocoscienza dei poeti Augustei', in: L. Belloni/G. Milanese/A. Porro (eds), *Studia classica Iohanni Tarditi oblate*, 2 vols., Milan, I.5–18.

Barchiesi, A. (1997), *The Poet and the Prince: Ovid and Augustan Discourse*, Berkeley.

Brugnoli, G. (1991), 'Anna Perenna', in: I. Gallo/L. Nicastri (eds.), *Cultura, poesia, ideologia nell'opera di Ovidio*, Napoli, 147–68.

Chiu, A. (2016), *Ovid's Women of the Year: Narratives of Roman Identity in the Fasti*, Ann Arbor.

Courtney, E. (1965), 'Ovidian and Non-Ovidian *Heroides*', *BICS* 12, 63–6.

Delz, J. (1994), 'Probleme in Ovids *Fasti*', *MH* 51, 88–96.

Döpp, S. (1969), *Virgilischer Einfluß im Werk Ovids*, München.

Feeney, D. (1992), '*Si licet et fas est*: Ovid's *Fasti* and the Problem of Free Speech under the Principate', in: A. Powell (ed.), *Roman poetry and propaganda in the age of Augustus*, London, 1–25.

Hinds, S.E. (1987), *The Metamorphosis of Persephone: Ovid & the Self-Conscious Muse*, Cambridge.

Hollis, A.S. (1977), *Ovid,* Ars Amatoria *Book 1*, Oxford.

Littlewood, R.J. (1980), 'Ovid and the Ides of March', in: C. Deroux (ed.), *Studies in Latin Literature and Roman History* 2, Brussels, 301–21.

Monhardt, S. (1994), 'Zu Ovids *Fast.* 3.557–8', *RhM* 137, 292–9.

Murgatroyd, P. (2005), *Mythical and Legendary Narrative in Ovid's Fasti*, Mnemosyne suppl. 263, Leiden.

Murgia, C.A. (1987), 'Ovid, *Fasti* 3.557–558', *CPh* 82, 151–3.

Peter, H. (1889), *Fastorum Libri Sex, für die Schule erklärt* (3rd edn.), Leipzig.

Pfaff-Reydellet, M. (2002), 'Anna Perenna et Jules César dans les *Fastes* d'Ovide: la mise en scène de l'apothéose', *MEFRA* 114, 937–67.

Porte, D. (1985), *L'étiologie religieuse dans les Fastes d'Ovide*, Paris.

Squire, M. (2013), 'Embodied Ambiguities on the Prima Porta Augustus', *Art History* 36, 242–79.

Tronchet, G. (2014), 'Trajectoire épique en an(n)amorphose (Ovide, *Fastes* 3.545–656)', *Dictynna* 11 [online].

Tristan Franklinos

Ovid, *ex Ponto* 4: An Intratextually Cohesive Book

The poems of the fourth book of Ovid's *Epistulae ex Ponto* are not infrequently held to have been arranged and published posthumously, firstly because of the absence of the structure of the *libellus* one might have expected in the light of that found in the first three books of the *Epistulae*;[1] secondly because of the (relatively) wide chronological range of the poems when compared with Ovid's other books of exilic poetry (AD 13–16);[2] and, thirdly because of the number of lines, which exceeds that of each of the other books of the *Tristia* and *ex Ponto* by a not insignificant degree.[3] The second and the third of these objections have been dealt with succinctly elsewhere.[4] In this paper, I will consider further the rôle played by the order of the poems—what Wulfram has referred to as 'des Pudels Kern',[5] the crux of the matter—in considering whether Ovid had a hand in arranging the *libellus*, and will demonstrate that an intratextual reading of the poems points to a cohesively arranged collection. To my mind, there is very little about Book 4 that suggests that the epistles were gathered together *sine ordine*, as Ovid fallaciously claims that those of Books 1–3 were (*Pont.* 3.9.53).

The final book of the *Epistulae ex Ponto* contains four poems addressed to one of the consuls of AD 14, Sextus Pompeius (4.1, 4.4, 4.5, and 4.15). The architectonic placement of 4.1 and 4.15 as first and penultimate poems of the *libellus*,[6]

My thanks to Stephen Harrison and Llewelyn Morgan for providing me with an opportunity to think about *Pont.* 4 in a 2015 seminar, and to Stephen Heyworth for his comments on an earlier draft of this paper. All translations are my own.

1 On the structure of *Pont.* 1–3, see, for example, Gaertner 2005, 2–5.

2 On the dating of *Pont.* 4, see Syme 1978, 42–4.

3 On the number of verses in Ovidian books, see Wulfram 2008, 260–1. For a more detailed overview of the arguments for posthumous publication, see Helzle 1989, 31–6.

4 Holzberg 1997, 197–200; Wulfram 2008, 259–62.

5 Wulfram 2008, 262.

6 Cf. the addresses to Maecenas in first and penultimate position of Horace's first book of *Epistles* (1.1 and 1.19), and of *Carm.* 1–3 (1.1 and 3.29). In both cases the penultimate poem addressed to Maecenas precedes a poem that is concerned with the afterlife of Horace's literary output; the same is true of *Pont.* 4.15 and 16 and the latter's treatment of Ovid's poetic renown. (Whether one believes that Horace's first three books of odes are to be treated as a unified corpus or not (cf. Hutchinson 2002), it is at least plausible to suggest that Ovid may thus have encountered them.)

https://doi.org/10.1515/9783110611021-018

and the diptych on Pompeius' consulship in 4.4 and 4.5,[7] have led to the suggestion— even by those who believe the book to have been posthumously arranged— that *Pont.* 4 is not entirely disordered. Such a view is supported by the central placement of 4.8, addressed to Suillius (Ovid's wife's son-in-law) and containing an appeal to Germanicus, which is followed by a poem —4.9— on the consulships of Graecinus and his brother, the former of whom is similarly encouraged to attempt to assuage the *principis ira* (4.9.51–2). This poem draws heavily on, and seems to answer to, the language and themes of the diptych on Pompeius' accession to the consulship.[8] The 'aba' cluster of poems (4.12, 13 and 14) addressed to two fellow-poets (Tuticanus, Carus, and Tuticanus again) is also suggestive of more than a little organisation, as is the placement of the final poem of the book. Addressed to an *Inuidus* and concerned with Ovid's poetic afterlife, poem 4.16 brings to a head one of the major themes of the *ex Ponto* in general—the preservation of one's *nomen*;[9] recalls Ovid's earlier reflections on his literary renown in closing sequences;[10] and, through its address to the Roman poets' equivalent of the baneful race of envy evoked in the *Aetia*,[11] underlines his continued adherence to the Callimachean aesthetic that he advertised with the description of his first poem to Pompeius as a *deductum carmen* (4.1.1).

In what follows I shall principally consider the opening run of poems, and how their intratextual relations point to a more careful construction of the *libellus* than even the architectonic aspects of arrangement that I have outlined already suggest.

7 Comparison is not infrequently made with *Amores* 2.7 and 8 on Cypassis (e.g. Helzle 2003, 45).

8 e.g.: *Pont.* 4.4.27–8~4.9.21–2; 4.5.17–22~4.9.43–8.

9 Ovid explains that there is no difference in the content of the *Epistulae ex Ponto* from that of the *Tristia*, but that *nomina* will be included (*Pont.* 1.1.17–18). He is *prima facie* referring to the names of his correspondents, but is also thus pointing to the renown that he will secure for them (and for himself) by their inclusion in his poetry (cf. Nagle (1980) 74–80). On Ovid's use of the term *nomen* to refer to his literary afterlife, see below; on the place of *nomina* in the Pontic epistles, see Gaertner 2005, 6–8, Tissol 2014, 18–23; and cf. Oliensis 1997 on (the absence of) *nomina* in the *Tristia*. Ovid's own *cognomen*—*Naso*—opens his *Epistulae* (1.1.1), and features conspicuously throughout; for the poet's use of *Naso* as his signature from the outset of his corpus, see Thorsen 2014, 39.

10 cf. *Am.* 1.15; *Am.* 3.15; *Met.* 15.871–9; *Tr.* 4.10.121–4.

11 Callimachus' Βασκανίης ὀλοὸν γένος (*Aet.* fr. 1.17 Harder); cf. *Ep.* 21.4 Pf and *Ap.* 105–12. On *Liuor* in Ovid, see Barchiesi 1997, 40–2.

1 *Leuis fortuna*

The opening of 4.4 consists of an *amplificatio* on what Helzle calls 'the positive aspect of fickle fortune';[12] it then goes on to explain how this applies to Ovid's particular situation. Though separated from his *domus*, his *patria*, and the *oculi* of his own, the poet is able to forget his lot and to think happy thoughts when prompted by some fitting *causa*, here the news of Pompeius' consulship, and the hope, as we discover in 4.5, that he will continue to have a care for Ovid.

> Nulla dies adeo est australibus umida nimbis,
> non intermissis ut fluat imber aquis;
> nec sterilis locus ullus ita est, ut non sit in illo
> mixta fere duris utilis herba rubis:
> nil adeo **fortuna** grauis miserabile fecit,
> ut minuant nulla gaudia parte malum.
> ecce domo patriaque carens oculisque meorum,
> naufragus in Getici litoris actus aquas,
> qua tamen inueni uultum diffundere causa
> possim, **fortunae** nec meminisse meae.
> *Pont.* 4.4.1–10

No day is so wet with southern rains that a shower pours with uninterrupted precipitation; no place is so infertile that no useful plant grows there among the rough brambles: weighty fortune has made naught so wretched that joys do not lessen its sadness in some part. See, lacking home, fatherland, and the sight of my kin, and driven as a wreck into the waters of the Getic shores, I have nevertheless found the cause by which I am able to gladden my face and not to be mindful of my lot.

This positive outlook is somewhat uncharacteristic of the poet in his exilic verse, and we may wonder why he adopts this rhetorical strategy. The idea that changeable *fortuna*, grievous –*grauis*– though she is, renders nothing so wretched (*miserabile*) that one is not capable of experiencing a little joy seems to me to respond to the suggestion, at the close of the preceding poem, that the anonymous *amicus ingratus* take care, as those things that seem *laeta* may become *tristia*.

> tu quoque fac timeas, et, quae tibi laeta uidentur,
> dum loqueris, fieri tristia posse puta.
> *Pont.* 4.3.57–8

You too should be afraid, and remember that what seems happy to you is able, as you speak, to become sad.

12 Helzle 1989, 108.

The contrasting relationship between 4.3 and 4.4, indeed, is marked. At the close of 4.4, Ovid asserts that his relegation would be made less tiresome were he to learn that Pompeius had recalled the poet's *nomen* in his wretched state (47–50). In 4.3, however, the man who was once Ovid's bosom friend no longer wishes even to seem to know Ovid (*nosse uideri*),[13] and asks of whom another speaks when the poet's *nomen* is mentioned (9–10).

> dum mea puppis erat ualida fundata carina,
>   qui mecum uelles currere, primus eras.
> nunc quia contraxit uultum Fortuna, recedis,
>   auxilio postquam scis opus esse tuo.
> dissimulas etiam, nec me uis nosse uideri,
>   quisque sit audito nomine Naso rogas.
>
> *Pont.* 4.3.5–10

> Whilst my ship had the foundation of a sure keel, you were the first to want to sail with me. Now, because Fortune has wrinkled her brow, you withdraw, after you realised that your help was needed. You dissemble too, nor do you wish to seem to know me, and you ask who Naso is when that name is heard.

Whilst Ovid hopes, in 4.4, that Pompeius may be willing to help him when his *fortuna* has taken a turn for the worse, the poet's *amicus ingratus* withdraws himself (*recedis*) when his *auxilium* is most needed (4.3.7–8). Ovid is bewildered by this (*quid facis, a demens?* (4.3.29)). He wonders why his erstwhile friend fails to grasp that by not helping him, he has denied himself even Ovid's sympathy, were his own *fortuna* to withdraw (*si…recedat* (4.3.29)).

> quid facis, a demens? cur, si Fortuna recedat,
>   naufragio lacrimas eripis ipse tuo?
>
> *Pont.* 4.3.29–30

> What are you doing, madman? Why, in case Fortune should abandon you, do you snatch tears from your own wreck?

---

13 This prolative use of *nosse* is recalled by Ovid a few lines later at 4.3.13 (*ille ego, qui primus tua seria nosse solebam*), where he speaks of his own erstwhile knowledge of the hardships of his now ungrateful friend; in both cases the infinitive opens the fifth foot of its hexameter. The contrast is emphasised further by the poet's use of *primus* of himself in 13 and 14, as opposed to of his *amicus* in 6.

Once a sure steersman (cf. 4.3.5),[14] Ovid characterises himself as a *naufragus* from the start of his exilic verse.[15] The use of this familiar trope of the *ingratus amicus* at 4.3.30 is recalled by Ovid at 4.4.8 (*naufragus in Getici litoris actus aquas*), where he speaks of himself, and again couples the imagery of shipwreck with the rôle played by *fortuna* in one's state of affairs. The poet is able to bring a smile to his face (*uultum diffundere* (4.4.9)) and to forget how grievous his *fortuna* is because of the favourable news that he receives regarding Pompeius' consulship. In so doing, he seems almost to have wiped the frown of which we hear at 4.3.7 (*contraxit uultum*) from *fortuna*'s brow. The smile that he gains apparently has a wry aspect to it too, as the poet seems to enjoy characterising fickle *fortuna* as *grauis* (4.4.5)—she who was so explicitly described as *leuis* in 4.3, and to whom his *amicus ingratus* is compared.

siue fui numquam carus, simulasse fateris,
seu non fingebas, inueniere leuis.
...
haec dea non stabili, quam sit leuis, orbe fatetur,
quem summum dubio sub pede semper habet.
quolibet est folio, quauis incertior aura:
par illi leuitas, improbe, sola tua est.

Pont. 4.3.19–20 & 31–4

If I was never dear to you, you confess that you lied; if you were not mendacious, your fickleness is found out...This goddess confesses how fickle she is by her own unstable wheel, the top of which she has ever under her unsure foot. Than any leaf, than any breeze she is more uncertain: equal to her fickleness is yours alone, faithless one.

The weight of her *dubius pes*, moreover, returns after the two poems on Pompeius' consulship, as *tenax fortuna* continues to obstruct Ovid's *uota* with her *malignus pes*, and he suffers a lot that is *miserabile* (cf. 4.4.5).

Quam legis, ex illis tibi uenit epistula, Brute,
Nasonem nolles in quibus esse locis.
sed tu quod nolles, uoluit miserabile fatum.
...
perstat enim Fortuna tenax uotisque malignum
opponit nostris insidiosa pedem.

Pont. 4.6.1–3 & 7–8

The letter which you read, Brutus, reached you from those places in which you do not wish Naso to be. But what you do not want, wretched fate does...For tenacious fortune persists and treacherously opposes her wicked foot to my wishes.

14 cf. *Ars* 1.772; 2.9–10; 3.99–100, 747–8; *Rem.* 811–12; *Fast.* 2.3, 863–4; 4.18.
15 e.g.: *Tr.* 1.2.52; 1.5.36; 1.6.7–8; 2.18; 5.9.17; *Pont.* 1.2.60; 2.2.126; 2.9.9.

Brutus, the addressee of 4.6, is not like the *ingratus* of 4.3: the former acknowledged Ovid when he had been harmed by *Fortuna iniqua*, unlike the greater part of his acquaintance.

> at, si quem laedi Fortuna cernis iniqua,
> mollior est animo femina nulla tuo.
> hoc ego praecipue sensi, cum magna meorum
> notitiam pars est infitiata mei.
> inmemor illorum, uestri non inmemor umquam,
> qui mala solliciti nostra leuatis, ero.
>
> *Pont.* 4.6.39–44

But, in the event that you see anyone harmed by iniquitous Fortune, gentler than your heart is no woman. I felt this keenly when a great part of my acquaintance denied any knowledge of me. Unmindful of them I shall be, but never unmindful of you who anxiously relieve my sorrows.

In the light of this kindness, Ovid will not be unmindful of him, and will secure Brutus a place of renown in his literary monument, unlike the *ingratus amicus* of 4.3 who remains unnamed lest he achieve some *fama* through mention of his *nomen*.

> nomine non utar, ne commendere querela
> quaeraturque tibi carmine fama meo.
>
> *Pont.* 4.3.3–4

Your name I shall not use, lest by my complaint you are advantaged and you obtain renown from my song.

The denial of any recognition to Ovid's *ingratus amicus* in *Pont.* 4.3, of any possibility of his being given a *nomen*, draws attention to the *nomina* given to more loyal friends in surrounding poems —Pompeius, Severus, Brutus, and the like. Later on in 4.3, indeed, *fama* is transformed, no longer referring to the renown that may be secured through verse, but to the messenger who informs Ovid of his friend's betrayal.

> uix equidem credo: sed et insultare iacenti
> te mihi nec uerbis parcere fama refert.
>
> *Pont.* 4.3.27–8

Scarcely do I believe it, but rumour tells me that you insult me down-trodden as I am, and are not sparing with words.

2 *Laeta Fama*

In *Pont.* 4.4, *Fama* is once again deployed as the bringer of news to the poet. In stark contrast to the preceding poem, however, Ovid has the winged deity explain that she is the *nuntia laetarum rerum*; there are some *gaudia* to be found even in exile, not just reports of further betrayals.

> nam mihi, cum fulua solus spatiarer harena,
> uisa est a tergo pinna dedisse sonum.
> respicio, neque erat corpus, quod cernere possem,
> uerba tamen sunt haec aure recepta mea:
> 'en ego laetarum uenio tibi nuntia rerum,
> Fama, per inmensas aere lapsa uias:
> consule Pompeio, quo non tibi carior alter,
> candidus et felix proximus annus erit.'
> dixit, et, ut laeto Pontum rumore repleuit,
> ad gentes alias hinc dea uertit iter.
> at mihi dilapsis inter noua gaudia curis
> excidit asperitas huius iniqua loci.
>
> *Pont.* 4.4.11–22

When I was strolling alone on the tawny sand, a wing seemed to make a sound behind me. I looked back: I could not see a body, but these words were heard by my ears: 'Lo, I, Renown, come to you as a messenger of happy events, having glided through the immeasurable paths of the air: since Pompeius will be consul, than whom none is dearer to you, the coming year will be bright and favourable.' She spoke thus and, when she had filled Pontus with glad tidings, she bent her course hence toward other peoples. For me cares fell away amongst new joys, and the iniquitous harshness of the place seemed to disappear.

Pompeius is to become consul at the start of the new year (23–4), and it is hoped that he will at some point turn his thoughts to his relegated friend, wondering how the poet fares. Word of such a situation would make Ovid's lot easier to bear (*mollius* (50)), as he hopes that the consul will intercede on his behalf so that he—a mere possession of his friend—may find a home nearer to Rome.[16]

> et detur amicius aruum,
> remque tuam ponas in meliore loco.
>
> *Pont.* 4.15.21–2

May a friendlier region be given to me, and may you place your possession in a better locale.

16 See below for Ovid's characterisation of himself as one of Pompeius' possessions.

Glad tidings have been conveyed to Ovid by *Fama* before in the exilic poetry, notably in *Pont.* 2.1 and 2.5, where news of Tiberius' triumph reaches Pontus, and, as in 4.4, he imagines the celebrations in Rome.[17] The particular characterisation of Ovid's visitor in *Pont.* 4.4, however, casts an especially auspicious light on the news that she brings. Playing with his readers' expectations, Ovid describes himself as walking alone on a beach in terms closely reminiscent of those used by the crow in the second book of the *Metamorphoses*.

> forma mihi nocuit. nam cum per litora lentis
> passibus, ut **so**leo, summa **spatiarer harena**,
> **uidit** et incaluit pelagi deus.
>
> *Met.* 2.572–4[18]

> My beauty harmed me. For when I was strolling, as was my custom, along the beach over the top of the sand, a god of the sea saw me and grew warm.

The crow (in her previous human form) is about to be raped by a god of the sea, and an attentive reader may wonder if the poet was about to receive an unwelcome visitation. There is, however, a change, as where it was the god that looked upon the daughter of Coroneus (*uidit*) in the *Metamorphoses*, it is Ovid's visitor who seems to appear to him (*uisa est*). This change points to another visitor that the poet has received whilst in exile, who also brought him good news.

In *Pont.* 3.3, Amor appears to the exile in a dream, promising that Caesar's anger will diminish, and that a more favourable hearing will be given to the poet's *uota* (83–4), just as Ovid is optimistic about an amelioration of his circumstances in *Pont.* 4.4.

---

17 The collocation *huc ... peruenit fama triumphi* is recalled from *Pont.* 2.1.1 at 2.5.27, referring in both instances to Ovid's receipt of news of Tiberius' triumph; also comparable is 2.9.3 (*Fama ... peruenit*).

18 This passage from the *Met.* itself alludes to Vergil's description of the crow walking along on the beach as a sign of rain (*tum cornix plena pluuiam uocat improba uoce / et* ***sola*** *in sicca secum* ***spatiatur harena*** (*G.* 1.388–9)). Keith 1992, 29–31 explicates Ovid's close linguistic reworking of the passage from the *Georgics*, but does not attempt any explanation as to why Ovid might have chosen this textual moment for his narrative in the *Metamorphoses*. One may wonder if he, tongue-in-cheek, is providing some sort of *aetion* for why Vergil's crow, walking on an empty seashore, might presage an outpouring of water: before her transformation, Coroneus, likewise on a desolate *litus*, was subjected to the onslaught of a watery *pelagi deus*. For the bird, as for the princess, the beach is somewhere it is likely to get wet. Such fanciful thoughts aside, it is worth noting that, where the adjective *sola* is concealed in the Alexandrian footnote *ut soleo* at *Met.* 2.573, it is restored as *solus* in *Pont.* 4.4.11, suggesting that Ovid had both passages in mind.

haec ego **uisus** eram puero dixisse uolucri,
hos **uisus** nobis ille dedisse sonos:
'per mea tela, faces, et per mea tela, sagittas,
per matrem iuro Caesareumque caput:
nil nisi concessum nos te didicisse magistro,
Artibus et nullum crimen inesse tuis.
...
ut tamen aspicerem consolarerque iacentem,
lapsa per inmensas est mea pinna **uias**...'
...
dixit, et aut ille est tenues dilapsus in auras,
coeperunt sensus aut uigilare mei.

Pont. 3.3.65–70, 77–8 & 93–4

These things I fancied that I said to the winged boy, and these utterances he seemed to make to me: 'By my weapons —torches— and by my weapons—shafts, by my mother I swear, and by Caesar's head: I learnt naught under your tutelage except what was permitted, and there is no crime in your *Artes*...nevertheless that I might look upon you and console you, downcast as you are, my wings have glided by immeasurable paths...'...He said this, and either he disappeared into thin air, or my senses began to awaken.

Recalling the dream-state in which he found himself in 3.3 through the use of *uisa* (4.4.12),[19] the poet claims that the flutter of a wing appears to make a sound behind him (cf. *pinna* at 3.3.78 and 4.4.12). The words used of the sound at 4.4.12 (*dedisse sonum*) are used of Amor's auspicious speech in 3.3, suggesting that the appearance of winged Fama to the elegist in 4.4 may in fact be a positive thing. Like the god of love before her, Ovid's visitor in 4.4 claims to have covered a significant distance (*per inmensas...uias* occurring in the same metrical *sedes* in both poems), and to have glided down to address him (cf. *lapsa* at 3.3.78 and 4.4.16); she too comes to look upon him, and to comfort him as Amor had done (*aspicerem consolarerque* (3.3.77)), such that the *asperitas loci* disappears (4.4.22).[20] Ovid finds himself amongst *noua gaudia* in 4.4, since his *curae* have slipped away

19 On the middle and passive of *uideo* used to mark dream sequences, especially in the elegists, see Scioli 2015, 24–54 with the review of Franklinos 2017.

20 The collocation *asperitas...loci* is used by Ovid in *Pont.* 4.14, the second poem addressed to Tuticanus, in which the poet explains that he holds no grudge against the land to which he has been relegated, only the people, yet wishes that the place could have been further from the frozen pole (61–2). In a list of those who have complained about their homeland as Ovid now complains of Tomi, he compares himself, *inter alios*, to Odysseus —that familiar *comparandus* for Ovid's exiled persona— and states that Ithaca's hero has himself provided evidence for her *asperitas* (*quis patriam sollerte magis dilexit Vlixe? / hoc tamen asperitas indice docta loci est* (35–6).

(*dilapsis* 4.4.21), recalling not only the arrival of Fama (*lapsa* (4.4.16)), but the departure of Amor from the mind's-eye of the poet at 3.3.93: *dilapsus in auras*.

3 Consuls and Caesars

In what follows in 4.4, Ovid imagines the scenes in Rome as Pompeius assumes his consulship,[21] fancying himself amongst the throng—*cernere iam uideor* (4.4.27), though he later admits (*non ego cernar* (43)) that, in his absence, he must rely on his mind's evocation of events.

> me miserum, turba quod non ego cernar in illa,
> nec poterunt istis lumina nostra frui.
> quod licet, absentem, qua possum, mente uidebo:
> aspiciet uultus consulis illa sui.
>
> *Pont.* 4.4.43–6

> Wretched me, that I shall not be seen in that crowd, nor will my eyes be able to enjoy those [sights]. It is allowed, however, that I shall see you in my mind's eye: this will see the features of its consul.

It is the case, however, that Ovid appears not only to rely on a mental image of what happens at Rome, but on his own account of the start of the consuls' term of office in *Fasti* 1.[22] The poet's inability to be present in Rome for such an event necessitates that he describe the event as imagined (e.g. *Pont.* 2.1), or that he suppose himself to be in the eternal city, as here or in *Pont.* 4.9—the poem on Graecinus' consulship that revisits lexical and thematic details of *Fasti* 1 and *Pont.* 4.4. The language with which he describes this supposition in 4.4 (*cernere iam uideor* (27)) recalls Ovid's response, in *Pont.* 2.8, to receiving images of Augustus, Tiberius, and Livia from Cotta Maximus.

> hunc [Augustum] ego cum spectem, uideor mihi cernere Romam,
> nam patriae faciem sustinet ille suae.
>
> *Pont.* 2.8.19–20

> As I look on Augustus, I seem to see Rome, for he encapsulates the likeness of our fatherland.

21 cf. the description of Tiberius' triumph in *Pont.* 2.1.

22 For an overview of points of contact, see Helzle 1989, 105–6, which is derived in large part from Du Quesnay 1976, 45–7.

The poet addresses his plaint to the images of the imperial family that he has been sent, as he is able to imagine himself supplicating them in person.

> parte leua minima nostras et contrahe poenas,
> daque, procul Scythico qui sit ab hoste, locum.
> *Pont.* 2.8.35–6

> Alleviate and decrease in some small part my punishment, and give me a situation far from the Scythian enemy.

Access to the emperor may not be granted to the exiled poet, but through a surrogate of Augustus (as in *Pont.* 2.8), or through an intermediary (as in *Pont.* 4.4 and 4.5), Ovid supposes that there is hope.

In *Pont.* 4.5, indeed, in a conceit familiar from his earlier exilic poetry,[23] the poet has his *leues elegi* go to Rome on his behalf with greetings for Pompeius whom he portrays as close to the imperial family and to the senatorial élite.

> aut, ubi erunt patres in Iulia templa uocati,
> de tanto dignis consule rebus aget,
> aut feret Augusto solitam natoque salutem,
> deque parum noto consulet officio,
> tempus et his uacuum Caesar Germanicus omne
> auferet: a magnis hunc colit ille deis.
> *Pont.* 4.5.21–6

> He will either, when the senators have been summoned to the Julian temple, debate affairs worthy of so great a consul, or he will bear accustomed greetings to Augustus and his son and will take counsel about a less familiar duty; Caesar Germanicus will claim all his time free from these concerns: the latter he reverences after the great gods.

Emphasis is given to the centrality of Pompeius' position in the upper echelons of Roman society as the collocation *patres...uocati* (4.5.21) recalls the speech that Ovid imagines is made by the consul as he assumed office in the course of a passage of 4.4 in which his favour amongst the Caesars is also implied.

> curia te excipiet, patresque e more uocati
> intendent aures ad tua uerba suas.
> hos ubi facundo tua uox hilarauerit ore,
> utque solet tulerit prospera uerba dies,
> egeris et meritas superis cum Caesare grates,
> qui causam, facias cur ita, saepe dabit.
> *Pont.* 4.4.35–40

23 e.g. *Tr.* 1.1; 3.7.

The senate will receive you, and the senators, summoned according to custom, will strain their ears to hear your words. When from eloquent mouth your voice has delighted them, and the day, as is customary, has brought auspicious words, you will give deserved thanks to the gods and to Caesar, who will often give you cause to do so.

It is this favour on which the poet's entreaties to the consul rely, as is made clear in *Pont.* 4.15, which opens with the assertion that anyone who remembers Ovid should know that he owes his life to the Caesars, and his *salus* to Pompeius.

Si quis adhuc usquam nostri non inmemor extat,
quidue relegatus Naso requirit agam,
Caesaribus uitam, Sexto debere salutem
me sciat: a superis hic mihi primus erit.

Pont. 4.15.1–4

If there is anyone anywhere who has not forgotten me, or asks how the relegated Ovid fares, may he know that I owe my life to the Caesars and my well-being to Sextus: after the gods he will be first as far as I am concerned.

This final poem addressed to the consul recalls *Pont.* 4.5 through the mention of Pompeius' *domus* as neighbouring the Forum Augustum itself.

protinus inde domus uobis Pompeia petatur:
non est Augusto iunctior ulla Foro.

Pont. 4.5.9–10

Straightway seek the home of Pompeius: none is nearer the Forum Augustum.

... quam domus Augusto continuata Foro...

Pont. 4.15.16

... as the home next to the Forum Augustum ...

The implicit physical proximity of Pompeius to the emperor adds force to the notion that the consul is likely to have a particular influence over the Caesars, and thus, since it is in their power to alter the poet's lot, Ovid asks his friend that he continue to pay homage to the rulers of Rome so that they might lessen his punishment.

et detur amicius aruum,
remque tuam ponas in meliore loco.
quod quoniam in dis est, tempta lenire precando
numina, perpetua quae pietate colis.

Pont. 4.15.21–4

May a friendlier region be given to me, and may you place your possession in a better locale. Since this is in the power of the gods, try to soften with prayer the deities whom you worship with unfaltering piety.

That being the case, one might be inclined to wonder what it is that Pompeius supposes that he is to get out of his efforts on Ovid's behalf. The answer seems to lie in an oddity of *Pont.* 4: in this passage of 4.15, as previously in the book, the poet characterises himself as Pompeius' possession —his *res* (22). In the final couplet of the first poem of the book, indeed, Ovid explains to his friend that he, the poet, is not the last of his friend's possessions (*pars rerum non ultima*).

unde, rogas forsan, fiducia tanta futuri
  sit mihi: quod fecit, quisque **tuetur opus.**
ut Venus artificis labor est et gloria Coi,
  aequoreo madidas quae premit imbre comas,
arcis ut Actaeae uel eburna uel aerea custos
  bellica Phidiaca stat dea facta manu,
uindicat ut Calamis laudem, quos fecit, equorum,
  ut similis uerae uacca Myronis **opus,**
sic ego pars rerum non ultima, Sexte, tuarum,
  tutelaeque feror munus **opus**que tuae.
Pont. 4.1.27–36

Whence, you might ask, do I have so great a faith in the future: because each man looks out for his creation. As Venus who presses her hair wet with the sea's spray is the toil and glory of the Coan artist, as the warring deity, guardian of the Acropolis, stands wrought in ivory and bronze by Phidias' hand, as Calamis claims the praise of the horses that he made, as the cow like unto truth is Myron's work, so I am not the last of your belongings, Sextus, and I am held to be the gift and work of your guardianship.

Ovid claims, rather, that he is the *munus* and *opus* of Pompeius' *tutela*. This final mention of *opus* is preceded by the assertion that Ovid has faith in his future (27), as each artist keeps watch over his own *opus* (28). Since, he claims, he is Pompeius' *opus*, he will be protected by his friend's watch (cf. *tuetur* (28) and *tutelae* (36)). He provides a list of four artists, familiar to the elegiac reader,[24] who have gained *gloria* and *laus* from their *opera*; with them he compares Pompeius. Since he has afforded Ovid *tutela*, and (the poet hopes) he will continue to do so, he too will gain *gloria* and *laus* from his undertaking, as his friend will secure his *nomen*

24 Apelles, Phidias, and Calamis appear together, *inter alios*, at Prop. 3.9.9–16; Myron is found at Prop. 2.31.7–8, and at *Ars* 3.219 along with Apelles' Venus, mentioned at 3.223–4 (*cum fieret, lapis asper erat; nunc, nobile signum, / nuda Venus madidas exprimit imbre comas*) in words which Ovid recalls at *Pont.* 4.4.30 (*madidas...premit imbre comas*).

by inscribing it into his verse. Such a reading of these lines is reinforced by the evident reworking, in the final couplet of *Pont.* 4.1, of a distich which Ovid had addressed to his wife in the final poem of the *Tristia,* in which he speaks of the monument that he has erected for her in his poetry. He explains that her *fama* is bound to his (*Tr.* 5.14.5), and that the *honos* she receives will not be insignificant, as she alone is the *tutela* of his affairs (*Tr.* 5.14.15–16).

Quanta tibi dederint nostri monimenta libelli,
  o mihi me coniunx carior, ipsa uides.
detrahat auctori multum fortuna licebit,
  tu tamen ingenio clara ferere meo;
dumque legar, pariter mecum tua fama legetur.
…
adde quod, ut rerum sola es tutela mearum,
  ad te non parui uenit honoris onus,
quod numquam uox est de te mihi muta, tuique
  indiciis debes esse superba uiri.
quae ne quis possit temeraria dicere, persta,
  et pariter serua meque piamque fidem.

Tr. 5.14.1–5 & 15–20

You yourself see how great a monument my books have given to you, wife dearer to me than myself. It is true that fortune has stolen much from their author, but you, famous, will be borne on by my genius; as long as I am read, your renown will be read with mine...Add that, since you are the only guardian of my affairs, a not insignificant burden of honour has come to you, because my voice is never silent about you, and you ought to be proud of your husband's witness. Lest anyone think this to be able to be said rashly, hold fast, and protect me and my reverent faith in equal part.

The poet asks his wife that she remain loyal and faithful to him, continuing to work in his interest, so that no one may suggest that the honour she is afforded by him was rashly given (*Tr.* 5.14.19–20). This same idea of reciprocity is prevalent in *Pont.* 4.

4 Grace and favour

In *Pont.* 4.1, indeed, Ovid asks Pompeius that he receive the well-spun poem, in which he is first given a *nomen* by his friend, as recompense for the poet's life (2). The grateful offering is to be added as the coping stone to Pompeius' deserts (*meritis* (4)), and Ovid hopes that his friend will not be angry with him for the gratitude shown him, for the *officium* discharged by the poet in this way.

Accipe, Pompei, deductum carmen ab illo,
    debitor est uitae qui tibi, Sexte, suae.
seu tu[25] non prohibes a me tua nomina poni,
    accedet **meritis** haec quoque summa tuis.
...
non potuit mea mens, quin esset grata, teneri:
    sit, precor, officio non grauis ira pio.
Pont. 4.1.1–4 & 7–8

Receive, Sextus Pompeius, a well-spun song from the one who owes you his life. If you do not forbid me to write your names, these will be the very coping stone of your deserts...My mind was not able to be restrained from being grateful: let not grievous anger, I beseech you, be your response to bounden duty.

He goes on to note that he will never be able to forget Pompeius (18),[26] hoping that his friend finds no *crimen* in his *officium*, and that he will receive *gratia*, albeit *leuis*, for his considerable undertakings (*meritis ... tantis*). Ovid insists on his gratitude (*gratus ero*) even if Pompeius is unwilling to receive it (22), since the latter was never slow to offer favours (*gratia*) to the poet.

da mihi (si quid ea est) hebetantem pectora Lethen,
    oblitus potero non tamen esse tui;
idque sinas oro, nec fastidita repellas
    uerba, nec officio crimen inesse putes,
et leuis haec **meritis** referatur gratia tantis;
    si minus, inuito te quoque gratus ero,
numquam pigra fuit nostris tua gratia rebus.
Pont. 4.1.17–23

Give me the waters of Lethe that dull the mind (if such a thing exists), and I shall not be able to forget you all the same. I beseech you to allow this, nor contemptuously to reject my words, nor to think there be any crime in my duty: may my slight gratitude be the due return for such great services. If you do not permit it, I shall be grateful even though you do not wish it: never was your grace slow in our affairs.

This lexical nexus of words such as *gratia*, *officium*, *merita*, and their cognates, recurs throughout *Pont.* 4, conspicuously in 4.5, another poem addressed to Pompeius, and in 4.8, addressed to Suillius, where Ovid is emboldened to call upon Germanicus himself.

25 Stephen Heyworth suggests reading *seu tu* for *qui seu*, as the transmitted relative pronoun is misleading after the *qui* of the preceding verse which has a different antecedent.
26 cf. 4.6.43–4 and the brief discussion above.

pro quibus ut **meritis** referatur gratia, iurat
se fore mancipii tempus in omne tui.
Pont. 4.5.39–40

That thanks be given for these services, he swears that he will be your slave for all time.

Littera sera quidem, studiis exculte Suilli,
huc tua peruenit, sed mihi grata tamen,
qua, pia si possit superos lenire rogando
gratia, laturum te mihi dicis opem.
ut iam nil praestes, animi sum factus amici
debitor, et **meritum** uelle iuuare uoco.
...
templa domus facient uobis urbesque beatae;
Naso suis opibus, carmine, gratus erit.
parua quidem fateor pro magnis munera reddi,
cum pro concessa uerba salute damus.
sed qui quam potuit dat maxima gratus abunde est,
et finem pietas contigit illa suum.
...
nec tamen officio uatum per carmina facto
principibus res est aptior ulla uiris.
Pont. 4.8.1–6, 33–8 & 43–4

Your letter, most urbane Suillius, though somewhat tardy in its arrival, is nevertheless pleasing to me, the one in which, if dutiful grace is able to mellow the gods by beseeching them, you said that you intended to bring me aid. Although you proffer nothing else, I have become indebted to your friendly nature, and I call the desire to help deserving...wealthy houses and cities will build temples for you and yours, Germanicus; Ovid will give thanks from his own store—with song. I confess, indeed, that small gifts are rendered for big, when I give words in exchange for the grant of well-being, but the man who gives as much as he is able is more than sufficiently thankful, and that service has achieved its end...nor indeed is anything more fitting for leading men than the duty fulfilled by the songs of poets.

Ovid promises servitude to Pompeius in thanksgiving for the latter's continued support in 4.5, and, in 4.8, explains to Germanicus that he will give thanks through song, as it is with this that he is endowed (34), and this that is most fitting to offer as one's bounden duty and service (*officio*) to the *principes uiri* (43–4).[27] Meanwhile, a sense of unity is given to the book by the occasional occurrence of these terms elsewhere: consider, for example, the officiosae *epistulae* that are sent between Ovid and Severus in 4.2. These epistolary prose exchanges

27 Note also that the use of *debitor* at 4.8.6 recalls Ovid's opening gambit at 4.1.2 (*debitor est uitae qui tibi, Sexte, suae*).

notwithstanding, Ovid is ashamed of the fact that he has not addressed a poetic epistle to Severus, since, as we have seen, gratitude for continued friendship is demonstrated by the author of the *Epistulae ex Ponto* through the inscription of a *nomen* in his verse.

> Quod legis, o uates magnorum maxime regum,
> uenit ab intonsis usque, Seuere, Getis;
> cuius adhuc nomen nostros **tacuisse** libellos,
> si modo permittis dicere uera, pudet.
> orba tamen numeris cessauit epistula numquam
> ire per alternas officiosa uices.
>
> *Pont.* 4.2.1–6

What you read, Severus, greatest poet of great kings, has come even from the unshorn Getae. It embarrasses me that hitherto my books have not mentioned your name (if you allow me to speak the truth), albeit that letters void of metre have never ceased dutifully to pass back and forth between us.

It is in the light of this that the use of the verb *tacuisse* at 4.2.3 is recalled by the poet in the opening of his next poem, addressed to the *amicus ingratus*, in which Ovid concludes that he will not mention his former acquaintance's *nomen* in case he gain any *fama* as a result.

> Conquerar, an **taceam**? ponam sine nomine crimen,
> an notum, qui sis, omnibus esse uelim?
> nomine non utar, ne commendere querela
> quaeraturque tibi carmine fama meo.
>
> *Pont.* 4.3.1–4

Should I complain, or be silent? Should I make a charge without your name, or should I want everyone to know who you are? Your name I shall not use, lest by my complaint you are advantaged and you obtain renown from my song.

The poet had asserted at the close of *Pont.* 3.9 that the pursuit of *gloria* was not the cause of his writing, but rather the hope of an amelioration of his circumstances through the continued *utilitas* of his correspondents, and the fulfilment of the *officium* owed to those who have helped him.

> da ueniam scriptis, quorum non gloria nobis
> causa sed utilitas officiumque fuit.
>
> *Pont.* 3.9.55–6

Pardon my writing, the purpose of which was not to achieve glory for myself, but was one of functionality and duty.

From an intratextual reading of the early poems in *Pont.* 4 that treats them as a carefully constructed unity, however, it seems clear that the *officium* that his readers merit on account of their support of his cause (their *utilitas* to him) necessarily results from the *gloria* that each of them may be granted by having their respective *nomina* inscribed in Ovid's text, and that such *gloria* is predicated on the success of the poet's verses themselves. One ought to pursue one's *studium*—one's adherence to the Muses—when it proves useful (*utiliter*), Severus is told by the poet at 4.2.47–8, since such *studium*, Ovid implies, results in *gloria.*

> excitat auditor studium, laudataque uirtus
> crescit, et inmensum gloria calcar habet.
>
> *Pont.* 4.2.35–6

An audience arouses one's devotion to work, and virtue that has been praised grows: renown has a mighty spur.

Bibliography

Barchiesi, A. (1997), *The Poet and the Prince: Ovid and Augustan Discourse*, Berkeley, CA.
Claassen, J.M. (2008), *Ovid Revisited: The Poet in Exile*, London.
Du Quesnay, I.M. Le M. (1976), 'Vergil's Fourth *Eclogue*', *PLLS* 1, 25–99.
Franklinos, T.E. (2017), Review of Scioli 2015, *CR* 67, 97–9.
Gaertner, J.F. (2005), *Ovid:* Epistulae ex Ponto, *Book I*, Oxford.
Helzle, M. (1989), *Publii Ovidii Nasonis Epistularum ex Ponto liber IV: A Commentary on Poems 1 to 7 and 16*, Hildesheim.
Helzle, M. (2003), *Ovids* Epistulae ex Ponto*: Buch I–II Kommentar*, Heidelberg.
Holzberg, N. (1997), *Ovid: Dichter und Werk*, Munich.
Hutchinson, G.O. (2002), 'The Publication and Individuality of Horace's *Odes* Books 1–3', *CQ* 52, 517–37.
Keith, A.M. (1992), *The Play of Fictions: Studies in Ovid's Metamorphoses Book 2*, Ann Arbor, MI.
McGowan, M.M. (2009), *Ovid in Exile: Power and Poetic Redress in the* Tristia *and* Epistulae ex Ponto, *Mnemosyne Supplement* 309, Leiden.
Nagle, B.R. (1980), *The Poetics of Exile: Program and Polemics in the Tristia and Epistulae ex Ponto of Ovid*, Collection Latomus 170, Brussels.
Oliensis, E. (1997), 'Return to Sender: The Rhetoric of *Nomina* in Ovid's *Tristia*', *Ramus* 26, 172–93.
Scioli, E. (2015), *Dream, Fantasy, and Visual Art in Roman Elegy*, Madison, WI/London.
Syme, R. (1978), *History in Ovid*, Oxford.
Thorsen, T.S. (2014), *Ovid's Early Poetry: From his Single* Heroides *to his* Remedia amoris, Cambridge.
Tissol, G. (2014), *Ovid: Epistulae ex Ponto Book I*, Cambridge.
Williams, G.D. (1994), *Banished Voices: Readings in Ovid's Exile Poetry*, Cambridge.
Wulfram, H. (2008), *Das römische Versepistelbuch: eine Gattungsanalyse*, Berlin.

Part VI: **Seneca: Prose and Poetry**

Christopher Trinacty

Nulla res est quae non eius quo nascitur notas reddat (*Nat.* 3.21.2): Intertext to Intratext in Senecan Prose and Poetry

This paper examines the way that Seneca manipulates language from intertexts in his works and how this process differs in his tragedies from his prose philosophy. In his writings, Seneca often features an intertext at an early point, the language of which will then become a leitmotiv for the work as a whole. These intertexts are emblematic of Seneca's writing style and show how Seneca imagines his genres, his readership, and, ultimately, his message. This paper focuses on two intertexts, from the *Thyestes* and the *Naturales Quaestiones,* in order to examine how the intratextual repetition of intertextual language functions. In each case, Seneca recontextualizes the language in his new generic environment and creates original interpretations through the fusion of source and target texts. The intratextual repetition not only provides structure to these works, but also helps to forge the ideal reader that Seneca desires. My paper stresses how the dramatic genre encourages a more 'open' interpretation of such intertexts.[1] The characters provide their own particular viewpoint on the language and their focalized views necessarily produce difference from the very act of repetition. Seneca's Stoic prose works often have a more 'closed' trajectory in which the intertexts are made to speak to the philosophical issues at hand. In the *Naturales Quaestiones*, I examine one of the earlier intertexts in the work (a nod to Ovid's *Metamorphoses*) and show how its repetitions throughout the work merge ethical and physical details. Seneca does this not only to emphasize the importance of the *Metamorphoses* to this opening book, but also to stress how scrutinizing *natura* includes scrutinizing the language used to describe *natura*. Such a practice highlights the way these two foundational facets of Stoicism are linked by the third of the triad, namely logic, which for Seneca revolves around the correct rhetorical use of language.

1 My use of 'open' and 'closed' here hearkens back to D. Fowler's works 'First Thoughts on Closure: Problems and Prospects,' (1989) and 'Second Thoughts on Closure,' (1997).

https://doi.org/10.1515/9783110611021-019

1 Horace's furious language

When the Fury emerges in the prologue of Seneca's *Thyestes*, she urges the ghost of Tantalus to incite his descendants to new crimes (*Thy.* 23–9):

perge, detestabilis
umbra, et penates impios furiis age.
certetur omni scelere et alterna vice
stringatur ensis. nec sit irarum modus
pudorve, mentes caecus instiget furor,
rabies parentum duret et longum *nefas*
eat in nepotes.

Go forth, hated ghost,
Stir up your foul household gods with fury.
Let them contend with every crime and let each one's sword
be wielded in turn. Let there be no limit to their anger,
and no shame, let blind madness goad their minds,
let the rage of parents endure and long-lasting evil
pass to the grandchildren.

Tarrant has admirably illuminated what makes this speech 'one of Seneca's most powerful pieces of writing, a sustained evocation of evil ceaseless in its operation and all-encompassing in its effects.'[2] Its literary make-up is also notable. Certain moments of the speech rework Ovid (*Thy.* 40–6 ~ *Met.* 1.144–50) and Vergil (*Thy.* 83–6 ~ *Aen.* 7.336–7),[3] but in this opening salvo a poem of Horace also looms large. Seneca's manipulation of the Horatian model reveals two fundamental aspects of his intertextual poetics, namely, (1) that intertextual language, once established, is repeated throughout a play to provide numerous recontextualized senses of the word, and (2) that the understanding of the full Horatian poem impacts how one must understand the intertext.[4] In this particular case it also shows how sensitive Seneca was to intratextual repetition in Horace's own poetry.[5]

---

2 Tarrant 1985, 23–67.

3 Schiesaro 2003, 32–4; Putnam 1995, 273.

4 For additional examples in Senecan tragedy, cf. Trinacty 2014, 188–90 (for Vergil's *Georgics* in the *Medea* and *Oedipus*), 225–7 (for Ovid's *Metamorphoses* and the *Oedipus*), and *passim*.

5 One can see a similar recognition in his *Medea*. Horace expands upon his own previous mention of the Medea story by repeating language from *Epode* 3.13–4: *hoc delibutis ulta donis paelicem / serpente fugit alite* in *Epode* 5 *fugit ulta paelicem* (*Epod.* 5.63). Seneca's Medea responds to Horace's representation —she will not endure being *inulta* at *Med.* 399, muses about vengeance against the *paelex* Creusa (*Med.* 920), and, when escaping, claims *sic fugere soleo* (*Med.* 1022).

The phrase *sit irarum modus / pudorve* replicates the opening of *C.* 1.24, where Horace asks, 'What restraint or limit should exist for grieving one so dear? Teach me songs of lamentation, Melpomene, to whom Father gave a pure voice with the cithara' *quis desiderio sit pudor aut modus / tam cari capitis?...* (*C.* 1.24.1–4). The collocation of *modus* and *pudor* is not common; Nisbet and Hubbard cite Martial 8.64.18 as the only other parallel.[6] The Horatian poem acts as a consolation to Vergil on the death of Quintilius, by offering advice[7] and calling attention to various views of the underworld –the boundary may be permeable (Orpheus as a particularly 'Vergilian' *exemplum*), but more likely Mercury herds all the shades and is not amenable to liberating the dead (*non lenis precibus fata recludere*, *C.* 1.24.17). These perspectives on the underworld are, of course, pertinent to the first act of Seneca's *Thyestes* in which the ghost of Tantalus is being driven to act by a denizen of Hades, and Seneca may be making the comment that welcome ghosts tend not to return (Quintilius, Eurydice), but in tragedy others will (Tantalus, Laius in *Oedipus*, Thyestes himself in *Agamemnon*). This opening language also resounds within the play as a whole.[8] The Fury impels Tantalus to disregard any limit or sense of shame in his anger (*irarum*), while Horace is asking the Muse (Melpomene) what the limit or restraint for missing a dear friend should be. Horace himself seems to be playing on the meanings of *pudor* and *modus* later in the poem, when he again features *Pudor* (*C.* 1.24.6), the personified god, and writes of Vergil's poetic skill 'even if you were to modulate the lyre more beautifully than Thracian Orpheus' *quid si Threicio blandius Orpheo / auditam moderere arboribus fidem* (*C.* 1.24.13–4). Thus the opening question may imply not only what limit is appropriate for mourning, but also which poetic meter (OLD s.v. *modus* 7).[9] Horace implies that his poem is a fitting tribute to Quintilius and, possibly, a better threnody than anything Vergil may have conceived or written.[10] If Quintilius was, for Horace, the embodiment of an honest friend and critic (cf. *Ars* 438–52), then Seneca's creative correction of Horace's language into a work exploring the limits

While many scholars have seen this final retort as an allusion to Euripides' *Medea*, Seneca may be thinking of Horace as well.

6 Nisbet and Hubbard 1970, *ad loc.*

7 See Thibodeau 2002–3 on the Epicurean overtones of this advice.

8 If the message of Horace's poem is ultimately that Vergil's song 'could not establish a connection between the living and the dead, not to speak of bringing the defunct back to life' (Putnam 2006, 106), then Seneca's ghost of Tantalus and the Fury would seem to belie this sentiment.

9 Cf. Putnam 1993, 127 explores the repetition of this term, concluding 'Horace's Virgil, however, though himself the grandest of singers, must practice not music's outgoing, charming modes but the delimitation of restraint on whatever poetic manifestation of grief he may choose to voice.'

10 If Vergil himself had written a mourning poem about Quintilius, cf. Khan 1967.

of *nefas* is an incisive and ironic move: after all, it is the final word of Horace's ode (*durum: sed levius fit patientia / quidquid corrigere est nefas*, *C*. 1.24.19–20).[11] Seneca is a perceptive reader of Horace: just as Horace intratextually resignifies terms in his short consolatory ode, so Seneca is interested in exploring the various connotations of *modus* and *pudor* in the tragic poetry of the *Thyestes* (his own metrical *modus*).

Schiesaro identifies the destabilization of *modus* and *pudor* as part of the Fury's 'language of subversion' that seeks to substitute *furor* and *nefas* in their place and explore the effects of a 'Fury-dominated world.'[12] Their use in a sentence dealing with the restraint of anger (*irarum*) befits *ira*'s crucial motivating force in the remainder of the play (180, 519, 1056).[13] Horace himself identifies *irae* with Thyestes at *C*. 1.16.17–8: 'Anger destroyed Thyestes in heavy ruin' (*irae Thyestem exitio gravi / stravere*). In both Horace and Seneca, then, the primary question of the work is limited by *pudor* and *modus*, i.e. the limits of *desiderium* for Horace, the limits of *ira* for Seneca. Seneca's repetition of these terms (*pudor*, 215, 891, 925; *modus* 198, 255, 279, 483, 1051–2) highlights their thematic importance for the subject matter of the play as a whole and acts as a further response to the initial intertext with Horace. For instance, in Atreus' *furor*-addled state, the fleeing sun is an indication of heavenly acceptance of his culinary creation, 'lest shame should get in the way / daylight has withdrawn' (*ne quid obstaret pudor*, / *dies recessit*, 890–1), a far cry from the Satelles' conception of a stable kingship 'where there is no shame, / care for law, righteousness, piety or faith, / rule is unstable' (*ubi non est pudor / nec cura iuris sanctitas pietas fides / instabile regnum est*, 215–7).[14] For Thyestes, *gravis pudor* (925) is the result of his exile and a feeling he attempts to banish when drunkenly celebrating his supposedly happy homecoming. This does not bode well because Atreus' own lack of *pudor* leads to the revenge he is able to inflict on Thyestes: the brothers become eerily similar here in their dismissal of *pudor*, which indicates that Atreus' reading of Thyestes' character is accurate.[15]

In addition, that scene of drunken revelry exposes that Thyestes is unable to maintain any sense of restraint in his success, a trait that Atreus recognizes

11 For more on Horace's view of Varus, cf. Brink 1971, *ad loc.*

12 Schiesaro 2003, 38–40. For more on *pudor* in Senecan philosophy and the *Phaedra*, cf. Wray 2015.

13 Cf. Tarrant 1985, *ad loc.*

14 The Satelles and the ghost of Tantalus act as blocking characters to the desires of Atreus and the Fury (respectively), and the repetition of the language of the prologue underlines the structural similarity in their roles.

15 Cf. *Thy*. 1104–10, where Atreus claims that Thyestes is anguished because he wishes that he had committed the same crime against Atreus.

earlier in the play 'Can he tolerate moderation when prospering' (*numquid secundis patitur in rebus modum*, 198). In like manner, Atreus thinks about his revenge in terms of such limits when he devises a plan 'beyond the limit of ordinary pain' (*nil quod doloris capiat assueti modum*, 255).[16] Seneca employs *modus* as Thyestes discusses his fear of Atreus 'what limit shall I set to my fear' (*timori quem meo statuam modum?*, 483) to accentuate that the dismissal of such fear leads to his entrapment (491–5). He should be afraid. This term, found first in the mouth of the Fury, lastly appears near the play's conclusion, when both brothers think about the crime, and the play, that has just occurred (*Thy.* 1050–3):

Th: genitor en natos premo
premorque natis! sceleris est aliquis modus!
At: Sceleri modus[17] debetur ubi facias scelus,
non ubi reponas.

Th: Mark how I, a father, press my sons
And am pressed by them! There is some limit to crime!
At: Limits for crime are owed when you do the crime,
Not when you pay it back.

If the Fury hopes at the beginning for there to be no limit to the hatred that afflicts this house, it is clear that Atreus has embodied her directives, which is suitable for a character who incessantly seeks to surpass the norm.[18] Seneca repeats this language throughout the *Thyestes* to show how the various characters define themselves through and against such limits and how these terms reflect upon their own self-control or lack thereof.

Seneca incorporates the intertext with Horace *C.* 1.24 near the opening of his play to show how the inability of restraining *nefas* and *ira* can lead to his tragic poetry. The 'songs of lamentation' (*lugubris cantus*, *C.* 1.24.2–3) that Horace asks Melpomene to produce are paralleled by the very creation of Seneca's tragedy and Atreus' own Fury-inspired metapoetic control of the narrative. The Fury acts as the Muse, taking over the role from Horace's Melpomene, traditionally the

---

16 He will tell the Satelles that this plan satisfies him (*hic placet poenae modus*, 279).

17 Davis 2003, 60 remarks on the way these characters use *modus* in different manners in this section 'Thyestes' concluding remark is particularly inept...if crime has a proper measure, it is because there is a balance of forces between the pressure exerted by his sons on Thyestes and by Thyestes on his sons. But Atreus takes him to mean, 'does crime have some limit.' (*Modus* means both 'measure' and 'limit'.) This of course he denies.'

18 Cf. Schiesaro 2003, 130–1.

Muse of tragedy.[19] Horace's incorporation of Vergilian language mirrors the impulse of Seneca in his employment of Horatian language in the prologue. In each case the poetic predecessor is evoked for the author to assert his own generic and thematic variation from the model.[20] If Horace examines poetry's ability for consolation and memorialization and Melpomene is used without reference to tragedy per se,[21] Seneca's tragic poetry is the conduit by which one discovers how *pudor* and *modus* are flimsy bonds to harness the power of *furor* and *ira*, but the proper genre of poetry for its expression. The Horatian intertext ultimately endorses Seneca's conception of his dramatic poetry, which views itself not only as a dialogue between authors, but also a dialectic between the characters over the fundamental meaning of language.

2 Form and fluidity: 'Among rational creatures there are gods and men, and creatures like Pythagoras' – Aristotle (frag. 192 Rose)

Intertexts appear throughout Seneca's prose works. As in his tragedies, these activate the reader's memory of previous works, often involve the Augustan poets, and raise questions of their applicability in their Senecan context. Notable moments such as that found above when an initial intertext continues to haunt the resulting narrative can be collected without much difficulty: an echo of *Aeneid* 5 at the opening of the *de Ira*, an evocation of Cicero when the narrator of the *Apocolocyntosis* offers his *modus operandi*, etc.[22] The letters delight in this as well and intimations of Horace's *Ep.* 1.11.27 (*caelum, non animum, mutant, qui trans mare currunt*) begin in the second letter of the collection (*Ep.* 2.1), only to be

19 Although Horace does not assign different spheres of poetry to different muses, it is clear that the trend is known by Seneca's time, cf. Prop. 3.3.33.

20 Cf. Lowrie 1994, 380 'Horace in one way tells Vergil that his association of the lyre with *elegos* in the figure of Orpheus will not account for his own more realistic version of the genre. In another, the last word of the poem answers its initial question...*Fas:* divine law, natural law, what can be spoken, what is poetic go hand in hand.' Of course the very question of what is *fas* and *nefas* is also integral to the *Thyestes*, cf. Schiesaro 2003, 36–45.

21 Nisbet and Hubbard 1970, *ad loc.*

22 Cf. *De Ira* 1.1.2 *decoris oblita* and *Aen.* 5.174 *oblitus decorisque...*; *De Vita Beata* 1.2: *conteretur vita inter errores* and Cato's *Mor.* Frag. 3= Gell. *N.A.* 11.2.6; *Apoc.* 1.1: *dicam quod mihi in buccam venerit* and Cic. Att. 14.7.2 (cf. Sen. *Ep.* 118.1); Ben. 1.1 and Cicero N.D. 1.43.5.

reiterated in *Ep.* 28 and 55.[23] In the *Naturales Quaestiones*, Seneca offers a preface for the work as a whole that is rich in such language. As scholars such as Hine and Williams have argued, the first book of the *Naturales Quaestiones* is what is commonly known as the third book.[24] Seneca opens this book as follows (*Nat.* 3.praef.1):

> Non praeterit me, Lucili virorum optime, quam magnarum rerum fundamenta ponam senex, qui mundum circumire constitui et causas secretaque eius eruere atque aliis noscenda prodere. quando tam multa consequar, tam sparsa colligam, tam occulta perspiciam?

> It does not escape me, best of men Lucilius, how I am laying the foundation of a great work. I, although an old man, have decided to survey the world and to draw out its causes and secrets and to publish what ought to be known to others. When will I pursue topics so many, collect topics so scattered, and contemplate topics so hidden?

This is the language of a new project and, notably, it features intertextual language that will be important for the complete work, but especially this book.[25]

While the concerns of the preface as a whole revolve around ethics and ethical improvement, the reader must also look at the movement that Seneca is encouraging, from a survey of the world (macroscopic) to a more specific delving into causes and then secrets (microscopic).[26] We are gradually moving from what can be seen by all to what can be found only with the application of *ratio* (to understand the causes) and a concerted effort to root out (*eruere*) nature's mysteries.[27] If this call for inspection is applied to the linguistic level (which I think it is

---

23 Cf. Richardson-Hay 2006, *ad* 2.1. Likewise, Seneca will quote Publilius Syrus at *Ep.* 9.21 and repeat the first half of the quote (*non est beatus*) later in his collection at *Ep.* 75.7 and 85.23. The resonance from its original mention carries over into those intertexts.

24 Codoñer Merino 1979, 1.xii–xxi; Hine 1981, 6–19; Williams 2012, 12–14 with full references.

25 For more on this preface, cf. Reydam-Schils 2005, 40–42; Inwood 2002, 126–28; Williams 2012, 29–37.

26 Note Seneca's novel use of *circumire* to mean 'to consider in detail' (s.v. *OLD* 7b). but movement (*ire*) is still implicit in the verb. To emphasize the reverse movement before beginning the *quaestio* proper, Seneca concludes his preface by stressing how one's scrutiny of 'hidden matters' will help when contemplating the external world as well (*in occultis exercitata subtilitas non erit in aperta deterior, Nat.* 3.praef.18). Honing one's *subtilitas* is important for interacting with the 'open' world as well.

27 Such 'rooting out' is found in the *Oedipus* as is the verb *noscere*, especially identified with Oedipus and his role as a riddle solver (*ambigua soli noscere Oedipodae datur,* 216). Seneca does not use the simple form *noscere* often in his works, but when he does it often is in relation to the Delphic oracle's injunction to 'know thyself' (*Dial.* 6.11.3, *Ep.* 94.28). The use of *causa* and *eruere*

meant to do), the reader is encouraged to pay attention to the specific words as well as to their more expansive syntax. The phraseology of this section strongly evokes Ovid's description of Pythagoras in his *Metamorphoses* (*Met.* 15.65–72):

> cumque animo et vigili perspexerat omnia cura,
> in medium discenda dabat coetusque silentum
> dictaque mirantum magni primordia mundi
> et rerum causas et quid natura docebat,
> quid deus, unde nives, quae fulminis esset origo,
> Iuppiter an venti discussa nube tonarent,
> quid quateret terras, qua sidera lege mearent,
> et quodcumque latet.

> Since he had contemplated everything with an alert and careful mind,
> he was giving out what ought to be learned openly and was teaching
> crowds silently marveling at his words the origin of the great universe
> and the causes of things and what their nature was, what the nature of god
> was, from where snow originates, whether Jupiter or winds thundered,
> when a cloud was split, what shook the earth, and by what law
> stars moved, and whatever else was hidden (from man's knowledge).

Linguistic recollections of *mundus, causa, perspicio* and similar content such as teaching this material to others initially attracted me to this passage.[28] Pythagoras' summary of topics also adumbrates a number of the topics of books in Seneca's *Naturales Quaestiones*: snowfall (4b), lightning and thunder (2), and earthquakes (6).[29] If the reader picked up this book expecting 'Inquiries of Nature', she might be surprised that little is mentioned in this ethical preface to indicate that Seneca is writing a work of meteorology until the preface concludes.[30] In effect, the intertext provides a nominal table of contents for the work as a whole and, if the reader picks up on the intertext, she will know what to expect as well as the rewards of unearthing 'whatever else was hidden' (*quodcumque latet*).[31]

---

at the conclusion of this book creates a telling ring-composition (*Nat.* 3.30.3) that shows Seneca's purposeful rhetorical composition.

28 Torre 2007, 54–5 also remarks on these similarities. Brown 1990, 319n.4 remarks that Ovid follows a generic didactic pattern in his list of topics.

29 The fact that Pythagoras never actually speaks about these matters in the Ovidian passage, whereas Seneca devotes books to these topics may also indicate Seneca's competitive 'completion' of subjects merely mentioned in Ovid.

30 This surprise technique is purposeful, cf. Henderson 2004, 6.

31 Note how the idea that there is something hidden reappears in Ovid (*quaeque diu latuere, canam, Met.* 15.147) and is picked up in Seneca, e.g. *Nat.* 7.30.4: *maxima pars mundi, deus, lateat.*

This opening recollection of *Metamorphoses* 15 is significant because it brings to the mind both the poetry of Ovid's epic and the figure of Pythagoras in particular. If the Horatian example above demonstrated how Seneca knew the complete Horatian poem and structured elements of his *Thyestes* as a response to that poem, this initial intertext in the *Naturales Quaestiones* tips the reader to acknowledge additional moments when Ovid's *Metamorphoses* and specifically 'Pythagorean'[32] topics appear in this book. The historical Pythagoras and his teachings might be considered to be an odd choice for an opening intertextual evocation.[33] Surely Aristotle's *Meteorologica* or even Lucretius' *De Rerum Natura* would be more expected at the opening of Seneca's monumental work on Stoic physics.[34] Feldherr, however, makes the valuable suggestion that 'Ovid's Pythagoras offers a comprehensive reading of the [*Metamorphoses*], and the act of assessing that reading allows each member of the poet's audience to retrace in turn her own experience of the work.'[35] In this vein, Seneca's reception of the *Metamorphoses* as a whole may be symbolically evoked by his recollection of Pythagoras' teaching at this moment, uniting scientific prose and epic poetry, the philosophical and the literary, and the *Naturales Quaestiones* and the *Metamorphoses*. The Ovidian reference emphasizes that change is ever present and this elemental fluidity is an aspect of his teaching that Seneca will highlight as his work continues. The subsequent quotations of Pythagoras as well as his continued intertextual presence insist on his applicability in matters ethical and physical. These recollections also stress the way that language will tie together these two areas and how previous literature will be redeployed actively to make those connections more emphatically.

Pythagoras' teachings in *Metamorphoses* 15 highlight his belief in vegetarianism, the transmigration of the soul, and the general elemental and temporal principle of flux (*omnia mutantur, nihil interit, Met.* 15.165; *cuncta fluunt,*

---

32 Ovid is conflating some of Pythagoras' ideas with those of Empedocles and Seneca will identify moments from Ovid's speech as Empedoclean (cf. Fantham 2004, 116). This conflation is the topic of Hardie 1995. Seneca mentions Pythagoras also at *Ep.* 90.6 and 108.17–19 where he mentions how Pythagorean teachings inspired him when young and led to his vegetarianism.

33 The question of the seriousness of Ovid's presentation of Pythagoras continues to vex scholars who see his speech as either central to the *Metamorphoses* or a comedic aberration, cf. Hardie 1995, 204 for a survey of opinions. Clearly, Seneca takes the passage seriously.

34 Myers 1994, 142–47 sees Ovid's Pythagoras as a direct response to Lucretius, so it is possible that Seneca is indirectly continuing the critique of Lucretius by evoking Pythagoras. Connors and Clendenon 2016, 176–82 stress that Pythagoras was also associated with caves and rivers, major topics of this book.

35 Feldherr 2010, 150. For Pythagoras as a self-conscious didactic poet, cf. Volk 2002, 64–68.

omnisque vagans formatur imago, Met. 15.178) – proved by the cycles of the day and night (*Met.* 15.186–98), seasons (*Met.* 15.199–213), and even the elements. A large segment of his speech (over one hundred lines) comprises a paradoxography of the miraculous qualities of water (*Met.* 15.259–360),[36] including some of the cosmological and mythical stories Ovid related earlier.[37] This detail didn't escape Seneca's notice: this book of the *Naturales Quaestiones* is concerned with terrestrial waters and quotations of this speech appear later in this book (now with philosophical elucidation).[38] Ovid's Pythagoras stresses that the four elements undergo continual change, 'even those things which we call elements do not persist' (*haec quoque non perstant, quae nos elementa vocamus, Met.* 15.237), an idea that Seneca expands further in his *Naturales Quaestiones*. Seneca's language draws on Ovid's account, especially when he claims 'everything arises from everything, air from water, water from air, fire from air, air from fire' (*fiunt omnia ex omnibus, ex aqua aër, ex aëre aqua, ignis ex aëre, ex igne aër*, 3.10.1), which clearly recollects Ovid's 'everything arises from these (elements) and falls back into them' (*omnia fiunt / ex ipsis et in ipsa cadunt*, 15.244–5).[39] Williams has stressed how the elemental interchangeability of this passage is programmatic for the topics of the *Naturales Quaestiones* as a whole, but it also points out how Ovid's Pythagoras is foundational for the physical theory that Seneca will stress throughout the *Naturales Quaestiones*.[40] If the first intertext was found in the more ethical preface, now we see Pythagoras' teachings involved in scientific proofs.

The importance of these intertexts is made manifest later in the book when Seneca quotes from Pythagoras' speech four times. Seneca flaunts his reading of this passage of Ovid and peppers his own explanation of miraculous waters with

36 See Myers 1994, 147–59 for more on paradoxography in Pythagoras' speech.

37 See Fantham 2004, 116 for these parallels (e.g. 15.251 ~ 1.35 on elemental flux and 15.319 ~ 4.285–7 on the spring of Salmacis). The repetition of elements from the opening of the *Met.* in Pythagoras' speech (e.g. 15.307–9 with the poem of *Met.* 1, cf. Myers 1994, 151) not only indicates 'the affinity of this thaumastic genre with his own stories' but a conscious reflection of beginning and ending and the cyclic movement Pythagoras espouses.

38 For Pythagoras many of these *mirabilia* simply seem to be listed for the sake of their wonder, while Seneca strives to verify how such 'wonders' are explicable if one understands Stoic physics. Williams 2012, *passim* stresses how Seneca's work strives throughout to normalize what is wonderful, frightening, and inexplicable with a 'rhetoric of necessity in nature's functioning' (44).

39 An intertext noted by Parroni 2002, *ad loc.*; and Berno 2012, 59–61.

40 Williams 2012, 19–20 on this passage's 'anticipatory or even programmatic form of coherence to...Seneca's tour through phenomena related to elemental fire, air, earth and water.' Ovid (and the Augustan poets in general) should be considered part of the 'community of scholars' for Seneca's doxographic sources (Hine 2006, 53).

quotations from Pythagoras' lecture. For Seneca, Ovid has provided the catalogue,[41] but not the reasons, and Seneca works hard in *Nat.* 3.20 to place, for example, Ovid's description of the Cicones' river (which turns your innards to marble) into the larger framework of waters that are *medicatum*, *Nat.* 3.20.3 caused by the various transformations of elements (*mutatione eius nascitur, in quam transfiguratus est, Nat.* 3.20.1) or influenced by soil composition and corruption. In doing so, the miraculous elements of Ovid's waters are downplayed and made part of the workings of Stoic *natura,* while endorsing aspects of *natura* that were found in Pythagoras' speech. A final quotation of this speech appears in *Nat.* 3.26, when Seneca is discussing the penchant of rivers to disappear and emerge elsewhere (*Nat.* 3.26.4 = *Met.* 15.273–76). For Seneca, this helps to prove his theory that veins of water move below the earth, for Ovid it was merely another example of nature's mutability. It also stresses the human analogy that Seneca provides for the earth with veins and arteries of air and water circulating below the surface (*Nat.* 3.15). Seneca's quotations reveal a more noticeable authorial control over the interpretation of the Ovidian material and his creative reuse of that material for his own specific physical theories.[42] He creates unity from the Pythagorean flux.

Seneca's interest in Pythagoras' speech concludes near the end of the book, when Seneca notably critiques Ovid's style during the flood passage. These concluding chapters, which describe the flood that will destroy the world, feature outright literary criticism about Ovid's own flood description (*Met.* 1), but the prominence of Ovid in the flood passage indicates how important he has been all along. It may also hint at a universal cycle, much like Pythagoras' theory (as Torre suggests),[43] and it certainly appears to endorse the Ovidian Jupiter's rationale for the flood (although now within a larger cosmic viewpoint).[44] By encompassing all

---

41 Seneca treats Ovid's waters in sequential order, but omits certain (more fabulous/mythological) stories, such as Salmacis and a tale involving Melampus and the daughters of Proetus.

42 Cf. Mazzoli 1970; Tarrant 2006, 2–3; and Ker 2015, 113–4 for more on Seneca's quotation of Augustan poetry. As Ker aptly states, 'Seneca's quotations are often the tips of icebergs' (114); in this case their use in this chapter reiterates how often that speech is important for this book as a whole.

43 Cf. Torre 2007, 58.

44 As Tarrant 2006, 4 points out, Seneca glosses Jupiter's decision to destroy mankind because of their wickedness (*Nat.* 3.28.2), and seems to update it to a near-future because of contemporary *mores*, cf. *Nat.* 3.29.5, 3.30.7–8 for further pessimistic statements about the deserved destruction of depraved humanity (cf. Mader 1983 for this rationale, Mazzoli 2005 for the rhetoric, and Volk 2006 for similarities between this passage and the *Thyestes*).

of Ovid's epic (albeit backwards)[45], there is a sense that Seneca can claim to have incorporated the entirety of Ovid's *Metamorphoses* here in the first book of his *Naturales Quaestiones*, taking from it some of its topics and its general theme of mutability, but now placed within his Stoic philosophical prose. Numerous scholars have remarked on Seneca's passage of literary criticism, but what is important for this paper is the way that Seneca concentrates his disparagement on certain pathetic passages of Ovid's rhetoric, yet continues to embellish his account with moments from Pythagoras' speech.[46] When explaining the various ways to understand the necessity of the flood, Seneca draws attention to the idea that the world is a living entity 'whether the world is an animal or a body governed by nature' (*sive animal est mundus, sive corpus natura gubernabile, Nat.* 3.29.2), which evokes Pythagoras' idea 'whether the earth is an animal and lives and has multiple blowholes for fire' (*sive est animal tellus et vivit habetque / spiramenta locis flammam exhalantia multis, Met.* 15.342–3).[47] This is, of course, true in as much as Seneca continually analogizes the earth in the book and indicates how such 'lessons' learned from Ovid's Pythagoras (in terms of mutability and figuring the earth as a living being) provide a rationale for the flood.[48] Seneca's explication and correction of Pythagoras occurs throughout this book and the language of Pythagoras' speech appears regularly to keep that speech in the mind of the reader. When the concluding flood narrative engages explicitly with Ovid's poetry and critiques its seriousness (*Nat.* 3.27.13), his *aemulatio* of such material is foregrounded. Certain lines *are* worthy,[49] the speech of Pythagoras becomes one of (if not *the*) major sources for this book and its blend of poetry and science is made to speak to the various concerns of *Naturales Quaestiones* 3.

If one follows the requisite circumspection urged at the opening of the work, one will see how the rhetoric there helps to make connections between sections

45 By beginning with intertexts from *Met.* 15 and concluding with quotations and analysis of the language of *Met.* 1.

46 E.g. *Nat.* 3.30.4~15.269, 3.28.2~15.390. The bibliography on this passage is vast, cf. Berno 2012, 64–5, n. 52; and Hine 2010, 109–10 for a survey.

47 Cf. Parroni 2002, *ad loc.*

48 Here it is used to specifically support Stoic ideas of the conflagration and fate, cf. *Nat.* 3.29.2. For more on analogy in Seneca's *Nat.*, cf. Armisen-Marchetti 2001, and Roby 2014. Roby points out how Seneca expects a reader well-versed in rhetoric and, while she does not mention intertextuality as part of the fictional nature of rhetorical modeling, I believe that this aspect highlights how her approach 'include[s] the creator and user of the model, showing how fiction can yield not just persuasive trickery, but genuine insight' (178).

49 Seneca will approve of *Met.* 1.285–90 with *magnifice haec* (3.27.14).

of the *Naturales Quaestiones* that may appear, at first glance, to be disparate.[50] The preface (as well as certain digressions) feature Seneca at his most ethical, while this final intertext and the later quotations are from moments in which Seneca is explicating Stoic physical theories. Intertexts, intratexts, and quotations spotlight the rhetorical texture of the work,[51] moments in which Seneca is referencing his own literary ability and ancestry, and act to unite the three strands of Stoic philosophy: physics, ethics, and logic.[52] While some may think that it is a stretch to conflate rhetoric and logic, when Seneca writes of logic (admittedly, not often)[53] it strongly resembles rhetoric, especially in its search for the correct use of language. For example, at *Ep.* 89.9, Seneca writes, 'The greatest authors, and the greatest number of authors, have asserted that there are three parts of philosophy: moral (*moralem*), natural (*naturalem*), and rational (*rationalem*).'[54] The 'rational' represents logic, but it is important that he goes on to define these as follows: 'The first orders the soul (*conponit animum*); the second investigates the nature of things (*rerum naturam scrutatur*), the third works out the essential meanings of words, their syntax, and the arguments which prevent falsehoods from creeping in and displacing truth' (*tertia proprietates verborum exigit et structuram et argumentationes, ne pro vero falsa subrepant*). As he continues, Seneca not only splits his discussion of logic into its parts (dialectic and rhetoric), but even has recourse to a quotation from Vergil to prove his point (*Ep.* 89.17 = *Aen.* 1.342). What is important about such logic is its persuasiveness and its application to one's conduct (*ad mores statim referas, Ep.* 89.18), as he goes on to

---

50 In this the intratextuality of the preface is stressed, when Seneca claims 'our acuteness, prepared on hidden things, will be no worse on open ones' (*in occultis exercitata subtilitas non erit in aperta deterior, Nat.* 3.praef.18) and its echo of the opening lines of the preface quoted *supra*. This repetition encourages the reader to open up her point of view to the visible natural phenomena that Seneca subsequently explores.

51 For more on the use of intertextuality in rhetoric of the time, cf. Sen. *Suas.* 3.5–7 and *Con.* 7.1.27.

52 The various analogies, such as the Stoic egg, or the orchard (logic is the wall, physics the tree, ethics the fruit) that link the three components can be found at S.E. *M* VII 17–19.

53 Cf. Barnes 1997, 12–23 concludes that the limited (and rather hostile) mentions of logic in Seneca indicate that he is hostile to logical trifling (syllogisms especially), but that he realizes it is an instrument to aid in the pursuit of Stoic physics.

54 Seneca's own philosophical writings often stress the workings of *ratio* and the *Nat.* certainly encourage the reader to exercise her *ratio* on the material. When considering philosophical models and the tendency of *ratio* to not be satisfied with the manifest world, Seneca employs similar language, *Ep.* 95.61: *ratio autem non impletur manifestis; maior eius pars pulchiorque in occultis est.* Hidden matters need models and doctrine to explain them, much like what we find detailed in *Nat.*, and the very inquiry into hidden matters is first emphasized at 3.praef.1 above.

illustrate in the remainder of the letter.[55] The rhetoric of Seneca's *Naturales Quaestiones* ultimately acts to bind the learning and the lessons of the books: intertexts lead to intratexts that help to order and reflect not just on the subject matter, but also on the proper hermeneutic method to appreciate and understand the natural world.[56] If the reader looks closely into the language and what is behind the language, that same reader may end up being able 'to see the entirety in her mind' (*animo omne vidisse*, 3.praef.10), which is, after all, the goal of the *Naturales Quaestiones* as a whole.[57]

3 Conclusion: *nulla res est quae non eius quo nascitur notas reddat*

After writing about how location and climate can affect the taste and composition of water, Seneca offers the general *sententia*: 'there is no matter which does not provide signs of that from which it was produced' *nulla res est quae non eius quo nascitur notas reddat* (*Nat.* 3.21.2). In terms of this paper, such a *sententia* can be read as a claim about the literary antecedents from which Seneca drew inspiration.[58] The works of tragedy and philosophy will provide 'signs' (*notas*) which will indicate their origins and influence the flavor of the works. These can be fleeting, but some abide. In the *Thyestes*, Horace's language continues to provide the basis for the characters' self-conceptions as well as the cycle of vengeance. Horace's own poetics of mourning becomes the engine for Seneca's poetics of violence and Horace's evocations of Vergil incite Seneca's own emulative evocations of Horace (and Vergil). The presence of Ovid in the *Naturales Quaestiones* may not be surprising, but the emphatic exploration of themes and topics, present as quotations and intertexts, then reframed as intratexts makes this work his most comprehensive response to Ovid's *Metamorphoses*. Pythagoras, whom Ovid describes as someone enduring self-exile on account of his hatred of a tyrant (*odioque tyrannidis exul / sponte erat*, *Met.* 15.61–2), may particularly evoke Seneca's own situation and his retirement from Nero at the time of writing *Naturales Quaestiones*. Seneca's intertexts and quotations of Pythagoras' speech show how he recontextualizes material from the Augustan poets to offer commentary on their works. In

55 Barnes 1997, 12–21 stresses this aspect about Seneca's use of logic.
56 As Seneca will say elsewhere, the goal of *ratio* is *secundum naturam suam vivere* (*Ep.* 41.8).
57 According to scholars such as Gunderson 2015, 68.
58 Cf. *Ep.* 84 for similar thoughts on the way one's influences will be revealed.

this case, his larger quest for 'nature's causes and secrets' (*causas secretaque eius eruere, Nat.* 3.praef.1)[59] willingly collects material from Ovid's great epic of change and mutability, but now reiterates how such elemental flux is part of *natura*'s larger workings and is fundamental to the correct perspective on nature. The rhetoric of Seneca's prose, which blends obvious 'literary' touches (quotations, the vivid description of the flood) with a more hidden architecture of intertextual and intratextual repetitions, enables the reader to acknowledge both the requisite skill and learning necessary to pursue this task and exemplifies the use of rhetorical logic to grasp Stoic physics and ethics.

Bibliography

Armisen-Marchetti, M. (2001), 'L'imaginaire analogique et la construction du savoir dans les Questions Naturelles de Sénèque', in: M. Courrént/J. Thomas (eds.), *Imaginaire et modes de construction du savoir antique dans les textes scientifiques et techniques*, Perpignan, 155–74.

Barnes, J. (1997), *Logic and the Imperial Stoa*, Leiden.

Berno, F.R. (2012), 'Non solo acqua. Elementi per un Diluvio Universale nel Terzo Libro Delle *Naturales Quaestiones*', in: M. Beretta/F. Citti/L. Pasetti (eds.), *Seneca e Le Scienze Naturali*, Florence, 49–68.

Brink, C.O. (1971), *Horace on Poetry: The 'Ars Poetica'*, Cambridge.

Brown, R.D. (1990), 'The Structural Function of the Song of Iopas', *HSCP* 93, 315–34.

Codoñer Merino, C. (1979), *L. Annaei Senecae Naturales Quaestiones*, 2 vol., Madrid.

Connors, C./Clendenon, C. (2016), 'Mapping Tartaros: Observation, Inference, and Belief in Ancient Greek and Roman Accounts of Karst Terrain', *CQ* 35.2, 147–88.

Davis, P.J. (2003), *Seneca: Thyestes*, London.

Fantham, E. (2004), *Ovid's Metamorphoses*, Oxford.

Feldherr, A. (2010), *Playing Gods: Ovid's Metamorphoses and the Politics of Fiction*, Princeton/Oxford.

Fowler, D. (1989), 'First Thoughts on Closure: Problems and Prospects', *MD* 22, 75–122.

Fowler, D. (1997), 'Second Thoughts on Closure', in: D.H. Roberts/F.M. Dunn/D.P. Fowler (eds.), *Classical Closure*, Princeton, 3–22.

Gunderson, E. (2015), *The Sublime Seneca: Ethics, Literature, Metaphysics*, Cambridge.

Hardie, P. (1995), 'The Speech of Pythagoras in Ovid *Metamorphoses* 15: Empedoclean Epos', *CQ* 45, 204–14.

Henderson, J. (2004), *Morals and Villas in Seneca's Letters: Places to Dwell*, Cambridge.

Hine, H. (1981), *An Edition with Commentary of Seneca, Natural Questions*, Book 2, New York.

59 Note how Seneca will reuse this language when speaking about quotations in his letters, 'I am accustomed to do this, Lucilius; from every quotation, even if it is very far away from philosophy, I try to root out something and make it useful.' *Hoc ego, Lucili, facere soleo: ex omni notione, etiam si philosophia longissime aversa est, eruere aliquid conor et utile efficere* (*Ep.* 58.26).

Hine, H. (2006), 'Rome, the Cosmos, and the Emperor in Seneca's 'Natural Questions'', *JRS* 96, 42–72.
Hine, H. (2010), 'Seneca's *Naturales Quaestiones* 1960–2005 (part 2)', *Lustrum* 52, 7–60.
Inwood, B. (2002), 'God and Human Knowledge in Seneca's *Natural Questions*', in: A. Laks/D. Frede (eds.), *Traditions of Theology: Studies in Hellenistic Theology, Its Background and Aftermath*, Leiden, 119–57.
Khan, H.A. (1967), 'Horace's Ode to Virgil on the Death of Quintilius: 1.24', *Latomus* 26, 107–17.
Ker, J. (2015), 'Seneca and Augustan Culture', in: S. Bartsch/A. Schiesaro (eds.), *The Cambridge Companion to Seneca*, Cambridge, 109–121.
Lowrie, M. (1994), 'Lyric's 'Elegos' and the Aristotelian Mean: Horace, 'C.' 1.24, 1.33, and 2.9', *CW* 87, 377–94.
Mader, G. (1983), 'Some Observations on the Senecan Götterdämmerung', *A Class* 26, 61–71.
Mazzoli, G. (1970), *Seneca e la Poesia*, Milan.
Mazzoli, G. (2005), 'La retorica del destino: la *demonstration diluvii* in Seneca, *nat. quaest.* III 27–30', *Pallas* 69, 167–78.
Myers, K.S. (1994), *Ovid's Causes: Cosmology and Aetiology in the Metamorphoses*, Ann Arbor MI.
Nisbet, R.G.M./M. Hubbard (eds.) (1970), *A Commentary on Horace Odes, Book I*, Oxford.
Parroni, P. (2002), *Seneca: Ricerche sulla Natura*, Milan.
Putnam, M.C.J. (1993), 'The Language of *Odes* 1.24', *CJ* 88, 123–35.
Putnam, M.C.J. (1995), *Virgil's Aeneid: Interpretation and Influence*, Chapel Hill.
Putnam, M.C.J. (2006), *Poetic Interplay: Catullus and Horace*, Princeton.
Reydams-Schils, G. (2005), *The Roman Stoics: Self, Responsibility, and Affection*, Chicago.
Richardson-Hay, C. (2006), *First Lessons: Book 1 of Seneca's* Epistulae Morales, *A Commentary*, Bern.
Roby, C.A. (2014), 'Seneca's Scientific Fictions: Models as Fictions in the *Natural Questions*', *JRS* 104, 155–80.
Schiesaro, A. (2003), *Passions in Play: Thyestes and the Dynamic of Senecan Drama*, Cambridge.
Tarrant, R.J. (1985), *Seneca's Thyestes*, Atlanta.
Tarrant, R.J. (2006), 'Seeing Seneca Whole', in: K. Volk/G.D. Williams (eds.), *Seeing Seneca Whole: Perspectives on Philosophy, Poetry and Politics*, Leiden, 1–18.
Thibodeau, P. (2002–3), 'Can Vergil cry? Epicureanism in Horace *Odes* 1.24', *CJ* 98, 243–56.
Torre, C. (2007), 'Tra Ovidio e Seneca: La Traccia Dell'Epos di Pitagora nel Programma Filosofico delle *Naturales Quaestiones*', in: A. Costazza (ed.), *La Poesia Filosofica*, Milan, 45–61.
Trinacty, C.V. (2014), *Senecan Tragedy and the Reception of Augustan Poetry*, Oxford.
Volk, K. (2002), *The Poetics of Latin Didactic: Lucretius, Vergil, Ovid, Manilius*, Oxford.
Volk, K. (2006), 'Cosmic Disruption in Seneca's *Thyestes:* Two Ways of Looking at an Eclipse', in: K. Volk/G.D. Williams, *Seeing Seneca Whole: Perspectives on Philosophy, Poetry and Politics*, Leiden, 183–200.
Williams, G. (2012), *The Cosmic Viewpoint: A Study of Seneca's Natural Questions*, Oxford.
Wray, D. (2015), 'Seneca's Shame', in: S. Bartsch/A. Schiesaro (eds.), *The Cambridge Companion to Seneca*, Cambridge, 199–211.

Stavros Frangoulidis

Intertextuality and Intratextuality: Euripides' *Iphigenia at Aulis* and Seneca's *Troades*

It is generally acknowledged that Seneca's *Troades*, composed of a double plot, draws its inspiration from two plays by Euripides: *Troades* and *Hecuba*, which depict the deaths of Astyanax and Polyxena respectively.[1] Yet the Roman playwright's treatment of the demise of the two youngsters is also replete with allusions to the sacrifice of Iphigenia. Inevitably, these allusions bring to mind a third Euripidean tragedy, namely *Iphigenia at Aulis* (*IA*). From such a perspective, the presence of Agamemnon's daughter may be read as part of Senecan intratextual poetics: we know that *IA* cannot have informed the Euripidean *Hecuba* or *Troades*, as it was written after them.[2]

With its thorough treatment of the way Iphigenia comes to be sacrificed, I would like to argue that *IA* may be regarded as an intertext for the Latin version of *Troades*. This is visible in a number of readily identifiable ways, most strikingly in the use of deception to trap and murder innocent youngsters, which is a crucial theme absent from the play's generally acknowledged models. The sustained presence of the *IA* text provides a prominent unifying thread to *Troades*.[3] The creative appropriation of *IA* in the Astyanax and Polyxena narratives further makes the latter intratextually related to the former, insofar as both rework the Euripidean model: Astyanax becomes a duplicate of Polyxena and vice-versa. This doubling of horror intensifies the calamity that has befallen the Trojans in the aftermath of war.

I wish to express my warmest thanks to David Konstan for his most valuable comments on an earlier version of this paper; and to Eleni Manolaraki, Thalia Papadopoulou and Poulheria Kyriakou for their useful suggestions. The Latin text and English translations are quoted from the Loeb edition of Fitch 2000. The text of *IA* is from the *OCT* edition by Diggle 1994, and the English translations from Morwood 1999.

1 E.g. Ράιος 2011, 54–5, who further observes the 'chiastic' combination of the Greek versions in Seneca's tragedy: *Hecuba*, *Troades–Troades*, *Hecuba*. The similarities between Euripides' *Troades* and Seneca's play of the same name are analyzed in detail by Phillippo 2007, 332–5.

2 I owe this observation to David Konstan *per litteras* (2017).

3 For a defense of the unity of Seneca's *Troades*, see Keulen 2001, 266–7. For the emotions of the Trojan women in the play, see the innovative essay by Fabre-Serris 2015, 100–18.

https://doi.org/10.1515/9783110611021-020

It should be noted, however, that Seneca alters the context and meaning of the *IA* in terms of his intertextual discourse, lending it an entirely new direction: whereas the sacrifice of Iphigenia in Euripides secures the passage to Troy and the prospect of victory and κλέος in war, in *Troades* two youngsters are sacrificed so as to ensure the total annihilation of Troy, and by extension the end of bloodshed between the Achaeans and the Trojans.[4] The Iphigenian connotations gain in significance if one considers that of the two deaths in the Euripidean *Hecuba* and *Troades*, only that of Polyxena is depicted as sacrifice.

Naturally enough, in discussing the evocation of Greek sources in Seneca's version of *Troades*, critics have also read allusions to fundamentals of the Iphigenia myth in terms of a repetition and regression that prevents the linear movement of history.[5] Yet little, if any, attention has been paid to the inclusion and adaptation of Euripides' *IA* within the entire narrative of Seneca's tragedy, as a means to underscore the atrocity of sacrificing two blameless youngsters in war to secure the eradication of Troy;[6] this innovative treatment of the *IA* intertext, as part of Seneca's intratextual strategy, also sustains the link between the play's two sub-plots. In what follows I shall focus on the incorporation and revitalization of the *IA* model, with a view to shedding light on Seneca's intertextual and intratextual poetics.

Appropriation of the model is triggered after the opening act, comprising Hecuba's dirge and the choral lament over the loss of Troy. In Euripides' *Hecuba* the chorus informs the title character that the fleet has been held up in port, but does not elaborate on the point. By contrast, Talthybius' employment in the Senecan play of the adverb '*semper*', 'always' (164), suggesting the repetition of *mora*,[7] may recall the intertext of *IA*, which offers the most comprehensive treatment of the delay at Aulis (especially 87–8). The major difference between the two plays is that in *IA* the warriors were anxious to sail for Troy, whereas in Seneca they wish to return home.

4 The theme of Troy's annihilation is also found in *Hecuba* and *Troades* by Euripides.

5 Shelton 2016, 205, n. 56 cites all allusions to the Iphigenia myth featured in the play. See also Schiesaro 2003, 193–4; Boyle 1994, 170–2, *passim*; Hanford 2014, 64–6; Colakis 1985, 153; Lawall 1982, 252; and Keulen 2001, 266–7.

6 Fantham 1982, 260 considers the idea of Polyxena being dressed in Greek bridal clothes as possibly deriving from Euripides' version of the pretext that brought Iphigenia to Aulis; Harrison 2015, 135–6, n. 44 points out that 'comparisons and contrasts with Euripides' *Iphigenia at Aulis* are obvious', but does not develop this idea any further. On the other hand, Penwill 2005, 89–90, 99 discusses allusions to the Iphigenia myth in Seneca's tragedy in relation to Lucretius' *DRN*. See also Schiesaro 2004, 200.

7 On the theme of delay in the play, see Schiesaro 2003, 191.

Interpreting events through the prism of the literary precedent set at Aulis, the Senecan chorus seeks to learn the identity of the divinity responsible for the delay, to which Talthybius responds that Achilles' shade has arisen from his tomb, castigating his fellow Achaeans for leaving without offering him a *γέρας* and ordering that Polyxena should be betrothed to his ashes (191–6).[8]

Achilles' ascent from the dead seems to be cast as a metaphorical birth:[9] the earth trembles, roars (172: *terra mugitu fremens concussa*) and cracks open (178: *scissa vallis*); the sea boils (176–7: *pontus / ... volvit vada*); the newly-opened chasm offers a passage to the world above (179–80: *hiatus ... pervium ad superos iter / ... praebet*); the hero's ghost rises from the deepest hollows of the earth (182: *emicuit ingens umbra*), and lightens Achilles' tomb (180: *tumulum levat*). This sequence of events directs attention to the *genesis* of a new play, after its apparent end, following Hecuba's dirge on the collapse of Troy and the ensuing choral lament both on the fallen city and implicitly on their own fortunes as war captives, since they are destined to be assigned as slaves to one of the Greek leaders (Act 1).[10]

The re-emergence of Achilles and the demand that Polyxena be given to him is also found in Euripides' *Hecuba*, albeit without any allusion to wedlock (109–15). The strong resonances of Aulis in the Senecan episode may also allow us to view the deceased hero's demand as reminiscent of Artemis in *IA*, when she requests that Agamemnon sacrifice his daughter (91–93). Here again, Seneca recontextualizes the signification of *IA*, for in Talthybius' narration, Achilles emerges into the upper world as a sign of his deep anger, so as to demand the sacrifice of Polyxena in person, unlike the Euripidean Artemis, whose will is communicated through Calchas, her earthly representative, obliging Agamemnon to sacrifice his daughter if he wishes to lead the expedition against Troy (92–3): καὶ πλοῦν τ' ἔσεσθαι καὶ κατασκαφὰς Φρυγῶν / θύσασι, μὴ θύσασι δ' οὐκ εἶναι τάδε ('and we could sail to Troy and sack the city if I performed this sacrifice, but if I did not sacrifice her it was not to be'). What is more, Achilles also aims to secure the progression of the tragic plot, even after his death, with a warning

8 As Fantuzzi 2012, 14 points out, Achilles has a special claim on Polyxena, as the last surviving virgin of Priam's daughters. That being said, the erotic undertones to her sacrifice must have been a rationalistic addition, originating in Hellenistic times and beginning with Lycophron.

9 For a detailed discussion of epic antecedents in the description of Achilles' ascent, see Trinacty 2014, 168–72.

10 This notion becomes clear from the *makarismos* of Priam (142–55 and 156–63). See the excellent discussion in Shelton 2016, 184–94. The decision to assign the captives to each Greek leader has already been taken, but the women are not yet aware of this information (208–9): *iam suum cuncti duces / tulere pretium* ('all leaders have taken their prize already').

metapoetically suggestive of the μῆνιν ... Ἀχιλῆος in the *Iliad* (193–4),[11] namely that neglecting his rights will prove as costly to the Achaeans as when he withdrew in anger from the battlefield. Such a threat points to the inevitability of Polyxena's murder, securing the continuation of the play.

The ensuing exchange between Pyrrhus and Agamemnon dramatizes the respective efforts made by the two characters to set the play in motion and so build on the literary antecedent, or halt this process and thereby the movement of plot. The confrontation is replete with resonances of Aulis, pointing to the intertextual presence of *IA* in Seneca's play: Pyrrhus recites his father's exploits, so as to validate his demand that Polyxena be offered up, given the fact that Agamemnon sacrificed his daughter at Aulis to reclaim Helen at the outset of the campaign against Troy (248–9):[12] *natam parens /... immolasti.* For his part, the king, now opting for wise rulership, tries to distance himself from his past, refusing to authorize the sacrifice on the grounds that more than enough reprisals have been exacted on Troy.[13] Agamemnon's literary past leaves him open to criticism: Pyrrhus rebukes the king for viewing the sacrifice of girls as *nefas* (therefore holding back the natural chain of events); but the king justifies his conduct as having been motivated by the good of the *patria* (332). In the hierarchy of Roman values, religion occupies a position still higher than that held by the fatherland. Hence, when the king scornfully refers to the circumstances of Achilles' death brought about by Paris, Pyrrhus' subsequent mention of the gods avoiding direct confrontation with Achilles (348) forces Agamemnon to reconsider and consult Calchas, the interpreter of the divine will, even though —in yet another allusion to Iphigenia— he admits that the seer's oracles are never in his favor.

The consultation with Calchas is absent from Euripides' *Troades*; it may thus be viewed as recasting the narrative on the expedition to Troy in *IA*.[14] This is signaled by the opening line of Calchas' prophecy, which explicitly states that the Fates will grant passage to the Danaans at the customary price, thus calling to mind the conditions at Aulis that enabled the fleet to sail (360). On this occasion, however, the Iphigenian connotations have been adjusted in terms of quantity to suggest that any repetition of the crime is worse and more savage than its model: in Euripides one victim is required to propitiate Artemis (89–91: Κάλχας δ' ὁ μάντις ... / ἀνεῖλεν Ἰφιγένειαν ... / Ἀρτέμιδι θῦσαι ('And Calchas the seer ...

11 Trinacty 2014, 170–1; Fantham 1982, 237–8.

12 See also Schiesaro 2003, 191–3; on the debate between Pyrrhus and Agamemnon, representing two different ways of exercising power in wartime, see Lauriola 2015, 56–7.

13 Schiesaro 2003, 191.

14 Schiesaro 2003, 192; Boyle 1994, 170–2.

announced that I had to sacrifice Iphigenia ... to Artemis');[15] but here the same prophet spells out that *fata* demand the sacrifice of two youngsters: dressed as an Achaean bride, Polyxena must be offered in marriage to Achilles' shade, and Astyanax must be hurled to his death. The command to execute both youngsters links their fortunes and affirms their intertextual relationship with *IA*.[16] What is more, this dialogue with the same intertext further accounts for the link between the two Senecan sub-plots, which may thus be read as intratextual doubles within Seneca's work. Polyxena is the last of Priam's children, while his grandson Astyanax is heir to the Trojan throne and therefore an incarnation of the kingdom's future. His demise, added to that of Polyxena, thus symbolizes the extinction of Priam's *domus* and therefore the end of Troy.

In Act III Andromache appears on stage, alarmed by a vision of her dead husband appearing in her sleep and ordering her to save their son (452–6). Hector is here rendered an intratextual double of Achilles' shade: both ascend from the lower world and foretell disasters yet to befall the defeated Trojans. In response to her husband's order, Andromache, with the assistance of an old companion, becomes mover of the action, fabricating a ruse to conceal Astyanax under the protection of his deceased father in Hector's tomb, which constitutes part of the stage-setting. She will then claim that he has perished in war, in a desperate attempt to save him and so preserve a future for the overpowered Trojans, even if in doing so she ironically foreshadows the boy's true fate.

The Achaeans charge Ulysses with obtaining the boy from his mother so as to implement the will of the *fata* and secure their homeward journey. Like Talthybius in Euripides' *Troades* (710–11), upon meeting Andromache, Ulysses states that he expresses the collective voice of the Achaeans, denying responsibility for the decision to have Astyanax killed (526–7). Yet Seneca's Ulysses goes further still, mentioning the oracle given by Calchas, which links the boy's death to the

---

15 Also 358–9. A similar increase of victims in terms of quantity appears in Seneca's *Thyestes*. Atreus' *scelus* in punishing his brother Thyestes by killing his brother's children and offering them as a meal to their father repeats a crime already witnessed in the past: that of Procne who butchers her son Itys and offers him as a meal to his father Tereus as punishment for raping her sister Philomela. The story is known from Ovid's *Metamorphoses* (6.412–674). Yet the Mycenaean version differs from its epic antecedent in terms of quantity. Instead of one victim, in *Thyestes* we have a banquet involving the murder of Thyestes' three children. On this see Frangoulidis 2017, 183 and further bibliography there.

16 A number of scholars see the twin fates of Polyxena and Astyanax as spoiling the Iphigenia parallelism. For a review of the relevant literature, see Keulen 2001, 266–7. Without elaborating on the point, the same author 2001, 266–7 also points out that the fortunes of the two youngsters establish several parallels and contrasts with the events at Aulis.

return voyage (528; 533). This validates a comparison of Andromache with Agamemnon in Euripides' *IA*, when he is informed of the divine demand that his daughter be sacrificed so as to raise the winds at Aulis (89–93).[17] Ulysses further adds a political motive for the murder, confirming the view that humans execute the divine will in accordance with their own reasoning:[18] if not killed, the boy will grow up to carry the war to Greek soil. Echoes of Agamemnon become even more explicit when Ulysses asks Andromache to endure the Achaean king's fate (555): *patere quod victor tulit* ('endure what the victor bore'). Yet again, the relevant scene in *IA* is substantially modified in the receiving text: while the Euripidean Agamemnon eventually agrees to sacrifice his daughter so as to enable the expedition against Troy to go ahead,[19] Seneca's Andromache refuses to surrender her son. This is evidenced by the performance of her meta-plot, in which she pretends to have no knowledge of her child's whereabouts.[20] What is more, in an obvious attempt to divert the focus away from the tomb itself, she mentions several places where her son might have been lost: in the countryside, the burning city or the wilderness (562–7). In entrusting her son to the protection of his father in the tomb, Andromache may also seem to reproduce Thetis' disguise of Achilles as a girl in Lycomedes' court, opting for her son to have a long life rather than let him go to war and meet a glorious death, as recounted in Ovid *Met.* 13.161–4.[21] Such a remark is backed up by Ulysses' relevant remark in his exchange with Andromache (568–9): *vicimus matrum dolos / etiam dearum* ('I have defeated the tricks of mothers, even goddesses'). The goddesses here include Thetis and her trickery. Andromache, however, binds herself by an oath as to the alleged truthfulness of her allegations and so, unlike Agamemnon, at least temporarily stalls the tragic plot (599–604).

Interaction with the *IA* intertext is further evidenced in Ulysses' subsequent deduction that the mother is lying, when he observes that her reaction is more indicative of fear than sorrow.[22] Employing the wiliness for which he is renowned in literature, he fabricates an ingenious ploy designed to instil fear in the mother

17 Also 358–9.

18 According to Lesky 1996, 85 humans carry out divine will on their own terms, which are distinct from those of the gods. This merging of divine and human motivation in one and the same act does not absolve humans of responsibility. A different view is advanced by Shelton 2016, 204–5.

19 Also 359–60.

20 In lines 564-691 Boyle 2017, 280 points out that Andromache plays the bereaved mother.

21 I owe this remark to Prof. S.J. Harrison. The contest between Ajax and Ulysses must feature in the *Armorum iudicium* by Pacuvius and Accius.

22 Fabre-Serris 2015, 110.

and gradually call her bluff with a view to obtaining the boy, who is the hallmark, so to speak, of the Iphigenian intertextual narrative.

In order to ascertain whether Astyanax really is dead, Ulysses informs Andromache of the cruel death originally planned for him (620–2). The trembling she displays leads him to believe that the boy is in fact alive (625); this in turn motivates a new bluff whereby Ulysses pretends that Astyanax has been found, and orders his arrest (627–30). The fact that Andromache looks around in terror at the location of the mound (631: *respicis*) enables him to sense that the boy is hiding in the tomb. This triggers a final bluff, in which Ulysses threatens to demolish Hector's tomb and therefore force Andromache to produce her son, even if he never truly plans to defile a sacred space (634–41).

The ruse employed to obtain Astyanax from his mother is absent from Euripides' *Troades*. The overall effect of the scene is to bring the Senecan Andromache, who has so far been seen as appropriating an intertextual Agamemnon, closer to the role of Clytemnestra as the victim of Agamemnon's ploy with the letter in *IA*.[23] In both cases the ruse is determined by the fact that it is otherwise impossible to obtain the child from the mother.

The inset text of *IA* is, yet again, reworked in order to convey the psychological anguish of the mother. Unlike Clytemnestra who brings her son and daughter to Aulis, Andromache faces the agonizing dilemma of whether to save her son and therefore let the ashes perish or to protect the ashes and therefore surrender her son. She ultimately resolves to carry forward her ruse to defend the tomb and save the life of her son, while openly claiming that she is fighting for Hector's ashes. The dilemma is non-existent: the safety of the child depends on the integrity of the tomb which also contains the ashes. Ulysses' new threat to demolish the mound (685) marks a key moment pointing to the victory of his ruse over that devised by Andromache: the mother eventually perceives the risks involved in defending the tomb for both son and husband and changes her strategy, begging Ulysses for mercy. Her plea confirms Ulysses' suspicions that the boy is living; it thus bears out the efficacy of the ploy, which is reminiscent of Agamemnon's success in obtaining the *virgo* from her mother through deception (704).[24]

The intertextual dialogue developed thus far is also seen after the emergence of the boy from his hideout. In Euripides' *Troades* Andromache hands her son over to Talthybius without second thoughts (782–9); but in the Roman play the mother puts forward her entreaties, having previously instructed her son to

---

23 Agamemnon later sends out a second letter to his wife, instructing her not to bring Iphigenia to the camp; but this *epistula* never reaches her because it is intercepted by Menelaus.

24 For a different assessment, see Stroh 2013, 443.

ignore his royal ancestry and beg for his life as a slave. In her own pleas, which also involve a rebuke of Ulysses (750–6), Andromache recalls the distraught Clytemnestra in *IA* when she learns the true plans of her husband and reproaches him while exhorting him to change his mind (1098–208). What is more, in clasping the victor's feet and begging for his life, Astyanax seems to be reworking Iphigenia's supplication of her father along with her young brother Orestes (1211–52). The connection also becomes clear in the way the respective leaders treat their suppliants: both Ulysses (736–8; also 593b) and Agamemnon (1266–8; also 1274–5) refuse to heed any entreaties - their priority is to prevent any future hostilities on Greek soil; and both the Ithacan (749) and the Argive king (1262–3) implicate Calchas in the process as a means of evading responsibility for the irrational decision of sacrificing innocent youngsters as a means of terminating the delay in port.[25]

The dialogic engagement of the two texts observed so far is further seen in the portrayal of the grieving mothers, following the refusal of Agamemnon and Ulysses to go against Calchas' wishes and spare the children. Andromache mourns the imminent death of her son. This brings to mind Clytemnestra in the Greek intertext, when she wails over the death of her daughter (1276–8); and Iphigenia sings a dirge on her death (1279–334). Yet a new context is served in Seneca's play. Informed by Achilles of the army's desire to sacrifice her for the sake of the expedition (1344–67), the Iphigenia in the Greek intertext eventually espouses the ideology of her father and wishes to give up her life to facilitate victory for her homeland (1390), while also trying to console her grief-stricken mother and forbidding her to fulfill the rites owed to the deceased (1437–8). On the other hand, in the Senecan play Astyanax reveals his immaturity by begging his mother for mercy in the midst of her dirge over his death while he is still alive, adding significantly to the horror of the act (792). Andromache is fully aware that all is now in vain, and so sends him off to be reunited with his father in the afterlife, having simultaneously acted out all rites owed to him as dead (802): *occurre patri* ('hurry to your father').

The intertextual interaction with *IA* is likewise apparent in the narrative of Polyxena's surrender. This effectively renders the Polyxena incident an intratext of that relating to Astyanax and vice-versa, insofar as both re-appropriate *IA* in the employment of trickery to ensnare and kill blameless youngsters as a prerequisite for departure.

25 On the theme of Astyanax as delaying the fleet in port and therefore as replicating the events at Aulis, see line 759: *ancoras classis legit*; and 813: *classis Argolicae moram*.

In Act IV Helen appears on stage, stating her reluctance to perform the duty imposed on her by the Achaeans. Following Calchas' instructions, she is to lure Polyxena into a false wedding to Pyrrhus and have her dressed in the Greek style, with the ultimate aim of sacrificing her on Achilles' tomb. In carrying out a task imposed by the Achaeans Helen appears as an intratextual double of Ulysses, who is charged with the task of obtaining the boy from his mother through deception. Only then will the army be able to sail from Troy. Helen is the sole dramatic character capable of playing out this role, due to her dual identity as both a Greek and Polyxena's sister-in-law.

The fact that in Euripides' *Hecuba* the Achaeans do not resort to trickery when obtaining Polyxena from her mother allows us to view the wedding ruse here as appropriating Agamemnon's deception in *IA*, when he writes to Clytemnestra asking her to bring Iphigenia to Aulis as a bride for Achilles (98–105 and 360–2). The intertext of *IA* is, once again, altered here, in keeping with the play's new context: Clytemnestra loses no time in obeying the order, as she has been fooled into thinking that her daughter will be married to a prominent fellow Achaean (607–30). In the Latin play too Hecuba remains silent, possibly because the survival of her only remaining daughter is the main priority, even if the girl is to be married to the murderer of her husband; but Andromache strongly reproaches Helen for the odd wedding proposal against the backdrop of a city laid waste by her disastrous union with Paris (888–902).

In her defense, Helen views her own lot as worse than that of the captives. Later, when commanding Andromache to prevail on Polyxena, she is brought to the verge of tears by the fact that she is torn between a sense of duty and the sympathy she feels for the plight of her sister-in-law (925–6): *vix lacrimas queo / retinere* ('I can scarcely hold back my tears'). Interaction with the Astyanax narrative lends Andromache the dramatic status of an intratextual double of Ulysses, once she observes a discrepancy between Helen's wedding proposal and her present weeping out of compassion for Polyxena; she infers that Helen's tears speak of a darker secret. Unlike Ulysses then, Helen is unable to carry her role to the end and reveals the truth (926), i.e. the command that the girl be wedded to Achilles in the afterlife. The bride's subsequent readiness to dress for the sacrificial killing, which she regards as preferable to marrying Pyrrhus (945–8), may point to Iphigenia, who, upon realizing the eagerness shown by the soldiers to go to war, declares herself ready to die for her country (1397): δίδωμι σῶμα τοὐμὸν Ἑλλάδι ('I give my body to Greece'). What is more, Polyxena's courage in the face of death, as Fabre-Serris correctly points out, invalidates Helen's assumption upon exhorting herself to play out her role that the wedding ruse will free her sister in law from the fear of death (869).[26] Yet the Euripidean intertext has been modified in the host-text: while Iphigenia altruistically offers her life up for the campaign at Troy, Polyxena views the sacrificial death planned for her as a release from hardship, ironically contributing to the annihilation of her homeland.

Turning to how the mothers of the young girls react, Clytemnestra becomes highly distraught when she learns of Iphigenia's resolve to die (1433–66); and Hecuba faints on learning similar news in Seneca's *Troades* (950–1): *at misera luctu mater audito stupet: / labefacta mens succubuit* ('but the unhappy mother is stunned to hear of her grief; her weakened mind has given way'). Yet, whereas in her sorrow Clytemnestra functions as a barrier to the Achaean objective, upon learning that the captive women have been allotted to new masters, Hecuba exhorts her daughter to rejoice at her own end in the awareness that death is ultimately preferable to life in captivity (967–8*): laetare, gaude, nata, quam vellet tuos / Cassandra thalamos, vellet Amndromache tuos!* ('rejoice, be glad, my daughter. How Cassandra or Andromache would wish your marriage!'). She thus functions as an intratextual double of Andromache, when she sends her son off to meet his father in the underworld (791), indirectly assisting the victors in their plan to destroy the city and its royal line.

The presence of multiple intertexts within the narrative of Seneca's tragedy helps us anticipate the fortunes of both Astyanax and Polyxena, on the basis of their treatment in the earlier Greek plays. The fact that in Euripides' *Troades* Astyanax's death is simply represented as politically motivated murder, devoid of any ritual connotations, invites comparison of the boy in the Latin play with the offering up of Iphigenia in *IA*. Reminiscent of her demise, the murder of Astyanax is explicitly framed by Seneca as a sacrificial ritual (1102; also 1006): *ad sacra*. The notion is further evidenced by two other instances: (1) at 634–5, Ulysses views the boy's fall from the crag as purification for the walls; and (2) at 1107, Andromache contrasts the Achaeans with Busiris, who may be notorious for performing human sacrifices, but who does not sprinkle his altars with a young boy's blood. And just as in *IA*, where the tragic heroine heads to the altar with an unflinching sense of purpose (1464), in Seneca's tragedy the young boy strides determinedly to the crag in a clear change of heart, perhaps due to his mother's earlier representation of his death as reunion with his father (1091–2).[27] Where the Euripidean Achilles recites prayers for victory at Calchas' instigation (1570–

26 See the excellent discussion in Fabre-Serris 2015, 113.

27 The bravery of the boy in meeting his death deeply moves the Achaean and Trojan onlookers; for the Roman audience in Seneca's time, the general sense of grief serves to cast the Achaeans in an even more hateful light.

6), in the Latin play Ulysses stands in for the *fatidicus* prophet, leading the prayers that summon the gods to the ritual, even if the boy preempts Ulysses' fatal push and jumps from the crag as a 'free choice of death' (1100–2).[28] In *IA* the *virgo* is reported to have vanished from the altar, perhaps after being spirited away by some divinity (1581–95), in terms which are taken as a positive omen for the expedition (1596–7).[29] Conversely, there is no solace for the Trojans in the loss of Astyanax: his end seals the fate of their city, as the boy symbolizes the best hope for the future.

Similar echoes are present in the sacrifice of Polyxena, Astyanax's intratextual double, as both victims courageously meet their death. In Euripides' *Hecuba* Polyxena is sacrificed at Achilles' tomb (518–82); but the presentation of her sacrifice by Seneca as a macabre wedding may allow comparison with the offering up of the heroine in *IA*. In line with Iphigenia, who perceives her death as nuptials (1398: οὖτοι γάμοι, 'This shall be ... my marriage'),[30] Seneca's Polyxena views her sacrifice in similar terms (948): *hoc thalamos putat* ('this she sees as marriage'). Associations between the two scenes are further backed up by the Greek style of Polyxena's dress.[31] The representation of both sacrifices in terms of a wedding intensifies the horror; the ritual celebrating the joys of union and the renewal of life here leads to the end of life. Iphigenia's mysterious removal from the altar is tantamount to a social death, as the *virgo* is lost forever for her parents and community, and Polyxena is brutally killed. Yet again, the intertext has been modified in the host-text: Iphigenia's disappearance marks the loss to be suffered by the Greeks for securing the expedition to Troy and the victory in war. Polyxena's atrocious death underscores the extirpation of the enemy stock and consequently of Troy (1127): *stirpem hostium*.

In *IA*, Clytemnestra's first reaction on hearing the account of her daughter's removal from the altar is to remain silent in disbelief, before claiming that the news may have been fabricated in a vain attempt to assuage her grief over the

28 On this scene, see the excellent discussion in Shelton 2016, 198.

29 The closing sequence in *IA*, containing Iphigenia's change of mind as well as part of the narrator's description of the sacrifice, is often viewed as a later addition. Insofar as Iphigenia's attitude is concerned, Kyriakou 2008, 247 points out that the original version is unlikely to have differed radically from the version handed down to us.

30 On the conflation of marriage and death as a topic in Greek Tragedy, see Rehm 1994. Earlier in the play the messenger relates a rumor by some soldiers: 'they are consecrating the young girl to Artemis, the ruler, in preparation for the wedding' (433–4): Ἀρτέμιδι προτελίζουσι τὴν νεάνιδα, / Αὐλίδος ἀνάσσῃ.

31 Harrison 2015, 135–6 points out that in myth too, Achilles was the intended spouse of Iphigenia; but unlike her, Polyxena needed to be dead.

loss of Iphigenia, and her anger at Agamemnon's trickery. This stance prefigures the transformation of the queen from a loyal wife to the avenger of her daughter's death, in the events to be played out when Agamemnon returns from the war in the Senecan play named after him, which is modeled on Aeschylus's *Agamemnon*.[32] This can be juxtaposed with the powerlessness of the captive Trojan mothers: Andromache submissively receives the horrific news of her son's death (1104–10), while Hecuba opts for death as a form of release from her troubles (1171–7).

In Euripides' *Hecuba* the winds blow following the narratives of the death of Polydorus and Hecuba's revenge on Polymestor, which is not directly linked to the return voyage. By contrast, in Seneca's *Troades*, the explicit order given to the enslaved to rush down to the sea as the fleet is departing (1178–9: *repetite celeri maria, captivae, gradu* ('head quickly towards the sea, you prisoners') could be seen as resonating with the lines of *IA* where Calchas commands the soldiers to board ship (1598–9): πᾶς τις ναυβάτης / χώρει τε πρὸς ναῦν ('so let every sailor ... go to his ship'). Both instructions are issued in the closing lines of the respective works, but in Seneca's tragedy this is the point that marks the final destruction of Troy, as if to mirror the events at Aulis prior to the beginning of the campaign.[33]

In the play's extra-dramatic events and in a remarkable change of fortune, as already echoed in Hecuba's dirge at the play's opening (5–6), the Achaeans are soon to take on the dramatic status of an intratextual double of the defeated Trojans: they will suffer great disasters at sea as atonement for their crimes. This fulfills Hecuba's earlier curse that they should meet rough seas to match their savage rituals (1005–6):[34] *precor / his digna sacris aequora* ('I pray for seas to match rituals like these'). The exegesis of the disasters as the outcome of the sacrificial ritual of a boy and girl discloses, yet again, Seneca's notable innovation on the tradition in which the disasters at sea are due to Athena for the rape of Cassandra at her temple and other atrocities committed by the Greeks during the sack of Troy.

On the basis of the above discussion, it can be concluded that in his narratives on the deaths of Astyanax and Polyxena, Seneca may not simply be drawing on Euripides' *Troades* and *Hecuba*, but also alluding to *IA*, which offers the most thorough treatment of the sacrifice of Iphigenia. The intertextual echoes of *IA* within the Roman play help establish a parallel between the beginning and end

32 See Frangoulidis 2016, 395–409.

33 Elsewhere in the Trojan War, murder as sacrifice is likewise seen in the story of Sinon, as recounted in Virgil's *Aeneid* 2.

34 The theme of rough seas in combination with the *nostos* theme first occurs at 995.

of the campaign against Troy. Thus the Latin play may be read as partaking in a rich intratextual dialogue between three model–texts. The sustained presence of *IA* within Seneca's *Troades* underlines the horror of human sacrifice and also maintains the unity of the two distinct sub-plots on Astyanax and Polyxena, rendering each a duplicate of the other in the sense that they appear to be re-working the fate of the Euripidean *virgo*. A new poetic objective is accomplished with the emphasis on the eradication of Priam's *domus* and by extension of Troy, through the inversion and re-contextualization of an intertext focusing on the optimistic prospect of victory and κλέος in war.

Bibliography

Bishop, D.T. (1972), 'Seneca's *Troades*: Dissolution of a Way of Life', *Rheinisches Museum für Philologie* 115, 329–37.

Boyle, A.J. (1994), *Seneca's Troades: Introduction, Text, Translation and Commentary*, Leeds.

Boyle, A.J. (2017), *Seneca, Thyestes*. Edited with Introduction, Translation and *Commentary*, Oxford.

Colakis, M. (1985), 'Life after Death in Seneca's *Troades*', *CW* 78, 149–55.

Corsaro, F. (1982), 'Il mito di Ifigenia e il Coro II delle *Troades* di Seneca', *Giornale Italiano di Filologia* 13, 145–66.

Damschen, G./Heil, A. (eds.) (2013), *Brill's Companion to Seneca: Philosopher and Dramatist*, Leiden.

Diggle, J. (ed.) (1994), *Euripidis Fabulae*, vol. III, OCT, Oxford.

Fabre-Serris, J. (2015), 'Women after War in Seneca's *Troades*. A Reflection of Emotions', in: J. Fabre-Serris/A. Keith (eds.), *Women & War in Antiquity*, Baltimore, 100–18.

Fantham, E. (1981), 'Seneca's *Troades* and *Agamemnon*: Continuity and Sequence', *CJ* 77, 118–29.

Fantham, E. Fantham, E. (1982), *Seneca's Troades. A Literary Introduction with Text, Translation and Commentary*, Princeton.

Fantuzzi, M. (2012), *Achilles in Love: Intertextual Studies*, Oxford.

Fitch, J.G. (ed., transl.) (2002), *Seneca: Hercules, Trojan Women, Phoenician Women, Medea, Phaedra*, Loeb Classical Library, Cambridge, MA/London.

Frangoulidis, S. (2016), 'Seneca's *Agamemnon*: Mycenaean Becoming Trojan', in: S. Frangoulidis/S. Harrison/G. Manuwald (eds.), *Roman Drama and its Contexts*, Berlin, 395–409.

Frangoulidis, S. (2017), 'Furia as *Auctor* in Seneca's *Thyestes*', *Trends in Classics* 9, 179–90.

Hanford, T. (2014), *Senecan Tragedy and Virgil's* Aeneid: *Repetition and Reversal*, PhD Diss., CUNY.

Harrison, G. (ed.) (2000), *Seneca in Performance*, London.

Harrison, G. (ed.) (2015), *Brill's Companion to Roman Tragedy*, Leiden.

Keulen, A.J. (2001), *L. Annaeus Seneca Troades: Introduction, Text and Commentary*, Leiden.

Kohn, T.D. (2013), *The Dramaturgy of Senecan Tragedy*, Ann Arbor, MI.

Kyriakou, P. (2008), 'Female *Kleos* in Euripides and his Predecessors', in: G. Avezzù (ed.), *Didaskaliae II*, Verona, 241–92.

Lauriola, R. (2015), 'Trojan Women', in: R. Lauriola/K.N. Demitriou (eds.), *Brill's Companion to the Reception of Euripides*, Leiden, 44–99.

Lawall, G.A. (1982), 'Death and Perspective in Seneca's *Troades*', *CJ* 77, 244–52.

Lesky, A. (1996), 'Decision and Responsibility in the Tragedy of Aeschylus', *JHS* 86, 78–85.
McAuley, M. (2015), *Reproducing Rome: Motherhood in Virgil, Ovid, Seneca, and Statius*, Oxford.
Morwood, J. (transl.) (1999), *Euripides: Iphigenia Among the Taurians, Bacchae, Iphigenia at Aulis, Rhesus*, with Introduction by Edith Hall, Oxford.
Motto, L.A./Clark, J.R. (1984), 'Seneca's *Troades*: Hecuba's Progress of Tribulation', *Estudios Classicos* 26, 273–81.
Penwill, J. (2005), 'Lucretian Reflections in Seneca's *Trojan Women*: The Function of the Second Choral Ode', *Antichthon* 39, 77–104.
Phillippo, S. (2007), '"A future for Astyanax": Alternative and Imagined Futures for Hector's Son in Classical and European Drama', *International Journal of the Classical Tradition* 14, 321–74.
Rehm, R. (1994), *Marriage to Death: The Conflation of Wedding and Funeral Rituals in Greek Tragedy*, Princeton.
Schiesaro, A. (2003), *The Passions in Play. Thyestes and the Dynamics of Senecan Drama*, Cambridge.
Shelton, J.-A. (2016), 'The Fall of Troy in Seneca's *Troades*', in: M.R. Bacharova/D. Dutsch/A. Suter (eds.), *The Fall of Cities in Mediterranean: Commemoration in Literature, Folk-Song and Liturgy*, Cambridge, 183–211.
Stroh, W. (2013), 'Troas', in: G. Damschen/A. Heil (eds.), *Brill's Companion to Seneca: Philosopher and Dramatist*, Leiden, 435–47.
Trinacty, C.V. (2014), *Senecan Tragedy and the Reception of Augustan Rome*, Oxford.
Volk, K. (2000), 'Putting Andromacha on Stage: A Performer's Perspective', in: G. Harrison (ed.), *Seneca in Performance*, London, 197–208.
Wilson, E. (transl.) (2010), *Seneca: Six Tragedies*, Oxford World's Classics, Oxford.
Zwierlein, O. (ed.) (1986), *L. Annaei Senecae Tragoediae*, OCT, Oxford.
Zyl Smit, B. van (2008), 'Seneca's Representation of Andromache and its Reception in French Drama', *Acta Classica* 51, 163–85.
Ράιος, Δ. (2011), *Σενέκα Φαίδρα. Εισαγωγή, κριτική έκδοση, μετάφραση, ερμηνευτική ανάλυση*, Ιωάννινα.

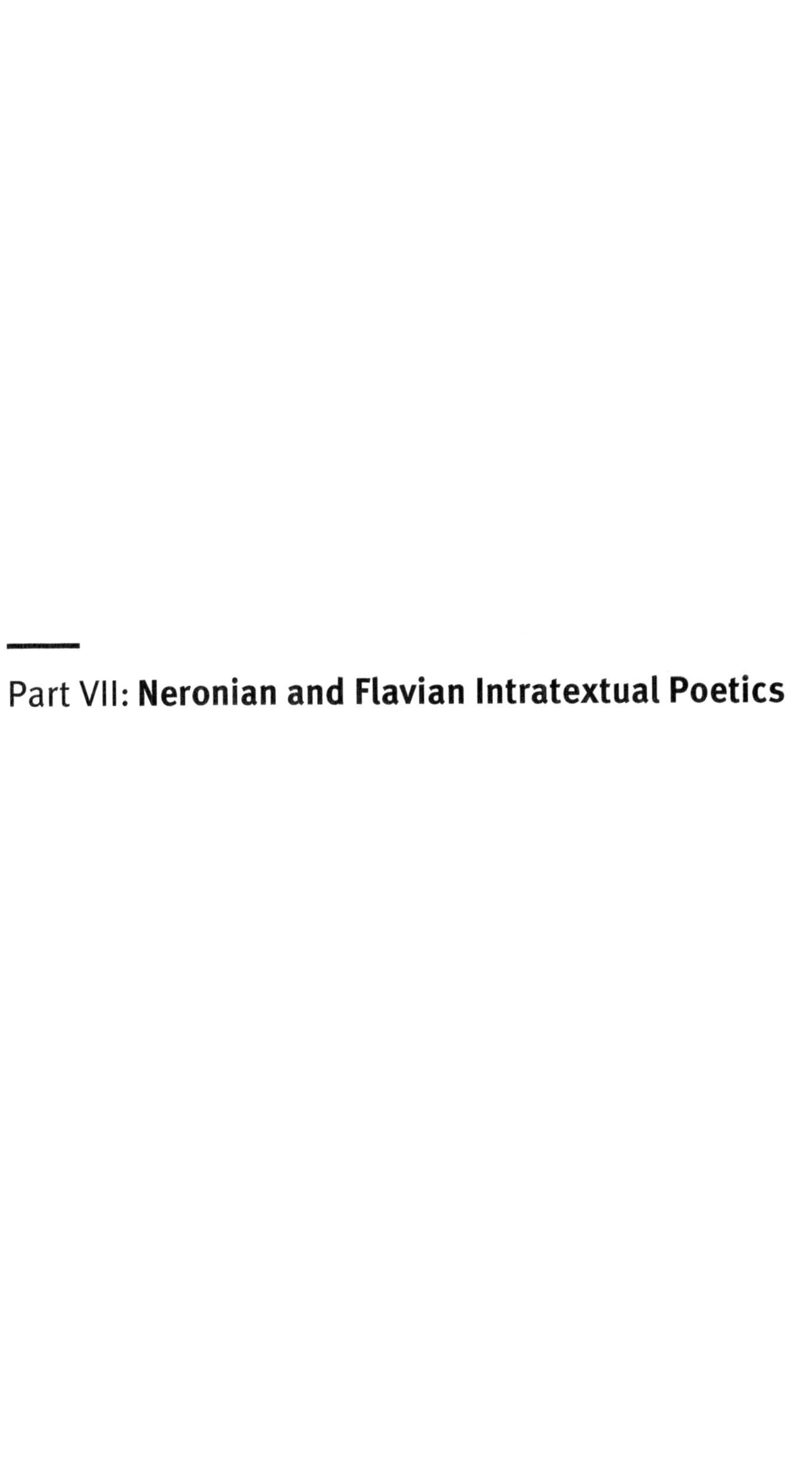

Part VII: **Neronian and Flavian Intratextual Poetics**

David Konstan

Praise and Flattery in the Latin Epic: A Case of Intratextuality

Why intratextuality?[1] That is, what does the approach so labeled add to what scholars of Latin literature have done all along in interpreting texts? The principal function of a literary theory is to inspire new ways of viewing a text; it is like a lens that allows certain features of the object to stand out in relief. A theory may invite attention to indications of race or gender, for example, or other social categories, or to the values that motivate characters in a work; it may highlight patterns of imagery (as the New Criticism did), or focus rather on contradictions in a text, whether with a view to resolving them or explaining why they are ineluctable (as deconstruction and certain styles of Marxist theory do). Examining how a work relates to a genre or to several genres at once is a matter of theory, as is a consideration of those cues within a text that indicate how it may have been performed, and reflecting in turn on what the context of such an imagined performance may suggest about the sense of the work itself. What, then, does intratextuality ask us to look at or for, and how does the angle of vision it represents affect our reading of a text? What kinds of works, moreover, yield up novel or interesting aspects when viewed from such a perspective? For not all objects are necessarily amenable to investigation by a given theory.

I will propose an example of a text that stands to be illuminated by an intratextual approach, but first let me lay out the lineaments of the method, as I understand it, so as to determine just what kinds of things it picks out for notice. The glossary in a recent lexicon of critical terms offers a crisp if not especially helpful definition of the word:

> **intratextuality:** Internal relations within a text, in contrast to intertextuality, which involves 'external' relations with other texts. Whilst the term intertextuality would normally be used to refer to links to other texts, a related kind of link is what might be called 'intratextuality' —involving internal relations within the text. Within a single code (e.g. a photographic code) these would be simply syntagmatic relationships (e.g. the relationship of the

1 This article benefitted from a fellowship at the Swedish Collegium for Advanced Study during the period 1 September to 16 December 2016, and from a fellowship at the Paris Institute for Advanced Studies (France), with the financial support of the French State managed by the Agence Nationale de la Recherche, programme 'Investissements d'avenir', (ANR-11-LABX-0027-01 Labex RFIEA+), during the period 1 February to 30 June 2017.

https://doi.org/10.1515/9783110611021-021

> image of one person to another within the same photograph). However, a text may involve several codes: a newspaper photograph, for instance, may have a caption
> (Chandler/Munday 2011, 225).

Despite the buzz words 'code' and 'syntagmatic', and the glance at relations across art forms, this formulation hardly distinguishes intratextuality from what classicists have comfortably done before the word was coined. One is inclined to exclaim, like M. Jourdain in Molière's play, 'Par ma foi! il y a plus de quarante ans que je dis de l'intertextualité sans que j'en susse rien!'[2]

Far more helpful is the description that Alison Sharrock has given us in the opening essay of the book edited by her and Helen Morales, which gave rise to the present conference:

> It is the hypothesis of intratextuality that a text's meaning grows not only out of the readings of its parts and its whole, but also out of readings of relationships between the parts, and the reading of those parts as parts, and parts as relationship…. [S]ometimes parts *don't* relate to each other in tidy and significant ways but stick out like sore thumbs. Intratextuality is about how bits need to be read in the light of other bits, but it is also about the bittiness of literature, as uncomfortable squareness-in-round-(w)holeness
> (Sharrock 2000, 6–7).

Sharrock's formulation summons the reader to notice not just relations among parts, but parts that seem on the face of it to be unassimilable to the whole. What is more, it is not the aim of intratextual criticism to integrate such parts into a coherent reading; they must remain separate not just formally but substantively: no salve or balm is to be applied to these swollen digits. Some parts of a text, to be sure, proclaim themselves as foreign or extraneous. One thinks of the prologues to Terence's comedies, which respond to attacks by rival poets or treat other contemporary matters. One might, of course, find connections between the prologues and the body of the plays, but such a critical operation, rewarding as it might be, moves in the contrary direction to that proposed by intratextuality, by demonstrating how self-evidently discrete parts of a work are in fact organically related to the whole. A more interesting case, perhaps, is the Euripidean prologue (and sometimes epilogue), which seems to stand apart from the dramatic action, violating the boundary constituted by the 'fourth wall' of the theater by directly addressing the audience, imparting information beyond the ken of the characters in the play. In this respect, it is something like the caption to a photograph, mentioned in the textbook definition of intratextual cross-coding.

2 Some at the conference spoke with a certain nostalgia of the 'retro' quality of the occasion, which seemed to hark back to an old-fashioned concern with Latin texts as literature.

Demonstrating the connection between a caption and a photograph, however, is hardly an exciting critical exercise, and the same may be said for similar operations on dramatic prologues. A more challenging inset piece is the postponed prologue, which by its position is more embedded in the drama; Menander offers several examples, and others are provided by the Roman adaptations of New Comedy (see Hunter 1985, 27–34). We may think in this connection of Aristotle's criticism of Euripides' choruses as *embolima* or extraneous insertions (*Poetics* 1456a25–32), which are so detached from the plot (*muthos*) of the play that they could as well come from an entirely different tragedy (cf. Nikolaidou-Arabatzi 2015). Aristotle prefers the chorus to function as another actor, in the manner, he says, of Sophocles, and to be part of the story rather than sing independent interludes that could be excised without in the least affecting the plot (a development in this direction occurred in New Comedy, where the choral intermezzi are simply indicated by the word *khorou*). The modern critic is drawn to eliciting the implicit relevance of such episodes, whether through verbal echoes or thematic analogies, but again, this is to deprive them of their alien quality and to render them fit subjects for conventional critical methods.

Perhaps the most radical example of such an apparently extraneous intervention in the body of a drama is the speech delivered by the *choragus* or sponsor in the middle of Plautus' *Curculio*, in which the actor ostentatiously refers to various monuments in the city of Rome, despite the setting of the comedy in Epidaurus.[3] The speech has been compared to the parabasis of Old Comedy, where such interruptions of the action were an acknowledged feature of the genre. Since there is no evidence of such intercalated speech in New Comedy, it is reasonably assumed that its presence in the *Curculio*, where it must have appeared out of place, is an invention of Plautus himself. The critic can assign various meanings to the episode, which may be regarded as bringing the Greek play home to Rome, or as emphasizing the distance between the ostensible location of the action and the site of its performance, among other possible functions. It nevertheless resists being absorbed into the action of the play, in part just because it seems to pertain to a different genre: as a pseudo-parabasis, it is anchored in the tradition of Aristophanic comedy, which marks it off as an intrusion from another domain. This vertical dimension, by which the choragus' monologue is construed in reference to a distinct tradition, serves to detach it from the horizontal plane of the text, opposing or defying the temptation to treat it as an integrated part of the drama. I would like to suggest that just this tension between the vertical allegiance, as it

3 Moore 1991, 462 calls it 'perhaps the strangest passage in all of Plautus'.

were, of the part and its planar context creates the opportunity for an intratextual interpretation.

Scholars have singled out various examples of quasi-independent sub-forms contained within broader literary genres, such as the lament in the Homeric epics (e.g., Tsagalis 2008, chap. 11) or hymns embedded in tragedy, which stand out like nuggets of precious metal in a chunk of ore. I would like to examine in similar terms a compositional element in Roman epic that has long troubled commentators, who have struggled either to isolate it entirely from the larger composition or, more rarely, to work it into the meaning of the work in one way or another. I am referring to the effusive praises of the emperor or other patron that are incorporated into the epics (and also other literary forms), which strike the modern reader as instances of servile flattery, scarcely compatible with the high seriousness of the genre, not to speak of what some critics have seen as the implicitly subversive message of the poems. They perhaps bear some resemblance to the fulsome dedicatory epistles that seventeenth- and eighteenth-century poets and novelists prefaced to their works. But these latter were plainly separate from the main text, and their authors generally stopped short of addressing their patrons as gods. The classical Latin eulogies are part and parcel of the poem, and in their gushing adoration seem as vacuous as the gesture of deference to the genius of Joseph Stalin that was obligatory in scientific publications in the Soviet Union during his reign. More particularly, how can one harmonize Lucan's *De bello civili*, which characterizes the founding father of the Julio-Claudian line, Julius Caesar himself, as an ambitious, self-interested wrecker of the ancient Roman constitution, with the over the top acclamation of Nero, who would order the poet to commit suicide even before he could finish his poem? Such an inset piece seems less an organic element in the work than an excrescence or tumor. Surely it is to be bracketed within the poem onto which it has been grafted as a wholly dispensable intrusion that disrupts the texture of the work.

It is to this text that I wish to apply the style of reading associated with intratextuality. I begin, however, with a brief look at another Latin epic, namely the *Achilleid* of Statius, which offers an illuminating comparison with Lucan's:[4]

Magnanimum Aeaciden formidatamque Tonanti
progeniem et patrio vetitam succedere caelo,
diva, refer. quamquam acta viri multum incluta cantu
Maeonio (sed plura vacant), nos ire per omnem
(sic amor est) heroa velis Scyroque latentem
Dulichia proferre tuba nec in Hectore tracto

4 Cf. Konstan 2016; the present comments depart somewhat from the interpretation offered there.

sistere, sed tota iuvenem deducere Troia.
tu modo, si veterem digno deplevimus haustu,
da fontes mihi, Phoebe, novos ac fronde secunda
necte comas: neque enim Aonium nemus advena pulso
nec mea nunc primis augescunt tempora vittis.
scit Dircaeus ager meque inter prisca parentum
nomina cumque suo numerant Amphione Thebae.
At tu, quem longe primum stupet Itala virtus
Graiaque, cui geminae florent vatumque ducumque
certatim laurus (olim dolet altera vinci),
da veniam ac trepidum patere hoc sudare parumper
pulvere: te longo necdum fidente paratu
molimur magnusque tibi praeludit Achilles.

Goddess, tell of great-hearted Aeacides and offspring feared of the Thunderer and forbidden to succeed to his father's heaven. The hero's deeds, 'tis true, are much famed in Maeonian song, but more are yet to celebrate. Be it your pleasure that I (so I crave) traverse the whole hero, bringing him forth by Dulichian trump as he hides in Scyros, nor stopping at Hector's drag, but singing the warrior through Troy's whole story. Only do you, Phoebus, grant me new founts if I have drained the old one with a worthy draught, and bind my hair with auspicious leafage; for no stranger do I knock at the Aonian grove, nor are these the first fillets to amplify my temples. The land of Dirce knows it, and Thebes numbers me among her forbears' ancient names along with her own Amphion. But you, the wonder of Italy's and Greece's manhood first by far, for whom the twin laurels of bards and captains flourish in rivalry (one of the twain is long since sad to be surpassed), give me good leave; suffer me in my eagerness to sweat awhile in this dust. On you I work in long and not yet confident preparing, and great Achilles is your prelude.

(trans. Shackleton-Bailey 2004).

The opening verses, which refer to Achilles as 'offspring feared of the Thunderer and forbidden to succeed to his father's heaven', can, I have argued, be understood as referring obliquely to Vespasian's decision to bypass Domitian as his successor and appoint Titus instead. If so, it might have awakened a bitter memory, since we are informed elsewhere of Domitian's resentment at this apparently deliberate slight. Achilles was, after all, not Jupiter's son but rather his great-grandson, and only in the vaguest sense did Jupiter deny him access to Olympus: we have to imagine that, had Jupiter not wedded Thetis to a mortal, Achilles would have surpassed his father and so replaced Jupiter as lord of the heavens. If this innuendo was present, are we to suppose that Domitian would have missed it —the emperor who is explicitly said to excel both in poetry and in war, even if his achievements in the latter outran those in the former? Did Domitian by this time —Statius was composing it in his final years, shortly before his own death and that of the emperor— cease to brood on his father's preference? Or was Statius emboldened by his own approaching death to take a risk and remind his readers of Vespasian's foresight in rejecting his now thoroughly paranoid son? Did Statius intend the fulsome praise of Domitian that follows, calling him 'the wonder of Italy's and Greece's manhood first by far', to be seen as conventional or formulaic, the obligatory laudation of the emperor, that would be understood as a mere formality and not as an integral part of the poem itself —a dedicatory epistle, as it were, but introduced into the opening verses of the poem itself?

These questions invite a critical approach that seeks to assess the political valence of the opening lines of the epic, and thereby to work them back into the text rather than detach them as part of a prefatory homage. But it is also possible to take the praise of Domitian rather as an unassimilated element, related intratextually to the rest of the poem as a not wholly integrated element that has its own standing and function. Statius has perhaps deliberately left the status of the eulogy open, both welding it to the body of the poem by the explicit comparison of Domitian to Achilles and framing it as a separable show piece of panegyric.

The practice of injecting praise of patrons into epic poetry did not, of course, begin with Statius, but in all likelihood goes all the way back to Ennius. Ennius was a foreigner: he was born in Calabria and brought to Rome by Cato the Elder, and he accompanied Marcus Fulvius Nobilior on his campaign to Aetolia in 189, perhaps with a view to celebrating his achievements; indeed, it is thought that the *Annales* originally ended with Book 15 and Fulvius' capture of Ambracia. Ennius acquired Roman citizenship thanks to Fulvius' son, Quintus, and it is plausible to suppose that the Fulvii were in some sense Ennius' patrons. Aulus Gellius (12.4) cites some verses from the seventh book of Ennius' *Annals* for their depiction of the ideal relationship between a man of lesser station and an upper-class friend (*hominis minoris erga amicum superiorem*), which were understood in antiquity to be a comment on Ennius' own relationship with Fulvius. There is no direct evidence for an outright eulogy of Fulvius, but we may note that Ennius begins his poem with an invocation to the Greek Muses rather than to the native Latin Camenae, and that Fulvius dedicated a temple to Hercules of the Muses, in which he is said to have placed a calendar or Fasti drawn up by himself (Macrobius *Sat.* 1.12.15) —a general and a writer, like Domitian, whose Fasti, moreover, could be said to complement Ennius' own annals (cf. King 2006, 31). Although much of what I have inferred about Ennius' treatment of Fulvius Nobilior in the *Annales* is speculative, it is worth considering the possibility that Statius, in his praise of Domitian, was casting an eye back as far as the glory days of the Republic.

I leapfrog over Virgil's tributes to Augustus in the *Aeneid*, since they are well enough known, although it is good to be reminded that even so great a critic as Robert Graves (1962) could find in the poem little more than servile propaganda, and take up what is perhaps the hardest case to stomach, that is, precisely Lucan's effusive eulogy of Nero.[5] Having begun his *Pharsalia* with a lurid description of the horrors of the war, Lucan proceeds:

quod si non aliam uenturo fata Neroni
inuenere uiam magnoque aeterna parantur
regna deis caelumque suo seruire Tonanti
non nisi saeuorum potuit post bella gigantum,
iam nihil, o superi, querimur; scelera ipsa nefasque
hac mercede placent. diros Pharsalia campos
inpleat et Poeni saturentur sanguine manes,
ultima funesta concurrant proelia Munda,
his, Caesar, Perusina fames Mutinaeque labores
accedant fatis et quas premit aspera classes
Leucas et ardenti seruilia bella sub Aetna,
multum Roma tamen debet ciuilibus armis
quod tibi res acta est. te, cum statione peracta
astra petes serus, praelati regia caeli
excipiet gaudente polo: seu sceptra tenere
seu te flammigeros Phoebi conscendere currus
telluremque nihil mutato sole timentem
igne uago lustrare iuuet, tibi numine ab omni
cedetur, iurisque tui natura relinquet
quis deus esse uelis, ubi regnum ponere mundi.
sed neque in Arctoo sedem tibi legeris orbe
nec polus auersi calidus qua uergitur Austri,
unde tuam uideas obliquo sidere Romam.
aetheris inmensi partem si presseris unam,
sentiet axis onus. librati pondera caeli
orbe tene medio; pars aetheris illa sereni
tota uacet nullaeque obstent a Caesare nubes.
tum genus humanum positis sibi consulat armis
inque uicem gens omnis amet; pax missa per orbem
ferrea belligeri conpescat limina Iani.
Sed mihi iam numen; nec, si te pectore vates
Accipio, Cirrhaea velim secreta moventem
Sollicitare deum Bacchumque avertere Nysa:
Tu satis ad vires Romana in carmina dandas.

Still, if Fate could find no other way for the advent of Nero; if an everlasting kingdom costs the gods dear and heaven could not be ruled by its sovran, the Thunderer, before the battle with the fierce Giants,—then we complain no more against the gods: even such crimes and

5 Cf. also Ovid's anticipation of Augustus' triumph over all peoples of the world, including the Parthians (*Ars Amatoria* 1.177–228), which he treats, however, as an opportunity for men to meet women in the game of love.

> such guilt are not too high a price to pay. Let Pharsalia heap her awful plains with dead; let the shade of the Carthaginian be glutted with carnage; let the last battle be joined at fatal Munda; and though to these be added the famine of Perusia and the horrors of Mutina, the ships overwhelmed near stormy Leucas and the war against slaves hard by the flames of Etna, yet Rome owes much to civil war, because what was done was done for you, Caesar. When your watch on earth is over and you seek the stars at last, the celestial palace you prefer will welcome you, and the sky will be glad. Whether you choose to wield Jove's sceptre, or to mount the fiery chariot of Phoebus and circle earth with your moving flame—earth unterrified by the transference of the sun; every god will give place to you, and Nature will leave it to you to determine what deity you wish to be, and where to establish your universal throne. But choose not your seat either in the Northern region or where the sultry sky of the opposing South sinks down: from these quarters your light would look aslant at your city of Rome. If you lean on any one part of boundless space, the axle of the sphere will be weighed down; maintain therefore the equipoise of heaven by remaining at the centre of the system. May that region of the sky be bright and clear, and may no clouds obstruct our view of Caesar! In that day let mankind lay down their arms and seek their own welfare, and let all nations love one another; let Peace fly over the earth and shut fast the iron gates of warlike Janus. But to me you are divine already; and if my breast receives you to inspire my verse, I would not care to trouble the god who rules mysterious Delphi, or to summon Bacchus from Nysa: you alone are sufficient to give strength to a Roman bard (trans. Duff 1928).

This is pretty ripe stuff, and many critics have supposed that it is totally dishonest, and even that Lucan meant it to be perceived as compulsory flattery by virtue of its very exaggeration. Others have taken the opposite view, and assumed that Lucan, like his uncle Seneca, may have had higher hopes of Nero in earlier times, and that the praise, over the top as it may be, is of a piece with Seneca's in his treatise on clemency.[6] Both interpretations look to relate the eulogy to the body of the text, albeit in contrasting ways, in the manner I intimated with respect to the opening verses of Statius' *Achilleid*.

If we approach it rather from an intratextual perspective, however, we may read the laudation of Nero as a separable set piece, or rather, both as part of Lucan's larger enterprise and at the same time detachable or at all events isolable, a foreign body, so to speak, but securely lodged in the corpus as a whole. Located near the beginning of the poem, it is reminiscent of the hymns that announced themselves as the foreword, as it were, to the recitations of archaic Greek epics.[7] In the Roman tradition, perhaps going back as far as Ennius, such praises of the gods were transformed into eulogies of great men whose achievements seemed

6 For irony, cf. Ahl 1976; the reaction to the subversive interpretation of Lucan has been equally energetic.

7 I owe this suggestion to Richard Janko.

almost divine. It has been suggested that Ennius' translation of Euhemerus' treatise, *The Sacred History*, in which the gods are regarded as posthumous elevations of mortal kings and heroes, suited the ambition of Roman aristocrats to achieve divine status after their deaths (one thinks of Scipio's dream at the conclusion of Cicero's *De republica*), a status to which Julius Caesar may have aspired even while still alive.[8] Instead of locating the hymn (or quasi-hymn) at the beginning of his epic, however, Lucan postponed it, somewhat in the manner of the delayed prologues in New Comedy. This dislocation binds it more closely to the poem itself, as opposed to the explicitly prefatory nature of the *Homeric Hymns*. The reader is thus required to work harder, so to speak, to extract the panegyric from its entrenched context, which is just the task that an intratextual approach beckons. Lucan's readers recognized such a graft when they saw it, because it was moored vertically to a tradition of isolable eulogies. If intertextuality invites the reader to absorb a foreign element into the text, intratextuality requires the contrary gesture of estranging an apparently integrated element in a text, making it foreign and resisting the temptation, always present, to reabsorb it into the work.[9]

An intratextual reading, then, defies the impulse to discover unity in a text, however strained it may be. In this respect, however, it may be closer to classical conceptions of the nature of a literary work than to modern values of internal coherence and consistency.[10] In Plato's *Phaedrus*, Socrates offers the earliest and perhaps best known statement of the idea that a good composition should have the organic unity of a living animal: 'But I think that you would at least say this, that every discourse [*logos*] should be composed like an animal, having a kind of

8 According to Servius Danielis (ad *Ecl.* 9.46), there was a statue of Julius Caesar on the Capitoline Hill, his head crowned by a golden star, bearing an inscription on the base that read: 'To Caesar, the Demi-God' (*eique in Capitolio statuam, super caput auream stellam habentem, posuit: inscriptum in basi fuit 'Caesari emitheo'*; cf. Sauron 1994, 246. Augustus, by contrast, refused to have his statue placed inside the Pantheon, as Agrippa had intended when he dedicated it in 25 BC (Dio Cassius 53.27.2–3); he preferred, in Sauron's words, a 'rupture avec l'héritage de son père César', and was content to represent himself as an 'emanation actuelle d'Apollon' (510). Note Lucan's insistence that Nero is already a god.

9 Oliensis 2002, reviewing Sharrock and Morales 2000, writes: 'If one were really, radically to resist unity, if one were seeking the best forum for the celebration of surface and discontinuity, one would circle back behind New Criticism and take up not the interpretive essay but the commentary. At one point Sharrock alludes to the commentary-tradition as a staple of classical training and as a "genre, more than any other" that "encourages fragmentation" (5)'. It might be better to say that the ancients read literary works as they read commentaries, attending to the discrete parts and their generic propriety.

10 There is a growing literature on inconsistencies in classical texts that treats them as pertaining to a different aesthetic from modern notions of unity; see, for example, O'Hara 2007.

body of its own, so as not to be either headless or footless but rather having mid-parts and extremities that, as they are written, suit one another and the whole' (*Phaedrus* 264C1–5).[11] Contrary to what might be a first impression, Plato was not thinking, I believe, of something like modern conceptions of literary unity, which favor an 'internally consistent thematic and dramatic development, analogous to biological growth', according to the *Encyclopedia Britannica* (s.v. 'organic unity'). I expect that he rather had in mind the structure of an oration, as laid out in rhetorical handbooks and in conformity with the practice of his time, which were divided more or less into a preamble or proem, narrative, proofs, and a conclusion or peroration (*exordium*, *narratio*, *partitio*, *confirmatio*, *refutatio*, and *peroratio*, in the more detailed Latin classification). In such a structure, each part has its own identity, which is not lost or submerged in the whole: a head remains a head, and does not blend with the foot. Intratextuality in a way hearkens back to this pre-romantic conception of unity, in which the parts resist, to a lesser or greater extent, assimilation into the larger composition; they insist on their separateness, even as they contribute —to the degree that they do— to the plan of the work as a whole.

We may consider also Horace's famous example of a poorly constructed painting in the *Ars poetica* (1–13):

humano capiti ceruicem pictor equinam
iungere si uelit et uarias inducere plumas
undique collatis membris, ut turpiter atrum
desinat in piscem mulier formosa superne,
spectatum admissi, risum teneatis, amici?
credite, Pisones, isti tabulae fore librum
persimilem, cuius, uelut aegri somnia, uanae
fingentur species, ut nec pes nec caput uni
reddatur formae. 'pictoribus atque poetis
quidlibet audendi semper fuit aequa potestas'.
scimus, et hanc ueniam petimusque damusque uicissim,
sed non ut placidis coeant immitia, non ut
serpentes auibus geminentur, tigribus agni.

If a painter had chosen to set a human head
On a horse's neck, covered a melding of limbs,
Everywhere, with multi-coloured plumage, so
That what was a lovely woman, at the top,
Ended repulsively in the tail of a black fish:

11 ἀλλὰ τόδε γε οἶμαί σε φάναι ἄν, δεῖν πάντα λόγον ὥσπερ ζῷον συνεστάναι σῶμά τι ἔχοντα αὐτὸν αὐτοῦ, ὥστε μήτε ἀκέφαλον εἶναι μήτε ἄπουν, ἀλλὰ μέσα τε ἔχειν καὶ ἄκρα, πρέποντα ἀλλήλοις καὶ τῷ ὅλῳ γεγραμμένα; my translation.

Asked to a viewing, could you stifle laughter, my friends?
Believe me, a book would be like such a picture,
Dear Pisos, if its idle fancies were so conceived
That neither its head nor foot could be related
To a unified form. 'But painters and poets
Have always shared the right to dare anything.'
I know it: I claim that licence, and grant it in turn:
But not so the wild and tame should ever mate,
Or snakes couple with birds, or lambs with tigers (trans. Kline).

Horace is not arguing that a poem or a work of art should have a single or integral meaning, but rather that the distinct parts should pertain to the same genus. In a literary work, a proem, for example, should suit the genre: the preface to a speech differs from the preamble to an epic or the prologue to a tragedy.[12] The adulation of Nero in Lucan's *De bello civili* should, on this conception of organic unity, be of the sort that is conventionally part of the genre (as, I have argued, an ancient reader would have recognized), rather than exhibit an ideological consistency with the presumed meaning of the work as a whole, something which classical critics did not in general seek to establish.[13]

Reading epic eulogies intratextually, then, is not a fancy name for the traditional attention to internal resonances in a text, nor for the posture of sitting on the fence and not deciding whether such cameos are honest or hypocritical —or both at once, in the hope that at least some readers would perceive irony to which the emperor himself would be deaf.[14] Romans were accustomed to admiring heroism on a grand scale, and developed the sub-genre of praise along its own lines, even if it appeared as a cameo in texts that cast such boldness in a darker light. Intratextuality proposes to view the parts of a whole as both separate and united, both apart and a part. This is the challenge to unity that Sharrock's formulation

---

12 Compare Lucretius' account (*De rerum natura* 5.878–924) of why centaurs and similar fabulous creatures that combine parts from different species cannot exist.

13 Some modern schools of criticism maintain that unity is better seen as an effect than as a property of literature; the apparent unity of a text papers over inconsistencies and contradictions that necessarily disrupt the surface coherence, whether because language itself is irremediably riddled with gaps, hiatuses, and semantic singularities or because literature can never entirely erase the rifts and fractures of class society, a view associated with Louis Althusser, Pierre Macherey, and Frederic Jameson (see Jameson 1981 for a good introduction to the approach). One must accordingly read texts 'symptomatically', treating contradictions as signs of repressed tensions in the work. The panegyrics embedded in Roman epics, however, do not require the critic's lens to be exposed: they are out in the open, not signs of unconscious stresses in the text but 'sore thumbs' that cannot be ignored.

14 For a dismissive treatment of intratextuality, along with other modernist terms, as mere obfuscation, see Friedrich 2003.

of intratextuality raises. When Julia Kristeva, who invented the word 'intertextuality', perceived that it was being used in ways that were little different from what previously had been called allusion (except that such references were not necessarily taken to be signs of authorial intent), she disowned the term.[15] We must be careful that intratextuality does not suffer the same fate and dissolve into the kind of close reading of resonances within a text that was the hallmark of the New Criticism.

Bibliography

Ahl, F. (1976), *Lucan: An Introduction*, Ithaca NY.

Chandler, D. / Munday, R. (eds.) (2011), *A Dictionary of Media and Communication*, Oxford.

Duff, J.D. (trans.) (1928), *Lucan: The Civil War*, Cambridge MA.

Encyclopaedia Brittanica, s.v. 'Organic Unity', online at global.britannica.com/art/organic-unity, accessed 29 June 2016.

Friedrich, R. (2003), 'Theorese and Science Envy in the Humanities: A New Take on the Two Cultures Divide', *Arion* 11, 33–50.

Graves, R. (1962), 'The Virgil Cult', *The Virginia Quarterly Review* 38, 13–37.

Hunter, R.L. (1985), *The New Comedy of Greece and Rome*, Cambridge.

Jameson, F. (1981), *The Political Unconscious: Narrative as a Socially Symbolic Act*, Ithaca NY.

King, R.J. (2006), *Desiring Rome: Male Subjectivity and Reading Ovid's Fasti*, Columbus.

Kline, A.S. (trans.), Horace *Ars Poetica*, available at http://www.poetryintranslation.com/PITBR/Latin/HoraceArsPoetica.htm#anchor_Toc98156240, accessed 1 June 2017.

Konstan, D. (2016), 'Doubting Domitian's Divinity: Statius *Achilleid* 1.1-2', in: I. Ziogas/P. Mitsis (eds.), *Wordplay and Powerplay in Latin Poetry*, Berlin, 377–86.

Kristeva, J. (1967), 'Bakhtine, le mot, le dialogue et le roman', *Critique* 239.

Kristeva, J. (1974), *La révolution de langage poétique*, Paris.

Moore, T.J. (1991), '*Palliata Togata*: Plautus, *Curculio* 462-86', *AJP* 112, 343–362.

Nikolaidou-Arabatzi, S. (2015), 'Choral Projections and *Embolima* in Euripides' Tragedies', *Greece & Rome* 62, 25–47.

O'Hara, J. (2007), *Inconsistency in Roman Epic: Studies in Catullus, Lucretius, Vergil, Ovid and Lucan*, Cambridge.

Oliensis, E. (2002), review of Sharrock and Morales 2000, *BMCR* 2002.06.21.

Sauron, G. (1994), *Quis Deum? L'expression plastique des idéologies politiques et religieuses à Rome*, Rome.

Shackleton-Bailey, D.R. (ed. and trans.) (2004), *Statius*, vol. 3, Cambridge MA.

Sharrock, A. (2000), 'Intratextuality: Text, Parts and (W)holes in Theory,' in: A. Sharrock/H. Morales (eds.), *Intratextuality: Greek and Roman Relations*, Oxford, 1–39.

Tsagalis, C. (2008), *The Oral Palimpsest: Exploring Intertextuality in the Homeric Epics*, Cambridge MA.

15 Kristeva first employed the term in Kristeva 1967 and renounced it in Kristeva 1974, 59–60.

Evangelos Karakasis

Lucan's Intra/Inter-textual Poetics: Deconstructing Caesar in Lucan

In contrast with Vergil, who begins his epic narrative from the early lines of the *Aeneid*'s proem,[1] Lucan turns to his main epic material, in other words the narrative of the historical events of the late Roman republic's second major civil war, on v. 183 of the *Bellum Civile*'s first book, the episode which retells Caesar's crossing of the Rubicon, in January of 49 B.C. The preceding verses, apart from the proem (vv. 1–7), are dedicated, on the one hand, to the 'encomium' of Nero (vv. 33–66),[2] and to a form of digression, of a mostly historiographical nature, that studies the reasons (vv. 8–32, 67–182) which according to Lucan resulted in the devastating civil war between Caesar and Pompey.

1 Objectives – Methodological observations

Many of the literary models of Lucan's epic narrative in the passage under examination have been noted by commentators on the *Bellum Civile* and the wider critical literature. However, a systematic intertextual/intra-textual (co-)reading of this particular passage, and of the epic as a whole, in order to examine in detail the mechanisms which create meaning on the level of use of sub-texts in Lucan's epic, is a desideratum. The objective, therefore, of the present paper is to examine the ways in which this passage converses both with preceding texts of the late republican and early imperial periods and with the contemporary literary production of Nero's reign, in order to inter-textually delineate Caesar's character. Within the context of the passage's epic narrative, methodologically we will need to discern, from a narratological perspective, two 'voices'; that of the epic narrator Lucan, who as the primary epic subjective narrator intervenes in the narrative and comments on the events, and the 'voice' of Caesar himself, or the words which the poet attributes to him and which the epic figure utters in the first person. My objective is to show that, while Caesar's 'voice' uses intertexts and symbolic political elements which present him in a favorable light as a new Aeneas

1 See Roche 2009, 92–3.

2 For the much-discussed matter of whether the praise of Nero in the *Bellum Civile* (vv. 33–66) is sincere or not, see mainly Roche 2009, 8, where the relating *status quaestionis* is given.

https://doi.org/10.1515/9783110611021-022

and, as a result, as the beacon of Augustan and Neronian imperial politics and ideology, the narrative 'voice' of the extra-textual narrator undermines this positive appraisal of the general on a parallel level, correlating Caesar with negatively charged figures of Roman history and Latin literature. The mechanisms of the intertextual 'deconstruction' of Caesar's image, along with the historical contextualization of this intertextual/intratextual subversion, are also examined in the present paper. Finally, I aim to attempt a meta-narrative reading of the description of the river Rubicon with its swollen waters as a metapoetic signifier of the transition to the main epic narrative.

2 Intertextual/intratextual delineation of Caesar

Let us examine more closely the aforementioned passage, in which, before crossing the Rubicon, a key boundary of Caesar's military action in Lucan's epic narrative as opposed to Caesar's historiography,[3] Caesar is presented as facing the phantasm of a personified Rome, which controls his movement towards the *Urbs* and attempts to impose limits on his military actions.

> Iam gelidas Caesar cursu superaverat Alpes
> ingentisque animo motus bellumque futurum
> ceperat. Ut ventum est parvi Rubiconis ad undas,
> ingens visa duci patriae trepidantis imago
> clara per obscuram vultu maestissima noctem
> turrigero canos effundens vertice crines
> caesarie lacera nudisque adstare lacertis
> et gemitu permixta loqui: 'Quo tenditis ultra?
> Quo fertis mea signa, viri? Si iure venitis,
> si cives, huc usque licet.' Tum perculit horror
> membra ducis, riguere comae gressumque coercens
> languor in extrema tenuit vestigia ripa.
> Mox ait: 'O magnae qui moenia prospicis urbis
> Tarpeia de rupe Tonans Phrygiique penates
> gentis Iuleae et rapti secreta Quirini
> et residens celsa Latiaris Iuppiter Alba
> Vestalesque foci summique o numinis instar
> Roma, fave coeptis. Non te furialibus armis
> persequor: en, adsum victor terraque marique
> Caesar, ubique tuus (liceat modo, nunc quoque) miles.

3 See Rondholz 2009, 434.

Ille erit ille nocens, qui me tibi fecerit hostem.'
Inde moras solvit belli tumidumque per amnem
signa tulit propere: sicut squalentibus arvis
aestiferae Libyes viso leo comminus hoste
subsedit dubius, totam dum colligit iram;
mox, ubi se saevae stimulavit verbere caudae
erexitque iubam et vasto grave murmur hiatu
infremuit, tum torta levis si lancea Mauri
haereat aut latum subeant venabula pectus,
per ferrum tanti securus vulneris exit.

And now Caesar had hastened across the frozen Alps and had conceived in his heart the great rebellion and the coming war. When he reached the little river Rubicon, the general saw a vision of his distressed country. Her mighty image was clearly seen in the darkness of night; her face expressed deep sorrow, and from her head, crowned with towers, the white hair streamed abroad; she stood beside him with tresses torn and arms bare, and her speech was broken by sobs: 'Whither do ye march further? and whither do ye bear my standards, ye warriors? If ye come as law-abiding citizens, here must ye stop.' Then trembling smote the leader's limbs, his hair stood on end, a faintness stopped his motion and fettered his feet on the edge of the river-bank. But soon he spoke: 'O God of thunder, who from the Tarpeian rock lookest out over the walls of the great city; O ye Trojan gods of the house of Iulus, and mysteries of Quirinus snatched from earth; O Jupiter of Latium, who dwellest on Alba's height, and ye fires of Vesta; and thou, O Rome, as sacred a name as any, smile on my enterprise; I do not attack thee in frantic warfare; behold me here, me Caesar, a conqueror by land and sea and everywhere thy champion, as I would be now also, were it possible. His, his shall be the guilt, who has made me thine enemy.' Then he loosed war from its bonds and carried his standards in haste over the swollen stream. So on the untilled fields of sultry Libya, when the lion sees his foe at hand, he crouches down at first uncertain till he gathers all his rage; but soon, when he has maddened himself with the cruel lash of his tail, and made his mane stand up, and sent forth a roar from his cavernous jaws, then, if the brandished lance of the nimble Moor stick in his flesh or a

> spear pierce his great chest, he passes on along the
> length of the weapon, careless of so sore a wound.
>
> 1.183–212[4]

The group of gods Caesar invokes here, i.e. at the beginning of his march on Rome (vv. 195–200), is particularly interesting:

> mox ait: 'o magnae qui moenia prospicis urbis
> Tarpeia de rupe Tonans Phrygiique penates
> gentis Iuleae et rapti secreta Quirini
> et residens celsa Latiaris Iuppiter Alba
> Vestalesque foci summique o numinis instar
> Roma, fave coeptis'.

The general, who is preparing to invade the *Urbs*, burn it down and confiscate its public treasury (*aerarium*), is presented as invoking deities that, in contrast, are related to the founding of Rome: the Phrygian gods, those deities which the proto-Roman hero Aeneas brought from Troy, Quirinus-Romulus, the founder of Rome, the Jupiter of Mount Alba in Latium, the region which Iulus-Ascanius, son of Aeneas, founded and whose inhabitants (i.e. of Alba Longa) were considered, according to one version of the legend, the mythical founders of Rome, and the Vestal Virgins with the 'holy light', whose duty was to keep lit the sacred flame which Aeneas had taken with him from Troy (see Braund 2009, 49–50).[5] These deities, who are directly related to Rome's founding, serve to show clearly the paradox inherent in a Roman's campaign against the city. In addition, however, as has been convincingly argued by P. Grimal (1970, 56–9) and D. Feeney (1991, 293–5), these deities constitute a historical anachronism, because as protectors of Rome they are distinctly related to the Julio-Claudian dynasty.[6] Caesar therefore seems to utilize a theological formation which is essentially a product of the historical trajectory he himself sets in motion.

However, what is perhaps of greater importance is the way some of the gods are directly related to the founder of the Roman *principatus*, Augustus himself. The temple of Jupiter Tonans was only built by Augustus in 22 B.C. near the

4 Translated by Duff 1928, 16–9.

5 See also Boels-Janssen 1995, 33–5; cf. also Getty 1940, 54–5; Ahl 1976, 210–1; Bernstein 2011, 266; Kimmerle 2015, 48–9. For the close association of Lucan's Caesar with Iuppiter Latiaris and Vesta through the alleged Trojan origin of the *Iulia gens*, see Ambühl 2015, 82 and n. 75.

6 Cf. also Tasler 1972, 20 and n. 1 with bibliography; Narducci 2002, 204; Sannicandro 2008, 223, Fantham, 2010, 56–7, Devillers 2010, 310; Dinter 2012 and n. 41; Day 2013, 122 and nn. 46, 48; Kimmerle 2015, 225–6 and n. 232.

Tarpeian Rock,[7] as a dedicatory offering to the father of the gods for saving the *princeps* from a lightning strike during the war against the Cantabri, and as a counterweight to the temple of Jupiter Optimus Maximus (cf. Suet. *Aug*. 29.3, 91.2); the temple of Quirinus was destroyed in a conflagration in 49 B.C. and was rebuilt by Augustus in 16 B.C.,[8] while Roma as a deity is also an innovation of the Augustan civil system.[9] Furthermore, the combined reference to Jupiter Tonans, Quirinus, Vesta and the household gods of Aeneas recalls the deities Ovid invokes at the end of the last book of his *Metamorphoses*,[10] which the poet calls on to delay the emperor's passing and who are directly connected with the program of religious and ceremonial rebirth of the first Roman *princeps* (vv. 861–70). Lucan's Caesar, as a result, associates himself not only with the deities who signify the birth of Rome, but also with the gods who are directly related to Augustus and are a part of his political and theological propaganda.[11] This association of Caesar with Augustus does not seem to be random, if one considers the political propaganda of the Neronian period and the policy of shaping the emperor's public image, as can be deduced both from the visual depictions of the emperor under the auspices of the imperial couple *par excellence* (Augustus – Livia), coins from the period with Augustan inscriptions, and from the texts of Lucan's contemporaries (mainly Seneca, esp. in *De Clementia,* and Calpurnius Siculus), and also from later authors, such as Tacitus, Suetonius and Cassius Dio (cf. 55.10.7, 61.9.5).[12] Nero was frequently described, but also presented himself, as the new Augustus (*imitatio Augusti*); in fact, he expressly stated that he would continue the policies of his illustrious predecessor: *ex Augusti praescripto imperaturum se professus* (Suet. *Ner*. 10.1, cf. also Suet. *Ner*. 12, 25, Tac. *Ann*. 13.4.1).[13]

The adoption by Caesar's 'voice' of Augustus's public image is continued with the phrase *en, adsum victor terraque marique* (v. 201). The combination of the phrase *terraque marique* with verbal nouns from *vincere* (*victor*, here) recalls the formula with which Augustus declares, as in this case, victory following

7 See Boels-Janssen 1995, 34; Roche 2009, 212; Day 2013, 123 and n. 49 vs. Wuilleumier/La Bonniec 1962, 46; Lebek 1976, 119 and n. 19.

8 See Getty 1940, 54–5; Roche 2009, 212.

9 See Feeney 1991, 293–4 (with the relevant bibliography in n. 172); Day 2013, 122 and n. 46; cf. also Getty 1964, 75, 81.

10 See Lebek 1976, 118; Feeney 1991, 292–3; Maes 2005, 22 and n. 56; Day 2013, 122 and n. 48; Ambühl 2015, 83 and n. 78.

11 Cf. Morford 1967, 78.

12 See Champlin 2003, 138–44, 307-8. Cf. also Neverov 1974, 80; Grant 1950, 79–87; Karakasis 2012, 494–500.

13 See Friedrich 1976, 147; Martin 2003, 75 and n. 7; Esposito 2009, 33–4 and n. 46 on page 33.

military operations and as a result the closing of the temple of the war god Janus in Rome (Aug. *R G.* 13: *cum [p]er totum i[mperium po]puli Roma[ni terra marique es]set parta victoriis pax*, text: A.E. Cooley 2009, 72).[14] The final closing of the temple of Janus during Augustus's reign took place in the context of the *pax* with the Parthians. In fact, this phrase, within the context of Nero's *imitatio Augusti*, is adopted on a coin produced in 64 A.D., on the occasion of the sealing of the *templum Iani* after Tiridates's subjugation and the *pax* with the Parthians.[15] Any positive connotations of the invocations to the deities on Caesar's part are invalidated by the conclusion of the apostrophe (v. 200: *Roma, fave coeptis*), which is only one verse ahead of the phrase *en, adsum victor terraque* and which, on the level of an intratextual reading, seems to decisively undermine Caesar's initial positive image with its 'Augustan connotations'. This phrase replicates the traitorous statement made by Pompey after his loss at the battle of Pharsalus in the 8th book (v. 322),[16] asking for the help of the Parthians, a traditional and important enemy of Rome, in the senatorial struggle against Caesar. Caesar, in other words, despite correlating himself, through his invocation, with both heroes and founding deities of Rome and with Augustus as victor over and enemy of the Parthians, on the intertextual level deconstructs this positive image by evoking Pompey and his anti-Roman behavior. With the appeal *Roma, fave coeptis*, Caesar's move against Rome (intratextually) is equivalent, at least to a certain extent, to a traitorous alliance with a long-standing enemy of the Romans, the Parthians, and therefore deconstructs Caesar's positive self-representation as Augustus – victor over the Parthians. The association of Caesar with the Parthians is, after all, further strengthened at the beginning of the narrative section of the march on Ariminium, where the speed of Caesar's movement is compared to the Balearic sling and the Parthian arrow (vv. 1.228–30). This subversion of Caesar's 'voice' is only beginning at this point, and is continued with greater consistency and on an inter-textual level in the episode's narrative frame.[17]

---

14 Cf. also Devillers 2010, 311. Roche 2009, 213–14 is of the view that the phrase *victor terraque marique* is 'a bitter inversion of Augustan rhetoric concerning the securing of universal peace'.

15 See Champlin 2003, 140.

16 See Wuilleumier/Le Bonniec 1962, 46; Getty 1964, 76–7; Morford 1967, 78; Ahl 1976, 171–2, 211; Bartsch 1997, 82; Sannicandro 2008, 223 and n. 8; Dinter 2012, 18; Tracy 2014, 25 and n. 20; Ambühl 2015, 205 and n. 71, Kimmerle 2015, 230.

17 It has been argued that v. 226: *procul hinc iam foedera sunto*, which Caesar delivers at the end of the narrative section concerning the crossing of the Rubicon, recalls v. 624 of the *Aeneid*'s 4th book, where the betrayed Dido wishes for eternal hatred between Carthaginians and Romans, *nullus amor populis nec foedera sunto* (see Maes 2005, 20–22; cf. also Roche 2009, 221; Kimmerle 2015, 231). However, the repetition of only two words (*foedera sunto*) within the context of a

3 The 'voice' of the narrative frame

Let us now turn our attention to the intertexts and the elements of political symbolism which the greater narrative frame, the 'voice' of the extra-textual narrator, recalls. While Caesar, with his own narrative 'voice', seems to adopt for himself the political image of Augustus, the epic narrator correlates the Roman general with Hannibal, a classic enemy of the Romans.[18] This link occurs at first with the reference to Caesar's crossing of the Alps (v. 183: *iam gelidas Caesar cursu superaverat Alpes*), as, according to the Roman mind, the crossing of this mountain range by Hannibal in 218 B.C. was the Carthaginian general's stand-out aggressive action. In fact, the language Lucan uses to describe Caesar's crossing of the Alps recalls, to a certain extent, the language of Livy, when he describes Hannibal's corresponding action (21.38.2, 21.41.15, *et al.*[19] —the use of the phrase *Alpes superare* in various syntactical positions, for example).

This resemblance is further strengthened by the comparison of Caesar to the image of the African lion (vv. 205–12). The image of a lion which commonly confronts a shepherd or a hunter is a familiar epic topos, which appears both in Homer and in Vergil,[20] Lucan's two basic epic templates. Within the context of the present reading, however, the description of the lion as Libyan, or, in other words, from the region of Africa where Hannibal originated, seems to be of particular significance.[21] Caesar, with his own narrative 'voice', will subsequently, in vv. 303–5 of the first book, compare himself to Hannibal. At this point in the narrative under examination, the resemblance occurs indirectly.

It has been convincingly argued that the description of Caesar in vv. 184–5: ***ingentis**que animo motus bellumque futurum* <u>*ceperat*</u> has Ovid's *Metamorphoses*

syntagm no less, where the future tense imperative is used, as is often in Latin literature in order to impart an archaistic flavor and a legal nature to the discourse, is not, in my opinion, sufficient material for an inter-textual correlation.

18 For the image of Caesar as the new Hannibal, common in Lucan, see mainly Ahl 1976, 107–12; Masters 1992, 1 and n. 1; Narducci 2002, 191–2, 207–17; Radicke 2004, 171–2; Braund 2009, 48; Uhle 2006, 448–52; Devillers 2010, 310 and n. 35; Myers 2011, 409–10; Day 2013, 117–8; Tzounakas 2013, 512–3 and n. 11; Ambühl 2015, 215 and n. 94; Kimmerle 2015, 230–1. Cf. also mainly Luc. 1.39, 1.255, 7.282–7 (Goebel 1981, 87), 7.408–9, 7.799–803. For Radicke 2004, 175–6, Caesar's crossing of the Rubicon has as its template the crossing of the river Padus (Po) by Hannibal, as is described in Livy (21.47.4–5), see also Rutz 1950, 151. Lucan's Caesar, as a result, is again identified with the Carthaginian general *par excellence*.

19 See Roche 2009, 204.

20 See Roche 2009, 216.

21 See Ahl, 1976, 199; Braund 2009, 51; Fratantuono 2012, 26.

1.166 as its model, a line describing Jupiter's rage,[22] ***ingentes*** *animo et dignas Iove* *concipit iras*. The supreme deity of the Ovidian passage under examination, with whom Lucan's Caesar is intertextually correlated, is depicted being carried away by his rage against Lycaon and rashly deciding to destroy the human race. Contrary to the *concilia deorum* of the epic tradition, which usually support an epic hero and his companions (see Anderson, 1997, 168; cf. also v. 173), the Ovidian council of the Gods is called in order to confirm the decision of a despotic and distant king of the gods. The Jupiter of the verse resembles Augustus, with the council resembling the submissive senatorial fathers. Olympus is also described in part as a divine counterpart to the aristocratic neighborhood of the Palatine hill (vv. 175–6).[23] It is possible, in fact, for this particular Ovidian *concilium* to be interpreted as a parody of the epic theme of the divine council, imitating a satire of Lucilius's first book.[24] Ovid's chief deity, therefore, to whom Lucan's Caesar 'alludes', is an unreasonable and despotic Jupiter, a parody of the symbol of the *princeps*. The satirical depiction of the council of the Gods also recalls another Neronian 'opposition text' against the *principatus* and his abuses, Seneca's *Apocolocyntosis* and its parody of the deceased Claudius. The intertextual references of the lines recall, as a result, passages which could have been interpreted as political parody and literature of political opposition.

The *Aeneid,* as the outstanding Roman epic, admittedly exerts a huge influence on the composition of the *Bellum Civile,* as Lucan's epic converses directly with Vergil's, to the extent that certain scholars believe the poetic *Bellum Civile* must be recognized as a sort of anti-*Aeneid* (see mainly Narducci 1979; 2002)[25]. Regardless of whether one accepts or does not accept this opinion, the close intertextual relationship between the *Bellum Civile* and the *Aeneid* and the decisive importance of the Vergilian epic for the deciphering of the Neronian epic's message is confirmed by the scholarly bibliography. Within this interpretational context, therefore, the theme of the *leo saucius* in the passage under examination, the image of the lion which is at first confused by the incoming attack (Luc. 1.206–7), alludes to Turnus from *Aeneid* 9.791–6,[26] who is compared in a similar way to a confused lion, when the forces of the Trojans attack him. On the other hand, the motherland's 'voice' in vv. 190–1 of Lucan's passage (*quo tenditis ultra? / quo fertis mea signa, viri?*), the anaphora, in other words, of *quo*, the repetition of the

22 See Pichon 1912, 233; Feeney 1991, 296; Roche 2009, 27, 205.
23 See Anderson 1997, 168–9, 172, 175. Cf. also Hill 1985, 176.
24 See Anderson 1997, 168.
25 See also Casali 2011, 81–2, where there is further bibliography. Cf. also Wensler 1989, 253.
26 See Roche 2009, 216; Devillers 2010, 312 and n. 47.

question introduced with *quo* and the phrase *quo tenditis*, recall the words of Mnestheus in the *Aeneid*'s specific intertext, in particular the verses in which he addresses the fleeing Trojans (Verg. *A*. 9.781: *et Mnestheus: 'quo deinde fugam, quo tenditis?' inquit*). While Caesar 'alludes' to Turnus from this Vergilian episode, the Patria in turn 'recalls' Turnus's adversary, the Trojan Mnestheus.[27] Also, the image of Caesar as an African lion who shakes his mane in rage (Luc. 1.208–9) 'alludes' at the same time to the image of Turnus in the first lines of the *Aeneid*'s last book (12. 4–9),[28] where once again the leader of the Rutuli is compared to a Carthaginian lion which, having been wounded, is depicted as shaking its mane. It should be noted here that within the context of a neo-historicist approach to the *Aeneid*, Turnus was convincingly interpreted as Augustus's enemy, Mark Antony.[29] The 'Augustan voice' of the epic hero is 'deconstructed' by the 'anti-Augustan' symbolism of the narrative frame's Vergilian intertext.

The ultimate Iliadic intertext, finally, also contributes, in turn, to the depiction of Caesar as an anti-Aeneas; a comparison to a wounded but counter-attacking lion is also found in *Iliad* 20. 164–75,[30] specifically the episode in which Achilles is compared to a lion and is advancing against Aeneas. This Iliadic episode seems to constitute a direct template of the passage under examination, as is evident from a series of details, shared between the two narratives. In both texts a lion is described, which a) at first avoids confrontation (*Il*. 20.166–7, Luc. 1.206–7), b) is attacked with a spear (*Il*. 20.167–8, Luc. 1.210–1), c) attacks in rage,

27 Cf. Maes 2005, 15–6, who convincingly claims that in the Vergilian epic, as is the case in Lucan's Patria, the syntagm *quo tenditis* appears in scenes (5.670, 8.113, 9.781) in which an epic hero (Ascanius/Iulus, Pallas, Mnestheas correspondingly) sees significant risk or dangerous foolishness in the plans of other characters in the epic narrative. See also Peluzzi 1999, 129; Willis 2011, 147–8 and n. 2.

28 See Getty 1940, 56; Wuilleumier/Le Bonniec 1962, 47; Morford 1967, 79 and n. 1; Ahl 1976, 105–6; Lebek 1976, 120–1; von Albrecht 1999, 240; Narducci 2002, 201–4; Radicke 2004, 174 and n. 76; Casamento 2005, 90–1 and n. 77; Uhle 2006, 448; Sannicandro 2008, 224 and n. 10; Roche 2009, 216; Devillers 2010, 312 and n. 47; Day 2013, 125. The theme of the lion also appears three times in Vergil's *Aeneid*, 9.339–41, 10.454–6, 10.723-8; cf. also Tarrant 2012, 85–6. In all three of these cases however we do not have the theme of the *leo saucius*, but simply the use of the comparison to the lion, in order to depict the forcefulness and savagery of the attacking epic hero (specifically Nisus, Turnus and Mezentius correspondingly).

29 See e.g. Smith 2005, 220. Cf. also Hardie 1998, 93 and n. 167.

30 See also Getty 1940, 56; Wuilleumier/Le Bonniec 1962, 47; Morford 1967, 79 and n. 1; Lebek 1976, 120; Radicke 2004, 174 and n. 76; Roche 2009, 216; Day 2013, 125. The passage 5.134–43 of the *Iliad* (cf. Roche *loc. cit.* and Tarrant 2012, 85–6), in which Diomedes is compared to a wounded lion does not seem to be an exact parallel to the passage in Lucan under examination, as the clear structural and thematic similarities noted between Lucan's *leo saucius* and the comparison of *Iliad* 20 (see above) are missing from *Iliad* 5.

signified by the beating of its tail and its threatening jaws (*Il.* 20.168–71, Luc. 1.208–10), and d) advances, finally, wounded, against his enemies, without fear of death (*Il.* 20.171–3, Luc. 1.210–2). Once again, Caesar is compared with figures hostile to Aeneas.[31] These particular intertextual heroes (Turnus, Achilles) and their untimely deaths within the context of the epic cycle where they belong, as in the case of the dead *leo saucius*,[32] can be further interpreted as historical symbols of Caesar's ultimate assassination.

The same historical symbols of an untimely end are evident in the next intertext, the episode of the eradication of the Fabii in the second book of Ovid's *Fasti* (2.193–242), which, as has been compellingly argued by M. Leigh (1997, 109 and n. 49; cf. also p. 218 and n. 69),[33] influenced Lucan in his description of the crossing of the Rubicon. The image of a small river which becomes a swollen torrent in the winter (Cremera (Ov. *Fast.* 2.205–6), Rubicon (Luc. 1.213–9)) due to rainfall and melting snow (Ov. *Fast.* 2.219–20,[34] Luc. 1.217–9), combined with the comparison to the attacking Libyan lion (Ov. *Fast.* 2.209–10, Luc. 1.205–12) shows the intertextual relationship between the (elegiac/epic) Ovid and the (epic) Lucan. The latter focuses on Caesar and his troops' military activity at the torrent of the Rubicon, exactly as Ovid does with the Fabii's military operations near the swollen Cremera, while Lucan's *dux* attacks like a lion, as do the Fabii against the Veientes. Despite their epic self-sacrifice, the 306 Fabii, who sacrificed themselves by attacking the Veientes, are not positively marked models, within the context of Ovid's narrative: crucially, the lack of *mora* which defines them, as it does Lucan's Caesar, contrasts with the *cunctatio* of their illustrious descendant during the 2nd Punic war (Q. Fabius Maximus, also known as *Cunctator*) and is essentially the reason for their destruction (they were defeated in 477 B.C. in an ambush, cf. Liv. 2.48.7–50.11).[35] In fact, as B. Harries notes (1991, 150–68), the epic forcefulness of the Fabii is undermined on an intertextual level by Ovid himself, with the narrative recalling negatively charged behaviors in the Vergilian epic (Nisus-Euryalus's disastrous venture, the *furor* of Mezentius *et al.*).

---

31 See Lebek 1976, 121; Day 2013, 125. Cf. also Fratantuono 2012, 24.

32 See Von Albrecht, 1970, 287. Cf. also Masters 1992, 2 and n. 5; Leigh 1997, 217–8 and n. 69 vs. Day 2013, 125 and n. 55.

33 See also Lebek 1976, 120 and n. 20.

34 See Robinson 2011, 191, where the similarity between the description of the rapidly flowing Cremera, on the one hand, and the current with which the forcefulness of the Fabii is paralleled, on the other, is convincingly noted (vv. 219–24). The comparison of the actions of the Fabii functions here as a form of reflection on Cremera's image.

35 Cf. Robinson 2011, 187–8.

On the level of political symbolism, the *domus Fabia*, which takes solely upon itself the burden of defending Rome, can function as a symbol of the *domus Augusta*, supporting the State during Augustus's later years.[36] Lucan's Caesar is therefore once again correlated with epic figures of a political nature, which are, however, weakened (also on the intertextual level), within the context of Ovid's elegiac narrative. Finally, as has been correctly shown by E. Fantham (1983, 213–4), the narrative of the Fabii in the form in which it survives today seems to be the result of a final treatment during the poet's years of exile in Tomi. Also, Maximus, whom Ovid addresses in v. 241, quite possibly includes along with Fabius Cunctator the poet's friend and contemporary Paullus Fabius Maximus, who is at the same time a familiar example of resistance against the despotic power of the imperial court of Tiberius, and whom, as was correctly noted by A. Barchiesi (1997, 144–52), Ovid encourages, through a coded literary message, to stay vigilant, be circumspect and act cautiously (obviously in contrast to the example set by his fifth-century ancestors). Lucan, as a result, chooses to 'allude' to an Augustan text of a poet victimized by imperial power, at the moment in fact that that poet urges his *amicus* to prudent political conduct, which will ensure (unlike the desperate forcefulness of his ancestors) his survival in the political arena of the early Julio-Claudian *principatus*.

Another intertext of negative connotations for the *leo saucius*/Lucan's Caesar can be found in Seneca's tragedy *Oedipus*, vv. 919–20.[37] At the beginning of the messenger's speech in the fifth act, in which the self-blinding of the accursed Oedipus is described, the *nuntius* compares the tainted king of Thebes, who has realized the *nefas* which he has committed, to a Libyan lion. The narrative parallels in the two passages are clear: both cases describe an enraged lion (Sen. *Oed.* 919–20, Luc. 1.207) in the Libyan countryside (Sen. *Oed.* 919: *qualis per arva Libycus insanit leo*, Luc. 1.205–6), with his mane erect (Sen. *Oed.* 920: *fulvam minaci fronte concutiens iubam*, Luc. 1.209–10). In Seneca, Oedipus conforms to the archetype of the tyrant-king. He is, in general, the main bearer of the negatively charged concept of *nefas*, which for the Romans already from the period of the triumvirates and the early Augustan years is a synonym of civil war,[38] and is the forefather of civil conflict, which is exemplified on the mythological level through his sons Eteocles and Polynices (cf. Sen. *Phoen.* 334–47, 353–5). In fact, the manner in which the king of Thebes is described in *Oedipus* resembles, as A. Boyle 2011

36 See Robinson 2011, 185.

37 See Getty 1940, 56; Wuilleumier/Le Bonniec 1962, 47; Morford 1967, 79 and n. 1; Lebek 1976, 121 and n. 21; Day 2013, 125 and n. 56; cf. also Schiesaro 2003, 124–6.

38 See Ganiban 2007, 34–5.

(1xxii) correctly argues, 'a Tacitean portrait of a Julio-Claudian emperor'. According to certain scholars, for whom the tragedy is not an early drama, but was written after 59 A.D., Seneca's Oedipus is a transparent allegory for the matricide Nero (vv. 1044–5).[39] If this hypothesis about the tragedy's dating is correct, and if Lucan was influenced in the description of his own wounded lion by Seneca's corresponding passage from *Oedipus*, then Lucan's Caesar is once again intertextually connected with negatively focalized figures: in this case the accursed Oedipus, before he blinded himself, the negatively charged tyrant-*princeps* of the Julii and Claudii, and possibly the matricide Nero.[40]

The description of the wounded lion's 'suicidal' behavior, his defying his wound and, as a result of his rage, his impaling the length of his body on the weapon that wounded him (v. 212: *per ferrum tanti securus* ***vulneris*** *exit*), has as its model, as P. Roche (2009, 29; cf. also n. 218) correctly notes, Seneca's reference to enraged barbarian forces in the *de Ira* (*Dial.* 5.2.6). At this point, however, the philosopher juxtaposes the Roman forces in battle with those of the barbarians, who are described negatively as self-destructive, as they 'gladly suffer wounds (*gaudent feriri*), fall on swords (*instare ferro*), charge into spears (*tela corpore urgere*) and perish from self-sustained wounds (*per suum* ***vulnus*** *exire*)'. The similarity in behavior between Lucan's lion and Seneca's barbarians is evident and is also supported on the linguistic level, due to similarities in expression. The result, however, of this inter-textual correlation is that Caesar, the moment he crosses the Rubicon, is painted as a barbarian, as a non-Roman, as someone who attacks Romans; in other words, as a *hostis patriae*.

On the level of intratextual analysis, the phrase *colligit iram* (v. 207), combined with the reference to Libya (*Libyes*, v. 206), alludes to the second book of the *Bellum Civile*, in particular to the description of the Marius/Sulla civil war by an elderly veteran-narrator;[41] there Lucan refers to Marius's years of activity in Africa and, in v. 93 (***Libycas*** *ibi colligit iras*), presents him developing similar feelings of hatred against Rome with those of her ancestral enemy, Libya,[42] i.e. Carthage (whose basic representative, its 'synecdochic hero' (a term used by

---

39 See Fitch 2004, 7 and n. 1. Cf. also Boyle 2011, 1xxii–1xxiii.

40 I would like, at this point, to note the great importance of the *recitationes*, i.e. the recitations of various literary texts, before their final publication, as a mechanism of literary imitation during Nero's rule. In this light, Lucan could have been influenced by the description of the *leo saucius* in Seneca's *Oedipus*, which could have been recited during a *recitatio* (and vice-versa), but had not yet been read as a published work.

41 See Fantham 1992, 98; Casamento 2005, 90–1, 109 and n. 24; Lowe 2010, 133; Bernstein 2011, 276 and n. 54; Myers 2011, 409–10.

42 Cf. Lowe 2010, 132.

P. Hardie 1993) is Hannibal) and its successor Numidia, the kingdom of Jugurtha. Through linguistic *imitatio*, Caesar, in crossing the Rubicon, is linked with Marius from the second book, another *hostis patriae*, who is, however, at the same time presented as the new Hannibal/Jugurtha, despite the latter's defeat at the hands of Marius's forces. This 'deconstruction' of Caesar as the new Hannibal is achieved by way of intratextual parallelisms.

Therefore, the Caesar of the narrative frame is correlated with historical and literary figures hostile to Rome and her mythical founder Aeneas, i.e. Achilles, Hannibal and Turnus, but also with the self-destructive Fabii of the Ovidian *Fasti*, the despotic *princeps* of Ovidian epic and Senecan tragedy, and *hostes patriae* on the field of battle. As a result, while Caesar's 'voice' invokes Aeneas (a familiar symbolic equivalent of the (Vergilian) Octavian, among others), his household gods and the sacred flame of his hearth, the Caesar of the epic narrator's 'voice' is presented as the anti-Aeneas,[43] as the new Iliadic Achilles at the exact moment when he attacks Aeneas, the subsequent forefather of the Romans, as the new Vergilian Turnus, who causes widespread destruction within the Trojan camp and therefore places the founding of the Roman race in jeopardy.

The negative connotations of the wider narrative frame do not end here, however. Researchers have called attention to several, mostly Vergilian, parallels to the 'epiphany' of the personified homeland, which in this passage most likely takes the form of Cybele (cf. Verg. *A.* 6.785)[44]/Tyche[45] with her tiered crown: the specter, for example, of the blood-stained Hector, who advises Aeneas in his sleep to abandon Troy (vv. 2.268–97), the epiphany of Venus to her son Aeneas (vv. 2.589–620), the shade of the dead Creusa, who predicts her husband Aeneas's future greatness (vv. 2.771–89), the voice of the dead Polydorus who speaks to Aeneas in the Thracian brushlands (vv. 3.22–68), the advice of the Penates to the sleeping Aeneas, who tell him to travel to Hesperia (vv. 3.147–71), and Apollo's appearance in the form of Butes and his advice to Ascanius to refrain from the imminent armed conflict (vv. 9.638–58).[46] On the other hand, there are

43 Cf. also Thompson/Bruère 1968, 9.

44 See mainly Getty 1964, 78–81; Thompson/Bruère 1968, 6–7; Peluzzi 1999, 141–9; Maes 2005, 4 and n. 12; Moretti 2007, 4–5; Aguirre 2008, 40; Sannicandro 2008, 227; Roche 2009, 208; Myers 2011, 413 and n. 56; Fratantuono 2012, 23 and the reservations by Kimmerle 2015, 225 and n. 230.

45 See Moretti 2007, 5–7.

46 See mainly Thompson/Bruère 1968, 6–7; Gagliardi 1989, 73; Masters 1992, 1–2 and n. 4 (with related bibliography); Peluzzi 1999, 128–31; Moretti 2007, 4; Anzinger 2007, 125; Penwill 2009, 89; Sannicandro 2008, 222 and nn. 3, 4, 225; Roche 2009, 23, 205–6. The scene with the personified homeland in the 1st book of the *Bellum Civile* seems in general to be based on the typology of (divine) message scenes of the Vergilian epic, see Maes 2005, esp. 6–13, 23.

those who suggest that the passage's model could also have been Iliadic (for example the epiphany of Athena to Achilles, 1.194–218, cf. also 21.211 ff. (Achilles-Scamander)),[47] Ennian (the conversation between Scipio and Patria, cf. Cic. *Fin.* 2.106),[48] Ovidian (Ov. *Fast.* 2.503–5)[49] or that Lucan could even have drawn inspiration from texts of rhetorical (*R.H.* 4.53.66 and the *conformatio* of Patria),[50] tragic (e.g. the association of the episode with the Theban tragic cycle (Caesar as Polynices and Patria as Iocasta)),[51] epistolographic ([Sal.] *Ad Caesarem senem de re publica* 13 and the dialogue of Patria and of the *parentes* with Caesar),[52] philosophical (Plat. *Crit.* 50b–54d and the laws as personified entities),[53] or historiographical/biographical generic nature. These last include Liv. 2.40.4–9 and the episode of Veturia's reproachful stance against the traitorous position of her son Coriolanus,[54] Liv. 21.22.6–9 and Hannibal's dream in the Hebrus region,[55] Suet. *Claud.* 1.2, D.C. 55.1.3–4 and the resistance of another female figure, non-Roman in this case, against Drusus's movement,[56] and female figures in German ethnographies, such as those which are later described in Tacitus, for example (*Germ.* 17)[57]).[58]

---

47 See Narducci 1980, 175; Lausberg 1985, 1589; Peluzzi 1999, 130; Devillers 2010, 303 and n. 1. Cf. also Green 1991, 238–9 for the relationship of Lucan's passage with Thetis and Achilles from the first Iliadic rhapsody (1.365–427), but also Agamemnon's dream in the 2nd book (2.23–4). Penwill 2009, 89 and n. 18, finally, suggests Hecabe's appeal to Hector for help in the 22nd book of the *Iliad* as a further parallel passage.

48 See Frings 1995, 118; Peluzzi 1999, 132; Devillers 2010, 303 and n. 1.

49 See Peluzzi 1999, 130.

50 See Jal 1963, 306; Narducci 1980, 175–6; Peluzzi 1999, 131; Radicke 2004, 173; Moretti 2007, 4; Devillers 2010, 303 and n. 1.

51 See Ambühl 2015, 197–211.

52 See Jal 1963, 306; Peluzzi 1999, 132; Devillers 2010, 303 and n. 1.

53 See Narducci 1980, 175 and n. 4.

54 See Henderson 1988, 139–40; Sannicandro 2008, 226–9.

55 See Sannicandro 2008, 225, Devillers 2010, 304–5, 310.

56 See Narducci 1980, 177–8; Radicke 2004, 173; cf. also Sannicandro 2008, 225; Penwill 2009, 88–9 and n. 18; Devillers 2010, 307–9. For the view that in this particular passage of the *Bellum Civile* Lucan was obviously influenced by the aforementioned anecdotal stories regarding Drusus, which could have been the main subject of the narrative both in the 142nd book of Livy's *Ab Urbe Condita* and in Albinovanus Pedo's poem in honor of Germanicus, son of Drusus, see also Peluzzi 1999, 141; Devillers 2010, 308.

57 See Narducci 1980, 177–8; cf. also Peluzzi 1999, 141–2; Aguirre 2008, 50; Devillers 2010, 308 and n. 20.

58 Brisset 1964, 87 convincingly sees in the passage the influence of Pompeian propaganda, according to which the senatorial government is one and the same with Rome; see also Gagliardi 1976, 83. Peluzzi 1999, 140–1 also convincingly asserts that the episode with the personified

This image of Lucan's personified homeland, which attempts to dissuade a citizen from anti-Roman behavior, does not occur in any other historic/literary source for the crossing of the Rubicon.[59] Despite any similarities to the aforementioned episodes, it mainly alludes to a passage in Cicero's first speech *In Catilinam* (1.18),[60] where, just as in Lucan's passage, the Patria, once again within the frame of a rhetorical personification, rebukes Catiline's anti-Roman position and demands his removal. Therefore, in this manner Caesar is also depicted as a new Catiline, and not in the Sallustian mold, where despite the *malum pravumque ingenium* (Sal. *Cat.* 5), he exhibits qualities that make him an ambiguous figure and occasionally give him an almost heroic nature, but as a Ciceronian Catiline, i.e. as the quintessence of the exceptionally negatively charged internal enemy of the city, who is presented as provoking a catastrophic civil conflict, just like Caesar. As was noted before, it has been convincingly argued that Lucan's Rome takes the form of Cybele, a goddess directly associated with the Augustan ideology and Augustus's theological policies. In the 6th book of the *Aeneid*, for example, and in the context of Anchises's celebratory prophecy to his son Aeneas in the Underworld, where Rome's future greatness, the apex of which is the *principatus* of Augustus, is predicted, Magna Mater is also mentioned (vv. 785–7). In fact, as R. Getty (1950, 1–12) convincingly suggested, Vergil, in the passage of the *Aeneid* under examination, correlates Rome, which boasts Augustus for her scion *par excellence* (*felix prole virum*, v. 784), with Cybele, who is also depicted as joyous over her son Jupiter (*laeta deum partu*, v. 786).[61] Augustus himself took pains to restore the temple of Cybele on the Palatine hill, after the destructive fire of 3

---

homeland functions as a counterweight to propaganda narratives in which the supernatural is at Caesar's service, cf. also Devillers 2010, 304 and n. 8. For the episode as an inversion of the theme of the victorious *Urbs* against external foes, see also Peluzzi 1999, 141, whereas for Patria employing arguments of a Republican coloring, cf. Kimmerle 2015, 225. For a comprehensive overview of the *status quaestionis* regarding Lucan's models within the context of the episode with the personified homeland, see mainly Peluzzi 1999, 128–37; also Kimmerle 2015, 223 and n. 226. Finally, Aguirre 2008, 31–60 advocates, through an exhaustive comparative study, that the passage under examination belongs to a literary genre he describes as 'Hero-Lady encounters' (see esp. p. 59).

59 See Tucker 1988, 247–8.

60 See Wuilleumier/Le Bonniec 1962, 44; Morford 1967, 78; Grimal 1970, 56; Frings 1995, 119; Boels-Jannsen 1995, 31; Peluzzi 1999, 131; Sannicandro 2008, 225; Penwill 2009, 87 and n. 17; Devillers 2010, 303 and n. 1; Bernstein 2011, 261. Cf. also Lebel 1976, 117 and n. 14. For a recent study of Ciceronian influence (namely Cicero's oratorical opus and epistolography) on Lucan's epic, see Galli 2015, 73–84.

61 See also Getty 1964, 78–9.

A.D.[62] Therefore, Cybele as a deity bears distinct Augustan connotations, and as a result her function in Lucan's passage under examination, as the *patria-Roma* which attempts to control Caesar's catastrophic actions, once again shows Caesar's role as an anti-Augustus.

4 Politics and ideology – Implicit criticism of the *princeps*/*principatus*?

It is true that a hostile stance toward Caesar is evident throughout the *Pharsalia*, and the present subversion of Caesar's 'voice' by the 'voice' of the narrative frame could be interpreted within the context of this generalized tactic. However, within the passage under examination this undermining involves a Caesar whose 'voice' correlates him with the imperial ideology, the figure and politics of Augustus (Aeneas), the model, in other words, for the Neronian *principatus*'s public image. In fact, this subversion is achieved largely through the adoption on the part of the epic narrator either of intertexts with clear 'anti-Augustan symbolic elements' (e.g. an association of Caesar with the Vergilian Turnus or the Ovidian *gens Fabia*, references to texts of an 'oppositional nature' against the imperial court's abuses), literary models clearly in the service of 'anti-Neronian propaganda' (Oedipus in Seneca's tragedy of the same name), or of a generally anti-Roman nature (Livy's Hannibal, Cicero's Catiline, the Homeric *Iliad's* Achilles).Therefore, do we have here an example of veiled confrontation between Lucan and Nero, or an attack on the imperial system in general? In other words, is Nero, according to Lucan, only superficially similar to Augustus, the Tyrant-Nero of the anti-Neronian literature who must be undermined? It is quite possible, as this passage does not seem to belong to the proem, which was written during the 'good years', when the relationship between Nero and Lucan, in all probability, had not deteriorated to a worrying degree. Those scholars who detect an anti-establishment position in Lucan's work in general, i.e. the adherents of the school of thought which supports Lucan's republican political ideology and which took its name ('the republic strikes back') from the second film of George Lucas's *Star Wars* trilogy, 'The Empire Strikes Back', could include the above interpretation in their argument. The same could be done by those critics who simply credit the

62 See Peluzzi 1999, 148–9.

poet with anti-Neronian sentiments and not a wider negative appraisal of the imperial system in its entirety.[63]

The intertextual (co-)reading of a text, a common practice in the field of Latin literature already from antiquity despite its modernist name, can offer to the model reader, or in any case to the informed reader, those analytical tools which offer the possibility of multiple readings and allow the production of a nuanced message. In fact, the often exceptionally complex nature and mechanics of this reading procedure seems to occasionally function as a safeguard, as a form of *dissimulatio*; it protects, in other words, the artist who attempts to criticize, if not always oppose, a largely authoritarian system of government, from direct accusations of perpetrating an obvious *crimen maiestatis*.

5 (Meta-)poetry: The commencement of the main epic

Let us turn our attention, finally, to the description of the river Rubicon and the second narrative of Caesar's crossing (1.213–27).[64]

> fonte cadit modico parvisque inpellitur undis
> puniceus Rubicon, cum fervida canduit aestas,
> perque imas serpit valles et Gallica certus
> limes ab Ausoniis disterminat arva colonis.
> tum vires praebebat hiemps atque auxerat undas
> tertia iam gravido pluvialis Cynthia cornu
> et madidis Euri resolutae flatibus Alpes.
> primus in obliquum sonipes opponitur amnem
> excepturus aquas; molli tum cetera rumpit
> turba vado faciles iam fracti fluminis undas.
> Caesar, ut adversam superato gurgite ripam
> attigit, Hesperiae vetitis et constitit arvis,
> 'hic' ait 'hic pacem temerataque iura relinquo;
> te, Fortuna, sequor. procul hinc iam foedera sunto;
> credidimus paci, utendum est iudice bello.'

63 In fact, the identification and study of the entirety of similar cases of inter-textual subversion of various narrative 'voices' throughout the *Bellum Civile* is, in my opinion, a scholarly desideratum and could potentially result in interesting conclusions regarding the variety and political implications of such a technique in Lucan.

64 See Masters 1992, 2–3; Penwill 2009, 87 and n. 16; Willis 2011, 147 and n. 1 for the problem of the 'second crossing' of the Rubicon. Cf. also Goerler 1976, 291–308, who supports the narration of the same event from two different viewpoints; both Caesar's and his troops' narrative focus are presented; see also Kimmerle 2015, 227–8, 248, in particular, for a representation of two more, opposing perspectives, namely an Augustan and a Republican standpoint.

> The ruddy river Rubicon glides through the bottom of the valleys and serves as a fixed landmark to divide the land of Gaul from the farms of Italy. Issuing from a modest spring, it runs with scanty stream in the heat of burning summer; but now it was swollen by winter; and its waters were increased by the third rising of a rainy moon with moisture-laden horn, and by Alpine snows which damp blasts of wind had melted. First the cavalry took station slantwise across the stream, to meet its flow; thus the current was broken, and the rest of the army forded the water with ease. When Caesar had crossed the stream and reached the Italian bank on the further side, he halted on the forbidden territory: "Here," he cried, 'here I leave peace behind me and legality which has been scorned already; henceforth I follow Fortune. Hereafter let me hear no more of agreements. In them I have put my trust long enough; now I must seek the arbitrament of war.'[65]

Emphasis is placed on the differences in the flow of the river Rubicon, whose spring (*fons*) is described as *modicus*; it normally flows at a low water level, but its waters are swollen and rush during Caesar's crossing. The typical adjective which describes the Rubicon under normal circumstances is, apart from the *puniceus*, which conveys the color of the river's red, muddy waters (cf. v. 214),[66] *parvus*[67] (cf. v. 185: *parvi Rubiconis ad undas*), as it is essentially the modern river Pisciatello, which springs from Monte Strigara and drains into the Adriatic after flowing for 31 km. As the epic narrator immediately makes clear in the verses under examination, the increase in the river's level is due to heavy rainfall and the melting of Alpine snow; conditions, in other words, which, following the *topos* of nature co-ordinating its manifestations with the flow of events, complicate Caesar's task even more and, as a result, show with even greater clarity the decisiveness of his character and the success of his military technique.

In interpreting the crossing of the Rubicon in Lucan, within the frame of the literary topos of the *poeta creator* (Lieberg 1982), J. Masters (1992, 6–8) argues

---

65 Translated by Duff 1928, 18–9.

66 Fratantuono 2012, 26–7 convincingly detects an etymological play in the use of the adjective. The description of the Rubicon as *puniceus* recalls the *Punicum* Caesar, who becomes a *hostis patriae*.

67 See Wuilleumier/Le Bonniec 1962, 44–5; Braund 2009, 48; Roche 2009, 206. Cf. Boels-Janssen 1995, 30.

that on the metapoetic level Caesar as the *dux* functions as a symbol of the epic poet, while on the other hand the personified Homeland, who attempts to halt the general's plans to cross the Rubicon and therefore to start the war, functions as the typical figure of the literary *revocatio* (cf., for example, Verg, *Ecl.* 6.3–5)[68], which attempts to dissuade the poet from the work he has already begun. The presence of the adjective *ingens* (see vv. 184 and 186) can also be interpreted as a metapoetic indicator of Lucan's epic endeavor (cf. Maes 2005, 10–1). Within the framework of these convincing metapoetic readings of the verses, the increase in the river's flow could also be associated with the narrative commencement of the main epic in the lines under examination. The image of the flooded and rushing torrent or the great (occasionally also murky) river is a familiar metapoetic symbol of high poetry both in Greek and Latin literature: a characteristic example is the symbolism of Pindar's poetry, which has epic connotations, as monte *decurrens velut amnis* (verse 5) in Horace, *Od.* 4.2.5–8 (cf. also Callim. *Apol.* 105–12, Ov. *Am.* 3.6, Stat. *Theb.* 3.671–6).[69] Furthermore, the sense of 'great' which is presented in the description of the passage under examination could, in the context of the reading presently being attempted, be combined with the concept of 'great' (*ingens*) which on the metalinguistic level is correlated, for the Roman (Callimachean) poetic theory in any case, with higher literary forms, such as epic and tragedy (cf., for example, Callim. *Aet.* 1.4, 18, 22–4 Pf., Verg. *Ecl.* 6.4–5, *et al.*).[70] It does not seem to be at random, then, that at the moment the epic narrative begins, Lucan adopts the meta-poetic indicator of the extensive rushing torrent with its poetological connotations of the *genus grande*.

68 See also Wimmel 1960, 135–42.

69 See Barchiesi 2001, 52–5; McNelis 2007, 79 and n. 11. One, of course, may come across rivers of epic meta-poetic connotations which, at the same time, up to a point also appear to be delaying forms of epic action. This is especially the case with Achelous in Ovid's *Metamorphoses*, postponing as it does, with his hurrying and swollen stream as Lucan's Rubicon, Theseus' warlike action (8.547–50); Lucan's Rubicon similarly functions as an obstacle to Caesar's military action (see Antoniadis, forthcoming). Even so, despite the *mora* it may cause to Caesar's military objectives, Rubicon all at once functions as the narrative turning point, from the introductory lines of mainly a rather historiographical character to the chiefly epic focus on the war action of the following verses (see above). What is more, even in the case of Ovid's Achelous, the stories that the river generates by putting off Theseus' bellicose deeds are simultaneously fraught with distinct epic markers in terms of the generically diversifying Ovidian epic. Despite the generic ambivalence flooding rivers may create in Latin literature, as a rule they bear noticeable generic connotations of the *genus grande*, epic in particular (see Barchiesi 2001, 50–5; cf. also Antoniadis *op. cit.*).

70 See Karakasis 2011, 76–8.

6 Conclusion

Lucan's narrative transition from his introductory remarks to the main epic narrative of the crossing of the Rubicon is signified through a familiar poetological marker, i.e. of the rushing torrent, which on the metapoetic level symbolizes the high-style poetry of the *genus grande*. In fact, by utilizing the episode of the crossing of the Rubicon, the epic narrator deconstructs on an inter-textual level the positive image which Caesar's 'voice', in attempting to present himself as the new Aeneas and as (the forerunner of) Augustus, projects for himself. Through various intertextual references to the Homeric, Vergilian and Ovidian *opus* and to Cicero's oratorical output, Livy's historical work, and Senecan tragedy and philosophical discourse, the epic narrator undermines Caesar's 'voice', painting him as an anti-Aeneas of Greek and Roman literary tradition, as a Ciceronian Catiline, as a reckless Ovidian Fabius, as a Livian Hannibal, and as a cursed Senecan Oedipus and barbarian. This is also achieved through the intratextual correlation of Caesar's endeavor not only with Pompey's anti-Roman stance in the eighth book of the epic, but also with Marius's internecine *irae* in the second book. This subversion of an epic figure immediately connected with the image of Aeneas/Augustus seems to have political connotations, given that within the frame of the political propaganda of the Neronian period, Nero combines his own public image with that of his illustrious predecessor, the founder of the Julio-Claudian dynasty. Therefore, this inter/intratextual subversion could also be interpreted as a form of subtle and as a result, relatively safe, criticism of the emperor.

Bibliography

Aguirre, M. (2008), 'The Grieving City: Lucan's Aged Rome and the Morphology of Sovereignty', *Neohelicon* 35, 31–60.

Ahl, F.M. (1976), *Lucan: An Introduction*, Ithaca, NY.

Albrecht, M. von (1970), 'Der Dichter Lucan und die epische Tradition', in: *Lucain. Entretiens Hardt* 15, 267–308.

Albrecht, M. von (1999), *Reading Epic. An Interpretative Introduction*, Leiden.

Ambühl, A. (2015), *Krieg und Bürgerkrieg bei Lucan und in der griechischen Literatur. Studien zur Rezeption der attischen Tragödie und der hellenistischen Dichtung im >Bellum civile<*, Berlin.

Anderson, W.S. (1997), *Ovid's Metamorphoses*. Books 1–5, Norman.

Antoniadis, T. (forthcoming), 'Between Intratext and Intertext: Water-Symbolism / Imagery and the Appropriation of Callimachus' "Assyrian River" in Post-Vergilian Epic (in the War-Narratives of Lucan, Valerius Flaccus and Statius)'.

Anzinger, S. (2007), *Schweigen im romischen Epos: zur Dramaturgie der Kommunikation bei Vergil, Lucan, Valerius Flaccus und Statius*, Berlin.

Barchiesi, A. (1997), *The Poet and the Prince. Ovid and Augustan Discourse*, Berkeley.
Barchiesi, A. (2001), *Speaking Volumes. Narrative and Intertext in Ovid and Other Latin Poets*, London.
Bartsch, S. (1997), *Ideology in Cold Blood. A Reading of Lucan's Civil War*, Cambridge, MA.
Bernstein, N.W. (2011), 'The Dead and Their Ghosts in the *Bellum Civile*: Lucan's Visions of History', in: P. Asso (ed.), *Brill's Companion to Lucan*, Leiden, 257–79.
Boels-Janssen, N. (1995), 'Le passage du Rubicon: Lucain, *Pharsale* 1, 183–205', *Vita Latin* 139, 27–37.
Boyle, A.J. (2011), *Seneca: Oedipus*, Oxford.
Braund, S. (1992), *Lucan: Civil War*, Oxford.
Braund, S. (2009), *A Lucan Reader: Selections from Civil War*, Mundelein, IL.
Brisset, J. (1964), *Les idées politiques de Lucain*, Paris.
Casali, S. (2011), 'The *Bellum Civile* as an Anti-*Aeneid*', in: P. Asso (ed.), *Brill's Companion to Lucan*, Leiden, 81–109.
Casamento, A. (2005), *La parola e la guerra. Rappresentazioni letterarie del Bellum Civile in Lucano*, Bologna.
Champlin, E. (2003), *Nero*, Cambridge, MA.
Cooley, A.E. (2009), *Res Gestae Divi Augusti: Text, Translation, and Commentary*, Cambridge.
Day, H.J.M. (2013), *Lucan and the Sublime. Power, Representation and Aesthetic Experience*, Cambridge.
Devillers, O. (2010), 'Le passage du Rubicon: Un itinéraire de l'information', in: O. Devillers/S. Franchet d'Esperey (eds.), *Lucain en débat. Rhetorique, poetique et histoire. Actes du Colloque international, Institut Ausonius (Pessac, 12–14 juin 2008)*, Bordeaux, 303–12.
Dinter, M.T. (2012), *Anatomizing Civil War: Studies in Lucan's Epic Technique*, Ann Arbor.
Duff, J.D. (1928), *Lucan. The Civil War*, Cambridge, MA.
Esposito, P. (2009), 'La profezia di Fauno nella I ecloga di Calpurnio Siculo', in: L. Landolfi/R. Oddo (eds.), *Fer propius tua lumina; giochi intertestuali nella poesia di Calpurnio Siculo*, Bologna, 13–39.
Fantham, E. (1983), 'Sexual Comedy in Ovid's *Fasti*: Sources and Motivation', *HSCPh* 87, 185–216.
Fantham, E. (1992), *Lucan: De Bello Civili*, Book II, Cambridge.
Fantham, E. (2010), 'Caesar's Voice and Caesarian Voices', in: N. Homke/C. Reitz (eds.), *Lucan's Bellum Civile: Between Epic Tradition and Aesthetic Innovation*, Berlin, 53–70.
Feeney, D.C. (1991), *The Gods in Epic. Poets and Critics of the Classical Tradition*, Oxford.
Fitch, J. (2004), *Seneca: Tragedies*, Cambridge, MA.
Fratantuono, L. (2012), *Madness Triumphant. A Reading of Lucan's Pharsalia*, Lanham, MD.
Friedrich, W. (1976), *Nachahmung und eigene Gestaltung in der bukolischen Dichtung des Titus Calpurnius Siculus*, Frankfurt.
Frings, I. (1995), 'Die Klage der Roma. Lukan I, 186ff. in der literarischen Tradition', *Eos* 83, 115–32.
Gagliardi, D. (1976), *Lucano: poeta della libertà*, Naples.
Gagliardi, D. (1989), *M. Annaei Lucani Belli Civilis Liber Primus*, Naples.
Galli, D. (2015), 'Lucano lettore di Cicerone', in: P. Esposito/C. Walde (eds.), *Letture e lettori di Lucano*, Pisa, 73–84.
Ganiban, R.T. (2007), *Statius and Virgil: The Thebaid and the Reinterpretation of the Aeneid*, Cambridge.
Getty, R.J. (1940), *Lucan. De Bello Civili I*, Cambridge.
Getty, R.J. (1950), 'Romulus, Roma, and Augustus in the Sixth Book of the *Aeneid*', *CPh* 45, 1–12.

Getty, R.J. (1964), 'Lucan and Caesar's Crossing of the Rubicon', in: M.F. Gyles/E.W. Davis (eds.), *Laudatores Temporis Acti. Studies in Memory of W.E. Caldwell Professor of History at the University of North Carolina by his Friends and Students*, Chapel Hill, 73–81.
Goebel, G. H. (1981), 'Rhetorical and Poetical Thinking in Lucan's Harrangues (7.250–382)', *TAPhA* 111, 79–94.
Goerler, W. (1976), 'Caesars Rubikon-Übergang in der Darstellung Lucans', in: H. Goergemanns/E.A. Schmidt (eds.), *Studien zum antiken Epos*, Meisenheim am Glan, 291–308.
Grant, M. (1950), *Roman Anniversary Issues*, Cambridge.
Green, C. M. C. (1991), '*stimulos dedit aemula virtus*: Lucan and Homer Reconsidered', *Phoenix* 45, 230–54.
Grimal, P. (1970), 'Le poète et l'histoire', in: *Lucain. Entretiens Hardt* 15, 51–118.
Hardie, P. (1993), *The Epic Successors of Virgil. A Study in the Dynamics of a Tradition*, Cambridge.
Hardie, P. (1998), *Virgil*, Oxford.
Harries, B. (1991), 'Ovid and the Fabii: *Fasti* 2.193–474', *CQ* 41, 150–68.
Henderson, J. (1988), 'Lucan/the Word at War', *Ramus* 16, 122–64.
Hill, D.E. (1985), *Ovid: Metamorphoses I-IV*, Warminster.
Jal, P. (1963), *La guerre civile a Rome: étude littéraire et morale*, Paris.
Karakasis, E. (2011), *Song Exchange in Roman Pastoral*, Berlin.
Karakasis, E. (2012), 'Βουκολική ποιητική και πανηγυρική ρητορική στα χρόνια του Νέρωνα: ποιμενική παράδοση και νεοτερικότητα στην πρώτη εκλογή του Καλπουρνίου του Σικελού', *Δωδώνη: Φιλολογία* 38–9, 468–513.
Kimmerle, N. (2015), *Lucan und der Prinzipat. Inkonsistenz und unzuverlässiges Erzählen im Bellum Civile*, Berlin.
Lausberg, M. (1985), 'Lucan und Homer', *ANRW* II. 32.3, 1565–622.
Lebek, W. D. (1976), *Lucans Pharsalia. Dichtungsstruktur und Zeitbezug*, Göttingen.
Leigh, M. (1997), *Lucan: Spectacle and Engagement*, Oxford.
Lieberg, G. (1982), *Poeta Creator*, Amsterdam.
Lowe, D.M. (2010), '*Medusa, Antaeus, and Caesar Libycus*', in: N. Hömke/C. Reitz (eds.), *Lucan's Bellum Civile: Between Epic Tradition and Aesthetic Innovation*, Berlin, 119–34.
Maes, Y. (2005), 'Starting Something Huge: *Pharsalia* I 183–193 and the Virgilian Intertext', in: C. Walde (ed.), *Lucan im 21. Jahrhundert = Lucan in the 21st Century = Lucano nei primi del XXI secolo*, München, 1–25.
Martin, B. (2003), 'Calpurnius Siculus: The Ultimate Imperial 'Toady'?', in: A.F. Basson/W.J. Dominik (eds.), *Literature, Art, History: Studies on Classical Antiquity and Tradition in Honour of W.J. Henderson*, Frankfurt, 73–90.
Masters, J. (1992), *Poetry and Civil War in Lucan's Bellum Civile*, Cambridge.
McNelis, C. (2007), *Statius'* Thebaid *and the Poetics of Civil War*, Cambridge.
Moretti, G. (2007), '*Patriae trepidantis imago:* La personificazione di Roma nella *Pharsalia* fra *ostentum* e disseminazione allegorica', *Camenae* 2, 1–18.
Morford, M.P.O. (1967), *The Poet Lucan: Studies in Rhetorical Epic*, Oxford.
Myers, M.Y. (2011), 'Lucan's Poetic Geographies: Center and Periphery in Civil War Epic', in: P. Asso (ed.), *Brill's Companion to Lucan*, Leiden, 399–415.
Narducci, E. (1979), *La provvidenza crudele. Lucano e la distruzione dei miti augustei*, Pisa.
Narducci, E. (1980), 'Cesare e la patria (Ipotesi su *Phars.* I 185–192)', *Maia* 32, 175–8.
Narducci, E. (2002), *Lucano. Un' epica contro l'impero, interpretazione della Pharsalia*, Roma/Bari.

Neverov, O. (1974), 'À propos de l'iconographie julio-claudienne. Les portraits de Néron à l' Hermitage', *GNS* 24, 79–87.

Penwill, J.L. (2009), 'The Double Visions of Pompey and Caesar', *Antichthon* 43, 79–96.

Peluzzi, E. (1999), '*Turrigero...uertice.* La Prosopopea della Patria in Lucano', in: P. Esposito/L. Nicastri (eds.), *Interpretare Lucano*, Naples, 127–55.

Pichon, R. (1912), *Les Sources de Lucain*, Paris.

Radicke, J. (2004), *Lucans poetische Technik: Studien zum historischen Epos*, Leiden.

Robinson, M. (2011), *A Commentary on Ovid's Fasti*, Book 2, Oxford.

Roche, P. (2009), *Lucan, De Bello Civili* Book 1, Oxford.

Rondholz, A. (2009), 'Crossing the Rubicon: A Historiographical Study', *Mnemosyne* 62, 432–50.

Rutz, W. (1950), Studien zur Kompositionskunst und zur epischen Technik Lucans, Diss., Kiel.

Sannicandro, L. (2008), I personaggi femminili della Pharsalia di Lucano, Diss., Padova.

Schiesaro, A. (2003), *The Passions in Play: Thyestes and the Dynamics of Senecan Drama*, Cambridge.

Smith, R.A. (2005), *The Primacy of Vision in Virgil's Aeneid*, Austin.

Tarrant, R. (2012), *Virgil: Aeneid Book XII*, Cambridge.

Tasler, W. (1972), *Die Reden in Lucans Pharsalia*, Bonn.

Thompson, L./Bruère, R.T. (1968), 'Lucan's Use of Virgilian Reminiscence', *CPh* 63, 1–21.

Tracy, J. (2014), *Lucan's Egyptian Civil War*, Cambridge.

Tucker, R.A. (1988), 'What Actually Happened at the Rubicon?', *Historia* 37, 245–8.

Tzounakas, S. (2013), 'Caesar as *hostis* in Lucan's *De bello civili*', *BStud.Lat.* 43, 510–25.

Uhle, T. (2006), 'Antaeus – Hannibal – Caesar. Beobachtungen zur Exkurstechnik Lucans am Beispiel des Antaeus-Exkursus (Lucan. 4.593-660)', *Hermes* 134, 442–54.

Wensler, A.F. (1989), 'Lucan und Livius zum Januar 49 v. Chr. Quellenkundliche Beobachtungen', *Historia* 38, 250–4.

Willis, I. (2011), *Now and Rome. Lucan and Vergil as Theorists of Politics and Space*, London.

Wimmel, W. (1960), *Kallimachos in Rom*, Wiesbaden.

Wuilleumier, P./Le Bonniec, H. (1962), *Lucain: Bellum Civile: Liber Primus = La Pharsale:Livre Premier*, Paris.

Theodore Antoniadis

Intratextuality via Philosophy: Contextualizing *ira* in Silius Italicus' *Punica* 1–2

1 Introduction

For many readers of the *Punica*, Hannibal's portrayal represents an amalgam of or even a conflict between Silius' historiographical and epic influences.[1] For some others, it rather serves or reflects the poet's strenuous endeavor to reconcile the Carthaginian general as an historical figure with outstanding models of epic heroism such as Homer's Achilles.[2] At the same time, Hannibal's unrelenting struggle against the Romans brings him closer to other 'exemplary villains' of Roman literary tradition such as Sallust's and Cicero's Catiline, Vergil's Mezentius, Lucan's Caesar, Statius' Capaneus and Seneca's Atreus.[3] Thus, as the recent study of Claire Stocks (2013) further illustrates, we are confronted here with probably the most 'intertextual' hero in Flavian epic, whose poetic incarnation is repeatedly crossing genre–boundaries.

On the other hand, discussion about Silius' attempt to reconstruct Hannibal's figure in his work may acquire a new interpretative twist, and actually a more 'intratextual' one, if viewed through a more philosophical perspective, as the text itself seems to be inviting us to do. So far, the intratextuality of the *Punica* has been found at the core of many critical studies and theories examining the thematic links between individual books or episodes in order to identify the epic's larger structure.[4] Taking *ira* as an intratextual 'marker' of generic identity, structure, characterization and plot since the wrath of Achilles in the *Iliad*, this paper will further apply Seneca's theory on anger as a tool first to 'compartmentalize' the text of *Punica* 1–2 into small 'Stoic chunks' and then try an alternative, more

1 Cf. Cic. *De Am.* 8.28, *Phil.* 5.25, *Sest.* 142; Nep. *Hannibal*; Hor. *Carm.* 4.4, *Epod.* 16; Liv. 21–30, Val. Max. 3.7 (ext.6), 5.1, 9.2 (ext.6), 9.6 (ext.2.) with Tipping 2010, 51–106 and Stocks 2013, 13–43, 81–6 who offer the most recent discussion of Hannibal's character in the *Punica* with view to the historiographic and literary tradition before Silius. Note also Nesselrath 1986, 204–10; Lucarini 2004, 106–11.
2 Asso 2010, 180–9 and Bassett 1966 have viewed Hercules as another possible model for Hannibal.
3 See in general Feeney 1982, 46–8; Marks 2010, 127–32.
4 Note especially Fröhlich 2000, 18–28 and Augoustakis 2009, 8–9 who gathers all the related scholarship.

https://doi.org/10.1515/9783110611021-023

'unified' reading of the 'anger motif' in these two books.[5] Given that for many readers Silius' narrative of the fall of Saguntum constitutes an 'epic within the epic',[6] such a 'case study' may help us reconsider the poem's *Makrostuktur* in view of the moral climate in which Silius actually began to write his epic or, at least, conceived it.[7]

2 Between *ira* and *virtus*: A very Senecan Hannibal

Before we focus on Hannibal's reflection in Books 1–2, though, let us ponder for a moment the passage of the *De Ira* that quite ostensibly sets the starting point for our discussion. In one of his frequent references to ruthless tyrants who indulged themselves in bloodshed even by killing people who steered clear of conflict, Seneca ends with Rome's utmost enemy (*De Ira* 2.5.1–4):[8]

> [1] Illud etiamnunc quaerendum est, ii qui uulgo saeuiunt et *sanguine humano gaudent*, an irascantur cum eos occidunt a quibus nec acceperunt iniuriam nec accepisse ipsos existimant ... [2] Haec non est *ira*, *feritas* est; non enim quia accepit iniuriam nocet, sed parata est dum noceat uel accipere [iniuriam], nec illi uerbera *lacerationesque* in ultionem petuntur sed in *uoluptatem* ... [4] *Hannibalem aiunt dixisse, cum fossam sanguine humano plenam uidisset*, «o formosum spectaculum!» Quanto pulchrius illi uisum esset, si flumen aliquod lacumque conplesset! Quid mirum si hoc maxime spectaculo caperis, [qui] *innatus sanguini* et ab infante caedibus admotus?

> [1] We must also enquire whether those whose cruelty knows no bounds, and who delight in shedding human blood, are angry when they kill people from whom they have received no injury, and whom they themselves do not think have done them any injury; ... [2] This is not anger, it is ferocity. For it does not do hurt because it has received injury, but is even willing to receive [injury], provided it may do hurt. It does not long to inflict stripes and mangle bodies to avenge its wrongs, but for its own pleasure ... [4] It is said that when Hannibal saw a trench full of human blood, he exclaimed, "O, what a lovely sight!" How much

5 Here I am following part of the introductory thoughts and terms on intratextuality found in Sharrock 2000, 1–27. On Stoicism in the *Punica* see Basset 1966; Vessey 1974; Billerbeck 1986; Matier 1990; Dominik 2010, 429–30.

6 See Vessey 1974 and Dominik 2003.

7 On the dating of the *Punica* see Fröhlich 2000, 9–18; Marks 2005, 287–8; Augoustakis 2009, 6–10; Wilson 2013, 7.

8 For the text of the *Punica* I have consulted Spaltenstein 1986 while translations are taken from Duff 1934 with some minor adaptations. Quotations from the *De Ira* are taken from Reynolds 1977. For the translations of *De Ira* I have mainly followed either Cooper 2005 or Kaster and Nussbaum 2010, as indicated.

more beautiful would he have thought it, if it had filled a river or a lake? Why should we wonder that you should be charmed with this sight above all others, you who were born in bloodshed and brought up amid slaughter from a child? (transl. Cooper)

To my knowledge, Stocks (2013, 32–3) is the only critic who, among other texts that provide us with an image of the 'Roman Hannibal', has also included this short reference to the Carthaginian general for its possible influence on the *Punica*.[9] For Stocks, Hannibal's proclaiming '*o formosum spectaculum*' in front of a ditch filled with human blood stigmatizes him as an 'epitome of cruelty'. In her own words (p. 32), 'accentuating Hannibal's supposed monstrosity *(innatus sanguine; De Ira* 2.5.4) suits Seneca's theme, but it shows too how far Rome's authors could go in shaping and sensationalizing Hannibal and his deeds to fit their purpose, whilst still making him recognizable to their readers'.[10] While this seems to be the case, Stocks does not go on to explore how this idea is applicable to Silius' narrative and especially with regard to the 'gory elements' that Hannibal's conduct 'intratextually' shares with that of his step–brother Hasdrubal. Such elements, as we shall see, have a 'programmatic' function that anticipates the Carthaginian savagery in books to come or even Hannibal's bitter end.

Already in the proem of the epic, Silius presents the Second Punic War as an account of the Barcids' familial vengeance against the Romans which obviously draws on the famous tradition of Dido's curse against Aeneas in Vergil's *Aeneid* (*Pun*. 1.17–19):

Tantarum *causas irarum odiumque* perenni
seruatum studio et mandata nepotibus arma
fas aperire mihi superasque recludere mentes.

The causes of such fierce anger, the hatred maintained with unabated fury, the war bequeathed by sire to son and by son to grandson—these things I am permitted to reveal, and to disclose the purposes of Heaven.

While there is no doubt that the strong influence of Dido's figure upon Hannibal reflects that of the *Aeneid* on the *Punica* as a whole,[11] Silius here appears to be

9 Tipping 2010 limits his attention to the *De Ira* in a single note (n.42, p. 67) where he connects Hannibal's excessive cruelty at *Pun*. 11.218–24 with Seneca's portrayal of furious tyrants in various passages of the *De Ira*. On this idea, see below.

10 As Neil Bernstein pointed out to me, Silius may also have combined Seneca's vignette about Hannibal with Vitellius' joy at Bedriacum (Tac. *Hist*. 2.70) in viewing the Roman dead.

11 Cf. Verg. *Aen*. 4.622–3: *tum uos, o Tyrii, stirpem et genus omne futurum/ exercete odiis*, 4.629: *pugnent ipsique nepotesque*, but see also Liv. 21.1.3, where the historian makes a similar remark. See further Feeney 1982, *ad loc*; Spaltenstein 1986, 1–2; Tipping 2010, 62; Stocks 2013, 82.

injecting into Hannibal's hatred (*odium*) against the Romans a philosophical potential that is mostly absent in Vergil's epic, but is critical for a more 'intratextual' reading of his work beyond the shadow of the *Aeneid*. The very fact that in the *Punica* we move from hatred to vengeance[12] should turn our attention to that treatise which employs vengeance as an essential feature that defines anger (*De Ira* 1.2.3b): *Ira est cupiditas ulciscendae iniuriae aut, ut ait Posidonius, cupiditas puniendi eius a quo te inique putes laesum*, 'Anger is the desire to take vengeance for a wrong or, as Posidonius says, the desire to punish the person by whom you reckon you were unjustly harmed' (transl. Kaster). For the readers of Silius' epic, this almost inexplicable passion for revenge, which, as *putes* suggests, may be committed against people innocent of wrongdoing,[13] might evoke the cruelty and blood–lust of the Carthaginians shown towards the people of Spain and the Saguntines in particular. From this point of view, the proem's *tantarum causas irarum* (17), apart from recollecting Juno's and/or Caesar's wrath in the *Aeneid* and the *Pharsalia* respectively,[14] seems to be projecting *ira* as an intratextual marker that applies an ethical/philosophical touch to the recurring symptoms of the Carthaginian cruelty in books 1–2 as well as throughout the epic.[15] This idea develops further as soon as the main protagonist enters the narrative (*Pun.* 1.38–41, 56–62):

Iamque deae cunctas sibi belliger induit *iras*
Hannibal: hunc audet solum componere fatis.
sanguineo tum laeta uiro atque in regna Latini
turbine mox saeuo uenientum haud inscia cladum,
...

12 On this idea see further Ahl *et al.* 1986, 2495 and Stocks 2013, 80–2.

13 Cf. also *De Ira* 1.1.3 : *Quidam ita finierunt: ira est incitatio animi ad nocendum ei qui aut nocuit aut nocere uoluit. Primum diximus cupiditatem esse poenae exigendae.* In examining the process through which the adfectus of ira arises at the beginning of Book 2 (1–4), Seneca refers again to the impression we have of having been wronged (*opinio iniuriae*) before we approve (*adsensus*) or not the necessity of taking revenge (*punire, ulcisci, dolorem reddere, vindicare, ultio, poena*). See further Monteleone 2013, 128; Kaster and Nussbaum 2010, 4–8.

14 Cf. *Aen.* 1.25–6: *necdum etiam causae irarum saeuique dolores / exciderant animo*, Luc. 1.67: *fert animus causas tantarum expromere rerum*. For other parallels from the *Aeneid* see the next note. On Silius' debt to Lucan see especially Marks 2010, 128–32.

15 It is noteworthy that in Book 1 *ira* is featured nine times in total, whereas it is found another fourteen times in Book 2 which is among the highest rates in the epic. Cf. *Pun.* 1. 17, 38, 101, 147, 169, 410, 451, 516, 690 (most of these occurrences are discussed below) and *Pun.* 2. 22, 45, 55, 139, 203, 208, 239, 242, 280, 328, 529, 539, 619, 672. On the almost proverbial Carthaginian cruelty as a defining, national trait cf. *Pun.* 1.170 (discussed below), 2.386, 11.44, 13.732 with Tipping 2010, 64 n. 33.

Ingenio *motus auidus* fideique sinister
is fuit, exuperans astu, sed *deuius aequi.*
armato nullus diuum pudor: *improba uirtus*
et pacis despectus honos, penitusque medullis
sanguinis humani flagrat sitis. His super, aeui
flore uirens *avet* Aegatis abolere, parentum
dedecus, ac Siculo demergere *foedera* ponto.

Now warlike Hannibal clothed himself with all the wrath of the goddess; his single arm she dared to match against destiny. Then, rejoicing in that man of blood, and aware of the fierce storm of disasters in store for the realm of Latinus ... By nature he was eager for action and faithless to his plighted word, a past master in cunning but a strayer from justice. Once armed, he had no respect for Heaven; he was brave for evil and despised the glory of peace; and a thirst for human blood burned in his inmost heart. Besides all this, his youthful vigour longed to blot out the Aegates, the shame of the last generation, and to drown the treaty of peace in the Sicilian sea.

Commentators have duly noted that Hannibal's representation as instrument of Juno's *ira* elaborates on the goddess's favouring of Carthage and fear of Rome in the *Aeneid* (1.12–32).[16] However, Silius' painstaking effort to append a divine motivation to Hannibal's wrath is followed by a gory sketch of the Carthaginian (40: *sanguineo...uiro*, 59–60: *sanguinis humani flagrat sitis*) that bears a far more realistic colour. One might think that Silius has in mind Seneca's portrayal of Hannibal as a bloodthirsty ruler with particular reference to his delight in front of a trench full of human blood (cf. *De Ira* 2.5.4, quoted above). This idea gains more 'intratextual' credit in the pleasure Hannibal takes at *Pun.* 10.449–53 in seeing the bloody battlefield after his victory at Cannae.[17] Moreover, Hannibal's craving for vengeance (61: *avet*) as a result of the Carthaginian defeat at sea in the First Punic War, along with his restless desire for war action (56: *motus auidus*), emphatically recall Seneca's definition of anger we have already seen (*De Ira* 1.2.3b) and, especially, his introductory account of anger as a passion that makes someone hungry for vengeance even at his own cost (*De Ira* 1.1.1):

16 Similarly, Juno's bitter soliloquy in intermediary lines 42–54 owes much to the Juno-monologues in the *Aeneid* (1.37–49; 7.293–322). In essence, Silius' Juno takes as her starting-point the establishment of the kingdom which Vergil's Juno had hoped to prevent. For the common elements between the two texts see Spaltenstein 1986, 8–11 and Feeney 1982, 49.

17 Cf. also *Pun.* 11.250–1 where the captured Decius accuses Hannibal of delighting in human blood. See n. 54 and Tipping 2010, 64 who also quotes Caesar's equally bloody portrait at Luc. 7.728–824.

> Ceteris enim aliquid quieti placidique inest, hic totus concitatus et in impetu est, doloris armorum, *sanguinis* suppliciorum minime humana *furens* cupiditate, dum alteri noceat sui neglegens, in ipsa *inruens* tela et *ultionis* secum *ultorem* tracturae *auidus*.

> All other passions have something calm and quiet about them; this one consists entirely in aroused assault. Raging with an inhuman desire to inflict pain in combat and shed blood in punishment, it cares nothing for itself provided it can harm the other: it throws itself upon the very weapons raised against it, hungry for a vengeance that will bring down the avenger too (transl. Kaster)

For Seneca, anger is all about hankering after vengeance even if this brings down the avenger himself (cf. also 1.5.3: *Ira, ut diximus, auida poenae est*). The emphatic use of the epithet *avidus* combined with so much war imagery invites us to trace the similar effects of vengeful rage on the most belligerent figure of the *Punica*.[18] Thus, we see Hannibal putting off the killing of Daunus in order to torture him at his leisure (1.451: *ad poenam lentae mandaverat irae* 'he reserved him to suffer the punishment of wrath deferred'). Similarly, he indulges to the full his fury in slaying Murrus (1.514–6: *sic Poenus pressumque ira simul exigit ensem / qua capuli statuere morae, teloque relato / horrida labentis perfunditur arma cruore*, 'clutching his sword in fury, he drove it home till the hilt stopped it; then he drew back the weapon, and his dread armour was drenched with the blood of the dying man'). Though his fury eventually brings him down, as he gets seriously wounded by Murrus' fighters (1.517–29), still he does not quit but takes deep-drawn breaths, groaning and murmuring at the same time, thereby exhibiting those symptoms that Seneca quite strikingly attributes to people who go into a frenzy of rage.[19]

The influence of Seneca's concept of *ira* together with its *inter*textual and *intra*textual implications becomes even more evident in Book 2. Before reaching its climax with the Saguntum massacre (see below), rage is exposed in Hannibal's

---

18 Hill 2004, 153 supplies a detailed account of Seneca's plays and dialogues where public and political figures are governed by an irrational and insatiable lust for power. Most characteristically, Alexander and his emulators are characterized as *avidi futuri* for their perverse desire to overcome every obstacle in order to achieve their goals. *Cf. Ep.* 91.18, 53.10, 57.12, 90.43; *Ph.* 215, 518–19, 1138–9; *Thy.* 453.

19 Cf. *Pun.* 1.530–2: *tum creber penitusque trahens suspiria sicco / fumat ab ore vapor, nisu elisus anhelo / auditur gemitus fractumque in casside murmur* ~*De Ira* 1.1.3–4: *crebra et uehementius acta suspiria, ita irascentium eadem signa sunt…spiritus coactus ac stridens, articulorum se ipsos torquentium sonus, gemitus mugitusque.* Cf. also *Pun.* 1.59–60: *penitusque medullis / sanguinis humani flagrat sitis* ~*De Ira*: 1.3.4: *Flagrant ac micant oculi, multus ore toto rubor exaestuante ab imis praecordiis sanguine.*

duel with Theron whom the Carthaginian kills in revenge for the demise of the Amazon Asbyte, his war companion (*Pun.* 2.239–43):

> gliscit Elissaeo *uiolentior ira tyranno*:
> 'Tu *solue* interea nobis, bone ianitor urbis,
> *supplicium*, ut pandas' inquit 'tua moenia leto.'
> nec plura effari sinit *ira*, rotatque coruscum
> mucronem;

> The wrath of the Tyrian leader waxed yet fiercer: "You, worthy keeper of the city's gates, pay your punishment to us for now so your death may lay open the walls", he says. Nor does rage let him speak further, and he whirls his flashing sword.

There are many features in this battle scene which evoke Hannibal's portrayal as we have already sketched it in Book 1 in connexion with Seneca's treatise. Although, as Bernstein notes in his commentary (2017, 128), violent anger (239: *violentior ira*, 242: *ira*) is a standard attribute of Hannibal in the tradition, the fact that the Carthaginian is fashioned as *tyrannus* (a noun that does not correspond to his status as leader of the Punic army) here is further indicative of Seneca's impact upon Silius' wording.[20] Apart from the possible influences from Atreus' malicious conduct in the *Thyestes* which will be discussed shortly, in the *De Ira* Seneca mentions many other tyrants as typical examples of characters who, blinded by anger because they think they have been harmed, seek revenge with a totally disproportionate *scelus*.[21] Moreover, Hannibal describes his revenge against Theron as a *supplicium* (241), applying to it one of Seneca's favourite terms for punishment.[22] That this punishment suggests a disproportionate *scelus* also here is confirmed in the very next scene when the Numidians, taking their own revenge for the death of their leader Asbyte, abuse Theron's corpse (2.266: *rapto ... corpore*) and burn his face (2.268: *ambusto ore genisque*).

Going back to Hannibal's opening portrayal in the *Punica*, the feature which most notably complements his rage is undeniably his notorious perfidy. This is at least what most commentators first read in *deuius aequi* (57), a phrase they

20 The noun is rarer in the *Aeneid* while in the *Metamorphoses* Ovid restricts its application to hated rulers. Silius applies it again to Hannibal in 1.239, 4.707, 5.202, 10.487, 11.31. See further Bernstein 2017, 128. Note also Hasdrubal's representation as another Atreus discussed below.

21 Note especially Seneca's frequent allusions to Caligula's violent temper and his repetitive outbursts in *De Ira* 1.20.4–5; 2.17.1, 2.20.1, 2.33.3–6, 2.36.3; 3.18.3-4, 3.19.1–5, 3.21.5. See further Monteleone 2014, 127; Tipping 2010, 67 n. 42.

22 Silius' phrasing (2.240–1: *solue ... supplicium*) recollects particularly *De Ira* 3.14.4: *suppliciis funeribusque soluentem. Supplicium* as a concept similar to *poena* is featured 15 times in *De Ira*, most strikingly in the preliminary account of anger (1.1.1: *sanguinis suppliciorum ... cupiditate*).

usually relate to various passages in Livy.[23] For a reader of the *De Ira*, though, such a wording may also recall the next part of Seneca's phenomenological description of anger discussed above: *uanis agitata causis (sc. ira), ad dispectum aequi uerique inhabilis* (*De Ira* 1.1.2), '(anger is) excited by trifling causes, awkward at perceiving what is true and just' (transl. Cooper).[24] In the *Punica* a similar notion seems to describe Hannibal's perverse fury against Rome as totally unjust, at least in the eyes of the narrator, who repeatedly puts the blame on the Carthaginians for breaking the treaties and the oaths. This idea suggests a pervasive motif throughout the first two books of the epic. We see it already in the proem (1.8–10: *ter Marte sinistro / iuratumque Ioui foedus conuentaque partum / Sidonii fregere duces*), in line 62 quoted above (*ac Siculo demergere foedera ponto*) and again in lines 268 (*rumpere foedera certus*), 296–7 (*Admouet abrupto flagrantia foedere ductor / Sidonius castra*, see below), 648–9 (*ruptique per enses / foederis*) or even in Hanno's speech to the Carthaginian senate (2.293: *ergo armis foedus fasque omne abrumpitur armis*, 297: *foedere rupto*).[25] In giving such prominence to Hannibal's perfidy, Silius, apart from following all those Roman authors who also reported Hannibal's attack on Saguntum as indicative of Carthaginian perjury,[26] seems to have also been influenced by another passage of *De Ira*. There Seneca refers to 'national crimes' committed by fickle governors who violate oaths and break treaties in the name of the 'might and the justice of the stronger' (*De Ira* 2.9.4): *Adde nunc publica periuria gentium et rupta foedera et in praedam ualidioris quidquid non resistebat abductum*, 'Add to this now the oaths of nations violated, treaties broken, the stronger taking off as booty whatever is too weak to resist'.

In the same direction, Hannibal's legendary *improba uirtus* (58), which has earned the lion's share of comments among Silius' readers, may in fact signify this lack of justice and especially of reasoning in the actions of an otherwise gifted general and a brave warrior.[27] According to Seneca, reasoning is

---

23 Cf. Liv. 21.4.9, 21.34.1, 27.26.2 with Tipping 2010, 52; Spaltenstein 1986, 12; Feeney 1982, 51–2.

24 Cf. also *De Ira* 2.9.1: *expulso melioris aequiorisque respectu quocumque uisum est libido se inpingit, nec furtiua iam scelera sunt.*

25 Cf. also *Pun.* 2.377: *auctorem* (sc. Hannibal) *violati foederis*; 2.451–2: *Hannibal abrupto transgressus foedere ripas / Poenorum populos Romana in bella uocabat.* For linguistic parallels in Vergil and Lucan see Vessey 1974, 28; Feeney 1982, 14; Bernstein 2017, *ad loc.*

26 See n. 23. For other parallels on Carthaginian perfidy, see Bernstein 2017, 149.

27 Silius appears to be particularly following Caesar's portrayal at Luc. 1.144–5: *sed nescia uirtus / stare loco, solusque pudor non vincere bello,* with Marks 2010, 129; Spaltenstein 1986, 13; Feeney 1982, 51–2. For different readings of Hannibal's *improba virtus* see von Albrecht 1964, 49–52; Kissel 1979, 88–95; Ahl *et al.* 1986, 2511–2; Tipping 2010, 61–73, 83-84; Stocks 2013, 71–75, 85–87 n. 23, 142.

fundamental to the *virtus* of any warrior whereas *ira* in itself is not only useless but may be disastrous (*De Ira* 1.9.1): *Deinde nihil habet (sc. ira) in se utile nec acuit animum ad res bellicas; numquam enim virtus vitio adiuvanda est se contenta*, 'Furthermore, anger has nothing useful about it and does not stir the mind to warlike deeds. Virtue should never be assisted by vice, but is sufficient in itself' (transl. Kaster).[28] Most significantly, when it comes to exemplars of such *virtus*, the philosopher lists most remarkably Fabius Maximus and Scipio Africanus who are among the major protagonists on the Roman side in the *Punica*.[29] In contrast, he is topping off his reference to Hannibal's blood lust (cited above) with a sardonic comment on his martial deeds (*De Ira* 2.5.4):

> Sequetur te fortuna crudelitati tuae per uiginti annos secunda dabitque oculis tuis gratum ubique spectaculum; uidebis istud et circa Trasumennum et circa Cannas et nouissime circa Carthaginem tuam.
>
> Fortune will follow you and favour your cruelty for twenty years, and will display to you everywhere the sight that you love. You will behold it both at Trasumene and at Cannae, and lastly at your own city of Carthage. (transl. Cooper)

Even if we cannot be sure whether Seneca's ironic rejection of Hannibal's warlike fury 'informs' the arrogance of the latter's *improba virtus* in the *Punica*, this idea gains more support later in Book 1 when Silius undermines Hannibal's glorious feats in similar fashion and tone. This takes place at the point already discussed when the Carthaginian is wounded but escapes death by chance and after Juno's intervention: *propius si pressa furenti / hasta foret, clausae starent mortalibus Alpes, / nec, Trasimenne, tuis nunc Allia cederet undis*. 'If the spear had pierced deeper into the fierce warrior, the Alps had been for ever closed to mortal men, and Allia would not now rank after the waters of Lake Trasimene' (*Pun*. 1.545–7). In both texts Hannibal's *improba virtus* is exemplified through his extreme fury and his equally extreme fortune.[30]

---

28 As Kaster and Nussbaum (2010) 80–1 note, this position was held by the Peripatetics, to whom Cicero attributes it at *Tusc. Disp*. 4.43. See also *De Ira* 1.11.8.

29 See *De Ira* 1.11.5–8 with Kaster and Nussbaum 2010, 106.

30 Conversely, it is the very stance of Marcus Fabius towards the Saguntines' urgent call for help at the end of Book 1 that epitomizes the pristine virtue of the old Romans in Stoic terms thereby distinguishing it from the avenging fury of the Carthaginians. 'Peering carefully into the future' (679: *caute speculator mente futuri*) and being 'very slow to provoke war' (680: *parcusque lacessere Martem*) the Cunctator encompasses a number of virtues that are distinctively Stoic and outdo Hannibal's *improba virtus*. Cf. *providus* (685), *praemeditans* (686) and *prospiciens* (688) with von Albrecht 1964, 69; Kissel 1979, 116–27; Ahl *et al*. 1986, 2523–31; Pomeroy 2010, 71–2.

All in all, while anger is a standard feature of most epic figures from Homer's Achilles to Lucan's Caesar, what we have seen so far is inviting us to view the Senecan intertext as an 'intratextual glue' that imparts coherence to Silius' thematization of Hannibal's rage in *Pun.* 1–2. Put simply, 'bloody' Hannibal is more vindictive, treacherous and unjust than his epic predecessors, sometimes quite inexplicably. Though his arrogance is shared by many epic protagonists, his fortune in escaping death is also quite striking in both writers. On a larger scale, though, Silius appears to 'programmatize' the evolution of Hannibal's self-destructive wrath against Rome in line with Seneca's definition of anger as a passion that brings down the avenger. Most characteristically, in the coda to the fall of Saguntum (2.696–707), the Carthaginian's gruesome destiny is prefigured as a due consequence of his unjust victory over the Saguntines (699: *non aequa…victoria*) and the violation of the treaties with Rome (2. 700–1: *audite, o gentes, neu rumpite foedera pacis / nec regnis postferte fidem*, 'hear, o nations, and do not break peace treaties nor set power above loyalty').[31]

3 Hasdrubal's *immedicabilis ira* (*Pun.* 1.144–81)

Let us see now how Silius' *intra*textuality is further exemplified and amplified via Seneca's conception of anger in the subsequent portrayal of Hasdrubal. The narrator interrupts Hannibal's entry into the epic to devote a rather extraneous passage of 37 lines to his step-brother Hasdrubal who was the first heir to the leadership of the Carthaginian army after Hamilcar's death. The depiction of Hasdrubal's appalling conduct towards the people of Spain, which will eventually bring about his downfall, creates an atmosphere of savagery that aptly sets the scene for Hannibal's similar period of rule (*Pun.* 1.144–50):

> Interea rerum Hasdrubali traduntur habenae,
> occidui qui solis opes et uulgus Hiberum
> Baeticolasque uiros *furiis* agitabat iniquis.
> tristia corda duci, simul immedicabilis ira,
> et fructus regni feritas erat; asper amore
> sanguinis, et metui demens credebat honorem,
> nec nota docilis poena satiare furores.

31 Hannibal's future is foreshadowed in similar terms at the conclusion of Scipio's *katabasis* in *Pun.* 13.868–93.

> Meanwhile the direction of affairs was handed over to Hasdrubal; and with unjust fury he harried the wealth of the western world, the people of Spain, and the dwellers beside the Baetis. The general's heart was unkind, and nothing could mitigate his ferocious temper; he relished the opportunity power gave him to be cruel. Thirst for blood hardened his heart; and he had the folly to believe that to be feared is glory. Nor was he willing to satiate his rage with ordinary punishments.

It is interesting that in their histories neither Livy nor Polybius confirm Silius' criticisms of Hasdrubal's baseless fury (146: *furiis…iniquis*), the unkindness of his heart (147: *tristia corda*) and, most significantly, his incurable anger (147: *immedicabilis ira*).[32] As such an unfavourable portrait rather deviates from Silius' primary historical sources or even contradicts them, Feeney (1982, 99) suggested that the poet here presents Hasdrubal as a typical paradigm of Carthaginian government. To be sure, Hasdrubal's ferocity supplements Hannibal's warlike tenor and injustice as seen already (cf. *iniquis*, 146~*devius aequi*, 57) and prefigures his overwhelming hatred of the Romans. Whereas this idea already points to another aspect of Silius' intratextuality, at the same time Hasdrubal's sketch displays some critical Stoic influences that commentators usually downplay. Feeney (1982, 100–1), for instance, notes that the reference to anger as a disease suggests a common metaphor in Seneca's writings, including a passage from the *De Ira* among his quotations.[33] However, he does not elaborate further on Silius' systematic application of comparable Stoic concepts to both Carthaginian leaders, as exemplified in the prominence the epicist lends also to Hasdrubal's cruelty and bloodthirstiness (148–9: *asper amore sanguinis*). This tendency can be explained at both the intertextual and intratextual level as Silius appears to exploit Seneca's reworking of the Stoic idea that 'bloody anger' is an incurable passion (Cf. *De Ira* 3.40.5: *iram…feram immanem sanguinariam, quae iam insanabilis est*, see n. 33), while at the same time he obviously recasts the gory image of Hannibal (cf. *Pun.* 1. 30, 60) which, as already seen, also echoes Seneca's reference to his notorious 'innate bloodthirstiness' at *De Ira* 2.5.1–4 (*innatus sanguini*). Similarly, Silius' emphasis on Hasdrubal's ferocity as a ruler in the intricate expression of

---

32 Quite the opposite, Livy 21.2.5 presents Hasdrubal as a rather mild and peaceful governor. Similarly Polybius 3.8.1–9.5 rather criticizes Fabius Pictor, the only historian who seems to have supplied a negative picture of Hasdrubal. See further Feeney 1982, 99; Spaltenstein 1986, 29; Karakasis 2018, 403–4.

33 Cf. *De Ira* 3.40.5 mentioned below and *Clem.* 1.17.1: *Morbis medemur nec irascimur; atqui et hic morbus est animi*; On *immedicabilis ira* note also *Pun.* 14.292–3: *Quae cernens ductor, postquam immedicabile uisum / seditio.*

line 148 (*fructus regni feritas erat*)[34] seems to reflect Seneca's recurrent attempt to distinguish the tyrants' cruelty from anger motivated by reason.[35] Furthermore, Hasdrubal's perverse wish to be feared (149: *metui demens credebat honorem,*) draws on the famous aphorism *oderint, dum metuant* from Accius' lost *Atreus* (203) which —not accidentally— Seneca quotes in the *De Ira* (1.20.4) as a typical stance of arrogant rulers, hinting especially at Caligula (cf. Suet. *Gaius* 30). Most strikingly, it is his fondness for novel punishments (150), as observed in the horrible treatment of Tagus (a noble Spanish governor), which corresponds to the figure of Atreus in Seneca's *Thyestes*. The Argive leader's similar obsession with the idea of an unprecedented crime has long established him as the malicious tyrant *par excellence*.[36] Once again though a recognizable Stoic subtext is endorsed with a double intratextual 'thrust', if one only remembers Hannibal, whom Silius repeatedly presents as a tyrant (cf. 2.239: *tyranno*, n. 20), sparing a Saguntine captive only to torture him at his leisure later, and exhausting his fury in finishing off Murrus (cf. *Pun*. 1.451, 515–6).

Most importantly, the impact of Seneca on Hasdrubal's story culminates with a scene of extreme violence that prefigures the savagery of the mass suicide which will take place in Saguntum before the invasion of the Carthaginians. The 'poetics of revenge' are re-enacted when Tagus' ignominious end instigates the fury of one of his slaves who assassinates Hasdrubal in reprisal for the death of his master (165–8). This in turn fuels the anger (169: *succensa ira*) of the Carthaginians who, in line with their leaders' tactics as *saevis gens laeta* (*Pun*. 1.170), make the avenger suffer a terrific number of tortures. Readers have already pointed out that these tortures evoke those Seneca mentions in *De Ira* 3.3.6 as resulting from people's obsession with diverse means of punishment.[37] The mutilation of the limbs (1.172–3: *lacerum scindentia*), in particular, probably

34 Feeney understands *fructus regni* (149) as something like "bonus" or "profit accruing" which is very close to the idea of delight Seneca's rulers take in punishing (*gaudent, voluptatem*).

35 Cf. *De Ira* 2.5.2 (quoted above): *Haec non est ira, feritas est*, 3.17.1: *Haec barbaris regibus feritas in ira fuit, quos nulla eruditio, nullus litterarum cultus inbuerat.*

36 Cf. especially Sen. *Thy*. 253–5, 267–70 with Feeney 1982, 101–2; Spaltenstein 1986, 29–30. Note also *De Ira* 3.20: *nouo genere poenae delectatus est.*

37 Cf. *De Ira* 3.3.6: *eculei et fidiculae et ergastula et cruces et circumdati defossis corporibus ignes et cadauera quoque trahens uncus, uaria uinculorum genera, uaria poenarum, lacerationes membrorum, inscriptiones frontis et bestiarum immanium caueae*. Feeney 1982, 116–17 notes the sadistic nature of the rack, the mutilation of limbs and the burning of buried bodies that feature in both torture scenes. For a detailed account of the Stoic elements embedded in the torture see Danesi-Marioni 1989. On this scene, see further Augoustakis 2010, 127–8 who points to some other aspects of Silius' intratextuality.

elaborates on Seneca's references to *lacerationes membrorum* (*De Ira* 3.3.6) and *lacerationesque in ultionem* (*De Ira* 2.5.2). If we further recall the defilement of Asbyte's corpse (2.266: *rapto … corpore*) and the burning of her face (2.268: *ambusto ore genisque*) by the Numidians, then Silius' 'gothic' touch is a structural force that initiates the revelation of the Carhaginian *ira* in terms that are distinctively Senecan.

To sum up, as far as intratextuality is concerned, in all of the scenes discussed so far the actions of the protagonists are constantly interwoven with the irrevocable effects of anger as a vengeful passion that, according to Seneca's doctrine, ultimately leads to self-destruction. This is what in essence adds coherence to Silius' narrative by connecting Hasdrubal with his own assassin and with Hannibal. At the end of the day, all protagonists fall victim to their uncontrollable anger. The first two will meet their death in due course, whereas Hannibal gets seriously injured. In his case, the consequences of his *ira* will only 'materialize' as we move towards the end of the epic.

4 Contextualizing *ira* with suicide

The passionate reaction of Tagus' slave culminates with a characteristic Stoic pose as he endures the tortures with laughter and pride: *mens intacta manet: superat ridetque dolores*, 'the man's spirit remained unbroken; he was the master still and scorned the suffering' (*Pun.* 1.179).[38] Not surprisingly, some readers have discerned here a 'Stoic martyr' who remains impervious to emotional and physical pain.[39] Viewed from this angle, such a stance actually suggests an early example of an honorable death tantamount to a 'well-considered' suicide. The fact that the slave appears more than ready to face death indicates that his initial reaction was more composed and rational than it seems at first reading. In other words, we are confronted with a suicide of Senecan style and Stoic import, a theme that Silius reworks in full scale when the Saguntines decide to take their own lives at the end of Book 2.

---

38 Cf. Val. Max. 3.3.7: *laetitiam tamen, quam ex uindicta ceperat, in ore constantissime retinuit* with Feeney 1982, 110.

39 See Danesi-Marioni 1989, 245. Torture is quite remarkably the central theme in one of the *Controversiae* (2.5) of Seneca the Elder, see especially Pagán 2007 and Feeney 1982, 111.

Based on an historical event with its own exemplary tradition,[40] Silius' account of the Fall of Saguntum (*Pun.* 2.457–707) has a considerable intertextual and intratextual scope that makes it one of the most sophisticated sections of the *Punica.*[41] It starts with the intervention of Hercules who, resenting Juno's plotting against the city he founded, asks for the assistance of Fides (*Pun.* 2.475–525). While several readings approach both the Tirynthian hero and Fides as 'personifications' of ethical concepts that are central to the *Punica*, it is also important to recognize the philosophical subtext in their words and posture.[42] Thus, for Vessey (1974, 29–30) Hercules' renowned labors on earth stand allegorically for the highest aspirations of the Stoics, while his triumphant *virtus* appears to be in stark contrast to Hannibal's notorious *improba virtus*. Moreover, designated as *Nemeae pacator* (*Pun.* 1.483), Hercules, an otherwise ambivalent figure in the *Punica*,[43] is allegedly established as a champion of peace and an anti–*ira* and anti–Hasdrubal/Hannibal figure (cf. *pacis despectus honos*, 59) in Senecan fashion.[44] On the other hand, Fides obviously exemplifies the loyalty and piety of the Saguntines. Her very presence stands in sharp contrast to Carthaginian perfidy, thereby justifying further Silius' multiple references to Hannibal's breaking of the *foedera*, discussed above. When it comes to her answer to Hercules' plea, though, the goddess becomes even more moralizing and critical (*Pun.* 2.498–506):

impia liqui
et, *quantum terrent, tantum metuentia regna*
ac furias auri nec uilia praemia fraudum
et super haec ritu horrificos ac *more ferarum*
uiuentis rapto populos *luxuque* solutum

40 Cf. Luc. 3.350ff.; Petron. *Sat.* 140.6; Juv. 15.113–15, where the Saguntines are commemorated as a paradigm of *fides* and *virtus*. See further von Albrecht 1964, 58–9; Bernstein 2016, 229 n. 5.
41 Suicide, in general, is a common theme in Flavian Epic. See further McGuire 1997, 185–248 and cf. especially the massacre on Lemnos in the *Argonautica* of Valerius Flaccus (2.98–241). On the suicide at Saguntum the bibliography is vast: Augoustakis 2010, 113–36; 2016, 285–7; Vessey 1974, 28–36; Küppers 1986, 164–70; McGuire 1990, 33–41; 1997, 207–19; Hardie 1993, 81–2; Dominik 2003; Stocks 2014, 106–21, 150–1, 155–6; Bernstein 2016, 235–44.
42 On the concept of *fides* and the role of Fides in the *Punica*, see von Albrecht 1964, 55–86; Kissel 1979, 96–102; Hardie 1993, 81–3; Pomeroy 2010. Bernstein 2016, 235–7 quotes Val. Max. 6.6 as a significant parallel. For the Homeric background of this scene, see Juhnke 1972, 192–3.
43 See Kissel 1979, 156–7 and Billerbeck 1986, 348 who regard Hercules as a helpless, unwise figure which perverts the Stoic standards. Asso 2010, 180–9 approaches Hercules as a model for Hannibal, whereas Tipping 2010, 20 finds him an 'uncontrolled and uncontrollable' figure.
44 Cf. with Vessey 1974, 29–30 Sen. *Ben.* 1.13 (comparing Hercules' virtus to the arrogance of Alexander the Great): *Hercules nihil sibi uicit; orbem terrarum transiuit non concupiscendo, sed iudicando, quid uinceret, malorum hostis, bonorum uindex, terrarum marisque pacator.*

omne decus multaque oppressum nocte *pudorem.*
uis colitur, iurisque locum sibi uindicat ensis,
et probris cessit uirtus.

I fled from impious kings, who themselves fear as much as they are feared, and the frenzy for gold, and the rich rewards of wickedness. I fled also from nations hateful in their customs and living by violence like wild beasts, where all honour is undermined by luxury, and where shame is buried in deep darkness. Force is worshipped, and the sword usurps the place of justice, and virtue has given place to crime.

Claiming that she was compelled to abandon earth because of the decadence of humankind, Fides emphatically condemns the acts of violence between nations and the wickedness of their rulers. For some readers this gloomy world of violence, greed and fear most pointedly reflects the atmosphere of Lucan's *De Bello Civili* and Statius' *Thebaid*, as both these epics focus on civil strife and its aftermath.[45] More generally, though, the domination of evil in the world was a standard topos in Stoic philosophy. It is omnipresent in Seneca's treatises, with the *De Ira* providing us again with some characteristic extracts.[46] Furthermore, Fides' speech and especially her reference to impious kings 'who themselves fear as much as they are feared' (2.499–500: *quantum terrent, tantum metuentia regna*) and to 'virtue which has given place to crime' (2.505: *probris cessit uirtus*) clearly mirrors –always through Seneca's eyes– Hasdrubal's Atreus-like despotism (1.149: *et metui demens credebat honorem*) and Hannibal's *improba virtus* (1.58).[47] Her words further point to the Carthaginians' lack of shame before the gods (cf. 1.58, 152–5~2.504) and their notorious disrespect for right and justice (cf. 1.57, 146, 303–4~2.503–4).[48] Fides' disavowal of nations living by violence like wild beasts (*more ferarum*–501) can be traced to Seneca's likening of enraged people to wild animals, except for the fact that the latter do not indulge in *mutua laceratio* as men do.[49] Additionally, Fides' criticism of luxury (*luxuque*–502) evokes a

45 Note the words of Pietas in Statius' *Thebaid* 11.465–70 with Dominik 2003, 493. McGuire (1997, 213–5) compares the killing during Sulla's proscriptions in Luc. 2.146–57 with the suicide scene in *Pun.* 2.617–38 (discussed below).
46 Cf. especially *De Ira* 3.24.2 with Vessey 1974, 59.
47 For other references to tyrants' crimes in the *Punica*, see 13.602, 16.533–4 with Bernstein (2017, 221) who quoting the similar figure of the malicious king in Seneca's tragedies cites *Oed.* 705–6, *Ag.* 60–1.
48 For Dominik (2003, 493) Fides' words foreshadow the gloomy atmosphere before the disaster at Cannae (8.243–57) and in the sibyl's prophecy of the death of Hannibal (13.853–67). Cf. also *Pun.* 13.602 and 16.533–4 with Bernstein's notes on 2.503–4.
49 See *De Ira* 2.8.3: *Ferarum iste conuentus est, nisi quod illae [bestiae] inter se placidae sunt morsuque similium abstinent, hi [uiri] mutua laceratione satiantur. [Hoc uno] ab animalibus mutis*

salient theme in Seneca's treatise often associated with anger, war and crimes or contrasted to hunger and thirst, as is the case of the besieged Saguntines (2.461–5).[50] What actually suggests a telling intratextuality, though, is that in *Punica* 11–13 Silius attributes Capua's decline to luxury, presenting even Hannibal himself and his troops as a victim of Capuan lavishness.[51]

Above all, as Dominik (2003, 486) has argued, Fides' confession in lines 510–12 that she cannot save the Saguntines despite their merits epitomizes the orthodox Stoic doctrine of Fate as an unbreakable chain of cause and effect. Thus, acting as a Stoic agent, Fides descends to Saguntum only to ensure that its citizens will take up arms and, remaining faithful to her and to Rome, will face their destiny undaunted. In other words, Fides wants them to celebrate their death, just as Tagus' slave did when he exhibited his own faith to his master (*Pun.* 2.516–8):

> tum fusa *medullis*
> implicat atque sui *flagrantem* inspirat amorem.
> arma uolunt temptantque aegros ad proelia nisus.

> Then, piercing even to their marrow, she filled them with a burning passion for herself. They call for arms and put forth their feeble efforts in battle.

Quite interestingly, Fides fuels the Saguntines' fury and warlike spirit in a way that most strikingly —and quite ironically— evokes the bloodthirsty Hannibal in *Pun.* 1.59–60: *penitusque medullis / sanguinis humani flagrat sitis.* Whereas the irony in their case is that blood is the outcome of their own sacrifice, Silius' poignant remark here is that *ira* in the form of madness is always involved whether one is killing enemies or one's own people. This idea is further employed as soon as, after Juno's arrangement, the Fury Tisiphone, disguised as Murrus' widow, drives the Saguntines to frenzy and forces them to commit parricide and almost every possible form of family crime before taking their own lives (*Pun.* 2.614–49, 655–80). Once again, it is mostly the predominance of *ira* (529, 539, 619, 672) and *furor*

---

differunt, quod illa mansuescunt alentibus, horum rabies ipsos a quibus est nutrita depascitur. For rabies cf. *Pun.* 2.620: *rabie.*

50 There are 24 references to luxury in Seneca's treatise, which constitute the highest frequency among his philosophical corpus. Cf. especially 2.25.3–4: *Nulla itaque res magis iracundiam alit quam luxuria intemperans et inpatiens;* 3.2.1: *Nullam transit aetatem, nullum hominum genus excipit. Quaedam gentes beneficio egestatis non nouere luxuriam*; note also 3.5.5, 3.40.2.

51 Cf. *Pun.* 11. 33–66, 351–5, 420–6 with Tipping 2010, 33 and 53. Valerius Maximus also cites Hannibal as a foreign exemplar of such vices as luxury and cruelty (cf. 9.1. *ext.* 1, 9.2.1 and 9.2.2 *ext.* 2). Jupiter refers to luxury that will affect the Romans too in his theodicy at *Pun.* 3.589–90. Note also Voluptas' words at *Pun.* 15.92–97.

(528, 623, 645, 657) that captures Seneca's concept of a dramatically evil world from which suicide appears to be the only decent escape.[52]

Though suicide is a recurring theme in Flavian epic (see n. 41), it is rather not by mere chance that a similar picture is embroidered in one of the gloomiest passages of the *De Ira* where parricide prevails among a series of crimes which have often wiped out cities and entire nations.[53] Recalling Seneca's almost monotonous pessimism about the human potential for moral behavior both at individual and collective level, Silius now seems to register Saguntum among those noble cities cast down by the anger not only of those gruesome leaders 'known to history as examples of grim destiny' but also of those men 'who took up weapons against their fathers'. Thus, it is not only Hannibal who is implicated here or, even more strikingly, Hasdrubal as the king who eventually 'exposed his royal throat to a slave's armed hand'; the Saguntines themselves who 'emptied their city', the Carthaginians who wiped Saguntum and its people out or even the Romans who abandoned it to its fate are also involved, depending on the 'nature' and the 'origin' of everyone's anger and furor. If we further take into account those readings comparing the Saguntum massacre with the besieged Capua in *Pun.* 13.281–394, where Fides together with an Erinys features again and another suicide takes place (13.296–8, 374–80) before the city's fall to the Roman troops, then we might reasonably register the concept of an overwhelmingly evil world together with its philosophical undertones among the structural themes of the *Punica*.[54]

---

52 As Augoustakis 2016, 287 rightly observes 'Silius emphasizes the emptiness of the city when the Carthaginians storm the citadel but also underscores the unleashing of Hannibal's tyrannical *ira* and *furor* as a result".

53 Cf. *Pun.* 2.609–95~*De Ira* 1.2.1–2 (underlined phrases include numerous verbal parallels and are discussed/rendered in the main text): *Videbis caedes ac uenena et reorum mutuas sordes et <u>urbium clades et totarum exitia gentium</u> et principum sub ciuili hasta capita uenalia et subiectas tectis faces nec intra moenia coercitos ignes sed ingentia spatia regionum hostili flamma relucentia. <u>Aspice nobilissimarum ciuitatum fundamenta uix notabilia: has ira deiecit</u>. Aspice solitudines per multa milia sine habitatore desertas: has ira exhausit. Aspice tot memoriae <u>proditos duces mali exempla fati</u>: alium ira in cubili suo confodit, alium intra sacra mensae iura percussit, alium intra leges celebrisque spectaculum fori lancinauit, <u>alium filii parricidio dare sanguinem iussit</u>, alium seruili manu regalem aperire iugulum, alium in cruce membra diffindere.*

54 See further von Albrecht 1964, 62; Kissel 1979, 97 n. 25; Cowan 2007, 26–30.

5 Conclusions

The limited scope of this essay cannot extend to all those cases in the following books where *ira* and irrational behavior link Seneca's philosophy and the introductory portrayal of the Carthaginian generals.[55] However, considering the warlike and equally despicable portrait of Caesar, who exhibits the same kind of fury against the people of Rome in the *Pharsalia*, we may now reasonably surmise that in sketching out his own 'delirious' protagonists Silius is basically following two of his contemporaries.[56] Thus, though *ira* furnishes 'intratextually' the plot, the structure and the character portrayal of many epics and, similarly, 'goriness' forms part of a long tradition of epic 'realism-naturalism', starting with Homeric battle scenes and taking a turn towards 'excess' with Lucan or Ovid, Silius has been found to push these features to their rhetorical and philosophical extremes. In this process, he might also be trying, more or less successfully, to move beyond the shadow of Vergil, who in his *Aeneid* often diversifies the epic tradition under the impact of both tragedy and philosophy, thereby making the epic discourse more subtle, morally complex and ambiguous and enriching it with all sorts of undertones coming from the reflexive heritage of those two genres.[57] In a similar fashion, Silius presents his main protagonist either as an embodiment of the anti-Stoic villain or as an alter-ego of Achilles, Caesar or even Dido. Supplemented intratextually by Hasdrubal and vice-versa, Hannibal further recalls Turnus or Mezentius, giving all possible twists to irrational fury and displaying the 'ne plus ultra' of epic anger. Yet, Silius does not subordinate his epic to philosophy/Stoicism. We are rather confronted with a kind of generic interplay between epic and philosophy that blends inter– textuality with intra– textuality. Nevertheless, there is at least one thing we can be less confident and more skeptical about when reading Silius' epic. No matter when he started or when he finished the composition of the *Punica*, Silius should be considered no more a Flavian than a Neronian poet, as Wilson (2013) has further argued. After all, maybe it is the *Zeitgeist* of Nero's Rome that informs the narrative of *Pun.* 1–2 with grotesque and 'gothic'

---

55 Most characteristically, when Hannibal first sees his son born during the siege at Saguntum, he recognizes the anger that they share. See *Pun.* 3.77: *irarum elementa mearum* with Stocks 2014, 103–32 and Bernstein 2017, 128. Later in the epic, in his arrogant response to Decius' stoic remarks on his predilection to might over right, Hannibal behaves with the same excessive anger that has so far typified him as a tyrant in Senecan terms. See *Pun.* 11.201–41 and n. 9.

56 See n. 14, 25, 27, 45. On other aspects of Lucan's influence on the Saguntum episode see Bernstein 2016, 237–8.

57 Discussion of this issue was fundamentally raised by Conte 1986, 97–207.

elements. The events of the year 68 might further account for the systematic working of *ira* along the epic's intra-textual axis in a way that marks the Carthaginian savagery and the concept of a 'decadent' world in these books and throughout the epic.[58]

Bibliography

Ahl, F./Davis, M.A./Pomeroy, A. (1986), 'Silius Italicus', in: *ANRW* 2.32.4, 2492–561.

Albrecht, M. von (1964), *Silius Italicus: Freiheit und Gebundenheit römischer Epik*, Amsterdam.

Antoniadis, T. (2015), 'Scelus Femineum: Adultery and Revenge in Valerius Flaccus' *Argonautica* Book 2 (98–241) and Seneca's *Agamemnon*', *Symbolae Osloenses* 89, 60–80.

Asso, P. (2010), 'Hercules as a Paradigm of Roman Heroism', in: A. Augoustakis (ed.), *Brill's Companion to Silius Italicus*, Leiden, 179–92.

Augoustakis, A. (2010), *Motherhood and the Other: Fashioning Female Power in Flavian Epic*, Oxford/New York.

Augoustakis, A. (2010), 'Silius Italicus, a Flavian poet', in: A. Augoustakis (ed.), *Brill's Companion to Silius Italicus*, Leiden, 3–23.

Augoustakis, A. (2016), 'Burial and Lament in Flavian Epic: Mothers, Fathers, Children', in: N. Manioti (ed.), *Family in Flavian Epic*, Leiden, 276–300.

Bassett, E.L. (1966), 'Hercules and the Hero of the Punica', in: L. Wallach (ed.), *The Classical Tradition. Studies in Honor of Harry Caplan*, Ithaca, 258–73.

Bernstein, N. (2016), 'Mutua vulnera: dying together in Silius' Saguntum', in: N. Manioti (ed.), *Family in Flavian Epic*, Leiden, 228–47.

Bernstein, N. (2017), *Silius Italicus, Punica 2: Text, Translation, and Commentary*, Oxford.

Billerbeck, M. (1983), 'Aspects of Stoicism in Flavian Epic', *PLLS* 5, 341–56.

Buckley, E.L. (2014), 'Valerius Flaccus and Seneca's Tragedies', in: G. Manuwald/M. Heerink (eds.), *The Companion to Valerius Flaccus*, Leiden, 307–25.

Conte, G.-B. (1986), *The Rhetoric of Imitation: Genre and Poetic Memory in Virgil and Other Latin Poets*, Ithaca/London.

Cooper, J.M./Procopé, J.F. (1995), *Seneca: Moral and Political Essays*, Cambridge.

Cowan, R. (2007), 'The Headless City: The Decline and Fall of Capua in Silius Italicus' Punica', ORA 1542, at http://ora.ouls.ox.ac.uk/objects/uuid%3Adceb6b5a-980c-46ca-ac9e-088615e7fbea (accessed 20 May 2017).

Danesi–Marioni, G. (1989), 'Un martirio stoico: Silio Italico, *Pun*. 1.169 sgg', *Prometheus* 15, 245–53.

Dominik, W.J. (2003), 'Hannibal at the Gates: Programmatising Rome and Romanitas in Silius Italicus' Punica 1 and 2', in: A.J. Boyle/W.J. Dominik (eds.), *Flavian Rome: Culture, Image, Text*, Leiden, 469–97.

Dominik, W.J. (2010), 'The Reception of Silius Italicus in Modern Scholarship', in: A. Augoustakis (ed.), *Brill's Companion to Silius Italicus*, Leiden, 425–47.

58 I am grateful to Professors Theodore Papanghelis and Neil Bernstein for their critical suggestions and remarks as well as to Evangelos Karakasis for our endless discussions on Silius from which this paper profited considerably.

Duff, J. (ed. and tr.) (1934), *Silius Italicus, Tiberius Catius Punica*, Cambridge.
Feeney, D. (1982), *A Commentary* on Silius Italicus *Book 1*, Diss. Oxford University.
Fillion-Lahille, J. (1984), *Le* De Ira *de Sénèque et la Philosophie Stoïcienne des Passion*, Paris.
Frölich, U. (2000), *Regulus, Archtyp römischer Fides: Das sechste Buch als Schlüssel zu den Punica des Silius Italicus*, Tübingen.
Griffin, M. (1976), *Seneca: A Philosopher in Politics*, Oxford.
Griffin, M. (2008), 'Imago Vitae Suae', in: J.G. Fitch (ed.), *Seneca*, Oxford/New York, 23–58.
Hardie, P. (1993), *The Epic Successors of Virgil: A Study in the Dynamics of a Tradition*, Cambridge.
Hill, T. (2004), *Ambitiosa Mors. Suicide and Self in Roman Thought and Literature*, New York/London.
Juhnke, H. (1972), *Homerisches in Römischer Epik Flavischer Zeit*, München.
Karakasis, E. (2018), 'Silius Italicus and Polybius: Quellenforschung and Silian Poetics', in: N. Miltsios/M. Tamiolaki (eds.), *Polybius and his Legacy*, Berlin, 401–15.
Kaster, R./Nussbaum, M. (2010), *Lucius Annaeus Seneca: Anger, Mercy, Revenge. The Complete Works of Lucius Annaeus Seneca*, Chicago/London.
Kaufman, D. (2014), 'Seneca on the Analysis and Therapy of Occurrent Emotions', in: M. Colish/J. Wildberger (eds.), *Seneca Philosophus*, Berlin/Boston, 111–33.
Kissel, W. (1979), *Das Geschichtsbild des Silius Italicus*, Frankfurt am Main.
Küppers, J. (1986), *Tantarum causas irarum. Untersuchugen zur Enleitenden Bücherdyade der Punica des Silius Italicus*, Berlin/New York.
Lucarini, C. (2004), 'Le Fonti Storiche di Silio Italico', *Athenaeum* 92, 103–26.
Marks, R. (2010), 'Silius and Lucan', in: A. Augoustakis (ed.), *Brill's Companion to Silius Italicus*, Leiden, 127–53.
Matier, K.O. (1990), 'Stoic Philosophy in Silius Italicus', *Akroterion* 35, 68–72.
McGuire, D.T. (1997), *Acts of Silence: Civil War, Tyranny, and Suicide in the Flavian Epics*, Hildesheim/New York.
Monteleone, M. (2014), 'De Ira', in: G. Damschen/A. Heil (eds.), *Brill's Companion to Seneca, Philosopher and Dramatist*, Leiden, 127–34.
Nesselrath, H.G. (1986), 'Zu den Quellen des Silius Italicus', *Hermes* 114, 203–30.
Pagán, V. (2007), 'Teaching Torture in Seneca Controversiae 2.5', *CJ* 103, 165–82.
Pomeroy, A. (2010), '*Fides* in Silius Italicus' *Punica*', in: F. Schaffenrat (ed.), *Silius Italicus: Akten der Innsbrucker Tagung vom 19–21. Juni 2008*, Frankfurt, 59–76.
Reynolds, L. (1977), *Seneca, Dialogi*, Oxford.
Ripoll, F. (1999), 'Silius Italicus et Valérius Flaccus', *REA* 101, 499–521.
Spaltenstein, F. (1986), *Commentaire des Punica de Silius. Italicus (livres 1 à 8)*, Geneva.
Stocks, C. (2014), *The Roman Hannibal: Remembering the Enemy in Silius Italicus' Punica*, Liverpool.
Tipping, B. (2010), *Exemplary Epic: Silius Italicus' Punica*, Oxford.
Van Hoof, L. (2007), 'Strategic Differences: Seneca and Plutarch on Controlling Anger', *Mnemosyne* 60, 59–86.
Vessey, D.W.T. (1974), 'Silius Italicus on the Fall of Saguntum', *CPh* 69, 28–36.
Vogt, K.M. (2006), 'Anger, Present Injustice and Future Revenge in Seneca's *De Ira*', in: K. Volk/G. Williams (eds.), *New Developments in Seneca Studies*, Leiden, 57–74.
Wilson, M. (2013), 'The Flavian Punica?', in: G. Manuwald/A. Voigt (eds.), *Flavian Epic Interactions*, Berlin, 13–28.

Christer Henriksén

Inside Epigram: Intratextuality in Martial's *Epigrams*, Book 10

In order to study intratextuality within a certain poet's corpus, we need a relatively substantial amount of text, preferably in the form in which it was originally published —a fact which applies to exceedingly few Greek and Roman epigrammatists. With the exception of the Posidippus papyrus (which was discovered as late as the 1990s), Greek epigram has survived mainly in anthologized form, which, while not making intratextual study entirely pointless, seriously hampers our capacity to interpret interrelations between individual poems by removing them from their original context. In Latin, there is, of course, Catullus, as long as we are willing to accept that the *Liber Catulli* that has come down to us is actually the poet's own redaction (which seems likely, whether we consider it to be a single book, or three separate books that have been joined together by an ancient editor).[1] But the most significant exception to these somewhat discouraging circumstances is the poet Martial, whose name has become synonymous with the entire genre. Martial made writing epigram his vocation; as far as we know, he never wrote anything else. And as has been sufficiently demonstrated in recent years, it was not the isolated epigram, but the epigram in the context of the book that was fundamentally important to Martial. As he famously said, *facile est epigrammata belle / scribere, sed librum scribere difficile est*: it's easy writing fancy epigrams, but making a book out of them is difficult (7.85.3–4). This programmatic statement encapsulates Martial's ambition: while devoting himself entirely to epigram, he did so in a way that made it possible for the most minuscule of poetical forms to challenge even epic: by ordering his epigrams into a twelve-book concept, equalling the *Aeneid* or the *Thebaid* in size, but entirely made up of short poems.

Martial's twelve books of epigrams are collections of, on the average, 98 poems, which, of course, is a very much larger number of items per book than in any other verse collection from antiquity. The sheer number, together with their myriad contents, has led some to regard a meaningful positioning of each poem within the book as effectively impossible and to take the view that these collections were put together more or less randomly, to some extent from epigrams previously circulated in *libelli* (short pamphlets). The structural devices used by Martial were seen as limited to the books' beginnings and ends. In between these

1 For the debate see e.g. Skinner (2007).

https://doi.org/10.1515/9783110611021-024

boundaries some epigrams were quite obviously connected in pairs or cycles, but there did not seem to be much else in the way of an overall plan.[2]

Since the middle of the twentieth century, this view has been gradually and eventually substantially revised, as scholars have identified certain thematic patterns that are distributed throughout books and seem to serve as a kind of skeleton.[3] Cycles, and even pairs of epigrams, have been found to spread over several books, tying them together as a unity. The most obvious instance is probably the large cycle on Domitian's Second Pannonian War that extends through Books 7, 8, and 9, making them the most tightly connected of Martial's books (Henriksén 2002). This fits very neatly with the suggestion that the twelve *Epigrammaton libri* are to be divided into four 'triads' of three books each (see in particular Holzberg 2002, 135–52). This approach is attractive and has much that argues in its favour, although further research needs to be done; naturally, it also opens up further intratextual possibilities.

For the present, though, we shall leave the overall book-concept open in favour of the intratextuality of individual poems within a single book, epigrams that at a first glance may seem to be randomly scattered without a guiding principle, like Seel's 'bunte Steinchen' (see n. 2). It is a fact, though, that every one of these 'coloured pebbles' sits in the place in which Martial himself put it, which effectively means that the arrangement was not arbitrary; even the sceptic would have to admit that if arbitrary, it would have been purposely arbitrary. Furthermore, it is also a fact that there will necessarily be a relation between adjacent poems within a book, whether of congruence or of contrast, or even of complete disassociation. This relation, or juxtaposition, is potentially an important structural principle for the book. A consistent application of the principle of juxtaposition has been termed concatenation, i.e., a connection of each poem to the next through thematic and lexical links. Such continuous linking has been suggested,

2 An extreme view is represented, e.g., by Otto Seel, who as late as 1961 said of Martial's *Epigrams*: 'Ist es nicht unangemessen, hier überhaubt von einem "Werk" als einer Einheit zu reden? Zweifellos: Diese fünfzehn Bücher sind ja doch nur das Resultat beliebiger und von nichts als dem jeweiligen zufälligen "Anfall" verursachter Anhäufung, ein Sack voll bunter Steinchen, Muscheln, Spielmarken' (Seel 1961, 73). Such a view is all the more remarkable as it postdates (by a significant margin) Karl Barwick's seminal work on 'cycles' in Martial's books (Barwick 1932, 1958).

3 The so-called *libellus*-theory, launched by Peter White (1974) and contradictory to the view of Martial's published books as meaningful and carefully designed units, was effectively refuted by Don Fowler twenty years later (Fowler 1995). The structural arrangement of the individual books is treated in the introductions to most modern commentaries; see also Scherf (2001).

for instance, for the entire book of Catullus in the actual form that it has come down to us.[4]

To the best of my knowledge, no-one has yet read an entire book of Martial from the perspective of concatenation, or any other principle for linking every epigram to another one. That, however, would have to be the subject of a monograph. In this paper, I will look at a series of poems from the *Epigrams* with the sole purpose of showing that Martial's epigrams form a tightly woven web of interlocking themes. The specimen will consist of the first twenty poems of Book 10, roughly a fifth of the book, up to the famous poem to Pliny (10.20).[5] From considerations of space, interpretation of the various poems will be limited to a bare minimum; for the same reason, there will be no in-depth discussion of what is actually the more important question, viz. what the epigrams may gain in meaning by this kind of contextualization.[6]

Book 10 is an odd bird in Martial's *corpus*, presented as a revised second edition, containing epigrams from the first but even more that are brand new. Chronologically, it places itself between books 11 and 12, with both of which it appears to have links at beginning and end.[7] The book opens with a four-line poem in elegiac couplets, in which the book itself advises the reader to read as much as (s)he likes, should it appear too long to her or him. While this may seem to undermine the whole concept of a coherent book structure, the poem actually links the beginning of Book 10 to the end of Book 11, which ends with three four-line poems about book length. It also creates a thematic link to 10.2, in which the poet talks about his book and its second edition in an address to the reader. This epigram introduces the theme of literary fame, presenting it as something that is harmed neither by time nor by theft (*at chartis nec furta nocent et saecula prosunt, / solaque non norunt haec monumenta mori*; 10.2.11–12). The adequacy of this statement, however, is immediately called in question by poem 3, which presents us with a poet who spreads aggressive lampoons under Martial's name.[8] This is a kind of poetry that Martial has always disclaimed right from the beginning of Book 1, and, in defence, he holds up his fame, his 'jewelled reputation', which

4 Claes (2002).

5 Book 10 is one of the —now very few— books that still lack a modern scholarly commentary.

6 Lorenz (2004) offers an interpretative reading of the opening sequence of Book 4, with discussions also of links from this sequence to epigrams later on in the same book.

7 See Lorenz (2002, 221–2).

8 *Vernaculorum dicta, sordidum dentem, / et foeda linguae probra circulatricis / ... poeta quidam clancularius spargit / et volt videri nostra* (10.3.1–2, 5–6).

has no need to be further corroborated by such nefarious means.[9] This motif of subject matter is continued in poem 4, one of Martial's more memorable attacks on mythological poetry, a favourite target of his: *Qui legis Oedipoden caligantemque Thyesten, / Colchidas et Scyllas, quid nisi monstra legis?* (10.4.1–2). The contrast to his own epigrams is expressed in a few well-turned lines: *Hoc lege, quod possit dicere vita 'Meum est'. / Non hic Centauros, non Gorgonas Harpyiasque / invenies: hominem pagina nostra sapit* (10.4.8–10). Like poem 3, then, poem 4 deals with poetry from which Martial very markedly dissociates himself. Poem 5 also continues the theme from no. 3: an anonymous 'despiser of matrons and magistrates' (*stolaeve purpuraeve contemptor*; 10.5.1) writes aggressive poems about respectable members of Roman society. Martial curses him elaborately in full assurance that he will eventually be forced to admit that the lampoons were his: *et cum fateri Furia iusserit verum, / prodente clamet conscientia "Scripsi"* (10.5.18–19). This poem not only picks up and varies the theme from no. 3 (false attribution and anonymous authorship respectively), but also functions as a pendant to no. 2, in which Martial shows the proper attitude by acknowledging his book as *decimi mihi cura libelli* (10.2.1).

These literary motives of fame, theft and subject matter are now put on hold as Martial inserts a pair of epigrams forming a *revocatio* for the emperor Trajan from the Rhine, a topic that he had previously developed on a grand scale for the emperor Domitian in Book 8. This is potentially interesting, as 10.6, which is the first poem in the book to refer to an emperor, only presents us with a 'Caesar'. The last time we heard of *Caesar* in Martial's *Epigrams* was in the grandiose 'false closure' to Book 9, the 24-line comparison between Hercules and Domitian (9.101). Reading book 10 in the place suggested by its number —after book 9— and without any further historical context, the reader might be excused to think that *Caesar* is still Domitian. Its companion piece, 10.7, serves to clarify matters by stating that the emperor in question is now Trajan.

Following the *revocatio* is another thematic break, as Martial introduces a single couplet on another favourite topic, an attack on an older female: the speaker does not want to marry Paula, as she is an old woman; he might consider it if she was older (*Nubere Paula cupit nobis, ego ducere Paulam / nolo: anus est. Vellem, si magis esset anus*; 10.8) —obviously so that before too long, he could hope to inherit her fortune. This poem may seem quite detached from its surroundings, but as we shall see, it has an important structural function and points

9 *Procul a libellis nigra sit meis fama, / quos rumor alba gemmeus vehit pinna: / cur ego laborem notus esse tam prave, / constare gratis cum silentium possit?* (10.3.9–12).

forward in several ways, on the thematic as well as on the lexical level; most importantly, perhaps, it introduces the topic of 'money'.

Now this new topic has been planted, Martial in poem 9 ends the theme of literature and literary fame in a concise and cynically humorous manner, stating that he enjoys international fame for his wit, which, as he studiously points out, is not impudent: *multo sale nec tamen protervo / notus gentibus ille Martialis / et notus populis* (10.9.2–4). This underlines the impossibility of him having written the libellous poems ascribed to him by the *poeta quidam* in poem 3, being also a repudiation of the anonymous lampoons written by the 'despiser of *stola* and purple' in poem 5. For all his renown, though, he is still less famous than the racehorse Andraemon (*non sum Andraemone notior caballo*; 10.9.5). So much for the rewards of literary genius.

Poems 2 to 9 form a thematically coherent opening sequence, and are clearly defined as such also by the choice of metre, as they introduce Martial's three principal metres alternating with each other: elegiacs / choliambics / elegiacs / choliambics – elegiacs / hendecasyllables / elegiacs / hendecasyllables.[10] This structure also sets poem 1 apart as an introductory piece, as it would otherwise break the parallel arrangement of metres.

With 10.10 begins a series of poems that deal with various aspects of wealth and *amicitia*. In this poem, the paradoxical nature of clientship is illustrated by a consul performing the cumbersome and humiliating duties of a client (*Cum tu, laurigeris annum qui fascibus intras, / mane salutator limina mille teras, / hic ego quid faciam?*; 10.10.1–3). The figure of the consul connects the poem to epigram 5, halfway to 10, in which Martial sharply criticized the figure of the *stolaeve purpuraeve contemptor*. This is the first instance within the book of parallel arrangement, a structural device which complements juxtaposition. The word *purpura*, representing the consulship, lexically links the poems by appearing both in the first line of 10.5 and in the last of 10.10 (*dimisit nostras purpura vestra togas*). However, the attitude towards the consul has changed between the two poems. For whereas the purple in 10.5 stood for a man who commanded respect, the reverse is rather the case in poem 10. And what about the speaker himself? Does he perhaps come dangerously close to doing what he criticized in poem 5? And should we perhaps remember that Martial has made fun of a *matrona*, the old and rich Paula, only in

---

10 10.9 even explicitly mentions distich and hendecasyllable as the basis for Martial's fame: *Undenis pedibusque syllabisque / et multo sale nec tamen protervo / notus gentibus ille Martialis* (10.9.1–3). The scazon is not mentioned here, but as it has been used in the previous section for poems the topic of which Martial wants to have nothing to do with, it is still present in the words *multo sale nec tamen protervo*.

poem 8? And is it really pure chance that the deplorable consul in 10.10 turns out to have the same name as this wealthy woman, being called *Paulus*? Of course, this is all too good to be coincidental; in this way, the first poem of the new series in several ways connects to the preceding one.

In epigram 11, we encounter Calliodorus who is eager to appear as a true friend, generous with his money and fond of comparing himself to mythological exempla of friendship, a link to 10.4. However, friendship cannot be bought; Orestes never gave Pylades anything, and what is more, *qui donat quamvis plurima, plura negat* (10.11.8). Close variations of the motif of gifts from the wealthy will appear in poems 15 and 17, and gifts of another kind will become important towards the end of the series.

10.12 introduces the second real person after Trajan, viz. the consular Domitius Apollinaris, a long-time patron of Martial, who receives a light-hearted farewell poem as he sets off to his native Vercellae in northern Italy. Here, then, is a *propemptikon* for a consular friend who goes in the opposite direction to the emperor, who received a *revocatio* from the north in poem 6 (halfway to 12, another instance of parallel arrangement). Mythical epithets provide a link to the previous poem, *Apollineae* for the town of Vercellae and *Phaethonteus* for the river Po. Apollinaris is told to enjoy as much sun as he can (*i precor et totos avida cute combibe soles*, 10.12.7), another link to poem 6, which presents Trajan as "gleaming with northern suns" (*coruscus solibus Arctois*, 10.6.1–2).

10.13 is a poem to one Manius, presented as a childhood friend of Martial and the cause why he longs for his native town in Spain. But there is no question of Martial going there (as Domitius did) —for as long as he knows that Manius returns his affections, any place will be home to both of them (or Rome, as Martial puts it: *in quocumque loco Roma duobus erit*; 10.13.10). The links to poem 12 are obvious: friendship, return to one's hometown, to which Domitius goes but Martial, by contrast, does not. Furthermore, Martial states that in Manius' company, he would love being a guest in African huts or Scythian cottages: these, of course, are standard geographical extremes, but the pentameter *et poteram Scythicas hospes amare casas* (10.13.8) conjures up the image of Ovid in exile, which we may be intended to bring with us into poem 14.

The protagonist of this poem, one Cotta, is extremely well off —the theme of wealth returns— and he does not hesitate to spend his money on extravagances. Nonetheless, at night he lies on the threshold of his haughty mistress, wets the door, deaf to his woes, with his tears and burns his breast with sighs. This, of course, is an almost parodic archetype of an elegiac poet. And the speaker can tell why he is so miserable —namely because all is well, *bene est* (10.14.10). I suggest that Martial here thematises the economic conditions of poets, another of his favourite complaints. Why does Cotta enter the role of the elegiac lover-poet? Not because he has any talent for it —but because he can afford it; talent is no longer a prerequisite for writing poetry, but rather economic independence. This, of course, becomes rather a paradox, as the precise opposite, rejection of wealth, is something of a guiding principle for a real elegist such as Tibullus (Maltby 2002, 115–17). And above it all, from the *Scythicae casae* of the preceding poem, looms another great elegiac poet, Ovid himself.

After poem 15, which varies the motif of wealth and friendship by inverting the situation from 10.11 —Crispus claims that he yields to none of the speaker's friends, but does not even give a loan, much less any gifts— we encounter the second single-couplet poem in this sequence in 10.16. A certain Aper has accidentally shot his well-dowered wife with an arrow, but in a game; the speaker concludes that Aper knows how to play games (*Dotatae uxori cor harundine fixit acuta, / sed dum ludit Aper: ludere novit Aper*). The connection to the previous single-couplet poem is clear, as both dwell on the death of a wife as a means to get at her wealth. And as these poems are nos. 8 and 16 respectively, we have here a third instance of parallel arrangement.

Via 10.17, another variation on gifts from wealthy 'friends' (Gaius promises lavish gifts but, when it comes to it, gives nothing), we arrive at 10.18, which starts paving the way for the poem to Pliny, treating as it does the practice of giving poems to a patron, in this case a certain Macer, curator of the Appian Way and soon to become propraetor of Dalmatia. Martial here addresses his own Muse, who wants to cheat Macer of his gift of poetry for the Saturnalia; this will not do, as Macer has asked for the poems himself. But it seems that the Muse wants to withhold the poems out of care for the Appian way; for what will happen to it, if Macer takes to reading Martial instead of the reports of the *mensores*?

Poem 19 then rounds off the theme of patrons by presenting a peculiar case, the patron who does not give dinners, nor sends presents, nor lends money — because he has none. Yet, he is cultivated by a throng of clients; thus, in the final poem of the series on wealth and friendship, we are invited to ask ourselves who are actually the worse, the patrons for their haughtiness or the clients for their foolishness (*Eheu! quam fatuae sunt tibi, Roma, togae!*; 10.19.4).

We thus arrive at 10.20, the poem to Pliny the Younger, in which Martial asks his Muse, now obviously more cooperative, to take a little book of poems through Rome to his house. After this list of perverted patrons and frustrated clients, Pliny easily stands out as a model. We know, too, that the poem was actually given to Pliny and that it was well received, as he chose to quote it in the letter to Cornelius Priscus in which he writes about Martial's death (*Ep.* 3.21.5).

To sum up, it should be fairly obvious that the first twenty poems of Martial's Book 10 contain two interconnected series, 2–9 (with no. 1 as an introductory poem) and 10–19. The opening series 2–9 highlights the theme of literary fame and its conditions, the pair of epigrams on Trajan and the single-couplet poem on Paula being inserted to break the continuity and herald the following series. This starts with poem 10, portraying the consul Paulus as a client, and is closed in no. 19 with another piece highlighting the absurdities of clientship. The poems in this series all present variations on the themes of wealth, friends, and friendship and are also held together by a common metre, the elegiac couplet, which here appears in an unusually long sequence of poems. The figure of the consul in 10.10 refers back to no. 5, and the leads from the pair on Trajan and the poem on Paula are picked up in poems whose numbers are exactly the double of their predecessors. The series leads up to the poem to Pliny, no. 20, with its 21 lines the longest so far. Money and friendship, or literary patronage, are presumably Martial's reasons for writing this poem, but importantly, he takes care not to include Pliny (or himself) in the preceding list of patrons and clients by suddenly changing the metre; while the entire series of poems on *amicitia* is written in elegiac couplets, the one to Pliny is in hendecasyllables.

As this short survey indicates, intratextuality is an important principle for Martial, who constantly refers to his own poems, locking them into each other in chains or parallels within his books, and in some cases also between them. Yet it has done little more than scratched the surface; a close sequential reading will reveal further structural devices. To give just one instance, rivers seem to play some kind of role in the design of Book 10. Poem 2 mentions the *pigra ... ingratae flumina Lethes* (10.2.8), no. 6 the Nile (*picti tunica Nilotide Mauri*, 10.6.8), no. 7 the Rhine and the Tiber (*Nympharum pater amniumque, Rhene / Thybris ... dominus*, 10.7.1 and 9), no. 12 the Po and the Nile (*Phaethontei ... arva Padi / Niliaco ... ore niger*, 10.12.2 and 12), no. 13 the Salo (*Salo Celtiber*, 10.13.1), no. 15 the Nile (*tua Niliacus rura colonus aret*, 10.15.6), and no. 17 the Tagus (*aurea ... divitis unda Tagi*, 10.17.4). The other poems do not mention rivers explicitly, but if we widen our view, we find references to water in no. 3 (the *amatrices ... aquas* of Hermaphroditus, 10.3.6), no. 5 (the *undas garruli senis*, sc. of Tantalus; 10.5.16), no. 14 (*Thetis* as metonymy for the sea; 10.14.4) and no. 20 (a statue of Orpheus at the top of a 'wet theatre', *Orphea ... udi vertice ... theatri*; 10.20.6–7). This means that in the opening series, only poems 3, 8 (the first single-couplet poem, looking forward to the second series) and 9 lack a direct reference to water. At this point, it becomes a matter of how far we are willing to push things to achieve a coherent system of references. As we have seen, in the final poem of the series Martial claims to be known *multo sale nec tamen protervo*, literally 'for much salt, though not impudent'. Obviously, *sal* is here primarily the usual metonymy for 'wit'. But the word is also, of course, equally common as a metonymy for the sea; thus, for instance, things can be submerged in *sal*, as in Quintus Curtius 9.9.20, where lands are described as *paulo ante profundo salo mersas*, 'a little before submerged in deep sea'. Martial may be exploiting this ambiguity when he says that Calliodorus considers himself a really funny chap and the only one to *multo permaduisse sale*, 'to have been thoroughly soaked in much *sal*' (6.44.2). As for the adjective *protervus*, it may be used of natural phenomena as shown by Horace's *Carm.* 1.26.2–3 *protervis ... ventis* ('violent winds'). So, if we are willing to go there, we may take Martial's *multo sale nec tamen protervo* as suggesting that he is known not only for much good-humoured wit, but also for much water – and as the water is not *protervus*, this may be the reason for its absence from poem 3. At the very least, we may note that Lorenz finds water to be a 'Leitmotif' also in Book 4, and points to its metapoetic connotations (see in particular Lorenz 2004, 264–5). Among other things, water is frequently presented as a threat to Martial's epigrams, which can be destroyed by being merged in water (cf., e.g., 9.58.7–8 *Nympharum templis quisquis sua carmina donat, / quid fieri libris debeat, ipse monet*; similarly 1.5). In this context, we may remember that Martial in 10.2.11–12 pointed out that theft does not harm his sheets and that time does them good, in short that these memorials are the only ones that do not know of death (see above); this comes out as rather a risky statement when there is, in fact, water, water everywhere (nor any drop to drink).

Bibliography

Barwick, K. (1932), 'Zur Kompositionstechnik und Erklärung Martials', *Philologus* 87, 63–79.

Barwick, K. (1958), 'Zyklen bei Martial und in den kleinen Gedichten des Catull', *Philologus* 102, 284–318.

Claes, P. (2002), *Concatenatio Catulliana. A New Reading of the Carmina*, Amsterdam.

Fowler, D.P. (1995), 'Martial and the Book', *Ramus-Critical Studies in Greek and Roman Literature* 24, 31–58.

Henriksén, C. (2002), 'The Augustan Domitian: Martial's Poetry on the Second Pannonian War and Horace's Fourth Book of *Odes*', *Philologus* 146, 318–38.

Holzberg, N. (2002), *Martial und das antike Epigramm*, Darmstadt.

Lorenz, S. (2002), *Erotik und Panegyrik. Martials epigrammatische Kaiser*, Classica Monacensia, Tübingen.

Lorenz, S. (2004), 'Waterscape with black and white: Epigrams, Cycles, and Webs in Martial's *Epigrammaton liber quartus*', *American Journal of Philology* 125, 255–78.

Maltby, R. (2002), *Tibullus, Elegies. Text, Introduction and Commentary*, Cambridge.

Scherf, J. (2001), *Untersuchungen zur Buchgestaltung Martials*, Beiträge zur Altertumskunde, München.

Seel, O. (1961), 'Ansatz zu einer Martial-Interpretation', *Antike und Abendland* 10, 53–76.

Skinner, M. (2007), 'Authorial Arrangement of the Collection: Debate Past and Present', in: M. Skinner (ed.), *A Companion to Catullus*, Oxford, 35–54.
White, P. (1974), 'The Presentation and Dedication of the *Silvae* and the *Epigrams*', *Journal of Roman Studies* 64, 40–61.

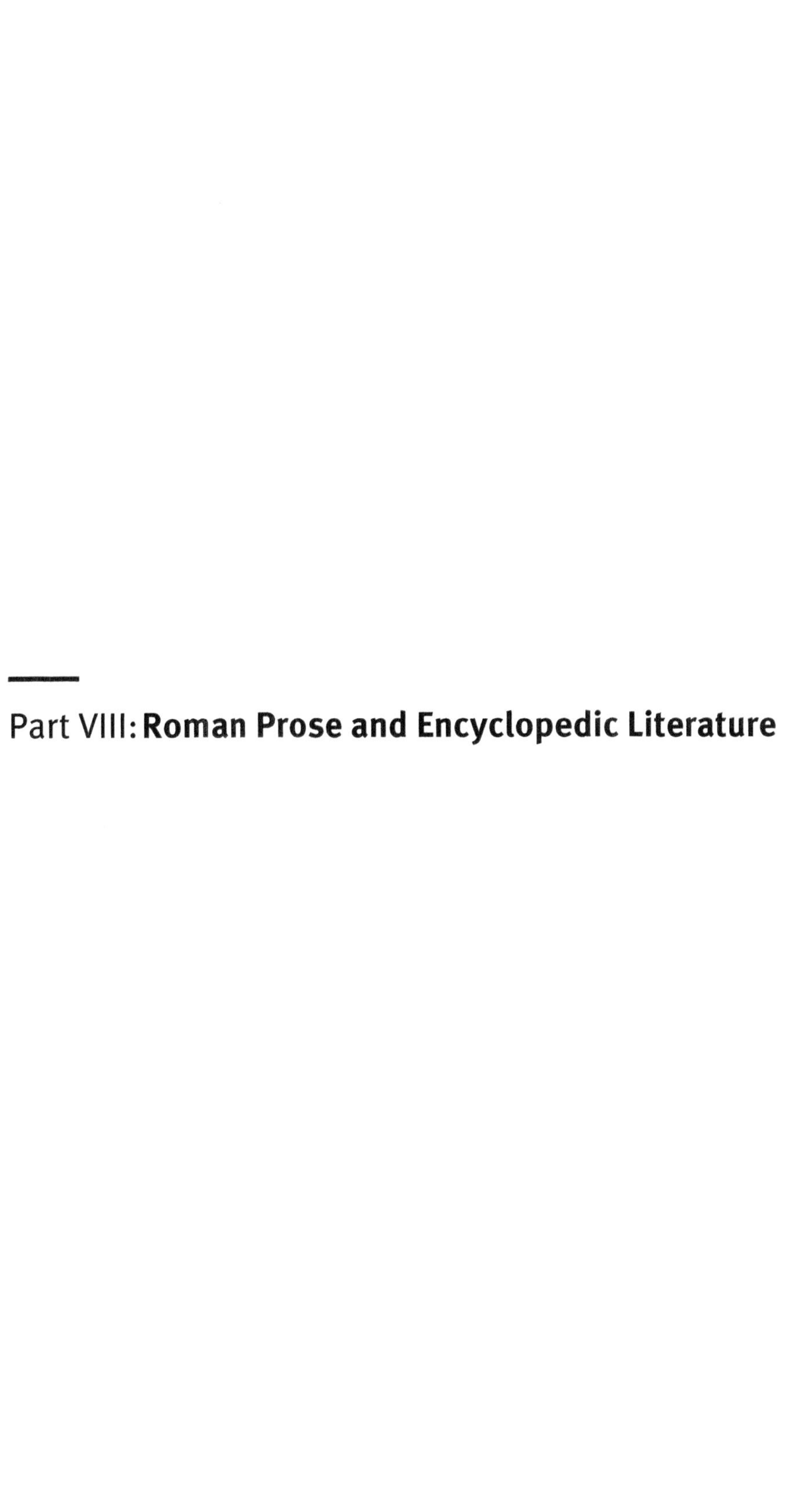

Part VIII: **Roman Prose and Encyclopedic Literature**

Gesine Manuwald

'Political Intratextuality' with regard to Cicero's Speeches

1 Introduction

Over the course of research on Cicero's writings it has long been noted that his speeches contain references to arguments advanced earlier and repetitions of points, that he refers to earlier speeches in later ones and that he comments on his speeches in treatises and letters. If one looks at such connections from the perspective of 'intratextuality',[1] therefore, one cannot restrict oneself to single speeches, but will have to consider the entire oratorical corpus: from the point of view of intratextuality[2] a 'text' can be defined as a single work or a text with paratexts or the entire oeuvre of a single author consisting of a number of self-contained works. The various manifestations of 'intratextuality' can thus be viewed as placed on a scale ranging from connections within a single work to links between several independent texts by the same author, when intratextuality approaches intertextuality.[3]

1 The main work on intratextuality with reference to ancient Greek and Roman texts is the collection edited by Sharrock/Morales (2000). The volume's framework and approach are outlined in Sharrock's (2000) introduction; this discussion is complemented by the methodological and theoretical observations in a review by Edmunds (2004). The essays in the volume apply different concepts of intratextuality to a range of selected texts. The collection includes an article on intratextuality in Cicero's *De re publica*, discussing intratextual relations within a single Ciceronian philosophical work (Fox 2000).

2 For a definition see e.g. Chandler/Munday, 2011, s.v. intratextuality: 'Internal relations within a text, in contrast to intertextuality, which involves 'external' relations with other texts. Within a single code (e.g. a photographic code) these would be simple syntagmatic relationships (e.g. the relationship of the image of one person to another within the same photograph). However, a text may involve several codes: a newspaper photograph, for instance, may have a caption (see anchorage).'

3 See Broich 1985, 49–50: 'Wenn die Bezüge von Texten auf einzelne Prätexte untersucht werden, dann handelt es sich bei den Prätexten in der Regel um Texte anderer Autoren. Es darf jedoch nicht übersehen werden, daß ein Text sich auch auf einen Text des gleichen Autors beziehen kann und daß dieses Phänomen ganz ähnliche Züge wie die Intertextualität aufweist. Hier ist zunächst der hin und wieder als Auto- oder Intratextualität bezeichnete Verweis eines Textes auf andere Stellen des gleichen Textes zu nennen. Gehen wir auf einer gedachten Skala einen Schritt weiter von der Intra- in Richtung auf die Intertextualität, so gelangen wir zu den für die Einzeltextanalyse ebenfalls wichtigen Verweisen eines Textes auf Nebentexte des gleichen Autors, wie z.B. Vor- und Nachworte, Erläuterungen in Briefen, Interviews und dergleichen.

https://doi.org/10.1515/9783110611021-025

Intratextual links to be observed with respect to Cicero's speeches predominantly rely on correspondences and consistency in the use of ideas and concepts. That, therefore, Cicero's individual speeches and further texts alluding to them can be seen as a coherent corpus and thus open to intratextual analysis, is a result of their shared themes and argumentative character. Obviously, there is a fundamental difference between speeches and comments in treatises and letters since the speeches were originally delivered orally on a particular occasion. What is available nowadays are the written versions, and they have been revised before publication (see section 4), even though the extent of the changes cannot be established with certainty. At any rate, as only the revised published versions are extant, it is almost impossible to explore in what way intratextual links within individual speeches may have arisen from positive or negative reactions among the audience at the point of delivery.[4] Thus, because the surviving written versions were composed after the event, noticeable intratextual connections in the extant versions are likely to have been created by the author on purpose. The different forms these can take, initially within a single speech and then across the oratorical oeuvre, shall be described in this case study, so that their functions can be analysed.[5]

2 Intratextual references within single speeches or groups of speeches

As for individual speeches, it can be inferred that written versions were typically more carefully constructed and polished than their delivered counterparts:[6] when Cicero says about the speech of thanks to the Senate given after his return from exile (57 BCE) that, because of the magnitude of the matter, it was delivered

Wiederum ein Stück näher in Richtung auf die Intertextualität sind solche Texte lokalisiert, die auf andere, eigenständige Texte des gleichen Autors verweisen.'

4 The opposite strategy, namely that Cicero changed his original tactic in the course of the delivery because of the hostile reactions of the audience, has been assumed for *Philippic Twelve* (Hall 2008 [2009]): the fact that this procedure is not immediately obvious might be seen as proof that Cicero turns the edited versions into coherent wholes.

5 Works by Cicero will be referred to by their titles only without the addition of the author's name. – Since this study is a brief consideration of structural principles rather than an analysis of specific passages, secondary literature on individual speeches will not be recorded and discussed in detail.

6 For some orators, however, Cicero claims in the *Brutus* and also in the *Orator* that they were better speakers than their written speeches indicate (e.g. *Brut.* 82; *Orat.* 132): this typically refers to their strengths in delivery, which are not replicated in the written text.

from a written text (*Planc.* 74), this indicates that for a speech delivered in the usual way comprehensive coverage and sophisticated structure could not always be guaranteed. The extant speech *Pro Milone* (52 BCE) is not the one given at the trial, as Cicero's appearance there was unsuccessful and not a great performance due to fear and frequent interruptions, but another that Cicero wrote as the proper speech for this occasion after the event, which was regarded as brilliant (Asc., pp. 41–42 Clark; Schol. Bob. *Arg. in Cic. Mil.* [p. 112 Stangl]; Plut. *Cic.* 35; Cass. Dio 40.54.2–4; 46.7.3). One reason why Cicero published speeches was to provide models for aspiring young orators, and he discussed the effectiveness and accuracy of certain phrases with Atticus before publication (see sections 4 and 6).

Accordingly, it is not unexpected that the extant (written) versions of speeches appear coherent and persuasive by means of intratextual references, though some of these are likely to have also been included in the oral version. In the orations on Catiline, delivered towards the end of his consular year (63 BCE), Cicero repeatedly presents Catiline and his followers as contemptible, irresponsible, non-human enemies of the Republic, without making an effort to discuss the reasons for their behaviour or offering alternatives, and announces that they should leave or have left Rome (e.g. *Cat.* 1.12–13; 1.20; 1.23; 2.1; 2.7–10; 2.12–14; 2.27; 3.3–4; 4.6). While Cicero only rarely marks the repetition or refers to events at an earlier stage in the process (*Cat.* 1.23; 2.12–14; 2.27, 3.3), the repeated negative characterization gradually creates a particular and consistent image of Catiline among the audience as well as of his opponent Cicero, and the appropriate reaction; this conditions them to agree to Cicero's policy and ensures a coherent argument and presentation of the situation. In addition, in the *First Catilinarian Oration* Cicero inserts two speeches of the personified *patria* to Catiline and to himself respectively (*Cat.* 1.18–19; 1.27–29): while both speeches are obviously products of Cicero's invention, the repeated structure invites a comparison between the two men without forcing Cicero to juxtapose their behaviour in his own voice.

Over the series of speeches Cicero's presentation varies and adapts to the circumstances in line with the developing situation; yet his main argument and his characterization of Catiline remain consistent throughout the group of four orations. This is probably not a coincidence since Cicero delivered more speeches in the context of the conflict with Catiline (e.g. at the meeting of the Senate when the *senatus consultum ultimum* was decreed: *Cat.* 1.3), but these are not extant, presumably because Cicero did not choose to write them up. On the other hand he regarded these four speeches as part of a consular corpus outlined in a letter to Atticus, which was meant to illustrate what he did and what he said as consul (*Att.* 2.1.3). The notion of viewing several speeches referring to a political event or a period in his life as a corpus (consular orations; *Philippic Orations*) is another indication that in Cicero's view a text may extend beyond a single speech and this may be indicated by internal links. In the *Philippic Orations* (44–43 BCE) too a consistent portrayal of Mark Antony is created by the repetition of his negative characteristics within the same speech and across speeches.

3 Intratextual references to oratorical activity across speeches

When, within oratorical corpora relating to the same incident, Cicero refers to statements made in earlier speeches or events connected with earlier speeches in later ones, these may serve to reinforce the argument in the new situation by appealing to consistency, often in combination with a particular interpretation of the original situation.

When Cicero reports the effect of *Philippic Three* to the People in *Philippic Four*, he tells them that Mark Antony has been declared a public enemy, if not in word, at any rate in actuality (*Phil.* 4.1). In fact, the motion Cicero put forward during the preceding meeting of the Senate (which was accepted) called for honours for generals and their armies who had opposed Mark Antony (*Phil.* 3.37–39); this could be interpreted as implying a denunciation of Mark Antony, but these consequences are not even indirectly stated in the adopted motion. Interpreting the decree of the Senate in the strong fashion of *Philippic Four* enables the orator to publicize the preferred reading of his intervention to the immediate and the wider contemporary audience and also to later readers of the group of speeches.

Again with reference to *Philippic Three*, Cicero says later in the struggle against Mark Antony that he was the first to recall liberty on that day (*Phil.* 14.19–20): this is another far-reaching interpretation of his efforts to make the Senate support Octavian and confront Mark Antony to avoid another dictatorship in Caesarian style, and again it contributes to creating an image of a consistent position in word and deed for Cicero.

Similarly to what he does in *Philippic Four*, during a slightly later sequence of discussions in the Senate extending over several days, Cicero's proposal to confront Mark Antony immediately was eventually turned down; instead, the Senate decreed the sending of an embassy to Mark Antony for negotiations. When reporting this outcome to the People in *Philippic Six*, Cicero claims that for three days almost everyone agreed with him, but that suddenly, on the present day, the majority followed another view for some reason (*Phil.* 6.3). Here Cicero could have referred back to his speeches given in the Senate; but since they were ultimately unsuccessful, he does not insert any intratextual references and instead keeps the report vague. This applies in particular to the description of the change of mind, so that there is no need to point out that in the end the Senate followed someone else's advice rather than Cicero's. The aim to counter the impression of defeat is pursued towards the end of the speech, when Cicero claims that he spent less effort in the meeting of the Senate earlier that day because he thought that it would be better if everyone agreed with him in twenty days' time than if he received criticism from a few at this point (*Phil.* 6.16). The speech Cicero gave in the Senate on that day is not included in the corpus of the *Philippics* and does not survive. Nevertheless, since Cicero strongly argued for speed rather than universal support at the beginning of the debate (*Phil.* 5), the statement sounds like a measure to obscure an unsuccessful initiative. Because in ongoing political discussions intratextual references also have a practical dimension related to an immediate aim, in cases where they were deployed unsuccessfully, they are not included or kept vague. Moreover, their insertion would affect the impression of a consistent and successful oratorical persona across Cicero's works.

Vice versa, when Cicero makes a strong statement and delivers speeches on the same issue both in the Senate and before the People, he sometimes emphasizes that he says the same in both settings (e.g. *Leg. agr.* 2.6; *Phil.* 6.5). Such comments create an oratorical link between the two elements of a pair of speeches; predominantly, they are meant to assure the audience that Cicero is a reliable and honest politician who does not change his mind and gives the same information to everyone even in difficult circumstances. An exact report of an earlier occasion is as much an element of political tactics as its suppression; the selection of procedure depends on the political context.[7]

Such tactics indicate that, besides reinforcement of arguments, intratextual links between different speeches, in the same corpus and beyond, mainly serve to create a consistent and successful image of the orator's persona or address any activities and incidents that might detract from it.

In another of the *Philippic Orations* Cicero feels prompted to explain that, contrary to his previous support for peace, he does not approve of peace with

7 On a single occasion Cicero seems to divide up material over several connected speeches, rather than repeating or interpreting what he said previously. In the *Agrarian Orations* (63 BCE) Cicero says in the speech in the Senate (*Leg. agr.* 1.21) about a particular argument that he will not deal with it in this speech, but will reserve it for the speech in the *contio* (*Leg. agr.* 2). This remark has been read as an allusion to an arrangement of these speeches as a corpus or as an element of an extended *praeteritio* (see Classen 1985, 367).

Mark Antony (*Phil.* 7.7–8). Because it means a move away from what he argued for in the past and what is regarded as the general preference, he expresses the new view in a long and complex sentence with a number of parenthetical comments and explanations before he reveals the main point at the very end. There is no reference to a particular preceding oratorical situation; instead, there is a comment on the general attitude emerging from Cicero's previous utterances and writings. Apparently, Cicero intends to create a coherent persona or at least to make changes of mind and policy plausible. Within the *Philippic Orations* Cicero comes back to the issue in later speeches and points out that there can only be apparent peace with Mark Antony and that he therefore opposed such a peace from the start of the conflict (*Phil.* 13.1–7; 14.20). Such remarks explain Cicero's position in relation to Mark Antony and make it appear consistent within this conflict.

Within the corpus of the *Agrarian Orations*, delivered when Cicero has just entered office as consul (63 BCE), Cicero notes at the beginning of the *Third Agrarian Oration*, given before the People, that he is forced to make this speech in justification of himself since false rumours had been spread about him and consequently some members of the audience had changed their attitude towards him in comparison with the *Second Agrarian Oration*, his inaugural speech to the People (*Leg. agr.* 3.1–3). While Cicero thereby justifies this speech and presents himself as the victim of something he will refute immediately, the reminder of the previous favourable attitude among the People (at least according to Cicero) suggests obliquely that there is no reason for a change of mind since Cicero is still their champion.

Comments on different oratorical appearances may also illustrate the orator's attitude over an extended period of time: after Cicero had established a reputation for himself as a defence advocate in his youth, he undertook his first prosecution in the trial against Verres in 70 BCE. In the *Divinatio in Caecilium*, the speech delivered during the selection of the preferred prosecutor before the actual trial, Cicero comments that he has acted for the defence for many years and people might therefore wonder why he is now aiming to act for the prosecution (*Div. in Caec.* 1). Here Cicero does not refer to a specific instance or a particular oratorical appearance, but rather to his oratorical career more generally: he acknowledges that his past behaviour in court cases has endowed him with a certain persona; as this is connected with the production of a particular type of speeches, it implies a reference to the (defence) speeches given so far and an indication that he is ready to go on to produce something different. The change of oratorical genre is not a mere literary decision, but rather prompted by the political circumstances. A similar justification, though not as elaborate since the situation is not as delicate, is offered when Cicero explains that he is giving his first speech before the People after becoming praetor in 66 BCE (*Leg. Man.* 2), as opposed to his previous speeches as an advocate.

Equally, where appropriate, Cicero emphasizes connections between his political appearances, usually with the implication that, as he was successful in the past, he will be so again in the present or future, and thus again works towards creating a consistent oratorical and political persona. For example, Cicero opens *Philippic Two*, composed in autumn 44 BCE, with the consideration that for the past twenty years nobody was an enemy of the Republic who was not also an enemy of Cicero; as the continuation of the argument reveals, he compares his present enemy Mark Antony to Catiline and Clodius in the past (*Phil.* 2.1). Later in the conflict Cicero claims that the People declared at a *contio* that by his initiatives against Mark Antony he had preserved the Republic a second time (*Phil.* 6.2). The point of comparison consists in his efforts in connection with the Catilinarian Conspiracy in 63 BCE; in the *Third Catilinarian Oration* Cicero reports to the People that he had been honoured for preserving the Republic (*Cat.* 3.15).

Cicero is able to link interventions at different times and against different individuals in this fashion, since he regards all his major opponents in a similar way and follows a comparable strategy in confronting them. He does not regard their different opinions or their planned activities as indications of structural problems or of the existence of different factions; instead he isolates these men as awful, non-human individuals who threaten the political system of the Republic. In response, he argues that these individuals will have to be eliminated; afterwards a return to the traditional and established system will be possible.

Accordingly, even if Cicero does not explicitly refer to the conflict with one opponent in a speech against another, there are intratextual connections owing to comparable tactics. This applies, for instance, to the speeches against Catiline in 63 BCE and those against Mark Antony in 44–43 BCE. Cicero does claim in one of the *Philippics* that Mark Antony is similar to Catiline only in crime, but not in industry (*Phil.* 4.15); yet this is meant to serve the argumentative purpose to make defeating Antony seem more achievable rather than indicating a major difference. Generally, the characterization of the two men and the arguments against them are comparable, though they are adapted to the different situations in that Mark Antony is commanding armies outside Rome while Catiline is stirring up a revolution within the city.

In both cases Cicero sets the great societal, juridical and political values offered by his side against the criminal and despicable features offered by the others (e.g. *Cat.* 2.25; *Phil.* 8.8–10). For each of the two men Cicero describes their negative character, demonstrated particularly by their sexual licentiousness and their squandering of money (e.g. *Cat.* 2.8; 2.10; *Phil.* 2.45; 2.67). Cicero stresses that the opponents cannot be regarded as Roman citizens and not even as human beings, rather as enemies and beasts (e.g. *Cat.* 2.12; 4.10; *Phil.* 3.12; 3.28; 4.12; 5.21; 6.7). Moreover, it is emphasized that it is not only they themselves who are of appalling character, but that they also surround themselves with followers who are like them or even worse (e.g. *Cat.* 2.7; *Phil.* 6.4).

4 References to speeches in letters

Since Cicero the orator was also a writer of letters and talks about his oratorical activity in letters (which in this context then assume the function of paratexts), there are cross-references across genres, and remarks on speeches in letters reveal details about the production process and how Cicero wanted them to be seen.

For instance, Cicero had an epistolary conversation with his friend M. Iunius Brutus about the *Philippics* (44–43 BCE): the preserved elements of the correspondence show that Cicero sent some of the speeches from this conflict to Brutus and jokingly called them '*Philippics*', presumably after the model of Demosthenes (*Att.* 2.1.3). Brutus confirmed that the two speeches he had read were of a quality to deserve this title and approved its use (*Ad Brut.* 2.3.4), so that Cicero gladly employed the name when sending another speech from the group (*Ad Brut.* 2.4.2). While this discussion is separated from the text of the speeches, in the context of Cicero's entire oeuvre it adds a further dimension to the orations: it demonstrates that Cicero wanted these speeches to be seen as comparable to those by Demosthenes, though it remains open whether this refers to the style, the respective political situation, or both.

Brutus' comments do not address details of these orations. Cicero's epistolary conversations with Atticus, on the other hand, include discussions of factual issues and individual stylistic points in orations (*Att.* 1.13.5; 15.13.1; 15.13.7 [= 15.13a.3]; 16.11.1–2). Cicero sometimes feels prompted to make changes in response to Atticus' suggestions; he almost expects him to provide such comments, uses him as a sounding board and is anxious with respect to Atticus' 'red pen' (*Att.* 16.11.1). Such conversations give insight into the production process and demonstrate that the text of speeches eventually circulated is not a spontaneous effusion, but one that has gone through several drafts and may incorporate suggestions from other people besides the author. The reflection of this process in Cicero's correspondence also means that some of the intratextual links across works do not refer to finished works, but their earlier stages. Since

Cicero may not have intended to publish all his letters to Atticus, it is not certain whether this phase of the composition process was meant to be an element of Cicero's public literary persona. At the same time this testimony demonstrates the care taken over the published version of speeches and thus the importance of this aspect as an element within Cicero's presentation of himself.

Atticus is also the addressee to whom Cicero sends a selection of speeches delivered in his consular year with an accompanying letter in 60 BCE; these he regards as his *orationes consulares* and as illustrating what he did and what he said as consul (*Att.* 2.1.3). The collection of these orations and the corresponding comments indicate that, despite some mock modesty, Cicero considered these speeches to be oratorically sophisticated and politically significant, and that he saw a close connection between his oratorical interventions and his political achievements. The list of consular orations given may encourage readers to see connections between speeches that they otherwise might not have linked apart from their shared date. In a later speech Cicero provides an overview of achievements during his consulship to distinguish himself from his opponent. In this context he mentions activities and results that are all linked to oratorical appearances; thus this summary functions as a kind of review of his major oratorical successes during his consulship (*Pis.* 3–5). By not letting them stand for themselves, but rather adding a particular presentation elsewhere in his oeuvre, the interpretation of these interventions and speeches becomes determined for later recipients, and they are explicitly integrated into the creation of Cicero's persona.

5 References to speeches in rhetorical treatises

Cicero as an author of rhetorical treatises could be regarded as different from Cicero the orator, though he writes on the basis of his own experience. Yet Cicero creates a link between the two as he frequently refers to examples from his own speeches in his rhetorical treatises; he thus in some way follows the principles outlined in the preface to book four of the anonymous *Rhetorica ad Herennium*, where the author argues that it is better to use one's own examples when explaining oratorical features, though he seems to think rather of invented examples (*Rhet. Her.* 4.1–10). Cicero's oeuvre can provide the required examples: he claims in the treatise *Orator* (46 BCE) that 'there is no kind of oratorical merit which is not found in our orations, if not in perfection, at least attempted and adumbrated' (trans. H.M. Hubbell), though this is qualified by comments in mock modesty. In the same context Cicero says that he does not quote detailed examples from his speeches since they are well known or easy to find (*Orat.* 102–104); such an assessment conveys confidence in his status as a well-known orator and indicates the view that intratextual references may help to build up a reputation.

These remarks follow after general comments on some of his speeches, illustrating the variety of styles used. Cicero says about the speech *De imperio Cn. Pompei* (66 BCE) that 'the task was to glorify Pompeius' and about *Pro Rabirio perduellionis reo* (63 BCE) that 'the whole principle of maintaining the dignity of the republic was at stake' (trans. H.M. Hubbell). These descriptions do not identify the legal issues addressed in these speeches; they rather single out the aspects Cicero chose to highlight when he turned these speeches into elements within a political controversy. The backward reference in the rhetorical treatise enables him to make this explicit and thus give pointers to the preferred reading.

Again, however, although the rhetorical treatises have less of an immediate political agenda than public speeches, the comments on earlier orations there convey a particular interpretation and therefore do not always match what Cicero says elsewhere. In *Orator*, when Cicero illustrates the effects of his vigorous style in dislodging opponents (*Orat.* 129), he claims that Catiline was struck dumb when accused by him in the Senate in 63 BCE, while he says elsewhere (*Mur.* 51 [63 BCE]) that Catiline made an answer (cf. also Sall. *Cat.* 31.6–32.1). The version in *Orator* is not necessarily a complete misrepresentation. Cicero stresses the overwhelming effect, since Catiline left the Senate immediately after his reply and did not meet with a favourable reception among the senators; thus Cicero disregards the initial reaction and emphasizes the effect of his own speech. A tendentious representation might become easier at some distance from the event; at any rate it contributes to creating an image of a successful Cicero for posterity.

Elsewhere in *Orator* Cicero provides examples from his speeches and quotes passages verbatim, almost exactly in the form in which they are transmitted for the speeches; he must have either remembered these phrases or had access to written versions (*Orat.* 107–108; 167; 225). On one of these occasions Cicero distances himself from his youthful exuberance (cf. *Brut.* 316), but still notes the applause received (*Orat.* 107–108). The repetition of these passages in the rhetorical treatise makes them more widely known and suggests that Cicero felt confident to promote them.

Some comments do not refer to particular speeches or phrases in speeches, but rather to an oratorical situation including the provoking of emotions in the audience by textual and paratextual elements. To illustrate the necessity to arouse the emotions of the audience, Cicero mentions his accusation speeches against Verres and his defence speeches. He obviously thinks that the written text sufficiently indicates the emotional atmosphere created by the speeches and that these orations are known or easily accessible to the audience of the dialogue.

Again he concludes the argument by stressing the variety in his speeches and their suitability as examples (*Orat.* 131–132). This method is a convenient way of providing an overview of his output and his abilities as an orator, and of indicating the breadth covered without taking the audience through a substantial sample of speeches, though they may thereby be encouraged to read some.

Similarly, elsewhere, Cicero does not quote extracts, but rather refers to passages from his speeches, briefly defined by their topics, as examples of instances where the use of rhythmical prose is appropriate (*Orat.* 210). Again Cicero stresses the variety of patterns in his orations, though he apologizes for this in mock modesty. He seems to assume that the audience is familiar with the details of the passages and to regard them as well-developed pieces. Since the examples mostly come from the second action against Verres, which was not delivered, Cicero would have had the chance to produce elaborate versions and the text would have been available in writing. The comments help to highlight aspects of the speeches that otherwise might have gone unnoticed, and to present Cicero as an orator who not only makes the appropriate argument in a political or juridical situation, but is also technically accomplished.

6 Conclusion

While some of the intratextual connections within individual speeches or across several speeches pointed out for Cicero in this brief overview might be regarded as general features of sophisticated oratory, the available evidence means that Cicero is the only Roman orator for whom they can be explored and interpreted as well as supplemented by comments in other literary genres. While it is known from remarks by ancient writers that other orators too had certain habits and preferred topics in composing their speeches,[8] these descriptions cannot be verified by surviving examples, and it is therefore uncertain whether such repetitions had a particular aim in the composition of each speech or across a person's oratorical and political or juridical activity. For Cicero, however, the extant material demonstrates that he exploits the opportunities provided by intratextual links, cross-references, self-comments and allusions both to further the argumentative aim of the respective pieces of writing and, across his oeuvre, to create a consistent

8 Quintilian records that the openings of many speeches by M. Valerius Messalla Corvinus included claims that he was weak, unprepared and no match for the talents of the opposing party (Quint. *Inst.* 4.1.8).

image of an oratorical persona, who produces highly-wrought, sought-after specimens of oratory and employs these successfully in political and juridical situations for the benefit of his countrymen and the Republic.[9]

Since, obviously, Cicero pursues a political agenda in his speeches, cross-references are not only determined by literary considerations, but also governed by political circumstances. Therefore Cicero may refer back to an earlier speech and its effect on a later occasion, but not accurately represent what he originally said since he exploits the renewed reference to give the earlier instance a particular interpretation conducive to his overall current aim. This may even trigger a reverse effect, so that recipients looking at the original text read it as Cicero later presented it when they have seen his interpretation first. Such references can be found in the later speeches within groups or in letters belonging roughly to the same period, when Cicero starts to comment on his oratorical appearances while the process is still ongoing, presumably to influence the next steps. Or they may occur in texts produced considerably later, presumably triggered by a concern to create a particular image for posterity.

In various works Cicero defines himself as an orator employing words as opposed to others using weapons; he thus creates a persona for himself based on separately available oratorical utterances (*Red. pop.* 20; *Fam.* 12.22.1). A qualitative element is added when he claims that he publishes written versions of his speeches, as he has been encouraged to do so by the enthusiasm of young men, and thus provides stylistic models (*Att.* 2.1.3; 4.2.2; *Brut.* 122–123). A similar effect of portraying himself as an accomplished and respected orator is achieved when Cicero reports the positive reaction to his speeches and indicates the hard work that has gone into composing them (*Brut.* 312). That Cicero establishes himself as an orator also on the basis of his written speeches becomes apparent when he refers to the available text of a speech as an example without mentioning further details (*Off.* 2.51). Such comments indicate that he regards all his oratorical works and the references to them as combining to create his oratorical persona.

Looking at Cicero's speeches from an intratextual point of view thus demonstrates how Cicero constantly works on creating a consistent image of himself as a successful and trustworthy orator and politician. Therefore one may conclude that intratextuality in the oeuvre of a politically active writer and applied to texts with a pragmatic function enhances the impression of unity and adds to the literary texture of the work, but predominantly is a convenient tool of controlling

9 Cicero's recognized fondness for the clausula *esse videatur* (Tac. *Dial.* 23.1) is too much of a technical element as to be relevant for a discussion of intratextuality.

reactions of the audience and —equally importantly in Cicero's case— of self-representation.[10]

Bibliography

Broich, U. (1985), 'Bezugsfelder der Intertextualität. Zur Einzeltextreferenz', in: U. Broich/M. Pfister (eds.), *Intertextualität. Formen, Funktionen, anglistische Fallstudien*, Tübingen (Konzepte der Sprach- und Literaturwissenschaft), 48–52.

Chandler, D./Munday, R. (eds.) (2001), *A Dictionary of Media and Communication*, Oxford.

Classen, C.J. (1985), *Recht – Rhetorik – Politik. Untersuchungen zu Ciceros rhetorischer Strategie*, Darmstadt; Italian translation: *Diritto, retorica, politica. La strategia retorica di Cicerone*, Bologna 1998 (Collezione di testi e studi, Linguistica e critica letteraria).

Edmunds, L. (2004), 'Review Article: Intratextuality: The Parts, The Wholes, and the Holes', *Vergilius* 50, 158–169.

Fox, M. (2000), 'Dialogue and Irony in Cicero: Reading *De Republica*', in: A. Sharrock/H. Morales (eds.), *Intratextuality. Greek and Roman Textual Relations*, Oxford, 263–286.

Hall, J. (2008 [2009]), 'The Rhetorical Design and Success of Cicero's *Twelfth Philippic*', in: T. Stevenson/M. Wilson (eds.), *Cicero's Philippics: History, Rhetoric and Ideology*, *Prudentia* 37 & 38, 282–304.

Sharrock, A./Morales, H. (eds.) (2000), *Intratextuality. Greek and Roman Textual Relations*, Oxford.

Sharrock, A. (2000), 'Intratextuality: Texts, Parts, and (W)holes in Theory', in: A. Sharrock/H. Morales (eds.), *Intratextuality. Greek and Roman Textual Relations*, Oxford, 1–39.

10 That 'intratextuality' has a political dimension was adumbrated in the volume edited by Sharrock/Morales (2000), but the potential manifestations were not explored within the scope of the case studies offered in that collection.

Therese Fuhrer

On the Economy of 'Sending and Receiving Information' in Roman Historiography

By the expression 'sending and receiving information' I am drawing on a term from the drama theory of Manfred Pfister (in German: *Informationsvergabe*) which is used to describe the communication structures internal and external to a drama or text and different degrees of 'awareness' (*Informiertheit*) and knowledge.[1] My adoption of theory and method from drama analysis for the analysis of historiographical texts can be justified as follows.

Firstly it is well known that ancient, and especially Roman, history-writing makes use of elements of structure and content drawn from drama; I am thinking primarily of Hayden White's thesis that by 'emplotment' the 'what' of the 'story' is given a logical and causal structure, and the 'why' of the occurrences is illuminated.[2] By dramatic structuring of a historical event, certain elements and episodes can be set in relation to each other, given meaning, and given a symbolic weight too. A semantically charged structure of this kind distinguishes the literary text from a mere report or from a presentation of the history of events that conforms to present-day scholarly criteria, which are not, or at least not *per se*, structured by an intratextual system of references.

Secondly the 'transmission of information' —not only within the context of drama theory— is one of the central tasks of historiography. However, in this case, the focus is on factual information that is delivered, on the one hand, to figures within the historical action represented, who —generally— exist in reality, and on the other hand to an audience interested in historical facts.

In what follows, consequently, I will try to describe the techniques of sending and receiving information in the representation of factual occurrences. In the title of my paper I speak of the 'economy of sending and receiving information' because my concern is to ask at which points in the text which and how much information is sent or received, which figures in the historiographical narrative are equipped with which knowledge and which 'point of view' is ascribed to them, to what extent an informational advantage and so a 'discrepant awareness' (*diskrepante Informiertheit*) arises among the actors internal to the text or with

1 See chapter 3, entitled 'Sending and receiving information', in Pfister ²1991, 40–102.
2 Best on this is Martínez/Scheffel ⁹2012, 155–9.

https://doi.org/10.1515/9783110611021-026

reference to the recipients (the readership),[3] and to what extent these differing degrees of knowledge are relevant for the production of a 'narrative meaning'.[4]

My study thus picks up a specific concern of research into intratextuality, namely the issue of what 'new' significance is created by a web of textual elements within the text as a whole, or a larger unit within it, that is not made explicit (for example through cross-references). For the analysis of historiographical texts this means, specifically: in what way is a piece of factual information charged with meaning, and 'repropositionalised', by the fact of its being revealed at several different points in a historical narrative?[5] I am thus asking to what extent the parallel and sequential positioning of statements that give information about a particular historical occurrence is relevant to the interpretation of the event represented in each case.[6] Taking the example of Sallust's *Bellum Catilinarium* I wish to show how a historiographical text can be re-semanticised by the economy of sending and receiving information, that is, how historical facts can be re-semanticised by the arrangement and breaking up (*hyperbaton*) of certain pieces of information, on the one hand, and on the other their juxtaposition alongside other pieces of information and the consequent creation of interfaces with other chains of events.

At the centre of the sequence of actions I have chosen from Sallust's monograph is Cicero's election as consul in 64 BC, through which Catiline's candidacy failed for a second time,[7] Catiline's second attempt and second defeat in 63 during Cicero's consulate, and the planning of the putsch and attempted assassination of Cicero (chapters 23–28). It thus concerns the questions of how the historian presents and arranges these particular events which were familiar to his readers both in his own time and in ours, what contexts he links them to, and what cast of characters he is working with. As well as the two protagonists in this episode,

3 On this see Pfister [2]1991, 49–56.

4 The term is taken from Martínez/Scheffel [9]2012, 157. See also Grethlein 2013, 1–26, who enquires specifically into the teleological sense of historiographical narrative; in my analysis, presented here, of a passage from Sallust's *Coniuratio*, however, the focus is on precisely the questioning of such a sense of history, or, to put it differently, the *telos* is interpreted as a collapse of order. Apt for my interpretation of the text is, rather, the remark of Sharrock 2000, 12: 'Intratextual irony may undermine the apparent monologic meaning of the text'.

5 So Sharrock 2000, 4 n. 8, with reference to Grigely 1995.

6 In contrast to the question of intertextual references to other texts, which are perceptible as hypotexts in the hypertext under investigation, in the investigation of the intratextual structuring the question of hyper- and hypotext remains open, or is not posed, since the two levels coincide; the hypotext that becomes effective at a particular point is at the same time the hypertext.

7 Still the best on this is Wimmel 1967; cf. also the brief summary of the factual details in Ramsey [2]2007, 15–21.

Cicero and Catiline, Sallust brings on stage the couple Q. Curius and Fulvia and – as it were, as a representative of other female figures– Sempronia. This lady Fulvia is not the famous wife of Clodius Pulcher, Scribonius Curio, and Mark Antony, but a lover of the conspirator Q. Curius,[8] who shall play the role of informant to Cicero in the course of the uncovering of the Catilinarian conspiracy.[9] In Sallust's monograph she is cast in the shade by Sempronia, whose captivating portrait is inserted after the report of Cicero's election as consul in 64 BC;[10] yet Fulvia's 'historical' significance becomes far more important for the dramaturgy of the events than that of the famous Sempronia, through the brief but repeated mentions of her, which can therefore be set in relation to each other.

The brief 'Fulvia narrative', which has not received much attention in research to date, immediately follows the famous 'blood scene' with which Sallust ends the gathering of the conspirators in 64 (*Catil.* 17 and 20–22), and immediately before the report of the election result (24) and the portrait of Sempronia (25), in *Catil.* 23:

> (1) Sed in ea coniuratione fuit Q. Curius ... (3) Erat ei cum Fulvia, muliere nobili, stupri vetus consuetudo. Quoi cum minus gratus esset, quia inopia minus largiri poterat, repente glorians maria montisque polliceri coepit et minari interdum ferro, ni sibi obnoxia foret, postremo ferocius agitare quam solitus erat. (4) At Fulvia insolentiae Curi causa cognita tale periculum rei publicae haud occultum habuit, sed sublato auctore de Catilinae coniuratione, quae quoque modo audierat, compluribus narravit.

> (1) Now one of the members of the conspiracy was Q. Curius ... (3) Fulvia, an aristocratic woman, had been his partner in promiscuity for some time, but he was no longer in her favour, because his limited resources had made him less generous. Suddenly he began to swagger and promise oceans and mountains, and to threaten her occasionally with his sword if she did not yield to him. Ultimately, he became much more ferocious than had been his custom. (4) But when Fulvia discovered the cause of Curius' abusiveness, she did not keep secret such a danger to the Republic. Hiding the name of her informant, she told many the details she had heard about Catiline's conspiracy.[11]

The member of the conspiracy Q. Curius, no longer able to meet the high financial demands of his lover Fulvia, makes promises to her, painting a prospect of immeasurable riches; at the same time he threatens her with violence when she

---

8 On this person cf. Ramsey ^{2}2007, 106.

9 The dates and 'facts' on Fulvia are surveyed by Pagán 2004, 41–6 and 144 n. 45 (with references to the sources) and Ramsey ^{2}2007, 128f.

10 The portrait also has the structural function of bridging the chronological jump into the year 63; on this see Ramsey ^{2}2007, 132.

11 The translation here and in what follows is that of Batstone 2010.

won't let him 'have his way with her'. When Fulvia discovers the reason for Curius' unwonted 'wild' (§ 3: *ferocius quam solitus*) and also improper behaviour (§ 4: *insolentia*), she tells several people what she has heard of the *Catilinae coniuratio*. By this, Sallust says, she made a decisive contribution to Cicero's electoral victory (§ 5): 'It was this event (*ea res*) that made men particularly eager to entrust the consulship to Cicero'.[12] The Roman nobility, now that they have seen the danger, are prepared to set aside both their resentment of the *homo novus* Cicero and their own pride (§ 6).

Through the fact that Fulvia has for years had an unmarried relationship with Q. Curius (§ 3: *stupri vetus consuetudo*) and has an interest in his financial solvency, she is characterised, like Sempronia, as an ideal-type of Rome's decadent society, but she is more than just another symptom of the ills of the state. Her appearance in the drama is given the role of a 'plot point' at both intra- and extradiegetic level by the fact that her revelations —intradiegetically— change the voters' picture of the candidate Sergius Catilina, and —extradiegetically, that is, in relation to the readers— unmask the social arrogance but also the fearfulness and self-interested thinking of the Roman elite.[13]

Fulvia, as a *mulier nobilis* (23.3), is herself a part of this decadent social stratum, the women of which are discredited yet further by the information that is placed ahead of the Sempronia chapter: Catiline —after his electoral defeat in 64— was counting on the greed of the women, whose habituation to luxury meant they could be bought; Catiline had wanted to make use of this in his plans for the putsch (*Catil.* 24.3f.).[14] Fulvia, moved by the same urge, had pushed her lover Curius to make promises to her and so, indirectly, to join Catiline. The fact that in Sallust's narrative it is precisely this figure who brings about Cicero's electoral victory, and so the suppression of the conspiracy,[15] is surely not insignificant and requires explanation, especially as Fulvia's part in Sallust's plot is not yet over.

---

12 23.5: *Ea res in primis studia hominum accendit ad consulatum mandandum M. Tullio Ciceroni.*

13 The term and concept of the 'plot point' derives from Field ^{4}2005, whose reflections on the screenplay are also illuminating for the analysis of literary texts.

14 24.3f.: *Mulieres etiam aliquot, quae primo ingentis sumptus stupro corporis toleraverant, post, ubi aetas tantummodo quaestui neque luxuriae modum fecerat, aes alienum grande conflaverant.* (4) *Per eas se Catilina credebat posse servitia urbana sollicitare, urbem incendere, viros earum vel adiungere sibi vel interficere.*

15 Ramsey ^{2}2007, 129f. evidently refers *ea res* to the voters' fear of Catiline, citing Appian (*Civ.* 2.2) and Plutarch (*Cic.* 11.2). Through the phrase *ea res in primis*, however, which can be related only to the preceding episode, what is decisive for Cicero's election in Sallust's text is not the fear of the conspiracy but the treachery of Fulvia, and consequently that which prompts the fear. That is jarring and is probably meant to be so; cf. Batstone 2010, 165 *ad loc.*: 'this is unlikely

At first Catiline evidently still intends to take power by legal means, and once again stands for the consulate in 63, as we are told straight after the Sempronia chapter; he relies on the support of Cicero's fellow consul C. Antonius and plots against Cicero (*Catil.* 26.1: *insidias parabat Ciceroni*). However, Cicero himself is no less devious (26.2f):

> (2) Neque illi tamen ad cavendum dolus aut astutiae deerant. (3) Namque a principio consulatus sui multa pollicendo per Fulviam effecerat, ut Q. Curius, de quo paulo ante memoravi, consilia Catilinae sibi proderet.

> (2) But, Cicero had sufficient guile and cunning to avoid them [i.e. the traps]. (3) At the beginning of his consulship, he made many promises and, through Fulvia, got Q. Curius, whom I mentioned above, to betray Catiline's plans to him.[16]

'With many promises' and 'through Fulvia' (*per Fulviam*) Cicero —who is now the serving consul— is able to get Curius to betray Catiline's plans to him. The result is well known: Cicero brings C. Antonius over to his side by swapping provinces, Catiline loses the election, and decides 'to go to war' (26.5: *constituit bellum facere*). In the night of November 6, in the house of Laeca, the assassination of Cicero is planned for the next morning (27.2–4). When Curius realises the danger the consul is in, he urgently warns him 'through Fulvia' (*per Fulviam*, 28.2):

> *Curius ubi intellegit, quantum periculum consuli inpendeat, propere per Fulviam Ciceroni dolum, qui parabatur, enuntiat.*

> When Curius heard the extent of the danger that hung over the consul, he quickly told Cicero through Fulvia of the treachery that was underway.

The assassination attempt fails (28.3). After the information, already given in ch. 26, that Cicero had by 'many promises through Fulvia' (*multa pollicendo per Fulviam*) got the conspirator Curius to betray Catiline's plans before the election (26.3), the phrase *per Fulviam*, repeated once again, reads like a reference to a well-worn procedure: Cicero is paying for information that Curius communicates to him through Fulvia, and in this way Curius is able to meet the demands of the

---

the sole reason for Cicero's success ... It is more likely that his success depended upon his skill as an advocate, his connections with leading members of the towns and Senate, and his contacts among the mercantile class.'

16 Here I have altered Batstone's translation, which makes Q. Curius the object of *multa pollicendo* ('he made many promises through Fulvia to Q. Curius'). The Latin text is ambiguous; it is only the intratextual reference to 23.3 (Curius ... *maria montisque polliceri coepit*) that makes Fulvia, rather, appear receptive to, and hence the recipient of, promises.

courtesan after all. Whereas in the first case Cicero exerts influence on Curius *per Fulviam*, in the second case it is Curius who informs Cicero *per Fulviam*.

In the dramaturgy of Sallust's depiction, at both 'plot points' Fulvia makes a decisive contribution to the fact that Catiline's plans were foiled in Rome. In Sallust's report she is the decisive pivot in the deflection of the 'danger' (23.4/28.2: *periculum*), and hence in saving the state and/or the consul Cicero; she is —within the text— responsible for communicating the decisive information. She does not do this from pure concern for the state or for the consul, but, as the intervening insertion of the portrait of Sempronia insinuates, because she represents the type of woman who, in order to maintain her extravagant lifestyle, could just as easily be instrumentalised by Catiline: she is spoilt, selfish, opportunistic, and venal, but now to the advantage of the state and/or Cicero, who, just like Catiline, takes advantage of this 'feminine weakness'. The procedure of sending and receiving information described in the text explains Cicero's advantage in knowledge, his electoral victory, and his rescue from Catiline's assassination attempt through his contact with a politically and historically insignificant (and fictitious?) figure, who takes on the role of pillar of the state, not in a moral sense but in a dramaturgical sense.

However, the process of sending and receiving information can be described succinctly also at the extra-textual level: through the few appearances that Sallust's text grants to this woman, who appears, as it were, like a 'pop-up' within the historical report of facts, Cicero and Fulvia are brought into a remarkable proximity —the consul and the courtesan, who ultimately come into direct contact. She is Cicero's confidante and this is made clear twice over through her dramaturgically important role (26.2/28.2: *per Fulviam*). The echoing repetition *per Fulviam* sets up an intratextual reference by which the narrative insinuates or —if we prefer not to ascribe a single meaning to the text— allows the inference that the consul and the demi-monde are collaborating. As this is an adulteress (23.3), the text also permits further speculations about the reciprocal relation of the pair, which however cannot be connected to either the literary picture of Cicero or the historical Cicero detectable through the sources.[17] However, with Fulvia's occasional 'stage appearances' ahead of Cicero's election at the climax of the crisis, the achievements of the 'great hero' are at the least relativised.[18]

---

17 According to Diod. 40.5 Fulvia reported what Curius had said to Cicero's wife Terentia; cf. Pagán 2004, 43f.

18 Here one can speak, with Malcolm Heath, of a 'centripetal way of reading', that is, of the attribution of 'symbolic or thematic relevance into the[ir] details', so Sharrock 2000, 17 (where 'their' refers to the 'ancient poets'' 'details').

The information management set up in the text, or, that is, the communicative economy of apparently marginal pieces of information addressed to the readers, their sparing positioning at certain points in the historiographical and, at the primary level, fact-oriented narrative, also suggest a certain interpretation of the historical occurrences: the key figures upholding the late Republic are not in a position to lead the state or save it, never mind to reform it.

Bibliography

Edition

C. Sallusti Crispi Catilina, Iugurtha, Historiarum Fragmenta Selecta, Appendix Sallustiana, rec. L.D. Reynolds, Oxford 1991.

Translation

Sallust, Catiline's Conspiracy, The Jugurthine War, Histories. A new translation by W.W. Batstone, Oxford 2010.

Books and Articles

Field, S. (^{4}2005), *Screenplay: The Foundations of Screenwriting*, New York.
Grethlein, J. (2013), *Experience and Teleology in Ancient Historiography. 'Futures Past' from Herodotus to Augustine*, Cambridge.
Grigely, J. (1995), *Textualterity: Art, Theory, and Textual Criticism*, Ann Arbor.
Martínez, M./Scheffel, M. (^{9}2012), *Einführung in die Erzähltheorie*, München.
Pagán, V.E. (2004), *Conspiracy Narratives in Roman History*, Austin.
Pfister, M. (^{2}1991), *The Theory and Analysis of Drama*, Cambridge.
Ramsey, J.T. (^{2}2007), *Sallust's bellum Catilinae*, edited with Introduction and Commentary, Oxford.
Sharrock, A. (2000), 'Intratextuality: Texts, Parts, and (W)holes in Theory', in: A. Sharrock/H. Morales (eds.), *Intratextuality. Greek and Roman Textual Relations*, Oxford, 1–39.
Wimmel, W. (1967), 'Die zeitlichen Vorwegnahmen in Sallusts "Catilina"', *Hermes* 95, 102–221.

Ulrike Egelhaaf-Gaiser

Saturnalian Riddles for Attic Nights: Intratextual Feasting with Aulus Gellius

1 Introduction: The problem

If the present volume were to be concerned with forms of intertextuality, the choice of an author such as Aulus Gellius would be self-explanatory. In the preface to the *Attic Nights*, the first-person narrator describes the careful sifting of numerous writings, the thoughtful excerpt, and the compilation of suitable scraps of information and 'common knowledge' as the defining features of his compendium[1] —which he offers as a service to very busy readers, who have only a limited amount of time at their disposal, and who therefore depend on the easy accessibility of a useful, and appealing, selection of literary excerpts.[2]

In view of these self-declared intentions, the intertextual questions arising from the *Noctes Atticae* are obvious and have been discussed at length in the literature.[3] The question of *intratextuality* on the other hand —instances of cross-referencing within the work itself— has barely played any part at all.[4] This deficit could have been caused by the fact that the *praefatio* puts such a glaring emphasis on the needs of the selective reader, whose ability to access particular passages with precision and at his/her own convenience was moreover enhanced by

The present paper has been prepared as part of the Sub-Project C 02, 'The Ancients Before Their Eyes: Religious and Antiquarian Transfer of Knowledge in the Educational Compendia of the Second Century BC', within the Collaborative Research Centre (SFB/CRC) 1136: 'Learning and Religion' funded by the German Research Foundation (DFG). This article was originally composed in German; I would like to thank Tina Jerke (Giessen) for the English translation.

1 Gel. *praef.* 2; cf. Gel. *praef.* 11.

2 Gel. *praef.* 12.

3 On the source criticism Mercklin 1860 and Holford-Strevens 2003, 65–80; Pausch 2004, 147–8 on the earlier research history; Astarita 1993, 28–31 attempts a hypothetical reconstruction of Gellius' method for creating and structuring his excerpts.

4 With this understanding of intratextuality in a narrow sense I follow the distinction underlined by Stocker 1998, 59, between intratextuality (internal relations within a text) and intertextuality (external relations with other texts). Accordingly, the definition suggested by Sharrock 2000, 10: 'intratextuality is offered in this volume as a way, albeit partial, of negotiating one's way around the textual system' would have to be amended to 'around the textual system *within one particular work of literature.*'

https://doi.org/10.1515/9783110611021-027

the inclusion of a table of contents and chapter headings.[5] Such a seemingly single-purpose presentation inevitably calls into question the very existence of intratextual connections beyond the undisputed referential axis of primary text and paratext[6] within the *Noctes Atticae* —and whether they can possibly perform their function in a situation where the text, as a rule, is not digested in its entirety. The problem is exacerbated by the insistence with which the author, in his preface, points to the arbitrary nature of his collection and the miscellaneous character of its content.[7] The apparently randomized sequence of the material in the *Noctes Atticae* contradicts the conventional principle of a linear progression in the material, and in the reader's experience of it.[8]

In my contribution, I would like to take a detailed look at the question of intratextuality, as it is exemplified in four *commentarii* that share a common theme through their interest in riddles. The focus will be on four forms of intratextual reference: 1. The relationship between chapter heading (*caput*) and body text, 2. The practice of providing missing information at a later location in the same chapter, 3. The deliberate fragmentation of thematic units[9] through the dispersal of related information over two separate commentaries, and 4. The option of a sequential study of the work across several books, as suggested by the list of contents first encountered by the newly recruited reader.

Our case study therefore aims to establish which of the mechanisms for orientation and reader guidance can be found in a miscellaneous volume such as the *Noctes Atticae*. This in turn poses the question whether in a fragmented work of this kind, dominated by excerpts, the creation of unity is in fact a key motivation.[10] Additionally, we need to verify the efficiency of the paratextual assistance offered for navigating the *Noctes Atticae*, and to what extent it is supplemented — or sabotaged— by additional pointers, or 'signposts', *within* the commentaries. Certainly, the collection resembles a labyrinthine maze at times,[11] its winding

5 Gel. praef. 25: *capita rerum, quae cuique commentario insunt, exposuimus hic universa, ut iam statim declaretur, quid quo in libro quaeri invenirique possit.*

6 For my line of enquiry, the two relevant subcategories of paratextual elements, as proposed by Genette 2001, are the preface (Genette 2001, 157–227) and the intertitles (Genette 2001, 281–303).

7 Gel. *praef.* 2: *usi autem sumus ordine rerum fortuito, quem antea in excerpendo feceramus*; cf. *praef.* 3. For an introduction to the 'haphazard order' cf. Holford-Strevens 2003, 27–47; on the tradition of 'disorderly' miscellaneous literature Vardi 2004, 169–79.

8 On narrative linearity and its deliberate undermining in certain textual genres Sharrock 2000, 9.

9 On the technique of fragmentation in literary texts Sharrock 2000, 11 and 18–19.

10 On the search for unity as an intuitive reader expectation Sharrock 2000, 21–2.

11 On the labyrinthine structure of particular works and its effect on their textual reception Sharrock 2000, 9.

paths navigable only to those who are determined to pursue their own, rigorous trial and error strategy of exploration.

How reliable, then, is the guidance provided by the contents-list, by the chapter headings and cross-references, how certain can readers be that they will be shown the correct path to follow? Do they receive unambiguous signals when they have reached the conclusion of their journey, and they can abandon their search? Or is the text ultimately structured in such a way as to remain impenetrable, to lure readers ever deeper into its intricate architecture and to trap them inside for as long as possible?

It is my contention that the *Noctes Atticae* invites the reader to participate in a subtle *Ergänzungsspiel* ('play with supplementation').[12] Even though Gellius lays out a number of different paths through the apparent clutter of his unsorted material, ultimately he rewards the diligent reader rather than the hasty one. As we shall see, at least *some* of the commentaries undermine the declarations of their paratexts: not only do they offer new aspects and, in doing so, expand the readers' horizons; they also surprise them with 'missing' pieces of the larger puzzle they can insert into gaps encountered elsewhere in the commentaries.[13] Unexpected 'lucky' finds such as these, and the instant gratification they afford, to me appear to be a form of authorial incentive; they appeal to readers to immerse themselves in a wide-ranging study of the work. How much (metaphorical) water this theory will hold in specific instances can only be determined by a close reading of the text. Let us therefore take the next step and turn the spotlight on to the two commentaries which deal with the light-hearted puzzle games played during the festivities of the Saturnalia.

2 Saturnalian riddles for Attic Nights

The two commentaries on the Roman Saturnalia are particularly well suited for a case study as they encapsulate and illustrate, in a sense almost ideally, the cultural and literary manifesto of the *Noctes Atticae*. Before we examine the above-mentioned forms of intratextual references in detail, I would like to sketch out, briefly, the way in which the general declarations of the proem find particular

---

12 On the concept of the *Ergänzungsspiel* as applied to the Hellenistic epigram Bing 2009, 85–6.

13 As previously observed by Maselli 1993 and Schröder 1999, 111–12, the contents of the commentaries are by no means fully revealed in the headings. Simply reading the *capita* will therefore not give an accurate impression of the body text. However, no attempt has to date been made to associate this peculiarity of the Gellian titles with the mechanisms of the literary puzzle.

application in the specific situation of the Saturnalian banquet: the chosen festive occasion already marks an exceptional period, the *one* temporary phase where all *officia* of the daily professional routine remain suspended, and regular social rules and norms are in abeyance.[14] The Saturnalia are therefore predestined to provide even the most duty-burdened members of the educated élite with an opportunity to indulge in some leisurely literary relaxation.[15]

During the carnivalesque holiday period, all class barriers are ritually lifted but the members of the upper classes —in our case the Athenian students— are still able to use the religious occasion to bolster their own social status:[16] on the one hand the host and his guests meet as equals, in contravention of the order of precedence usually in place around the table,[17] which is reflected in the practice of mutual invitations (Gel. 18,2,3) and festive meals jointly financed (Gel. 18,13,4 and 6). On the other hand, the Roman students keep to themselves in their foreign Greek environment, and in demonstrative demarcation from the usual amusements associated with the festival —opulent feasts, colourful goings-on in the streets, cheap joke gifts, and boisterous games of dice[18]— they content themselves

14 The particular status of the Roman Saturnalia as an ancient form of carnival has been emphasized by numerous scholars: fundamental are Versnel 1993, 136–48 and 153–7; Scullard 1985, 287–90; Leary 2014, 8. Generally considered to be among the most significant features of the Saturnalia are their marked liminal qualities, an exuberant festive joy, complete with bacchanalian banquets and joke presents, the time-limited reversal of the social order, or at least the levelling of class boundaries, an indulgence in otherwise prohibited activities (e.g. games of dice), and the associated social 'safety-valve' function.

15 Cf. the *aliis negotiis occupati* in Gel. *praef.* 12. As previously noted by Keulen 2009, 40, exemplary discussions among Imperial scholars in the *Noctes Atticae* are explicitly, and with conspicuous frequency, set during the limited periods of *otium*, thus e.g. in Gel. 11,3,1; 14,5,1; 19,8,1 and 19,8,15; 19,9,1.

16 The attempt to achieve social distinction is particularly apparent in the introduction of Gel. 18,2,1, with not one but two references to the adequacy of the nightly entertainment programme, and the apologetic quotation from the philosopher Musonius: *Saturnalia Athenis agitabamus hilare prorsum ac modeste, non, ut dicitur, remittentes animum – nam 'remittere' inquit Musonius 'animum quasi amittere est' – sed demulcentes eum paulum atque laxantes iucundis honestisque sermonum inlectationibus*; a similar attitude is demonstrated in Plin. *Ep.* 2,17,24; Sen. *Ep.* 8,1–4.

17 Thus in Gel. 2,22 (symposium and patronizing after-dinner speech by Favorinus); Gel. 7,13 (literary 'presents' at the symposium of the philosopher Taurus); Gel. 17,8 (*quaestio convivialis* staged by the host Taurus in his own house).

18 An —albeit faintly sketched— tableau of the festive joys associated with the Saturnalia can be gleaned from Martial's epigrams and Lucian's *Saturnalia*, e.g. Mart. 11,2; 11,6; 11,15; 13,1; Lucian *Sat.* 2;4;18.

with a frugal meal[19] and 'amusing sophistries and enigmas', as befits their station.[20]

More than any other festival in Rome, the Saturnalia were linked to learning and literature.[21] As the first-person narrator of the *Noctes Atticae* points out, it was the *literary* delicatessen which dominated the Saturnalia of his student days at Athens. In terms of content, the riddles cover not all,[22] but many, of the central themes of the work as a whole.[23] The tasks of the game listed in Gel. 18,2,6 include the discussion of an opaque line of poetry, or a subject from the more distant past, the explication of a philosophical tenet or a dialectical fallacy, a rare term or an ambiguous tense. With the introduction of philology, history, and philosophy, it seems, almost effortlessly but hardly by accident, three core concerns of the *Noctes Atticae* are laid out before us.

Perhaps even more important than the content or subject, however, is the mode (the *how*) of the intellectual challenge, which is presented to the reader as a cheerful entertainment: the narrator is keen to stress that the riddles were 'amusing rather than perplexing'.[24] The commentaries set during the Saturnalia thus attempt to play down the effort of acquiring an education and demonstrating one's command of it, presenting it instead as a triviality that is both harmless and entertaining. In this they follow the exact strategy of the proem, where in a similar display of gracious understatement, and close verbal assonance, the reader is invited to sample the —on the whole— easily digestible rather than 'knotty and troublesome' contents of the *Noctes Atticae*.[25]

---

19 Gel. 18,2,3: *qui et cenulam ordine suo curabat*; Gel. 18,13,4: *cenula curabatur omnibus*.

20 On the tradition of the Saturnalian puzzles see Ov. *Tr.* 2,481–2; Suet. *Aug.* 75; *Anth. Pal.* 286 Riese. See also Leary 2014, 10–12.

21 The amalgamation of learning and religion finds succinct, programmatic expression in a letter Cicero addressed to his friend Atticus, in which he sums up the topics of the conversation in the formula σπουδαῖον οὐδὲν *in sermone*, φιλόλογα *multa* (*Att.* 13,52,2).

22 Missing in particular are legal aspects, which play a major part in Gellius; see for instance Gel. 2,12; 2,24; 4,3; 11,18. Nevertheless, the detailed descriptions of the rules of the game (see Gel. 18,2,3–5; 18,13,2–4 and 6) can certainly be understood as a humorous equivalent of the official laws; this is supported by the enactment, in jest, of a 'Saturnalian Law', which is also attested in Lucian *Sat.* 18.

23 Already noted by Beall 1988, 64.

24 Gel. 18,2,6: *aut sententia poetae veteris lepide obscura, non anxie*.

25 Gel. *praef.* 13. The systematic self-diminution and the 'playful authority' it helped to establish are rightly seen by Keulen 2009, 18–20 and 46–58, as an effective trademark strategy of the *Noctes Atticae*.

The light-hearted parties with friends also combine two strands of literary traditions from Greece and Rome:[26] one of them being the ideal of the 'feast of words' is being reactivated —known as a *logôdeipnon* since Plato and documented in the opening dialogue of the *Phaedrus*.[27] The other, in Gellius' commentary 18,2, reflects the thoroughly Roman tradition: like no other Roman festival, the Saturnalia found a broad echo[28] in prose and poetry and virtually created their own sub-genre.[29] When in Gellius the invited guests each receive a laurel crown and an old book as tokens of their victory, after successfully completing their set task, it symbolizes the intertwining of the common practice of honouring the victor of a literary competition and the exchange of gifts during the Saturnalia – for it is on the occasion of this festival that poets would present their friends and patrons with a book (preferably from their own pen).[30]

The narrator moreover adapts his description of the puzzle game to the specific occasion of the Saturnalia by emphasizing its playful, accidental nature: he tells us that the tasks were assigned to each guest through the luck of the draw, or as he puts it, 'each one of us cast them before the company in his turn, like knuckle-bones or dice.'[31] At first glance, therefore, the sequence of questions appears just as arbitrary as the miscellaneous array of *commentarii* promised in the proem.[32] What arouses our suspicion, however, is the narrator's apparent eagerness to sabotage the impression that the affair is left purely to chance by offering a detailed explanation of the rules:[33] if such strict rules[34] exist even for the rounds

---

26 Visible in the direct juxtaposition of the ancient Roman national festival and the Greek capital of learning (Gel. 18,2,1: *Saturnalia Athenis*; 18,13,1: *Saturnalibus Athenis*) and in the colourful mixture of Greek and Roman literary puzzles and authors (including excerpts from Ennius, Plato, and Hesiod) and book prizes. Astarita 1993, 67, has already commented on the close intermingling of both cultures of learning in the Saturnalian commentaries.

27 Pl. *Phdr.* 227a–b.

28 A good overview of prominent Saturnalian texts can be found in Döpp 1993.

29 Candidates, in particular, are the self-contained books 13 and 14 of Martial's epigrams, which are entirely devoted to the Saturnalia, the *Saturnalia* of the satirist Lucian, the late ancient *Saturnalia* of Macrobius and the *Aenigmata* of Symphosius.

30 Catul. 14; Stat. *Silv.* 4,9; Mart. 4,14; 5,18; 10,18.

31 Gel. 18,2,3: *rem locumque dicendi sors dabat*; Gel. 18,13,2: *Saturnalibus Athenis alea quadam festiva et honesta lusitabamus huiuscemodi ... captiones, quae sophismata appellantur, mente agitabamus easque quasi talos aut tesserulas in medium vice sua quisque iaciebamus*; Gel. 18,13,6: *ritu aleatorio*. On the conventional association of the Saturnalia (and Saturnalian poetry) with the game of dice and the luckless Mart. 12,62 and 13,1.

32 Gel. *praef.* 2 and above n. 8.

33 Gel. 18,2,3–5; 18,13,2–4 and n. 7.

34 A decidedly sympotic set of rules can also be found elsewhere, in other commentaries, for instance in Gel. 2,22; 7,13; 13,11; 17,8. The particular features —especially the greater license

of merry puzzle-solving in the topsy-turvy world of the Saturnalia, surely we must assume that a similar set of rigorous regulations is in place for the *Noctes Atticae*.

One final argument for the highly self-referential character of the Saturnalian commentaries is provided by the fourth riddle mentioned in Gel. 18,2, which demands an aetiological explanation for mutual invitations among patricians (on the occasion of the *ludi Megalenses*) and among plebeians (during the *ludi Cereales*). In this question we not only find a miniature version of the round-robin gatherings staged by the students during the Saturnalia, but these festive rounds now become themselves the subject of the playful, educated puzzle game. The pronounced mise-en-abyme effect is moreover placed exactly at the centre of the seven tasks, which are quoted verbatim. We must therefore assume that behind the ostensibly random series there is a hidden structural principle and a formal pattern at work which observant readers, availing themselves of the intratextual evidence, can and must discover.

In our quest to trace the postulated technique presumably employed by the narrator, of guiding the reader with covert clues, we will first take a closer look at the commentary 18,2.

3 Who speaks truth? Knowledge test with rules

Any attempt to approach the commentary 18,2 must by definition begin with the summarizing chapter heading, or lemma: *Cuiusmodi quaestionum certationibus Saturnalicia ludicra Athenis agitare soliti simus; atque inibi inspersa quaedam sophismatia et aenigmata oblectatoria.*

The heading is bipartite: the first section prepares the reader for an entertaining, competitive game of questions-and-answers, with which the narrator claims to have celebrated the Saturnalia with friends during their long-gone Athenian student days. The second part complements these *quaestiones* with fallacious arguments, or sophistries (*sophismatia*), and amusing riddles (*aenigmata*) interspersed among them.

---

compared to formal everyday life— of the sympotic space are pointed out by Keulen 2009, 204. Heusch 2011, 390–2 defines the symposium as the central space for the competitive situation and the 'social game', in which the [male] members of the cultural élites had to follow strict rules to prove their social aptitude. Both positions, taken together, paint an accurate picture of the ambivalences of the *convivium*, where in the course of an evening, the participants would ostentatiously play down and *at the same time* reaffirm the prevailing class boundaries and rivalries.

The relationship of heading and text turns out to be unproblematic. A close reading of the commentary confirms that the reader's expectations are fulfilled in their entirety. In the first third of the *commentarius* 18,2,1–6 the setting is established with a description of the festive gatherings and a detailed run-down of the rules of the game. The list of the questions posed in the past then takes up the largest, and central, space (18,2,7–14). The scattering of a number of riddles, as mentioned in the heading, can also be verified. The third of a total of seven *quaestiones* presents the reader with three fallacies (*captiones*). The round of riddles then leads to the final award ceremony, in which Saturn, like the invited guests, receives a crown to honour his victory, because one of the three questions could not be solved by any of the human guests present at the time (18,2,15).

For our intratextual enquiry, the following observation is of particular importance: the original game is repeated and brought forward into the present; the narrator only cites the questions without supplying the answers. Readers may now feel encouraged to take up the invitation and join in the game alongside the students of old. At the bottom of the list of riddles we can even compare our own successes with those of the historical guests who, after all, failed as a group to solve one of the seven riddles.

For this one unsolved riddle the narrator now picks up the initiative and offers his —belated— full-length, 'maximum' solution: first he gives us the precise location, Book 13 of Ennius' *Annals*, and on top of that he adds the precise wording of the line in question.[35] The supplementary information conveys two messages to the reader: 1) the narrator presents himself as an 'exemplary student'[36] who —as the text suggests— cannot bear the thought of lacking the answer to a harmless riddle, and who attempts to expunge the disgrace with the diligent study of the ancient authors. 2) The example set by the narrator confronts the reader with the implicit challenge to become active in a similar fashion, and the hidden incentive is there as well: if the readers for their part succeed in solving similar riddles that still remain unanswered, they can at least take their imaginary seat among their equals in the original group of riddlers and revellers.

In our search for overarching patterns in the casual sequence of tasks, it is also remarkable that the supplementary part, without further ado, transforms the

35 This comprehensive attribution of the quote is consistent with Gellius' usual practice of making a precise record of his sources, see Astarita 1993, 23–6. Rare exceptions prove the rule, obviously with a view to encouraging the reader to take an active interest in researching the story for themselves; see below chapter 5 and n. 50.

36 An in-depth study of the preferred self-representation of the narrator figure 'Gellius' as a model student is offered by Neumann 2015.

allegedly coincidental series into a meaningful structure: since the narrator refuses to divulge his answer to the fifth riddle before the end of the commentary, the game played by the party of revellers is opened and closed, in cyclical fashion, with a verbatim quotation from Ennius.[37]

With this unexpected structural reinforcement in a text ostensibly arranged at random, the added value of the supplement is far from exhausted: not only do the two citations from Ennius, in *combination*, create the characteristic tension inherent in the game, the act of 'empuzzlement', between what is and what appears to be, but they also illustrate the cognitive process from the setting of the task to its final resolution. The introductory quotation (18,2,7) uses a clever pun to focus on the verb *frustrari*, implicitly reflecting the confusion of the person trying to solve the riddle, as would have been intended by the person setting the task. The second Ennius quotation (18,2,15) —hardly less premeditated— deals with the Old Roman verb *verare* (an equivalent of the phrase *vera dicere*). It therefore appears to confirm, in the act of reading, the deeper claim to veracity of the 'seeing' poet (*vates*): the 'truth-telling' quotation has led the reader to the correct solution for the one remaining puzzle question. The message of the quotation and the 'enlightenment' of the reader, who is participating in the festive guessing game, merge into one.

Not the least of the first-person narrator's interests in adding the supplement is the promotion of his *Noctes Atticae*. By including the supplementary solution he confirms that beyond the original ancient sources, it is the contemporary encyclopaedic and compilatory works in particular which condense the sum of all knowledge and thus commend themselves for research purposes. Through their colourful choice of topics they cover a wide spectrum of knowledge, and as the preface makes it clear,[38] thanks to their paratextual aids to navigation, they provide quick and convenient access to answers for a multitude of questions. The excerpts of the *Noctes Atticae*, implicitly, present themselves as a formidable alternative to a complete —and quite impossible— study of all fundamentally important works, certainly for the busy reader. Nevertheless, the usefulness of the compendium, fully affirmed in the commentary 18,2, seems anything but certain if we widen the scope of our investigation to include the second commentary with a Saturnalian theme.

---

37 A nifty structural side effect arising from the enlightening list of puzzles is that its cyclical composition is mirrored in the shape of the victory crowns.

38 Gel. *praef.* 25.

4 You are not what I am: Clever *captiones* with comeuppance

In terms of content, the commentary 18,13 is closely related to the text discussed above; its structure is analogous. Like the previous commentary, 18,13 evokes at first the cheerful puzzle game during the Saturnalia and explains the rules (18,13,1–4), but they now contain a remarkable innovation: in contrast to *NA* 18,2, the guests bring money to the playful gathering. Depending on the quality of his answer, each guest either receives a coin from the community pot or must pay into it; the collected sum is used to pay for the meal. After the narrator has then recited a number of tasks (18,13,5) he concludes his commentary with the narrative of an illuminating example: the last third of the text (18,13,7–8) is dedicated to the account of the Cynic philosopher Diogenes making a witty response to a provocative catch question posed by an anonymous dialectic philosopher.

Clearly the second commentary presents us with a variation and an extension of the cheerful Saturnalian puzzle games already discussed in 18,2: the close connection is indicated without the slightest attempt at subtlety in the nearly identical repetition of the first two words (18,2,1: *Saturnalia Athenis*; 18,13,1: *Saturnalibus Athenis*). At the same time the second commentary limits and intensifies the message: no longer are we invited to choose from the entire spectrum of questions and riddles, but we must focus on the idiosyncrasies of the fallacy. Formerly a casual element in the text, the problem of the fallacy now becomes the central theme, while the new fine for rejected solutions adds further intrigue. As an interesting aside, the narrator has replaced the final excerpt from Ennius' *Annals* with an amusing anecdote.[39]

For the reader of both commentaries, their structural and thematic relationship is practically self-evident: the same material has obviously, and deliberately, been spread across two textual segments separated by physical space. The fact that Gellius has indeed created made-to-measure gaps in the earlier text to be filled with building blocks from the second commentary becomes apparent if we take a closer look at the sophism that is so ingeniously resolved by Diogenes. The exactly same catch question aimed at the victim's manly pride, 'You are not what I am, are you?' was already among the three sample questions listed by the narrator in 18,2 —albeit without a successful solution. Eleven commentaries later

39 In a somewhat more underhand manner, the passage also demonstrates how a fallacy, repackaged as a short narrative, can possibly be reinserted into the conversation where the opportunity presents itself.

we receive the missing information in the form of an instructional anecdote that shows us how we can respond to the challenge. The question-and-answer game in the manner of the Saturnalian gatherings is thus not confined to a single location in the text; it stretches across textual boundaries. Question and 'casual' answer are part of, and give shape to, the larger whole.

Another finding is therefore all the more surprising: a direct comparison of the two headings reveals that while Gellius does, with a certain regularity, employ the *caput* to point out textual analogies to his readers,[40] in the case of the Saturnalia he foregoes any such unequivocal explanation: in the heading for 18,13, the festive occasion is studiously disregarded, and the introduction is curtailed to comprise a single sentence.[41] It mentions only the concluding anecdote, even though in the body text itself Diogenes' encounter is cited merely as an afterthought to the problems of the Saturnalia.[42] Not only does the paratext which precedes it elevate the seemingly insignificant addendum to the status of a key topic, but it also omits the first half of the commentary as if it did not exist at all.

It appears as if the author had allowed himself to be guided by two competing interests in the layout of the chapter headings. On the one hand the aim would have been to direct the readers' attention to Diogenes' witty response;[43] the indication that the anecdote will yield a helpful solution for dealing with catch questions is already present in the heading. But beyond the correct answer it also offers something of value in return, suggested in the use of the judicial term *talio* (retaliation):[44] not only does Diogenes teach students and readers how to expose the logical weakness of a fallacy, and thus how to avoid the fine (*multa*) at the Saturnalia, he also shows how such a challenge can be rebutted, and the opponent be made to pay back his debt 'in kind' even outside the Saturnalian context. The playful penalty (*talio*, retaliation) —whether in the material or in the verbal

40 Both the *caput* and the first sentence of Gel. 2,9 refer the reader back to the commentary immediately preceding it, which is based on the same work by Plutarch; the *caput* for Gel. 9,14 follows a similar strategy with its explicit mention of Claudius Quadrigarius, whose work has already been analyzed in Gel. 9,13. The *capita* of both Gel. 4,3 and 4,4 advertise the shared subject of dowries.

41 Gel. 18,13 *caput: Quali talione Diogenes philosophus usus sit pertemptatus a dialectico quodam sophismatio inpudenti.*

42 Gel. 18,13,7: *Libet autem dicere, quam facete Diogenes sophisma id genus, quod supra dixi, a quodam dialectico ex Platonis diatriba per contumeliam propositum remuneratus sit.*

43 The *capita* do indeed quite often contain an important aid to interpreting the body text, and they seek to direct the reader's attention to it, see Maselli 1993, 35.

44 On the predominant use of the term ('retaliation') in legal contexts see Gel. 20,1,18, and 35.

sense— thus serves as a piece of practical advice and as a bracket linking heading and body text as well as the two narrative units of the commentary.

On the other hand the narrow focus of the heading, apart from pointing to the solution of the problem, also has the opposite effect of deceiving the reader, because the *caput* turns out to be self-referential in that it describes the successful response to catch questions as the subject of the commentary, while leaving the reader 'clueless' about the situational context of the question as a quintessential Saturnalian pastime. Above all else, however, the heading denies to the reader the one unique marker —in the list of contents— which would have pointed to the thematic relationship between the two commentaries 18,2 and 18,13. Such a glaring lacuna undoubtedly diminished the reader's ability to make optimum use of the book. In this, the heading blatantly contradicts the promise of the proem which states that we can expect from each heading a reliable summary of the contents of the commentary. Such a deliberate act of deception ultimately calls into question the very point —the raison d'être— of the work itself.

Why then does Gellius in the preface promote his work as a service for the busy reader when that promise is then promptly undermined by his paratexts? A plausible explanation to me seems to be the assumption of a second authorial intention competing with the aims of accessibility and efficiency. I see this second, parallel purpose in the text itself providing continual incentives for the reader to study the work in the broadest and most attentive fashion possible. The mere recapitulation of a crystal-clear, step-by-step solution may be helpful for superficial readers or those in a hurry, but by the same token it does not inspire the ambitious reader who is actively engaging with the text.[45] A genuine search for clues, that will only lead to a successful conclusion if separate commentaries are compared and contrasted with great care, will no doubt be more satisfying to the second type of reader: it challenges their mental acuity and encourages them to 'dig deeper', that is, to continue with their extensive, and intensive, in-depth study of the text.

Our theory of a playful 'empuzzlement' —the scattering of related pieces of information throughout the work with the purpose of creating an intratextual riddle— draws additional support from the fact that the discovery of the referential relationship between the *capita* of 18,2 and 18,13 still stands even without a second mention of the Saturnalia. The term *sophismation*, which occurs in both headings, and only there, indicates a thematic overlap between the two commentaries. Apparently, with a view to sharpening the readers' eye for this common

45 On the concept of such a 'strong', active reader who creates meaning Beer 2014, 59.

theme, and to tickling their curiosity, Gellius even chose to mark the occasion with this particular —and exclusive— neologism.[46]

If our assumption is correct, and we are here being invited to an intratextual game of 'puzzle solving', we must face the inevitable question of to what extent this observation can be applied to our overall understanding of the *Noctes Atticae*. Are we looking at a situation that is unique to these two commentaries because of their Saturnalian background? Or are we looking at a fundamental structural principle underlying the Gellian work? In the latter case, we ought to be able to trace the observed technique at various locations throughout the book: the simultaneous deception and instruction of the reader by means of markers in the text, even though they may be veiled and inconspicuous.[47] It remains for us, in the next and final section, to arrive at a definitive answer.

5 The *Noctes Atticae* as a serial game of discovery and *Ergänzungsspiel*

A complete survey of the *Noctes Atticae* does indeed confirm that the two Saturnalia-themed commentaries are embedded in a complex system of intratextual references. The attentive reader, who follows the trail laid out by the narrator, will thus have a choice of several options for an extended study of the work relating to 'riddles and catch questions': in view of the intertextual evidence we have uncovered for the *sophismation*, it seems reasonable to speculate that the second category of light-hearted diversion listed alongside it in the *caput* of 18,2 might hold a similar significance. The phrase *aenigma oblectatorium* is, after all, another neologism[48] that might have been introduced with similar intentions.

Starting with a quick glance at the table of contents, purely for orientation, the reader's eye would instantly be drawn to the commentary 12,6 (*de aenigmate*), which does prove to be relevant in more ways than one. Firstly, it reaffirms the

46 As has previously been observed by Maselli 1993, 23, in an overview of linguistic innovations, which for him are instruments that are being used deliberately to engage the reader.

47 A parallel to our *commentaries* concerning Saturnalian riddles are Gel. 5,3 and 5,10, both narrating an anecdote of the sophist Protagoras. Again the connection between both commentaries is not marked in the headings, but becomes evident only in the texts: there Protagoras is characterized two times as *acerrimus sophistarum* (Gel. 5,3,7 and 5,10,3). Beside that evident intratexutal marker there is also a link of content, since the second anecdote confirms and carries forward the first one.

48 On the conspicuous neologism *oblectatorius* Maselli 1993, 23.

strategy of a deliberate 'empuzzlement' of the text, to encourage in-depth investigation. The meaning behind the laconic title (by far the shortest *caput* in the *Noctes Atticae*)[49] can only be gleaned from reading the commentary: the text beneath the heading begins with a definition of the term *aenigma* and then quotes a puzzle. However, in proceeding from one to the other, the narrator is adamant that he will not divulge the solution so as to stimulate the reader's own 'ingenuity' at problem solving. The result, he assures us, can be verified by referring to Book 2 of Varro's *De lingua Latina*. Thus, by giving us a definition of the term and a concrete example, the first commentary moreover functions as a meta-linguistic manual, an introduction to the literary puzzle of the *Noctes Atticae*. We are being alerted, implicitly, to be on the lookout for possible encounters with similarly playful questions and riddles, and their 'hidden' answers, throughout the book.[50]

More than riddles in the strictest sense, it is catch questions, or sophistries (and related forms such as syllogisms, arguments *a contrario*, axioms, and paradoxical arguments), commonly found in the logic and dialectic of Stoicism, that play a critical role in a whole series of commentaries.[51] Of relevance to us is the fact that the contents of these commentaries are by no means, as a rule, revealed in the heading: in some, albeit very rare, instances they play hide and seek with the reader.[52]

This strategy is particularly apparent in Gel. 16,2: the heading promises a critical discussion of the law (*lex*) underlying dialectical debates.[53] In order to explain the dialecticians' set of rules, the narrator then cites two exemplary fallacies (Gel. 16,2,5–11). The second of these contains a hidden puzzle piece which the readers —if they identify it as such— can reactivate in the Saturnalian commentary 18,2: here, the exact same sophistic question is brought up again, with minimal variation in the wording, but *without* the solution. The *Ergänzungsspiel*

---

49 Thus already Maselli 1993, 21.

50 Thus for instance in Gel. 12,11 the narrator creates a literary puzzle for the reader at the end of the body text by pretending (rather unconvincingly) to have forgotten the name of a poet from whom he then proceeds to quote a line verbatim.

51 Thus in Gel. 2,7 and 2,8; 5,10 and 5,11; 7,13; 16,2; 16,8; 17,12; 18,1; on this see the earlier observations by Astarita 1993, 106–109. Keulen 2009, 158–62 has rightly pointed out that such playful activity in educated circles would have been consistent in particular with the interests of Antonine literature on account of its interactive and competitive nature; it also affirms the self-referential character of the relevant commentaries on the subject. Similarly Beer 2014, 64–8 on the contemporary context of the Second Sophistic.

52 In Gel. 2,7, for instance, the discussion of a 'quibbling' conclusion can only be accessed through the body text; ditto for Gel. 18,1, where the keyword *captio* is not mentioned in the title.

53 Gel. 16,2 *caput: cuiusmodi sit lex apud dialecticos percontandi disserendique; et quae sit eius legis reprehensio.*

linking 18,2 and 18,13 can thus be extended backwards, as it were, and be applied to link 16,2 and 18,2 in a similar fashion.

The path to success, however, is markedly more difficult here, because the space separating the two linked references is now much wider than in our first example: two whole books rather than eleven commentaries. Additionally, there is no conspicuous word in the heading to point to the connection; only a supremely scrupulous reader will be able to deduce an intratextual relationship. That reader would have to be aware of fallacies as a typical domain of dialecticians and expect to find them treated in the commentary under the neutral heading of Gel. 16,2. He would also have to recognize precisely these *captiones* in the synonymous neologism *sophismation* from Gel. 18,2 and, finally, confirm the accuracy of his or her assumptions through a close reading of both key passages. Alternatively, the 'recycled' fallacy could of course reveal itself through a full linear reading of books 16–18; the reader would then however have to possess a remarkable capacity for recalling minute details from previous chapters.

In view of these complications we must address the question as to whether a miscellany such as the *Noctes Atticae* can actually be trusted to sustain an extended and elaborate cross-reference of the type we have identified: are we indeed looking at a fully intentional marker, to 'tease' the reader? Perhaps Gellius inadvertently used a well-known fallacy more than once to illustrate a point?[54] The possibility cannot be dismissed outright. However, it can be argued that there are other, similarly unobtrusive passages in the commentaries where diffuse clues invite the reader to undertake an in-depth interrogation of the work.[55]

Readers will moreover feel encouraged to look for thematic overlap among the three commentaries the very moment they recognize the two recurring catch questions as an intratextual sequence ('Do you, or do you not, have what you have not lost?' in 16,2 and 18,2; 'What I am, that you are not' in 18,2 and 18,13). Their sleuthing will garner a twofold reward: firstly, they will discover that Gel. 16,2 lays down a methodical foundation, with its systematic analysis of the dialectic question-and-answer technique, while at the same time according a serious component to the playful trick questions of the Saturnalia. And secondly, the

54 The fact that Seneca, in *Ep.* 45,7 and 49,8, sees no need to quote the full *captio*, is an indication of its popularity: 'What you have not lost, that you have', was a widely known catch question.

55 The careful laying down of such a trail of intertextual 'crumbs' can be observed, for example, in the commentaries Gel. 14,7 and 18,4: both conclude with the vague remark from the narrator that he has already written on the subject 'in another place' and is therefore not providing any further details. A general remark of this type obviously appeals to ambitious, assiduous readers —who are willing to immerse themselves in a full-scale hunt for clues throughout the *Noctes Atticae*.

narrator is growing ever more confident of his ability to solve the catch questions, from his somewhat apodictic advice in Gel. 16,2, not to answer any question from a dialectician, and thus to avoid being caught in a trap, to his expectation in Gel. 18,2,9 of a successful resolution to the compromising question, and finally, in Gel. 18,13, the spectacular culmination of this expectation in Diogenes' ingenious 're-taliation'.

6 Conclusion

By lining up the three commentaries we *can* create a coherent mini-series. In doing so, however, we must keep in mind that this chain could be extended at any time with additional links: likely candidates might be Gel. 12,6 on the enigma (*de aenigmate*), or the commentary 7,13, which describes the sparkling discussion of *quaestiones* at the dinner table of the philosopher Taurus. A serial approach to the work thus allows the readers to choose which path they wish to pursue, and where to set a suitable end point. In our case, while concrete, applicable knowledge about riddles, *quaestiones*, and fallacies is indeed being communicated, serial readers will first and foremost be encouraged, in the sense of an intratextual *Ergänzungsspiel*, to engage extensively, and intensively, with the contents of the *Noctes Atticae* —which in turn allows the work to fulfil its self-declared, programmatic ambition: to serve as 'a kind of literary storehouse' (*penus litterarum*).[56]

Bibliography

Astarita, M.L. (1993), *La cultura nelle 'Noctes Atticae'*, Catania.
Beall, S.M. (1988), Civilis eruditio. *Style and Content in the* Attic Nights *of Aulus Gellius*, Ann Arbor.
Beer, B. (2014), 'Schwache Erzähler, starke Leser. Zum erzählerischen Programm im Vorwort von Gellius' *Noctes Atticae*', *A&A* 60, 51–69.
Bing, P. (2009), '*Ergänzungsspiel* in the Epigrams of Callimachus', in: *id.*, *The Scroll and the Marble, Studies in Reading and Reception in Hellenistic Poetry*, Ann Arbor, 85–105.
Döpp, S. (1993), 'Saturnalien und lateinische Literatur', in: S. Döpp (ed.), *Karnevaleske Phänomene in antiken und nachantiken Kulturen und Literaturen*, BAC 13, Trier, 145–77.
Genette, G. (2001), *Paratexte. Das Buch vom Beiwerk des Buches*, Frankfurt.
Heusch, C. (2011), *Die Macht der memoria. Die 'Noctes Atticae' des Aulus Gellius im Licht der Erinnerungskultur des 2. Jahrhunderts n. Chr.*, UaLG 104, Berlin.

56 Gel. *praef.* 2.

Holford-Strevens, L. (2003), *Aulus Gellius. An Antonine Scholar and his Achievement*, Revised edn., Oxford.
Keulen, W. (2009), *Gellius the Satirist. Roman Cultural Authority in Attic Nights*, *MnS* 297, Leiden/Boston.
Leary, T.J. (2014), *Symphosius. The Aenigmata. An Intoduction, Text and Commentary*, London/New Delhi/New York/Sydney.
Maselli, G. (1993), 'Osservazioni sui "lemmata" delle "Noctes Atticae",' *Orpheus* n.s. 14, 18–39.
Mercklin, L. (1860), 'Die Citiermethode und Quellenbenutzung des A. Gellius in den Noctes Atticae', *JbClPh* Suppl. 3, H. 5, 633–710.
Neumann, C. (2015), *Der perfekte Schüler. Die Figur des Aulus Gellius in den* Noctes Atticae, Master thesis, Göttingen.
Pausch, D. (2004), *Biographie und Bildungskultur. Personendarstellungen bei Plinius dem Jüngeren, Gellius und Sueton*, Millennium-Studien 4, Berlin/New York.
Schröder, B.-J. (1999), *Titel und Text. Zur Entwicklung lateinischer Gedichtüberschriften*, UaLG 54, Berlin.
Scullard, H.H. (1985), *Römische Feste. Kalender und Kult*, Kulturgeschichte der antiken Welt 5, Mainz.
Sharrock, A. (2000), 'Intratextuality. Texts, Parts, and (W)holes in Theory', in: A. Sharrock/H. Morales (eds.), *Intratextuality: Greek and Roman textual relations*, Oxford, 1–39.
Stocker, P. (1998), *Theorie der intertextuellen Lektüre. Modelle und Fallstudien*, Paderborn.
Vardi, A. (2004), 'Genre, Conventions, and Cultural Programme in Gellius' *Noctes Atticae*', in: L. Holford-Strevens/A. Vardi (eds.), *The Worlds of Aulus Gellius*, Oxford, 159–86.
Versnel, H.S. (1993), *Transition and Reversal in Myth and Ritual*, Studies in Greek and Roman Religion 6, Vol. 2, Leiden/New York/Cologne.

Part IX: **Rounding off Intratextuality: Greece and Rome**

Richard Hunter

Regius urget: Hellenising Thoughts on Latin Intratextuality

This paper* briefly considers three aspects of the Greek background reflected both in the 'intratextuality' of Latin literature and in some modern discussions of what that term might mean. The three case-studies are overlapping in their concerns, as is, I hope, appropriate for the subject of this volume.

1 Empedocles and Horace

Any discussion of 'intratextuality' in ancient literature must, sooner or later, turn to the opening and closing of Horace's *Ars Poetica*:

> humano capiti ceruicem pictor equinam
> iungere si uelit et uarias inducere plumas
> undique collatis membris, ut turpiter atrum
> desinat in piscem mulier formosa superne,
> spectatum admissi risum teneatis amici?
> credite, Pisones, isti tabulae fore librum
> persimilem, cuius, uelut aegri somnia, uanae
> fingentur species, ut nec pes nec caput uni
> reddatur formae. 'pictoribus atque poetis
> quidlibet audendi semper fuit aequa potestas.'
> scimus, et hanc ueniam petimusque damusque uicissim,
> sed non ut placidis coeant immitia, non ut
> serpentes auibus geminentur, tigribus agni.
>
> Horace, *Ars Poetica* 1–13

> Imagine a painter who wanted to combine a horse's neck with a human head, and then clothe a miscellaneous collection of limbs with various kinds of feathers, so that what started out at the top as a beautiful woman ended in a hideously ugly fish. If you, friends, were invited to the private view, could you help laughing? Let me tell you, Pisones, a book whose different features are made up at random like a sick man's dreams, with no unified form to have a head or a tail, is exactly like that picture. Painters and poets have always enjoyed recognised rights to venture on what they will. Yes we know; indeed, we ask and

* An earlier version of this essay was delivered as the closing lecture at the 'Intratextuality' conference in Thessaloniki in May 2017. In accordance with tradition, I have not sought to remove all traces of its origin in an oral performance.

https://doi.org/10.1515/9783110611021-028

grant this permission turn and turn about. But it doesn't mean that fierce and gentle can be united, snakes paired with birds or lambs with tigers.

(trans. D.A. Russell, adapted)

ut mala quem scabies aut morbus regius urget
aut fanaticus error et iracunda Diana,
uesanum tetigisse timent fugiuntque poetam,
qui sapiunt; agitant pueri incautique sequuntur.
hic dum sublimis uersus ructatur et errat,
si ueluti merulis intentus decidit auceps
in puteum foueamue, licet 'succurrite' longum
clamet 'io ciues', non sit qui tollere curet.
si curet quis opem ferre et demittere funem,
'qui scis an prudens huc se deiecerit atque
seruari nolit?' dicam, Siculique poetae
narrabo interitum. deus inmortalis haberi
dum cupit Empedocles, ardentem frigidus Aetnam
insiluit. sit ius liceatque perire poetis;
inuitum qui seruat, idem facit occidenti.
nec semel hoc fecit nec, si retractus erit, iam
fiet homo et ponet famosae mortis amorem.
nec satis apparet cur uersus factitet, utrum
minxerit in patrios cineres, an triste bidental
mouerit incestus; certe furit, ac uelut ursus,
obiectos caueae ualuit si frangere clatros,
indoctum doctumque fugat recitator acerbus;
quem uero arripuit, tenet occiditque legendo,
non missura cutem nisi plena cruoris hirudo.

Horace, *Ars Poetica* 453–76

Men of sense are afraid to touch a mad poet and give him a wide berth. He's like a man suffering from a nasty itch, or the jaundice, or fanaticism, or Diana's wrath. Boys chase him and follow him round incautiously. And if, while he's belching out his lofty lines and wandering round, he happens to fall into a well or a pit, like a fowler intent on his birds, then, however long he shouts 'Help! Help! Fellow citizens, help!' there'll be no one to bother to pick him up. And if anyone should trouble to help and let down a rope, my question will be, 'How do you know that he didn't throw himself down deliberately? Are you sure he wants to be saved?' And I shall tell the tale of the Sicilian poet. Empedocles wanted to be regarded as an immortal god, and so he jumped, cool as you like, into burning Etna. Let poets have the right and privilege of death. To save a man against his will is the same as killing him. This isn't the only time he's done it. If he's pulled out now, he won't become human or lay aside his love of a notorious end. It's far from clear why he keeps writing poetry. Has the villain pissed on his father's ashes? Or disturbed the grim site of a lightning-strike? Anyway, he's raving, and his harsh readings put learned and unlearned alike to flight, like a bear that's broken the bars of his cage. If he catches anyone, he holds on and kills him with reading. He's a real leech that won't let go of the skin till it's full of blood.

(trans. D.A. Russell)

The relationships between the way in which literary works or corpora begin and end is one of the big intratextual questions: as T.S. Eliot ought to have said, do our ends *ever* know our beginnings? Let me begin, however, at the beginning. It might be asked more often than it is *why* the *amici* of v.5 will inevitably laugh at what Charles Brink has christened 'a grotesque';[1] which of the traditional causes of laughter is appropriate here?[2] The usual answer, and one which must at least in part be important to Horace, is that this is a bonding form of laughter for *amici* (including ourselves) who recognise the lack of πρέπον when they see it and also the linkage in critical theory between unity and beauty.[3] Nevertheless there is a real discontinuity here. This painter, so often labelled 'inept' etc in modern criticism,[4] apparently *wants* to paint a grotesque (*uelit* v.2). Who then, we should ask, is focalising *turpiter* in v. 3?: the standard view, of course, is that this is 'Horace's judgement',[5] but can we be sure that *turpiter* does not describe the effect at which the painter is actually aiming? So too, can we be absolutely sure that *ut* in v. 3 does not (or could not) introduce a purpose clause rather than a result clause or even (so Brink, citing Wickham) a clause of 'added qualification'; if so, this painter might in fact be delighted when his work is received with laughter (even the laughter of Horace's *amici*, perhaps provoked by thoughts of which the painter would not approve). The clear implication which follows that *poets* produce such 'grotesque' effects unwittingly and would not welcome audience laughter must be set against this opening ambiguity. Horace's painter may be operating within an entirely different critical structure than the one Horace will adopt (however loosely) in the rest of the poem, and this needs to be borne in mind in any assessment of the intratextual relation between the opening and the rest; moreover, as the ending will make clear, it is not just painters who can operate *extra leges*. Far from pointing unambiguously to a similarity between painters and poets (v. 9), the opening passage at least seems to draw from and contribute to that other ancient discourse about the difference in potential between poetry (or literature more broadly) and the plastic and representational arts. Horace sets himself up as critic and judge (v. 11), but some people just could not care less – and that irony might itself be thought very Horatian.

1 But see, e.g., Schwindt 2014.

2 Cf. (briefly) Beard 2014, 37–9; Beard does not discuss the opening of the *AP* in her book.

3 For a more nuanced answer cf., e.g., Oliensis 1998, 201.

4 Not untypical is Citroni 2009, 19, 'a glaring example of an artistic failure, clearly recognizable as such, immediately and intuitively ...'.

5 Oliensis 1998, 201.

The opening 'grotesque' gives way at the end to a blood-sucking leech, no longer the stuff of a sick man's dreams (v. 7) or Plato's worst nightmares, but instead a small singularity, utterly focused, utterly *simplex et unum*, almost utterly self-reliant (leeches are hermaphroditic), a creation designed by nature to have (at least to the naked eye) no head, neck or tail (never mind feathers), but to have a very clear purpose, and to leave no room for *risus*, a creature which – like poetry – claims to have medicinal properties, but ends up killing you. The long recognised ring-composition and variation which frames the *Ars Poetica* is richly meaningful.[6] The friends let in to view the painting at the beginning suggest also the audience for a *recitatio* of poetry, and that implied audience becomes real at the end, as the mad poet latches (or rather 'leeches') on to some one – rather like the 'boor' in *Sat.* 1.9[7] or Eumolpus in the *Satyrica* – and recites him to death, as at this moment we are listening to the *AP* and just wishing it would end .... Poetry needs audiences – just as a leech – needs a blood-filled host; but the audience for poetry, unlike the leech's host, needs to make critical choices, needs to engage more than passively with the give and take of poetic creation.

The mad poet-*recitator*-leech, who operates *extra leges artis* like the opening painter (who may or may not be 'mad'), had already been exemplified by Empedocles, who, paradoxically or not, had prayed to the gods to avoid μανίη in what he sang (fr. 3 = D44 L-M).[8] Empedocles threw himself into Etna, but he does not disappear from Horace's poem. The image of the (medicinal) leech has something to do with the famous opening passage of the *Katharmoi*, in which Empedocles claims healing powers:

ὦ φίλοι, οἳ μέγα ἄστυ κατὰ ξανθοῦ Ἀκράγαντος
ναίετ' ἀν' ἄκρα πόλεος, ἀγαθῶν μελεδήμονες ἔργων,
ξείνων αἰδοῖοι λιμένες, κακότητος ἄπειροι,
χαίρετ'· ἐγὼ δ' ὑμῖν θεὸς ἄμβροτος, οὐκέτι θνητός
πωλεῦμαι μετὰ πᾶσι τετιμένος, ὥσπερ ἔοικα,
ταινίαις τε περίστεπτος στέφεσίν τε θαλείοις.
<πᾶσι δὲ> τοῖς ἂν ἵκωμαι ἄστεα τηλεθάοντα,
ἀνδράσιν ἠδὲ γυναιξί, σεβίζομαι· οἱ δ' ἅμ' ἕπονται
μυρίοι ἐξερέοντες, ὅπηι πρὸς κέρδος ἀταρπός,
οἱ μὲν μαντοσυνέων κεχρημένοι, οἱ δ' ἐπὶ νούσων
παντοίων ἐπύθοντο κλυεῖν εὐηκέα βάξιν,
δηρὸν δὴ χαλεπῆισι πεπαρμένοι <ἀμφ' ὀδύνηισιν>.

Empedocles fr. 112 D–K = D4 L–M

6 On the ring-composition of the *Ars* cf., e.g., Russell 2006, 339, Oliensis 1998, 215–18, Laird 2007, 137.

7 Cf., e.g., Oliensis 1998, 218–19.

8 For the abbreviation L–M cf. the bibliography, under Laks–Most.

> Friends, who live in the great city of the yellow Acragas, up on the heights of the citadel, caring for good deeds, I give you greetings. An immortal god, mortal no more, I go about honoured by all, as is fitting, crowned with ribbons and fresh garlands; <and by all> whom I come upon as I enter their prospering towns, by men and women, I am revered. They follow me in their thousands, asking where lies the road to profit, some desiring prophecies, while others ask to hear the word of healing for every kind of illness, long transfixed by harsh <pains>. (trans. KRS 1983, 313[9])

In introducing this fragment, Diogenes Laertius (8.61) reports that Heraclides Ponticus called Empedocles 'a doctor and a prophet' (P16 L–M), just as Satyrus described him as 'a doctor and excellent orator' (P24 L–M); Empedocles was credited in antiquity with medical treatises in both verse and prose (P25b, 26 L-M), and Hippocratic writers treat him as a rival (cf., e.g., *Ancient Medicine* 20, *Nature of Man* 1). The ancients were as familiar as we are with jokes about how doctors ('leeches', in an archaic English usage) kill as many as they cure, and this lies behind *occidit* in v. 475; the Romans certainly knew that the use of medicinal leeches for blood-letting was potentially fatal (Pliny, *HN* 32.123). Empedocles himself, however, had claimed to be able to teach how to 'bring the strength of a dead man out of Hades' (fr. 111 D–K = D43 L–M), and the sudden Horatian transformation from a bear to a leech was a mere bagatelle for a poet who had been 'a boy, a girl, a bush, a bird and a fish' (fr. 117 D–K = D13 L–M) and who claimed magical powers which could turn nature upside down (fr 111 D–K = D43 L–M).

If Empedocles brings up the rear, he is also there at the beginning, for both the opening description and vv. 7–9 can, as Philip Hardie has pointed out,[10] hardly fail to recall Empedocles' zoogony:

> Ἐμπεδοκλῆς τὰς πρώτας γενέσεις τῶν ζώιων καὶ φυτῶν μηδαμῶς ὁλοκλήρους γενέσθαι, ἀσυμφυέσι δὲ τοῖς μορίοις διεζευγμένας, τὰς δὲ δευτέρας συμφυομένων τῶν μερῶν εἰδωλοφανεῖς, τὰς δὲ τρίτας τῶν ἀλληλοφυῶν κτλ.
>
> Empedocles A 72 D–K = D151 L–M

> Empedocles: the first generations of animals and plants were not at all born as complete entities, but were disconnected, with parts that had not grown together; the second ones, when the parts had grown together, had the appearance of phantasms; the third ones, when the parts had grown in conformity with one another ...
>
> (trans. L–M)

9 For the abbreviation KRS cf. the bibliography.

10 Hardie 2018 (originally a conference paper from some years earlier). Hardie's argument is picked up by Tamás 2014, 188–90.

ἧι πολλαὶ μὲν κόρσαι ἀναύχενες ἐβλάστησαν,
γυμνοὶ δ' ἐπλάζοντο βραχίονες εὔνιδες ὤμων,
ὄμματά τ' οἶ' ἐπλανᾶτο πενητεύοντα μετώπων.
Empedocles B 57 D–K = D154 L–M

Here sprang up many faces without necks, arms wandered without shoulders, unattached, and eyes strayed alone, in need of foreheads.
(trans. KRS 1983, 303)

πολλὰ μὲν ἀμφιπρόσωπα καὶ ἀμφίστερνα φύεσθαι,
βουγενῆ ἀνδρόπρωιρα, τὰ δ' ἔμπαλιν ἐξανατέλλειν
ἀνδροφυῆ βούκρανα, μεμειγμένα τῆι μὲν ἀπ' ἀνδρῶν
τῆι δὲ γυναικοφυῆ σκιεροῖς ἠσκημένα γυίοις.
Empedocles B 61 D–K = D156 L–M

Many creatures were born with faces and breasts on both sides, man-faced ox-progeny, while others again sprang forth as ox-headed offspring of man, creatures compounded partly of male, partly of female, and fitted with shadowy parts.
(trans. KRS 1983, 304)

The Empedoclean texture is in fact very thick in Horace's opening verses. Horace's 'dreams of a sick man' reflect the same original as Aetius' εἰδωλοφανεῖς (31 A 72 D–K), a word which could have appeared in a hexameter, or it may even be more to the Horatian point to recall Circe's Empedoclean pets in the fourth book of Apollonius' *Argonautica*:

θῆρες δ', οὐ θήρεσσιν ἐοικότες ὠμηστῆισιν
οὐδὲ μὲν οὐδ' ἄνδρεσσιν ὅλον δέμας, ἄλλο δ' ἀπ' ἄλλων
συμμιγέες μελέων, κίον ἀθρόοι, ἠύτε μῆλα
ἐκ σταθμῶν ἅλις εἶσιν ὀπηδεύοντα νομῆι.
τοίους καὶ προτέρους ἐξ ἰλύος ἐβλάστησε
χθὼν αὐτὴ μικτοῖσιν ἀρηρεμένους μελέεσσιν,
οὔπω διψαλέωι μάλ' ὑπ' ἠέρι πιληθεῖσα
οὐδέ πω ἀζαλέοιο βολαῖς τόσον ἠελίοιο
ἰκμάδας αἰνυμένη· τὰ δ' ἐπὶ στίχας ἤγαγεν αἰών
συγκρίνας. τὼς οἵ γε φυὴν ἀίδηλοι ἕποντο,
ἥρωας δ' ἕλε θάμβος ἀπείριτον.
Apollonius Rhodius, *Argonautica* 4.672–82

Her beasts – which were not entirely like flesh-devouring beasts, nor like men, but rather a jumble of different limbs – all came with her, like a large flock of sheep which follow the shepherd out of the stalls. Similar to these were the creatures which in earlier times the earth itself had created out of the mud, pieced together from a jumble of limbs, before it had been properly solidified by the thirsty air or the rays of the parching sun had eliminated sufficient moisture. Time then sorted these out by grouping them into proper categories. Similarly unidentifiable were the forms which followed after Circe and caused the heroes amazed astonishment.

Horace's *undique conlatis membris* is, however Lucretian, virtually a translation of ἄλλο δ' ἀπ' ἄλλων / συμμιγέες μελέων.[11] Moreover, when the Argonauts come upon Circe she is just purifying herself from a nightmare such as a (really) sick man might have had. I also wonder whether *amici* in *AP* 5 picks up ὦ φίλοι, the opening word of the *Purifications* (see above), which also perhaps became a recurrent mode of address in the poem (cf. fr. 114 D–K = D6 L–M); the echo helps to confirm that, whatever the syntax of *amici*, we are to feel ourselves, not just the Pisones, addressed here. Even Horace, after all, has – as many critics have recognised — more than a little of the Empedoclean leech within. The whole opening description of a painter reverses, as Philip Hardie also noted, a famous Empedoclean simile (fr. 23 D–K = D60 L–M) of skilled painters who can 'fashion shapes similar to all things, creating trees and men and women, wild animals and birds and fish nourished in the water and long-lived gods', but not apparently all jumbled together.[12] Horace's *Ars Poetica* (though that, of course, might not have been the original title) thus begins with a description of the apparent abandonment of all *ars* in a passage which unsurprisingly exhibits, through a remarkable 'window allusion' (and many other things), *ars poetica* to the highest degree.[13]

As a 'didactic poet', and one given such a prominent place by Lucretius, Empedocles was a very important part of Horace's heritage in the *Ars*, functioning to some extent both like and unlike the figure of Lucilius in *Satires* 1. Moreover, Empedocles hovers on the edges of the ancient and modern critical traditions, which can never really make up their minds whether he is a poet or a philosopher; Aristotle is of course the key figure here.[14] Empedocles poses Horatian questions, or rather poses challenges to Horatian positions; v. 470, *nec satis adparet cur uersus factitet*, is a Horatian spin precisely on Aristotelian and other debates about 'philosophical poetry'. Empedocles serves Horace in more than one way, just as he can also help us to read 'intratextually'. When, for example, our suspicions about the Empedoclean colour of the opening of the poem appear to be confirmed by the end, we re-read and the two passages become somehow re-inforcing. Details

---

11 Hardie 2009, 140–1 suggests that Ovid drew on this passage of *Arg.* 4 in the Pythagorean discourse in *Met.* 15.

12 This catalogue appears to be formulaic in Empedocles, cf. D73.270–2 L–M. It is perhaps worthy of note that the author of the Hippocratic *On Ancient Medicine* 20 claims that what has been written about the origins of man by Empedocles and others has less to do with medicine than with γραφική, which seems most naturally understood as 'painting'. Bad painting and bad medicine frame the *Ars Poetica*. On Empedocles fr. 23 D–K cf. Iribarren 2013.

13 On the opening verses see, in addition to the commentaries and the works I have cited elsewhere, Schwindt 2014; Gantar 1964; Frischer 1991, 68–74; Geue 2014, 152–3.

14 Cf. Hunter forthcoming.

always come in and out of focus, at both macro- and micro- levels. So it is, for example, that once we get explicitly to the story of Empedocles we realise that *ructatur* in v. 457 is preparing us for Mt Etna, whereas *errat* in the same verse (and cf. *error* in v. 454) becomes (*inter alia*) a specific reference to the central place of 'wandering' in Empedocles' account of souls:

> τῶν καὶ ἐγὼ νῦν εἰμι, φυγὰς θεόθεν καὶ ἀλήτης,
> Νείκει μαινομένωι πίσυνος.
>
> Empedocles fr. 115.13–14 D–K = D10.13–14 L–M

> I too am now one of them, an exile from the divine and a wanderer, who trusted in crazed Strife.

Empedocles was a 'wandering poet' in a very particular way.

2 Intratextual unities

A leitmotif of all discussion of 'intratextuality' is how the term self-consciously plays with its relationship with its older sister, 'intertextuality' (the original IT girl); Horace's use of Empedocles in the opening of the *Ars Poetica* well illustrates how this issue, if not the modern terms, were well understood in antiquity. Consider one of the earliest surviving explicitly intratextual observations. In 1.97.2 Thucydides explains his 'digression' on Athenian power as follows:

> ἔγραψα δὲ αὐτὰ καὶ τὴν ἐκβολὴν τοῦ λόγου ἐποιησάμην διὰ τόδε, ὅτι τοῖς πρὸ ἐμοῦ ἅπασιν ἐκλιπὲς τοῦτο ἦν τὸ χωρίον καὶ ἢ τὰ πρὸ τῶν Μηδικῶν Ἑλληνικὰ ξυνετίθεσαν ἢ αὐτὰ τὰ Μηδικά· τούτων δὲ ὅσπερ καὶ ἥψατο ἐν τῆι Ἀττικῆι ξυγγραφῆι Ἑλλάνικος, βραχέως τε καὶ τοῖς χρόνοις οὐκ ἀκριβῶς ἐπεμνήσθη. ἅμα δὲ καὶ τῆς ἀρχῆς ἀπόδειξιν ἔχει τῆς τῶν Ἀθηναίων ἐν οἵωι τρόπωι κατέστη.
>
> Thucydides 1.97.2

> I have recorded these things and have made this digression from my narrative for the following reason: this theme was neglected by everyone before me, who composed their work either about Greek affairs before the Persian Wars or about the Persian Wars themselves. The man who did touch on these matters in his *Atthis* was Hellanicus, but he dealt with it only briefly and was inaccurate in his chronology. At the same time my account serves as an exposition of how the Athenian empire was established.
>
> (trans. Mynott)

The intratextual dynamic, the relationship, as Alison Sharrock put it in her Introduction to Sharrock-Morales 2000, between parts and (w)holes, is here governed by a very clear intertextual imperative, the need to make good a gap (ἐκλιπές is almost a perfect translation for 'gap'), not in Thucydides' own work, but in that of his predecessors. The part is indeed related to the (w)hole, but it is someone else's (w)hole. That relationship between inter- and intra-textuality may also be (in part) why the modern pursuit of intratextual questions has always seemed to matter more to Latinists than to their Hellenist colleagues. If there is any reality behind this impression, it may be that that big sister again, intertextuality, hangs from the very beginning over Latin literature and its study much more importantly (and threateningly) than she does over Greek literature. There is a real question here about the different kinds of problems posed by the two literatures and about what role 'intratextuality' can play in helping us to make discussion of those differences as sharp as possible. It is not, of course, that Greek literature is any less 'intertextual' (or indeed 'intratextual'), it is just differently so. Antiquity's most quintessentially 'intratextual' readers were in fact probably the scholars whose work lies behind the epitomized notes which make up our corpus of Homeric scholia. They always read for part and (w)hole, and they read with extraordinarily sensitive eyes and noses for what was unusual and seemed to disturb the perfection of the surface. To that perfect surface I will return.

Thucydides' term for his 'digression', ἐκβολή, is one of a familiar cluster of terms which suggest that a *logos* is a path or a journey, one with twists and turns, with stopping and starting, as well as a hoped-for destination. Other examples include ἐκτροπή and, above all, πλάνη, 'wandering', a term which may or may not have something to do with the structure and story of the *Odyssey*. At the opening of the *Laws*, for example, Plato's Athenian Stranger proposes entertainment for the journey ahead:

> προσδοκῶ οὐκ ἂν ἀηδῶς περί τε πολιτείας τὰ νῦν καὶ νόμων τὴν διατριβήν, λέγοντάς τε καὶ ἀκούοντας ἅμα κατὰ τὴν πορείαν, ποιήσασθαι. πάντως δ' ἥ γε ἐκ Κνωσοῦ ὁδὸς εἰς τὸ τοῦ Διὸς ἄντρον καὶ ἱερόν, ὡς ἀκούομεν, ἱκανή, καὶ ἀνάπαυλαι κατὰ τὴν ὁδόν, ὡς εἰκός, πνίγους ὄντος τὰ νῦν, ἐν τοῖς ὑψηλοῖς δένδρεσίν εἰσι σκιαραί, καὶ ταῖς ἡλικίαις πρέπον ἂν ἡμῶν εἴη τὸ διαναπαύεσθαι πυκνὰ ἐν αὐταῖς, λόγοις τε ἀλλήλους παραμυθουμένους τὴν ὁδὸν ἅπασαν οὕτω μετὰ ῥαιστώνης διαπερᾶναι.
> ΚΛ. Καὶ μὴν ἔστιν γε, ὦ ξένε, προϊόντι κυπαρίττων τε ἐν τοῖς ἄλσεσιν ὕψη καὶ κάλλη θαυμάσια, καὶ λειμῶνες ἐν οἷσιν ἀναπαυόμενοι διατρίβοιμεν ἄν.
> ΑΘ. Ὀρθῶς λέγεις.
> ΚΛ. Πάνυ μὲν οὖν· ἰδόντες δὲ μᾶλλον φήσομεν. ἀλλ' ἴωμεν ἀγαθῆι τύχηι.
> ΑΘ. Ταῦτ' εἴη. καί μοι λέγε· κατὰ τί τὰ συσσίτιά τε ὑμῖν συντέταχεν ὁ νόμος καὶ τὰ γυμνάσια καὶ τὴν τῶν ὅπλων ἕξιν;
>
> Plato, *Laws* 1.625a6-c7

Athenian: ... I suspect that you would not be unwilling for us to proceed on our way by contributing and listening to discussion on constitutions and laws. Certainly, the road from Knossos to the cave and shrine of Zeus is, so we are told, not short, and in this heat there

> will doubtless be shaded resting-places provided by the tall trees; there we can often rest, as men of our age should do, and by cheering ourselves with discourse we can thus complete the journey in some ease.
> *Cleinias*: Indeed, stranger, as you proceed you find in the groves tall and wonderfully beautiful cypress-trees, and meadows where we can rest and discuss.
> *Ath.*: Excellent idea!
> *Cleinias*: Indeed, and when we have seen them we shall agree all the more. Well, let's be off!
> *Ath.*: Fine! Now tell me: why does the law ordain your common messes and the gymnasia and the nature of your arms?

Reading the *Laws* will be a long journey, one requiring resting-places. A few years ago I suggested that Plato is here also alluding playfully to the *locus amoenus* of the *Phaedrus*, already famous by the time of the *Laws*, as a passage which had already come to be seen as quintessentially intratextual, that is as marking structures within the *Phaedrus*.[15] Be that as it may, allusions from one part of a writer's corpus to another is today how 'intratextuality' is largely understood (when it is) in several countries (notably Germany), and here of course writers such as Cicero, Ovid and Horace offer very rich pickings indeed.[16]

One passage to be placed alongside Thucydides 1.97.2 is the famous Herodotus 4.30:

> θωμάζω δέ (προσθήκας γὰρ δή μοι ὁ λόγος ἐξ ἀρχῆς ἐδίζητο) ὅ τι ἐν τῆι Ἠλείηι πάσηι χώρηι οὐ δυνέαται γίνεσθαι ἡμίονοι, οὔτε ψυχροῦ τοῦ χώρου ἐόντος οὔτε ἄλλου φανεροῦ αἰτίου οὐδενός·
>
> Herodotus 4.30.1

> But I wonder at the fact (for it was the way of my *logos* from the beginning to seek out additions) that in the whole of Elis no mules can be conceived although the country is not cold, nor is there any evident cause ....
>
> trans. Godley, adapted

The *logos*, whether that be the whole work, in whatever shape it was when Herodotus wrote this chapter, or just 'the Scythian *logos*', 'has from the beginning been seeking προσθῆκαι'. We can debate what is meant by the Greek term and by what form of critical orthopedics we are to distinguish 'prosthetic' from 'natural' limbs, but what is clear is that Herodotus' intratextual consciousness is on open display here: the habits of the mules of Elis might be digressive to the habits of Scythian mules and hornless oxen, but what is the real *logos*, the 'path' if you like, of the Scythian *logos*? Herodotus is clearly already playing with audience

15 Hunter 2012, 193–4.
16 Cf. Scheidegger Lämmle 2016.

expectations about the nature of extended narrative journeys and, in particular, with expectations about what we might as well call 'unity'. Moreover, the verb ἐδίζητο suggests that the *logos* has a life of its own, it is not content with any simple, pre-ordered narrative path.

In the context of unity, τὸ ἕν, the language of searching almost inevitably suggests Parmenides, who set before us two ὁδοὶ διζήσιος, though one is not really a followable path at all (B2 = D6 L–M, B6.3 = D7.3 L–M, B7.2 = D8.2 L–M); those who foolishly follow the imaginary path of 'what is not' are characterized by 'wandering minds' (πλαγκτὸς νόος, B6.6 = D7.7 L–M, B8.53 = D8.59 L–M), whereas the true perfect reality of 'what is' exists by necessity (ἀνάγκη, B8.16, 30 = D8.21, 35 L–M), lacks nothing (B8.33 = D8.38) and may be compared to a perfectly-rounded ball:

> αὐτὰρ ἐπεὶ πεῖρας πύματον, τετελεσμένον ἐστί
> πάντοθεν, εὐκύκλου σφαίρης ἐναλίγκιον ὄγκωι,
> μεσσόθεν ἰσοπαλὲς πάντηι· τὸ γὰρ οὔτε τι μεῖζον
> οὔτε τι βαιότερον πελέναι χρεόν ἐστι τῆι ἢ τῆι.
> οὔτε γὰρ οὐκ ἐὸν ἔστι, τό κεν παύοι μιν ἱκνεῖσθαι
> εἰς ὁμόν, οὔτ' ἐὸν ἔστιν ὅπως εἴη κεν ἐόντος
> τῆι μᾶλλον τῆι δ' ἧσσον, ἐπεὶ πᾶν ἐστιν ἄσυλον·
> οἷ γὰρ πάντοθεν ἶσον, ὁμῶς ἐν πείρασι κύρει.
>
> Parmenides B8.42–9 D–K = D8.47-53 L–M

> But since there is a furthest limit, it is perfected, like the bulk of a ball well-rounded on every side, equally balanced in every direction from the centre. For it needs must not be somewhat more or somewhat less here or there. For neither is it non-existent, which would stop it from reaching its like, nor is it existent in such a way that there would be more being here, less there, since it is all inviolate: for being equal to itself on every side, it lies uniformly within its limits.
>
> (trans. KRS 1983, 252–3)

We do not (necessarily) have to believe that Parmenides' poem is the origin of the intratextual turn, but a concern with whether everything in a text is in fact μεσσόθεν ἰσοπαλὲς πάντηι, 'equally balanced in every direction from the centre', was presumably not far away when intratextuality was conceived. Parmenides shows us, moreover, that any temptation we might have had to think of intratextuality as only a 'textual' phenomenon is misplaced; Parmenides can serve to remind us that textual structures may be understood as imitations of metaphysical structures which govern what is intelligible. If that sounds a bit too much like 'popularised Plato' for comfort, then I can only plead that we can hardly keep Plato out of this discussion, whether it be readers or writers with whom we are concerned. In the context of the former, we may think that the tripartition of the soul has a particular significance in considering *how* we read; the soul-chariot of the *Phaedrus*, in which the two horses pull in opposite directions, is in fact by no means the worst image for the reading experience. As for the creation of texts, perhaps the most famous intratextual discussion of them all, one that Horace certainly picks up, along with Empedocles, at the head of the *AP*, is indeed Platonic:

> οὐ χύδην δοκεῖ βεβλῆσθαι τὰ τοῦ λόγου; ἢ φαίνεται τὸ δεύτερον εἰρημένον ἔκ τινος ἀνάγκης δεύτερον δεῖν τεθῆναι, ἤ τι ἄλλο τῶν ῥηθέντων; ἐμοὶ μὲν γὰρ ἔδοξεν, ὡς μηδὲν εἰδότι, οὐκ ἀγεννῶς τὸ ἐπιὸν εἰρῆσθαι τῶι γράφοντι· σὺ δ' ἔχεις τινὰ ἀνάγκην λογογραφικὴν ἧι ταῦτα ἐκεῖνος οὕτως ἐφεξῆς παρ' ἄλληλα ἔθηκεν; ... ἀλλὰ τόδε γε οἶμαί σε φάναι ἄν, δεῖν πάντα λόγον ὥσπερ ζῶιον συνεστάναι σῶμά τι ἔχοντα αὐτὸν αὑτοῦ, ὥστε μήτε ἀκέφαλον εἶναι μήτε ἄπουν, ἀλλὰ μέσα τε ἔχειν καὶ ἄκρα, πρέποντα ἀλλήλοις καὶ τῶι ὅλωι γεγραμμένα.
>
> Plato, *Phaedrus* 264b4–c3

> Don't you think the parts of the discourse are thrown out helter-skelter? Or does it seem to you that the second topic had to be put second for any cogent reason, or that any of the other things he says are so placed? It seemed to me, who am wholly ignorant, that the writer uttered boldly whatever occurred to him. Do you know any logographic necessity why he arranged his topics in this order? ... But I do think you will agree to this, that every discourse must be organized, like a living being, with a body of its own, as it were, so as not to be headless or footless, but to have a middle and extremities, composed in fitting relation to each other and to the whole.
>
> (trans. Fowler, adapted)

No lengthy discussion of this famous passage is necessary, however difficult it is to catch its tone. For Neoplatonists, Socrates' observations were quite literally a godsend. In his commentary on the *Phaedrus* Hermeias (p. 231 Couvreur) notes that 'beauty and the good' are the result of unity, and associates this with the fact that beauty (κάλλος) is not really beautiful if there is no 'unification' (ἕνωσις) of the parts. We will think of the opening of the *Ars Poetica* again. So too, this passage of the *Phaedrus*, like Parmenides' denial of change, reminds us that the unity which intratextual studies interrogate is also fundamental to classicism and ideas of the classical, best illustrated by Plato's account of perfect beauty in the *Symposium*:[17]

> πρῶτον μὲν ἀεὶ ὂν καὶ οὔτε γιγνόμενον οὔτε ἀπολλύμενον, οὔτε αὐξανόμενον οὔτε φθίνον, ἔπειτα οὐ τῆι μὲν καλόν, τῆι δ' αἰσχρόν, οὐδὲ τοτὲ μέν, τοτὲ δὲ οὔ, οὐδὲ πρὸς μὲν τὸ καλόν, πρὸς δὲ τὸ αἰσχρόν, οὐδ' ἔνθα μὲν καλόν, ἔνθα δὲ αἰσχρόν, ὡς τισὶ μὲν ὂν καλόν, τισὶ δὲ αἰσχρόν· οὐδ' αὖ φαντασθήσεται αὐτῶι τὸ καλὸν οἷον πρόσωπόν τι οὐδὲ χεῖρες οὐδὲ ἄλλο οὐδὲν ὧν σῶμα μετέχει, οὐδέ τις λόγος οὐδέ τις ἐπιστήμη, οὐδέ που ὂν ἐν ἑτέρωι τινι, οἷον

17 Cf. further Hunter 2015.

ἐν ζώωι ἢ ἐν γῆι ἢ ἐν οὐρανῶι ἢ ἔν τωι ἄλλωι, ἀλλ' αὐτὸ καθ' αὑτὸ μεθ' αὑτοῦ μονοειδὲς ἀεὶ ὄν, τὰ δὲ ἄλλα πάντα καλὰ ἐκείνου μετέχοντα τρόπον τινὰ τοιοῦτον, οἷον γιγνομένων τε τῶν ἄλλων καὶ ἀπολλυμένων μηδὲν ἐκεῖνο μήτε τι πλέον μήτε ἔλαττον γίγνεσθαι μηδὲ πάσχειν μηδέν.

Plato, *Symposium* 210e5–211b5

It is eternal; it does not come to be or cease to be, and it does not increase or diminish. It is not beautiful in one respect and ugly in another, or beautiful at one time but not at another, or beautiful in one setting but ugly in another, or beautiful here and ugly elsewhere, depending on how people find it. The lover will not perceive beauty as a face or hands or any other physical feature, or as a piece of reasoning or knowledge, and he will not perceive it as being anywhere else either – in something like a creature or the earth or the heavens. No, he will perceive it in itself and by itself, constant in form and eternal, and he will see that every beautiful object somehow partakes of it, but in such a way that their coming to be and ceasing to be do not increase or diminish it at all, and it remains entirely unaffected.

Unsurprisingly perhaps, intratextual studies point us to a far larger set of questions than the agenda they set for themselves.

3 Plotting necessity

Socrates' insistence, perhaps an inheritance from Parmenides, that there should be a λογογραφικὴ ἀνάγκη (Plato, *Phaedrus* 264b8), which is to determine the proper order of things in a speech, as it does in a living creature, is of particular importance in this context. The laughter which greets the composite animal at the start of Horace's *AP* is in part – by a familiar theory of the laughable – a recognition precisely that 'the necessary' has been breached. As far as poetry is concerned, we are very familiar with the idea that necessity, like fate, can function as a way of expressing authorial decisions about otherwise surprising features of narrative:

ἀλλά, θεαί, πῶς τῆσδε παρὲξ ἁλὸς ἀμφί τε γαῖαν
Αὐσονίην νήσους τε Λιγυστίδας, αἳ καλέονται
Στοιχάδες, Ἀργῴης περιώσια σήματα νηός
νημερτὲς πέφαται; τίς ἀπόπροθι τόσσον ἀνάγκη
καὶ χρειὼ σφ' ἐκόμισσε; τίνες σφέας ἤγαγον αὖραι;

Apollonius Rhodius, *Argonautica* 4.552–6

How is it, goddesses, that beyond this sea, in the Ausonian land and the Ligurian islands called Stoichades, many clear traces of the *Argo*'s voyage appear? What necessity and need took them so far away? What winds directed them?

As so often, the later developments familiar from Hellenistic and Roman epic are developments from Homer. Let me illustrate this with two examples from Odysseus' narration in *Odyssey* 10. After the terrified Eurylochus has reported to him about the disappearance of their comrades who went to Circe's house and has urged flight, Odysseus allows him to stay by the ship, whereas he himself 'must' take the same path that they did, κρατερὴ δέ μοι ἔπλετ' ἀνάγκη (*Od.* 10.273). Odysseus, of course, is presenting himself to the Phaeacians as a caring leader, just as he had earlier in the book with the description of how he killed a large deer in order to allow his men to eat. Moreover, Odysseus is driven by that mixture of inquisitiveness and desire for honour which leads him constantly to seek out, rather than to avoid, dangerous situations.[18] From Homer's point of view, however, there is another 'necessity' driving Odysseus' decision, namely the 'necessity' that Odysseus meets Circe; as often, then, poetic 'necessity' is not simple, and the movement of the plot, the relationship and ordering of the parts, is multiply determined.[19] After Odysseus and his men have spent a year with Circe, it is time to go, and Circe knows it:

> ὣς ἐφάμην, ἡ δ' αὐτίκ' ἀμείβετο δῖα θεάων·
> 'διογενὲς Λαερτιάδη, πολυμήχαν' Ὀδυσσεῦ,
> μηκέτι νῦν ἀέκοντες ἐμῶι ἐνὶ μίμνετε οἴκωι.
> ἀλλ' ἄλλην χρὴ πρῶτον ὁδὸν τελέσαι καὶ ἱκέσθαι
> εἰς Ἀΐδαο δόμους καὶ ἐπαινῆς Περσεφονείης
> ψυχῆι χρησομένους Θηβαίου Τειρεσίαο,
> μάντιος ἀλαοῦ, τοῦ τε φρένες ἔμπεδοί εἰσι·'
>
> Homer, *Odyssey* 10.487–93

> So I spoke, and the splendid goddess straightway made answer: 'Son of Laertes, Zeus-born, Odysseus of many devices, stay no longer in my house against your will; but you must first complete another journey, and come to the house of Hades and dread Persephone, to consult the spirit of Theban Teiresias, the blind seer, whose mind is firm as before'.

Generations of students have been asked to discuss 'Why does Odysseus have to go to the Underworld?' (particularly in view of what actually happens there), and very few teachers will accept 'Because Circe tells him he has to' as a full and proper answer. Nevertheless, this is, in summary, what the Homeric narrative pattern offers us. Heubeck's observation in the Oxford commentary, 'The divine

---

18 According to Dio Chrysostom (52.11–12), Odysseus was made to reflect upon this φιλοτιμία in the prologue of Euripides' *Philoctetes*.

19 Another aspect of this nest of issues which deserves fuller treatment is the grammarians' use, amply attested in the scholia, of 'necessity' as an argument in discussions of the *athetesis* of Homeric verses.

authority of Circe ... provides convincing motivation for the journey to Hades, which could not be omitted from the series of adventures ...', acknowledges, but utterly mistakes, the nature of the ποιητικὴ ἀνάγκη operative here. Part of that λογογραφικὴ or indeed ποιητικὴ ἀνάγκη is what we might call μυθικὴ ἀνάγκη, and some of the implications of this will form the final case-study of this paper.

One of the most famous structural (or indeed 'intratextual') problems in Greek drama is posed by Euripides' *Heracles Furens*. After Heracles has taken his revenge on the tyrannical usurper Lykos, Iris and Lyssa ('Madness') enter and Iris, speaking for Hera, reports that Heracles must now suffer and she rides roughshod over Lyssa's protests; Lyssa acknowledges that she must follow Hera's instructions — ἀναγκαίως ἔχει are her words (v. 859). Many critics believe that Euripides here innovates in placing Heracles' madness after the labours, but – be that as it may – it is (again) poetic and mythic 'necessity' which is strongly advertised. Euripides is not just being 'clever' in making his Lyssa seek to offer 'rational' *parainesis* and *nouthetesis* to apparently 'irrational' powers, but he is setting us to wonder just what sort of 'necessity' is driving this μῦθος, particularly as Iris has already explained (vv. 827–9) that, before the labours had been completed, Heracles had been saved by 'necessity (τὸ χρή) and the intervention of Zeus'. In the *Poetics* Aristotle privileged μῦθοι in which what was done and said unfolded in a pattern driven by 'probability or necessity', which is why poetry, which concerns itself with τὰ καθόλου, is 'more philosophical and more serious (σπουδαιότερον) than history' (1451b5–9); Aristotle's 'necessity' is not (necessarily) the 'necessity' of any tragic plot which has survived,[20] but this is by no means the only case where we find the impetus for an important critical idea of the *Poetics* already foreshadowed in fifth-century drama itself. The voluminous modern debate about the 'unitary' or 'broken' status of the *muthos* in the *Heracles* (cf. the survey in Bond's introduction to his edition) are the aftershocks of Aristotle's systematisations, although they are not always acknowledged as such.

Heracles is indeed a figure around whom questions of μυθικὴ ἀνάγκη readily cluster. Aristotle also famously criticises the 'errors' of poets 'who have written *Heracleids*, *Theseids*, and such poems, who think that since Heracles was one individual (εἷς), the *muthos* must also be (εἶναι προσήκειν) unitary (εἷς)' (1451a19–22). The action of Euripides' play is set against the background of the series of Heracles' labours, which are twice catalogued in the play in very different modes and at very different length, vv. 359–435, 1270–80; from the perspective of later criticism, the juxtaposition might be seen as that between an expansive epic 'telling', or indeed cataloguing, of Heracles and a dramatic one. Aristotle wanted epic

20 There is a huge bibliography: Halliwell 1986, 98–106 is a good place to start.

to be as close to his ideal of tragedy as he could make it, and he found his wish fulfilled in (as well as created by) Homer, but here again the seeds of the idea of two different ways of telling can already be sensed in drama itself. If Aeschylus thought of his tragedies as 'slices' (τεμάχη) from Homer's 'great feasts' (T 112 Radt), then Euripides' drama is a 'slice' from the 'great feast' of Heraclean myth; the relation between narrative epic and drama, more generally, is probably characterized as well in this fashion as in any other.

The *Heracles* has not exhausted its surprises for, after the killing of the children, Heracles responds to Theseus' attempted consolation in yet more famous verses:

> οἴμοι· πάρεργα < > τάδ' ἔστ' ἐμῶν κακῶν·
> ἐγὼ δὲ τοὺς θεοὺς οὔτε λέκτρ' ἃ μὴ θέμις
> στέργειν νομίζω δεσμά τ' ἐξάπτειν χεροῖν
> οὔτ' ἠξίωσα πώποτ' οὔτε πείσομαι
> οὐδ' ἄλλον ἄλλου δεσπότην πεφυκέναι.
> δεῖται γὰρ ὁ θεός, εἴπερ ἔστ' ὀρθῶς θεός,
> οὐδενός· ἀοιδῶν οἵδε δύστηνοι λόγοι.
>
> Euripides, *Heracles* 1340–6

> Alas! this is quite beside the question of my troubles. For my part, I do not believe that the gods indulge in sexual unions which are not right; and as for putting bonds on hands, I have never thought that worthy of belief, nor will I now be so persuaded, nor again that one god is naturally lord and master of another. For the deity, if he be really such, has no wants; these are miserable tales of the poets.
>
> (trans. Coleridge, adapted)

These verses seem to deny the very foundations of the play we have been watching, let alone Heracles' own bitter view expressed immediately before (vv. 1303–10); a rehearsal of modern critical approaches to this problem would itself make for a slender volume on 'intratextuality'.[21] Godfrey Bond's rightly standard commentary is, however, a good place to start: 'These lines ... must be taken firmly in their context as a direct and detailed answer to the argument of Theseus ... Heracles' arguments must not be removed from their context... In particular [1341–2] should not be taken from the context of incest between gods and used to deny Zeus' intercourse with Alcmena and his fathering of Heracles ...These lines must not be taken as Heracles' considered views: that way lie delusions like Verrall's rationalistic explanation of the play. Heracles is not an academic philosopher who has thought out the implications of everything he says ... 1341–6 may well

21 There is a helpful survey in Brown 1978.

represent Euripides' own considered view; but that is another matter ...' (Bond then continues with a helpful note about the possible influence of Xenophanes). 'Incest' in fact is not at issue here, but let us not quibble.[22] It is, however, worth insisting[23] that Theseus' own arguments do not really fit the case he needs to make:

οὐδεὶς δὲ θνητῶν ταῖς τύχαις ἀκήρατος,
οὐ θεῶν, ἀοιδῶν εἴπερ οὐ ψευδεῖς λόγοι.
οὐ λέκτρ' ἐν ἀλλήλοισιν, ὧν οὐδεὶς νόμος,
συνῆψαν; οὐ δεσμοῖσι διὰ τυραννίδα
πατέρας ἐκηλίδωσαν; ἀλλ' οἰκοῦσ' ὅμως
Ὄλυμπον ἠνέσχοντό θ' ἡμαρτηκότες.
καίτοι τί φήσεις, εἰ σὺ μὲν θνητὸς γεγὼς
φέρεις ὑπέρφευ τὰς τύχας, θεοὶ δὲ μή;

Euripides, *Heracles* 1314–21

There is no mortal who is unravaged by misfortune, nor any god either, if what poets sing is true. Have not those whom the law forbids slept with one another? Have they not defiled their own fathers with chains to gain sovereign power? Still they inhabit Olympus and brave the issue of their crimes. And yet what shall you say in your defence, if you, a mortal, take your fate excessively hard, while they, as gods, do not?

(trans. Coleridge, adapted)

Theseus apparently needs Olympian 'parallels' for Heracles' killings or, at the very least, for violent outrages against φίλοι, which have not had serious consequences; although putting chains on your father is not a course of action to be recommended, it is hardly on a par with what has happened to Heracles. Moreover, gods cannot die, and that is the course of action on which Heracles seems set. To put the killing of the children down to τύχη or to consider it as just a

22 Bond apparently derives his notion that 'incest' is involved from Theseus' claim at 1315–17, to which Heracles is responding, that 'if the tales of bards are not false', the gods λέκτρ' ἐν ἀλλήλοισιν, ὧν οὐδεὶς νόμος, / συνῆψαν; in his note on that passage Bond observes that the reference is 'to incestuous intercourse like that of Zeus and his young sister Hera or Ares and Aphrodite'. It is, however, at least doubtful that Zeus and Hera are in fact evoked here; in the first instance it is probably Ares and Aphrodite from *Odyssey* 8 of whom we first think, and although by some genealogies they are half-brother and half-sister (through their common father Zeus), there is, I think, no suggestion in the song of Demodocus that we are to think of their relationship as incestuous, as well as adulterous, despite some shared diction between *Il.* 14.295–6 and *Od.* 8.268–70. However closely Heracles' declaration in 1341–2 rewrites Theseus' assertion of 1316–17, it is (I think) not easy to erase all reference to Heracles' own parentage from 1341–2; many of the audience may remember Amphitryon's harsh charge against Zeus at 344–5.

23 Cf. Brown 1978, 24.

'misfortune' (1314, 1321) also hardly seems to fit the case; when Heracles echoes Theseus' language at 1357, τῆι τύχηι δουλευτέον, the bitterness is hard to ignore.[24] When Heracles apparently dismisses Theseus' arguments from the Olympians as πάρεργα ... ἐμῶν κακῶν, it is hard not to sympathise.

The exchange between Theseus and Heracles, then, is characterized by a dramatization of rhetorical practice, in which the relationship between argument and exemplum (Theseus) and argument and generalization (Heracles) was always subject to the contingencies of the moment. To insist, as Godfrey Bond does (above), on 'context' simply means that we ought always to be asking 'which context?'. In this case, too narrow a focus on 'the immediate (dramatic) context' and upon Heracles' character conceals what is really at stake here. In rejecting the consolation which 'the wretched tales of poets' were so often used to provide, in many different rhetorical contexts, Heracles rejects a literary and cultural practice which for us begins with Homer. Achilles urges Priam to eat and wait until morning before seeing Hector's corpse, and he tells him how Niobe ate, though she had lost twelve children to Apollo and Artemis. To this story Priam makes no response; the silence is deafening. Heracles is different, and Theseus is a less frightening proposition than the still very fragile Achilles (we cannot, I think, imagine Priam telling Achilles that he finds no comfort whatsoever in the story of Niobe), but time too has moved on. This Heracles inhabits a world which, for many decades, had given serious thought to how poetry and myth work in the world and to the nature of the gods; the intratextual fractures in the surface of the text which are the product of that reflection point us towards the very complex relationship between literature and the culture out of which it grew.[25]

Bibliography

Beard, M. (2014), *Laughter in Ancient Rome*, Berkeley.

Bond, G.W. (1981), *Euripides, Heracles. With Introduction and Commentary*, Oxford.

Brink, C.O. (1971), *Horace on Poetry. The* "Ars Poetica", Cambridge.

Brown, A.L. (1978), 'Wretched Tales of Poets: Euripides, *Heracles* 1340–6', *Proceedings of the Cambridge Philological Society* 24, 22–30.

Citroni, M. (2009), 'Horace's *Ars Poetica* and the Marvellous', in: P. Hardie (ed.), *Paradox and the Marvellous in Augustan Literature and Culture*, Oxford, 19–40. a.

---

24 Cf. the similar bitterness of the earlier 1263, Ζεὺς δ', ὅστις ὁ Ζεύς κτλ.

25 Another development which would have to be taken into account in any proper survey of 'intratextual dynamics' in the late fifth and fourth centuries would be the rise of the anthological habit and the practice of poetic citation. Parts of wholes could now have a life of their own, and that expectation may even have coloured composition.

Frischer, B.D. (1991), *Shifting Paradigms: New Approaches to Horace's* Ars Poetica, Atlanta.
Gantar, K. (1964), 'Die Anfangsverse und die Komposition der horazischen Epistel über die Dichtkunst', *Symbolae Osloenses* 39, 89–98.
Geue, T. (2014), 'Editing the Opposition: Horace's *Ars Politica*', *Materiali e Discussioni* 72, 143–72.
Halliwell, S. (1986), *Aristotle's Poetics*, London.
Hardie, P. (2009), *Lucretian Receptions: History, The Sublime, Knowledge*, Cambridge.
Hardie, P. (2018), 'Horace et le sublime empédocléen', in: S. Franchet d'Esperey/C. Lévy (eds.), *Les Présocratiques et la literature latine*, Paris, 263–82.
Heubeck, A./Hoekstra, A. (1990), *A Commentary on Homer's Odyssey*. Volume II. Books IX–XVI, Oxford.
Hunter, R. (2012), *Plato and the Traditions of Ancient Literature. The Silent Stream*, Cambridge.
Hunter, R. (2015), 'The Idea of the Classical in Classical Antiquity', *Proceedings of the Academy of Athens* 90, 51–68.
Hunter, R. (forthcoming), 'Hesiod and the Presocratics: A Hellenistic Perspective?', in: H. Köning/L. Iribarren (eds.), *Hesiod and the Presocratics*.
Iribarren, L. (2013), 'Les peintres d'Empédocle (DK 31 B23): enjeux et portée d'une analogie préplatonicienne' *Philosophie antique* 13, 83–115.
KRS=Kirk, G.S./Raven, J.E./Schofield, M. (eds.) (1983), *The Presocratic Philosophers*, 2nd edn., Cambridge.
Laird, A. (2007), 'The *Ars Poetica*', in: S. Harrison (ed.), *The Cambridge Companion to Horace*, Cambridge, 132–43.
Laks, A./Most, G.W. (eds.) (2016), *Early Greek Philosophy*, Cambridge MA.
Oliensis, E. (1998), *Horace and the Rhetoric of Authority*, Cambridge.
Russell, D.A. (2006), '*Ars Poetica*', in: A. Laird (ed.), *Oxford Readings in Ancient Literary Criticism*, Oxford, 325–45.
Scheidegger Lämmle, C. (2016), *Werkpolitik in der Antike: Studien zu Cicero, Vergil, Horaz und Ovid*, Munich.
Schwindt, J.P. (2014), 'Ordo and Insanity: On the Pathogenesis of Horace's *Ars poetica*', *Materiali e Discussioni* 72, 55–70.
Sharrock, A./Morales, H. (eds.) (2000), *Intratextuality: Greek and Roman Textual Relations*, Oxford.
Tamás, A. (2014), 'Reading Ovid Reading Horace. The Empedoclean Drive in the *Ars poetica*', *Materiali e Discussioni* 72, 173–92.

List of Contributors

Theodore Antoniadis is Assistant Professor of Latin at the Aristotle University of Thessaloniki. He has studied Classics at the Universities of Thessaloniki (BA 1999, PhD 2007) and Toronto (MA 2000). His doctoral dissertation, *The Rhetoric of Belatedness: A Running Commentary on Ovid's* Amores (Thessaloniki, 2009) as well as a translation of Lucretius' *De Rerum Natura* have been published in Greek. He has published various articles on Seneca's works and Flavian Epic in classical journals, and is currently working on a monograph-length study of Silius Italicus' *Punica*.

Ulrike Egelhaaf-Gaiser has been since 2008 Professor of Classics/Latin Philology at the University of Göttingen. Her publications combine the fields of Roman religion and cultural history with the methods of literary studies and refer as well to questions of intertextuality and intermediality. Current research projects focus on the interplay of religion and education in the *Quaestiones Graecae et Romanae* of Plutarch and the *Noctes Atticae* of Gellius, on the role of the *miles gloriosus* in the cultural background of the second century and on the concept of authorial leadership in the letters of Horace and Seneca.

Jacqueline Fabre-Serris is Professor of Latin Literature at the University of Lille. She has published on Classical Latin literature, especially on Gallus and Augustan poetry, on mythology and mythography. She has special interests in gender and genre, intertextuality, and reception of Antiquity. She is co-director of the electronic reviews *Dictynna*, *Eugesta*, and *Polymnia*, and of a series on mythography published by Les Presses universitaires du Septentrion.

Stavros Frangoulidis is Professor of Latin at the Aristotle University of Thessaloniki. He has written on Roman comedy, Senecan tragedy and the Latin novel; with Theodore Papanghelis, Gesine Manuwald and Stephen Harrison he has edited several volumes on Latin literature for *Trends in Classics*. His books include: *Handlung und Nebenhandlung: Theater, Metatheater und Gattungsbewusstein in der römischen Komödie* (1997); *Roles and Performances in Apuleius'* Metamorphoses (2001); and *Witches, Isis and Narrative: Approaches to Magic in Apuleius'* Metamorphoses (2008).

Tristan E. Franklinos is a British Academy Postdoctoral Fellow in Classics at the University of Oxford and a Junior Research Fellow at Trinity College, Oxford. His principal research interests lie in the area of Latin poetry of the first centuries BC and AD, especially that of the elegists and the *Appendix Vergiliana*.

Therese Fuhrer has held Chairs of Latin at the Universities of Trier, Zurich, Freiburg, the Free University of Berlin, and since 2013 at the LMU Munich. She is currently engaged in a number of major research projects in the field of Roman rhetoric, on the authorial voice and on Roman Carthage in Latin literature. She is the author of several books, as e.g. (with Martin Hose) *Das antike Drama*, München 2017; (with Simone Adam) *Augustinus, Contra Academicos, De beata vita, De ordine* (Bibliotheca Teubneriana 2022), Berlin/Boston 2017.

Laurel Fulkerson is Professor of Classics and Associate Dean at FSU in Tallahassee, Florida. Her published work focuses on the elegiac poets, especially Ovid, and on the emotions in antiquity. Among other books, she is the author of *No Regrets: Remorse in Classical Antiquity* (2013) and *A Literary Commentary on the Elegies of the Appendix Tibulliana* (2017).

Philip Hardie is a Senior Research Fellow at Trinity College, Cambridge, and Honorary Professor of Latin in the University of Cambridge. He was formerly (2002–6) Corpus Christi Professor of the Latin Language and Literature, University of Oxford. He is a Fellow of the British Academy, a Member of the Academia Europaea, and an Honorary Fellow of the Australian Academy of the Humanities. He was the Sather Professor at the University of California at Berkeley in Spring 2016. He is the author of *Virgil's Aeneid: Cosmos and Imperium* (Oxford 1986); *The Epic Successors of Virgil* (Cambridge 1993); *Virgil Aeneid 9* (Cambridge Greek and Latin Classics, Cambridge 1994); *Ovid's Poetics of Illusion* (Cambridge 2002); *Lucretian Receptions. History, The Sublime, Knowledge* (Cambridge 2009); *Rumour and Renown. Representations of Fama in Western Literature* (Cambridge 2012); *The Last Trojan Hero: A Cultural History of Virgil's Aeneid* (I B Tauris 2014); and *Ovidio Metamorfosi* vol. 6 *Libri XIII-XV* (Fondazione Valla 2015). He is editor of *The Cambridge Companion to Ovid* (2002), co-editor (with Stuart Gillespie) of *The Cambridge Companion to Lucretius* (2007), and co-editor (with Patrick Cheney) of *The Oxford History of Classical Reception in English Literature* vol. 2: *1558–1660* (Oxford 2015).

Stephen Harrison is Fellow and Tutor in Classics at Corpus Christi College, Oxford and Professor of Latin Literature in the University of Oxford. He is author and/or editor of many books on Latin literature and its reception, most recently a commentary on Horace *Odes* 2 (CUP) and *Victorian Horace: Classics and Class* (Bloomsbury), both 2017.

Christer Henriksén is Professor of Latin at Uppsala University. He is the author of *A Commentary on Martial, Epigrams Book 9* (OUP), editor of the forthcoming *A Companion to Ancient Epigram* (Wiley/Blackwell), and has written a number of articles on Martial, Statius, and Latin epigraphic epigram; he has also published on Latin and Greek epigraphy in general. His research interests further include Latin metre and Augustan poetry.

S.J. Heyworth has been Bowra Fellow and Tutor in Classics at Wadham College, Oxford since 1988; he is Professor of Latin in the University. In 2007 he issued a new edition of Propertius in the Oxford Classical Text series together with a detailed textual commentary entitled *Cynthia*. With James Morwood he has produced literary and grammatical commentaries on Propertius 3 (2011), and *Aeneid* 3 (2017). His main focus is now on Ovid's *Fasti*: a commentary on book 3 will appear shortly in the Cambridge Greek and Latin Classics series, to be followed by an Oxford Classical Text of the whole poem.

Richard Hunter is Regius Professor of Greek at the University of Cambridge and a Fellow of Trinity College. His most recent books are *Plato and the Traditions of Ancient Literature: the silent stream* (2012), *Hesiodic Voices: Studies in the Ancient Reception of Hesiod's Works and Days* (2014), *Apollonius of Rhodes, Argonautica IV* (2015), and *The Measure of Homer* (2018). He is an Editor of *Cambridge Greek and Latin Classics* and *Cambridge Classical Studies*, a Fellow of the British Academy, a Foreign Fellow of the Academy of Athens and a Fellow of the Australian Academy of the Humanities.

Evangelos Karakasis is Associate Professor of Latin at the University of Ioannina. He is the author of the following monographs: *Terence and the Language of Roman Comedy* (Cambridge, 2005, 2008), *Song Exchange in Roman Pastoral* (Berlin, 2011) and *Calpurnius Siculus: A Neronian Poet in Rome* (Berlin, 2016) as well as of several papers on Roman comedy, pastoral, elegy/lyric poetry, epic and reception. He is also the editor of *Singing in the Shadow … Pastoral Encounters in Post-Vergilian Poetry* (*Trends in Classics* 4.1, Berlin, 2012) and, with I.N. Perysinakis, of *Plautine Trends: Studies in Plautine Comedy and its Reception* (Berlin, 2015). He is currently completing a monograph on post-Calpurnian Roman Pastoral.

George Kazantzidis (D.Phil 2011, Oxford) is Assistant Professor of Latin Literature at the University of Patras. His research interests lie in the history of mental illness and the history of emotions in classical antiquity. He has recently published articles on the emotion of disgust in Hippocratic medicine and on the topic of insanity in Greek and Roman paradoxography. A volume on hope (*elpis, spes*) in antiquity (co-edited with Dimos Spatharas) is forthcoming in 2018, in the subseries *Ancient Emotions*, hosted by *Trends in Classics* for De Gruyter. He is currently working on a book project, provisionally entitled: 'Paradoxography in Greek and Roman Antiquity: Medical Science, Horror, and the Sublime'.

Alison Keith teaches Classics and Women's Studies at the University of Toronto and currently serves as the Director of the Jackman Humanities Institute there. Her research focuses on the intersection of gender and genre in Latin literature: she has written books on Ovid's *Metamorphoses*, Latin epic, and Propertius, and edited volumes on the reception of Ovid's *Metamorphoses*, Roman dress, and Latin elegy and Hellenistic epigram. She is currently completing a book on Vergil for IB Tauris in their series 'Understanding Classics'. Ongoing projects include a commentary on the fourth book of Ovid's *Metamorphoses* for Cambridge University Press and a monograph on the reception of Ovid's *Metamorphoses* in Flavian epic.

Wolfgang Kofler studied Classical Philology in Innsbruck, Tübingen and Heidelberg. From 2009 to 2012 he held the chair of Latin at the University of Freiburg im Breisgau; since 2012 he has been Professor of Latin and Neo-Latin literature at the University of Innsbruck. His main areas of research are Hellenistic and Augustan poetry, epic, epigrams, Neo-Latin and the history of reception.

David Konstan is Professor of Classics at New York University. Among his publications are *Greek Comedy and Ideology* (Oxford, 1995); *Friendship in the Classical World* (Cambridge, 1997); *Pity Transformed* (London, 2001); *The Emotions of the Ancient Greeks: Studies in Aristotle and Classical Literature* (Toronto, 2006); *'A Life Worthy of the Gods': The Materialist Psychology of Epicurus* (Las Vegas, 2008); *Before Forgiveness: The Origins of a Moral Idea* (Cambridge, 2010); and *Beauty: The Fortunes of an Ancient Greek Idea* (Oxford, 2014). He is a past president of the American Philological Association (now the Society for Classical Studies), and a vice president of the Bristol Institute of Greece, Rome & the Classical Tradition. He is a fellow of the American Academy of Arts and Sciences and an honorary fellow of the Australian Academy of the Humanities.

Martin Korenjak was born in 1971 in Wels (Austria). He studied Classical Philology and Linguistics at Innsbruck and Heidelberg (1990–96), worked as research assistant at Innsbruck (1997–2003) and was Professor of Classical Philology at Bern (2003–09), before returning to Innsbruck in 2009. Since 2011, he works there partly for the University and partly for the Ludwig Boltzmann Institute for Neolatin Studies. His research areas include Greek and Latin poetry, rhetoric, literary theory and criticism, the reception of classical antiquity and Neolatin literature.

Giuseppe La Bua is Associate Professor of Latin Literature at the Department of Ancient World Studies at La Sapienza University of Rome. He has extensively published on religion and literature in the Roman world, Latin hymns, Ciceronian rhetoric and oratory, Augustan poetry, Ovid, and the Latin prose panegyrics. In 2010 he edited a collective volume on Ovid's *Fasti*. His book on the reception of Cicero's speeches in ancient education and scholarship (*Cicero and Roman Education. The Reception of the Speeches and Ancient Scholarship*) is in preparation for the Cambridge University Press.

Michèle Lowrie is the Andrew W. Mellon Professor of Classics and the College at the University of Chicago. She has published *Horace's Narrative Odes* (OUP 1997), *Writing, Performance, and Authority in Augustan Rome* (OUP 2009), and edited *Oxford Readings in Classical Studies: Horace's Odes and Epodes* (OUP 2009) and *Exemplarity and Singularity: Thinking through Particulars in Philosophy, Literature, and Law* (Routledge 2015), among other volumes.

Gesine Manuwald is Professor of Latin at University College London. Her research interests include Cicero's speeches, Roman drama, Roman epic and the reception of antiquity, especially in Neo-Latin literature. Her publications include commentaries on Cicero's *Philippics* (2007) and *Agrarian Speeches* (2018), a volume on Cicero (2015) and an edited collection on *The Afterlife of Cicero* (2016).

Theodore D. Papanghelis is Professor of Latin at the Aristotle University. He has published monographs, articles and translations in both English and Greek and has co-edited *A Companion to Apollonius Rhodius* (Brill) and *A Companion to Greek and Latin Pastoral* (Brill) with Antonios Rengakos and Marco Fantuzzi, respectively. He has just finished a Greek verse translation of Virgil's *Aeneid*.

Christine Perkell is Professor of Classics at Emory University. She is the author of *The Poet's Truth: A Study of the Poet in Virgil's Georgics*; *Reading Vergil's Aeneid: An Interpretive Guide* (ed. and contributor); *Vergil Aeneid 3 A Commentary*; *'Critical Theory,' and other entries* in: *The Virgil Encyclopedia*; *Vergil Aeneid 12: A Commentary*, forthcoming; she is editor of *Vergilius* (2013–8).

Alison Sharrock is Professor of Classics at the University of Manchester. She is the author of *Seduction and Repetition in Ovid's Ars Amatoria II* (Oxford, 1994) and *Reading Roman Comedy: Poetics and Playfulness in Plautus and Terence* (Cambridge, 2009), as well as of edited books and articles across Latin verse literature from the Republic to the early Empire. She is particularly interested in theoretical approaches to classical literature, including feminism, genre theory, narratology, and the construction of meaning.

Thea S. Thorsen is Associate Professor of Classics at NTNU, Trondheim, Norway. She is the author of several books, including *Ovid's Early Poetry* (2014) and editor and contributor to several volumes, including *The Cambridge Companion to Latin Love Elegy* (2013) and *Roman Receptions* *of Sappho* (with Stephen Harrison, forthcoming with Oxford University Press). Her metrical translations of Ovid's entire erotic-elegiac output are the first ever into Norwegian (2001–2009).

Gail Trimble is Associate Professor in Classical Languages and Literature at the University of Oxford and Brown Fellow and Tutor in Classics at Trinity College. Her commentary on Catullus 64, with newly edited text, is forthcoming in the Cambridge University Press 'orange' series, Cambridge Classical Texts and Commentaries. Her wider research interests focus on Latin poetry and literary form: she has published book chapters on Catullus, Virgil, Ovid and the history of scholarship, and is co-editing a forthcoming volume on *metalepsis* in Classical literature.

Christopher Trinacty is Associate Professor of Classics at Oberlin College. He is currently writing a commentary on Seneca's *Naturales Quaestiones 3* and has published widely on Senecan tragedy, the reception of Seneca, and Augustan poetry.

Chrysanthe Tsitsiou-Chelidoni is Assistant Professor of Latin Literature at the Aristotle University of Thessaloniki. Her book *Ovid, 'Metamorphosen' Buch VIII. Narrative Technik und literarischer Kontext* (2003) is based on her PhD (University of Heidelberg). Her publications are in the field of Augustan poetry and Roman historiography. Her research interests include ancient rhetoric and ancient and modern literary criticism.

General Index

https://doi.org/10.1515/9783110611021-029

Index Locorum

The list of passages includes ancient sources. Fragmentary texts are cited by the number and name of modern editor only. The relevant editions of both ancient sources and fragmentary texts are to be found in the bibliography accompanying each article. Abbreviations for ancient works are those of *LSJ* and *OLD*.

https://doi.org/10.1515/9783110611021-030